"Auschwitz is still with us. Both its immeasurably cruel reality and what it represents still stalk and haunt us after half a century. Indeed, the shadow of Auschwitz will no doubt follow us—and should follow us—as long as human memory endures.

In this absorbing book Rubenstein and Roth return to the old questions but in a new way, and they raise new and troublesome questions in an unavoidable way. This is a volume every thoughtful person, regardless of field or faith, needs to read and ponder."

—Harvey Cox
Hollis Professor of Divinity
Harvard University

"This excellent book discusses the Holocaust in all its essential dimensions: its historical, cultural, and ideological context; its political and bureaucratic development; its devastating impact on victims and survivors; the responses of the Christian churches; its evocation in art, music, and literature; and its impact on contemporary religion, philosophy, and ethics. Complex, detailed, and occasionally provocative, it will appeal to students, generalists, and specialists from many fields."

—Susan Zuccotti
Author, *Under His Very Windows: The Vatican and the Holocaust in Italy*

This analysis of the Holocaust is complex yet lucid, the narrative is comprehensive and detailed, the research both thorough and fully current. No other study deals as centrally with the main historical issues of the Holocaust while at the same time exploring its significance from religious, philosophical, and artistic points of view.

—J. Michael Phayer
Professor of History Emeritus
Marquette University

"This definitive study of the Holocaust and its religious and ethical implications is now updated, reflecting significant advances in scholarship during the past two decades. With attention to film, literature and architecture, the Goldhagen debate, the role of the Vatican, and women's experience in the Holocaust, the book provides an excellent survey of the Holocaust's place in the intellectual and social history of the twentieth century. Long a popular choice for college courses on the Holocaust and genocide, *Approaches to Auschwitz* is now even better suited to helping students consider how these world-shattering events must affect our way of thinking, acting, and believing in a post-Holocaust world."

—Stephen R. Haynes
Associate Professor of Religious Studies
Rhodes College, Memphis, Tennessee

"This revised edition of Rubenstein and Roth's original 1987 edition of *Approaches to Auschwitz*, beautifully written, lucid, challenging, and inspiring all at once, is a *tour de force*, an engaging, comprehensive, humane work of precise, critical scholarship. The authors have distilled and critiqued some of the best and most thought provoking historical, literary, and theological scholarship about the Holocaust while at the same time making their own scholarly contributio

will force all of us to rethink how we approach this 'unthinkable but unavoidable' horrific event of the twentieth century."

—Carol Rittner RSM,
Distinguished Professor of Holocaust & Genocide Studies
The Richard Stockton College of New Jersey

"*Approaches to Auschwitz* is arguably the most comprehensive and adept overview of the state of Holocaust scholarship currently available. Although the book is deceptive in its simplicity, Roth and Rubenstein provide demanding insights, and draw from a wide range of disciplines. Through a combination of history, theology, philosophy, sociology, political science, psychology, and art, they examine the long and troubling historical context in which the Holocaust took place, set the text of its convoluted evolution within the latest scholarship, and provide analyses of its consequences that demonstrate its overwhelming demands. They do not shirk from demonstrating the complexity of the history of the Holocaust and its consequences, preferring to explore difficult questions than provide easy answers. *Approaches to Auschwitz* is ideal as a course text, accessible to read from cover to cover, and a useful reference tool too. Every student of the Holocaust should digest this book thoroughly—it is a must for every serious reader of the Holocaust."

—Stephen D. Smith
Founding Director of the Aegis Trust and the Beth Shalom Holocaust Centre,
United Kingdom

"In the new and fully revised edition of *Approaches to Auschwitz,* John K. Roth and Richard L. Rubenstein have renewed, intensified, and enhanced what had been one of the most respected texts on the Holocaust. Built on the foundation of the original, the new work has incorporated seamlessly the findings of almost two decades of research in a book that approaches Auschwitz from the vantage point of art and literature, film and theology, and history and psychology.

Rubenstein and Roth demonstrate that the best way to approach the Holocaust is with fear and trembling and to seek understanding in diverse fields, for each discipline provides greater insight into the experience of the victims and the psychology of the perpetrators. They treat testimony with the utmost of respect and heed the work of other scholars, even those with whom they disagree, who have toiled—as they—to comprehend the incomprehensible.

The work encompasses a deep understanding of antisemitism in its religious origins and of the Enlightenment and its ambiguous and ambivalent attitude toward the Jews. Its reach is breathtaking, its achievements substantial. *Approaches to Auschwitz* is written with passion and sensitivity. It is the mature work of seasoned scholars who have worked at understanding the Holocaust and its implications for decades and who never backed away from tough conclusions. Their contribution is lucid and will shape the understanding of both students and scholars, challenging both to broaden their reach and deepen their understanding."

—Michael Berenbaum
Adjunct Professor of Theology and Director of the Sigi Ziering Institute, University of Judaism. Former President of the Survivors of the Shoah Visual History Foundation. Former Project Director of the United States Holocaust Memorial Museum

# Approaches to Auschwitz:
# The Holocaust and Its Legacy

## *Revised Edition*

Richard L. Rubenstein
and
John K. Roth

Westminster John Knox Press
LOUISVILLE • LONDON

Book design by Sharon Adams
Cover design © 2003 Eric Handel/LMNOP

The cover photograph is of Auschwitz-Birkenau © Hulton-Deutsch Collection/CORBIS.

The cover inset is taken from the stained-glass window *The Last Journey,* which is in Beth Shalom in Nottinghamshire, Britain's first Holocaust memorial. This window was designed and made by Roman Halter and his daughter Aviva Halter. The image is based on a photograph that was taken by an SS man in 1944 in Auschwitz-Birkenau. It depicts a grandmother with three little children. They are moving toward the gas chambers.

Roman Halter is a survivor of the Lodz ghetto, Auschwitz-Birkenau, the Nazi camp at Stutthoff, and slave labor in a Dresden munitions factory, where he endured the bombings on 13–14 February 1945.

The authors gratefully acknowledge the assistance of Betty Rogers Rubenstein for the discussion of Holocaust-related art in this book.

*Second edition*
Published by Westminster John Knox Press
Louisville, Kentucky

This book is printed on acid-free paper that meets the American National Standards Institute Z39.48 standard. ♾

PRINTED IN THE UNITED STATES OF AMERICA

04 05 06 07 08 09 10 11 12 — 10 9 8 7 6 5 4 3 2

**Library of Congress Cataloging-in-Publication Data**

Rubenstein, Richard L.
    Approaches to Auschwitz : the Holocaust and its legacy / Richard L.
Rubenstein and John K. Roth. — Rev. ed.
        p. cm.
    Includes bibliographical references and index.
    ISBN 0-664-22353-2 (alk. paper)
        1. Holocaust, Jewish (1939–1945)—Causes.    2. Antisemitism—History.    3. Christianity and antisemitism.    4. Holocaust (Christian theology)    5. Holocaust (Jewish theology)
6. Auschwitz (Concentration camp)    I. Roth, John K.    II. Title.

D804.3 .R79 2003
940.53'18—dc21                                                                                      2002193398

To
Betty and Lyn

*Many waters cannot quench love,
neither can floods drown it.*

*The Song of Solomon 8:7*

*Today people know*
*have known for several years*
*that this dot on the map*
*is Auschwitz*
*This much they know*
*as for the rest*
*they think they know.*
                    Charlotte Delbo,
                        *Auschwitz and After*

# Contents

Preface and Acknowledgments     ix

Prologue: What Is the Holocaust?     1

**PART ONE: HOLOCAUST ORIGINS**     23

1   The Jew as Outsider: The Greco-Roman
and Early Christian Worlds     25

2   The Triumph of Christianity
and the "Teaching of Contempt"     49

3   The Irony of Emancipation: France
and the Dreyfus Affair     71

4   Toward Total Domination     97

**PART TWO: THE NAZIS IN POWER**     119

5   "Rational Antisemitism"     121

6   War and the Final Solution     143

7   "A Racial Struggle of Pitiless Severity"     167

8   "Priority over All Other Matters"     185

**PART THREE: RESPONSES TO THE HOLOCAUST**     215

9   Victims and Survivors     217

10   Their Brothers' Keepers? Christians,
Churches, and Jews     249

**11**   What Can—and Cannot—Be Said? Artistic
         and Literary Responses to the Holocaust                       291

**12**   God and History: Philosophical and Religious
         Responses to the Holocaust                                    327

**Epilogue: Business as Usual? Ethics after the Holocaust**            **355**

**Notes**                                                              **379**

**A Chronology of Crucial Holocaust-Related Events**                   **453**

**Select Bibliography**                                                **457**

**Index**                                                              **461**

# Preface and Acknowledgments

On 4 May 1961, Dr. Aharon Peretz, a survivor of the Kovno ghetto, gave testimony in Jerusalem during the postwar trial of Adolf Eichmann, one of the Holocaust's chief perpetrators. Peretz described how the Germans rounded up Lithuanian Jews, including several thousand children who were driven to a killing site and then shot to death. He remembered one moment in particular:

> A mother whose three children had been taken away—she went up to this automobile and shouted at the German, "Give me the children," and he said, "You may have one." And she went up into that automobile, and all three children looked at her and stretched out their hands. Of course, all of them wanted to go with their mother, and the mother didn't know which child to select and she went down alone, and she left the car.[1]

No one book can fully encompass the Holocaust and its legacy, because that catastrophe included an incomprehensible number of episodes akin to the one that Dr. Peretz recalled in May 1961. Each of those events differed, because men, women, and children perished one by one, just as every killer, bystander, or rescuer was an individual with all the complex relationships and circumstances that such identity entails. As Charlotte Delbo, a survivor of Auschwitz, reminds us in the passage selected for this book's epigraph, we can know where Auschwitz is located. We can even know much about what happened there, how and why those things took place, but our knowledge is not without remainder. "This much they know," she wrote; "as for the rest they think they know."[2] The Holocaust compels attention. When given the full attention its gravity deserves, that disaster also requires considered judgment, lest we think we know more than we do or can.

The Holocaust and its legacy are so vast that, at best, there can be only selective narratives and analyses about it. Done well, they more or less weave together reliable glimpses, documented perspectives, focused but not all-embracing slices from a destruction process that swept through a continent from 1933 to 1945. This melancholy work is done not to achieve an unattainable mastery but, as the historian Raul Hilberg says, "lest all be relinquished and forgotten."[3]

People study the Holocaust because it happened, but not only for that reason. They study it for ethical, political, and religious reasons that are rooted in a longing for a safer and more humane world. After Auschwitz, that longing no longer permits much in the way of optimistic talk about "civilization." Unless that word is redeemed by deeds of caring and justice, silence about civilization's grandeur can only be broken with mournful irony. *Approaches to Auschwitz* shows how easy it is for decency and good intentions to fail against ruthless power that is intent on genocidal destruction. When the killing stopped, moreover, the Holocaust was not over. So quickly, and in such devastating ways, the Holocaust swept away good things. Its legacy, and the purpose this book tries to serve, should be a never-forgotten warning to take nothing good for granted.

Since 1987, when *Approaches to Auschwitz* was first published, scholarship about the Holocaust has grown immensely in quantity, scope, and complexity. It reflects daunting questions, which, in turn, create heated controversies that writing about the Holocaust can scarcely avoid: Where to begin? What to emphasize or leave out? How strongly to claim that one's account explains what took place? Where to end, and what, if anything, to conclude? Keeping those questions in mind, this second edition has been thoroughly revised so that the book not only reflects the best scholarship at the time of our writing but also focuses the authors' current thinking about the history and implications of the Holocaust. Between us, that thinking has been going on for decades. We believe that it has been enhanced by the fact that one of us is Jewish, the other Christian.

The revision can be compared to the remodeling of an older house. The foundation stands, the exterior walls remain, the basic structure holds, but the interior has been extensively reworked and upgraded. This edition places renewed emphasis on religious factors in the roots of the Holocaust and on the ethical, religious, and political implications of the Holocaust as well. The latter themes are illustrated in some detail by the book's interpretation of the responses of the churches during the Holocaust. These features distinguish *Approaches to Auschwitz* from many other books about the Holocaust. At the same time, the second edition devotes more attention than the first to Holocaust history, including an emphasis on the way in which the Holocaust was embedded in World War II. Updated sections on film, art, and literature can be found as well. We trust that the book will be of interest to the general reader, but it is designed especially for undergraduate teaching. With twelve chapters, plus prologue and epilogue, the book can fit well into semester-length courses.

We owe thanks to a great many people who helped to make this new edition possible. They include scores of scholars—many of them named in the notes and bibliography—whose research informed out understanding. In addition, friends who have used the book in their teaching urged us to recreate it. Alan Berger, Carol Rittner, and especially Michael Berenbaum were particularly helpful in that regard. Susan Zuccotti, as well as Berenbaum, read the manuscript carefully and helped us to polish it. We thank them for encouragement and support, underscoring that in no way are they accountable for the book's deficiencies, which are entirely our responsibility. At Westminster John Knox Press, our editors, Jack Keller, Daniel Braden, Donald McKim, and Hermann Weinlick, provided the sound counsel and expert assistance that nurtured our writing and brought it to completion. At Claremont McKenna College, the Gould Center for Humanistic Studies, directed by Jonathan Petropoulos, kindly provided funds for the book's index. The art historian Betty Rogers Rubenstein generously contributed her expertise by writing on Holocaust art for chapter 11, which focuses on artistic and literary responses to the Holocaust. She also suggested that Roman Halter's art should grace the book's cover. A remarkable artist, Halter is a Holocaust survivor who endured the Lodz ghetto, Auschwitz-Birkenau, Stutthoff, and slave labor in a Dresden munitions factory, where he survived the bombing on 13–14 February 1945. "The Last Journey," his stained-glass version of a 1944 Nazi photograph from Auschwitz-Birkenau, depicts a Jewish grandmother walking with little children, including perhaps an infant cradled under her arm. They are on the way to death in the gas chambers.[4] No words, no book, can ensure that journeys akin to that one will ever end, but we have written with the conviction that they must and the hope that they will.

# Prologue

# What Is the Holocaust?

*Within the ranks of the perpetrators, the one premise that shaped all the orders, letters, and reports from 1933 to 1945 was the maxim that Jews must be removed from German spheres of life.*
Raul Hilberg, *Sources of Holocaust Research: An Analysis*

On 23 February 1930, an erstwhile law student died in Berlin at the age of twenty-three. Like many other young men in the Germany of his day, Horst Wessel, the son of a Lutheran clergyman, rebelled against his bourgeois upbringing and in 1926 joined the *Nationalsozialistische Deutsche Arbeiterpartei* (NSDAP), the National Socialist German Workers' Party. As a member of the Nazi Party's "Brownshirts" (*Sturmabteilung* [SA], storm troopers), Wessel's political activities included participation in bloody street battles with Communists. Meanwhile, in 1929 Wessel had moved in with Erna Jaenicke, a prostitute with whom he was having an affair. When their rent went unpaid, the couple's landlady, a Frau Salm, sought to evict them by enlisting help from her late husband's Communist associates. Much more than an eviction took place. When Wessel opened the door on the night of 14 January 1930, he was confronted by Jaenicke's former pimp, Ali Höhler, a member of the rival Communist Red Front Fighters' League. Höhler's gunshot left Wessel mortally wounded.[1]

History frequently pivots around small events. Horst Wessel's demise is a case in point. His death would have been inconsequential, had he not written a poem sometime before. Entitled "*Die Fahne hoch*" (Raise high the flag), the poem had been published in the 23 September 1929 issue of *Der Angriff* (The attack), a Nazi newspaper edited by Joseph Goebbels. Set to music, Wessel's verse had also become part of a Nazi marching song. While Wessel lay dying, Goebbels, the mastermind behind Nazi propaganda, saw an opportunity to turn a lovers' triangle

1

into martyrdom and political power. Wessel's lyric paid homage to those who had given their lives for the Nazi cause. Arranging to have the "Horst Wessel Song" sung at the conclusion of a political rally, Goebbels envisioned that it would become the Nazis' battle hymn. He was correct.

That same February, a Jewish doctor named Sigmund Freud went about his work in Vienna. Only a few weeks earlier, he had finished a small book that would be among his most famous. In English it is called *Civilization and Its Discontents*. Among its final words are these: "Men have gained control over the forces of nature to such an extent that with their help they would have no difficulty in exterminating one another to the last man."[2] Freud was also correct. Horst Wessel's song would help to prove the point.

As the Nazis sang in the Berlin *Sportpalast* on a winter night in 1930, an infant destined to be at least as well known as Freud was fast asleep.[3] The revolution glimpsed by Freud's premonition and rallied by Wessel's song would profoundly mark this Jewish girl, whose name was Anne Frank. Years later she lived for months in her Amsterdam hiding place writing the diary that is still read by millions. One of its last entries, dated 15 July 1944, testifies, "I see the world being slowly transformed into a wilderness, I hear the approaching thunder that, one day, will destroy us too, I feel the suffering of millions." Anne Frank also affirmed that "people are truly good at heart," and she went on to say that her gloomy forecast would not be the last word. "When I look up at the sky," she wrote, "I somehow feel that everything will change for the better, that this cruelty too shall end, that peace and tranquility will return once more."[4] Anne Frank was correct, too, but how far is not clear. She was right about the gloomy part, as her deportation to Auschwitz and eventual death in the Nazi camp at Bergen-Belsen bear witness. As for the rest, perhaps the best one can say is that the jury is still out.

Horst Wessel, Sigmund Freud, and Anne Frank—these people never met. Yet they are linked together in ways that we ignore at our peril in the twenty-first century, which has the potential to be even more lethal than the blood-drenched twentieth century turned out to be. What links them is the Holocaust.

## WHAT DOES THE HOLOCAUST SIGNIFY?

World War II claimed the lives of fifty million people, more than half of them civilians.[5] Operating largely under the cover of war, the Third Reich's system of concentration camps, murder squadrons, and killing centers took millions of defenseless human lives, between five and six million Jews among them.[6] As we understand the Holocaust, it was the systematic, state-organized persecution and murder of approximately six million Jews by Nazi Germany and its collaborators. The Nazi intent was to rid Europe, if not the world, of Jews. Hitler went far in fulfilling that goal; two-thirds of Europe's Jews were dead by the end of World War II. Thus, the Holocaust refers primarily, but not exclusively, to the Nazi destruction of the European Jews, because Nazi Germany's murderous policies destroyed millions of other defenseless people, including Roma and Sinti (Gypsies) and Polish citizens as well as homosexuals, the handicapped, Jehovah's Witnesses, and other political and religious dissidents within Germany itself.[7] For racial, cultural, or political reasons, members of these groups became Nazi targets in ways that were related to but not identical with the Jews' fate under Hitler. Additionally, in their German captivity, which ruthlessly disregarded international conventions pertaining to civilized treatment of war prisoners, an estimated 3.3 million Soviet POWs lost their lives to starvation, inadequate medical treatment, forced marches, or outright murder.[8] Some further allusions to Freud, Wessel, and Anne Frank will clarify these facts and illustrate the scope of meaning reflected by the word *Holocaust* in the following chapters.

The event designated as the Holocaust is named by more than one term. Many of Horst Wessel's peers, for example, took part in what the Nazis eventually called the Final Solution (*die Endlösung*). Wessel's friends had lived through a period when hopes for imperial expansion were shattered by Germany's humiliating defeat in World War I. The aftermath was political and economic instability coupled with yearnings for a renewed sense of German identity, honor, and empire. The Nazis' political instincts capitalized on these conditions. Nazi tactics included an ideological campaign that implicated the Jews in all of Germany's problems. Jews, the Nazis proclaimed, were undesirable and unwanted.

Nazi propaganda accorded Jews this status not because they were impoverished. Nor were Germany's Jews uneducated, unskilled, or unproductive. People can be unwanted for those reasons, of course, and some of the Nazis' Jewish victims fitted into such categories. Most, especially in Germany, did not. On the contrary, they were able men and women. Thus, the Holocaust reveals that it can be as easy for talented people to lose their places in the world as it is for those who cannot cope with civilization's complexities. Even those who facilitate and adapt to the modern world may be spewed out by it. Whenever and wherever a definable population—for whatever reason—can find no viable place in the society it inhabits, that population's very existence may be at risk. In the Nazis' case, their antisemitic racism determined that Jews should have no place in German society. That determination culminated in the Final Solution.

The Nazi outlook insisted that Germany faced a serious "Jewish question" that had to be answered. One way or another, it was claimed, the Jews were a population that had to be eliminated from German society. From the Nazi perspective, the elimination of an unwanted and undesirable Jewish presence required governmental takeover and intervention. Even then, however, what it would mean to solve Germany's "Jewish problem" was not completely clear, for as governments implement solutions aimed at population elimination, the measures can range from segregation and incarceration, to eviction and expulsion, and ultimately to outright extermination. The Nazis planned brutal treatment for groups they labeled inferior, including even German citizens who were physically or mentally enfeebled, but in the Nazis' racial hierarchy, Jews were the lowest of the low. After experimenting with various population-riddance techniques that failed to achieve the desired results, the National Socialists unblinkingly embraced the most radical alternative to answer their Jewish question—the Final Solution, which decreed systematic, state-sponsored total annihilation.

The line that moved from Horst Wessel's song to a clear definition of "the Jewish problem" in Germany, then to gas chambers in death camps, was neither simple nor direct. As Karl Schleunes describes it, the road to Auschwitz was twisted.[9] But a road there was, and interpreting the signs that map it shows why and how an entire people came to be so unwanted that no effort was spared to destroy them. Such investigations pertain not only to the 1930s and 1940s. They take us back into the European and American past and then forward to our own day and beyond as we seek to identify peoples and forces struggling through scenarios that have striking similarities. The Holocaust points to a reality larger than itself. By referring to the Nazis' particular attempt to destroy the Jews, the term also puts us on the trail of tracking forces still with us that can bring to power those who find systematic population elimination—more or less radical as circumstances require or permit—to be the most expedient means for achieving "solutions" for the problems that they perceive.

*Shoah*, a Hebrew word, also names the Holocaust. The preferred name in Israel and in some European countries, it signifies catastrophic destruction. According to Uriel Tal, *shoah* was used by Polish Jews as early as 1940 to designate their plight under Hitler. The roots of this word, however, go back much further. Indeed, they are biblical. The term is found in the Psalms, in Isaiah's prophecies, and in Job's lamentations. Its meanings are multiple. Sometimes the word denotes dangers that threaten Israel from surrounding nations; at other times it refers to individual distress and desolation. If catastrophic destruction is signified in each case, Tal argues, "all Biblical meanings of the term *shoah* clearly imply Divine judgment and retribution."[10] Those ancient meanings, however, are called into question by the Final Solution. In contemporary usage *shoah* conveys the old sense of destruction but adds profound elements of fragmentation and questioning where religious tradition is concerned.

Freud's best-known book about religion is *The Future of an Illusion*. "In the long run," he wrote, "nothing can withstand reason and experience, and the contradiction religion offers to both is only too palpable." If Freud believed it would be "an indubitable advantage to leave God out of the question altogether, and to admit honestly the purely human origin of all cultural laws and institutions," he also knew that religion had long been a ruling factor in human society. In particular, he acknowledged, religion had "contributed much toward restraining the asocial instincts."[11] But not enough, Freud believed, for even the best intentions toward mastery of aggression and self-destruction created hostility as well.

It is moot whether one can leave God out of the question altogether where *shoah* is concerned, but it is certain that religion must occupy a central place in any reliable scholarly approach to Auschwitz. It must do so from a perspective that incorporates history, politics, economics, and sociology. Such a perspective can be developed only by taking seriously what men and women have believed about themselves, their people, and their destinies. At least in that sense, God is present in the *Shoah*. Here again the particularity of an event—the loss of six million Jewish lives under Hitler, as well as the loss of millions of other people—sends out waves that move back and forth in time. The *Shoah* prods one to understand Jewish singularity, a history of volatile anti-Jewish sentiment in Christianity, and the impact of the Holocaust, not only on Jewish and Christian religious consciousness that follows after, but also on human self-understanding generally.

The Nazis named the Holocaust before the worst took place. While their Final Solution was under way, its Jewish targets sensed catastrophe, usually too late, and they were correct: the *Shoah* happened. Both the Final Solution and the *Shoah* are more commonly known as the Holocaust—the term began to achieve prominence in the 1950s—but like the others, that name did not appear out of thin air either. Contemporary dictionaries define *holocaust* as a great or complete devastation or destruction, especially by fire. Its definitions indicate that *holocaust* can also refer to any mass slaughter or reckless destruction of life. The term has a long, nonreligious history. In secular contexts, however, the word was sparsely used; it tended to be reserved for especially disastrous events. By no means was it explicitly invented to designate Nazi Germany's mass murder of the Jews.

The story behind the word *holocaust*, however, does involve other features—problematic ones, some would say. *Holocaust* is derived from the Greek *holókaustos*, meaning "burnt whole." Once more, biblical roots become important. In the Septuagint, a Greek translation of Jewish Scripture dating from the third century B.C.E. (before the common era), *holókauston* is used for the Hebrew *olah*, which literally means "what is brought up." (In the later Latin Vulgate translation, the biblical term becomes *holocaustum*.) In context, the Hebrew *olah* refers to a sacrifice, often specifically to "an offering made by fire unto the Lord." These connections can suggest that the destruction of the European Jews has special religious significance, but that outlook, to say the least, is contested. Some critics protest that the Final Solution should not be called the Holocaust precisely because the latter term conveys religious connotations that are repulsive. Walter Laqueur, for example, is not alone when he finds *Holocaust* a "singularly inappropriate" name, arguing tersely that "it was not the intention of the Nazis to make a sacrifice of this kind, and the position of the Jews was not that of a ritual victim."[12] Nevertheless, Laqueur also acknowledges that "in the English-speaking world the word is so deeply rooted that it is impractical to deviate from it."[13] No name can do justice to the destruction of Jewish life attempted by Nazi Germany. It is practical to use the term *Holocaust* because this disaster was an unprecedented mass slaughter in which the burning of bodies and the scattering of ashes revealed the perpetrators' conviction that Jews should disappear without a trace.

Horst Wessel and Sigmund Freud testify that history involves powerful social forces that dwarf individuals. Those powers of domination must be studied on a macrocosmic level if they are to be grasped adequately at all. At the same time, history's drama is also enacted by individual persons. What those individuals choose and fail to choose, how they act and fail to act make a great deal of difference. Individuals have an identity because of the social reality into which they are born, but how they shape their identities in response can vastly alter those circumstances. The stories of people who survived and people who died—victims, killers, rescuers, and those who stood by—are essential, too, for trying to fathom the Holocaust. Only by keeping individuals in focus can one avoid the oversimplifications of sweeping generalizations or identify the exceptions that prove a rule.

The Holocaust, then, means Final Solution and catastrophe. Strictly speaking, it neither begins nor ends with Jews. The history of human conduct is longer than that of Jewish history; the implications of both reach well beyond Jewish destiny, too. And yet Jewish particularity remains at the center of this story. Jewish contributions to civilization, and the prices paid for them, show what the scope of human conduct can be and prod us to ask, For what is it worthwhile to live or die?

## HOW HAS THE HOLOCAUST BEEN INTERPRETED?

Names for an event have different meanings. Likewise, the Holocaust itself calls forth varied interpretations. Even to mention all of them here is impossible, but consider some of the more important ones to delineate further the perspective found in this book. The burgeoning scholarship and reflection on the Holocaust appear in many languages. No one can master them all, but in English works at least three main trends should be singled out. They correspond to our themes of Final Solution, catastrophe, and mass slaughter designed to eliminate Jewish life without a trace.

First, approaching the Holocaust as Final Solution puts a priority on documenting the steps that brought Adolf Hitler and his Nazi followers to power and then took Nazi Germany to war and the annihilation of Jewish life in Auschwitz and other killing centers. Few works have been more influential in this regard that Raul Hilberg's *The Destruction of the European Jews* (1961, revised 1985 and 2003). Hilberg concentrates on the German side. His analysis implicates virtually every segment of German society in a process that moved from definition of its Jewish targets to concentration and seizure of them and then to their ultimate destruction. Although they differ from Hilberg in significant ways, younger interpreters continue to explore paths related to those he pioneered. Often at odds, Christopher Browning (*Ordinary Men*, 1992, and *Nazi Policy, Jewish Workers, German Killers*, 2000) and Daniel Goldhagen (*Hitler's Willing Executioners*, 1996) belong in this tradition, and so does Robert Gellately (*Backing Hitler*, 2001) along with a recent generation of German historians—Götz Aly, Wolfgang Benz, Ulrich Herbert, Christian Gerlach, Peter Longerich, and Dieter Pohl among them—whose writings are becoming better known and more influential in the English-speaking world. Some scholars situate the Holocaust in the broad contexts of Western civilization and European history, an approach illustrated by

Jonathan Glover (*Humanity: A Moral History of the Twentieth Century*, 1999) and Mark Mazower (*Dark Continent: Europe's Twentieth Century*, 1998). Others place the Holocaust specifically within the history of the Third Reich or World War II. Michael Burleigh (*The Third Reich: A New History*, 2000) and Gerhard Weinberg (*A World at Arms: A Global History of World War II*, 1994) are only two examples. Still others—for instance, Doris Bergen (*War and Genocide: A Concise History of the Holocaust*, 2002), Debórah Dwork and Robert Jan van Pelt (*Holocaust: A History*, 2002), John Weiss (*Ideology of Death: Why the Holocaust Happened in Germany*, 1996), and Robert Wistrich (*Hitler and the Holocaust*, 2001) provide significant overviews, but the emphasis placed on the Holocaust still comes primarily from a perspective oriented toward Nazi aims and policies.

Another strand of this historical scholarship places much more emphasis on Jewish experience. If Hilberg and his successors drive home the National Socialists' ability to overcome nearly every obstacle that stood between them and annihilation of the Jews, historians such as Yehuda Bauer (*A History of the Holocaust*, 1982, revised 2001, and *Rethinking the Holocaust*, 2001), Michael Berenbaum (*The World Must Know*, 1993), Lucy Dawidowicz (*The War against the Jews*, 1975), Saul Friedländer (*Nazi Germany and the Jews*, 1997), and Martin Gilbert (*The Holocaust: A History of the Jews of Europe during the Second World War*, 1985, and *Never Again: A History of the Holocaust*, 2000) show how the Jews, against all odds, tried to continue their Jewish lives. Collectively, all of these studies rightly maintain that a firm grounding in history—broadly conceived to include politics, economics, and social change—is fundamental in any sound approach to the Holocaust.

When initially confronted by the horror of Auschwitz, one may ask, how could it happen? Historical research reveals how and, to a large extent, why the Final Solution *did* happen. The story is millennia long. In special ways, religion marks it indelibly, bringing the makings of catastrophe. Those ingredients lodge in tensions between two groups, one spawned from the other, who have seen themselves as God's chosen people. A second major trend of Holocaust-related scholarship focuses specifically on these Jewish-Christian relationships. It tends to see the Holocaust as the culmination of religiously inspired antisemitism.[14] Historians of religion, philosophers, and theologians—some Jewish, others Christian—such as Victoria Barnett, Doris Bergen, Harry James Cargas, A. Roy and Alice Eckardt, Emil Fackenheim, Susannah Heschel, Steven Katz, David Kertzer, Franklin Littell, John Pawlikowski, Paul van Buren, and Robert Wistrich have made major contributions to this part of Holocaust studies, which also includes the perennially "hot" topic of the role of the churches, and especially the Vatican, during the Holocaust years.

The past casts shadows on the future of religion. Littell, for example, finds the Christian tradition so drenched in guilt as to face an unprecedented credibility crisis.[15] Meanwhile Jewish religious leadership continues to share Fackenheim's perplexity concerning "God's presence in history."[16] What is at stake in such studies, however, is not restricted to religion alone. To play a variation on Freud's

theme, human consciousness may encounter multiple illusions via the Holocaust, religious factors counting as only one of their dimensions, and the future
may not be too bright as a result. Science, medicine, law, technology, education,
professional skills of all kinds—these were also instrumental in unleashing catastrophe during the Third Reich. Religious influences figured into those relationships, just as today uncertainty about where human power may lead is attended
by clashing gods who vie for loyalty.

Loyalty and competition for it were key ingredients that led to mass slaughter and thus to the acts of individuals. So a third major body of reflection on the
Holocaust deals with the particular men and women who enacted and went
through the process of destruction. Biographies of Hitler, for instance, continue
to multiply. Ian Kershaw's two-volume *Hitler* (1998, 2000) is only one striking
example. Additional insight about the perpetrators can be obtained not only from
the volumes of court proceedings from postwar trials such as those at Nuremberg, but also—to name only four examples—from the writings of Rudolph Höss
and from interviews conducted with Franz Stangl, men who managed the killing
centers at Auschwitz and Treblinka respectively, as well as from the diary of Joseph
Goebbels and the calendar of Heinrich Himmler, the latter the Nazi leader who
has aptly been called the Holocaust's architect.

Several memoirs by Jewish survivors, such as Elie Wiesel's *Night* and Primo
Levi's *Survival in Auschwitz* (both appeared in the late 1950s), have become clas-
sics. Their relatively early accounts are now joined by a wide range of testimony—
one remarkable case is Victor Klemperer's two-volume diary, *I Will Bear Witness*,
which was published in English in 1998–99—including tens of thousands of oral
histories that have been recorded by the Survivors of the Shoah Visual History
Foundation and other archives. Significantly, the memoirs and scholarship about
them include the perspectives of women much more than was the case as recently
as the early 1990s. Charlotte Delbo and Etty Hillesum, Ida Fink and Gerda Klein
are only a few of the women whose eyewitness testimony sheds indispensable
light on the Holocaust and its legacy. Fact is illuminated by fiction too. Story-
tellers such as Tadeusz Borowski (*This Way for the Gas, Ladies and Gentlemen*,
1959); Imre Kertész (*Fateless*, 1975), who won the 2002 Nobel Prize in Literature; Carl Friedman (*Nightfather*, 1991); and Sara Nomberg-Przytyk (*Auschwitz:
True Tales from a Grotesque Land*, 1985) provoke and deepen their readers' inquiry
and understanding. They do so by exploring the Jews' struggle to survive as well
as the fact that the Holocaust left its mark on non-Jews and on generations that
live beyond the years of those who inflicted, perished, or narrowly escaped mass
murder.

The Holocaust is defined largely by the stories that are told about it. Whether
factual or fictional, historically documented or symbolically expressed, these narratives from and about individual persons remain to check and to be balanced by
the insights provided by scholarly treatments that take a broader view. With their
emphasis on particularity, such approaches are a necessary ingredient to explo-
rations of the Holocaust as Final Solution and catastrophe.

## HOW SHALL WE INTERPRET THE HOLOCAUST?

The Holocaust is too vast for any book to describe completely, any theory to explain fully, or for any interpretation to grasp entirely. This event defies every effort to produce a master narrative about it. As a result, varied approaches to the Holocaust are unavoidable and necessary. Even if none can complete the inquiry that the Holocaust's questions make essential, a plurality of perspectives can help to advance comprehension that will always fall short of finality. Governed by this understanding, *Approaches to Auschwitz* begins in antiquity.

The Third Reich lasted from 1933 to 1945. Auschwitz, which in key ways epitomizes the Holocaust's lethal climax, functioned as a labor and death camp from 1940 through 1944. But these momentous years were centuries in the making. So it is crucial to keep this question in mind: Why did the Holocaust fail to occur before the 1940s? For most of their history, Jews have been viewed as an alien presence by those around them. Hence, the first major part of this book, which tracks the historical roots of the Holocaust, begins in the Greco-Roman and early Christian worlds, specifically with the Jewish experience of being "outsiders" in those circumstances. While emphasizing the objective innocence of the victims, plus the hideous disparity between the merit of Jewish life and its treatment by non-Jews (Gentiles) in the West, we find—contrary to some conventional interpretations—that it is less helpful to regard Jews as passive objects on whom Gentiles have visited antisemitism irrationally than to see the historical situation as a seething conflict involving active parties on all sides. In a word, Jews and Christians could not help but disconfirm each other's religious traditions. The unhappy effects of that tragic fact escalated and mutated until the world reached Auschwitz.

Since the triumph of Christianity over Rome in the fourth century, Raul Hilberg emphasizes, there have been three fundamental anti-Jewish policies: conversion, expulsion, and annihilation. "The second," says Hilberg, "appeared as an alternative to the first, and the third emerged as an alternative to the second. . . . The missionaries of Christianity had said in effect: You have no right to live among us as Jews. The secular rulers who followed had proclaimed: You have no right to live among us. The German Nazis at last decreed: You have no right to live."[17]

This dynamic will become evident as we outline the Jewish situation in Europe from the triumph of Christianity, through the Middle Ages, to the eve of the French Revolution. Although constantly on precarious ground religiously and culturally, owing to their refusal to embrace the dominant majority's Christian ways, Jews had some security because those same ways mitigated against systematic mass murder. Perhaps even more importantly, we shall suggest, at this time the Jews of Europe could find a place where they were an economically complementary population. They were not, however, destined indefinitely to be an elite minority that filled needed commercial and professional roles left vacant by the dominant population.

Modernization of Europe's economy was, as some have called it, the great transformation.[18] Displacing the social structures and mores of subsistence agriculture, a revolutionary form of human consciousness evolved toward preeminence from the sixteenth century onward. Bent on liberation from the dead hand of the past, its yearnings for progress emphasized organization, industrialization, and specialization—all driven by the Enlightenment's rational methods, which stressed efficiency and cost-effectiveness. Modernization brought forth mass production, but that activity not only resulted in more manufactured goods and wider trade than ever before; it also enhanced the food supply. Populations grew, though not necessarily because they were needed. In fact, the great transformation made overpopulation a persistent threat to the system, especially in a changing value environment that increasingly calculated the worth of everything by the price it could fetch in the marketplace, an outcome that tended to make money more important than persons.

One outcome was the denial in practice, if not in theory, that there is anything sacred about human life. Rather, it is simply another component to be calculated in cost-benefit analysis. Such thinking, unfortunately, contains no credible restraint to its own excesses. Furthermore, vast dislocations attended the modernizing process. In addition to mass production, it led to mass migration and mass politics. In due course, modernization became a factor—by no means the only factor but a significant one nonetheless—in mass murder. Steps on the way were found in political upheavals such as the French Revolution. In some regions, these Enlightenment efforts emancipated the Jews, but the irony of the long run was that no group would pay more dearly for the modernization of Europe's economy and society than the Jews.

Having traced some of the early historical roots of the Holocaust in part 1, we focus more explicitly on Nazi-Jewish relations in part 2. Although significant exceptions to the rule could be found, Jews, largely helpless to prevent their fate, became increasingly unwanted during the nineteenth century, their competition in the marketplace unwelcome because, official decrees to the contrary notwithstanding, Jews were still an alien minority. By the end of the nineteenth century, those attitudes were reflected in biological, racial, and nationalistic theories that transmuted older anti-Jewish sentiments into new forms of political anti-semitism. They were also manifest in a series of devastating Russian pogroms carried out in the 1880s with the blessing of a state that wanted to rid itself of Jews. The political leaders of czarist Russia in the late nineteenth century pursued a goal not entirely different from that of the Nazis. Only the means employed were less radical and less systematic. The social, economic, and political forces unleashed by accelerating modernization in Europe had already moved far along to seal the fate of European Jewry several decades in advance of Hitler's rise to power. Meanwhile, population pressures made the last quarter of the nineteenth century a period of mass emigration from Europe generally. Open frontiers around the world, many pioneered by imperialistic interests, provided essential safety valves. But as these openings disappeared in the twentieth century, European space for Jews, emancipated or not, would become disastrously hard to find.

Engineered by the Prussian leader Otto von Bismarck, the unification of Germany in 1871, coupled with the Russian pogroms of 1881, formed one fateful watershed for Europe's Jews. World War I created another; inaugurating the twentieth century as the most lethal thus far in human history, it made massive killing a politically acceptable method for modern states to use in restructuring society. In addition, when the Germans interpreted their own defeat as a "stab in the back" fomented by a Jewish world conspiracy, the stage was set for the beginnings of the Nazi Party and the emergence of its political messiah, Adolf Hitler. As the Great Depression struck, European nationalism never waned. Fascism was on the rise, and Jewish circumstances became increasingly problematic. Particularly in Poland, which had by far the largest Jewish population of any European nation between the two world wars, the situation for Jews worsened every year. Gradually caught in the closing vise between a Poland that wanted its Jews to leave and a Germany that would eventually murder them, millions of eastern European Jews learned to their sorrow what the Jewish political scientist Hannah Arendt would mean when, following Max Weber, she referred to Jews as a pariah people.[19] That category consists of persons with no country of their own, who may be granted privileges but lack the fundamental rights guaranteed to a society's full members. Hitler's regime removed every privilege from the Jews' pariah status. Without political citizenship, stripped of their membership in any community ready and able to defend their rights, the Jews had no rights whatsoever, a fact that bears a sober warning: no consideration of abstract "human rights" impeded the National Socialists' state-sponsored program of systematic population elimination. The Jews became an utterly unwanted population to be diminished by expulsion, if not by death. Before Hitler finished, approximately six million of the nine million Jews in Europe in 1939 were dead, and more than 90 percent of Poland's 3.3 million Jews perished. Our study of the Holocaust therefore convinces us that it is imperative to explore how and why a people can become so helplessly isolated. Failure to do so obscures both the Holocaust's unprecedented character and how that uniqueness is part of a much larger and continuous social pattern.

When the Nazis came to power in 1933, they counted the fully Jewish population of Germany to be approximately 550,000—about 1 percent of the nation's total—including some 50,000 nonreligious Jews who still fitted Nazi racial criteria. Beyond those numbers were an estimated additional 750,000 Jewish-Germans of mixed ancestry, many converts to Christianity among them. The Nazis' commitment to antisemitism was clear, but their practical policies toward Jews were not. It is one thing to have antisemitic feelings and quite another to make those feelings effective in a political regime. Hence it took time for the Nazis to work out a coherent anti-Jewish program.[20] From 1933 to 1938 hoodlum violence mixed with "paper violence," but increasingly the latter proved decisive in ways that the former could not. With the help of an expanding bureaucracy to expedite such matters, German Jews were dismissed from government positions, eliminated from professions and from commerce, and stripped of basic legal protection. The objective behind this paper violence was not harassment and degradation for their own sake, but rather to drive Jews out of Germany, albeit with as little as possible in their possession.

The outbreak of World War II in September 1939 required new strategies because it foreclosed opportunities for expulsion of Jews and eventually brought millions of additional Jews under German authority in eastern Europe and the Soviet Union. From the Nazi viewpoint, this war was a "holy" struggle aimed at giving the Germanic peoples their rightful dominion over the European continent. Populations that did not belong were either to serve Germans as slaves or to be eliminated or both.[21] As mobile death squadrons *(Einsatzgruppen)* fanned out with advancing German troops all along the eastern front, attention behind the lines went to a strategy of ghettoization, which would ultimately feed the slave labor and death camps of the Reich. Nazi Germany destroyed countless victims—for example, Slavs, Poles, Gypsies, Russian prisoners of war, homosexuals, the physically handicapped, and the mentally ill—but the Jews, ranking lowest in Hitler's racial hierarchy, were especially targeted. Nazi Germany's policy toward these people, aimed at total domination, was symbolized by orders "to dig mass graves, strip, climb into the graves, lie down over the layer of corpses already murdered and await the final *coup de grace.*"[22]

Under German domination, the ghettoized Jewish communities had to organize themselves. The dilemma that faced the leadership was how to survive when one could do so neither by total compliance with Nazi commands nor by violent resistance against them. The vast majority of Europe's Jews perished in the process, though not without resistance. Some did survive the ghettos and the camps. The story of their struggle has much to teach us—not least because that struggle took place against a regime that pursued bureaucratically organized, systematic domination that exceeded moral comprehension. The Jews had developed survival strategies of compliance and endurance that had worked against less radical threats in the past. These techniques, sadly, were no match for the power of Hitler's German state. What was unimaginable then but not now—the Final Solution—took place.

Although Nazi Germany did not parade their death camps openly, the extermination of the Jews was no secret either. Dissemination of Holocaust-related news was complicated, however, not only because the Nazi regime suppressed the truth, but also because such reports as did exist could not readily be repeated with impunity or seemed so horrible as to be beyond belief. In short, one could learn the truth and yet disguise, doubt, dismiss, or deny it; and even when one surmised or knew that a report was authentic, questions remained about what, if anything, should or could be done. Thus, the third major portion of our study concentrates on responses to the Holocaust, then and now. That story includes an examination of the ways in which Christian churches reacted to Hitler's policies. Although exceptions exist, a majority of Christian institutions and individuals either stood by as the Holocaust unfolded or actively contributed to the Jews' demise. But if Christian complicity is part of the catastrophe represented by Auschwitz, religious institutions were not alone in failing to do all that they could to alleviate the plight of persecuted minorities. Western governments knew about "the Jewish problem," even talked about it during the 1930s, but generally did little to relax restrictive immigration policies in favor of Jewish refugees. Intent though the Allies were on refusing Hitler victory during the war, serious questions remain as to whether they did everything possible to minimize Nazi Germany's toll on the Jews. Nor were business communities and the professions left with clean hands. Granted new freedom to experiment by the Nazis, German science made unprecedented use of human subjects, destroying most of them in the process. Under Hitler, German industry capitalized on the fact that profit can be made from human misery. It modernized slavery, finding ways to get the most for the least by working people to death. Moreover, the Nazi experiment proved that a highly advanced society, steeped in music, art, philosophy, and literature, is not immune to propaganda that teaches people to kill.

A common reaction greets such revelations with dismay: such realities should not be, but if they did occur they must surely be an aberration, a deviation from the norm. We advance a different thesis. Without question the Holocaust remains shocking, and it is so because it did not have to be. But it is equally important to understand how irresistible the Holocaust was, how rational were the responses of standing by that characterized so many of the institutions and individuals of the Western world. Here we must make a special effort not to be misunderstood. In arguing for the irresistability of the Holocaust and for the rationality of responses of the sort that have been mentioned, our intention is not to condone or to legitimize mass death. Quite the contrary, our points instead are, first, that any tendency to see the Holocaust and the responses concurrent to it as purely contingent or irrational ignores the fact that there was a certain logic, at once forceful and compelling, at work within them. Second, it is crucial to see how the content of that logic developed and unfolded, because only by doing so can one become clear about the modern powers of destruction that threaten human life and about what is necessary to check them.

Nazi Germany laid waste to defenseless life—that much is clear. What is more problematic is whether the Holocaust was a crime and, if so, in what senses. Postwar trials held by the victorious Allies and by the Israelis provide verdicts in the affirmative, but the fact remains that had the Nazis triumphed instead, the world might have concluded otherwise. One issue, then, is whether the reality of law and morality that transcends the boundaries established by political power has itself been victimized by Auschwitz. Practically speaking, answers to that question depend on what individuals and societies believe. True, those beliefs do not determine reality completely, for the existence of God or of normative principles may not depend on us at all. Nonetheless, it does appear that the efficacy of God's reality or of moral principles that govern human conduct may indeed depend on human convictions that God is real and that norms exist which cannot be violated with impunity. In spite of the ultimate defeat of the Nazis, what they did to the Jews is sufficient to drive home a telling point, namely, that the rights of the defeated dead are of precious little consequence. Functionally, normative status belongs much more to decisions governed by power politics and cost-effective economics, which tend to hold nothing sacred unless it is expedient to do so.

Literature, art, and film—some of it produced during the Holocaust, much of it coming after—have much to teach us about such dilemmas and about the struggle that continues to determine what values shall have priority. The Holocaust cannot be encountered without despair over the power of many traditional views about the good, the true, and the beautiful to sustain themselves against the might of human destructiveness. And yet that is not the whole story. Dark though it remains, the Holocaust did not extinguish human goodness, including the perseverance to suffer and die for matters of faith and to survive to fight for the insistence that nobody should be condemned to a fate like the one that befell European Jewry under Hitler. The range of possibility is wide in such matters. The literature, art, and film of the Holocaust help us to explore it and to see something worthwhile about ourselves along the way.

In particular, Holocaust-related literature often raises questions about the silence of God, which reveals once again the centrality of religious factors in understanding the Holocaust. The question is whether belief in God, at least in terms of the ways that Jews and Christians have tended to think about divinity, can be credible after the Holocaust. Put otherwise, the Holocaust appears to be a season of the "death of God," which is not a factual claim but a metaphor, utilizing the vocabulary of religion, to point out the Holocaust's shattering spiritual impact. No sensitive religious thinker can approach Auschwitz without sharing in that experience. How Christians and Jews respond to it, and how their responses affect what they say to one another in a post-Holocaust setting, constitutes an important chapter in the quest for identity undertaken by individuals and groups in a post-Holocaust world. Such a world, to use Max Weber's term, is largely "disenchanted." That is, our lives are not obviously those of children of God, and the powers that actually govern our world are not divine. Rationalization and intellectualization reduce creation to naturalistic categories, moral absolutes to relativistic conventions, and inalienable human rights to boundaries established by those who have the power to define social reality. Although religious conviction lives on after the Holocaust—more intense and authentic in some circles, more extreme and violence-prone in others—there can be little doubt that the Holocaust has left the world more profane and less sacred than before. That fact is not cause for celebration, because it may mean that human life is worth less than it used to be.

Finally, the legacy of the Holocaust is a staggering human agenda for the future. Today's world is one in which the credibility of traditional moral and religious norms has been threatened perhaps beyond repair. And yet this world contains a population that continues to grow enormous. As it does so, the specter of scarcity has not been banished. If the twentieth century was one of "progress," as we were so often told, a more realistic appraisal finds that many of its advances cheapened life and enhanced capabilities and even reasons for destroying it. Do we have the resources, individually and collectively, to check such forces, if not to turn them around? Our book ends by reflecting on those questions.

## WHAT CAN BE DONE?

*3 Governing Theses*

At least three governing theses emerge from the preceding outline of the way in which this book interprets the Holocaust. First, to grasp both the Holocaust's distinctiveness and its place in a larger and continuing social evolution, attention must focus on the fact that some populations have come to be judged so unwanted that attempts to eliminate them follow. Any people may fall into this category. They actually do so when, for any reason, they cannot find a viable role in the society they inhabit. The primary forces that put Jews in this condition within the Third Reich were religious, cultural, and racial. The Jews' very existence was radically incompatible with the racially antisemitic objectives that Nazi Germany pursued once it launched a war of imperialistic expansion that entailed ethnic cleansing and population riddance. When people become sufficiently unwanted, one solution to that problem is expulsion. The Final Solution is to kill them. Second, the Holocaust-as-catastrophe is best characterized by the fact that Nazi Germany revealed a potential for bureaucratically organized, systematic domination that exceeded the comprehension of the liberal, enlightened imagination of the day. That power resulted in a radical state-sponsored program of population elimination, a fact that helps to define the Holocaust's continuities and discontinuities with events before and after. Third, it is crucial to understand that the ensuing destruction of defenseless lives—both by the overt killers and by those who stood by—was "rational," not in terms of some absolute standard of value, but in the sense that it had a compelling logic of its own.

To the extent that these propositions are valid, humankind faces a profoundly problematic future. It includes fundamental uncertainties about morality and law, about state power and "progress," about wealth and well-being, about God and religion, and about unwanted people, an issue that will be exacerbated as the world's population continues to grow and more people cannot find gainful employment. A fourth thesis waits to be found in this labyrinth, and it may be located by reflection on what can be done. One thing that can be done is *genocide,* which was an all-but-inevitable consequence of the National Socialist emphases on antisemitism, German nationalism, and biologically based politics that stressed "racial purity" and conquest of new territory for the German people.[23] Often used in conjunction with the Holocaust, *genocide* is a relatively recent term. It was coined in the 1940s by Raphael Lemkin, a Jewish lawyer who fled from Poland during the Holocaust. Initially defining *genocide* to mean "the destruction of a nation or of an ethnic group," Lemkin observed that the term denoted "an old practice in its modern development," for the plight of the Jews under Hitler was not a simple repetition of past historical patterns.[24]

*"genocide"*

Lemkin played an important role in moving the United Nations to adopt its 1948 Convention on the Prevention and Punishment of the Crime of Genocide. That document defined genocide as

*Def of genocide*

> any of the following acts committed with intent to destroy, in whole or in part, a national, ethnical, racial or religious group, as such: a. Killing members of the group; b. Causing serious bodily or mental harm to members of the group; c. Deliberately inflicting on the group conditions of life calculated to bring about its physical destruction in whole or in part; d. Imposing measures intended to prevent births within the group; e. Forcibly transferring children of the group to another group.

In addition, the UN Convention provided that punishable acts should include not only genocide itself but also "conspiracy to commit genocide; direct and public incitement to genocide; attempt to commit genocide; complicity in genocide."

*Possible forms of Genocide*

Nazi Germany's destruction of European Jewry was genocide, or nothing could be. That fact, however, did not mean that everyone was satisfied to have the Holocaust classified under such a broad and ambiguous category. Debates still ensue about the Holocaust's unique or unprecedented character.[25] They reflect the fact that genocide covers a multitude of atrocities. The destruction of a nation or of an ethnic group can happen, for example, through deprivation of the means to live and procreate or through outright killing. In short, the methods of genocide can be diverse. Even killing can be slow and indirect—starvation, for instance—as well as quick and immediate. The destruction process, moreover, can be as subtle as it is prolonged. Procedures to curtail birth rates and to increase mortality can have a genocidal effect over time. Eventually a people can also disappear if their culture is decimated by eliminating intellectual leadership, dismantling institutions, and suppressing literacy.[26]

Variations on the theme of genocide also include another basic distinction. There is a difference between genocide understood as the annihilation of a national, religious, or ethnic identity and a more radical form that makes no exceptions for the giving up of such identity through assimilation or conversion. The difference is that between seeing the potential victim of genocide as having a fixed and immutable nature versus one that could be altered by choice or acculturation. Furthermore, genocide covers more or less extreme cases of depopulation. There is no precise measurement of when a people has been functionally destroyed, nor is it always crystal clear when an attempt in that direction is under way.

The Jews were permanent Nazi targets. They lacked any options for changing their identities to guarantee their safety within the Third Reich. Nazi propaganda portrayed the Jews as less than subhuman, in fact, as not human at all. They were considered disgusting, parasitic vermin and at the same time the embodiment of absolute evil that must be eliminated to complete the Nazi drama of salvation. Nazi aims toward the Jews were neither restricted to specific territory nor based primarily on what Jews had done. Simply to be born a Jew sufficed to give one a Nazi death sentence. Hence the Jews were the only group Hitler destined for *total* destruction by unrelenting, mass murder. Arguments for the Holocaust's distinctiveness do not depend primarily on the number of Jewish victims or even on the way in which they were killed. Rather, as Steven T. Katz maintains, the crucial point is that "never before has a state set out, as a matter of intentional principle and actualized policy, to annihilate physically every man, woman, and child belonging to a specific people. . . . Only in the Third Reich was such all-inclusive, non-compromising, unmitigated murder intended."[27]

Hitler and his followers, of course, were not the first people who wanted thoroughly to eliminate the Jews from their midst. The Nazis, however, were quite ready to resort to measures to ensure this end absolutely, whereas their predecessors lacked the wherewithal and/or the resolution to do so. To some extent, the means necessary to achieve the Nazis' goal had ample precedents. The *implementation* of these means to achieve the Final Solution was National Socialism's unprecedented contribution. These considerations make clear that events much milder than the Holocaust can be cases of genocide. At the very least, then, it is appropriate to see Hitler's destruction of the Jews as an extreme case of genocide, as "the farthest point of the continuum." As such, Yehuda Bauer suggests, a special designation is appropriate. "Holocaust" can designate the murder of the Jews carried out by Hitler. It can also be "a generic name for an ideologically motivated planned total murder of a whole people," which, thanks to Hitler, can never again be the unthinkable possibility that it once was.[28] As Bauer sums up the point, "although the Holocaust has no precedent, it could become one."[29]

Only in the twentieth century under Hitler and the Nazis did the direct and total killing of a people biologically and racially identified as Jewish become an implemented human intention. Closely related but not identical practices have been pursued before and since. It is no exaggeration to say ours is an age of genocide, a claim supported by the dreary fact that post-Holocaust genocides have taken place with regularity: Unleashed by Pol Pot and the Khmer Rouge, the Cambodian genocide (1975–79) took two million lives. In 1987–88, Saddam Hussein's regime murdered 100,000 Iraqi Kurds. Serbian onslaughts destroyed 200,000 Bosnians between 1992 and 1995. In Rwanda, Hutus slaughtered 800,000 Tutsis in 1994, a gruesome task accomplished in only a hundred days. It is a good question whether genocide will ever end. Meanwhile, the repetition of genocide drives home Emil Fackenheim's conviction that the Holocaust remains an "epoch-making event."[30] To continue with that theme, consider two prior attempts at population elimination, not to show that one genocide is worse than another—which would be morally abhorrent—but to clarify further some similarities and differences.

First, especially in the nineteenth century, the westward expansion of American hegemony across much of the North American continent wreaked havoc on Native American life. The United States census of 1890, for example, counted an all-time low of about 250,000 Native Americans, down from approximately 400,000 in 1850, and one that some scholars take to be a full 95 percent lower than the North American population of indigenous people in the year 1500,

before European colonization began.[31] Primarily disease, but also forced reloca-
tions (often to marginal land), treaties negotiated and then broken by the American government, military actions—all of these took an immense toll on Native
American life. Some of the devastation is attributable to intentions that are rightly
called genocidal. Nevertheless, the differences between nineteenth-century U.S.
government policies toward Native Americans and Nazi Germany's twentieth-
century policies toward Jews are substantial and significant. Missionizing efforts
toward the Indians, for instance, and the establishment of reservations show that
American intentions—lethal though they often were—stopped short of a Final
Solution, which could have been accomplished if American policy had aimed that
way. Such points are made not to minimize the history of the devastation of
Native American life in the United States, but to clarify how civilization has
"advanced" to new levels of destructive consciousness in our own day.

The Armenian genocide (1915–18), which has been called "the first of the
modern ideologically-motivated genocides,"[32] provides a second benchmark. In
1853 Czar Nicholas I of Russia labeled the Ottoman Empire the "sick man" of
Europe. This crumbling regime had once stretched mightily from Persia to Hungary, but it had become a congeries of nationalities without an adequate base of
unity that could enable it to compete with the nationalistic yearnings that were rising in other European states. The Armenians, a Christian minority in the empire's
predominantly Muslim culture, had long been present in Ottoman territory, especially in the provinces of Anatolia. In the late nineteenth century, as the Armenians began to assert themselves collectively, they increasingly became the targets of
pogroms and massacres unleashed during the reign of Sultan Abdul-Hamid II.
Between 100,000 and 200,000 Armenians were killed in 1895–96 alone.

The empire's continuing decline and the authoritarian rule of Abdul-Hamid
led to revolution in 1908. Promising "Freedom, Justice, Equality, Fraternity," the
ascendancy of the Young Turks and their party, the Committee of Union and
Progress (CUP), was welcomed at first by Turks and Armenians alike. Political
instability remained, however, and by 1913 a dominant CUP faction determined
that the old Ottoman Empire was finished and that the future depended on unit-
ing the Turkish people in a homogeneous nation-state. Finding cultural pluralism
contrary to their modern, ultranationalistic Turkish aims, this group, headed by a
triumvirate of CUP leaders—Enver Pasha, Jemal Pasha, and, most importantly,
Talaat Pasha (also known as Talaat Bey), the chief initiator of the Armenian genocide—seized control in 1913. The resulting dictatorship proved extremely hostile
to the Armenians.

World War I began in August 1914. Concerned to thwart Russian influence,
Turkey entered the conflict as an ally of Germany and Austria-Hungary on
2 November. By the winter of 1914–15, the Turks were in combat against Russian units along a front that included Turkish provinces with a substantial Armenian population. War set the stage for decisive steps in the "Turkification" process.
Following orders issues by Talaat, during the night of 23–24 April 1915—Armenians usually hold their genocide observances on 24 April—some 250 Armenian

*Umbluse of obligation → term to keep in mind*

leaders were rounded up in the capital city of Constantinople (present-day Istanbul) and soon were murdered. Important though it was, this action was not the first in the destruction process. About eight weeks earlier, for example, the CUP's executive committee had telegraphed to regional governors its intention to "exterminate all Armenians living in Turkey, without allowing a single one to remain alive."[33] With Talaat's authorization, deportations that were death sentences targeted the Armenians, who, under the pretext of disloyalty, were either annihilated straightaway or brutally marched off to die in the desert. From Talaat's perspective, there could be no Armenian exceptions, for those who might be "innocent" today could well be "guilty" tomorrow.[34] The available evidence makes clear that this massive destruction of Armenian life was as premeditated as it was thorough. As in all genocidal situations, death statistics cannot be exact, but reliable estimates indicate that, by the end of World War I in 1918, the genocide had destroyed about half of the approximately two million Armenians who had lived in Turkey three years earlier.[35]

The geographic, demographic, and technological scale of Turkish ambitions was more modest than that of the Nazis later, and the Turks lacked the detailed biological and demonizing ideology that informed Hitler's policies toward the Jews. But present in the disaster was a Turkish calculation of means and ends in which premeditated genocide of a radical kind emerged as the remedy of choice. One point to underscore is that genocide, which can scarcely happen without government sponsorship, becomes a remedy of choice—typically under the cover of war—when the powers-that-be deem it desirable or imperative to eliminate a population that challenges the economic, political, cultural, or religious values of the politically dominant group. In this sense, genocide can be *rational*. Lest we be misunderstood, it must be emphasized again that speaking of rationality in this way is *not* to condone genocide. On the contrary, recognition that genocide can be "rational" in the sense of being the most efficient, economical way to solve a "problem" is to raise urgent questions about the "progress" and political power that human energy has achieved.

In the cases of both the Armenians and the Jews, a basic condition for genocide had been in place for centuries. As Helen Fein says, both of these minorities "had been decreed by the dominant group that was to perpetrate the crime to be outside the sanctified universe of obligation—that circle of people with reciprocal obligations to protect each other whose bonds arose from their relation to a deity or sacred source of authority."[36] At least in the case of the Jews, of course, this being "outside" had certain components that for centuries left Jews "inside" as well. Christian consciousness could find a place for Jews as potential converts. Pariah status, therefore, could still leave one a place of sorts; it did not necessarily entail mass death. Yet before National Socialism was through, that lethal outcome followed.

Clearly, the Holocaust had much to do with religion, so much so, in fact, that no account of that event's distinctiveness can be adequate if it neglects several points that go beyond those that have been made above on this topic: First, although the Nazis were anti-Christian racists and the Christian church had stopped well short of systematic annihilation of the Jewish people, Christian hostility toward Jews remains a factor essential for any sound attempt to explain how and why the Holocaust happened. Second, when considered in relation to other genocides before or during the twentieth century, that fact supports the realization that no genocide other than the Holocaust is so deeply connected with the traditions of biblical religion, which have played dominant parts in Western civilization. Third, the links between biblical religion, especially Christianity, and the Holocaust clarify why that catastrophe resonates so profoundly in Western consciousness, non-Jewish as well as Jewish. For those who are affected, one way or another, by biblical religion, what happens to the Jews attracts much more than ordinary interest. For example, there are responses to the Holocaust that reflect what Stephen R. Haynes calls the "witness-people myth," the belief that whatever happens to the Jews, for good or ill, involves God's providential justice.[37] According to Haynes, the witness-people myth is especially "a deep structure in the Christian imagination," which involves "a complex of ideas and symbols that, often precritically and unconsciously, informs ideas about Jews among persons who share a cultural heritage or world view."[38]

To elaborate on Haynes's insights, the witness-people myth has its roots in the biblical doctrine that God chose Israel as God's people by bestowing upon them a covenant stipulating that Israel's fidelity would be rewarded by divine protection as surely as infidelity would be harshly punished. As the next chapter will detail, after the destruction of Jerusalem in the year 70, the rabbis interpreted that event as God's punishment for Israel's failing to keep the commandments. Christian thinkers of the same period agreed that the destruction of Jerusalem was divine punishment, but they argued that the rejection of Jesus as Lord and Messiah was God's motive for allowing the Romans to lay waste Jerusalem and the Holy Temple. According to their interpretations, the Jew could regain God's favor only by truly embracing the Christian faith. As long as the Jews refused, God would condemn them to the suffering, humiliation, and indignity of exile. The suffering of the "witness people" was thus understood as a confirmation of Christian faith, and Jews were seen as *justly* paying a bitter price for their refusal to accept the truth as understood by Christianity.

Given the enormous weight both Judaism and Christianity have placed on the interpretation of Jewish disaster as an expression of God's justice and providence, it was scarcely avoidable that both Jews and Christians would respond to the Holocaust in terms of their respective traditions. It is possible, for instance, for Christians to view the Armenian genocide or the Pol Pot massacres in Cambodia as purely secular events, without raising the question of whether transcendent religious meaning involving "chosen people" is at stake. Not so the Holocaust—almost inevitably it elicits some form of religious interpretation or inquiry, even among many people who are not particularly "religious" but who are still affected by deep structures of imagination such as Haynes identifies in his analysis of the witness-people myth. Never before in Jewish history had there been a catastrophe of such magnitude as the Holocaust. If one believes, as most Jews and Christians do, in a God who is the ultimate author of the drama of history, then the question of divine involvement in the Holocaust is bound to arise. Part of its distinctiveness, then, pivots around the religious impulses that contributed to the Holocaust and the unavoidably religious questions and responses it evokes.

The Armenian genocide and the Jewish Holocaust were distinctively twentieth-century phenomena rooted in ancient traditions that yielded pariah status but also required factors that came to fruition only in recent decades. The Armenian disaster happened because the calculating rationality of the Young Turks determined that the most cost-effective way to establish a modern Turkish state entailed extermination of a minority group. The Nazis made similar calculations to facilitate their aims for the Third Reich. The difference was that their efforts sought a European continent and ultimately an entire world that would be *judenrein,* cleansed of Jews altogether. That goal was practically conceivable only through a sophisticated, bureaucratic orchestration of modern technology and transportation, coupled with a German willingness to commit unspeakable atrocities in the process. Nazi Germany was ready when the twentieth century brought the required elements together in an environment of economic upheaval and global warfare.

Knowing what has been done takes us back to the question what can be done. In particular, is there anything that study about the Holocaust can accomplish to make human life less under threat, to keep genocidal tendencies at bay? Many advocates of study about the Holocaust think that the answer can be yes. Unfortunately, the evidence in favor of such a view is not overwhelming. In the twenty-first century, when the Holocaust is studied by more people than ever before, it is arguable whether the threats of genocidal depopulation have diminished in any significant way.

Study about the Holocaust can provide some understanding of what happened in a particular time and place, why it happened, and how that catastrophe fits into a broader historical pattern. Such understanding, unfortunately, does not constitute a map for the present and the future, at least not one to guarantee that people will stem the tides that kill. It does show something about the strength of those tides—for example, the fact that those who control the use of violence in any political regime can go far in acting with impunity against others within their jurisdiction. Study of the Holocaust, then, should be undertaken without sanguine illusions. It reveals a world more complex, more obsessed with power, more difficult to humanize than one might have guessed before.

The result is that the Holocaust leaves us with tortuous questions. What priorities shall we establish? What ends shall we seek? Which ones are realistic and which ones are naive? What shall count as good? Where can courage be found? Can the individual do anything that matters? Are communities of moral concern significant anymore? What does the twentieth-first century have in store? What will become of humanity?

We started with the question "What is the Holocaust?" It will rise up again at the end, for responses to it hang in suspense. The Holocaust was Final Solution, catastrophe, the massive destruction of defenseless life. All the forces that made it so are still at large in the world, some of them with greater power than ever. The issue is whether there are other powers too, and whether they can muster enough authority to keep the Holocaust from being a prelude to something worse, which ultimately might include extinction of human life through biological and nuclear war.

Horst Wessel's song honored the dead, but it moved men and women to kill. That song may be silent now, but there are others to take its place. They form the counterpoint to Anne Frank's diary, which still moves people to bring out the good that she saw within the human heart. In *Civilization and Its Discontents,* the struggle between Eros and death was Sigmund Freud's concern. His study works in between, trying to discern what makes people love and hate. No one can be sure that attempts to understand the Holocaust will change anything very much, just as Freud could not be sure that his research would have a happy outcome. Indeed the study of final solutions, catastrophes, and massive destruction of defenseless life may produce despair or even help to show the way for turning potential victims into corpses. But without seeing what Horst Wessel's song can do, it is also unlikely that Anne Frank's diary can be read without a sentimentality that obscures its power to yield a more realistic and intense yearning that might conserve life, that might help to foster the right of all persons to a place of dignity within their communities. A fourth thesis that lurks in the Holocaust and its aftermath is this: in spite of all the risks involved in seeking to understand approaches to Auschwitz, we can ill afford not to make the effort.

# PART ONE
# HOLOCAUST ORIGINS

# Chapter 1

# The Jew as Outsider:
# The Greco-Roman
# and Early Christian Worlds

*Jews must always be special cases in products of the Christian imagination, because of the uniquely ambivalent place which the Jewish people inhabit there.*

Stephen R. Haynes, *Reluctant Witnesses:*
*Jews and the Christian Imagination*

Holocaust history begins in a world that had no Jews at all. This fact suggests that the Holocaust leaves some questions beyond answering, for the path that must be followed to explore how Auschwitz came to be will not finally lay to rest issues about why existence is structured so that Auschwitz was possible. Granted, philosophical, scientific, and theological theories are not lacking to respond to that ultimate "Why?" and some of them make more sense than others. But it is also true that the more one learns about the Holocaust, the more understandable it becomes, the more one may be left to wonder. Such claims deny neither that the Holocaust is thoroughly a historical event nor that historical inquiry can go far in explaining how that catastrophe happened. Nevertheless, comprehension of the Holocaust has limits, partly because of our finite and fallible human capacities and partly because the event raises questions and possesses implications that are more than history can contain.

"Man," said the French philosopher Albert Camus, "is not entirely to blame; it was not he who started history; nor is he entirely innocent, since he continues it."[1] Jewish history, which has so distinctively marked the world, is a case in point.[2] The biblical accounts of creation in Genesis, for example, do not identify Adam and Eve as Jews. Whether one takes them to be actual persons or mythic figures, they are man and woman in a pre-Jewish world. And yet that appraisal is not all that must be said, for the story of Adam and Eve is also a Jewish story,

25

one that begins an ancient account that ponders why there are Jews as well as why the world and its human life exist.

## A PEOPLE SET APART

Genesis, the first of five biblical books forming the Pentateuch or the Torah, which constitutes the most important part of Judaism's Scripture, is a blending of oral and written instruction much older than the final written codification that scholars place around 550 B.C.E. Insofar as it hinges on that written testament, Jewish identity is a human creation forged as tribes of diverse origin blended their shared experiences and memories into a unifying, articulated self-consciousness. But these experiences and memories, and even their articulation in a final written form, are not solely the results of conscious choices. Events and experiences happen to people; the forces of life are not completely under human control but instead move in and through us partly at their own bidding. Jews do not account for themselves any more than Adam (man) and Eve (woman) can do so.

Religiously speaking, Jews have affirmed that God accounts for their existence. We shall see some of the awesome effects that have followed from that conviction, but first let us probe a gray zone where the world vacillated between having and not having "the Jewish question." Even the best recent scholarship cannot fix the dates precisely, but biblical history appears to begin between the year 2000 B.C.E. and 1900 B.C.E. At some point in the early centuries of that millennium, tribes of people, eventually led by a patriarchal figure whom tradition calls Abraham, migrated southwestward from Haran in Mesopotamia into the land of Canaan.[3] No one is sure why these journeys occurred, but the biblical tradition asserts it was because Abraham felt that his God had so directed. Lured by a divine promise that he would become the father of a great people, Abraham and his seminomadic followers stopped at the site of Shechem. There, the Bible tells us, God promised to give the surrounding land to Abraham's offspring. Periodic famines kept these people on the move. Under Abraham's successors, Isaac and then Jacob (the latter eventually identified as Israel), they moved about the hill country of Canaan until hard times once more drove them southwest, this time into Egypt.

A majority of modern biblical scholars regard these accounts not as literal historical records but as a reconstruction brought about as a congeries of strangers formed a community by adopting a common faith at Sinai. As the well-known stories of the Exodus and the theophany at Sinai are recounted in Scripture, the "Hebrews" who were enslaved in Egypt appear to share common tribal and religious roots.[4] In reality, the Bible offers ample hints that the group who escaped from Egypt with Moses did not possess a common inheritance. For example, referring to Moses's band in the wilderness, Scripture speaks of "the rabble that was among them" (Num. 11:4).

For several centuries before the Exodus, people from Canaan and Syria had entered Egypt, some as hostages and prisoners of war, some as merchants, and some who had been forced to take up residence in Egypt after engaging in activities hostile to their Egyptian overlords. The name "Hebrews," then, probably designated a number of alien peoples who shared a common condition and social location in Egypt but were from varied backgrounds. Each group of resident aliens retained something of its own identity, especially insofar as their indigenous religious traditions involved elements of ancestor worship. Not all were slaves, but their situation tended to deteriorate over time. In some respects, the situation of the Hebrews was similar to that of members of a modern multiethnic metropolis, in which diverse groups share common problems in the present but remain distinct because of differences in origin, religion, and culture. Once unified, they explained their experience by the cycle of stories involving Abraham, Isaac, Jacob, and even Moses himself. When Moses arrived on the scene, however, the Hebrews were less than Jewish.

Restricted to biblical sources, which draw on oral tradition and myth, biographical data about Moses is imprecise, but it seems likely that he was a charismatic leader born during the reign of Seti I, Pharaoh of Egypt (1308–1290 B.C.E.). Tradition has it that Seti I, fearing that the Hebrew slave population was becoming too large, decided for reasons of security to limit its growth by eliminating all newborn Hebrew males. Moses survived. According to Scripture, he was put into the Nile in a reed basket fashioned by his mother, and then he was discovered and adopted by an Egyptian princess. Although nurtured in the Pharaoh's court, Moses also identified with those who were oppressed. Thus, when he took revenge on an Egyptian soldier who killed one of them, he had to seek refuge in the desert.

Again, no one knows with certainty what happened to Moses as he lived there with a tribe called the Midianites. The Bible, however, speaks of Moses's encountering a strangely burning bush. The bush was not consumed. Instead, as Moses approached to discern it better, he was left with the conviction that the God called Yahweh ("The One who causes to be") was directing him to return to Egypt and to liberate the captives. Conviction was mixed with reluctance and skepticism about this mission, but Moses went, and under his leadership the Hebrew clans fled.

Until this time, the Hebrews probably shared a common yearning for liberation and a common hatred of their overlords but little else. This was enough to unify them for the escape. As soon as they were beyond the reach of the Egyptians, however, a compelling basis for unity beyond shared antipathy and a desire to flee had to be found if the band of fugitives and outcasts was to survive the natural and human hazards of the wilderness. Fortunately, the escape provided a further shared experience, the Exodus itself.

In the ancient Near East, where the distinction between group membership and religious identity was unknown, there could be only one basis for communal unity. The diverse peoples could become a single people only if they were united by a common God who was the author of their shared experience. This new basis for unifying the ethnically diverse band was proclaimed in the prologue to the Ten Commandments: "'I am the LORD your God, who brought you out of the land of Egypt, out of the house of slavery'" (Exod. 20:2).

The God of the new religion, moreover, had to be one whose power exceeded that of Pharaoh, the Egyptian god-king. Nor could any of the diverse peoples among the escapees claim that its particular ancestral god (or gods) was the true God of the entire band without arousing the mistrust and hostility of the others. Ancestral gods were an impediment to unity. The Hebrews shared a common historical experience more than kinship. Only a God who was regarded as the author of their shared experience could unify them. The Bible reflects this emphasis: "'You shall have no other gods before me. . . . for I the LORD your God am a jealous God'" (Exod. 20:3, 5).

Yahweh's insistence on exclusive worship had both political and religious implications. It united those who accepted worship of Yahweh into a community and barred them from returning to the disuniting worship of their ancestral gods. *After* they had been unified under the new God, it was natural for the assorted peoples to claim that they had been kin all along and to read back elements of continuity between their common God and their ancestral gods. Hence, Yahweh, the God of Moses, was identified as the God of Abraham, Isaac, and Jacob, too.

Thus, in the desert at Mount Sinai, probably in the thirteenth century B.C.E., the Hebrews, though still far from being a people united under an earthly king, took formative steps toward a distinctive identity. Their unifying pact with Yahweh, it is crucial to underscore, was a *covenant*. This agreement presented through Moses to the people by Yahweh, set forth the terms of an agreement that bound God and the Hebrews together, albeit on an asymmetrical footing. God's deliverance of the people from Egyptian bondage, Moses told them, had not been an end in itself. God expected something more: "'Now therefore, if you obey my voice and keep my covenant, you shall be my treasured possession out of all the peoples. Indeed, the whole earth is mine, but you shall be for me a priestly kingdom and a holy nation'" (Exod. 19:5–6). The people accepted this status of being God's chosen people. It was the proper response to their liberation.

We can better understand this crucial action of covenant and election by noting that the structure of the biblical covenant between God and the followers of Moses resembles that between a suzerain and his vassals in Hittite treaties of the fourteenth and thirteenth centuries B.C.E. In these treaties, the ruler grants his vassal protection but stipulates what is expected of the vassal in return. In both the Hittite and the biblical versions, blessings and curses, the former as reward for compliance and the latter as dire consequences of disobedience and rebellion, are emphasized.

In the Hittite world the solemnity of these pacts was often dramatized in elaborate ceremonies. Biblical scholars note that the account in Deuteronomy reflects the procedure of such a treaty ceremony. A recital of the historical events that moved the vassal to enter into the covenant is followed by proclamation of the law to be obeyed, then by a statement of mutual obligations between God and Israel, and finally by the crucial blessings and curses. Although the Hebrews were not yet politically united, they had become one people in agreeing to obey the commandments of their God. Having entered this covenant, the people were warned that disobedience could not take place with impunity, for Yahweh is a jealous God who tolerates no rivals.

Did God or only Moses speak at Sinai? Did divine revelation bring Jewish identity to the fore, or was that consciousness forged more by forces of human politics that used religious ingredients to secure a base of power? The historical record can be read in more than one way, but of this much we can be sure: the existence of a Jewish people who fell under Hitler's threat three thousand years later does depend on the tradition that God acted in history in the Exodus and at Sinai. That action, moreover, singled out a people whose destiny would not only be linked with the land of Israel but also would set them apart from every other human group that has walked the face of the earth. With Moses, if not with God, the world received "the Jewish question." Nothing would ever be the same again.

## ANTI-JEWISH POLICIES
## IN THE GRECO-ROMAN WORLD

Space permits no detailed account of the next millennium of Jewish history. Suffice it to say that Moses did not live to enter the "promised land" of Canaan, the land of Israel, which came to be construed as part of the pact between Yahweh and the Hebrew tribes or Israelites. Joshua succeeded in dominating that territory, but pressure from hostile elements remained intense. In waging wars of defense, however, the Israelite confederation was ultimately solidified under its first king, Saul, and later under the more expansive rule of David and Solomon (ca. 1000–922 B.C.E.). For a time an Israelite empire prospered, but Solomon's death brought political division, and two states emerged: Israel in the north and Judah in the south. Existing in a buffer zone between Egypt and Mesopotamia, these small powers were constantly threatened by political struggle in the Middle East. In 722 the northern kingdom fell to the Assyrians. When the Babylonians seized hegemony from the Assyrians, Jerusalem and the southern kingdom fell to them in 587/586, and the Jews were dispersed and exiled. A century later, under Persian rule, they were permitted to return to their homeland. Jerusalem and the Temple were restored. Politically, Jewish life remained under Persian authority until the conquests of Alexander the Great (356–323 B.C.E.) brought Jews under Greek control.

Jewish life has enriched human experience in countless ways and out of all proportion to its numbers. Yet, viewed in one way, these ancient Jews seem singularly unimportant in the world's history. Admittedly their ways of life differed from other groups around them, but their political power was less than overwhelming. Most people knew little about them. It would even be hard to document that Jews were consistently singled out for special discrimination and persecution in the world of pre-Christian antiquity. This is not to say that they were specially favored or even that there was nothing to approximate either the anti-Judaism that emerged from the triumph of Christianity or the racially oriented antisemitism that would follow in nineteenth- and twentieth-century Europe. Some of the seeds of that hostility were planted in the Greco-Roman era prior to the birth of Christianity. It will be well to note them.

As we do so, let us take a moment to clarify some concepts. Uses of the term "antisemitism" are now so frequent that one might suppose them to be of long standing. In fact, the term was first popularized in the late 1870s by a German racist ideologue and journalist named Wilhelm Marr.[5] He employed it in speaking about the largely secular anti-Jewish political campaigns that were widespread in Europe at the time. The word derives from an eighteenth-century etymological analysis that differentiated between languages with "Aryan" roots and those with "Semitic" ones. This distinction, in turn, led to the assumption—a false one—that there are corresponding racial groups. Under this rubric, Jews became Semites, paving the way for Marr's usage. He might have used the conventional German *Judenhass*, but that way of referring to Jew-hatred carried religious connotations that Marr wanted to de-emphasize in favor of racial ones. Apparently more "scientific," the term *Antisemitismus* caught on and eventually became a way of speaking about all the forms of hostility experienced by the Jews throughout history. Antisemitism, then, is both one thing and many.[6] Hatred of Jews is at its heart, but the driving motives behind that hatred can be diverse: economic, political, racial, religious, social, and mixtures in between. To reckon with antisemitism, then, is to do much more than to deal with "prejudice," for its causes reach deep down into fundamental social, economic, and religious structures.

Religious, and therefore social, factors became an ancient seedbed for modern antisemitism, as Alexander the Great sought to bring his empire under the domination of Greek culture. As far as the Jews were concerned, that policy had impact not only in the Jews' ancient homeland but also upon the now widely scattered Jewish enclaves that could be found throughout the Mediterranean world. Jewish immigration—much of it forced by exile, but some of it voluntary—had for centuries dispersed this people, and even when there was opportunity to return to the homeland, significant numbers decided that their interests were best served by remaining in the Diaspora. Some of these Jews assimilated completely. In most cases, however, a Jewish identity that differentiated Jew from non-Jew (Gentile) was sustained. The decision to remain different, needless to say, could lead to friction between a Jewish minority and any dominant power whose aspirations for empire were predicated on cultural homogeneity. It should be noted, however, that Jews who had migrated to the East did not generally experience such tension. In both China and India, for example, Jews led essentially peaceful lives as a group. In particular, they experienced none of the violence that would be the fate of the Jews later on in Christian and, to a lesser degree, in Muslim lands.

Where Greek power dominated, the typical view held that anything non-Greek was barbarian. Thus, a people who worshiped but one God exclusively— and that one intolerant of any rivals and therefore very different from those of the Greeks—might not do so with impunity. Religious belief, moreover, never stops with theological affirmation. It penetrates into cultural practices, and thus the Jews were different once again in their observance of a special Sabbath, in their rites of circumcision, in their restrictions on diet and marriage, and in their conviction that Jerusalem was the holy city.

Cultural collision could hardly be avoided, and one of its early scenes was in the Egyptian city of Alexandria, which was becoming a commercial and intellectual center. Alexander himself invited Jews to settle there. Thousands accepted, and many of them prospered while occupying a specially designated area where they could live by their own religious law. Resentment, however, was not far behind. Fueled by Egyptian dislike of tolerance shown to the Jews and by Jewish refusal to accommodate to Greek religious and social standards, an early form of antisemitism found a home in Alexandria. The basic charge was that Jews were misanthropic, distrustful, and hateful toward other peoples, a libel whose virulence would spread and intensify with time.

Tension between Greek and Jewish ways was not restricted to the Diaspora. Greek culture had made substantial inroads in the Jews' Holy Land. Matters came to a head in 167 B.C.E., when the Syrian ruler Antiochus IV Epiphanes took harsh measures to speed up that process among the Jews. Under his rule, Jews faced a death sentence if they circumcised their sons or observed the Sabbath. In addition to forcing Jews to eat forbidden foods and to take part in pagan rituals, Antiochus desecrated the Temple in Jerusalem and then rededicated it to Zeus. Antiochus had gone too far. Led by Judah the Maccabee, a successful revolt ensued. Purification and restoration of the Temple, now commemorated by the Jewish holiday of Hanukkah, occurred in 164 B.C.E. Both within the Jewish homeland and in the Diaspora the hellenizing trends were reversed. A Jewish revival ensued, replete with an expansionist war led by the Judean John Hyrcanus, who forcibly converted some of the vanquished. During his rule (135–104), the Pharisees and Sadducees, parties both religious and political, achieved prominence.

Jewish successes, however, did not mean that all was well. If the ethical demands of Jewish monotheism attracted voluntary converts in the now declining and even decadent Greek world, these gains were hardly welcomed by everyone. Gentile intellectuals especially launched anti-Jewish attacks, alleging that Jews hated strangers and were absurdly superstitious; they practiced ritual murder, but they were also atheists. Tension mounted, although its seeds would not produce their most devastating harvest until much later.

The influence of Greek culture outlasted the political might of Alexander the Great. After his death in 323, the Mediterranean political situation was destabilized, even though the powers vying for authority were united by strands of Greek culture. By the beginning of the second century B.C.E., however, Rome had filled the power vacuum. Soon Roman authority dominated the Mediterranean world. How did this development affect Jewish life?

What occurred was basically a continuation of relationships as they had been under Greek dominance. Certainly in the pre-Christian era there was no official state antisemitism on the part of the Romans. Although Jewish and Roman religious practices differed greatly, Jews were, if anything, granted special legal and religious privileges in a regime that was quite tolerant of religious diversity. Thus, a large Jewish community in Rome, second in size in the Diaspora during the first century B.C.E. only to that of Alexandria, could enter the city's business life, win converts, and participate in political life. So long as the Jews posed no serious threat to the government's stability, their lives were reasonably secure. A continuing vilification of Jews by intellectuals remained a concern, but those views, fraught with political dangers though they were, did not come to dominate official government policy at the time.

Nevertheless, Jewish life under Roman authority could hardly be described as tranquil. The first anti-Jewish pogrom, for example, may have occurred in Alexandria during Caligula's reign in 38 C.E. Somewhat later, in Antioch, Ephesus, and numerous cities bordering on Palestine, as the Romans now called the region that contained the former Jewish homeland, the Jews experienced outbreaks of violence, often provoked because of Jewish refusal to join mainstream religious practices. Inside Palestine itself, the situation was not more comfortable. By mid-century many Jews found the burden of Roman rule intolerable, and none more so than the nationalists known as Zealots. Open rebellion broke out, and at first the Jews were successful. By August 70, however, Roman power, which abhorred political insurrection and was efficient at crushing it, had prevailed, and the Temple in Jerusalem was in ruins. The last Jewish stronghold, Masada, fell three years later. The Jews who died there—nearly a thousand men, women, and children—did so by their own hand rather than permitting the Romans to enslave or kill them. Shortly there will be more to say about the fall of Jerusalem, but for now suffice it to note that a less militant Jewish population survived. Under the leadership of Rabbi Yochanan ben Zakkai, the Jewish religion was transmuted. It centered no longer on sacrifices at the Temple presided over by hereditary priests. Instead, local synagogues, which would produce a rabbinic civilization stressing study, the sanctity of life, and obedience to God's will as it came to be interpreted by scribes and sages throughout the centuries, rose to the fore. Still, Jewish visions of independence were not dead altogether. Under the emperor Trajan and again under Hadrian there were Jewish rebellions—the Kitos War (115–17) and the Bar Kokhba War (132–35), respectively—against Roman power. With the crushing of these revolts, Israel's life as an effective political force in antiquity came to an end.

To summarize the major points that should be drawn from the historical sketch set forth above, it is clear, first, that there was a two-way relationship between Jews and Gentiles in the pre-Christian world. While Jews were complementary from an economic point of view, their ways of life were still alien, not in superficial ways, but in terms of the most fundamental social, political, and religious matters. Second, although the balance of power was always heavily weighted in favor of non-Jews, the Jews remained a minority people primarily because they chose to be, and they did so not least because of a religious persua-

Separatism and Elitism

sion that they were chosen by God for a special purpose and destiny. Their covenant with God could not be violated with impunity, or so many of them believed. One result of sustaining this covenant was that Jewish life could understandably be perceived as foreign to the dominant political and cultural forces of the day. That status could not be held with impunity either; it was a step toward making the Jews tragically unwanted and vulnerable.

It should come as no surprise that tensions might build to the point of hatred and violence, unless one holds a view of human society more protean, or of human nature more sanguine, than history makes credible. At the same time, however, it is important to note what did not transpire in these ancient civilizations. Plenty of vilification and brutality could be found—more than an estimated million Jews lost their lives in the Judeo-Roman War of 66–70 alone—but the antisemitism that existed then was not mainly engendered by racism or economic hostility, nor did it involve unrelenting elimination of political rights, let alone a systematic plan for total Jewish annihilation. It can even be argued that this early antisemitism was not primarily theological—at least not in the sense that would emerge once Christian power took hold—although the early anti-Jewish feeling did have much to do with a Jewish separatism and yearning for independence that was rooted in religious practice.

If there was no enduring state antisemitism in antiquity, despite the extreme violence of the Jewish rebellions against Roman rule, it must still be underscored that a potent antisemitic mood was in the air from the third century B.C.E. onward. Primarily cultural though it was, its attitudes exacerbated the pariah status of Jews, leaving them vulnerable in a struggle for survival against the Romans. Those struggles left the Jews largely landless and powerless. Their fate would become still more precarious as Jewish history came to be read through Christian eyes. To that account we turn next.

## THE BIRTH OF CHRISTIANITY AND THE BEGINNING OF THE JEWISH-CHRISTIAN SCHISM

The birth of Jesus and the birth of Christianity are not identical, although the narratives about the former in the Gospels of Matthew and Luke do bring the two close together. According to the New Testament book of Acts, it was at Antioch, some time after the death of Jesus, that Jesus' disciples for the first time were called Christians. The span between events and written records of them may not have been stretched out so far as in the cases of Moses and the Pentateuch, but there is a gap between the historical Jesus and the Christian New Testament. The earliest of those canonical writings are some of the letters by Paul, and they precede by only a few years the first of the Synoptic Gospels, Mark, which is dated approximately 70 C.E. Along with the accounts by Matthew and Luke, Mark appears to draw on an earlier source, often named Q, which may have been in existence by mid-century. The birth narratives, then, are far from being eyewitness accounts of historical events, but clearly they are the accounts of witnesses who heard and saw something special in Jesus of Nazareth and testified about it. The fact that they did so changed the world no less than the liberation of Hebrew slaves from their Egyptian bondage.

Jesus, whose name is the Greek form of the Hebrew name Joshua or Y'ho'shua (meaning "the Lord saves"), preached a message proclaiming the imminent coming of the kingdom of God and the conditions for inclusion in it. Neither Jesus nor his early followers intended to establish a new religion, although their intentions did entail purification and reform of the Jewish faith. As his public ministry continued, however, some of Jesus' disciples began to view him as the Messiah traditionally promised to the Jews by God. The coming of the Messiah, foreshadowed centuries before in the prophetic writings of Isaiah and Jeremiah and fervently longed for throughout Jewish domination by the Romans, would redeem Israel and bring in the kingdom of God. How and when this divinely appointed king would carry out his work was a matter of diverse conjecture, and Jesus was not alone in having messianic expectations placed upon him.

To be regarded in this way was a mixed blessing, for Jewish and Roman leaders alike knew that subversive agitation might breed in such thinking. Thus, when Jesus eventually made his way from Galilee to Jerusalem, danger was real. How much danger no human mind could have known in advance; what ensued left the world shaken. What really happened to Jesus during those seven days is no easy matter to discern, for the claims are so varied, the testimonies so conflicting, and the resulting controversies so acrimonious throughout history that the interpretations about the facts, let alone the facts themselves, are among the elements that decisively changed the human condition. Stating the matter as simply and as neutrally as possible, the following outline can highlight some of the points that are the most crucial for linking Jesus' demise with Auschwitz.

Following the Gospel narratives—which means that one must be alert to the interpretive points that the writers wish to make at least as much as one must be concerned to piece together a chronology of factual occurrence—Jesus entered Jerusalem amid a popular demonstration by his followers near the time of Passover, the Jewish holiday that celebrates the Exodus, toward the end of the reign of Pontius Pilate, the Roman governor of Palestine from 26 to 36. At such a time, both nationalistic and eschatological hopes ran high, and there can be little doubt that some of Jesus' followers—and assuredly the later interpreters—regarded Jesus' entry into the city as a sign that the kingdom of God might indeed be at hand and that Jesus himself would be instrumental in its arrival.

Such feelings were intensified by the next recorded episode, which finds Jesus driving the money changers and sellers of sacrificial animals from the Temple. Such commercial practices, carefully restricted to the outer court of the Temple, were quite acceptable to most Jews, but Jesus cleansed it nonetheless. Not surprisingly, such actions raised questions about Jesus' authority. Thus, whether the ensuing events happened as written, the Synoptic Gospel narratives follow the cleansing of the Temple with a series of parables, discussions, and speeches that pushed the conflict between Jesus and his opponents to new heights when he predicted the destruction of Jerusalem and the Temple.

The official religious leadership of the Jews, the New Testament reports, now felt compelled to intervene, and such steps were taken on the night after Jesus shared a last meal with his followers. The precise date of this supper—prior to, after, or precisely on the first night of the Passover celebration—is disputed. A pre-Passover dating seems safest, even though it is clear that the later interpreters wanted to identify Jesus as closely as possible with the lambs that were slaughtered for the festival. In any case, Jesus was arrested and brought before the Jewish high court (Sanhedrin).

At this point the historical facts blur even more. The Gospels offer a picture of a nighttime trial replete with false witnesses, Jesus' confession that he is the Messiah, and a death sentence for him on the charge of blasphemy. The literary effect is to contrast the messianic Jesus with the rage, cruelty, and falsehood of his opponents. These stories, however, cannot be taken simply at face value. Jewish procedure was certainly at variance with the New Testament's version of Jesus' case. It is noteworthy that nowhere is there an instance of anyone else ever having been accused of blasphemy and sentenced to death by the Jewish authorities because of messianic claims, even though such claims were not uncommon. Add to this the fact that if Jesus had committed blasphemy, the Jews had the right to execute him but would have done so by stoning. Instead, Jesus was turned over to Pontius Pilate, the Roman governor, and ultimately crucified, a form of punishment that was exclusively the prerogative of Roman courts of law and reserved for political criminals.

Roman, not Jewish, power put Jesus to death.[7] An uneasy governor, Pontius Pilate, saw Jesus' execution as the most expedient way to deal with a Jewish messianic pretender who might have a further destabilizing effect in a city that was already chaotic enough during the Passover season. If Pilate's decision to eliminate Jesus as a political suspect was encouraged and welcomed by some of the Jewish leadership for similar reasons, their numbers were small, and by no means did they represent the feelings of the entire Jewish populace, many of whom shared Jesus' antipathy toward the pro-Roman Temple leadership. According to the New Testament, however, Pilate did not accede completely to the wishes of those Jewish leaders. Overriding their protests, he insisted that the identifying inscription on Jesus' cross should read "Jesus of Nazareth, the King of the Jews" (John 19:19). Whether historical fact or literary device, the point would not be missed by Christian readers: Pilate's irony allegedly conveyed the truth, but Jewish blindness was so extreme that it killed the redemption of Israel.

Jesus was a thoroughly observant Jew.[8] He opposed neither the written nor the oral law, although his interpretations differed from those of some Jewish leaders. His emphasis was on love of one's neighbor, on the need for repentance, on liberation for the oppressed. He eschewed violence and was repaid with a violent death that left his followers dismayed and scattered. Indeed his demise would probably have given him no more than a footnote in history, had it not been for the fact that his disciples came to believe—and were able to convince others—that Jesus was resurrected from death.

For a time the followers of Jesus also continued to be practicing Jews, but with the difference that they believed the Messiah, expected by all observant Jews, had actually come in Jesus of Nazareth. Moreover, their experience at the Jewish feast of Shavuot (Pentecost), which commemorated the giving of the Law at Mount Sinai, left them convinced that Jesus remained spiritually present among them and that his return to rule over God's kingdom on earth would not be long in coming. These beliefs were expressed and celebrated in worship that closely resembled existing Jewish rituals even while they were supplemented by scriptural interpretations that pointed to Jesus as the Messiah (the Christ in Greek) and by a commemoration of Jesus' last supper with his disciples prior to the crucifixion, which focused attention on Jesus' continuing presence and expected return.

It is crucial to note that from the outset an ardent missionary zeal characterized these early Jewish Christians. Their efforts to win converts aimed first at their fellow Jews. Jewish authorities wavered between toleration of the new sect and repression of it, but competing religious beliefs bred animosity within the ranks of the Jews themselves. One dimension of struggle revolved around the issue of whether being a follower of Jesus necessitated one's first being a Jew. The view that came to dominate—represented initially by Peter and then even more powerfully by Paul, who formerly had been a Jewish persecutor of Christians—was negative. Gentiles, without becoming observant Jews, could be Christians. The result was that Christianity spread, establishing communities in Rome itself by the time of Paul's execution there in 64.

Under Paul's influence, the Christian message offered to the Gentiles exerted considerable attraction.[9] Especially among the poor and enslaved, an emphasis on equality before God, on love and charity, coupled with an exclusive sense of chosenness or election that embraced the believer who confessed Jesus as Lord, provided a hope for eternal life and therefore a status on earth that was welcome. But these benefits were not without cost, for in their early years communities of Christians were targets of Roman persecution, accused, as Jews have been, of threatening social order and political stability.

In spite of persecution, Christianity grew. One cause and effect of that growth was the emergence of written narratives about Jesus. These writings had both instructive and evangelistic purposes. They also had to deal with some ticklish problems. None was more crucial than the issue of who bore responsibility for the crucifixion of Jesus. That issue was critical because it was precisely at this juncture that the relationships among Christians, their elder Jewish siblings, and the prevailing Roman authorities stood out in boldest relief. To emphasize Rome's responsibility in Jesus' death could have unfortunate results by intensifying suspicion that the followers of Jesus were indeed undesirable anti-Roman elements. It is not accidental, therefore, that the Gospels united in playing down Pilate's role in favor of a much stronger portrayal of nearly fanatical Jewish thirst for Jesus' blood.

Other reasons for such an interpretation are not far to find, nor should they be particularly shocking when one remembers that Christianity was carved out of Jewish religious experience in such a way that each posed a threat to the other, a threat made more intense, not less, by their extremely close relationships. Already we have noted that the Jewish establishment did not always welcome Christians with open arms. By the year 90 C.E. most Jews had made a definitive religious break with Christians, who were now considered to be the greatest apostates from Judaism. Christians would more than return the favor. One crucial way of doing so involved the destruction of Jerusalem and the Temple at the end of the Judeo-Roman War in 70. We return now to that event.

## THE FALL OF JERUSALEM AND THE ROOTS OF THE HOLOCAUST

The Judeo-Roman War of 66–70 C.E. and its aftermath can be seen as the Holocaust of ancient times. Rebellion against Rome broke out in Palestine in the year 66. Under normal circumstances, Rome would have been able to subdue the revolt in a few weeks. In war, however, events seldom unfold as expected. The Jewish revolt became a bloody conflict that dragged on for four long years. As the Romans overcame the Jews, slaughter, plunder, famine, and desolation were the order of the day. Of overwhelming importance for Jewish destiny was the destruction of Jerusalem's Holy Temple. The Talmud records that for seven years after the fall of Jerusalem "the nations of the world cultivated their vineyards with no other manure than the blood of Israel."

The Jewish historian Josephus records that 1,197,000 Jews were killed or taken captive by the Romans.[10] Nevertheless, Rome had no interest in exterminating the Jews as did the German government under Hitler. The victor's interest was so to reconstitute the Jewish community that it would henceforth submit peacefully to Roman rule. This objective could be accomplished only by a radical transformation of the Jewish community's religious and political leadership. Those who had led the Jewish people before the war were no longer acceptable to the Romans. The old aristocracy and the hereditary priesthood were excluded from any leadership role in the reconstituted community. So too were the Zealots, who were chiefly responsible for starting and sustaining the war. Only one group was acceptable to Rome: the pacifist wing of the Pharisees under Rabbi Yochanan ben Zakkai, who was known to have opposed the war and to have counseled a policy of submission to Caesar.[11]

Yochanan's counsel was bitterly opposed by the Zealots, who were initially convinced that God would enable them to overcome their world-conquering foe. Yochanan and his disciples were more realistic. They understood that it was impossible for the Jews to defeat Rome. Moreover, they saw no pressing reason why they should defeat Rome, believing that the ultimate fate of the Jewish people was not dependent upon military strength but on reverent obedience to God's

law. As long as Rome permitted the Jews religious autonomy, Yochanan was willing to accept Caesar's rule.[12]

The legend of how the leadership of the Jewish community passed to the Pharisees is recorded in an ancient tradition that has been ingrained in the consciousness of every rabbi, whether Orthodox or liberal, to this day. The tradition
has undoubtedly been embellished. Nevertheless, it reveals a great deal about the
psychology and character of Judaism. According to the legend, Yochanan determined to escape during the siege of Jerusalem and to save what he could.[13]
Because Jewish law forbade keeping the dead in Jerusalem for even a single night,
Yochanan's followers were able to carry their master out of the city in a coffin,
pretending that he was dead. Once outside the city, Yochanan was brought to
Vespasian, the Roman commander and soon-to-be emperor. When the future
emperor asked Yochanan what, in effect, were his terms, Yochanan is said to have
replied, "I ask nothing of you save [the rabbinical academy at] Yavneh, where I
might go and teach my disciples and there establish a house of prayer and perform all the commandments."[14] In the face of the catastrophic defeat of his own
community and the victor's overwhelming power, Yochanan wanted only a center of religious learning and prayer.

There was wisdom in Yochanan's choice of surrender and petition for a center of learning and prayer. Prolonged resistance could have been suicidal and devastating for the future of Judaism. Having fought a long and bloody war, the
Romans had no intention of permitting the reconstitution of a Jewish power base
capable of challenging them in a future crisis. The Romans wanted a submissive
community that would be incapable of again becoming a military threat. Because
they were scholars rather than soldiers, Yochanan and his rabbinic colleagues were
eminently suited to lead a conquered Jewish community. It must be stressed,
however, that Yochanan was neither a turncoat nor a crass collaborationist. In the
midst of utter defeat, he was realistic and determined to save what he regarded as
essential for the preservation of Judaism.

An agreement was struck between the Romans and the Pharisees. The Pharisees foreswore all resort to the use of power in their dealings with their Roman
overlords. The Romans permitted the defeated community religious autonomy.
Within a relatively short period, a majority of the Jews would cease to live in the
homeland of their ancestors, but wherever they dwelt, they were to be led by the
disciples and heirs of religious leaders originally placed in power by their conquerors. This outcome does not mean that the rabbis came to lead the Jews
against the people's will. On the contrary, no other group within Judaism had a
viable program for coping with the conditions in which the Jews found themselves after 70. Still, those conditions would not have existed, had it not been for
a catastrophic military defeat.

After becoming the leaders of the Jewish community, the rabbis claimed that
they were the heirs of biblical Judaism, a claim that most Jews accept to this day.
Nevertheless, as a result of the fall of Jerusalem, the Jewish people experienced a
religious revolution that was to affect Jewish life for the next two thousand years.

Instead of an altar of stone upon which bloody offerings were made, Jewish religious life emphasized the bloodless study of a book. The Jews were taught by their rabbis to turn inward and, through a life of study and prayer, to become reconciled to their God. And so it came to pass that a brave and warlike people who had dared to enter into combat with the world's greatest empire forsook the sword for the Book. Every aspect of future Jewish life was decisively shaped by that political arrangement between Rome and the rabbis.

By surrendering to the Romans, Yochanan took a calculated risk that Caesar could be trusted. The Zealots were unwilling to trust Caesar. When it became apparent that Jerusalem's fall was inevitable, the Zealots, led by Eleazar ben Yair, withdrew to the mountain stronghold of Masada, where they held out until May 73. Finally, Eleazar exhorted his followers to kill themselves rather than surrender. For Eleazar, a life of utter powerlessness was not worth living. The historian Josephus records that Eleazar, anticipating the degradations a powerless people would have to endure, told his followers, "Wretched will be the young, whose strong bodies can sustain many tortures; wretched, too, the old, whose age cannot endure afflictions! One man will see his wife dragged away by violence, another hear the voice of his child crying to a father whose hands are bound."[15]

According to Josephus, all 960 defenders of Masada, with the exception of a few women and children, died by their own hands or those of kin. At Masada the Zealots preferred death to life in a world where their lives would be entirely dependent upon the whim of hostile strangers. By contrast, the rabbis were prepared not only to accept the risks of powerlessness but to create a religious culture predicated upon the disciplined renunciation of the use of force. Such a policy entailed the necessity of submitting at regular intervals to acts of murderous aggression. Yochanan and his spiritual heirs trained the Jews so to live that their defenselessness became their only defense. Periodically, they were abused and slaughtered, but somehow a remnant managed to survive until the twentieth century, when a new kind of Caesar arose, a Caesar who was determined to exterminate every single Jew within his grasp. Unlike the Caesars of old, the new Caesar respected no limits. The Jews were essentially without defense against the assembly-line methods he used to annihilate them. In his worst nightmares, Yochanan could not have imagined what was to be the fate of his people nineteen centuries after he helped to set them on the path of powerlessness.

Other long-range consequences of the fall of Jerusalem are important to our story as well. Before 70, many Jews had settled outside of Palestine. After 70, the process of out-migration became irreversible. Within a relatively short period, the majority of the Jews came to live in other people's lands. As a minority, the Jews were compelled to maintain themselves by doing work which complemented that of the indigenous majority. Although generalizing for all Jewish communities over a period of almost two millennia is difficult, typically the Jews served as a "middle-man minority," that is, as merchants, traders, artisans, physicians, and moneylenders. The religion of the Book gave the Jews the skills of literacy and calculation required to survive as an economically complementary population in

a world where commerce was poorly developed. These roles were especially valuable after the breakdown of the Roman Empire and the beginnings of the feudal
Middle Ages. As a rule, Jews were permitted to settle wherever the need for their
skills outweighed the natural hostility felt by an indigenous population toward a
community of strangers.

In significant ways, the fact that the Jews were strangers facilitated the development of their role in commerce. Success in commerce requires impersonal calculation. Merchants must be able to calculate accurately the profit required to remain
in business. They cannot put emotional considerations of kinship solidarity ahead
of financial calculation. Simply put, merchants must to a certain extent treat every
person impersonally, that is, as a stranger. It is, however, difficult to treat one's own
kin or fellow villagers impersonally. Claims of kinship and mutual support are too
insistent to be ignored. That is why in many precapitalist cultures, commerce and
the professions have often been carried on by ethnic minorities, such as—from time
to time—the Chinese in southeast Asia; the Indians and Pakistanis in Kenya,
Uganda, and other parts of Africa; the Armenians in the urban areas of Turkey; and
the ethnic Germans in eastern Europe. Sometimes religious differentiation can have
comparable results, as was the case in France after the Reformation. For centuries
France's small Protestant community has been disproportionately represented in
banking and finance. Only with the arrival of an economic system such as capitalism, in which all persons are treated more or less impersonally, at least in business
and finance, have members of the indigenous majority taken over the commercial,
professional, and financial roles formerly played by ethnic minorities. Whenever
such transformations have taken place in relatively homogeneous societies, whether
in Africa, Asia, or Europe, a movement has arisen among the majority calling for
the elimination of the "middle-man" minority.

Success in commerce seldom enhances an ethnic minority's popularity, especially among those majority populations in which business and finance are poorly
understood. There is almost always the suspicion that the minority is somehow
engaged in sharp or dishonest business practices, a common reaction of con-
sumers to business persons in any society. This pattern was particularly evident
in the case of medieval Jews in Christian countries where usury was regarded as
a greater sin than adultery. Jews were identified both with Judas, the disciple who
for money betrayed his Master with a kiss, and with the devil, the very opposite
of all that Christ stands for. It is hardly accidental that in precapitalist societies
one usually finds a strong distaste for commerce and a preference on the part of
elite members of the majority for what are the considered more "honorable"
careers. Had it not been for the defeat of 70, the Jews would undoubtedly have
shared the same distaste for commerce and money lending and a preference on
the part of elite members of the majority for more "honorable" careers. As it was,
they had no choice but to do whatever work was available to them.

Rabbinic Judaism was not the only new religious tradition to emerge as a consequence of the fall of Jerusalem. Gentile Christianity as we know it also came
into being as a direct consequence of that event. The importance of the fall of

Jerusalem for both Judaism and Christianity has been stated succinctly by the late Norman Perrin, a distinguished New Testament scholar:

> The destruction of Jerusalem and the Temple by the Gentiles sent a shock wave through the Jewish-Christian world whose importance it is impossible to exaggerate. Indeed, much of the subsequent literature both of Judaism and Christianity took the form it did precisely in an attempt to come to terms with the catastrophe of A.D. 70.[16]

Before the fall of Jerusalem, the Christian church was essentially Jewish in leadership, with Jerusalem as its headquarters. After 70, Rome became the church's spiritual center, as the church divested itself of its Jewish leadership and became the essentially Gentile church it remains until this day. The fall of Jerusalem and its immediate aftermath marked the final parting of the ways for the two religious communities.

Many scholars share our opinion that the Gospels contain extensive evidence of the Christian response to the fall of Jerusalem.[17] At least three and possibly all of the Gospels are thought to have been written after the fall of Jerusalem. Some scholars assign a date before 70 for the writing of Mark, generally agreed to be the oldest Gospel, but even these scholars seldom date it before 66, the year the Judeo-Roman War began. In any event, early Christians came to agree that the fall of Jerusalem was a terrible punishment visited by God upon the Jewish people for having rejected Jesus and for having been responsible for his crucifixion.

The classical response of the post-70 church to the fall of Jerusalem is anticipated in the parable of the Wicked Tenants, the tale of the householder who planted a vineyard, "leased it to tenants and went to another country" (Matt. 21:33). When the land rents fell due, he sent three servants, one after another, to collect from the tenants. The wicked tenants assaulted the first and murdered the second and third servants. Finally, the landlord sent his own son to collect the rents. He too was killed. As Matthew tells the story, Jesus asks his listeners, "'Now when the owner of the vineyard comes, what will he do to those tenants?'" Significantly, Jesus' listeners themselves reply, "'He will put those wretches to a miserable death, and lease the vineyard to other tenants who will give him the produce at the harvest time'" (Matt. 21:40–41).

The parable of the Wicked Tenants is immediately followed in Matthew by the parable of the Marriage Feast. In this parable Jesus is depicted as likening the kingdom of heaven to a marriage feast given by a king for his son. Twice the king sent forth his servants to invite the guests. On both occasions those invited refused to come. Some even dared to abuse and kill the messengers. Jesus is then reported as saying, "'The king was enraged. He sent his troops, destroyed those murderers, and burned their city'" (Matt. 22:7). According to most scholars, both of these passages contain clear references to the fall of Jerusalem and were composed as a response to that event.[18]

Perhaps the most intense expression in the Gospels of the view that Jewish misfortune is a manifestation of God's punitive wrath is to be found in the terrible scene found only in Matthew in which Pontius Pilate, finding no fault in Jesus, nevertheless condemns him to death to appease the Jewish mob, washes his hands before the crowd, and proclaims, "'I am innocent of this man's blood'" (Matt. 27:24). Matthew describes the response as follows: "Then *the people as a whole* answered, 'His blood be on us and on our children'" (Matt. 27:25, italics added).

A political motive seems evident for the Gospels' insistence that the Jews rather than the Romans were wholly responsible for the crucifixion. The church had every reason to dissociate itself from the defeated rebels against the victorious empire. It became necessary to tell the story of the trial and execution of Jesus in such a way that Jesus was not portrayed as yet another Jewish insurrectionist. Hence, in the Gospels the Jews are clearly depicted as the real villains at Jesus' trial. By contrast, the Romans are exculpated.[19]

The moral is clear. It is constantly reiterated. No difference of opinion separates the Jewish Christianity of Matthew from the Gentile Christianity of Mark and Luke. *The Gospel writers agree that the Temple was destroyed, Jerusalem ruined, and the Jewish nation slaughtered, not by the profane strength of the Roman empire, but by a just, righteous, all-powerful, avenging God, who was determined to teach the Jews the true cost of rejecting God's Son.*

Nor was the young church alone in interpreting the Jewish catastrophe as God's punishment. Another tradition tells of Yochanan's seeing a desperately hungry Jewish girl on the road to Emmaus. Out of desperation for something to eat, she was extracting undigested barleycorn from the excrement dropped by an Arab's horse. Some time later, alluding to Deuteronomy 28:47–48, he commented to his disciples about what he had seen: "Because you did not serve the Lord your God when you had plenty, therefore you shall serve your enemy in hunger and thirst. Because you did not serve the Lord . . . by reason of the abundance of all things, therefore you shall serve your enemy in want of all things."[20]

Yochanan had a clear theology of history. In many respects it was very much like that of his Christian contemporaries, which is scarcely surprising. Both the Jews and the Christians were nurtured spiritually by Scripture to believe that God is the sovereign Lord of history who controls the destiny of all nations. Both traditions affirmed that God had entered into a covenant with a chosen people and that Israel's ruin was explained by her failure to keep the covenant and God's inevitable response. Where they differed was in the view each held of the sin for which Israel had been chastised. As noted, the Christians believed that Jerusalem fell because the Jews had rejected Jesus Christ. For the rabbis, Jerusalem fell because the nation failed to obey God's commandments as they were interpreted by the Pharisees.

After the twentieth-century Holocaust, theologians began to seek for the religious meaning, if any, in that event. That effort became known as Holocaust theology. Nevertheless, crucial elements of such theology are as old as the fall of Jerusalem if not older. Moreover, insofar as the Gospels are concerned with the religious interpretation of the fall of Jerusalem, they can be seen as the oldest classical expression of a kind of Christian Holocaust theology, just as Rabbi Yochanan's interpretation of the same event constitutes ancient rabbinic expression of themes that influence Jewish Holocaust theology. There are, of course, even older attempts to

offer a religious interpretation for catastrophic Jewish misfortune, namely, the interpretation by the prophets of the capture of Jerusalem by the Babylonians in 587/586
B.C.E. Taken together, all of these interpretations form the scriptural basis and, as
we shall see, the dilemmas for both Jewish and Christian Holocaust theology.

Let us look for a moment more closely at the "Holocaust theology" of the
Gospels. In the aftermath of the Judeo-Roman War, Christians had no doubt that
Jesus himself had pronounced the dire judgment against Jerusalem ascribed to
him in the New Testament. In this respect, the Gospel writers were following a
tradition that can be traced back to Moses and the prophets. Consider, for example, the biblical words attributed to Moses when he gives expression to the idea
that Israel is a nation chosen by God:

> "It was not because you were more numerous than any other people that the
> LORD set his heart on you and chose you—for you were the fewest of all
> peoples. It was because the LORD loved you and kept the oath that he swore
> to your ancestors, that the LORD has brought you out with a mighty hand,
> and redeemed you from the house of slavery, from the hand of Pharaoh king
> of Egypt. Know therefore that the LORD your God is God, the faithful God
> who maintains covenant loyalty with those who love him and keep his com-
> mandments, to a thousand generations, *and who repays in their own person
> those who reject him. He does not delay but repays in their own person those who
> reject him.* " (Deut. 7:7–10, italics added)

Consider also the words of the prophet Amos:

> Hear this word that the LORD has spoken against you, O people of Israel,
> against the whole family that I brought up out of the land of Egypt:
>
>> You only have I known
>> of all the families of the earth:
>> *therefore I will punish you
>> for all your iniquities.*
>> (Amos 3:1–2, italics added)

Finally, note the words of Micah, as he declares to the rulers of Israel what are
to be the consequences of infidelity to the covenant:

>> Hear this, you rulers of the house of Jacob
>> and chiefs of the house of Israel,    *holy temple*
>> who abhor justice
>> and pervert all equity,
>> who build Zion with blood
>> and Jerusalem with wrong!
>>
>> . . . . . . . . .
>>
>> *Therefore because of you
>> Zion shall be plowed as a field;
>> Jerusalem shall become a heap of ruins,
>> and the mountain of the house a wooded height.*
>> (Mic. 3:9–10, 12, italics added)

The "house" to which Micah refers is, of course, the Holy Temple.

Thus, a firm scriptural basis was already available for the view that the destruction of Jerusalem was God's punishment. All that was sacred to the young church encouraged Christians to interpret the Jewish catastrophe as incontrovertible evidence of God's rejection of the Jews and their religious institutions. The unparalleled misery of the defeated Jews seemed to confirm Christians in their belief that the church rather than the synagogue was the true successor of the fallen Temple.

Consider, for example, the situation of thoughtful Gentile Christians in Rome about the year 75. Even those who did not have direct contact with the Jews knew that the Jewish mainstream had actively rejected such distinctively Christian beliefs as Jesus' messianic status, atoning death, resurrection, and heavenly lordship. Christians regarded these beliefs as decisive for their eternal salvation. Moreover, Jewish unbelief was no small matter, because it came from people who were kin to Jesus and shared with Christians a common faith in the authority of Scripture. Because of their superior numbers at first, Jews could and often did express their rejection of Christian belief with harsh and undiplomatic arguments, as well as with outright persecution of those Christians who had not broken completely with the Jewish community. Such conduct was bound to be a source of anger to Christians. Today, as a result of the findings of social psychologists in the field of cognitive dissonance, we are able to understand how a group is likely to respond to those who present disconfirming information or who seek to discredit beliefs in which the group has a very strong emotional investment.[21] The social-psychological theory of cognitive dissonance holds that if a person or a group has an important stake in an item of information that does not fit together psychologically with a second item of information, an attempt will be made to make the dissonant items consistent with each other. This process is known as dissonance reduction. An obvious method of dissonance reduction is to discredit the source of the dissonant item of information. An even more radical method would be to eliminate the source entirely. Both methods have been employed in the history of religion. Nevertheless, one must remember that the fundamental motive for even the most abusive attempts at dissonance reduction is the defense of the integrity of values or beliefs that are perceived as indispensable to the survival of one's community.

We see this process of dissonance reduction at work in the Gospel of John, where Jesus is depicted as condemning Jews who do not believe in his mission. The community that produced the Gospel of John in the 80s or 90s C.E. consisted of Jewish-Christians or Jews become Christians. More than sixty times, however, far more often than in the Synoptic Gospels (Matthew, Mark, and Luke) taken together, John uses *hoi Ioudaioi*—"the Jews," as that Greek phrase has typically been translated—and often "the Jews" are vilified as benighted disbelievers who are hostile to God's grace and truth. Biblical scholars—Christians and Jews alike—have been working diligently to produce translations that are both more accurate and less destructive. Recent scholarship clarifies that the negative rhetoric about "the Jews" that is attributed to Jesus in the Gospel of John would not refer

to the Jewish people as a whole but to some Jewish leaders and synagogue authorities in a particular context. Unfortunately, centuries-long reading and interpretation of the Johannine text did not reflect those important qualifications.

Although the Gospel of John's negative references to "the Jews" have by no
means been removed from Christian consciousness, thanks to recent biblical
scholarship the context of those polemics is better understood than it was for
more than nineteen centuries.[22] The Gospel of John reflects the Christian side—
one side—of a disputatious competition between Jewish Christians and Jews who
were reconstituting Judaism in the wake of the disastrous revolt against Roman
rule a few decades earlier. In that situation, Jewish Christians—especially those
of the Johannine community—who seemed an internal threat to Jewish tradition, took offense when they were treated accordingly in the synagogue. The
Gospel of John, including its polemics against "the Jews," reflected and emerged
from this family fight. Those polemics, in short, say more about developments
late in the first century C.E. than they do about the Jesus of history.

By the end of that century, the split between the early church and the synagogue had become wide and deep. As Christianity spread in the predominantly
non-Jewish Mediterranean world, John's Gospel was read in ways that lost sight
of the details of that Jewish family fight and the divorce it produced, but the reading still pitted Christians against "the Jews" in an "us" versus "them" schism. That
estrangement had disastrous consequences, largely because of the especially hostile portrayal found in the eighth chapter of John's Gospel, which shows how
severe the Johannine school was prepared to be in dealing with the vexing problem of Jewish unbelief a few years after the fall of Jerusalem. Jesus is depicted as
saying to Jews who challenge his authority:

> "If God were your Father, you would love me, for I came from God and now
> I am here. I did not come on my own, but he sent me. Why do you not
> understand what I say? It is because you cannot accept my word. *You are
> from your father the devil, and you choose to do your father's desires.* . . . Who-
> ever is from God hears the words of God. The reason you do not hear them
> is that you are not from God." (John 8:42–44, 47, italics added)

From the perspective of social psychology, the author(s) of this highly important passage in the Gospel of John are attempting to discredit the disconfirming
other. Apart from all consideration of class, ethnic, and economic conflict
between believing Jews and Christians, there has always been an enormous potential for mutual hostility in the profound challenge each faith poses for some of
the most deeply held beliefs of the other.

The passage we have cited from the Gospel of John attributes a satanic character to those Jews who reject Jesus. The motives for such an attribution are understandable in the light of the theory of cognitive dissonance. The issue dividing
mainstream Judaism and Christianity was not negotiable. Either Jesus was or was
not the Messiah. In the apocalyptic atmosphere of the Judeo-Roman War and its
aftermath, Christians did not hesitate to defame those who rejected Jesus. After

all, they were convinced that the salvation of humanity was at stake. Still, the defamation was destined to have tragic consequences for the next two thousand years. There is no defamation of comparable severity of one religion by another. The ascription of a satanic nature to Jews had the effect of legitimating even the most obscene violence against them. If every single man, woman, and child of the Jewish community is of the devil—and this is one implication of the defamation as it was typically understood—then no one need have any qualms about how Jews are treated. Whatever violence is perpetrated against them can be defended as consistent with God's judgment. Nor, as we shall see, were the National Socialists reticent about using versions of this legitimation for their antisemitism.

Given the fateful conflict between Christianity and mainstream Judaism, Christians living in the last decades of the first Christian century had every motive to regard the fall of Jerusalem as an expression of divine judgment against the Jews. If the events demonstrated that the unbelieving Jews had been rejected by God, Christians had no reason to be concerned with Jewish arguments against faith in Jesus as the Messiah. Thus, *the supreme Jewish disaster of ancient times was quite plausibly seen by Christians as empirical confirmation of the faith which the Jews had rejected.*

Moreover, if one applies the categories of the Christian thought world to the Nazi Holocaust, that event can be interpreted as further punishment of the Jews for having rejected Jesus. As a matter of fact, no other interpretation of the Holocaust is strictly consistent with the classical Christian theology of history.[23] This fact will be of special importance when we consider the role of the Christian church in the rise of modern antisemitism and the vexing question of the response of the Christian churches to the Holocaust. We will be unable to avoid the question of the extent to which belief in the divine origin and justice of catastrophic Jewish misfortune influenced the behavior of Christian leaders in the period culminating in the Holocaust. The question is important because, as we have seen, the view that Jewish disaster confirmed Christian truth was not peripheral to Christianity but was an overwhelmingly important component in the birth of the Gentile church. Nevertheless, at no time in the two-thousand-year history of the encounter between the church and the synagogue did the church ever have extermination of the Jews as its objective.

The fall of Jerusalem affected the Holocaust of modern times in yet another way. The fundamental assumption motivating Yochanan's decision to submit to Rome was his belief that Caesar and his heirs could be trusted not to use their power to destroy the Jews and Judaism as long as the Jews honored their part of the agreement. For two thousand years, Yochanan's calculated risk was justified. Even the Catholic monarchs of Spain, Ferdinand and Isabella, permitted the Jews to leave when they decided to eliminate Spain's Jewish population in 1492. The arrangement between the Jews and Caesar finally broke down in the twentieth century. As the legally constituted leader of the German Reich, Adolf Hitler was an heir to the power and authority of Caesar. It was he who finally used the power renounced by the Pharisees to seek the degradation and annihilation of every single Jew within his grasp. Under National Socialism the government of Germany no longer had any interest in Jewish submission, as did Vespasian and his successors. With more logic than humanity, the wartime National Socialist elite understood that they had the power to bring about a Final Solution to the Jewish question, that the problem of an unwanted population could be "solved" by extermination. *The extermination of the Jews during World War II must thus be seen as part of the price, albeit long delayed, that the Jewish community paid for having lost the war against Rome in 70. What the Zealots feared, and much worse, came to full fruition in the Europe of World War II.*

Year 50 Germans of Jerusalem — — do you have to become Jewish before joining the Christian ??? church/group

# Chapter 2

# The Triumph of Christianity and the "Teaching of Contempt"

*Let them [the Jews] survive, but not thrive! . . . Ultimately, history would show that such double-edged ambivalence is impossible to sustain without disastrous consequences.*

James Carroll, *Constantine's Sword: The Church and the Jews*

A century after the death of Jesus, the schism between Christians and Jews was well defined. Each group struggled for life and influence as a minority in an empire that had reason to look askance at both. Neither group was above trying to curry Roman favor at the expense of the other, and both competed persistently for converts. Christians claimed to be the true heirs of the promises God first made to Israel. To Jews such claims were anathema. Taking Jesus to be the Messiah and gradually even to be a divine being, the very incarnation of God, Christians could regard Jews as blind and even perverse, fully deserving of every misfortune that befell them, not least because that misfortune might manifest God's judgment. By and large, Jews were neither impressed nor persuaded by such indictments, but they were definitely opposed to them, and the conviction that their own way was the true one was driven deeper. Perhaps involuntarily but nonetheless unavoidably pitted together as rivals who disconfirmed each other, neither side had the upper hand, but both held uncertain status under Roman authority. That latter situation, however, would soon change dramatically. As a result, Christians and Jews would continue as rivals, but henceforth the power between them would become radically asymmetrical. Even less than before would Jews be able to choose with impunity to be different. Certainly both the Jewish and the Christian religions have a better face than the one we have been tracing, but the Holocaust is the night side of history's cunning, and thus we must continue to see how the rivalry of Christians and Jews led both groups toward the Nazi death camps.

49

## FROM THE CHURCH FATHERS TO THE REFORMATION

Christian power increased during the second century after the death of Jesus, but that of the Roman Empire rapidly declined. Civil war was almost continuous by the middle half of the third century. Several strong emperors halted the decline. One of them was Constantine (280–337), who converted to Christianity early in the fourth century. Whatever Constantine's motives, political considerations were not missing from them. Although Christians constituted only about 10 percent of the empire's population at the time, they had put together a vital and dynamic organization, the Christian church. For some time, it had functioned almost as a state within a state. The church handled disputes, provided for the poor, maintained lines of communication from place to place, in addition to making headway toward canonizing its own sacred writings into a New Testament and rationalizing its fundamental doctrines. These developments took place gradually, and the effect was less than tidy and systematic, but by Constantine's time nearly every city in the empire had its bishop and body of priests. One of them, the bishop of Rome, had asserted his authority to be the spiritual leader of the entire church. By wedding himself to the Christian faith and its institutions, Constantine strengthened his political grip. From its origins as a Jewish sect and an underground movement targeted by Roman persecution, suffering its worst devastations only a century earlier, Christianity had triumphed as the state religion.

These developments did not bode well for Jews, and one of the reasons was that, as Christians worked to ground their faith firmly in Roman soil, considerable attention continued to be paid to the relationships between Christianity and the Jewish tradition. Historically, Jewish unbelief was regarded by the Christian church as a far more serious matter than that of any other group of believers because Christians—then and now—have always recognized that their religion has a special relationship to Judaism and to the Jewish people. Unlike the pagan religions of ancient times, Judaism, Christianity, and Islam have based their fundamental claims on the belief that certain events took place in history. In the case of Christianity, the historical setting of its foundation is asserted to be in the days of Caesar Augustus, and the fate of Jesus was decided in a trial conducted by an identifiable Roman official, Pontius Pilate.

Notice next that if two or more eyewitnesses to an event are asked to recount the event after the fact, there is a high probability that they will not tell exactly the same story. The probability of different stories being told will be enormously increased if one or several of the witnesses assert that the event involved decisive divine intervention and other witnesses claim that no such thing took place. That result is precisely what happened with testimony regarding Jesus of Nazareth. Unfortunately for the Jews, there was no way that the Christian church could accept the dominant Jewish interpretation of events surrounding Jesus of Nazareth, for Christians affirmed precisely what Jews rejected: namely, that Jesus is Lord, the Messiah, and that the revelation given to the Jewish patriarchs—

Abraham, Isaac, and Jacob—as well as to Moses and the prophets, prefigured and came to its fulfillment in Jesus. In sum, Christianity has historically understood itself as the religion God intended Judaism to be, but, owing to a failure of understanding or will, the Jews were incapable of receiving God's most precious gift.

What eventually emerged was a more structured, more official Christian position toward Jews, one that scholars now identify as a "teaching of contempt."[1] Built upon foundations that extend back into pre-Christian antiquity, and advanced by the first-century competition between the two rival faiths, this *adversos Judaeos* tradition or anti-Judaism, as it is sometimes called, achieved ever greater influence as Christian authority and Roman power joined hands, an outcome that led eventually to an essentially Christian civilization in Europe and the Western world.[2] As will become clearer in what follows, the anti-Judaic teaching of contempt—its vestiges still exist—pivots around *supersessionism*, a term derived from the Latin *supersedēre* (to sit on). Citing the theologian Mary Boys as his source, Padraic O'Hare identifies supersessionism's defining features as follows: "(1) revelation in Jesus Christ supersedes the revelation to Israel; (2) the New Testament fulfills the Old Testament; (3) the church replaces the Jews as God's people; (4) Judaism is obsolete; its covenant abrogated; (5) post-exilic Judaism was legalistic; (6) the Jews did not heed the warning of the prophets; (7) the Jews did not understand the prophecies about Jesus; (8) the Jews were Christ killers."[3] In a word, supersession means, with a vengeance, that Christianity allegedly trumps Judaism.

We have noted how Jews and Christians created dissonance for each other. Each tradition claimed to possess accurate and exclusive knowledge of God's will. That will, moreover, they took to be decisively revealed in particular events and through particular persons. They agreed on some of these matters but just enough to make their disagreements enormous, for each tradition looked forward to a time when all persons would acknowledge and serve its truth, something that could be done only if people abandoned one tradition for the other. Existing in such close proximity, mutual disconfirmation sowed seeds of doubt and threatened each other's established beliefs, values, and sanctioned modes of behavior. One function of religious leaders and teachers is precisely to reduce such dissonance for their people. Both camps worked hard to achieve that end. Jews, for example, could and did argue convincingly that Jesus simply did not qualify as the messiah, let alone as God incarnate, an analysis reinforced by the fact that Jesus was, after all, one of their own. To Christian ears, that strategy defamed Jesus intolerably. So, a favorite dissonance-reducing strategy employed by Christians was to elaborate the defamation of Jewish character. For instance, through the teachings of church fathers such as Justin, Tertullian, Origen, Gregory of Nyssa, and John Chrysostom, a theology of supersession or displacement insisted on pariah status for Jews.

At least two claims were central to this perspective: first, God was essentially finished with the Jews; second, the Christian church had replaced the Jewish people as a new Israel with a special historic destiny. To make the case, a variety of arguments and charges were made. One approach was to look at Jewish rejection of Jesus not as an isolated instance but rather as the gravest and ultimate example of age-old Jewish perversity. Jewish history, it was claimed, had been a repetition of apostasy that resulted even in the shunning and killing of prophets sent by God to correct Jewish evildoing. Indeed the Torah was given to Jews not as a blessing but as a check on their viciousness. Of course, there were exceptions. Not all Jews fitted this description, but the ones who did not were the forerunners of the Christian church, not the patriarchs of Jewish failure.

The decisive Jewish sin, the indictment continued, was the willful murder of the Messiah. For this deicide no retribution could be too great, and thus all Jewish favor with God was lost. No more were the Jews a chosen people, except in the sense that they had been cast permanently into exile. Their Holy City ravaged, their Temple ruined, neither would be rebuilt. Jewish misery would continue to the end of time. One hope remained. When Jesus returned in glory, Jews would have a final chance to repent, a teaching that also gave impetus to conversion attempts whose success could count as evidence that the kingdom was not far off.

The language in which such views were expressed was often impassioned, especially in the eastern regions of the Roman world where Christians encountered Jews in the greatest number and were at times persuaded to give up their Christianity in favor of Judaism. Gregory of Nyssa (331–96), for instance, spoke of Jews as "murderers of the Lord, assassins of the prophets, rebels and detesters of God, they outrage the Law, resist grace, repudiate the faith of their fathers. Companions of the devil, race of vipers, informers, calumniators, darkeners of the mind, pharisaic leaven, Sanhedrin of demons, accursed, detested, lapidators, enemies of all that is beautiful." Somewhat later in Antioch, where Christians were probably tempted to associate with the numerous and influential Jews of that city, John Chrysostom (344–407) sermonized as follows: "Brothel and theater, the synagogue is also a cave of pirates and the lair of wild beasts. . . . Living for their belly, mouth forever gaping, the Jews behave no better than hogs and goats in their lewd grossness and the excesses of their gluttony. They can do one thing only: gorge themselves with food and drink."[4]

Anti-Jewish polemics were not an end in themselves. They also served to undergird Christian triumphalism, the sense that Christians were favored partners in a new covenant that would vindicate Christian faith and God's sovereignty. By putting Jews down, Christians thought they exalted themselves. But in spite of rhetoric that often knew no bounds, Christian restraint toward Jews remained important too. Under pagan Roman law, Jews had been both Roman citizens and a protected national group with a right to their own forms of worship. The policies of Christian Rome minimized Jewish freedom—for example, severe laws were passed against Jewish attempts to convert Christians and against interference with Christian attempts to convert Jews—but within prescribed boundaries Jewish existence and religious practices were permitted.

In sum, ancient Christian logic entailed a volatile ambivalence about Jews. If Jews were to be permitted to dwell in the midst of Christians, under no circumstances were they to be permitted to lead the faithful astray. At stake was the credibility of the foundations of the Christian faith. On the other hand, although Jews were a dissonance-producing threat and as such hated and attacked, they could also be useful. Their existence as outsiders made plain that the church was victorious. Their conversion to Christianity provided a potential for further corroboration of Christianity's triumph. For those who failed to see the light, God's punishing justice would suffice. Implicitly if not explicitly, then, the aim—never unrelated to an awareness that Jews were a disconfirming threat—was essentially to rid Christendom of Jews. If the church's methods could never have been those of National Socialism, nonetheless implications of its theology about the Jews were not lost on those who made way for Auschwitz.

Christian hostility toward Jews was not simply the result of gratuitous malice vented by an immoral rabble. Nor is the facile explanation that the church was intrinsically evil or psychologically demented an adequate account. Rabble, corruption, and psychological pathology there were. The more telling fact to reckon with, however, is that the most thoroughly anti-Jewish positions were advanced by the church's greatest saints and most rational thinkers. Some of them have been  mentioned before, but Jewish-Christian circumstances from the beginning of the medieval period until the eve of the French Revolution can be illuminated in outline by observing attitudes toward Jews held by Augustine (354–430) and by the Protestant reformer Martin Luther (1483–1546). Among other things, these examples suggest that every tendency to interpret antisemitism merely as an expression of a psychological disorder on the part of its advocates is a misleading simplification. Such interpretations overlook the fact that, insofar as Jews persisted as disconfirming "others," Christians had substantive reasons, as logical as they were unfortunate, for anti-Jewish hostility. Christians also had the power to dictate what status that hostility would entail for the Jewish minority. Let there be no misunderstanding: that hostility was deplorable. Yet even the extremity of Christian vilification of Jews suggests how deep-seated the reasons for it were and how seriously they were taken. The anti-Jewish stance of leading Christian thinkers can best be explained by the desire to defend what they regarded as supremely important, the authority and integrity of their religious tradition. The point is not to claim that these tactics were morally justifiable or that they were consistent with all Christian teachings. It is to claim that a logic governed Christian anti-Judaism just as later on a developed rationale would govern Nazi efforts to destroy Europe's Jews.

Augustine of Hippo remains an intellectual giant in Western civilization. His formative influence on Christian theology was profound, and no Christian thinker between Paul and Thomas Aquinas exerted greater influence. *The City of God* is Augustine's magisterial theology of history, and in it the Jews play a fundamental role. Augustine could not withhold all affection for the Jewish people, because God's work of redemption had been carried on through their history, culminating in the crucifixion and resurrection of Jesus. At the same time, Augustine identified Jews as enemies of the church. Their dispersion and misery were the results of blind refusal to acknowledge Christian truth. By permitting their continued existence, however, God's grace to Christians was all the more evident, for the dispersed Jews remained as a witness-people.[5] Their ongoing history and fate testified to the necessity and significance of Christ's coming; the misery of their experience also underwrote the conviction that God's power cannot be mocked. Augustine still enjoined Christians to love Jews and thus to lead them to Christ, but Christian ambivalence toward Jews persisted. Since Jews were potential converts, the official view was usually that their lives should be spared. Debasing Jewish life, however, was much less discouraged, for Jewish suffering appeared to vindicate the church's authority. That authority entailed that Jewish resistance to Christian pressures for conversion would not be permitted with impunity. The church, for example, asserted itself in the legal domain to ensure that Christian-Jewish contacts would be carefully regulated. Intermarriage was prohibited. Jews were excluded from the army, from most administrative posts, and from the legal profession. Commerce remained open to them, however, and many moved into those fields, eventually fulfilling economic functions that gave them a protected political status even as they were restricted in their rights.

By the fifth century centralized Roman authority was in decline, the political map of Christendom destabilized. It is impossible, therefore, to make statements that apply to Jewish life without exception, but until the eleventh century Jews and Christians coexisted without much change under terms we have been describing. That situation, however, was not to last. A major turning point occurred in 1096, when crusading Christian fervor to recapture Palestine's holy places from Islamic forces took its toll on the Jews as well. Massacres followed as Christians also sought to purify their European territory in early versions of what would now be called "ethnic cleansing." Following on the heels of those blood-baths, Jews were obliged by the Fourth Lateran Council (1215) to wear specially marked clothing. Different styles developed, but in France the insignia was a yellow patch, the precursor of the yellow star later decreed by the Nazis. In the popular imagination, Jews became increasingly identified with Satan. Both cause and effect of that pernicious belief was the "blood libel," a charge that still raises its ugly head periodically. It alleged that Jews murdered Christian children so that Christian blood could be used at the Passover meal, which was portrayed as a demonic, inverted caricature of Christ's Last Supper and Holy Communion. Jews were also falsely accused of poisoning wells and, worse still, of desecrating the body of Christ by despoiling the bread and wine that Christians took to become Christ himself in the sacrament of the Mass. Jews were held responsible too for the plagues and famines that ravaged Europe in the fourteenth and fifteenth centuries. Pogroms exacted payment in blood for these "crimes." Outright expulsion occurred as well—from England in 1290, from France beginning in 1306, and from Spain in 1492. The reasons for these and related departures, however, were more complex than appeals to irrational Jew hatred and random violence suggest. They often hinged decisively on economics.

For centuries most European Jews had lived in western and central Europe, but that pattern shifted as Jews were increasingly forced east. Why they headed

*Nostra Aetate → Oct 28 1965 -- Second Vatican Council -- discusses Church's Relation to other Religions -- Jews and Christians unified as one under Jesus -- Jews not to blame.

in that direction is clarified by recalling that Europe's medieval economy was pre-capitalist. Far more agrarian than urban, it aimed much less toward investment for industrial production and profit making than toward subsistence. Because farming and ownership of land were not open to Jews, they tended to work in certain commercial and professional roles that were needed but not filled by the dominant majority, often because ecclesiastical law and tradition restricted financial dealings. As merchants, traders, and moneylenders, the Jews' marketplace activities rarely won them esteem, but at least the Jews had a place, because they served a complementary economic function. The Jewish situation in western and central Europe, however, began to deteriorate as the subsistence economy of the feudal period was displaced by nascent forms of capitalism and industrialization. This transformation led to the emergence of an indigenous commercial class; it competed with Jews who occupied similar roles. Predictably the "outsiders" lost more often than they won.

Shunted into marginal enterprises—peddling and pawnbroking, for example—many Jews in western and central Europe were squeezed economically to such an extent that they found it necessary to seek their livelihood elsewhere. The economically backward regions of eastern Europe provided a safety valve. There Jews could once again make a decent living by filling needed commercial roles in an economy still largely agrarian and subsistence-oriented. Yet, if Jews were once again an economically complementary population, that status still left them vulnerable. In Poland, to cite one case, Jewish life achieved remarkable autonomy, prestige, and influence from the early sixteenth century until the middle of the seventeenth century, a period when the Jewish population grew from about 15,000 to an estimated 300,000. However, the 1648 anti-Polish uprising led by the Cossack chieftain Bogdan Chmielnicki unleashed a series of events that also brought Russian and Swedish invaders into Poland. The Jews paid double. They were savaged by Poland's enemies and then by the Poles themselves on the grounds that they had aided the invaders. Jews were killed in the tens of thousands. Nevertheless, the number of Jews generally would continue to grow, reaching approximately 750,000 in Poland and 1.25 million in Europe overall by the middle of the eighteenth century.[6] Meanwhile, modernizing trends that took over in western Europe also worked their way east. Those developments contributed to making millions of Polish and Russian Jews unwanted, which, in turn, eventually helped to set them up for the Final Solution.

- Papal Bull = issued murder by Church / any issue by church

## MARTIN LUTHER, THE PROTESTANT REFORMATION, AND THE ENLIGHTENMENT

As the sixteenth century dawned, the philosopher Erasmus (ca. 1466–1536) spoke perceptively about Europe generally when he observed that "if it is the part of a good Christian to detest the Jews, then we are all good Christians."[7] By then, anti-Jewish feeling had diversified and intensified as economic and broadly cultural

Christian Church → better if have focused on Mary/Jesus as Jews as well as Christian peoples prejudice supplemented its basically religious beginnings in Christendom. All of these forces, plus others of a particular political significance, would conspire to make the Reformation a crucial time in Jewish destiny. Sometimes Protestant-Catholic rivalry gave Jews room in which they could maneuver to their advantage, but it can scarcely be said that Jewish security in Christendom was permanently enhanced, let alone guaranteed, by the Protestant Reformation and the Catholic Counter-Reformation that soon followed.

Protestant rebellion against Roman Catholicism produced two main branches. Though not the earliest, one was inspired by Geneva's John Calvin (1509–64). His version of the Reformation flourished in western European areas from which Jews had already emigrated in large numbers, which may help to account for the relatively low degree of anti-Jewish sentiment in his outlook. In any case, with motives that were political and economic as well as religious, the Christians who followed Calvin not only emphasized individual enterprise and responsibility and energetic political action, but also identified their strug-gle and mission with that of the biblical Jews. Their outlook tended to favor Jews more than was the case with Martin Luther and his German followers. Particu-larly in areas where Calvin's influence prevailed—parts of France, the Nether-lands, and eventually North America—a relatively tolerant attitude toward Jews could be found.

Luther's theology emphasized justification by faith in Christ, not by human works that would earn God's grace. This position led him to criticize a Roman church that seemed to have incorporated a "works righteousness" into its piety, replete with an emphasis on penance, pilgrimages, and indulgences that might win one favor in heaven. Luther's challenge to Rome included a fear of political anarchy and an awareness that the triumph of his religious reform depended on political power. Thus, although Luther wrote treatises about the limitation of such power and about the need for rulers to be in harmony with God's will, he also sided with political might that was friendly to his cause and urged obedience to it. Add to those facts the realization that Luther's political consciousness included seeds that would later flower into German nationalism, and it is not hard to see that his legacy is mixed in the light of Auschwitz.

On the Jewish question, Luther's attitudes were at first ambivalent and then overtly hostile. In the 1520s Luther primarily wanted to convert Jews. Indeed part of his attack on papal Catholicism was that it had treated Jews wrongly, so much so that in a 1523 pamphlet, significantly titled "Jesus Christ Was Born a Jew," he would write, "If I had been a Jew, I should have preferred to turn pig before I became a Christian, seeing how these imbeciles and ignorant louts govern and teach the Christian faith. They have treated the Jews as if they were dogs and not men. They have done nothing but persecute them." In addition, he identified the Jews as "the blood relatives, the cousins and brothers of Our Lord," and then went on to say that "if His blood and flesh could be boasted of, the Jews belong to Jesus Christ much more than we do. . . . We must welcome them in friendship, let them live and work with us, and they will be of one heart with us."[8]

Luther hoped that milder treatment might produce Jewish conversion. When those hopes did not prevail, his policy changed. His antisemitic booklet *On the Jews and Their Lies* (1543) advocated the destruction of Jewish synagogues and houses, confiscation of their religious books, restriction of their worship, and even their expulsion. By refusing to see the light and embrace the Christian faith, the Jews called into question the truth of the Christian faith, including its trust that God had raised Jesus from death and guaranteed eternal life to those who believed in him. Some scholars think that Luther advocated these extreme measures still hoping that at least a few Jews might be brought to their senses and realize that Christian conversion was the only way, but it also seems clear that Luther's patience with Jewish intransigence had run out. At the time, his writings on the subject were not widely circulated, but four centuries later the Nazis would make public Luther's largely forgotten text, capitalizing on it in ways that Luther could not have anticipated or imagined. Whether those ways would have surprised him altogether must remain an unanswered question.[9]

The five-hundredth anniversary of Luther's birth was observed in 1983. Luther was nine years old when Columbus discovered the New World, but Luther did as much to discover the new world of the spirit as Columbus did to discover the territorial New World. If, as many historians and sociologists of religion maintain, the modern world is in large measure an unintended consequence of religious and cultural forces arising out of the Protestant Reformation, Luther can be seen as one of its seminal creators. Consider further, then, the extent to which he contributed to one of the darker aspects of modernity, antisemitic genocide.

According to Ernst Troeltsch (1865–1923), an insightful social scientist and an influential interpreter of the history of Christian thought, the new element in the Protestant theology initiated by Luther was "the special content of the conception of grace."[10] Before Luther, grace had normally been regarded as a mystical reality imparted through the sacraments. Protestantism came to regard grace as "a Divine temper of faith, conviction, spirit, knowledge, and trust . . . discerned as the loving will of God which brings with it the forgiveness of sins."[11] As a consequence, according to Troeltsch, Protestant Christianity became primarily a matter of faith and conviction. This development was, as we shall see, of enormous importance in shaping Luther's attitude toward the Jews. By putting the whole weight of his religious commitment on faith, it became supremely important for Luther to discredit any group that might challenge his belief system.

Luther was convinced that no institution or ritual could enable sinful human beings to ascend to the supernatural. Without extranatural intervention, no human institution, not even the church, could rescue humanity from the dreadful fate that awaits all creatures. Persons in their ordinary sinful state without God are hopelessly lost. No atheistic existentialist ever held a bleaker image of the human condition than Luther's image of humankind without God. Luther once commented that he would rather be a sow than be a person without Christ, because a sow does not have the fear and the anxiety to which humanity is condemned after the fall.

Luther's unique contribution to the religious thought of his time was to insist that, though humanity's fallen nature is hopelessly cut off from God, nevertheless the graciousness and righteousness of God are such that sinful persons can be reconciled to God. However, such a reconciliation is entirely dependent on what God, not a person, does. Moreover, the good news whereby we learn of this reconciliation is to be found solely in Scripture, whose central message and true meaning, according to Luther, is God's justification of humanity in and through Jesus Christ.

Notice what transpired: Luther abandoned the medieval hope that persons can rise from a natural to a supernatural state through this-worldly means, whether of religion or reason. Everything now depends upon the truth of Scripture's account of God's promises. Luther tells us that Christians are assured that Christ is the "ruling Messiah." He then adds, "If this were not so, then God's word and promise would be a lie."[12] For Luther and those who follow him, if his reading of Scripture is without foundation, then there is no hope of salvation for any human being. Yet it was precisely his reading of Scripture that was challenged not only by Jews but by many Christians as well. Some way had to be found to meet the challenge.

Luther's "immense simplification in doctrine," to use Troeltsch's phrase, significantly aggravated the hazard of Jews living in regions subject to Lutheran influence.[13] Perhaps we can understand this better if we imagine that in the year 1540, three years before Luther wrote *On the Jews and Their Lies*, a delegation of Chinese had been living in Saxony and entered into dialogue with him. If Luther had told this imaginary delegation of his faith in redemption through Christ as revealed in the Gospels, they might have responded: "Dr. Luther, we really do not know what you are talking about. We know about enlightenment and we know about the cycle of dependent causation, but we do not know about your Christ, nor do we know anything about the God you say speaks to people through your holy books."

Without doubt Luther would have been disturbed and annoyed, but it is unlikely that his annoyance would have been remotely as strong as was his annoyance with the Jews. Luther published *On the Jews and Their Lies* in response to a Jewish challenge to his interpretation of Scripture.[14] Luther was moved to write the treatise as a result of a letter he received from Count Wolf Schlick zu Falkenau in which the latter enclosed a polemical treatise by a rabbi who had criticized Luther's earlier work "Against the Sabbatarians" (1538). The count requested that Luther answer the rabbi's treatise, which is no longer extant.[15] Thus, Luther's most important and most hostile anti-Jewish document was a response to a Jewish challenge against his own reading of the Bible.

There is, of course, a very important reason why Luther was far more hostile to the Jews than he would have been to the Chinese. Unlike the Chinese, the Jews agreed with Luther that God was the ultimate ground of biblical authority. Both Luther and the Jews regarded the human condition as fallen and in need of divine redemption. However, an unbridgeable gap existed in their understanding of how

Jesus
Vs
Luther

redemption was to take place. For the Jews, redemption would ultimately result from compliance with the will of God as revealed in Scripture and as interpreted by the rabbis. For Luther, the Jewish belief was not only mistaken but perverse and demonic. To rely upon human works, such as those required by Jewish religious practice, was to make precisely the kind of spiritual error that had been fostered by the Roman Catholic Church in its insistence that the sacraments were the path to salvation. Moreover, the Jewish error was compounded by rejection of Christ as the Redeemer. Thus, the Jews were far more offensive to Luther than any other religious community. Having reduced all of Christian hope to a scripturally based faith in Jesus Christ, Luther could hardly have been expected to look kindly upon exponents of a tradition that used Scripture itself to deny what for Luther had become his sole assurance of salvation. If the Jews were right, Luther had nothing to hope for save the sow's fate, absent the sow's blessed ignorance.

By contrast, Judaism constituted far less of a challenge to Roman Catholicism than it did to Luther, because of the totality of religion, culture, and tradition that served to undergird the medieval church. Jews may have challenged some aspects of Catholic belief in the Middle Ages, but they were in no position to challenge the imposing edifice of medieval Christian civilization as a whole. Ironically, when Luther reduced the religious foundations of Christianity to faith in Christ as revealed in Scripture, he added greater weight to the Jewish challenge and thus to the Jewish danger. Not only had Luther reduced religious hope to a single source, the Bible, but he had chosen the one source the Jews were best able to challenge. Jewish scholars were at home in their ancestral language, the first language of Scripture, and they were the people into whose midst Jesus of Nazareth had been born.

Luther's *On the Jews and Their Lies* begins by stating that the interpretation of Scripture is the fundamental area of conflict between him and the Jews. "I have received a treatise in which a Jew engages in dialogue with a Christian," he wrote. Luther complained that the Jew "dares to pervert the scriptural passages which we cite in testimony to our faith, concerning our Lord Christ and Mary his mother, and to interpret them quite differently. With this argument he thinks he can destroy the basis of our faith."[16] Consequently, much of *On the Jews and Their Lies* is given to Luther's refutation of the Jewish interpretation of Scripture. Moreover, Luther was altogether clear concerning what was at stake in this dispute: if the Jewish interpretation is correct, Christian faith in Christ's redemption is without foundation. Luther's fundamental motive for his attack was thus the defense of his reading of Christian faith.

In the treatise, Luther asserts that he is neither interested in quarreling with the Jews nor really in attempting to convert them. Whatever hopes he may have had at an earlier period for their conversion through persuasion have long since been abandoned. Only their dire straits might cause some to change, but even that prospect is dim. "They have failed," he writes, "to learn any lesson from the terrible distress that has been theirs for over fourteen hundred years in exile."[17] Nevertheless, Luther counseled those Christians who have reason to enter into dialogue with Jews to offer their religious rivals the following proof of their errors:

> But if you have to or want to talk with them, do not say any more than this: "Listen, Jew, are you aware that Jerusalem and your sovereignty, together with your temple and priesthood, have been destroyed for over 1,460 years?" . . . Let the Jews bite on this nut and dispute this question as long as they wish.
>
> For such ruthless wrath of God is sufficient evidence that they assuredly have erred and gone astray. . . . For one dare not regard God as so cruel that he would punish his own people so long, so terribly, so unmercifully, and in addition keep silent, comforting them neither with words nor with deeds, and fixing no time limit and no end to it. Who would have faith, hope, or love toward such a God? Therefore this work of wrath is proof that the Jews, surely rejected by God, are no longer his people, and neither is he any longer their God. . . .
>
> In short, as has already been said, do not engage much in debate with Jews about the articles of our faith. . . . There is no hope until they reach the point where their misery finally makes them pliable and they are forced to confess that the Messiah has come, and that he is our Jesus.[18]

For Luther, as for so many Christian thinkers both ancient and modern, the best refutation of the Jewish reading of Scripture is Jewish misfortune. Luther's argument was not unlike that of the prophets, save that the prophets were lovingly admonishing their own community, whereas there was no love in Luther's description of those he regarded as enemies and strangers. Had the Jews understood God's revelation and conformed to the divine will, none of their terrible sufferings would have taken place. Luther argued that a just God would never have visited so horrible a fate on those who are truly God's people. Hence, Luther saw only one hope for the Jews: their fate would become so miserable that a few might see the light and accept Christ as their Savior.

There is little doubt how Luther would have interpreted the Holocaust: he would have seen it as decisive proof of God's rejection of the Jews. Nor is it surprising that, when the theologians of the German Lutheran Church met in Darmstadt in 1948, three years after the Holocaust, they proclaimed that the Holocaust was a divine punishment and called upon the Jews to halt their rejection and ongoing crucifixion of Christ.[19] Whatever the motives of the theologians in releasing this document, they were undoubtedly speaking in the spirit of the founder of their church.

Although Luther's arguments were harsh and although contemporary Lutherans, at least in North America, have dissociated themselves from the overtly antisemitic aspects of his writings, it must be recognized that this position vis-à-vis Judaism conforms to the classical position of Christendom.[20] Luther explicitly derived from Scripture his position that Jewish misfortune is proof of Christian truth and Jewish error:

> Well, let the Jews regard our Lord Jesus as they will. We behold the fulfillment of the words spoken by him in Luke 21 [:20, 22–23f.]: "But when you

see Jerusalem surrounded by armies, then know that its desolation has come
near . . . for these are days of vengeance. For great distress shall be upon the
earth and wrath upon this people."[21]

One must sadly observe, moreover, that Luther's polemical use of history to
discredit the Jewish interpretation of Scripture was by no means without a measure of methodological justification. Both Judaism and Christianity have traditionally claimed exclusive knowledge of God's revelation. The Jewish-Christian
controversy was fundamentally concerned with the historical question of what
God had actually done in relation to Israel and, through Israel, for all of humanity. Jews could scarcely expect their rabbis to reject publicly the Christian view of
God's action in history without arousing a strong Christian response. In view of
the overwhelming weight that Luther placed upon Scripture as the sole source
of revealed truth, it was unavoidable that he would attempt to argue from history to discredit Judaism. For Luther to have taken the secular view that honorable people can sincerely disagree on ultimate questions would have been to
render doubtful the sole foundation for his hope of redemption.

Unfortunately, Luther's theological polemic led him, as well as other great
Christian spiritual leaders, to defame Judaism in terms more radical than those
with which any other religious community had ever attempted to discredit a rival.
For Luther, the bottom line was that the Jews and their religion ended up being
radically evil. Put differently, for Luther the Jews are of the devil, and Luther took
the devil to be real, not metaphorical. Here are some characteristic expressions of
his views on the subject:

I advise you not to enter their synagogue; all devils might dismember and
devour you there. . . . For he who cannot hear or bear to hear God's word
is not of God's people. And if they are not God's people, then they are the
devil's people.[22]

You cannot learn anything from them except how to misunderstand the
divine commandments. . . .
        Therefore be on your guard against the Jews, knowing that wherever they
have their synagogues, nothing is found but a den of devils in which sheer
self-glory, conceit, lies, blasphemy, and defaming of God and men are practiced most maliciously.[23]

In yet another passage, Luther expressed himself in a similar vein:

They are real liars and bloodhounds. . . . Their heart's most ardent sighing
and yearning and hoping is set on the day on which they can deal with us
Gentiles as they did with the Gentiles in Persia at the time of Esther. . . .
The sun has never shone on a more bloodthirsty and vengeful people than
they are who imagine that they are God's people who have been commissioned and commanded to murder and to slay the Gentiles. In fact, the most
important thing that they expect of their Messiah is that he will murder and
kill the entire world with their sword.[24]

At the beginning of the twentieth century, a fabricated document entitled *The Protocols of the Elders of Zion* first appeared in Russia. It "revealed" a detailed plot by international Jewry to undermine Christianity and to establish Jewish dominion over the world. Few writings have done more to fuel antisemitic fires; historians of the Holocaust have shown that this document provided antisemites with a "warrant for genocide."[25] The *Protocols* was widely disseminated throughout Europe between the end of World War I and the beginning of World War II. Much to Hitler's delight, the American industrialist Henry Ford gave the *Protocols* extensive publicity.[26] Its distribution, which continues in the twenty-first century—especially among Islamic fundamentalists—contributed to a climate of opinion in which the elimination of the Jews was seen as beneficial. Nevertheless, even the *Protocols* did not go as far as did Luther, who accused the Jews of plotting genocide against the Gentile world. Moreover, Luther was not content with verbal aggression. He actively sought the expulsion of the Jews from Saxony, an effort which succeeded in 1536. When the edict was partly rescinded two years later, Luther was vehement in his opposition. In his very last sermon, preached on 15 February 1546, he demanded the expulsion of the Jews from Germany.[27]

Nor had Luther refrained from advocating overt violence against the Jews and their institutions:

> We are at fault in not slaying them. Rather we allow them to live freely in our midst despite all their murdering, cursing, blaspheming, lying, and defaming. . . .
> What shall we Christians do with this rejected and condemned people, the Jews? Since they live among us, we dare not tolerate their conduct, now that we are aware of their lying and reviling and blaspheming. . . . I shall give you my sincere advice:
> First, to set fire to their synagogues or schools and to bury and cover with dirt whatever will not burn, so that no man will ever again see a stone or a cinder of them. This is to be done in honor of our Lord and of Christendom, so that God might see that we are Christians, and do not condone or knowingly tolerate such public lying, cursing, and blaspheming of his Son and of his Christians. . . .
> In Deuteronomy 13[:12ff.] Moses writes that any city that is given to idolatry shall be totally destroyed by fire, and nothing of it shall be preserved. If he were alive today, he would be the first to set fire to the synagogues and houses of the Jews. . . .
> Second, I advise that their houses also be razed and destroyed. For they pursue in them the same aims as in their synagogues.[28]

Although Luther continues at length in much the same spirit, there is little need to follow him further. It is significant, however, to note a comment that the Lutheran editor of the American translation of Luther's works offers about this passage:

> It is impossible to publish Luther's treatise today . . . without noting how similar to his proposals were the actions of the National Socialist regime in Germany in the 1930's and 1940's. On the night of November 9–10, 1938,

*[handwritten margin note: Fabricated by Antisemites in Russia]*

> the so-called *Kristallnacht,* for example, . . . synagogues in all parts of Germany, together with many Jewish homes and shops, were burned to the ground. . . . In subsequently undertaking the physical annihilation of the Jews, however, the Nazis surpassed even Luther's severity.[29]

While the editor's embarrassment at Luther's call to overt violence is obvious, especially in view of the events of World War II, he has apparently overlooked the fact that Luther had written, "We are at fault in not slaying them."

What shall we make of this religiously legitimated incitement to homicidal violence? For many Jews, passages such as the ones we have quoted from Luther are evidence of a moral flaw at the heart of Christianity and most especially in the stature of Luther himself. For many post-Holocaust Christians, including members and leaders of Lutheran churches, the passages are an embarrassment. In the 1930s, however, *On the Jews and Their Lies* occasioned little embarrassment in German Lutheran circles. When the treatise was published in the Munich edition of 1936, the German editors claimed approvingly that *On the Jews and Their Lies* was the arsenal from which antisemitism had drawn its weapons.[30] Other leading German Lutherans of the period, including Bishop Otto Dibelius (1880–1967), who was to serve as president of the World Council of Churches in 1965, saw the National Socialist policies toward the Jews as the fulfillment of Luther's program.[31] Leaving aside the issue of active support for National Socialism's antisemitic policies, no European church during the period 1933–45 was more silent or indifferent to the known fate of the Jews than the German Lutheran Church.[32]

However one views Luther's writings on the Jews, he was without doubt one of the most influential religious leaders of all time. The sheer violence of the position taken by so dominant a figure points to an important, though often neglected, aspect of Christian antisemitism: the crucial question is not why mean-spirited or malicious people were so violently anti-Jewish but why some of the greatest thinkers and most pious saints within Christianity adopted that posture.

Briefly stated, the answer would appear to be that Luther, and others like him, felt compelled to negate and discredit the disconfirming other to maintain the credibility of those religious beliefs and values that were of absolutely fundamental importance to him. Because Judaism and Christianity have a common scriptural inheritance, the Jew can be for Christianity the disconfirming other par excellence, as indeed the Christian can be the disconfirming other par excellence for Judaism. The related problems of dissonance reduction and the disconfirming other had an especial urgency for Luther because of the overwhelming importance of his distinctive reading of Scripture for his whole religious system. If that reading proved mistaken, he had nothing left. Luther thus had little option but to attempt to convince, discredit, or eliminate the Jew as the disconfirming other. To convince meant to seek to convert; to discredit involved religious defamation such as the canard that the Jews were incarnations of the devil; to eliminate meant expulsion or mass murder. At the very least, Luther was compelled to defame the Jews and Judaism so as to minimize the credibility of their reading of Scripture and to combat their failure to accept Jesus as the Messiah. A practical consequence of the need to discredit or eliminate the disconfirming other is that, in the process, the other is always in danger of becoming wholly alien, that is, wholly outside of the universe of moral obligation of those whose values he or she challenges. This result is especially likely when, as in the case of the Jews, the other is identified with the devil. Such an identification can have the effect of religiously legitimating any conceivable violence, even extermination camps.

Furthermore, notice that Luther's attack was not an isolated phenomenon but arose out of the exclusivistic tendencies common to all of the world's major monotheistic religions: Judaism, Christianity, and Islam. For practical reasons, the exclusivism can be softened and played down, but each of these traditions contains the seeds of a resurgence of exclusivistic intolerance and violence on the part of those who claim that they are defending the true meaning of their tradition.[33] The exclusivism is grounded in Scripture. Admittedly, Scripture can be read so as to minimize the problem, but there does not seem to be any way to eliminate the exclusivistic component altogether. Neither Protestantism, Roman Catholicism, Judaism, nor Islam appears able wholly to abandon the claim that it alone is the true faith.

In a complex, interdependent world, there are, we trust, better solutions to the problem of the disconfirming other than Luther's. Yet we had best be warned by Luther's example. In times of minimal social stress, exclusivistic religions can normally live in relative peace with each other, especially when the power relations between them are clearly defined. Unfortunately, as the early twenty-first century has confirmed, we have all too many examples of periods of heightened social stress in which religious and communal strife has been intensified to the point of large-scale intergroup violence. The Reformation was such a time; so too was World War II. Moreover, intergroup violence has all too frequently received religious legitimation. Luther's sixteenth-century demonization of the Jews and Judaism, which reiterated the view of the Jews found in the Christian Gospels, gave sacred sanction in the twentieth century to a view of the Jews as enemies wholly outside of any conceivable German universe of moral obligation. Thus, it is hardly surprising that the German churches did not protest explicitly against the stripping of Jewish citizenship rights, the forcible deportation to the east of Jews whose families had lived in Germany for centuries, or the widely known, state-sponsored, systematic extermination of Europe's Jews. Germany was by no means the only country without effective religious protest against the extermination project, and Luther was hardly original in his virulent demonization of the Jews. Nevertheless, Luther made the Bible available to the Germans in their native tongue and did more to shape the religious life of his nation than any other figure in German history. He did not create the gas chambers. He did, however, contribute significantly to their indispensable precondition, the denial of the Jews' humanity and their transformation into Satan's children. What makes his contribution to the Holocaust especially ironic was the nature of his motives. Luther's fundamental interest was the defense of Christian faith. It was the historic misfortune of the Jews that their religious civilization challenged that faith. This challenge did not automatically make them candidates for the gas chambers. It did result, however, in the legitimation of their treatment as satanic nonpersons to whom German Christians felt themselves bound by no moral obligation.

The date when Hitler gave public notice of his intention to exterminate the Jews remains a matter of scholarly debate. Arguably, it was no later than his Reichstag speech of 30 January 1939 in which he proclaimed to the whole world, "Today I will once more be a prophet: If international Jewish financiers in and outside Europe should succeed in plunging the nations once more into a world war, then the result will be not the Bolshevization of the earth, and thus the victory of Jewry, but the annihilation of the Jewish race in Europe!"[34] In the winter of 1938–39, Hitler and the National Socialists wanted war and were far advanced in preparing for it. Therefore, Hitler could be interpreted as saying, in effect, "I intend to go to war and, before it is over, I intend to exterminate the Jews in Europe." As it became apparent that this was one promise Hitler meant to keep, German Lutheranism was neither able nor apparently much interested in defining the mass destructiveness as morally out of bounds. Even three years after the war, German Lutheran theologians could keep silent in the face of the monumental tragedy but felt compelled to proclaim the Holocaust as God's punishment of the people who continued to crucify Christ.

The full danger inherent in the Jewish challenge to Luther's Protestant interpretation of the Bible did not become apparent until World War II. More immediately, however, the Reformation also put at risk those Jews who resided in the Catholic strongholds of Europe, where the effects of the Counter-Reformation were being felt. The Counter-Reformation was not of help to Jews, for in spite of the later Luther's anti-Jewish posture, Roman Catholic leaders suspected that Jews were among those behind the Protestant challenge to Rome's authority. In Spain, for example, not only had the staunchly Catholic King Ferdinand and Queen Isabella criminalized the practice of Islam during their "purification" of Spain, but also stern Roman Catholic measures were directed at Jews who had recently—and often forcibly—converted to Christianity. Those Jews who refused conversion had already been expelled, but discrimination remained for those who had become Christian. Some Jews had converted on an external basis only; they continued their Jewish ways in secret. These *Marranos* (pigs), as they came to be called, were ferreted out by the Inquisition. Its measures, however, were judged insufficient to guarantee the cultural and religious homogeneity that Spain sought. One result was the 1547 Statute of Toledo, which mandated a test of "blood purity" (*limpieza de sangre*).

The initial *limpieza* law restricted those of Jewish blood from leadership roles in Toledo's cathedral. The broad implication, however, was that Jews, even if converted, were ineradicably stained. Soon the Spanish Inquisition expanded and extended "blood purity" law so that people of Jewish ancestry were excluded not only from religious offices but also from certain guilds as well as from some military, municipal, and educational roles. This Spanish example was not yet one of a full-blown, free-standing antisemitic racism, since the concern about Jewish blood was more the effect of a suspicion about religious impurity than a cause of discrimination in its own right. Nevertheless, the *limpieza* legislation represented a significant advance in the logic of hostility directed against the Jews. It would make even the racial nature of Nazi antisemitism, which has often been contrasted with Christian anti-Judaism, less than completely unprecedented in relation to some Christian practices.

Meanwhile, Cardinal Gian Pietro Caraffa, former head of the Holy Office of the Inquisition, became Pope Paul IV in 1555.[35] His Counter-Reformation reign was short, lasting only until his death in 1559, but especially for Jews it was decisive. Paul IV's earliest papal acts included support for *limpieza de sangre* legislation and the issuing of *Cum Nimis Absurdum*, the edict he proclaimed on 12 July 1555. In territory under Vatican authority, Jews were prohibited from owning land. Apart from menial exceptions, the edict also restricted Jewish entry to professions and trades. Taxes for Jews were increased; clothing and badge requirements for Jews were to be enforced. The list of ordinances was extensive, but no measure was more crucial than the one that required the establishment of Jewish ghettos, including one that was soon established in Rome. Defined by a wall whose construction the Jews themselves had to finance, that ghetto's cramped confines would provide their required Roman quarters until late in the nineteenth century. Much earlier, the Fourth Lateran Council (1215) had called for measures, including ghettoization, similar to those stipulated in *Cum Nimis Absurdum*. Jewish ghettos had been set up in various European cities, but enforcement of ghettoization had been irregular. Consequently, Pope Paul IV's ordinance was, in James Carroll's words, a milestone: "Never before had a decree ordering the establishment of a Jewish quarter been issued with such seriousness of intent, and never before, as subsequent history would show, was such a mandate to be so rigorously enforced. And never before had such a mandate been issued by a pope."[36] Later popes waxed and waned in their enthusiasm for measures of the kind promulgated by Pope Paul IV. Nevertheless, until emancipation reversed the trend more than three centuries later, his example meant, in Carroll's words once more, that "Jews in Christendom were to live in the ghetto."[37]

The Reformation fragmented Christian authority in Europe. For Jews it was never more than a mixed blessing, although the Reformation did nurture some forces that would *apparently*—and that term must be underscored—make their lot vastly better. Depressed by the continuous warfare between Catholics and Protestants and between the rapidly multiplying Protestant sects, but greatly impressed both by the power of human reason reflected in the mathematical and scientific advances of the time and by the economic possibilities that they might produce, a new class of bourgeois intellectuals became openly critical of Christianity and of the old order in general. In tandem with the economic developments discussed earlier, their Enlightenment outlook made its initial and most forceful impact in western and central Europe—especially in England and France and to a lesser extent in German and Italian regions. Only later did it find its way east. Not entirely welcome, because its ways tended to undermine religious tradition and long-established social structures, the Enlightenment's optimistic promises to liberate people from fear, superstition, and the dead hand of the past nonetheless made a powerfully winning appeal.

To conclude, however, that such a perspective was simply a reaction against Western religion would be mistaken. A more adequate interpretation is that these Enlightenment sentiments were a logical outcome of fundamental motifs in both Judaism and Christianity. Indeed, the beginnings of the modern secular world are located here. Arguably, given history's development, only those who believed in God's unique sovereignty could abandon religious belief in magic, spirits, and gods, and rationally conceive a world almost as subject to humanity's sovereign mastery as people were to God's. The paradoxical precondition of the rationalizing and secularized attitude that has effectively eliminated religious and ethical values from so many of the economic and productive processes of the modern world was a religious revolution. The biblical accounts of creation, for example, describe a natural order devoid of magical forces or gods that people must appease. If it is true that one must stand on proper terms with God, who both transcends the world and remains sovereign over it, still the forces of nature are ones that humanity can understand and instrumentalize even if they cannot be controlled completely. In addition, worldly principalities and political authorities have no divinity. Kings and queens are human; divinity is God's alone.

The Christian teaching of incarnation established a distinctive link between God and the world—one that the Catholic Mass and its doctrine of transubstantiation underwrote—but the emphasis remained on the difference between God and the world. At the same time, although both Jewish and Christian traditions have stressed that men and women sin against God, both religions also incorporate strands that strongly urge the use of the human mind to reason and resolve, to produce and progress, to criticize and calculate. Western religion, therefore, and the secularizing drive of the Enlightenment are more like two sides of one coin than they are simple opposites. Together they yielded—sometimes by design, sometimes inadvertently—a marked emphasis on knowledge as power, which, in turn, placed a premium on instrumental, problem-solving rationality. Because knowledge is power, the irony was that the advances of practical rationality could be used for any ends determined by those intelligent enough to master its methods and wily enough to succeed in the struggle to control its direction. Thus, as the cunning of history has unfolded, human reason is less the queen who rules economic and political might and more their handmaiden instead. Unintended and unnecessary though they may have been, the consequences resulting from Western religion and the Enlightenment would include National Socialism's Final Solution of the so-called Jewish question.[38]

Meanwhile, one of the Enlightenment's major themes was the conviction that Christians and Jews share a common humanity and basic human rights, and by the late eighteenth century, secular ideas about human equality, religious toleration, and basic civil liberties were becoming more widespread in Western civilization. These ideas lent force to the view that citizenship should belong to all inhabitants of a certain territory, regardless of their class or religion. Coming earlier in France (1789–91) and the Netherlands (1796) than in Austria-Hungary (1867), Germany (1871), or Russia (1917), emancipation gradually expanded civic equality for Europe's Jews. Restrictions of ghetto life relaxed partly because capitalism was encouraging an economic system in which usury was permissible, international connections indispensable, and concern to maximize profits so intense as to transcend some of the animosity of ethnic prejudice and religious difference. Assimilation without discarding Jewish identity, if one chose to keep it, no longer seemed impossible. But once again it must be emphasized that the state of the Jewish question in Europe was anything but uniform. As the French Revolution of 1789 approached, the eighteenth century contained pogroms—they would persist and even escalate in some parts of Europe in the nineteenth century—as well as pro-Jewish philosophes.

Jewish emancipation was never welcomed universally, and it was resisted with devastating success, as the Holocaust eventually showed. Even some of the secular intellectuals during the Enlightenment used their pro-Jewish pronouncements more as a means to embarrass and discredit Christian authority than honestly to advance the Jewish cause. Others were openly antisemitic too, sharing Voltaire's outspoken opinion in 1756 that Jews are "an ignorant and barbarous people, who have long united the most sordid avarice with the most detestable superstition and the most invincible hatred for every people by whom they are tolerated and enriched." Voltaire thought the Jews were a threat to European culture. "Still," he conceded, "we ought not to burn them."[39] Suspicions that the Jews were ultimately an alien people, who would subvert new nation-states, diversified and intensified antisemitism yet again by giving it a secular footing. From that base, antisemitism could gnaw away at emancipation, permitting it to exist in letter but not necessarily in spirit.

In a word, emancipation had numerous strings attached. As Count Stanislas de Clermont-Tonnerre, a strong advocate for Jewish civil rights, put the point in the French National Assembly's citizenship debate on 23 December 1789: "The Jews should be denied everything as a nation, but granted everything as individuals. . . . It is intolerable that the Jews should become a separate political formation or class in the country. Every one of them must individually become a citizen; if they do not want this, they must inform us and we shall then be compelled to expel them. The existence of a nation within a nation is unacceptable to our country."[40] Clermont-Tonnerre's view, which was widely shared by those who were favorably disposed to Jewish emancipation, meant that Jews must largely set aside their peculiar ways and become, in effect, much less Jewish. Even if the Jews did so, however, it did not follow that they would be fully accepted in the regimes where their newly gained citizenship placed them. Anti-Jewish feeling had not disappeared. Emancipated and assimilated Jews could still be regarded with suspicion and hostility precisely because they were perceived to be receiving and taking advantages that they had not earned and did not deserve.

Once more, Jews would pay double. They would be damned if they did assimilate and damned if they did not.[41]

Later on we shall see in greater detail how these developments advanced approaches to Auschwitz. For now, let this chapter conclude by taking stock of three major points highlighted in its survey of historical background for the Holocaust. First, Jewish history is the story of a people who chose to be different and, often to their disadvantage, were stamped as such by the majority populations around them. As an alien people in Christendom, European Jews possessed little power. Although commonly under duress, Jewish culture and religious life still endured and sometimes prospered there. Indeed, far from succumbing to pressures from the Gentile majority, Jewish life proved amazingly resilient and energetic.[42] While preserving Jewish uniqueness, this vitality made Jews readily identifiable. It also made them vulnerable just to the degree that they were politically powerless. Too foreign from the majority, under Nazi rule they were destined to become an unwanted population ruthlessly targeted for elimination. That fact should stand as a warning to any who take cultural pluralism for granted or who glibly think that separation from the majority ethos may not exact a heavy cost.

Second, during the period under examination in this chapter, persecutions and massacres conspired with Christian desires for the Jews eventually to disappear through conversion, but they were not yet targeted by systematic, state-sponsored policies aimed at their total extermination. The reasons include the fact that the Jewish religion gave birth to a rival Christian faith whose power in the West depended not only on repressing Jewish existence but also on sustaining it for spiritual and economic purposes. Thus, although Jews were vilified and segregated, those measures did not seek a murderous total annihilation of Jewish life. However, if Christianity alone would never have been sufficient to cause the Holocaust, it must be said that Christian authority proved unable, if not unwilling, to prevent the Nazi state from murdering two-thirds of European Jewry. The Nazis and their collaborators used religious history, and specifically Christian teachings about Jews, to obtain precedents for many of the measures that they exacted against the Jews. Without the anti-Jewish feeling that Christianity sustained for centuries, moreover, it is barely conceivable that Nazi Germany would have targeted the Jews for annihilation. Christianity's historic hostility toward Jews certainly belongs high on any list of conditions that were necessary for the Holocaust to take place.

Third, anti-Jewish feeling waxed and waned over the centuries, but in Christendom it diversified, too. Economic and cultural elements were incorporated in addition to the religious. Racial overtones and aspects of suspicion that were primarily nationalistic and secular began to intrude as well. So long as Jews could be seen as potential Christian converts and/or as a complementary economic population, their vulnerability was at least reduced. Conversely, as the former consideration became less important in a West secularized by forces latent in its own religious traditions, as well as by the Enlightenment, the latter status took on greater import. Unfortunately, the chances for Jews to occupy an economically complementary status also diminished as Europe's economy modernized and as political nationalism flourished. Still, as we leave this chapter, it could be argued that circumstances were looking relatively better than they had been for the estimated 1.5 million Jews who inhabited Europe in the late eighteenth century, a number that would approach nine million early in the twentieth century.[43] That appraisal, sadly, would prove to be an illusion within the lull before the storm. Why that storm broke out in all its twentieth-century fury should be clearer now, but the list of reasons awaits further additions. Probably it always shall.

# Chapter 3

# The Irony of Emancipation:
# France and the Dreyfus Affair

*George Mosse pointed out long ago that if one were situated in Europe in the 1890s and asked to name the country most dangerous for the Jews, one might easily settle upon France.*

Michael R. Marrus, *The Holocaust in History*

In 1879–80, about the time that the German journalist Wilhelm Marr coined the term *antisemitism*, an influential German historian, Heinrich von Treitschke (1834–96), published a series of articles on the theme "Ein Wort über unser Judentum" (A word about our Jewry).[1] A committed nationalist who was deeply concerned about the future of Germany, which had achieved unification under Otto von Bismarck and Kaiser Wilhelm I only in 1871, Treitschke urged the emancipated German Jews "to make up their minds without reservation to be Germans." Treitschke continued: "There will always be Jews who are nothing else but German-speaking orientals," but Jews must "show some respect for the faith, the customs and the feelings of the German people which has long ago atoned for old injustice and given them human and civil rights." Only then, he indicated, would it be possible to reverse the justifiable complaint that Germans were making: "Die Juden sind unser Unglück" (The Jews are our misfortune).

Less than forty years after his death, Treitschke's fateful phrase would be inscribed on banners at Nazi rallies. The historian Daniel Jonah Goldhagen regards Treitschke's phrase and the uses to which it was put as evidence for his controversial thesis that Germans harbored a pre-Nazi "eliminationist anti-semitism" that was "powerful enough to have set Hitler and the German nation on an exterminationist course."[2] Later there will be more to say about Goldhagen's thesis, but at the time of Treitschke's death in 1896 it was not clear that German or Austrian antisemitism put European Jews most at risk. Arguably that

71

dubious distinction belonged to czarist Russia or, even more plausibly, to France, a view supported by the late George Mosse, an eminent scholar of the Third Reich's origins, who once made the following observation: "Ironically, before the First World War, it was France rather than Germany or Austria that seemed likely to become the home of a successful racist and National Socialist movement."[3]

Analyses such as Mosse's in no way deny that it took Nazi Germany to unleash the Holocaust. Nevertheless, the specific circumstances in which that disaster took place were prefigured by European reactions against Jewish emancipation. In the 1890s, those reactions became acute in France, particularly in the case of Captain Alfred Dreyfus (1859–1935). More than a century later, France is home for some six hundred thousand Jews—about 350,000 live in Paris—which makes its Jewish population the largest of any European country and the third largest in the world. It was in France, moreover, that European Jews were first emancipated. Significantly, equal citizenship for German Jews was first proclaimed in 1808, when French forces under Napoleon conquered western regions of that land. (When Napoleon was defeated, the German emancipation was largely rescinded. Further attempts to emancipate German Jews in 1848 did not last either. Only in 1871 did the Jews of Germany acquire close to full legal and civil equality.) Yet France is also home to Jean-Marie Le Pen's *Le Front National*, the largest twenty-first-century fascist movement in Europe. In addition, France's Holocaust-related history includes the collaborationist Vichy government (1940–44), whose anti-Jewish legislation was at times more radical than Nazi Germany's. Still further, the historical record shows that roundups by French police dispatched about eighty thousand Jews from France, most of them refugees and immigrants, to their deaths at Auschwitz and other German killing centers in the East.[4] As this chapter argues, French reactions to Jewish emancipation, including the so-called *L'Affaire Dreyfus* (Dreyfus Affair), played key parts in what Robert Wistrich identifies as "a kind of dress-rehearsal for the mob politics of Nazi-style anti-Semitism," which, in turn, promoted Hitler's genocidal attack on the world's Jews.[5]

## THE RATIONALIZATION OF POLITICS AND ECONOMICS

The political status of Jews first became a matter of public controversy during the French Revolution, which erupted in 1789. Before the Revolution, Europeans generally agreed that Jews were to be treated as a distinctive community of religious and cultural outsiders. Where Jews were permitted at all, they were subject to strict constraints on the ways in which they earned a living and conducted their affairs. Nowhere in Europe did they have a voice in public affairs outside of their own community. The decision to grant them civic equality was radical, and it took an economic, social, and political revolution to bring it about.

At the time of the Revolution, fewer than fifty thousand Jews lived in France, only about five hundred of whom resided in Paris.[6] Some eight thousand Jews of

Marrano ancestry lived in southern France. Many of them were descendants of Spanish Jews who had outwardly converted to Christianity in the 1490s when all openly believing Jews were expelled from Spain. Most of the "New Christians," as they were called, remained secretly Jewish. In France they reverted to open practice of their ancestral faith. They were, however, far better adjusted to the society and culture of their neighbors than were the forty thousand French Jews who lived in the Rhineland province of Alsace. Alsace had been part of the Germanic Holy Roman Empire until it was annexed to France by King Louis XIV in 1648. The language of Alsace's Jewish population was a local variation of Yiddish, the Hebrew-German-Slavic dialect spoken throughout central and eastern Europe.

As we have noted, during the Middle Ages the economy of Europe was predominantly agrarian and feudal. In many locations nonagrarian pursuits, such as trade and money lending, were carried on by Jews. The economic role of the Jews thus complemented that of the non-Jewish population. However, as western Europe began its long process of transformation to an urbanized, money economy in which even agriculture was industrialized and rationalized, non-Jews began to compete with Jews in those areas of economic activity in which Jews had previously played an important role.

Because of the greater power of Christian competitors, most Jews were forced to leave the increasingly modern economies of western Europe and seek their livelihood in eastern Europe. There a relatively primitive, subsistence agrarian economy persisted until the nineteenth century. As long as this condition continued, Jews remained an economically complementary class within the larger eastern European population. Because they were needed, political authorities were less likely to seek their elimination than was the case when the economy began to modernize and large numbers of non-Jewish competitors made their appearance.[7]

While the transition to an impersonal money economy enlarged the area of economic conflict between Jews and the increasing number of urbanized, middle-class non-Jews, it also lessened the importance of *inherited status* as a determinant of social and economic rank. In a money economy an individual's background tends to be less important than his or her financial resources. The diminishing practical value of inherited status helped to incite the French Revolution, whose motto, "Liberty, Equality, and Fraternity," was rooted in the realities of the new economy and in the related philosophies of the Enlightenment as well.

An important aim of the Enlightenment was the rationalization of politics. In general, Enlightenment philosophers were hostile to religion, which they tended to see as a vestige of a superstitious past. They were also hostile to religion because of the support given by the church to the old royalist order, known after the Revolution as *l'ancien régime*. Throughout French history, periods of tension and conflict marked relations between the throne and the altar; nevertheless, both institutions shared a view of France as a Christian commonwealth. By contrast, a strong anti-Christian, anticlerical bias was evident in the writings of many of the Enlightenment thinkers, the most important of whom included François-Marie Arouet (Voltaire). As noted, however, this bias did not produce greater

*[margin note: Ideas led to emancipation]*

*[margin note: New Idea]*

sympathy for Judaism. Voltaire, for example, despised Judaism as the source of Christianity and for its polemical attitude toward Greco-Roman paganism. He regarded the Jews as a community alienated from the rest of humankind and practicing a primitive, superstitious religion.[8] Nevertheless, the Enlightenment had the practical effect of fostering Jewish emancipation, because it advocated the elimination of religion from the political sphere. Ironically, Enlightenment rationality had the further consequence of fostering the growth of racism. Before the Enlightenment, opposition to the Jews was religiously motivated. By relegating religion to the private sphere, the Enlightenment did not eliminate public hostility. On the contrary, it encouraged the growth of nonreligious reasons for antisemitism. Race eventually became the most decisive.

When Jewish emancipation was debated in the French National Assembly during the Revolution, the majority of the philosophes favored it. Simultaneously, they expected the emancipated Jews to divest themselves of their inherited "superstitions" and become more like their fellow citizens in language, culture, and vocational distribution. Thus, acceptance of the Jews as French citizens was conditional on their becoming "new people." Unfortunately, the expectation carried with it the seeds of future mischief. Because of the diversity of social, political, and religious values held by the French, no Jewish cultural transformation could satisfy more than a fraction of the French populace. Indeed, for many French citizens nothing the Jews could do would make a difference. The historian Arthur Hertzberg has aptly described the dilemma faced by emancipated French Jews:

*[margin note: By BS]*

> This "new Jew" had been born into a society which asked him to keep proving that he was worthy of belonging to it. Unfortunately, this "new Jew" was never quite told exactly what he had to prove and before which tribunal. Franz Kafka has described this phenomenon in his novel *The Trial.* The hero, and the victim, of this tale is K., who feels burdened by crimes which he wished he knew how to define and who keeps hoping to find the judges who would read him the charges, or at least accept his pleas of guilt.[9]

*[margin note: guilty w/o an explanation -- why? b/c you are Jewish]*

Another important motive for Jewish emancipation was the conviction that rational economic growth would be seriously impeded were France's widely divergent regions and classes to retain their own distinctive laws and standards. Before the Revolution, France had neither a common system of weights and measures nor a common currency. Internal tariffs between provinces imposed stringent limitations on commercial development. Economic rationalization required a measure of economic, political, social, and even linguistic *homogenization*, such as the introduction of a single system of weights and measures (the metric system), a universal system of education controlled from Paris, and a common currency for all of France. In the political sphere, homogenization was a consequence of the Revolution's assertion of the equality of all citizens. The Revolution discarded as irrelevant, at least before the law, all of the differences of culture, ethnicity, religion, and class that had been decisive in determining a person's status in *l'ancien régime*. All French people became *citizens* rather than members of different estates. The destruction of the traditional social hierarchy, a process which had begun even before the Revolution, contributed greatly toward the eventual creation of mass society.

As soon as the leveling of status was seriously under way, it was almost inevitable that the special status of the Jews would be abolished, albeit reluctantly, and Jews declared free and equal citizens of the French Republic. The more assimilated Jews of the south were granted French citizenship on 28 January 1790. The vote in the Assemblée Nationale was quite close, 374–280. Moreover, the vote was taken when most of the clergy in the Assemblée, who were known to be opposed, had left the chamber. Emancipation of the Jews of the north was opposed with great vehemence in Alsace, where hostility to the Jews as petty traders, moneylenders, and aliens was especially virulent. Nevertheless, this second emancipation passed on 27 September 1791.

In spite of emancipation, serious religious, social, and cultural differences remained between the Jews and their fellow French citizens. Jews and non-Jews had different historical memories, vocational distributions, and religious backgrounds. Of great importance was the fact that the vast majority of the French population was of peasant and Roman Catholic origin. Insofar as the equality and fraternity of French citizens was based upon some measure of homogeneity of origin and outlook, the Jews did not share in that homogeneity.

## OPPOSITION TO EMANCIPATION

For an understanding of the Holocaust, it is important to note that Jewish emancipation in France was bitterly fought by the Roman Catholic Church and by those royalist circles opposed to the breakdown of traditional society. The church  emphatically rejected a conception of secular society in which Jews and Protestants could enjoy the same political rights as Catholics. With some notable exceptions, the Roman Catholic Church actively supported the antisemitic movements in France from the time of the French Revolution until the beginning of World War II.

In fairness, we repeat that the church never advocated a policy of extermination as did the National Socialists. However, under twentieth-century conditions, exclusion of a group from membership in the community in which it lives can be functionally equivalent to a death sentence. As long as the earth contained relatively open territories to which people could migrate, group expulsion constituted a harsh way of dealing with an unwanted community, but it did not involve the threat of extermination. Unfortunately, those circumstances have changed. The progress of "civilization" entailed that there are no longer relatively open territories. Almost every part of the earth is controlled by a political state capable of limiting the right of permanent residence to those whom political authorities deem acceptable. When France's Catholic Church initiated a campaign to deny citizenship rights to France's Jews, it played an important part in a process whose lethal consequences could only be fully understood in the aftermath of the Holocaust.

Although the nineteenth-century French Catholic Church was normally allied to right-wing political movements, French antisemitism was as much a phenomenon of the left as of the right. In spite of the shortcomings of the old order, every person had a fixed and relatively secure place within it. Although personal status was caste-determined, cooperation rather than individualistic competition was the predominant social value, especially among peasants and artisans. The communitarian values of the old order were destroyed by the Revolution. Although the Revolution ended the caste system, it brought a radically new attitude toward political and social morality, which can best be characterized as *possessive individualism*.[10] In place of the old cooperative spirit, people found themselves in competition with their peers. Although far fewer peasants left the land for the city in nineteenth-century France than in England, fierce competition for jobs often had the effect of driving urban wages down to the barest subsistence level. As wealth increased for some, so did social misery for others.

Initially, the new spirit of competition suited the interests of France's commercial and professional classes. Before the Revolution an archaic socioeconomic system prevented the bourgeoisie, a class possessed of talent, ambition, and energy, from creating a modern economy. With the triumph of the Revolution, this class was free to make full use of its talents. The triumph of the bourgeoisie can also be described as the victory of the city over the countryside or the victory of the world of human artifice over nature. Indeed, according to the *Oxford English Dictionary*, the word *bourgeois* originally denoted "a citizen of a city or burgh, as distinguished from a peasant on the one hand and a nobleman on the other." The Jews had no option but to concentrate in the cities and pursue professional or bourgeois occupations. Even after the Revolution removed their civic disabilities, the French Jews had neither the experience nor the social connections with which to enter agriculture. Nor were the Jews welcomed into the ranks of French labor. They were an urbanized people whose experience had been in trade, commerce, and finance. Moreover, the extreme marginality of their situation compelled them to become individualistic competitors in those fields that were open to them.

When the Jews in France entered urban, middle-class occupations, they gained a new enemy, the French left, in addition to their old enemies: the nobility, clergy, and peasantry.[11] Charles Fourier (1772–1837) was one of the earliest of a long line of French socialist antisemites.[12] His hostility to the Jews had something of a time-bomb effect. France was the original homeland of socialist thought and, hence, of socialist antisemitism. Until the twentieth century, for example, French socialists were generally hostile to Marxism on the twin grounds that Karl Marx was a German and, although baptized, of Jewish origin. Incidentally, Marx's Jewish origin did not prevent him from adopting an attitude of extreme hostility to Jews and Judaism, which he regarded as key sources of the capitalist society he hoped to overthrow.[13]

Rejecting the individualism fostered by the Revolution, Fourier advocated organizing society into a system of utopian communities known as "phalansteries." Because these communities were to be agrarian and self-sufficient, they were not expected to need trade, finance, or commerce, the principal areas of Jewish economic activity. However, unlike later antisemites who favored violent measures, Fourier proposed that Jews be forced to engage in agriculture and other forms of "productive" activity. Toward the end of his career, he took a somewhat milder view, advocating the return of the Jews to Palestine where, with help from the wealthy Rothschild family, he thought they might create their own "phalansteries."

In the next generation, Fourier's antisemitism was intensified by another of France's leading socialist thinkers, Pierre-Joseph Proudhon (1809–65), who was one of Karl Marx's most important critics. His publicly expressed anti-Jewish sentiments were relatively mild, but his private sentiments were violent. The following entries from Proudhon's notebooks, which were published in 1961, are instructive:

> *Jews*—Write an article about this race which poisons everything by meddling everywhere without ever joining itself to another people.—Demand their expulsion from France, with the exception of individuals married to Frenchwomen.—Abolish the synagogues; don't admit them to any kind of employment; pursue finally the abolition of this cult.
> It is not for nothing that the Christians call them deicides. The Jew is the enemy of the human race. One must send this race back to Asia or exterminate it. . . . By fire or fusion, or by expulsion the Jew must disappear. . . . Tolerate the aged who are no longer able to give birth to offspring.
> *Work to be done*—What the peoples of the Middle Ages hated by instinct, I hate upon reflection and irrevocably.[14]

In the nineteenth century, Proudhon kept his thoughts about extermination to himself. In World War II such thoughts would become public policy.

According to George Lichtheim, a historian of socialism, "Proudhon had the countryman's dislike and distrust for that side of modern civilization which rests upon the subjugation of nature."[15] Socialists such as Fourier, who advocated that Jews be compelled to engage in agriculture, ignored the obvious fact that every year more and more peasants were unable to sustain themselves and were forced to migrate to the cities. Those who found work in the cities were as likely to be engaged in trade, finance, commerce, the professions, and public administration as in what antiurban romantics regarded as "productive" labor. The demand that Jews seek work in the countryside was clearly counter to the basic trends of modern civilization, which fostered ever greater urbanization.

In addition, the universal tendency toward urbanization that characterizes modern civilization had a distinctive character in France. For a young person of ambition, especially in literature, the arts, and journalism, France had and still has only one dominant city, Paris. To be successful meant success in Paris. Jews participated in the gravitation of talent to the capital city. At the time of the Revolution, Paris's Jewish population numbered about five hundred; twenty years later nearly three thousand Jews lived there. By 1869, the year before the Franco-Prussian War, there were approximately thirty thousand. After the war, many Jewish families chose to leave Alsace and settle in the capital. By 1871, two-thirds of the nation's sixty thousand Jews lived in Paris.[16]

Because of their urban concentration, Jews were more visible to France's opinion and decision makers than their minuscule numbers would otherwise have warranted. The proportion of Jews to the total population was only one in six hundred. Nevertheless, their presence in the cities, especially Paris, was noted and resented by many of the non-Jewish immigrants from the countryside, who tended to regard the Jews as an unwelcome, alien presence.

Before 1870 most urban Jews were quite poor, but there were important exceptions, the most important being banking families such as the Rothschilds and the Foulds. Some Jews also prospered in the theater, literature, journalism, law, medicine, and after 1870 in Republican politics. Unfortunately, between 1870 and 1900 France experienced a serious "overproduction of intellectuals."[17] The glut was caused in large measure by the democratization of higher education under the Third French Republic, the government that came to power after 1870. Universities were free and overcrowded, especially after 1891, when the length of compulsory military service was reduced for students in graduate and professional schools. In addition to the overproduction of intellectuals, an analogous "overproduction" of doctors, lawyers, engineers, and commercial artists developed. The situation was further exacerbated by the fact that the surplus professionals and intellectuals were predominantly lower middle-class in origin, which meant that they lacked sufficient capital to start their own businesses. Their training constituted their main hope to attain a securely comfortable livelihood. The oversupply of trained people was especially evident in journalism. In 1900 the newspapers of Paris employed more than 125,000 people.[18] With so great a surplus, wages were low, opportunities for advancement almost nil. The situation was no better in other professions. Fewer than half of the nation's doctors, lawyers, and engineers could be considered even moderately prosperous. Army officers received salaries wholly inadequate for the style of life they were supposed to maintain. Competition for promotion was bitter. Pensions were low. Widows of officers were left with little protection. Even priests were hard pressed, especially in the rural areas. Such problems, however, were hardly unique to France.

## GROWING RESENTMENT

Every developing country has experienced the migration of dislocated peasants to urban areas, the rapid growth of the proletariat, the development of an unpredictable and impersonal labor market, the enlargement of educated and professional classes beyond the nation's absorptive capacity, and the expansion of capital requirements that are both necessary for economic success and beyond the resources of the average small businessperson. In almost every developing country, conditions such as these have yielded a large number of articulate, educated men and women who have become deeply resentful at a society in which they can find no viable place. Moreover, transition to a modern economy has been almost universally attended by exploitative child labor, mass unemployment, and vast urban slums, with all of their accompanying social pathology. In France, those whose frustrated careers made them resentful had only to look around them to conclude that theirs was a hopelessly corrupt society. France's small Jewish population was blamed as the source of the corruption. This pattern, and many others we are noting, would repeat itself in Germany, particularly after World War I.

Middle-class French resentment was intensified by the fact that the French were less inclined to emigrate than were the British, Irish, Germans, Norwegians, Swedes, Italians, and many other Europeans. France thus lacked the population safety valve possessed by almost every other European nation. Between 1846 and 1932, 18 million people emigrated from Great Britain and Ireland; 14.2 million people left their homes in Russia, many to colonize Siberia; 5.2 million left Austria-Hungary; and about 5 million emigrated from Germany. Many of these people came to the United States. By contrast, only 520,000 left France during this period.[19]

Other elements tended to increase French embitterment. For instance, France became a republic for the third time in 1870. Nevertheless, a very important segment of the French people did not regard the republican government as legitimate. In most countries, conservatives tend to be a force for stability. This was not true in France after its defeat by Germany in 1870 or in Germany after its defeat in 1918. In France the officer corps, the clergy, and the upper bourgeoisie included many people who despised the Republic and were vehemently antisemitic. Nor were these sentiments restricted to the upper strata of French society. They were shared by almost everyone who felt he or she had been injured by the new order.

Anticipating what would happen in Weimar Germany after World War I, those who rejected the legitimacy of the Republic tended to depict the Jews as its principal beneficiaries. Indeed, French Jews perceived themselves as having benefited from the Revolution insofar as they had been granted full citizenship. Other groups in society perceived the Jews as having prospered at their expense. Jews had little choice but to pursue careers in those fields that opened up as France modernized. Those fields tended to offer the greatest rewards for success. In addition to trade, Jews were found in industry, the professions, banking, and finance, where successful members of their community were highly visible even when the numbers were small. Thus, those who saw themselves as injured by modernization tended to see the Jews as both responsible for and profiting from what they regarded as an illegitimate social order.

The situation in France was in strong contrast to that in Great Britain. In spite of the harsh social abuses that attended the British industrial revolution, that development took place under a government that was almost universally regarded as legitimate. Moreover, the Church of England, the aristocracy, and the armed forces saw themselves as the leaders of the established order, not its enemies. There was a poisonous element in French politics that grew stronger as the nineteenth century drew to a close.

The identification of the Jews with the hated world of modernity was evident in the themes of many of France's antisemitic writers. Alphonse Toussenel's 1845 book *Les Juifs rois de l'epoque* (The Jews, kings of the time) depicted the minuscule Jewish community as an alien presence controlling France. Toussenel was especially bitter about "Rothschild's railroads," a response to the fact that the Rothschild banking house had provided much of the investment capital for the building of French railroads. In 1869, Henri Gougenot des Mousseaux, another antisemitic author, produced a book entitled *Le Juif, le judaisme, et le judaisation des peuple chretiens* (The Jew, Judaism, and the judaization of the Christian people). Where Toussenel saw Jewish commerce and finance controlling France, Mousseaux claimed that the Jews had successfully used the ideals of the Enlightenment to overthrow Catholic France.

Blaming the Jews for the fall of *l'ancien régime* echoed an earlier complaint by Catholic leaders who had depicted the Revolution as the consequence of a secret conspiracy of anti-Catholic Freemasons. According to the historian Robert F. Byrnes, from 1865 on there was a tendency on the part of the French right to ascribe the French Revolution to the workings of occult forces.[20] Pope Leo XIII, usually a force for moderation, saw the Masons as an anti-Christian force. On 20 August 1884, he issued a decree of the Inquisition identifying the Oddfellows, the Knights of Pythias, and the Sons of Temperance as "the synagogue of Satan."[21]

It was natural for those who wanted to restore some, if not all, of the features of *l'ancien regime* to resort to a conspiracy theory to explain both its fall and the onset of the modern period. To have admitted that the old order could not have survived the challenge of modernization would have been an act of self-criticism that opponents of the Republic were not prepared to make. Once the conspiracy theory gained acceptance in Catholic circles, it was to assert that the Jews controlled the Masons and finally to blame the Revolution on the Jews, who were accused by French antisemites of being "kings" of the new epoch.

The defeat of France by Germany in 1870 and the subsequent German annexation of Alsace-Lorraine added to French bitterness. Like the Weimar Republic, which preceded Hitler's rule in Germany, the Third French Republic was born in military defeat. Furthermore, the defeat of 1870 was followed by some of the worst civil violence that Europe had ever seen. Infuriated by the French surrender to the Germans, thousands of Parisian workers set up the Paris Commune. This development so enraged and frightened Adolphe Thiers's promonarchist government, which had supplanted the regime of Emperor Louis Napoleon, that in the week of 21–28 May 1871 more than twenty thousand Parisians who had fought for the Commune were put to death by government troops. Another fifty thousand were arrested. The hatreds thus engendered were to poison the Third French Republic from its inception in military defeat to its demise when Nazi Germany occupied France in 1940.

It was only a matter of time until the Jews were blamed for the defeat of 1870. Before this happened, a new Roman Catholic bank, the Union Générale, failed in 1882. The bank had been founded in 1878 by Eugene Bontoux, formerly a Rothschild employee. Many of France's leading banks were under Protestant control. Bontoux promised to break what he called the banking monopoly of Jews and Protestants. He received Catholic support that was enthusiastic and widespread. For four years the bank was very successful. However, in 1882 it failed as a result of Bontoux's ill-advised attempts to support the price of the stock of the Suez Canal Company in a rapidly declining market. The failure caused great hardship to its Catholic depositors and investors. Bontoux fled to Spain, where he blamed the failure on the Jews, in particular, the Rothschilds. Many French Catholics readily believed him.

French antisemitism was greatly strengthened by Édouard Drumont's two-volume work *La France Juive* (Jewish France), which was published on 14 April 1886. The book was praised in the Catholic press and quickly went through several editions. As was more or less typical with professional antisemites, Drumont was of lower middle-class origins. Born in Paris in 1844, he was the son of a minor bureaucrat who died when Drumont was seventeen. The young man did not go to university but gained employment in the Paris city hall. After six months he quit and tried journalism. From 1869 to 1885, underpaid and unrecognized, Drumont worked for *Chronique Illustrée*, a left-of-center paper owned by a Jewish family. He also shared with many of his fellow antisemites a yearning for "the old France." Where Toussenel saw the new railroads as a monumental scar on the face of his beloved France, Drumont hated both electric lighting and the new Eiffel Tower, which he regarded as defacing Paris.

The success of Drumont's book encouraged the appearance of many others. Within a short time, the Jews became the scapegoat for all of France's many ills. But in the case of Drumont, there was a modern element to his antisemitism. Where previously antisemites had been either socialist or Christian, Drumont tried to unite conservative Christians and left-wing socialists in a single movement. This alliance, however, proved precarious. As long as attention was focused on what the antisemites were against, unity was a possibility; but neither Drumont nor his allies could agree on a program to cope with the problems of a France that was now beginning to industrialize at a slow but accelerating pace.

Another important development was the founding in 1883 of a new Catholic newspaper, *La Croix* (The Cross), sponsored by the Assumptionist Fathers, a new French order that was especially devoted to the Sacred Heart of Jesus. This order was responsible for the construction of the world-famous Basilica of Sacré Coeur on Montmartre. *La Croix* was the first newspaper to praise Drumont's book. The paper's antisemitism intensified as its circulation rose. In 1889 its circulation was eleven thousand. By 1893 it had reached 180,000. In addition, it published various Sunday and weekly editions whose total circulation reached two million in 1894.

As we discuss Catholic antisemitism in the period following the Franco-Prussian War, we note a further source of bitterness for French Catholics: the unification of Italy and the destruction of the temporal power of the pope.[22] In 1867 the Italian patriot Giuseppe Garibaldi (1807–82) led a march on Rome, hoping to wrest control of the city from the papacy. Emperor Napoleon III of France sent an expeditionary force that successfully defended the Papal States. However, after the Germans defeated Napoleon III in 1870, the Italians seized control of Rome with only token resistance. Pope Pius IX became the "prisoner of the Vatican," refusing to leave his small enclave or to recognize Rome as the capital of united Italy.

Traditionally, French Catholics had seen themselves as the pope's protectors. As long as Napoleon III was emperor, the new Italian state was prevented from seizing Rome; but after their defeat by the Germans, the French were incapable of protecting the pope. The situation was aggravated by the fact that the kingdom of Italy enjoyed the protection of Bismarck's Protestant German empire. French Catholics thus tended to equate their own defeat with the pope's and to see both as the result of the triumph of Protestantism and godless modernism over Catholic Christianity. Such attitudes provided fertile fields for antisemitism as well.

Yet another element in Catholic antisemitism from 1789 to 1945 was the fact that the Roman Catholic Church regarded itself, with considerable justice, as the most important institutional victim of the French Revolution. It viewed the Revolution as an unmitigated social and political catastrophe. It could not accept a secular political order in which Judaism and Protestantism enjoyed a legal status equal to its own. Viewing itself as the one true church, the Roman Catholic Church felt obligated to undo what it regarded as the damage done by the Revolution. It sought to restore a Roman Catholic commonwealth in which Jews and Protestants would be relegated to inferior status. Nevertheless, it would be inaccurate to see the church's hostility toward the Jew as motivated by gratuitous malice. The church's Jewish policy was consistent with its vision of the good society, which could only be Roman Catholic. In some, though not all, parts of Europe, the Roman Catholic Church was prepared to suffer the Jews to live as protected pariahs. Nevertheless, it was not prepared to grant a political voice to those who had no stake in the maintenance of a Christian commonwealth.

The Roman Catholic Church's nineteenth-century antisemitic policy did not have extermination as its objective. The church was attempting to restore the status quo ante, the hierarchically ordered Christian society that preceded the French Revolution. Condemning the Jews to pariah status was consistent with those aims, whose fundamental principles embraced legalized social stratification. Pariah status, in turn, encouraged Jewish emigration. Migration always involved hardship, but there were places to which the Jews could go. When Hitler came to power in 1933, migration was no longer such a viable option. Once World War II began in September 1939, it was even less so for Europe's Jews. Nevertheless, in spite of the altered situation, most leading Christians failed to understand that the status quo ante could not be restored and that, under twentieth-century conditions, to strip a group of political rights could easily result in something far worse than forced emigration or pariah status. Nor were the

Catholic and Protestant churches alone in failing to comprehend the changed conditions. Most of the leaders of the Jewish community in both eastern and western Europe were equally incapable of discerning the changes.

## THE JEW AS JUDAS

The Jewish question intensified as a French political issue in 1894 when Captain Alfred Dreyfus was arrested and tried for treason.[23] Dreyfus was a member of a wealthy Jewish textile manufacturing family from Mulhouse in Alsace, which had been ceded to Germany in 1871, when Dreyfus was twelve. The German occupation heightened the family's staunchly French identity. Eventually that identity would make Dreyfus the only Jewish member of the French army's General Staff, but at a time when almost every officer of consequence was antirepublican and antisemitic. Moreover, the French officer corps had its "old-boy network" consisting of officers who prepared for the École Polytechnique at a Jesuit preparatory school on the Rue des Postes in Paris. Known as "Postards," they controlled advancement within the officer corps. Non-Postards could advance on the basis of superior scholarship and behavior, but they could never hope to be part of the army's inner circle.[24]

Dreyfus was a target from the moment of his original appointment to the General Staff in January 1893. The appointment drew strong protests in *La Croix* and *La Libre Parole* (Free Speech), a new paper established by Drumont in 1892. Drumont's paper conducted an abusive campaign against Jewish army officers. In one issue he published the names of Jewish officers and claimed that they were potential traitors.

There was at least one real traitor among the French officer corps, but it took several years before a significant sector of the French public realized that the traitor was not Jewish. Toward the end of the summer of 1894, the traitor delivered to Colonel Maximilien von Schwartzkoppen, the German military attaché in Paris, a number of documents containing French military secrets. There was also a handwritten bordereau or memorandum itemizing some of the documents. Reports about this document remain clouded; probably it was stolen from Schwartzkoppen's papers by a French secret agent who worked in the German embassy. In late September, the bordereau reached Major Hubert Henry, an officer in the Statistical Section of the General Staff's Deuxième Bureau. The Deuxième Bureau was the army's intelligence agency; the Statistical Section was its counterespionage arm.

Once Henry had shared the find with his superior, Colonel Jean Sandherr, an Alsatian who was known to be bitterly antisemitic, the hunt for the bordereau's author began. The evidence was not crystal clear, but less than thorough handwriting analysis eventually suggested that Dreyfus might be the culprit, a possibility that Sandherr readily accepted. Charged with treason, Dreyfus was arrested on 15 October. Harassing interrogations attempted to extract a confession, but

Dreyfus insisted that he was innocent. Meanwhile, realizing that the high-stakes situation included the army's honor, not to mention individual careers, the General Staff decided against publicizing the breach of security revealed by the bordereau. In late October, however, word about the situation leaked out. Some evidence suggests that Henry secretly contacted Drumont's newspaper, *La Libre Parole*. If Henry's role in that part of the Dreyfus Affair remains uncertain, *La Libre Parole*'s does not. On 1 November it announced Dreyfus's arrest. A few days later, on 10 November, the paper portrayed a hook-nosed "Judas Dreyfus" wearing a spiked German helmet.[25] When more of the press joined the attack, a court-martial could not be avoided.

Convened on 19 December 1894, the court was composed of a Postard network that was strongly inclined to find the Jew guilty. Nevertheless, at the end of the first day of the trial's closed sessions, both Dreyfus's demeanor and the lack of any supporting evidence to support the charges (they depended entirely on the undated and unsigned bordereau, which did not fit Dreyfus's handwriting as closely as his detractors hoped) began to raise doubts about his alleged guilt. Determined to avoid an acquittal, General Auguste Mercier, the minister of war, and Colonel Sandherr quickly put together a secret file containing additional "evidence." Some of this "evidence" was fabricated; none of it was more than circumstantial. On the trial's third and final day—without the knowledge of Dreyfus's defense attorney, Edgar Demange, a prominent Roman Catholic lawyer who firmly believed in Dreyfus's innocence—this file was given to the judges. Not only did the "evidence" lack merit, but also it was contrary to France's military and civil law to withhold evidence from the accused. Nevertheless, on 22 December Dreyfus was convicted as charged and sentenced to public degradation and life imprisonment.

Dreyfus's prison sentence was to be served in solitary confinement on Devil's Island, a desolate former leper colony situated off the coast of South America. He was imprisoned there on 14 April 1895, but first the captain's public degradation had to take place in Paris. This highly charged event was originally scheduled for 4 January 1895, a Friday. Second thoughts determined that it would be more fitting for the ceremony to be held on the Jewish Sabbath. So it was that on 5 January the Paris parade ground of the École Militaire was the venue for a ten-minute ritual of humiliation, which was witnessed by several thousand French troops, a large number of dignitaries, including the papal nuncio to France, and a crowd of curious onlookers, estimated at twenty thousand, who tried to catch a glimpse of the spectacle. Dreyfus was stripped of his rank: the gold epaulets were torn from his shoulders; the red stripes on his trousers, which identified him as a General Staff officer, were cut away and his sword broken and thrown to the ground. Shouts of "Death to the Jews!" added their ominous rage to the scene. As Dreyfus was marched past the assembled troops, who represented every regiment in the Paris garrison, he repeatedly declared, "I am innocent. Long live France!"[26] In the aftermath the press magnified the crowd's death curses. "It was not an individual who was degraded here for an individual crime," Drumont's *La Libre*

*Parole* proclaimed. "The shame of an entire race was bared in its nakedness." *La Croix* took a more invidious religious approach: "His cry of 'Long live France!' was the kiss of Judas Iscariot."[27] The Dreyfus trial had become the trial of all of France's Jews. Nor was *La Croix* alone in identifying Dreyfus with Judas. As Colonel Sandherr watched Dreyfus's degradation, he said to a young French diplomat, "That race has done . . . nothing but betray. Remember they betrayed Christ!"[28]

*La Croix*'s identification of Dreyfus with Judas linked the affair with one of the deepest sources of antisemitism in the Western world. According to the Christian New Testament, Judas betrayed Jesus for thirty pieces of silver and did so with a kiss. The moral of the identification is clear: like Judas, Jews can never be trusted even when they appear trustworthy.[29] Thus, the condemnation of Dreyfus as a traitor released powerful mythic themes that had always stood barely beneath the surface of the Christian image of the Jew. Colonel Sandherr's readiness to believe in Dreyfus's guilt was due in some measure to the power of the Judas image. Dreyfus's conviction, based on fabrication and illegality though it was, reinforced that image.

The identification of the Jew with Judas would have an even greater influence on German politics after Germany's defeat in World War I. Both the French Third Republic and the German Weimar Republic were born in military defeat, and defeated nations often find it easier to believe that they were betrayed rather than defeated by the enemy. It was the Jews' misfortune that the Judas myth served to convince many of the French that the Jews had betrayed them to the Germans, while convincing many Germans in 1918 that the Jews had betrayed them to the French and their allies.

Early on, Mercier, Sandherr, and most of their colleagues were strongly inclined to believe the worst of Dreyfus. Before the leak to the press took place, however, there arguably may have been no conspiracy to ruin him. But after *La Libre Parole* made an issue of Dreyfus's secret incarceration, the army had the strongest motive to find Dreyfus guilty. Its inner circle would not be blemished if the officer who had sold secrets to the Germans turned out to be a Jewish outsider. Furthermore, Dreyfus's guilt could only reinforce the position of those officers who believed that France was a Roman Catholic country and that it was a mistake to grant French citizenship to Jews.

If the army had reason to ensure Dreyfus's conviction, Dreyfus had every motive for loyalty to France. The psychological impossibility of Dreyfus's having betrayed his trust was spelled out by Theodor Herzl (1860–1904), the founder of modern Zionism, in a conversation with the Italian military attaché Colonel Alessandro Panizzardi: "A Jew who has opened a career of honor as a general staff officer cannot commit such a crime. . . . As a consequence of their long civic dishonor, Jews have an often pathological desire for honor; and a Jewish officer is in this respect a Jew to the nth power."[30] Mutual espionage interests connected Panizzardi and Schwartzkoppen, the German military attaché. The Italian knew far more about the Dreyfus case than he could reveal to Herzl at the time.

Fifteen months after the court-martial, the French government changed. General Mercier was no longer minister of war. Lieutenant Colonel Georges Picquart, another Alsatian, succeeded Sandherr as head of the Deuxième Bureau's Statistical Section. Picquart soon became aware that Major Ferdinand Walsin-Esterhazy, a debt-ridden officer of shady reputation who was related to one of Hungary's greatest families, was in frequent and problematical contact with Schwartzkoppen.[31] Then, in late August 1896, Picquart had reason to study two letters that Esterhazy had written. The handwriting seemed familiar. His suspicion aroused, Picquart compared Esterhazy's letters with a facsimile of the bordereau that was in his possession.[32] It was unmistakable, Picquart concluded; Esterhazy had written the bordereau, and Dreyfus was innocent. Although Picquart disliked Dreyfus and was personally antisemitic, he immediately took the discovery to his superiors. Picquart was told to forget the whole affair—too many reputations were at stake—but, as we will see, he refused.

About the same time, in September 1896, Mathieu Dreyfus, Alfred's brother, decided to revive interest in the case. He did so by publishing a false report in *The South Wales Argus*, a Welsh newspaper. This story claimed that Alfred had escaped from Devil's Island. The hoax succeeded, and not least because the antisemitic press maintained that a secret Jewish "syndicate" had conspired to buy off Dreyfus's guards. Once again, *L'Affaire Dreyfus* was front-page news.

Picquart thought that the least damage to the army would result from an admission of error in the Dreyfus case. His colleagues and superiors disagreed. Some remained honestly convinced that Dreyfus was guilty, perhaps in collaboration with Esterhazy, but those who had fabricated evidence were beyond the point of return. Their strategy was to admit nothing and to leak damaging "evidence" to friendly journalists. One such leak appeared on 15 September in *L'Éclair* (Lightning), a newspaper that frequently reflected army opinion. Through an article in *L'Éclair*, the army let it be known that Dreyfus had not been convicted on the slender evidence of the bordereau but on the basis of evidence "secretly handed to the judges of the court" without the knowledge of the defense attorney. Among the "evidence" cited was a message that French intelligence had intercepted. A key document in the secret file that had condemned Dreyfus, this message from Schwartzkoppen to Panizzardi referred to French military plans that had been left with him for the Italian by "that scoundrel D." The initial D did not, in fact, refer to Dreyfus, but his opponents conveniently claimed that it did. *L'Éclair* went further, revising its quotation of the leaked text to read explicitly "that animal Dreyfus."[33] Since no one engaged in espionage would have identified by name so valuable an asset as a General Staff officer, it was apparent that the "evidence" was suspect. Moreover, the army had unwittingly admitted that Dreyfus's trial had been conducted illegally. Lucie Dreyfus, the prisoner's wife, petitioned for a new trial but was ignored. Nevertheless, public interest in the case continued to grow.

By the late autumn of 1896, Picquart, who knew too much and thus endangered the General Staff, had been sent on a series of missions that would keep him away from Paris for some time. These postings eventually, and intentionally, put him in harm's way in Algeria and Tunisia. Meanwhile Picquart's responsibilities in the Statistical Section fell to Hubert Henry, whose loyalty to the army was unquestionable. He wanted further evidence to strengthen the case against Dreyfus. With the help of a French agent within the German embassy, he fabricated a pivotal piece of correspondence from Panizzardi to Schwartzkoppen, which used Panizzardi's forged handwriting to incriminate Dreyfus. This particular forgery, one of several produced by Henry, became known as the *faux Henry* or false Henry document.

When Picquart realized that the General Staff had exiled him, he wrote to Louis Leblois, a lawyer friend, detailing the evidence for Dreyfus's innocence and Esterhazy's guilt. He asked the lawyer to keep the letter secret, but to reveal its contents to the president of France should he, Picquart, die. Leblois could not contain himself. He told the vice president of the French senate, Auguste Scheurer-Kestner, a widely respected Protestant political figure, what he had learned from Picquart, pledging him to secrecy concerning the latter's involvement.

Scheurer-Kestner privately shared his doubts about the Dreyfus case with the French president and minister of war. Meanwhile, among the army's many mistakes was the publication of a photographic facsimile of the bordereau. Esterhazy's handwriting was recognized by a banker named Castro, one of many people who had unpleasant dealings with him. The banker, who had letters from Esterhazy, sent the correspondence to Mathieu Dreyfus, Alfred's brother, who on 15 November 1897 formally denounced Esterhazy to the minister of war as the author of the bordereau. Mathieu's letter was published the next day in the French newspaper *Le Figaro*. Esterhazy suffered further damage to his unraveling reputation when a copy of a letter he had written to a former mistress also came into the hands of Mathieu Dreyfus, who published it in *Le Figaro* on 28 November. "I am absolutely convinced that these people [the French] are not worth the ammunition it would take to kill them," Esterhazy had written, "I would kill one hundred thousand Frenchmen with pleasure."[34]

## THE MYTH OF CONSPIRACY

In spite of the 1897 revelations, the newspapers were filled with further "proofs" of Dreyfus's guilt and the existence of a secret Jewish "syndicate" whose objective was to free Dreyfus, degrade the Christian Esterhazy, and ultimately to destroy France. These reports were a variant of the myth of a Jewish conspiracy to dominate the world that had been depicted in another forgery, *The Protocols of the Elders of Zion*. The idea of a secret Jewish conspiracy was related, in turn, to the identification of the Jew with Judas. *By accusing the Jews of being a group secretly conspiring to conquer the world, it became possible to see any atrocity committed against them as an act of self-defense.* The conspiracy myth thus helped to create the moral and psychological climate in which genocide became an acceptable political policy.

The conspiracy theory of politics, the idea that behind the public facade of politics a determined minority has conspired secretly to control the political order, was applied to the Freemasons, who were held responsible for the French

Revolution, before it was applied in France to the Jews. In an earlier period, witches were alleged to be in league with the devil to destroy Christian society. French Protestants were also the object of such theories. Although a numerically small community, they controlled much of France's banking system and were sometimes accused of seeking to control all of France by means of their capital. Moreover, the left was just as capable of using the theory as the right. Toward the end of the nineteenth century, it was widely held in left-wing and even moderate Republican circles that the Jesuits were seeking to control France and much of Europe through the confessional and their influence on education.

Although men and women have engaged in conspiracies since the beginning of recorded history, the use of the conspiracy theory in mass politics can be seen as related to the bureaucratic centralization of government in which unknown, anonymous officials have the power to make decisions affecting the lives and property of millions of their fellow citizens. Sociologists and political theorists have commented on the tendency of bureaucrats to insist on the secret nature of their work.[35] Moreover, nowhere is bureaucratic secrecy more important than in the workings of intelligence agencies such as France's nineteenth-century Deuxième Bureau or the Central Intelligence Agency (CIA) of our own time. In many situations, there are perfectly valid reasons for bureaucratic secrecy. Nevertheless, the claim of executive privilege has been frequently abused to cover up administrative mistakes, cost overruns, and even crimes. An important consequence of bureaucratic secrecy and anonymity is a widespread feeling among ordinary citizens that they are governed by unseen forces beyond their control.

In the premodern period, the relations between those who govern and the governed usually had a personal element. People owed their allegiance to a *person*, the local lord and his agents in the first instance, the monarch at the highest level. In the modern period, political loyalty took on an abstract and impersonal character. Loyalty was due to the *nation*, the *state*, or the *constitution* instead of a person. In modern bureaucracies, the official's fundamental responsibility is to carry out his or her assigned tasks without regard to the personalities of superiors, the nature of the task, or those affected for better or for worse by its implementation.

Sociologists have argued that well-functioning bureaucracies constitute an advance in administrative rationality in complex mass societies. While this is undoubtedly true, as with so many other advances in functional rationality, bureaucratic rationality has had ironic, irrational consequences. Since few citizens can discern who really governs beneath the public facade of politics, all sorts of myths concerning invisible political conspiracies can find believers. In the case of the Jews, their concentration in the capital city, their strangeness, their command of financial resources, and the distrust in which they were held resulted in the accusation that they were conspiring to control Christian France. As noted, the consequences of the conspiracy theory were deadly for the Jews. Having been effectively depicted as a menace to public order and security, their elimination from the body politic was widely accepted as a public benefit. Ironically, far from being conspiratorial, most French Jews, like their German counterparts, were apolitical. They were interested in full political acceptance but not necessarily in politics itself. The majority of those active in the Jewish community were too frightened by the Dreyfus affair to take an active role in securing justice.

When Mathieu Dreyfus denounced Esterhazy, an official investigation became necessary. The army would have been content to have a private investigation and to retire Esterhazy quietly. Esterhazy, who was hardly the model of prudence, insisted on nothing less than complete vindication. A court-martial became unavoidable. By this time, however, the army was too deeply implicated in forgery for Esterhazy's guilt or innocence to be judged on its merits. As the institution that guaranteed the security of the state against foreign enemies, the army had a claim on the loyalty and trust of all French citizens. Some believed that the fate of a single officer was less important than maintaining the respect of the army. Some indeed held that it was Dreyfus's duty to accept his sentence as a good soldier in the service of France. Thus, even Dreyfus's insistence on his innocence was taken as proof that he was not a true Frenchman. A similar argument was used in the Soviet Union in the 1930s by Stalin's secret police to persuade faithful Communists to confess crimes they did not commit. Many people prefer order above justice.

After a brief two-day trial, held in closed sessions for purported reasons of national security, Esterhazy was acquitted on 11 January 1898. Too much was at stake to permit any other verdict, but the acquittal moved Émile Zola (1840–1902), France's eminent novelist, to publish an open letter to the president of the Republic. With its title, *J'accuse!* emblazoned across the front page in a black banner headline, the letter appeared in a special edition of three hundred thousand copies of the French newspaper *L'Aurore* on 13 January.[36] Zola accused the army of deliberately falsifying evidence, willfully perpetrating a miscarriage of justice, and committing judicial crime by convicting Dreyfus contrary to French law. Zola challenged the authorities to try him, which they did—for libel—in February. A crucial moment in the Zola trial came when Brigadier General Georges de Pellieux insisted that, in addition to the bordereau, the evidence against Dreyfus included a letter allegedly written by Panizzardi to Schwartzkoppen assuring the German that, if asked, Panizzardi would deny all knowledge of Dreyfus. This was the *faux Henry* document. When called as a witness, Picquart declared the document a forgery. Nevertheless, Zola was found guilty. Only after his death would Zola be fully vindicated when the High Court of Appeals cleared Dreyfus of wrongdoing. Meanwhile, in late February 1898, Picquart was dishonorably discharged from the army. In the eyes of his brother officers, he had become a disloyal "whistle blower."

## A NATIONAL OBSESSION

Zola's involvement made the Dreyfus case a renewed national obsession. One French diplomat wrote, "Whatever you may say or do, you are classed as a friend or enemy of the Jews and the Army."[37] Hostesses wrote on their invitations that the affair was not to be discussed. Antisemitism increased. On 5 February 1898 *La Civiltà Cattolica*, the official publication of the Jesuit order in Rome and an authoritative voice of Vatican sentiment, expressed the opinion that "[t]he Jew was created by God to serve as a spy wherever treason is in preparation." The journal saw only one cure for the situation, the victory of antisemitism:

> Thus, anti-Semitism will become, as it should, economic, political, and national. The Jews allege an error of justice. The true error was, however, that of the *Constituante* which accorded them French nationality. That law has to be revoked. . . . Not only in France, but in Germany, Austria, and Italy as well, the Jews are to be excluded from the nation.
>
> Then the old harmony will be re-established and the peoples will again find their lost happiness.[38]

The Vatican secretary of state, Cardinal Mariano Rampolla, expressed the opinion that every French citizen was duty-bound to stand by the French premier Félix-Jules Méline "in his anti-Semitic endeavors."[39] In France itself, the antisemitic campaign was led by Drumont and the Assumptionist Fathers who published *La Croix*. There were riots. Jewish stores were plundered in several French cities.

A strange turning point came with the appointment of Godefroy Cavaignac as minister of war in June 1898. Cavaignac made it clear that he was certain of Dreyfus's guilt. He acknowledged that Esterhazy had committed treason as well. In fact, he thought that Dreyfus and Esterhazy were confederates. Then, on 7 July, Cavaignac went to the Chamber of Deputies to make a speech about the Dreyfus affair. Assuring the Chamber that he was convinced of Dreyfus's guilt, he read the *faux Henry* document, which he regarded as genuine and decisive evidence.[40] When news of Cavaignac's widely publicized speech reached Picquart, he told the minister of war that the document was a forgery. Infuriated, Cavaignac had Picquart arrested for disclosing secret papers and eleven months of imprisonment followed. Not wanting to be caught off guard, Cavaignac also ordered a careful examination of the Deuxième Bureau's dossier on Dreyfus to assure himself of the authenticity of its documents. The aide reported back that the *faux Henry* document was a crudely pasted forgery. Cavaignac, who had acted in good faith, was understandably furious. On 30 August, Henry was brought to Cavaignac and admitted the forgery; his arrest and imprisonment followed. A brief communiqué was issued stating that Henry had confessed to writing the letter in which Dreyfus had been named. The next day Henry was found dead in his prison cell. He had apparently committed suicide by slitting his throat.

News of Henry's demise created a sensation. Dreyfus's retrial was now inevitable. The anti-Dreyfusards were momentarily in disarray but quickly regrouped, largely as a result of an extraordinary posthumous defense of Henry by Charles Maurras (1863–1952), a young royalist.[41] Maurras praised Henry for having had the initiative and courage to do what was required, even if it meant falsifying documents. He praised Henry's suicide as a sacrifice for a noble cause, pledging himself and his friends to avenge his blood.

As we have seen, the mythic identification of Dreyfus with Judas Iscariot was never far from the surface in the Dreyfus affair. Maurras's tribute to Henry completed the myth. By characterizing Henry's suicide as a sacrificial death and by pledging vengeance for Henry's blood, Maurras brought the emotional power of the image of Christ crucified into the affair. With Henry's death, the affair gained a strange sort of a Christ figure in addition to its Judas. Moreover, the implicit identification of Henry with the crucified Christ reflected the sense of victimization the French felt after their defeat and the loss of Alsace-Lorraine in 1871. French Catholics also strongly identified with the pope, who had been stripped of temporal possessions because of the unification of Italy and was now known as "the prisoner of the Vatican." Dreyfus was thus cast as the Judas who betrayed France to the Germans and whose followers were determined further to weaken an already assaulted church.

In the initial stages of the Dreyfus affair, Maurras had entertained the possibility that Dreyfus might be innocent. He nevertheless faulted Dreyfus and his family for putting the individual well-being of the accused over the honor and reputation of the army. In Maurras's view, Dreyfus—even if innocent—should have endured his degradation for the sake of the institution to which France had entrusted her security. In Maurras's eyes, however, nothing could really make Dreyfus a Frenchman. At best, Dreyfus, the Jews, Protestants, and Freemasons were *metics*, resident aliens, owing France no permanent allegiance and dwelling in France only because of the lure of commerce. By contrast, Henry was depicted as a true soldier of France.

For Maurras, the Revolution of 1789 and the emancipation of the Jews were profound mistakes that he proposed to correct by founding in 1899 a new right-wing antisemitic movement called *Action Française*, which played an important role in French life until 1944.[42] Under Maurrus's leadership, *Action Française* would incite anti-Jewish sentiment and enthusiastically support the racist, anti-semitic legislation of collaborationist Vichy France during World War II. After the war, Maurrus was found guilty of collaboration with Nazi Germany and sentenced to life imprisonment. Meanwhile, the young Maurras's distinction between the alleged selfish individualism of Dreyfus and the sacrificial selflessness of Henry was consistent with his indictment of the values of modern France. For Maurras, only a Catholic France ruled by a hereditary monarch could successfully end the warring conflicts that plagued the Third Republic. Maurras also distinguished between what he called the *pays légal*, the legal country, and the *pays réal*, the real France. He held that while the Revolution had mistakenly granted the Jews legal rights, no law could transform a people of alien origin and religion into true French persons. The question that Maurras was unprepared to deal with was the one that had initially prompted the emancipation of the Jews in 1789. To create a modern state, the French had abolished separate legal status for distinct groups within the population. In the case of the Jews, the only alternative to granting them equality was to eliminate them from the population altogether. This would have meant either expulsion or extermination. In 1789 extermination of an entire community was not a serious political alternative. Even in 1900 French antisemites were more interested in controlling Jewish access to political office, social rank, and economic and professional activity than they were in more radical measures, although voices calling for the death of the Jews were being raised both in mob demonstrations and by well-placed individuals.

After Henry's death, the call for a massacre of the Jews was frequently expressed in Drumont's *La Libre Parole*. Drumont established a Henry memorial fund to support the widow and children of the deceased. The names of the contributors were listed daily as the fund grew. Some donors gave their reasons for contributing. A number of priests and army officers called for a massacre of the Jews, recalling with pride the massacre of French Huguenots, instigated by Catherine de Medici, which began on St. Bartholomew's night, 24 August 1572. The massacre, which Catherine justified as being in the interest of public safety, continued until 3 October in the provinces. An estimated fifty thousand Protestants were slaughtered. Whether those who called for the elimination of the Jews were fully conscious of the consequences of their politics, they were in fact preparing the basis for collaboration in, if not actual implementation of, the extermination of the Jews. Moreover, those who called for the slaughter of the Jews at the time of the Dreyfus affair were doing more than indulging homicidal fantasies. Their program had as its model a concrete event in French history.

By his literary transformation of a forger into a sacrificial victim, Maurras succeeded in creating a viable myth that enabled the army to keep its sense of honor intact. He was also able to reinforce antisemitism within military and clerical ranks. Moreover, although the Vatican under Pope Leo XIII was increasingly uncomfortable with the possible diplomatic fallout from the church's support of the anti-Dreyfusards, the Holy Office, with the approval of the pope, rejected the efforts of English Catholic leaders to get the pope to join his predecessors—Innocent IV, Gregory X, Martin V, and Paul III—in denouncing the increasingly prevalent ritual murder or "blood libel" accusation, which alleged that the Jews tortured and murdered young Christian boys in order to use their blood for ritual purposes, especially in the Passover meal.[43]

The Dreyfus case dragged on after Henry's suicide, but the issues had been clarified. On one side were those who fought against what they regarded as an intolerable miscarriage of justice. On the other were those who were convinced that the legacy of 1789 had been a catastrophic mistake. They insisted that nothing must be done to harm the two institutions—the army and the church—that embodied the true spirit of France. Initially, the socialists were either indifferent or hostile to Dreyfus, partly in keeping with the traditional antisemitism of the French left. However, led by Jean Jaurès, most eventually came to see that what was really at stake was the survival of the legacy of the French Revolution.

Dreyfus was brought back from Devil's Island, and a second court-martial was convened in the military-base town of Rennes on 7 August 1899. There was, however, no possibility that a military court would reverse the first court-martial. Had it done so, it would have found one man innocent but, by implication, General Auguste Mercier, minister of war at the beginning of the affair, and a goodly number of General Staff officers guilty of obstructing justice. This the court would not do. On 9 September, by a vote of five to two, Dreyfus was again found guilty of treason. It was obvious that the verdict had less to do with Dreyfus's guilt or innocence than with the political impossibility of going against the army high command. Because of "extenuating circumstances," his sentence was reduced to ten years, five of which he had already served. The verdict represented an impossible compromise. Ten years' imprisonment is too light a sentence for a traitor and too severe for an innocent man.

The trial itself attracted worldwide attention, and the verdict was almost universally condemned. The nineteenth century was drawing to a close, although the twentieth century can be said to have begun in France with the Dreyfus trial. Prime Minister Rene Waldeck-Rousseau had let it be known that he would not let a guilty verdict stand. There was also fear that the Paris Exposition scheduled for 1900 would be widely boycotted. On 19 September 1899, Dreyfus accepted the pardon granted by Émile Loubet, the president of France. Late in the next year, on 27 December, a general amnesty was declared for all those involved.

Some of the most important Dreyfusards were vehemently opposed to Dreyfus's accepting a pardon. One pardons a guilty person; an innocent person needs no pardon. Ironically, Dreyfus had never been a Dreyfusard. He did not understand the political implications of the controversy that had engulfed his life. He had only one desire—to establish his innocence and rehabilitate his career. In any event, a return to the hell of Devil's Island was more than this prematurely aged man could endure. Dreyfus had endured enough. The generals also had experienced enough. They were willing to accept the amnesty. The files on the embarrassing case could be closed, and the army could get on with its business.

Picquart was embittered by the amnesty. It placed him beyond the reach of his enemies on the General Staff, but he could not accept the permanent blemish on his honor that anything less than complete vindication could bring. He demanded justice, but to no avail. Mathieu Dreyfus would not let matters rest either. He wanted to know why the judges at Rennes had voted as they did. In October 1903 a government report acknowledged that the use of fabricated evidence to secure Dreyfus's conviction in the first court-martial had also taken place in the second trial. The second trial had been as bogus as the first. Subsequently, on 25 November Dreyfus petitioned the minister of justice for a new trial. A month later the case was referred to the Cour de Cassation (High Court of Appeal), a civilian court. Strictly speaking, the case should have been referred to a third court-martial, but there was apprehension lest there be a third conviction. More than two years of hearings and deliberations followed, but on 12 July 1906 the High Court annulled the Rennes verdict. Along with Picquart, Dreyfus was rehabilitated, although the French army did not officially reverse its judgments against him until 1995. Dreyfus was promoted to the rank of major and made a member of the Legion of Honor. Picquart was promoted to brigadier general, the rank he normally would have had. In October 1906 Georges Clemenceau, who had been among Dreyfus's vicious detractors before rallying to his cause in 1897—he edited *L'Aurore* when Zola published *J'Accuse* in it—became France's prime minister. His first appointments included naming Picquart minister of war.

## ANTICIPATIONS OF AUSCHWITZ

Coming at the end of the nineteenth century, the Dreyfus affair can be seen as a curtain raiser for the far more destructive acts of antisemitism that would follow only a few decades later. In the years that followed the trial, the aim of the French right was to put an end to the society created by the French Revolution. In 1936 Charles Maurras was elected to the Académie Française. His election gave him a stamp of approval from the nation's most illustrious intellectual and literary leaders. When the Germans defeated France in 1940, Marshal Henri Philippe Pétain (1856–1951), an old Postard who had been a young officer at the time of the Dreyfus affair and subsequently France's chief military hero from World War I, became the head of the Vichy-based French state, which did the Germans' bidding. Early on, according to Eugen Weber, "Pétain's policy seemed to reflect ideas that Maurras had spent his life trying to teach the French."[44] Without much prompting from the Germans, Pétain's regime enthusiastically initiated the kind of antisemitic legislation the French right had sought for decades. When the Germans implemented the Final Solution in France, almost all of the work of rounding up Jews for deportation to the death camps was done by the obliging French bureaucracy and police force. Maurras's antisemitism had led him to collaborate with the Germans in World War II. When the Free French convicted him of treason in 1945, he cried out in the court room, "*C'est la revanche de Dreyfus*" [This is the revenge of Dreyfus].

Two journalists with very different loyalties had observed the Dreyfus affair. One of history's ironies is their shared conclusion that the French Revolution's emancipation of the Jews was unworkable. Charles Maurras was one of the journalists. The other was Theodor Herzl, the founder of modern political Zionism. As the Paris correspondent of the Viennese newspaper *Neue Freie Presse*, Herzl had followed the Dreyfus case and had witnessed Dreyfus's degradation. He heard the mob shout, "Death to the Jews!" Originally an assimilated Jew who believed in the viability of emancipation, Herzl reversed his opinion. Reinforcing his rejection of emancipation and assimilation as solutions to Europe's Jewish problem, "the Dreyfus case," he said, "made me a Zionist."[45] Maurras wanted forcibly to eliminate the Jews from Europe; Herzl believed that it was imperative for the Jews voluntarily to remove themselves from Europe through the creation of their own state.

On 17 January 1896, a year after Dreyfus's official degradation, Herzl succinctly analyzed the causes of modern antisemitism and the difference between modern and traditional antisemitism:

The Jewish Question still exists. It would be foolish to deny it. It exists wherever Jews live in perceptible numbers. Where it does not yet exist, it will be
brought by Jews in the course of their migrations. . . .

Only an ignorant man would mistake modern antisemitism for an exact
repetition of the Jew-baiting of the past. . . . In the principal countries where
antisemitism prevails, it does so as a result of the emancipation of the Jews.
When civilized nations awoke to the inhumanity of exclusive legislation,
and enfranchised us—our enfranchisement came too late. For we had, curi-
ously enough, developed while in the Ghetto into a bourgeois people, and
we stepped out of it only to enter into fierce competition with the middle
classes.[46]

As the twentieth century began, Herzl was pessimistic about the Jewish future
in Europe. If the Jews prospered, they would arouse envy and hatred; if they sank
into poverty, they would be regarded as contemptible and useless. If they sought
refuge in a new land that was not fully their own, even one with little antisemitism, their increasing numbers would create the very affliction from which
they had fled. There was still hope for the Jews, Herzl believed, but only in a state
of their own. Herzl was prophetic. Nevertheless, as farseeing as his grim analysis
proved to be, it erred on the side of optimism. The final catastrophe was unthinkable even to him.

Herzl died in 1904. He saw neither the Holocaust nor the establishment of
the state of Israel. As for Alfred Dreyfus, he served his country in World War I,
and then he and his family—arguably the best known Jews in France—lived quietly in Paris, where he died in 1935. By the time of the German occupation of
France, most members of the extended Dreyfus family were in the United States
or England. Along with his aging widow, Lucie, whose identity was unknown to
the Catholic nuns who sheltered her in their convent, four of Dreyfus's grandchildren remained in wartime France and joined Resistance organizations.[47]
Before Lucie Dreyfus died on 14 December 1945, she learned how antisemitism
had snared one of her granddaughters. Arrested for a curfew violation, Madeleine
Dreyfus Lévy had been kept in custody when the authorities became aware of her
name. She was deported in November 1943. Three months later the consequences latent in *L'Affaire Dreyfus* were evident: Alfred Dreyfus's granddaughter
had perished in Auschwitz.

# Chapter 4

# Toward Total Domination

*The new regime made no bones about using coercion in many forms against its declared enemies, but it also sought the consent and support of the people at every turn. . . . Consent and coercion were inextricably entwined throughout the history of the Third Reich, partly because most of the coercion and terror was used against specific individuals, minorities, and social groups for whom the people had little sympathy.*

Robert Gellately, *Backing Hitler: Consent and Coercion in Nazi Germany*

Approaches to Auschwitz were not confined to German soil. In the late nineteenth century, they included avenues of military intrigue in Paris. They would also involve the streets of provincial Austrian towns and vast expanses of Russian-dominated eastern Europe. The Dreyfus affair drew Theodore Herzl, the founder of modern Zionism, west from Vienna. In France he witnessed a reaction against the emancipation of Jews initiated by the French Revolution and the Enlightenment. That reaction would spread with lethal consequences for the Jews. Indeed, the Dreyfus affair was only one of several decisive indications that the twentieth century would take a greater proportionate toll on Jewish life than any other. Unfortunately, these signs could not be read with complete clarity at the time. They foreshadowed the Holocaust nonetheless.

## THE RUSSIAN SOLUTION TO THE JEWISH PROBLEM

From the beginning of the sixteenth century, Europe's Jewish population was located predominantly in eastern areas—especially Poland, Lithuania, and Russia.

Population estimates for 1825 show that of the 2.7 million Jews in Europe, about 460,000 lived in western and central Europe, the remainder in eastern and south-eastern areas of the continent. In 1900, European Jews numbered nearly nine million. By that time, only about 15 percent of them lived in Europe's western and central regions. For a time, eastern Europe had provided Jews with opportunities to earn a decent livelihood that they had lost in the west, but the economic necessity that drove Jews into Poland and the Russian-dominated east was not complemented by opportunities that would last indefinitely. The economy of eastern Europe was to witness development later but roughly comparable to that of the west. A pattern of displacement of the Jews by the dominant majority was repeated in the east, but with the added difficulty that fewer readily accessible havens were available. Crucial to this process was the land reform that came to Poland and Russia in 1846 and 1861, respectively. These steps emancipated some forty-eight million serfs. Their freedom, however, proved to be a mixed blessing. The division of the land could not produce a livelihood for all of the growing population. Millions of peasants turned to the towns and cities in the hope of maintaining themselves, but the industrial base was not sufficient to provide them with work. Unemployment was rife. In Russia and even more so in Poland, it affected Jews in multiple ways. The rationalization of agriculture into large, cost-effective units, for example, displaced many Jews from the agrarian villages. Others found themselves competing with non-Jews in trade and commerce. Still others found themselves thrust into urban centers with an equally desperate non-Jewish proletariat. All the while, Jewish numbers were growing. Throw in a strong dose of antisemitism, which had long been an important factor in these regions, and it becomes apparent that pressures were mounting to explosive levels.

The year 1881 was a watershed for the fate of the Jews. On 13 March (new calendar[1]) revolutionary terrorists assassinated Czar Alexander II. Influential government circles blamed the Jews, whose population in Russia was approximately five million at the time of the czar's death. The first in a series of murderous pogroms began on 27 April. The violence recurred from 1903 to 1906 and again between 1917 and 1921 during the Russian civil war. Significantly, the pogroms of 1881–84 can be called state-sponsored. Mobs acted with impunity. The target population did not receive the normal protection of the law until the Russian intention was unmistakable: Jews should go elsewhere. By the tens of thousands, Jews got the message, and a westward exodus began. Discriminatory laws affected those who stayed behind. Particularly noteworthy were the "May Laws" of 1882, which severely restricted Jewish movement and opportunity within areas under Russian jurisdiction. The intent of these measures was to make life so uncomfortable for the Jews that they would leave—voluntarily if not because the law required them to do so.

In sum, by laying the groundwork for the capitalist transformation of eastern European agriculture, emancipation created the conditions for the beginnings of a small but growing indigenous middle class. As this class developed, the Russian government, traditionally hostile to the Jews, had even less reason to tolerate a minority that was seen as foreign to the nation's ethnic and religious consensus. The ultimate aim of Russian policy in the aftermath of the events of 1881 was the total disappearance of Jewish life from Russia.

No one understood that aim better than Konstantin Petrovich Pobedonostsev (1827–1907), a highly influential bureaucrat who zealously advocated the Russification of all non-Russian minorities. Responding to a group of Jewish petitioners in 1898, he stated succinctly the Russian solution to the Jewish problem: "One third will die out, one third will leave the country, and one third will be completely dissolved in the surrounding population."[2] Thus, decades before World War II, Russian policymakers articulated essentially the same goal with respect to the Jews as did the early National Socialists. There was, of course, an important difference between the means even a modernizing bureaucrat like Pobedonostsev was prepared to use before World War I and those employed by the German state during World War II. Even as Pobedonostsev propounded his Russian solution, however, events destined to close the gap between means and ends were under way.[3]

## HITLER AND WORLD WAR I

When Pobedonostsev set forth his Russian solution, Adolf Hitler (1889–1945) was a nine-year-old schoolboy in the obscure Austrian village of Lambach. No one could have guessed that he would become a dominant world figure, let alone that his infamy would have so much to do with the Jews. Biographies of Hitler and controversies about his history abound.[4] So in lieu of summarizing his life, let us note some salient details that put him on paths to the Holocaust. Consider, first, that Bismarck's creation of a unified German empire in 1871—the same year the German Jews were emancipated—was followed by a decade of economic depression. Already those conditions exacerbated tensions in Germany and Austria between Jews and non-Jews. To make matters worse, unsettled conditions led large numbers of eastern European Jews to immigrate to Berlin, Vienna, and other major population centers. In 1846, for example, 3,739 Jews lived in Vienna; in 1900 there were 176,000. In 1852, 11,840 Jews lived in Berlin; by 1890 there were 108,044, some 5 percent of the city's population. Concurrent with the Jewish influx, which heightened tensions, an important emigration was afoot. Between 1871 and 1885 approximately 3.5 percent of the entire population, 1,678,202 Germans, went to the United States. The peak of this *Auswanderung*—250,000 persons—occurred in the crucial period of 1881–82.

In 1891, ten years after the beginning of the decisive Russian pogroms, Leo von Caprivi, Bismarck's successor as chancellor of the German Reich, observed that "Germany must export goods or people."[5] Caprivi understood the classic dilemma of production and consumption that besets every modern technological society. Germany's ability to produce exceeded her capacity to consume.

Without foreign markets, Germany would be faced with an unacceptable level of mass unemployment at home. Over the long run such destabilization could not be tolerated.

For a time, emigration of its native population was considered the normal, acceptable method of population control in Germany. Reliable estimates show that about six million people left Germany in the nineteenth and early twentieth centuries.[6] Specifically for the period 1846–1932, there were 4.9 million departures from Germany, another 5.2 million from Austria-Hungary.[7]

Amidst these massive population movements, Hitler, 18, headed for Vienna to find his way in the world. His hopes did not pan out. Denied admission to the Vienna Academy of Fine Arts, he also lost his beloved mother to cancer—she had been attended by a Jewish physician—in December 1908. Five years of embittered Viennese wandering ensued. Hitler observed the Jewish population, now full of unassimilated eastern arrivals. They struck him as alien in every way. Later he would identify their presence as a major factor in forcing Germans out of a place that he considered was rightfully theirs. For the present, intent German nationalist that he was, the young Hitler could no longer abide Vienna and the polyglot Hapsburg Empire it epitomized. In May 1913 he left for Munich.

Recalled to Austria in February 1914 to be examined for military service, Hitler was rejected as too weak and unfit. But when war broke out in August, he volunteered and was accepted for service in a Bavarian infantry regiment. Wounded twice, he served with distinction, winning the Iron Cross (First and Second Class). In October 1918, Hitler was badly gassed. By the time he recovered, Germany had obtained an armistice. Along with many other Germans, Hitler was stunned by the capitulation. The intensity of his belief that the nation had been "stabbed in the back," betrayed specifically by Jewish interests from within, was matched only by the fervor of his disdain for the conditions imposed on Germany by the Treaty of Versailles.

Hitler's violent antisemitism and its eventual outcome, the Holocaust, must be seen against the horizon of the unprecedented magnitude of violence perpetrated in the twentieth century. No century in human history can match the twentieth in the sheer number of human beings slaughtered as a direct consequence of the political activity of the great states. The figures can never be exact, but demographic research suggests that the twentieth century's toll included more than two hundred million humanly inflicted deaths.[8]

Twentieth-century mass slaughter began in earnest with World War I, Europe's first industrial war. Some 8.5 million soldiers were killed—another 21 million were wounded—in a war that included massive artillery barrages and poison gas attacks. Between five and six thousand people were killed every day during more than fifteen hundred days of warfare.[9] On the worst of those days—1 July 1916 during the First Battle of the Somme—the British army's casualties alone numbered more than fifty-seven thousand. The Great War, as it was called at the time, was the first truly modern war of the century. The civilian societies of both the Allied and the Central powers (Germany, Austria-Hungary, and the

Ottoman Empire) were organized in such a way that millions of ordinary people were withdrawn from their normal occupations, supplied with weapons of unprecedented destructiveness, and dispatched to the battlefields where they slaughtered one another en masse. Without the systematic organization of both population and industry, it would have been impossible to wage the kind of mass war that was fought.

A mass war has its own logic. Such warfare differs immensely from the almost ritualistic and symbolic contests of compact units of military professionals that formerly waged war on their countries' behalf. Diego de Velasquez's magnificent painting *The Surrender of Breda* (25 June 1625), which hangs in Madrid's Prado Museum, suggests how European wars were once fought: With the troops of both sides facing each other, the Dutch commander Justin of Nassau bows as he surrenders the keys of Breda, a crucial Dutch city, to the Spanish commander, the Genoese general Ambrogio Spinola. Spinola has dismounted from his horse and has placed his right hand on the shoulder of Justin as he accepts the keys. Spinola's gesture suggests mutual respect and knightly comradeship. The victor knows that things could have gone the other way. He is also convinced that the victory belongs to God. By contrast, at the end of World War II, Hermann Göring (Reichsmarschall and chief of the *Luftwaffe*, the German air force), Field Marshall Wilhelm Keitel (chief of staff of the *Wehrmacht* High Command), and General Alfred Jodl (chief of operations for the High Command) were among the members of the senior Nazi military leadership condemned to death by the International Military Tribunal in Nuremberg on 1 October 1946 for "crimes against humanity." The execution method—hanging—was no different than the one that might be inflicted on common criminals. Göring escaped that fate by committing suicide.

Modern warfare is scarcely conducive to knightly comradeship. The objective is often to annihilate the enemy's armed forces. In essence, that is what General Erich von Falkenhayn, the German commander, attempted at World War I's battle of Verdun (21 February–July 1916). Falkenhayn's objective was to destroy as many of the enemy as possible.[10] His strategy foreshadowed military strategies that would provide the context for the death camps of World War II. Meanwhile, Falkenhayn could not slaughter the French in huge numbers without suffering a comparable loss of his own men. The battle of Verdun laid waste to about four hundred thousand men on each side during a five-month battle. By the end of 1916, a French counteroffensive left the battle lines more or less where they had been at the beginning of the German attack in February.

Apparently, the German military and civilian authorities did not consider so great a human sacrifice too high a price to pay for the victory they sought. It is somewhat easier to understand the resolve of the French to take their losses. They were convinced that their national existence was at stake. No comparable danger threatened the Germans. They were the attackers who were determined to win the war no matter what the cost. From the perspective of subsequent history, Verdun offered a hint of the extent to which Germany's leaders regarded even their own people as expendable. If the German leaders were prepared to sacrifice their own people on so vast a scale, they were not likely to be concerned about the fate of populations they deemed their enemies; and by 1939 the overwhelming majority of the German people were convinced that the Jews were their most dangerous mortal enemies.[11] Nevertheless, there is an important difference between the Germans' actions at Verdun in 1916 and their policies during World War II. Although there is little evidence that the Germans would have intensified their violence against their adversaries had they won World War I, *the Germans' intentions in World War II, especially in relation to eastern Europe, aimed at the permanent enslavement, if not annihilation, of their enemies.*

Meanwhile, the Germans were not alone in their indifference to the fate of large numbers of their own men during the campaigns of World War I. On 1 July 1916, General Sir Douglas Haig launched the First Battle of the Somme. By the end of the first day, the British casualties numbered almost sixty thousand (twenty thousand dead) and included half of all of the officers assigned to the battle. Refusing to desist, Haig was determined to break through the German lines at any cost, but the British offensive failed. The British lines had moved forward only five miles. Casualty estimates for the entire battle included 650,000 Germans, 420,000 British, and 195,000 French, a toll that had been taken for nothing.[12]

Haig and the British High Command learned little from the disaster at the Somme. In the summer of 1917, Haig began the Passchendaele Campaign (31 July–November), the last of three major battles fought in the area of Ypres, Belgium.[13] Predictably heavy rain turned the terrain into a muddy swamp. As the war of attrition wore on, the Germans bombarded Haig's troops with high-explosive shells and released canisters of deadly chlorine gas as well. The gas included agents—"sneezing gas"—that made it difficult to use the gas-mask technology that by then had been developed to thwart the effectiveness of such attacks. (Referred to as "mustard gas," owing to its chlorine-derived yellowish-green color, gas as a tool of warfare had been initiated by the Germans on 22 April 1915 during the Second Battle of Ypres. Subsequently, both sides frequently resorted to gas attacks.) Haig still refused to call a halt until 6 November, when the Allies finally took what was left of the utterly destroyed village of Passchendaele. In three months of brutal fighting, the combined Allied and German casualties totaled some 850,000, including the death of 300,000 British, Australians, and Canadians and about 250,000 Germans. Ninety thousand British or Australian bodies were never identified; forty-two thousand were never recovered at all, having been blown to bits or drowned in the hideous morass.[14]

Undoubtedly, military leaders such as Falkenhayn and Haig were convinced that they had the best of reasons for permitting the slaughter of their own troops. Both men had been entrusted with the most awesome of responsibilities, the command decisions affecting the lives of their respective nation's fighting men during wartime. The process by which they were selected was neither frivolous nor fortuitous. In a moment of extreme national crisis they were regarded as the best available commanders. Under the circumstances, their military decisions cannot be regarded as solely personal. They were chosen because they were trusted to make the right decisions. Those decisions were accepted. The British and the German generals made the same decision: their country's young men were expendable.

The death statistics do not begin to convey the carnage experienced on both sides. During much of the war, the armies carried on the battle from trenches that were bitterly cold in winter, often flooded by rain, plagued by rats, stench-filled with excrement and decaying body parts from the dead. The order to move out of the trenches on the attack was often a mass death sentence that the troops could refuse only if they were prepared to face the more disgraceful death of execution by their comrades for "deserting." The surviving troops often faced an arguably worse fate—crippling dismemberment and disfigurement that made it difficult for them to look in the mirror or to return to "normal" civilian life, if indeed such a life was possible after the mass slaughter.

The war had begun with combatants on both sides—including Adolf Hitler—under the illusion that theirs was a heroic enterprise that promised glory unattainable in their humdrum civilian lives. Horror's reality soon overtook them. Soldiers on both sides developed their own subculture, which was contemptuous of both the traditional officer corps and the civilian leaders at home.[15] The gulf between ordinary soldiers and the traditional officer corps was nowhere more evident than in Haig's persistent refusal to visit the wounded. Although Haig cold-bloodedly gave the orders that resulted in the death of hundreds of thousands of his fellow countrymen, his son reported that Field Marshal Haig "felt it was his duty to refrain from visiting the casualty clearing stations because these visits made him physically ill."[16] Apparently it was easier for Haig to give impersonal commands than to confront their very human consequences.

It did not take long for those who had endured the slaughter to become alienated from their fellow citizens at home and even to feel they had more in common with enemy soldiers at the front, who at least shared their terrible experiences.[17] On the home front, politicians, propagandists, and recruiters glorified war and depicted the soldiers as noble, self-sacrificing heroes. The mixture of mud, death, dismemberment, and stench at the front yielded no such conviction. When the war was over, the surviving, battle-hardened conscripts were expected to return home to "normal" life, but four years of war had changed both "home" and the veterans. Having fought for their countries in a way that was unimaginable to those who remained behind, they became increasingly convinced that their trench experience gave them a prerogative to change society.[18] Above all, frontline soldiers had to make sense of their senseless experience not only to endure the unendurable but to achieve a modicum of meaning and sanity in the aftermath. As we shall see, Hitler and many of his staunchest followers found in National Socialist ideology and antisemitism the meaning they sought.

As the historian Omer Bartov has pointed out, the frontline soldiers developed a new understanding of "soldiers' glory." It came to mean "enduring the most degrading, inhuman conditions, under constant threat of death and while regularly killing others, without losing one's good humor, composure, and humanity."[19] Atrocities that the soldiers had inflicted and endured came to be regarded as an elevating experience rather than as an abomination. During the interwar period (1919–39), moreover, the memory of the mass killing played a decisive role in national politics, although the meaning ascribed to the war was very different in Britain and especially France, on the one hand, and in defeated Germany, on the other. In the aftermath of World War I, as Bartov has observed, the French saw themselves very largely as a *community of suffering* "unified by common pain and sorrow, bound together by horror, determined to prevent such wars from ever happening again."[20] By contrast, Germany's veterans saw themselves as a *Kampfgemeinschaft* (battle community). They turned the despair of the war's aftermath—Germany had lost European and colonial territory, as well as millions of lives, and been forced to sign what was taken to be a humiliating peace treaty—into a prelude for a new Germany.[21] Unexpected, shocking, and unnecessary though the 1918 defeat had been, the German veterans and other "true Germans," who shared the right kind of *inneres Erlebnis* (inner experience) even though they might not have served at the front, would form a renewed *Volksgemeinschaft* (national community). Ensuring that the setback of 1918 was only temporary, it would take revenge on Germany's enemies and make the nation triumphant.

In the 1920s and 1930s France's reaction to the horror of the Great War, much of which had taken place on her soil, emphasized avoiding another war.[22] Among Germany's veterans and those who regretted that they had been too young to fight, the dominant attitudes were very different. They closely fitted Hitler's conviction that decisive steps must be taken to avenge Germany's defeat, overturn the hated Versailles *Diktat*, and smash those who had been responsible for the *Dolchstoss* (stab in the back) that had brought the nation down.[23] With respect to the "stab in the back," after four years of death, dismemberment, and destruction, it was impossible for the German soldiers to believe that *they* had lost the war. They became convinced that more than the Allies military power was responsible. As the veterans, joined by many like-minded Germans, came to see the situation, there must have been betrayal from within.[24] There were plenty of potential scapegoats—left-wing politicians and pacifists, for example—but Jews, sharing neither ethnic nor religious roots with the majority, were the best candidates.

As a relatively powerless minority, the Jews could not fight back effectively when German blame was heaped upon them for allegedly starting the war, surreptitiously engineering Germany's defeat, bringing about the Bolshevik Revolution, and using it to create political, social, and religious chaos throughout Europe. Never mind that German Jews had been eager to prove their loyalty to their imagined fatherland by bravery in battle. Out of a community of some 600,000, about 100,000 German Jews served in the German military.[25] Twelve thousand of them lost their lives on the battlefield but to no avail. Jews were too convenient a scapegoat, the only scapegoat who could unify all other German groups in a common sense of belonging: whatever their religious affiliation, their class status, or their political convictions, they were *not* Jews.[26]

Meanwhile, although the ending of World War I seemed once more to leave Hitler's hopes in ruins, the war, in fact, gave his life renewed purpose, and not least because it focused and intensified his antisemitism in postwar Munich, the city that did more than any other to give birth to National Socialism. There, for example, Hitler witnessed a series of left-wing attempts, led largely by marginalized, irreligious Jews, to bring about an enduring socialist revolution in Catholic, conservative Bavaria. They failed, but not without leaving a lasting impression on Hitler and also on Archbishop Eugenio Pacelli, later Pope Pius XII, who was the papal nuncio to Bavaria at the time.

Munich was also a principal gathering place for White Russian refugees who brought with them *The Protocols of the Elders of Zion*, the infamous forgery that inflamed anti-Jewish hatred by purporting to reveal a Jewish conspiracy to rule the world. Translated into German and English, the book was given worldwide dissemination. When the White Russians depicted Bolshevism as an assault by alien Jews on the essence of European Christian civilization, the very conspiracy to which the *Protocols* referred, the visibility of Jewish leadership in the short-lived Bavarian Socialist Republic and the even briefer Soviet republics lent credibility to the accusations. The impact of these events should not be overlooked in accounting for Hitler's linking of antisemitism and anticommunism.

## THE EMERGENCE OF THE NAZI PARTY AND ITS IDEOLOGY

No sooner had the guns of the Great War fallen silent than various German groups resolved that the enormous blood sacrifice would somehow be made good in the future.[27] Antisemitism figured strongly in many of these groups. A case in point was an obscure organization called the *Deutsche Arbeiterpartei* (DAP; German Workers' Party), which Anton Drexler, a Munich railroad worker, had founded in January 1919. Still in the army, Adolf Hitler had been assigned—ironically, as it turned out—to investigate radical political activity. His orders put him in contact with the DAP in September 1919. Finding that its ideas coincided with many of his own, Hitler became member number 555 (the DAP's numbering system began at 501 to magnify its size). Less than two years later, on 29 July 1921, he gained dictatorial control of the renamed *Nationalsozialistische Deutsche Arbeiterpartei* (NSDAP; National Socialist German Workers' Party).

Capitalizing on Hitler's powerful rhetorical talents, the NSDAP was six thousand members strong by the following summer. Its development included a paramilitary arm known as the *Sturmabteilung* (SA, or storm troopers), which was organized by Hermann Göring (1893–1946), an ace pilot from World War I, and under the command of former army captain Ernst Röhm (1887–1934). The SA drew its membership largely from right-wing war veterans and other Germans who distrusted the postwar Weimar Republic's democratic leanings. Wishfully thinking that the Weimar Republic was near collapse, on 8–9 November 1923

Hitler and his followers attempted a takeover of the Bavarian state. His plan was a disaster but only in the short run. Sentenced to five years in Landsberg Prison, Hitler served nine months before he was released. He was back on the streets by Christmas 1924. In the meanwhile he had put his comfortable prison term to good use by starting to write one of the twentieth century's most influential books, *Mein Kampf* (My Struggle). By 1933 *Mein Kampf* had sold more than one million copies. The five-hundredth printing took place in 1939, and by 1945 sales had reached ten million copies. The royalties made Hitler wealthy.

In *Mein Kampf* Hitler reckoned that nature's basic law is that of eternal struggle in which conflict is the means to greatness.[28] In addition, Hitler found two other natural laws that he regarded as vitally important, the laws of heredity and self-preservation. Nature, he contended, balks at the mixing of species in reproduction. It also preserves the strongest while eliminating the weakest. Human life is not exempt from nature's ruthless process, which always takes the shortest, most efficient path in selections that destine the strongest for life. The crucial difference, however, is that human beings can know—indeed they must know—that their individual and social existence unfolds in an arena of unending mortal struggle. The strong, therefore, will not flinch from embracing a principle that was self-evident to Hitler, namely, that national survival may well depend on utterly ruthless aggression and violence. Crucial in those considerations, Hitler urged, is the additional fact that a people's survival and movement toward excellence depend on geography. Sufficient land (*Lebensraum*) is essential for a vital people and for the purity of its way of life.[29] To achieve greatness and the space it requires, brutal means may be necessary. A people's spirit is tested as it is required to apply maximum force in subduing its enemies.

The links between these aspects of Hitler's worldview and his virulent antisemitism are not hard to find. In fact, the two components were interfused. Nature and history, thought Hitler, are of one piece. Early on he was driven by the conviction that human existence and the allegedly racially superior German people were threatened by racial pollution. Thus Poles, Russians, Ukrainians, and other Slavic peoples, as well as "defective" Germans or "asocials" (for example, the mentally retarded, the physically handicapped, homosexuals, and criminals), would become Hitler's targets. Topping this list, however, was the racial enemy Hitler regarded as the most unrelenting of all: the Jews. In a word, *Mein Kampf* testifies that wherever Hitler saw a threat to the ethnic and national survival he prized, wherever he sensed an obstacle to the geographical expansion he craved, he ultimately blamed the Jews. Following Hitler's lead, Nazi propaganda portrayed Jews in multiple negative ways: the Jew is conspiratorial, greedy, immoral, satanic, parasitic, Bolshevist, and, above all, so threatening racially that a Jewish presence in Germany was a problem that must be solved.

In sum, the Jewish race was alleged to have subverted, plundered, and infected the very people who, according to Hitler, deserved to dominate the world. Nazism's vision was politically messianic, and in that sense it was full of religious undercurrents and overtones. As Nazi ideology saw it, the Germans' struggle against the Jew had nothing less than cosmic stakes. Defeating the Jews was both a political challenge and a metaphysical one. As the historian Saul Friedländer has rightly argued, Hitler and his followers were not advocating run-of-the-mill hostility toward Jews but *redemptive antisemitism*.[30] The Nazis, Hitler believed, could and would provide the requisite force to eliminate Jewish pollution of the German bloodstream and to ensure the redemption of Germany.

The reasons Germans joined the Nazi Party or eventually voted for Hitler were diverse. Party members and the Nazi electorate came from varied classes. Nazism attracted them because it took a strong stand against communism, or because other parties did not back their economic and political interests and the Nazis promised to do so. The part played by antisemitism has been the subject of much debate among historians, but this much is clear: without antisemitism, neither Nazism, Hitler's dictatorship, nor the Holocaust was possible. Absent antisemitism, there can be no credible account of why the Holocaust happened. On the other hand, if there is an ideology steeped in racial antisemitism, a dedicated cadre of political leaders who are profoundly committed to it, and a populace that eventually is willing to follow where those leaders and their ideology take them, then one can go far in explaining why the Holocaust happened. Yehuda Bauer hits the mark on this point: "When you want something badly, you try to translate your desire into reality. That is precisely what the Germans did: they were possessed by a racist ideology, and they enacted it."[31]

Although the formula is true—no ideology equals no Holocaust—credible explanations of the Holocaust cannot be reduced to simplifications. Accordingly, Daniel Goldhagen's proposition is problematic when he argues that, long before the Nazis came to power, an "eliminationist antisemitism" so permeated German society and culture that the vast majority desired the total elimination of the Jews. If Goldhagen means that the German people, early on, wanted the Final Solution, the evidence is not on his side. Yet his account wins support when he argues that Nazi Germany did arrive at a point "where an enormous number of ordinary, representative Germans became—and most of the rest of their fellow Germans were fit to be—Hitler's willing executioners."[32] Meanwhile, while antisemitism was not the major factor in accounting for Nazi voter appeal, Hitler never lost sight of its centrality to his objectives. Antisemitism was at the core of all of his thought and action. Moreover, his political intuitions—including his idealism about Germany's future—and his antisemitism served each other well. He sensed effectively when and how to stress "the Jewish question" and when and how to downplay it. Depending on his audience, Hitler ramped up or reined in his anti-Jewish rhetoric. Once he and his like-minded Nazis were in the saddle, they practiced what they preached, and the appeal of their "idealism," along with its strict policing measures, was widespread.

The early Nazi Party contained disputing factions that included different degrees of antisemitism, but by 1926 Hitler quelled the most contentious of them. Assisted by Göring, Joseph Goebbels (1897–1945), and Heinrich Himmler (1900–1945), he put behind him the defeat suffered in the 1923 Munich putsch. At that time the NSDAP had about 55,000 members. Briefly banned from German politics, the party fell into disarray, but Hitler, vowing to pursue parliamentary means to power (a strategy that increased his credibility, because most Germans deplored Nazi street fighting), relaunched it in February 1925. Membership had fallen to 27,000 after the failed coup; by 1928 the decline had been reversed and 108,000 Germans belonged.[33]

Those gains, however, did not immediately translate into ballot-box success. After the 1923 hyperinflation, the German economy stabilized considerably. The Nazis won only twelve seats in the 1928 Reichstag elections. They would not achieve major political gains until the world was plunged into the severe depression whose origins included the American stock-market crash in October 1929. During the winter of 1929–30, more than three million Germans (14 percent of the population) were jobless. By the autumn of 1932, five million were out of work, a figure that climbed to six million by January 1933. The Weimar Republic's economic woes—industrial production fell 42 percent from 1929 to 1932—benefitted the Nazis. Party membership doubled from 1928 to 1930. In September 1930, the Nazis won their first major breakthrough in Germany's national elections: nearly 6.4 million votes and 107 seats (out of 577) in the Reichstag, which made their delegation second only to the Social Democrats.

Hitler did not belabor the Jewish question per se, but Nazi rhetoric skillfully alluded to alleged Jewish contributions to the evils that were of greatest concern to voters, such as the continuing limits imposed on Germany by the Versailles Treaty, communism, and the economic instability of the Depression. To Hitler and the Nazis, Jewishness was primarily a matter of race, but he did not confine it strictly to that realm. Non-Jews might also be considered "spiritual Jews" insofar as they identified with democracy, socialism, or internationalism, which were among the causes Hitler identified as "Jewish." Such people also became his targets. Hitler's popularity, however, did not increase primarily because of his anti-semitism. Sarah Gordon puts the point succinctly: "Middle-class and other voters did not vote for Hitler because he promised to exterminate European Jewry. Neither did they vote for him because he promised to tear up the constitution, impose a police state, destroy trade unions, eradicate rival political parties, or cripple the churches."[34] Yet when he got the requisite power, and the German people by consent or coercion gave him his way, these were the things that Hitler went on to do.

## CLOSING AND OPENING DOORS

The Nazis' strong showing in the 1930 elections not only firmed up Hitler's control of the Nazi Party but also made him a major political figure in Germany at an auspicious moment. For the Weimar Republic, which was never greatly loved by the large number of Germans who regarded it as foisted on them by the victorious Allies after World War I, was becoming wracked by factionalism that weakened it beyond recovery. Hitler's domination of Germany was not far off.

Before we reach that part of the story, however, it will be well to observe what was happening concurrently in Poland, where so much of Hitler's Final Solution of the Jewish question was to take place, as well as in the United States.

In the 1920s, a flood of eastern European immigrants provoked an explicitly anti-Jewish response in the United States Congress. The Report of the Congressional Committee on Immigration entitled "Temporary Suspension of Immigration" (dated 6 December 1920) was concerned almost exclusively with bringing Jewish immigration to a halt. The report cited the published statement of a "commissioner of the Hebrew Sheltering and Aid Society of America": "If there were in existence a ship that could hold 3,000,000 human beings, the 3,000,000 Jews of Poland would board it to escape to America."[35] In 1924, the year the membership of the racist and antisemitic Ku Klux Klan reached an all-time high, Congress passed the Johnson-Reed Act (also known as the Immigration Act of 1924). By restricting immigration to 2 percent of each foreign-born group in the United States as of the 1890 census, the law's intent was to curtail sharply new waves of immigration from southern and eastern Europe and to favor immigration from northern and western Europe. Subsequent congressional action in 1929 set the total annual immigration quota at 150,000. Only 20,000 of that number was allotted to southern and eastern Europe and Asia. These restrictive policies would not be reversed until 1965, when Congress passed immigration legislation that removed quotas based on national origins. Meanwhile, the effects of the Immigration Act of 1924 meant, for example, that quotas for 1938 would accommodate 27,370 persons from Germany (including Austria); 6,524 from Poland; 2,712 from the Soviet Union; 869 from Hungary; and 377 from Romania. Doors for Jews were closing on both sides of the Atlantic.

The 1919 statement that all three million Polish Jews would emigrate to America if they could was undoubtedly an exaggeration. Still, the vast majority did want to leave, for the political and economic situation of the Jews of Poland, the European country with by far the largest number of Jews in the period between the wars, deteriorated year by year. The restoration of Polish independence in 1918 was accompanied by a violent wave of antisemitism. Thousands of Jews had fought for Poland's freedom, but typically the Jews were regarded by the Poles as unassimilable foreigners. That hostility was intensified by the fact that the Jewish population was increasingly urban, giving Jews a disproportionate and highly visible representation in Poland's cities, whereas the Polish population was predominantly rural. In addition to the miserable conditions of the Polish peasants, between seven and eight million Poles were unemployed or woefully underemployed in a country of 32.5 million.[36]

The Polish government reacted to the economic predicament by enacting a series of ever more stringent measures designed to transfer whatever jobs and resources there were from Jewish to Polish hands. The downward mobility of the Jews was immediately evident in government-sponsored agencies. After 1918, Jews were barred from positions in all state bureaus and state-owned enterprises. At no time did the Polish government attempt effectively to expand the economy so that both Jews and Poles might be gainfully employed. In addition, the anti-Jewish measures were actively supported by Poland's Roman Catholic Church, which regarded the Jews as agents of secularization, liberalism, and bolshevism. Roman Catholic faith was regarded as an indispensable component of authentic Polish identity, and religious hatred of the Jews attained a virulence of far greater intensity in Poland than in almost any other European country.[37]

Unknowingly, as the 1930s began, the Jews of eastern Europe were entering a death trap from which there would be no escape. As was the case elsewhere, Poland was determined to make life as miserable as possible for them as a way of inducing them to leave. At the same time, the German forces that were to murder the Jews were in the process of formation. For the vast majority of Europe's Jews, emigration had ceased to be an option. Even Palestine would soon be restricted when the British issued the White Paper of May 1939, which limited immigration to a total of seventy-five thousand between 1939 and 1944.

Nevertheless, while the Polish and the National Socialist governments shared a common aim in their Jewish policy, few Poles in the 1920s and 1930s seriously entertained the possibility of establishing a system of mass extermination camps in their country. The Poles were neither modern nor secular enough to plan and execute a systematic program of mass extermination. Under Adolf Hitler and the Nazis, the Germans were.

Although Hitler, an Austrian, had led the Nazi party for almost ten years, he did not become a German citizen until mid-February 1932. At that time the Nazis needed to field a candidate against the Weimar Republic's incumbent president, eighty-five-year-old Field Marshal Paul von Hindenburg, a World War I hero. Hitler, the only Nazi with a chance to win, had to be naturalized before he became eligible to run. In a Germany wracked by economic depression and political chaos—six million Germans were unemployed—Hitler campaigned "For Freedom and Bread," hoping a beleaguered lower middle class and idealistic youth would bring him victory. Hindenburg, perceived by moderate Germans as the last bulwark between communism or Nazism, defeated Hitler by more than seven million votes. The splintering of the electorate, however, was sufficient to force a runoff, since Hindenburg had not received a majority. The field marshal won the second round, but only after Hitler narrowed the margin by nearly 1.2 million votes.

Hindenburg's victory brought Germany neither peace nor unity. The Weimar Republic's parliamentary system, never a tower of strength, had been especially shaky since September 1930, when it became clear that no government could successfully rule Germany without Nazi support. On 31 July 1932, elections for the Reichstag brought the Nazis nearly fourteen million votes (37 percent of the total and 230 Reichstag seats), more than half a million more than the combined total of the Nazis' two closest rivals, the Social Democrats and the Communists. Braced by this showing, Hitler was determined to be chancellor, the chief executive of the German government. Political opponents still had sufficient strength to frustrate Hitler's ambition, and the tide turned against him—momentarily.

Hitler's refusal to join any coalition government forced new elections, which were held on 6 November 1932, at a time when the world's economic crisis was starting to subside. The election results were far from those that the National Socialists desired: the NSDAP got two million votes fewer than it had polled in July. Although the Nazis remained the largest party in the Reichstag, they had lost thirty-four seats. Their momentum seemed to be stalling. A stunned and discouraged Hitler wrote at the end of 1932: "I have given up all hope. Nothing will ever come of my dreams."[38] Rarely has a self-appraisal been so inaccurate.

Faced by the prospect that no sustainable government would emerge after the November election, Hindenburg was persuaded to invoke emergency dictatorial power granted him under the Weimar constitution to prevent an overthrow of democratic order. Ironically, when he reluctantly made Hitler chancellor—a man he despised—Hindenburg ensured the very result his action was supposed to forestall.

Hitler had not seized power. In fact, the power he craved had nearly eluded him. Instead, power was handed to him by German industrialists, military leaders, and right-wing politicians. They thought they could control Hitler, who, in turn, would control the labor unions and stem the leftist tide that seemed about to engulf German society. Another self-appraisal backfired; this time it was not Hitler's. The Nazis moved quickly to consolidate their gains. Strides in that direction were made when secretly inspired Nazi arson at the Reichstag on 27 February 1933—the Communists were blamed—enabled the Nazis to persuade President Hindenburg to curtail civil rights "for the protection of the People and the State." On 23 March 1933, the Reichstag passed the so-called "Enabling Act," which gave Hitler direct legislative power to enact laws and conduct foreign policy without the Reichstag's consent. The act was Hitler's means of gaining absolute dictatorial power "legally." Passage was crucial to Hitler's claim to govern as Germany's legitimate leader, but passage was dependent on the votes of the Catholic Center Party, the only remaining democratic party. The party's leadership opposed passage but nevertheless voted for it at the insistence of Monsignor Ludwig Kaas, the party's president and a close confidant of Cardinal Eugenio Pacelli, papal secretary of state and later Pope Pius XII. Kaas later admitted that a deal was in the making in which the Center Party would vote for the Enabling Act, an act of political suicide that ended democratic opposition to Hitler, in exchange for the government's agreement to negotiate a concordat with the Vatican on favorable terms, a topic to which we return later.[39]

The Nazi regime's power was unassailable when the Enabling Act was renewed on its original expiration date, 1 April 1937. (Hitler made the Act perpetual in 1943.[40]) On 14 July 1933, for example, the NSDAP was established by law as the sole legitimate political party in Germany. Three months later, Hitler announced his intention to withdraw Germany from the League of Nations, calling for a plebiscite on the issue on 12 November, the day after the anniversary of the armistice that had ended World War I. With Hindenburg's ambivalent support, Hitler's policy was overwhelmingly endorsed. A few weeks later, another decree made the NSDAP "the representative of the German state idea and indissolubly linked to the state."[41]

Hitler could well have imagined that the dissolution of his dreams just a year before had now reversed itself so that the vision of *Mein Kampf* would be realized: "The German Reich as a state must embrace all Germans and has the task, not only of assembling and preserving the most valuable stocks of basic racial elements in this people, but slowly and surely of raising them to a dominant position."[42] Implicit in these views was the need for additional territory (*Lebensraum*), cleansed of allegedly inferior racial elements, in which the enlarged German *Volksgemeinschaft*, an ethnically and culturally homogeneous community, could flex its muscle with room enough for all who belonged and no room for those who did not.

## THE TWISTED ROAD TO AUSCHWITZ

Obviously, the Jews were excluded from Hitler's "most valuable stocks of basic racial elements." Instead he took them to be an absolutely unwanted population, completely at odds—racially, culturally, and not least of all economically—with his vision for a redeemed Germany. Recall that Hitler grew up in the heyday of a pan-German nationalism fueled by Bismarck's unification of Germany in 1871. Also significant was the depression of 1873–79. Taking a heavy toll, the depression left economic disturbance in its wake. As history testifies, economic instability typically intensifies ethnic and religious intolerance. The lower middle class in Germany and Austria had been especially hard hit. Like their counterparts elsewhere, these people were often the victims, not the beneficiaries, of economic modernization. Handicapped in competition with well-financed, large-scale enterprises, they were threatened with proletarianization and, in hard times, with unemployment. Even the resumption of an upward trend in the business cycle left these artisans, small retail merchants, and small farmers disadvantaged in comparison to the owners, managers, and laborers in much larger financial and industrial concerns. Blame for the disparity was often laid at Jewish doorsteps.[43] One should not underestimate the determination of a politically active sector of the indigenous German middle class to eliminate a competing economic group regarded as alien to both the national and the religious consensus. Although it is not the whole story, Europe's Jews were unwanted, not so much because they were unemployed, but because they were regarded as a threat by a more powerful group that feared its own downward mobility.

As a young man, Hitler watched thousands of eastern European Jews emigrating from Russia and Poland to the urban centers of Germany and Austria. During the same period, record numbers of ethnic Germans, their economic prospects in decline, emigrated from their native lands to North and South America to find a better life. When Hitler put this equation together, he concluded that, as far as Germans were concerned, the Jews would forever be unwelcome competition, never an economically complementary population. From that perspective, he found the Jews damnable on all sides. It struck him that Jews who were not squeezing Germans in a power struggle to make ends meet had surely exploited them in achieving financial success. Other Jews, he reasoned, threatened to destabilize traditional German society by their liberal democratic leanings, if not by embracing various forms of Marxist socialism or communism. Hitler was not alone in holding such views. They thrived and not only among his lower-middle-class contemporaries, whose social and economic standing grew still more precarious in the 1920s and the early 1930s.

During this time, Jews understandably identified with the ideas and interests that seemed best to serve their needs. Thus they tended to equate modern functional rationality with pluralism, liberalism, and tolerance. Meanwhile their non-Jewish counterparts in the German-speaking world were attracted to forms of modernity that stressed cultural homogeneity, standardization, and centralization. Thus what the Jews hoped for in the way of a pluralistic community, influential members of the dominant majority took to be no community at all, but a congeries of atomized strangers. These Germans sought to restore older bonds of community based upon kinship and shared origins. The irony, of course, was that the emancipation of Europe's Jews had appeared to offer them civic equality, but as a leveling measure it did away with official recognition of very real differences in tradition, culture, and function among the diverse elements of the population. It was only a question of time before voices were heard demanding the elimination of those whose differences could not be leveled. In spite of, or even because of, their claim to be good Germans, Jews fitted into that category. Racial nationalism offered the lower middle class in particular an appealing political program, for it legitimated hostility toward the hated Jewish competitor while providing an ideological basis for community with the owners of large-scale business and the managers of large-scale government, with whom they were inextricably related in any case.

When the National Socialists proclaimed, "Die Juden sind unser Unglück" (The Jews are our misfortune), the message of unreconcilable differences resonated. In Hitler's cry to create a single Aryan neotribe—a project both elicited and nurtured by such tools of modern technology as high finance, industry, bureaucracy, transportation, and wireless communication—millions found the National Socialists articulating what they had long been feeling. They rallied loyally, for from their perspective National Socialism sought to restore civic unity and altruism. The Nazi appeal was all the stronger because it was not based on an abstract religious or humanitarian ideal of human solidarity in general, but rather on dreams rooted in specifically German blood and soil. As a result, pieces were falling in place to ensure that the situation for European Jewry would prove disastrous.

Hostility engendered by economic competition did much to lead the way to Auschwitz and other Nazi death factories. Thus, young German lawyers, doctors, and other professionals saw the expulsion of their Jewish counterparts as a welcome, once-in-a-lifetime opportunity for rapid professional advancement.[44] Yet the road to Auschwitz was anything but straight and narrow. First, it was not easy to remove Jews from the German economy, because they were so deeply and legally embedded in it. Eventually the National Socialists would develop the administrative apparatus to manage a thoroughgoing destruction process. That process defined its victims, concentrated them, and then destroyed them—expropriating their wealth, energy, and personal effects along the way. Although not always foreseen, the process exhibited an inherent pattern, a logic of its own, but in the early stages difficulties arose in arriving at a systematic and coherent Jewish policy.

According to Karl A. Schleunes, during the initial years of Hitler's rule "the Nazis stumbled toward something resembling a Final Solution to the Jewish Problem. The Final Solution as it emerged in 1941 and 1942 was not the product of a grand design. In fact, when the Nazis came to power, they had no specific plans for a solution of any sort. They were certain only that a solution was necessary: This commitment carried the Nazi system along the twisted road to Auschwitz."[45] It is arguable whether the Nazis had "no specific plans for a solution of any sort," as Schleunes contends, but his basic point—the early Nazi initiatives lacked clarity and coordination—is valid. For instance, as far back as 29 April 1920, Hitler said, "We will carry on the struggle until the last Jew is removed from the German Reich." He frequently reiterated the fact that such "removal" (*Entfernung*) was one of his top priorities.[46] The precise meaning of these beliefs, however, as well as the means for carrying them out could be defined in various ways. As the Swiss historian Philippe Burrin suggests, early on and until those ambiguities were removed, Hitler "did not have a plan, but only an obsession: to cleanse the Reich of the Jews within its borders."[47]

On 30 January 1939, the sixth anniversary of his appointment as Germany's chancellor, Hitler spoke to the Reichstag about the future of Europe and the fate of European Jewry in particular. The evening's two-and-a-half hour speech included his by then familiar anti-Jewish tirades, but on this occasion Hitler's menacing forecasts were more ominous than usual. "If the international Jewish financiers in and outside Europe should succeed in plunging the nations once more into a world war," Hitler insisted, "then the result will not be the Bolshevization of the earth, and thus the victory of Jewry, but the annihilation [*Vernichtung*] of the Jewish race in Europe."[48] Historians debate the meaning of this statement: Was it a clear and explicit signal that Hitler intended mass murder as the Final Solution for the Third Reich's Jewish problem? If it was such a signal, how long had Hitler consciously held that intention? Detailed conclusive answers to those questions are unlikely to be found. Certainly no one can climb into Hitler's mind to obtain them. But to anticipate in summary form topics to be developed further in upcoming chapters, the best historical research makes the following points clear: (1) No later than the end of 1941, the intention to annihilate the European Jews was being rapidly and systematically implemented by Nazi Germany. (2) Although no document containing Hitler's order for the Final Solution has ever been found—probably because no such written order existed—

the systematic destruction of European Jewry was a policy so vast in its scope and implications that the decision to enact it had to be Hitler's. In short, no Hitler, no Holocaust. (3) If Hitler intended mass murder for the European Jews in 1939, or even earlier, he was in no position to implement that intention until war—including the absolute loyalty of the German people as their wartime commander—gave him the opportunity. (4) Throughout the 1930s, actual Nazi policy did not consist of mass murder for Jews. "Until the late 1930s," as Robert Gellately cogently argues, "antisemitism was not the primary concern of the public, most Germans were not rabidly antisemitic, and pushing out the Jews was not the top priority of the German state."⁴ Early in his leadership of Nazi Germany, Hitler had other priorities and had to contend with many problems all at once. Unification of his own party was among them.

Hitler carried out a revolution in Germany more through legal channels than through violence. The Nazi regime did not hesitate to use coercion and terror against its enemies, but, as Gellately convincingly explains, it also successfully "sought the consent and support of the people at every turn."⁵⁰ It was in Hitler's long-range interests to continue on that path, for he had come to power with the promise to restore rather than to destroy traditional German society, and he attracted industrial and military support for that reason. On the other hand, Hitler's Nazi Party followers included many who had taken his revolutionary rhetoric, especially the parts about the Jews, with great seriousness. Once the Nazis gained power, those elements had to be placated or at least reckoned with. Of particular importance in this regard was the SA [*Sturmabteilung*].

The SA was under the leadership of Captain Ernst Röhm, one of Hitler's close friends from the Nazi Party's earliest days. One commentator describes him as "a curious mixture of military reformer and Bavarian crook, . . . who, more than any other one man, was responsible for launching Hitler . . . into German Politics."⁵¹ First organized in the summer of 1921, its membership drawn from disgruntled World War I veterans, the SA would have 4.5. million members by June 1934, which made its forces much larger than Germany's post–World War I army. Far from securing Nazi Germany's interests, however, Hitler and many other party leaders—to say nothing of the allies Hitler needed from German industry and the military—saw Röhm and the SA as threats to stability, particularly because it was Röhm's ambition to make the SA the true army of the Third Reich.

In the spring and early summer of 1934, another complication arose. President Hindenburg had given his blessing to most Nazi initiatives, but the old man's health was failing. Hitler had to protect his flanks. If Röhm's SA was not checked, the army's generals and other strong conservative forces in industry and the civil service might use Hindenburg's death as the occasion to check or even to end Hitler's authority. Well aware that the army welcomed his goal of German rearmament, Hitler concluded correctly that Germany's military leadership would support his desire to become Hindenburg's successor if the SA's threat was removed. The so-called Night of the Long Knives, a bloodbath ordered by Hitler, ensued on 30 June–1 July 1934. The exact number of people who were killed during this purge remains uncertain. Among the murdered, however, were not only Röhm and other senior SA men but also conservatives who were perceived as threats who might try to depose Hitler and restore monarchy in Germany.

A key figure in the Röhm purge was Heinrich Himmler, who headed the black-shirted SS (*Schutzstaffel*, or protection squad). Organized in the summer of 1925 as Hitler's personal guard unit, the SS was part of the SA for a time. When Himmler took command in January 1929, the now more independent SS consisted of a few hundred men. By the spring of 1934, it had already become everything that the SA was not—a disciplined, armed elite of more than 50,000 men who were intensely loyal to Hitler. At this time, Himmler's influence expanded further as he gained increasing control of Nazi Germany's political police, whose main branches included the SD (*Sicherheitsdienst*, or security and intelligence service) and the Gestapo (*Geheime Staatspolizei*, or secret state police).

Once his rival Röhm was out of the way, Himmler reaped the benefits. For its part in the purge, his SS got full independence from the SA, a move that enhanced Himmler's authority. Meanwhile, Himmler had bestowed some rewards of his own. On 4 July, for example, he appointed Theodore Eicke, commandant of the Dachau concentration camp—the earliest camp of its kind, Dachau opened in March 1933—as inspector of concentration camps. Eicke, who had followed Himmler's execution order by personally murdering Röhm, instituted in other camps the systematically brutal methods of control and punishment that had characterized his administration at Dachau. With the help of Eicke and other SS subordinates, Himmler soon controlled a vast state security empire. In this capacity, Himmler would use his SS and police power to become a key architect of the destruction of the European Jews.

While Himmler expanded his power, Hitler still had to shore up his political authority. The Röhm purge had removed threats to that authority, but it left Hitler with the need to explain what had happened and why. Hitler's strategy was to argue that Röhm and his closest SA associates were guilty of treasonous activity and sexual deviance—Röhm was a homosexual—and to portray himself as a protector whose intervention had saved German integrity as well as lives. Speaking to the Reichstag on 13 July, Hitler took responsibility for the purge, referring to himself as the "highest judge of the German people," and affirmed that "in the State there is only one bearer of arms, and that is the Army; there is only one bearer of the political will, and that is the National Socialist Party."[52] The army leadership's satisfaction in hearing that proclamation was matched by the Reichstag's applause as it passed a law legitimating the purge as "emergency defense measures of the state."

Hitler's good fortune continued. He received a congratulatory telegram from Hindenburg, who wrote that Hitler had "nipped treason in the bud" and "saved the nation from serious danger." But an even bigger reward was his on the morning of 2 August when Hindenburg died. With the plan already arranged, a government announcement was made within an hour of Hindenburg's death: the offices of president and chancellor were to be merged. Hitler would be Nazi Party chief, head of state, and supreme commander of the armed forces as well. He was now the nation's ultimate authority. Signaling that fact on the same day, German soldiers took a personal oath of loyalty to Hitler: "I swear before God this sacred oath: I will render unconditional obedience to Adolf Hitler, the Führer of the German nation and people, Supreme Commander of the Armed Forces, and will be ready as a brave soldier to risk my life at any time for this oath."

Less than three weeks later, the German people were given an opportunity to ratify Hitler's new position and the title by which he was to be known—Führer  and Reich Chancellor. The turnout for this plebiscite was more than 95 percent of the 45.5 million people who could vote. Thirty-eight million Germans—about 90 percent of the votes cast—said yes. Not every German agreed, however. More than four million voted no. In addition, about 870,000 defaced voting papers turned up. Nevertheless, Hitler went to the 1934 Nazi Party rally at Nuremberg much more confident than he was when the year began. As Hitler received the accolades of the Nazi Party congress that September, he had survived internal challenges to his personal power that would not reach a comparable magnitude until a near-miss assassination attempt in July 1944.

PART TWO
**THE NAZIS IN POWER**

# Chapter 5

# "Rational Antisemitism"

> The Third Reich was certainly not a lawless state. On the contrary, the Nazi regime insisted that it was defending law and order against the forces of anarchy, and this claim was vital to its popularity and self-image. Over four thousand statutes, decrees and ordinances were issued in the first three years of the Third Reich in the official law bulletin of the Reich alone.
>
> Mark Mazower, *Dark Continent: Europe's Twentieth Century*

The preceding chapter's discussion of Hitler's rise to power necessarily glossed over important details concerning the twisted road to Auschwitz. Retracing some steps can fill them in. As early as 1919, for example, Hitler distinguished "rational antisemitism" from "antisemitism on purely emotional grounds." He wrote,

> Anti-Semitism on purely emotional grounds will find its ultimate expression in the form of pogroms. Rational anti-Semitism, however, must lead to a systematic legal opposition and elimination of the special privileges which Jews hold, in contrast to the other aliens living among us. . . . Its final objective must unswervingly be the removal [*Entfernung*] of the Jews altogether.[1]

The occasion for this reflection—Hitler's first explicit writing about the Jews—was a letter to Adolf Gemlich in September 1919. Gemlich had participated in a postwar troop instruction course that Hitler taught in conjunction with his position in the army's information department; his task was to inculcate German soldiers with the proper nationalist and anticommunist attitudes. Gemlich wrote to ask for clarification about the "Jewish question." Hitler's letter to Gemlich explained, first, that "Jewry is unqualifiedly a racial association and not a religious association. . . . Its influence will bring about the racial tuberculosis of

Racial 121
Tuberculosis

the people." Hitler then drew his distinction, as indicated above, between the types of antisemitism.

Although Hitler's letter advocated "rational antisemitism" as the preferred method of solving the Jewish problem, his writings and speeches in the 1920s and early 1930s expressed in murderously vituperative and demagogic language hatred and rage that were also key parts of his redemptive antisemitism. One theme dominates both his writings and his speeches: *The Jews are the most potent force for radical evil in history. They are engaged in a vast conspiracy to dominate the world and destroy European civilization. They are responsible for Germany's defeat in the First World War and the Bolshevik Revolution, as well as for all of the moral, financial, political, and social problems that have beset Germany and the world since.* In the second chapter of *Mein Kampf,* Hitler linked a messianic response to his apocalyptic image of the alleged Jewish danger: "If, with the help of his Marxist creed, the Jew is victorious over the other peoples of the world, his crown will be the funeral wreath of humanity and this planet will, as it did thousands of years ago, move through the ether devoid of men." Hitler concludes this chapter: "Hence today I believe that I am acting in accordance with the will of the Almighty Creator: *by defending myself against the Jew, I am fighting for the work of the Lord.*"[2] His proposed cure was equally simple and extreme: eliminate the Jew once and for all.

Nevertheless, Hitler knew when to tone down his message. When he sought the financial and political support of industrialists, financiers, and former military officers of high rank, he moderated or omitted entirely his customary diatribes against the Jews.[3] He recognized the need to incite hatred, but he also knew that his war against the Jews could not be won by random violence and hooliganism. Instead, it would have to be a deliberately calculated campaign organized and sustained over time. In late 1932, for example, plans for implementing the Nazi anti-Jewish program were surprisingly modest: If the party received an absolute majority in the forthcoming elections, Jews would be deprived of their rights by newly enacted legal statutes. On the other hand, if the Nazis were compelled to share power, they intended to undermine Jewish rights by administrative means. Such caution was not shared by the SA, which by March 1933 had launched an anti-Jewish campaign of its own, replete with boycotts of Jewish businesses, street fighting, random brutality, and murder. These wildcat actions, which lacked central direction even from the SA itself, served to vent some spleen but brought more distress than comfort to a Nazi regime seeking to stabilize its authority over German life.

In the early years of the Weimar Republic, Hitler's preference for "rational," "legal" antisemitism was widely shared by a relatively small hard core of radical Jew-haters, largely young people who had yet to commit themselves politically. Like Hitler, they regarded the Jews as the source of all evil. Many ultimately found a home in the Nazi Party, but they committed few acts of overt anti-Jewish violence, especially when compared with the almost daily street clashes between Nazis and Communists.[4] They were, however, strongly influenced by the steadily intensifying campaign of antisemitic defamation that included the translation and publication of *The Protocols of the Elders of Zion* and allegations that Jews practiced ritual murder. In addition, there were incidents almost every night of desecration of Jewish cemeteries and synagogues, usually perpetrated by youths not directly attached to the organized political right. The German historian Ulrich Herbert argues that these desecrations demonstrated a serious potential for murderous aggression against Jews. Lurking barely beneath the surface, this potential was held in check during the Weimar years by the threat of social ostracism and legal prosecution.[5]

Herbert stresses the importance of a "passive antisemitism" that fed on wartime developments, military defeat, and the rise of Bolshevism. As he sees the situation, during the Weimar period many "respectable" Germans regarded the Jews as aliens who possessed especially unpleasant traits, were allegedly allied with Germany's enemies, and profited from the war, the inflation, and the depression.[6] While most Germans were not members of the Nazi Party and were averse to participation in street brawls, they were ready to accept the Nazi program of depriving Jews of their rights and were even willing to lend a hand. These attitudes were especially strong in the Protestant church.[7]

Particularly in one sector of German life—the universities—radical antisemitism gained an early and powerful ascendancy, and it was there that the future leaders of the Third Reich were being trained. By 1921 the *Deutschen Hochschulring*, the organization that united most of the traditional student organizations in German universities, had made the "Jewish question" a central issue. Students of Jewish descent, whether practicing Jews or Christians, were barred from membership on racial grounds. When the Prussian government contested the exclusion, the *Hochschulring* held a referendum in 1926. Seventy-seven percent of the Prussian students voted to maintain the exclusion.[8]

This student antisemitism was both radical and racist. It was also elitist and opposed to the "vulgar antisemitism" of the SA's crude assaults on Jews and their property. The students became convinced that the Jewish problem was to be solved in a cold, "dispassionate" manner through legal and bureaucratic measures rather than riots and pogroms. According to Herbert, the antisemitism of the "wild-eyed fanatics" was nowhere as important or as dangerous a factor in German politics as the antisemitism of the university students. The latter "achieved something like respectability" in the 1920s and was "no longer identified solely with the abusive and pogrom antisemitism that even the radical *völkisch* students held in contempt."[9]

There is a direct link between the leadership cadres of the *Hochschulring* in the 1920s and early 1930s and the leadership cadres of the Security Police and the SD, identified by Herbert as "the genocide's active core."[10] Approximately two-thirds of this group were of the generation born between 1903 and 1915.[11] Two-thirds of the Security Police and SD leadership had university degrees and one-third had earned doctorates, very largely in law, and had been active in one or more *völkisch* or ultranationalistic groups as students.[12] They came not from the dregs of German society but from the middle and upper classes. According to Herbert, "before 1933 they had undergone a political socialization that synthesized generational self-consciousness and political radicalism (which meant particularly: radical, race-based antisemitism) into a formative world-view."[13] These were the men who played leading parts in the deportation and ghettoization of the Jews and in the organization of industrialized mass murder during World War II.

In Hitler's first months of power, Nazi hooliganism was rife. If it served a useful purpose by intimidating Hitler's nonsupporters, this terrorism also eluded the control that Hitler needed to advance his own aims, not to mention eroding confidence in his promises to maintain law and order. As a step toward rationalizing the terror process, a secret police force, the Gestapo, was organized under Göring's authority in March and April 1933. Meanwhile appeals for discipline went largely unheeded by the SA, prompting Hitler to seek a way to let it flex some muscle, but in a way that would not be counterproductive to the Nazi effort to undermine Jewish status administratively. A nationwide boycott against Jews in the business world and the professions appeared to be a way out.

In response to foreign protests against Nazi violence and discrimination against Jews and to the threat of a worldwide movement to boycott German goods—Nazi propagandists claimed that Jews were behind the agitation—the German boycott of Jewish business and commerce was to be enforced by the SA and other local party units, who would push concurrently for the development of a quota system to restrict the number of Jews in the various professions.[14] As the boycott was announced, however, Hitler found himself in a bind. Prices dropped dramatically on the Berlin stock exchange, creating troublesome anxiety among his nonparty supporters. At the same time, Hitler could not afford to lose face with the Nazis, and with the SA in particular, by calling off the action. Compromise led to plans for a one-day boycott. Meanwhile Goebbels worked to minimize lost prestige through the means available to him as head of the newly formed Ministry of Public Enlightenment and Propaganda. On Saturday, 1 April 1933, the boycott went into effect, but only in fits and starts and without discipline. It was cancelled before the day was over.

Adverse reaction from foreign governments was substantial. Ironically, however, the failure of this attempt worked to Hitler's advantage. It showed that the party radicals, who had been given responsibility for implementing the boycott, were seriously wanting as formulators and executors of anti-Jewish policies. More importantly, it became clear that the boycott strategy, especially if it had been successful, would have exacted a price far greater than any gains it could have achieved. A systematic boycott of Jewish business would have been far too disruptive to the German economy. The Nazis needed to stabilize and nurture the economy, not put it under further threat. Thus, more rational calculations about how to deal with the Jewish question would be required.

Neither random violence nor hastily contrived and ill-administered programs provided effective anti-Jewish measures. None of those lessons were lost on Hitler and his closest associates, but it took time to clarify their meanings and to put their implications into practice. One other crucial problem came to light as well. Insofar as the Nazis' propaganda picture of the Jews led them to envision a worldwide Jewish economic conspiracy, they also believed that a boycott against German Jews would take foreign heat off the Nazi regime. When that assumption proved false, some Nazi leaders realized that their own propaganda might be blinding them. Henceforth more accurate insight about Jewish life, inside Germany and abroad, would be essential.

## PAPER VIOLENCE

Hitler appears moderate on the Jewish question in 1933 when compared to some of his followers in the SA. Nevertheless, it is a mistake to think that his antisemitism was ever less than radical. Hitler's moderation was rooted in tactical considerations, not in benign intentions; thus the April 1933 boycott's failure did not blur his general aim of "removing" the last Jew from the German Reich. The issue was how best to define and accomplish that goal. If direct economic intervention fell short, perhaps a more solid entrenchment of Nazi political power would open the avenue of "paper violence."

As already noted, the passage of the Enabling Act on 23 March 1933 was a decisive breakthrough for Hitler. This action by the Reichstag gave Hitler power to legislate and govern by decree, including the latitude to set aside provisions in the Weimar constitution that guaranteed legal equality for all citizens. It was not left to Hitler alone, however, to use law against the Jews. Advice was forthcoming from all sectors of the Nazi Party. Two weeks after the Enabling Act was in place, on 7 April, the Nazis enacted the Law for the Restoration of the Professional Civil Service. Its third paragraph, which came to be known as the "Aryan paragraph," targeted Jews by requiring that "civil servants of non-Aryan descent must retire." One law followed another. In the early months of the Nazi regime, anti-Jewish laws were enacted on an almost daily basis. Multiplying into the thousands, they defined, segregated, and impoverished the German Jews.

On the night of 10 May 1933—a hundred days after Hitler had become chancellor—"paper violence" of a different but related kind took place when more than twenty thousand books were burned in the *Opernplatz* (Opera House Square) opposite the Humboldt University in Berlin.[15] This event was not an isolated incident. In some thirty German university towns, brown-shirted German students along with many of their professors purged "un-German" writings from libraries and shops and set them ablaze. Enthusiastic crowds witnessed the spectacle, which was launched with torchlight parades and accented by speeches by Goebbels and others proclaiming the death of "Jewish intellectualism" and the purification of German culture.

As a precondition for burning, "Jewish books" had to be identified. Likewise, the anti-Jewish laws, which aimed at a thorough racial separation between Jews and Germans, could not be systematically implemented unless one knew to whom they applied. The Nazis wrestled long and hard with the critical problem of defining who was a Jew. The definition issue was complicated, because Nazi ideology made Jewishness a matter of blood. Paradoxically, however, these racial lines could be determined only by reference to religious identity.[16] Thus, not only would decisions have to be made concerning the amount of Jewish blood that was sufficient to make one a target of discrimination under the law, but also determinations as to a person's religious heritage would become essential—for Gentiles as well as for Jews—in answering questions about bloodlines. As the historian Michael Burleigh points out, "state registry offices only covered the period since 1875," which meant that "the regime relied upon ecclesiastical records to trace ancestry or conversions from Judaism to Christianity, essential to the identification of racial Jews living as 'non-Aryan' Christians."[17] The task of certifying ancestry fell on priests and pastors as well as clerks and archivists. The process led to an expanding network of investigations and bureaucratic offices that became one of the hallmarks of Nazi Germany's racial state.

Early attempts at definition utilized the term "non-Aryan." While intended to target Jews exclusively—the crucial regulation of 11 April 1933 defined a "non-Aryan" as a person who had a Jewish parent or a Jewish grandparent—both the category and its definition were too imprecise. "Jew" was the specific designation that had to be refined, but not until 14 November 1935 was a more detailed definition announced. Stipulated in what was known as the First Implementation Order to the Reich Citizenship Law, that definition distinguished between full Jews and part-Jews, and its purpose was to make a person's status unalterable. Basically, a person was fully Jewish if he or she had three or four Jewish grandparents. That criterion, however, did not cover everyone who possessed Jewish blood. Thus further calculations were needed: if a person had two fully Jewish grandparents, then he or she was a part-Jew—specifically a *Mischling* (mixed breed)—provided the person (1) did not belong to the Jewish community (practice Judaism) at the time of the promulgation of the Reich Citizenship Law (15 September 1935) or thereafter; (2) was not married to a Jew at the time of the promulgation of the Reich Citizenship Law or thereafter; (3) was not born from a marriage concluded by a Jew after 15 September 1935; (4) was not born after 31 July 1936 as the result of extramarital intercourse involving a Jew. Failure to meet any of these criteria meant that an individual with two fully Jewish grandparents was also identified as a full Jew. The *Mischling* category was eventually refined to distinguish between first and second degrees, the latter classification referring to persons who had only one fully Jewish grandparent and met the four conditions noted above. *Mischlinge* were subject to discrimination, but they were less at risk than those classified as full Jews.

The complexity of these definitions, not to mention the range of detail covered by the various anti-Jewish laws, was far removed from the uncoordinated physical violence the SA longed to unleash. A campaign of "paper violence" required instead a vast bureaucratic network, a web of offices to plan, interpret, implement, and enforce the required actions. The twisted road to Auschwitz was engineered neither by Hitler alone nor solely by his Nazi Party. Its construction enlisted, in the words of Raul Hilberg, "an ever larger number of agencies, party offices, business enterprises, and military commands. . . . The machinery of destruction was the organized community in one of its special roles."[18]

Hitler understood intuitively what the German sociologist Max Weber had noted twenty years earlier: in a modern state the power to achieve political domination rests with the forces that control bureaucracy. As Hitler rose to power, he inherited and directed a sophisticated German civil service that was willing to serve its master and was capable of efficient operations on complex problems. Indeed, once nudged into action—in this case dealing with the Jewish problem— it would take the wishes of its leaders to heart and calculate the most effective ways of implementing them. Instead of helping those in peril, the apparatus of government worked to increase their defenselessness and then to get rid of them. In carrying out such steps, the German bureaucracy was not acting atypically when compared to other modern states that have existed before or since. But the skill with which the German system carried out its mandate does reveal the extent to which state power can threaten people for whom it no longer wishes to care. This is not to say that the German bureaucracy was a monolith that worked single-mindedly to rid the Reich of Jews; nor did German bureaucrats unanimously formulate one basic anti-Jewish plan and set it inexorably into motion. The destruction process that culminated in death camps moved step by step. Here it faltered; there it was confused. Sometimes costly unintended consequences emerged, and on a few occasions it may have been subverted from within by officials such as Bernhard Loesner, who drafted legislation so that it touched fewer Jews rather than more.[19] But the destruction process never relented. As long as Nazi power lasted, the bureaucracy that served it remained in motion too. Without it, there could have been no Final Solution.

Meanwhile, legislative measures against German Jews proved less effective than the Nazis hoped. Those tactics left the more violence-oriented factions of the party unsatisfied, but those who sought a more orderly handling of the problem were also troubled, because the qualifications attached to some of the laws exempted too many Jews. For example, the earliest laws exempted the very few "non-Aryan" officials who had been employed in the civil service on or before 1 August 1914, and special provisions held for Jewish veterans of World War I. Joseph Goebbels effectively regulated cultural activities so that Jews were excluded from film production, literary publication, broadcasting, and the press. Still, as 1933 drew to a close, even Jewish observers could say that, although many German Jews had lost their economic base for existence, a tolerable Jewish future seemed possible in Germany. Coupled with the fact that relatively little legislative action was taken against the Jews in 1934, the purging of the Röhm elements in the Nazi Party also portended a moderating climate for Jewish life. Indeed several thousand Jews who had fled Germany returned home in early 1935.[20]

The calm was deceptive. In May 1935 Hitler reintroduced general military conscription as part of his rearmament plan. Jews, however, were considered unfit for service. If that decision was a relief to some, it caused profound humiliation for others, and not without reason, because especially in Germany, where military service was honored and provided opportunities to enhance one's prestige, this action was a further step toward making Jews second-class citizens. Much more extensive anti-Jewish legislation appeared in conjunction with the Nazi Party rally at Nuremberg later in the year. The Nuremberg Laws, passed unanimously by the Reichstag on 15 September, contained two fundamental provisions.

First, the Reich Citizenship Law stated that German citizenship belonged only to those of "German or related blood." This part of the law did not mention Jews explicitly, but the intention was clear: henceforth Jews would be guests or subjects only. Moreover, even blood was an insufficient condition for citizenship. It was to be granted by certificate, and that certification was to be functionally controlled by the Nazi Party. Receipt and retention of citizenship, then, depended less on an inalienable right and more on approved conduct.

Second, the Law for the Protection of German Blood and Honor explicitly prohibited marriage and extramarital sexual relations between Jews and persons of "German or related blood." Also outlawed were the employment of German female servants under 45 years of age in Jewish households and display of the Reich flag by Jews. Such decrees, once buttressed by the November definitions of full Jew and *Mischling*, established race as the fundamental legal principle in German life and put Jews even more at the mercy of the German state, especially when one notes that the November definitions gave all of the state's anti-Jewish measures a more precise focus.

The legislative phase of the Nazis' anti-Jewish campaign put German Jews under duress by severing social contacts between Jews and Germans; imposing restrictions on housing, movement, and work; creating identification measures; and establishing Jewish administrative mechanisms for helping to carry out the various decrees. But these steps were not enough to produce the Holocaust. While the Nuremberg Laws were pivotal in the legislative phase, the enforcement of such decrees and the others that came before and after—at least until late 1938—would not have eradicated the ongoing existence of a Jewish community in Germany, second class though it surely would have been. Hitler and the Nazi leadership became aware of that fact, which left them far from their professed goals of making German life *judenrein* (Jew-free). Thus, as the Nazis used law against the Jews, it proved to be a two-edged sword. If law kept order and spiked the damaging side effects of random violence, it also constrained the Nazis. By itself, law offered no Final Solution.

Wanting to be certain that the 1936 Olympic Games would be on German soil, the National Socialists soft-pedaled their anti-Jewish policies in late 1935 and 1936.[21] But having used the Olympics successfully to showcase the Reich, the Nazis had to do more to satisfy the racial purists. Pressure to stifle Jewish participation in the German economy intensified, and thousands of small Jewish businesses began to be liquidated after harassment by local Nazis. The German economy as a whole, however, was still not vigorous enough to permit tampering with all Jewish businesses, disconcerting though it may have been to the Nazi rank and file to see major Jewish firms continuing to prosper while the "little man" had to battle to make ends meet. Major legislation to excise Jewish economic influence from German life was forthcoming, but it was developed with caution.

Prior to November 1938 Nazi strategies included barring Jews from the professions and working to "Aryanize" the German economy. Jewish businesses—so defined if they were owned by or under the dominant influence of Jews—would be sold "voluntarily" to private German interests. At least three types of pressure encouraged such sales: Germans were urged to boycott Jewish firms, Jewish access to raw materials was restricted, and the depressing effects of these measures were psychologically sufficient to nurture Jewish fear that already troubled circumstances could always take a turn for the worse. Nevertheless, the Nazi policies once again were less than optimally effective. In April 1938, for example, some forty-three thousand Jewish firms still did business in Germany. Therefore, additional steps were taken to facilitate compulsory Aryanization, which became effective that autumn. A more rigorous definition identified any business enterprise as Jewish if, to cite only some provisions of the decree, it had a Jewish proprietor, involved a Jewish partner, or included Jews among its board of directors on or after 1 January 1938. Other actions set termination dates for many small Jewish firms. Licenses were taken away from Jewish doctors, and Jewish lawyers were prohibited from practicing after 31 December. In November and December the vise tightened further. Jewish retail establishments were to be dissolved and liquidated by the end of the year, and on 3 December 1938 another decree provided that all Jews could be required to sell or liquidate industrial and real estate holdings within a stated time. By 1939 the German Jews, now numbering little more than half of the approximately 550,000 who resided in Germany at the time of Hitler's victory in 1933, were increasingly impoverished. Jewish professionals and ordinary workers alike found outlets for their labor restricted, and much Jewish capital was now in German hands. Even German Jewish communal organizations could no longer own property or act as legal entities. And yet despite the Nazi attempts at apartheid and economic discrimination, the Jewish problem remained. Indeed, two events made it worse for the Nazis, moving them to find new paths for ridding the Reich of Jews.

## THE LAST YEAR OF PEACE

Late in the afternoon of 29 September 1938, British Prime Minister Neville Chamberlain received a hero's welcome as he returned to London. Earlier that day he had joined Benito Mussolini of Italy, Édouard Daladier of France, and Hitler in signing the Munich Agreement, which permitted the Nazis to annex the predominantly ethnic German border territories of Czechoslovakia (known as the Sudetenland) in exchange for Hitler's promise that no further territorial demands would follow. "I believe," said Chamberlain of his pact with Hitler, "it is peace in our time." Daladier was less optimistic. When he returned to Paris after signing the Munich Agreement, Daladier expected to be met by outraged demonstrations because of having caved in to Hitler. Instead, he was greeted by cheering crowds who were delighted that war had been avoided, even if the cost was betrayal of an ally. Depressed, Daladier pointed to the crowd and whispered, "The idiots!"

War was never far from Hitler's mind nor from the core of the Nazi program. The fate of the Jews hung in the balance, because Hitler believed that Jews must be eliminated from Germany to avoid the repetition of an alleged Jewish "stab in the back" that would thwart the military effort. The Nazi goal of a racial utopia required war both to validate German superiority and to create an empire. From the outset of Hitler's rule, he worked to place the Reich on a war footing, not least because doing so relieved Germany's unemployment problem, which was largely solved by 1938. After the 1936 Olympic Games, Hitler directed Göring to implement a Four-Year Plan that called, in part, for invading Czechoslovakia, following the annexation of the Führer's native Austria. Hitler stuck to his timetable. On 12 March 1938, after months of intimidation and threats supported by Austrian Nazis, the German army occupied Austria without resistance while the world watched. Hundreds of thousands of enthusiastic Viennese greeted Hitler's triumphal arrival. "As Führer and chancellor of the German nation and Reich," he proclaimed on 15 March, "I now report to history that my homeland has joined the German Reich."

For our purpose perhaps the most significant fact about the *Anschluss* (annexation of Austria) is that it brought some two hundred thousand Austrian Jews under the swastika. Since 1933 Nazi policies had not succeeded in eliminating that many Jews from Germany itself. Thus, the *Anschluss* considerably increased the magnitude of the Nazis' Jewish problem. National Socialist strategies, of course, had aimed at making life so uncomfortable for German Jews that they would be prompted to get out, but these tactics had not succeeded completely. The dimensions of the Jewish problem created by the *Anschluss* called for more effective measures. Austria became a laboratory to test them. One of those put in charge was a young, recently promoted *Untersturmführer* (second lieutenant) in the SS. This rising expert on Jewish affairs was Adolf Eichmann (1906–62).

Able to work in a relatively unencumbered fashion, Eichmann initiated an assembly-line technique of forced emigration for Austrian Jews. Heretofore in Germany, emigration, like "Aryanization," had been "voluntary" although very desirable from the Nazi point of view. Incentives to make that "choice" remained mixed, however, because Nazi policies also levied heavy taxes against Jews who left. In addition, the red tape to be negotiated was considerable, consuming weeks before a Jew could exit. Thus, some German Jews believed the lesser of evils was to stay put and to hope that things would improve or at least not get worse. Under Eichmann's administration, the Central Office for Jewish Emigration got its program under way in Austria during the spring of 1938. Softened up by a reign of terror far greater than any the German Jews had endured, the Austrian Jews were eager to leave. Eichmann's policies were costly for Jewish victims from an economic standpoint, but they speeded up the emigration process immensely. As one Jewish leader, Dr. Franz Meyer, testified in the Eichmann trial in Israel (1961), Eichmann's procedure could be compared to "a flour mill tied in with a bakery. You put a Jew in at one end . . . [and] he comes out at the other with no money, no rights, only a passport saying: You must leave the country within two weeks; otherwise you will go to a concentration camp."[23] If that account is over-simplified, still in six months' time Eichmann removed nearly forty-five thousand Jews from Austria. By May 1939, some one hundred thousand—more than half of Austria's Jewish population—had left. As Schleunes says, Eichmann demonstrated "that appropriate bureaucratic and organizational measures rendered the Jewish problem amenable to solution."[24] Neither his plans nor his personal administrative skills went unnoticed by the Nazi leadership, for he was eventually put in charge of the deportations that took Jews from every quarter of Europe to the death camps.

We shall return to Eichmann's status in the SS, as well as to some of the problems that were produced by his Austrian policy of forced emigration, but let us first consider another momentous event, the November Pogrom (or the so-called *Kristallnacht*), which took place eight months after the Anschluss. In addition to the tens of thousands of German Jews who still resided in Germany in 1938, the presence of nearly seventy thousand Polish Jews inside German borders was an embarrassment to the Nazi policy of making Germany *judenrein*. That embarrassment was aggravated when the Polish government, fearful that Polish Jews in Austria and Germany might return to Poland, announced on 31 March that all Polish citizens living outside of Poland must have their papers approved by Polish consulates or lose their Polish citizenship. Polish antisemitism, less modern and secular than the German but hardly less intense, was fueled by a religious hatred as virulent as in any part of Europe. The antisemitism of Polish policy became clear when Polish Jews, upon appearing at Polish consulates, were denied the stamp of approval. The Nazis could also read the handwriting on the wall: Germany would soon be burdened by a large community of Polish Jews rendered stateless by action of the Polish government.[25] The Nazis could see that stateless Jews would be wanted by no one. Ridding Germany of them by emigration would be extremely difficult.

The Poles established 31 October 1938 as the last date for Polish nationals to obtain the necessary consular approval. When the Germans learned that Polish policy would indeed prevent Polish Jews from reentering Poland, thereby rendering them stateless, the German Foreign Ministry decided that expulsion would have to follow. By 28 October the Gestapo was rounding up Polish Jews and shipping them to the Polish frontier, but the Poles were unwilling to accept them. Blocked from Poland, unable to return to Germany, detained in hideous conditions, these Jews found themselves in a hapless no-man's-land. An uneasy compromise was reached after several days. The Poles accepted most of the refugees; others were allowed to return to Germany. Matters were anything but settled, however, especially when a seventeen-year-old refugee, living clandestinely in

Paris at the time, learned that his parents were among the Jews who had been expelled from Germany.

Herschel Grynszpan decided to take action, but he scarcely could have anticipated the consequences of his decision. On 7 November, after buying a pistol, he went to the German embassy. There he asked to see an official. His request took him to the office of the German diplomat Ernst vom Rath. Grynszpan shot him. The news broke in Germany without any special flourishes—until 9 November, when the press announced that vom Rath had died the previous afternoon. Under Goebbels's direction, the press editorialized that Jews in Germany ought to be identified with the crime and that punishment would follow.

The ensuing "punishment" has come to be known as *Kristallnacht* (9–10 November), the "night of broken glass," a nationwide, staged orgy of communal violence. For several months the idea of a mass pogrom in Germany had been in the air. The *Sicherheitsdienst* (SD) had explicitly recommended "the controlled and purposeful use of violence" in a memorandum of January 1937.[26] A synagogue in Munich had been torched on 9 June 1938 and another in Nuremberg on 10 August.[27] Especially during the night of 9–10 November, but in some places as late as 13 November, more than 1,000 Jewish places of worship were devastated, many of them burnt down while German firefighters either stood by or protected non-Jewish property, and 7,500 Jewish shops destroyed.[28] As communications networks—radio and teleprinters, for example—spread word of the pogrom, Jews throughout the Reich were terrorized—often beaten, sometimes raped or killed. This violence was anything but spontaneous. For example, at 1:20 a.m. on 10 November, Himmler's right-hand man Reinhard Heydrich (1904–42, head of the SD) transmitted secret instructions to the Gestapo and SD. Under the heading "Measures against Jews Tonight," his directive stated that "demonstrations against the Jews are to be expected in all parts of the Reich." It went on to authorize the burning of synagogues and the destruction of Jewish businesses and apartments—so long as German lives and properties were not endangered—and to make clear that "the demonstrations are not to be prevented by the police." Furthermore, "as soon as the course of events during the night permits the release of the officials required, as many Jews in all districts, especially the rich, as can be accommodated in existing prisons are to be arrested." Subsequently they would be sent to "the appropriate concentration camps."[29] In the days that followed, more than 20,000 Jewish men, ages 16–60, were arrested and sent to the Dachau, Buchenwald, and Sachsenhausen concentration camps.[30] Property damage totaled hundreds of millions of marks.

Many Germans, by no means only the police and SD, perpetrated the November Pogrom, including the SS, the SA, and vandalizing mobs who wreaked much of the havoc. They were turned loose by a Goebbels speech in Munich during the fifteenth anniversary celebration of Hitler's Beer Hall Putsch (9 November 1923) after the Führer agreed that "the SA should be allowed to have its final fling."[31] The "fling" was a multiple disaster. Although the pogrom was an extremely harsh blow against Germany's Jews, *Kristallnacht* led to the resolution of a power strug-

gle among the Nazi leadership, which in the long run would have even more devastating effects on the Jews. *Kristallnacht* had caught Göring and Himmler off
guard. In addition to wanting to block a Goebbels power play, they were convinced that street violence was counterproductive, not least of all economically.
The Göring-Himmler argument carried the day. Hitler delegated to Göring
responsibility for solving the "Jewish problem." As the influence of Goebbels and
the radical wing of the party declined, the need for a decisive, coordinated, and
rational anti-Jewish policy became ever clearer.

There was no repetition of *Kristallnacht* in Germany. Instead increasingly
punitive—even sadistic—legal measures were put in place, with the intention of
speeding up forced emigration. On 12 November Göring issued orders—decided
upon by Hitler on 10 November—stipulating that the insurance payments for
damage done to Jewish property would be confiscated by the Reich and that the
Jews would bear all the costs involved in repairing their businesses.[32] They were
also required to complete the demolition of their synagogues at their own
expense. Humiliating restrictions were imposed to segregate Jews on trains. In
addition, a crippling fine of one billion reichmarks was imposed on the increasingly impoverished Jewish community.[33] On the same day Göring decreed the
cessation of Jewish business as of 1 January 1939. Jews were required to sell their
businesses, equity holdings, land, and art works. In the case of art, although there
was some selling of art works at fire-sale prices, wholesale confiscation was the
norm.[34] On 15 November all Jewish children still in German schools were
expelled. On 19 November the state general welfare system barred Jews. On 3
December Jews were deprived of their driver's licenses.

On 6 December Göring addressed key Reich officials (*Gauleiter* or district
leaders) at a meeting in which he set forth official policy concerning the Jews.
The speech made clear that Göring was acting on orders that Hitler had given
him two days earlier.[35] He told the *Gauleiters* that there would be no punishment
for deeds committed out of a "hatred for the Jews" on 9 and 10 November, but
that "purely criminal acts" involving personal gain would be prosecuted. He further declared that Jewish life in Germany was to be made so unpleasant that the
Jews would make every effort to leave. Forced emigration had the highest priority, and Heydrich was directed to implement in Germany a program like the one
established by his subordinate Adolf Eichmann in Austria. This policy, of course,
was consistent with the state-sponsored sadism and destructiveness of *Kristallnacht* and its aftermath. On 28 December Göring directed that Jews be gradually moved into "Jews' houses," a process further facilitated on 30 April 1939,
when Aryan landlords were given the right to break their leases with Jewish tenants upon approval of local authorities.[36] By concentrating the Jews in identifiable locations, establishment of "Jews' houses" facilitated the soon-to-be-taken
steps to round up and remove them entirely from Germany.

On 12 November 1938, Göring had remarked that "I would not like to be a
Jew in Germany."[37] The undisguised, state-sponsored public violence of the
November Pogrom and its aftermath revealed to everyone in Germany that there

were few, if any, limits to the measures the German government was prepared to perpetrate against the Jews. Significantly, there was no outcry from the German public or judiciary.[38] Other than complaints about the "unnecessary destruction of property" and the untidy character of the rioting, the German public was indifferent to the fate of the Jews. As long as it avoided indecorous public acts, the government now understood that it could murder the Jews with impunity.[39] Although that step was not yet taken, the experts in the controlled use of terror and bureaucratic pressure had finally suppressed the impetus to random violence. The road to Auschwitz had become more open, less twisted. As Debórah Dwork and Robert Jan van Pelt aptly sum up the point, "[t]he pogrom of 9 November 1938 was the end of the beginning; the 10th of November was the beginning of the end."[40]

## "THE MOST FANTASTIC ASSOCIATION OF MEN IMAGINABLE"

As Nazi Germany tightened its grip on the Jews in 1933–39, men such as Himmler, Heydrich, and Eichmann came increasingly to the fore, along with the organization they represented, the SS (*Schutzstaffel,* Protective Squad). The development of the SS and the emergence of a clearly defined policy toward the Jews were closely linked and warrant attention, for the Holocaust bears the unmistakable mark of this "order of the 'Death's Head,'" which Heinz Höhne aptly called "the most fantastic association of men imaginable."[41]

Formed in April 1925, the SS was originally a select group of SA members armed to protect Hitler, top party leaders, and party meetings. It numbered fewer than three hundred members—compared to some sixty thousand in the SA—in January 1929, when Hitler named Heinrich Himmler *Reichsführer-SS.*[42] Twenty-eight at the time, Himmler was a former school teacher and chicken farmer who had climbed the Nazi ladder, serving as the NSDAP deputy Gauleiter (district leader) of Lower Bavaria for a time and then as deputy leader of the SS. As Himmler began to transform the SS into an elite, racially pure cadre that would take direction solely from Hitler, it became clear that along with his mystical devotion to German blood and soil were the makings of a "cold professional policeman who possessed an almost instinctual understanding of the use of power."[43] Always serving Hitler's desires faithfully, that understanding usually advanced Himmler's ambitions as well.

Fearing the threats posed by the power of the SA, Hitler counted increasingly on Himmler's help, committing to him and his men, who numbered about three thousand by the end of 1930, the task of carrying out police duties within the party. To help him with this assignment, Himmler turned in 1931 to Reinhard Heydrich, four years his junior, whose antipathy toward Jews may have been fueled by the desire to disarm the false but persistent allegation that his own family tree contained Jewish blood. Heydrich proceeded to develop a secret security branch within the SS, the *Sicherheitsdienst* (SD). It became an awesome intelligence and surveillance system whose network eventually extended to all of Nazi-occupied Europe.

Spurred by economic unrest, SS membership leaped to fifty thousand by the end of 1932 and then to two hundred thousand a year later. However, only after the purges of 1934 did Himmler and Heydrich secure the independence of the SS from the SA. Meanwhile the first concentration camps began to appear in Nazi Germany. The earliest, set up by Himmler in March 1933, stood not far from Munich, near the town of Dachau. *SS-Oberführer* (Senior Colonel) Theodor Eicke and his *Totenkopfverbände* (death-head units, so named for the skull and crossbones insignia on their uniforms) were in charge. Like all institutions of their kind, before and since, these proliferating camps provided a way to incarcerate people who had committed no crime and could not be confined through the normal workings of the criminal code, but whom the state nevertheless wanted to eliminate either temporarily or permanently without necessarily killing them. Put differently, in contrast to normal prisons, concentration camps tend to be extralegal institutions of incarceration for the guiltless but unwanted.[44]

Whoever controlled such weapons had vast power, not least because, as Robert Gellately has documented, there was nothing secret about the concentration camps.[45] Their existence openly publicized, the camps were successfully promoted by the Nazi regime as essential for removing undesirables from the German population. The camps also ensured that the German mainstream would stay in line. At first there was no central administration for the Nazi camps. Himmler won, however, when the secret police or Gestapo, formed originally by Göring, came under his authority. Henceforth the camps were in Himmler's jurisdiction as well. Now the inspector for concentration camps, Eicke consolidated them and introduced uniform procedures. After World War II began, Eicke was succeeded by Richard Glücks and then by Oswald Pohl, who presided when the camp apparatus operated at its zenith.

The SS, SD, and Gestapo, which became an arm of the larger *Sicherheitspolizei* (security police), had overlapping spheres of influence that no organizational chart could map adequately, but the fact was (and it got Hitler's official stamp of approval on 17 June 1936) that Himmler was both *Chef der Deutschen Polizei* (Chief of the German Police) and *Reichsführer-SS*. As the oath taken by every SS man upon induction made plain ("I swear to you, Adolf Hitler, as Führer and Chancellor of the German Reich, loyalty and valor. I pledge to you and to the superiors whom you will appoint obedience unto death, so help me God."), Himmler could unleash means of physical coercion and instruments of terror far more devastating than any that the SA's emotional, ad hoc violence could muster.

In the early months of the Nazi reign, Jewish matters were not a priority on the SS agenda. By the summer of 1936, however, Himmler and Heydrich had consolidated their authority and an expanded SD bureaucracy developed a special department on Jewish affairs (subsection II-112). Adolf Eichmann worked in this area.[46] Raised in Upper Austria, Eichmann had joined the Nazi Party in

April 1932, just after his twenty-sixth birthday. When the Nazi Party was declared illegal by Austrian Chancellor Engelbert Dollfuss, Eichmann returned to his native Germany and subsequently joined the SS in 1933. Learning that a new section of the SS, the *Sicherheitsdienst*, wanted recruits, Eichmann applied and found himself assigned to gather information about Freemasonry, a fraternal order that leading Nazis suspected was part of an international Jewish conspiracy, as the notorious forgery *The Protocols of the Elders of Zion* had claimed.

In 1935 Eichmann was directed to concentrate on the "Jewish problem." Studying its various dimensions, he emerged as something of an "expert" on Jewish affairs, a fact that distinguished him from most National Socialists, who actually knew very little about Jewish history and culture. In particular, Eichmann studied Zionism and became convinced that forced emigration was probably the most expedient solution for the Jewish question. Because Eichmann's superiors discerned that this young man also had organizational talent, his knowledge, philosophy, and skill would make him a decisive figure in the destruction process.

Eichmann is best known for organizing the transports that took Jews to the death camps, but in 1937 his efforts were directed toward Jewish emigration. Eichmann realized that greater pressure had to be brought against Jews to convince them to leave Germany. Simultaneously conditions that would permit their leaving had to be expedited. This meant that Jews must retain sufficient financial resources so that other countries would be more willing to take them. That consideration meant, in turn, that Nazi antisemitic propaganda might have to be toned down. However, neither Eichmann nor the SS alone controlled Jewish policy at this time. Competing Nazi views were still transmitting conflicting signals to German Jews. For example, an important consideration was the question of what steps the Nazi regime would take to help ensure that Jews had a place to go. Eichmann, for example, spent considerable energy working on Jewish emigration to Palestine. Those efforts, however, were undertaken with misgivings, shared by Hitler, that it might be unwise to allow the concentration of too many Jews in any one place outside of Germany, let alone to enhance the possibility of a Jewish state. Such fears, indeed, promoted suspicion that even forced emigration might not be an adequate solution for the Jewish question. Something more permanent would emerge as necessary, but not yet. Eichmann's successful Austrian experiments in this area, coupled with the mixed results of the *Kristallnacht* pogrom, kept alive the basic, if unclearly articulated, Nazi aims at this time—to eliminate Jews from the German economy and then to drive them out of the Reich—even as they helped to make SS expertise dominant in Jewish affairs.

Not until 31 July 1941 did Heydrich receive official authorization from Göring, then Hitler's chief deputy, that he should make "all necessary preparations with regard to organizational, technical and material matters for bringing about a complete solution [*Gesamtlösung*] of the Jewish question within the German sphere of influence in Europe." The master plan for carrying out this "final solution [*Endlösung*] of the Jewish question" was to be submitted to Göring "in the near future."[47] Most likely, Göring approved a text that Heydrich himself had drafted in March

1941 to ensure that jurisdiction over the "Jewish question" would reside unmistakably under the direction of Himmler and Heydrich. Furthermore, the language of this text was ambiguous; it did not explicitly mention or authorize specific procedures but was instead, in Raul Hilberg's words, "an authorization to invent."[48] Significantly, the context for invention by then included mass shootings of Jews in eastern Europe, plus the fact that Hitler had been speaking about "the annihilation of the Jewish race in Europe" at least since his speech to the Reichstag on 30 January 1939. Such rhetoric and the actual development and implementation of policy, however, did not yet coincide altogether, because Göring's authorization to Heydrich in late July 1941 called for supplementing "the task that was assigned to you on 24 January 1939," which was to promote Jewish "emigration and evacuation in the most suitable way." The bottom line remained, however, that Heydrich and Himmler had been given considerable latitude to plan and control the fate of the Jews. Not only was Eichmann's Austrian model put into effect in Germany, but also a decisive step had been taken to centralize implementation of Jewish policy and to locate responsibility for it within the SS. Eichmann's reward for services already rendered took him first to Prague, where he was to oversee the deportation of some three hundred thousand Jews who had to be dealt with after Hitler gained control of Czechoslovakia; then to Berlin, to head the Reich Central Office for Jewish Emigration; and finally in 1941 to section IV-B-4 of the *Reichssicherheitshauptamt* (Reich Security Main Office; RSHA), where as head of Jewish Evacuation Affairs he organized Europeanwide transports to the killing centers that Nazi Germany established on Polish soil.

The evolution of Eichmann's career illustrates the SS's role in an ever intensifying destruction process. As Eichmann first rose to influence, forced emigration and an advance of SS authority in Jewish affairs moved to center stage. But with the expansion of German power in Austria and Czechoslovakia before World War II, and then further encompassing vast areas of Europe when the Nazi *Blitzkrieg* followed, forced emigration or resettlement by outright deportation became impossible, due to the sheer size of the Jewish population and also to logistical difficulties in wartime. To illustrate, on the eve of World War II, Poland's Jewish community, the largest in Europe, numbered nearly 3.5 million. Another 2.7 million Jews eventually came under Nazi control after Hitler invaded the Soviet Union. Add to those figures the Jewish population in central and western Europe, and the Nazis would eventually have some nine million unwanted Jews on their hands in the midst of huge military operations.

According to historian Hans-Günter Adler, in the summer of 1940 the phrase "Final Solution" was already in use but did not yet refer to extermination in the sense of systematic murder.[49] In the fall of 1939, Hitler, Himmler, and Heydrich had planned to create a "Jewish reservation of Lublin" in eastern Poland, but that project was abandoned when it proved incompatible with other military and economic objectives. After the fall of France in June 1940, the idea of using the island of Madagascar, then a French colony, as a dumping ground for Europe's Jews was considered for a time. On 15 August 1940, Eichmann's office presented a plan to deport four million Jews to the island.[50] As would be the case with all the Nazi deportation schemes, little if any thought was given to how the deportees were expected to survive. Had they been carried out, initiatives such as the Madagascar plan were tantamount to a mass death sentence for Jews. Although in retrospect that plan appears utterly fantastic, at the time there was some reason to believe that it could be successfully implemented. With France and her North African empire defeated and England's imminent defeat confidently expected, Germany's leaders saw themselves as about to dominate Europe, the Mediterranean, and Africa. The Soviet Union was temporarily allied to Germany, and in case of war the USSR was expected to be speedily defeated in a "five-month campaign."[51] There were even discussions in Hitler's chancellery concerning future governorships in "German East Africa." In due time, however, it became apparent that the Madagascar project was not feasible. Other methods of population elimination to assure a *judenrein* Nazi empire had to be found. This concern led some SS scientists to experiment with techniques for mass sterilization. Under the cover of war, that same concern led other segments of the SS to see cold-blooded mass murder as the solution.

## THE FAILURE OF EMIGRATION

None of the National Socialist strategies in the prewar 1930s—boycott, discriminatory legislation, Aryanization, forced emigration—proved to be a satisfactory "solution" to the Jewish problem, partly because the "problem" itself remained ill-defined. Was the issue one of separating Jews from Germans through apartheid, as biological antisemitism insisted and as the pogroms of the SA demanded? Or was it simply to eliminate Jews as an economic influence? Or was the only "solution" one in which Jews physically left German soil altogether in ways that would make their return inconceivable?

Movement toward the latter conclusion was steady, but that evolution took time, and its direction was not obvious when the Nazis came to power. Moreover, Hitler himself seems not always to have played a decisive directing role, waiting instead to see how the struggles would turn out between the competing factions he had helped to create, and commissioning the SS to prepare a coordinated effort against the Jews only after it prevailed late in 1938. At no time, however, did either Hitler or his followers ever consider the possibility that the Jewish problem was not decisive. On the contrary, as each measure brought further difficulties, "a more extreme approach appeared to be the only alternative to the less-than-total solutions which had proved unsatisfactory or unworkable."[52] One reason why forced emigration proved to be both unsatisfactory and unworkable, thus necessitating a more extreme approach, was simply that the nations of the world chose not to open their doors to the potential Jewish refugees.

In the late 1970s and early 1980s, a number of "boat people," mostly from southeast Asia and the Caribbean, were driven from their homelands and left to drift and die without a port of entry. These "homeless, tempest-tost" refugees were different from those the Jewish poet Emma Lazarus had in mind when she wrote the poem now etched at the base of the Statue of Liberty in New York harbor. And yet those Asian and Latino victims were not so different either. The hordes of people who emigrated—some voluntarily, others choicelessly—from Europe to America in the nineteenth century, for example, might have been "boat people" too, had there not been a safety valve, a place to go where they could make a new start. These people, like their more recent counterparts, were in some sense unwanted people, whose presence in their native lands was no longer socially or economically valued or at least did not seem very promising. The great difference is that so many of them found new homes. Some of the Jewish refugees created by Nazi policies in the 1930s did too. Most did not.

Numerous factors beyond the Nazis' control thwarted their plans for forced emigration. The global economic depression with its accompanying mass unemployment, to cite one factor, persisted well into the late 1930s. Many nations did not want to add to their burdens by needlessly enlarging their populations, especially when doing so entailed acceptance of Jews left impoverished by Nazi expropriation and emigration taxes. Although Zionist agencies worked at occupational retraining for German Jews, their predominantly professional and business skills were a disadvantage in a competitive situation where countries often favored immigrants with craft and industrial skills. A rising average age among German Jews was also an obstacle, since most countries tended to prefer youth and to discriminate against the elderly. Antisemitic feeling in other nations clearly stood behind most of these obstacles to emigration. Meanwhile most German Jews also thought of themselves as thoroughly German. Until *Kristallnacht*, many settled for second-class status at home rather than an uncertain future elsewhere.[53]

The feasibility of emigration as a solution to the Jewish question depended on the availability and willingness of other nations to take Jews. That fact, in turn, slowed down the process from the Nazi viewpoint, because the exit process had to be handled in an ordered and legal manner that would not tax already strained international goodwill too far. When Eichmann speeded up the process in Austria, his success created a critical refugee problem. Jewish agencies such as the American Joint Distribution Committee devoted their energies to meeting the need. In particular, Zionist organizations in Palestine—where the Jewish population numbered about 180,000 in 1933—worked to bring Jewish refugees to the *Yishuv* (settlement), as the Jewish community there was called. Hope that assistance might come from other quarters was prompted by U.S. President Franklin D. Roosevelt's call for an international conference on refugee problems, which convened on 6 July 1938 at the French resort of Evian-les-Baines on Lake Geneva, near the Swiss border.[54]

Representatives from thirty-two nations, plus delegates from thirty-nine private relief agencies (twenty-one of them Jewish) came to the Evian conference. The Nazis permitted representation from the German and Austrian Jewish communities. Upon hearing the Jewish accounts, the nations in attendance quickly discerned that, short of doing nothing at all, their efforts would have to be directed at alleviating conditions within Germany. Otherwise they would have to open their doors to the refugees, which most were unwilling to do. In fact, the American invitation to the conference included the assumption that non-German governments would not have to foot the bill for any necessary emigration and stated explicitly that "no country would be expected to receive a greater number of emigrants than is permitted by its *existing* legislation."[55] Although the delegates expressed sympathy for the Jewish refugees, they also made excuses. The doors of their countries would not be opened. After nine days of deliberations, the fact remained that the world was divided into two camps—one that wanted to be rid of Jews and one that would not accept them. The *Völkischer Beobachter*, the official newspaper of the Nazi Party crowed triumphantly, "Nobody wants them!"[56]

A Swiss delegate to the conference had expressed concern about the threat of a flood of refugees into his country, stemming from the Austrian *Anschluss* and the fact that the Swiss and German governments had no visa requirements between them. Subsequently, after the Swiss applied further pressure during the summer of 1938, the German government specified that all German passports belonging to Jews were to be stamped with a large red J. By the end of the year, every Jew in the Reich was also required to have a special identification card available at all times. Such measures abetted the cause of anti-Jewish discrimination outside of Germany as well as within.

Jewish persecution reached new heights in Germany during the summer of 1938. Meanwhile substantial numbers of Jews did flee. By the middle of 1938 about a third of the emigrants—approximately forty-five thousand since Hitler's takeover—had found their way to the Jewish community in Palestine. Most went in accord with the August 1933 *Haavara* (transfer) Agreement that had been negotiated between the German economic ministry, the Zionist Organization of Germany, and the Anglo-Palestine Bank. Basically, these arrangements worked as follows: German restrictions prevented Jews from taking their money abroad, but their assets could be placed in special blocked bank accounts. These funds then paid German exporters for merchandise, including agricultural and industrial machinery, that went to the Middle East. Some of the goods were sold to Jewish enterprises in Palestine, but the market included Arab areas too. The proceeds from these sales were deposited in the Anglo-Palestine Bank. When the Jewish emigrants arrived, they received a partial reimbursement in pounds sterling from the Jewish Agency, a semiautonomous arm of the World Zionist Organization.[57]

In 1933 the Zionists were the only Jewish group that was convinced that Jewish life was finished in Germany and that Palestine offered the best hope for a Jewish revival. Palestine's Jewish population, however, was too small, the territory's infrastructure too undeveloped, and British and Arab interests in the region too hostile to make a Jewish state viable. Nevertheless, the Nazis and the Zionists recognized a temporary convergence of interests. Through the Haavara Agreement, Germany could profit from exports and better employment as it got rid of a sizable portion of her Jewish population, and Jewish Palestine could get both the people and the resources necessary for the eventual creation of a Jewish state. Although the agreement was much criticized by many Jews because it weakened boycott threats against the Nazi regime, the transfer program continued until World War II.

Even with the Haavara Agreement, however, Jewish emigration to Palestine was no easy matter. For one thing, the British wanted to stabilize the Middle East to ensure control of the Suez Canal, its passage to India. So British power in the region acceded to Arab pressures restricting Jewish immigration to Palestine in the second half of the 1930s.[58] Specifically, the British issued their White Paper on Palestine on 17 May 1939. Terminating the promise to establish a Jewish national homeland in Palestine, which had been announced in the Balfour Declaration of 2 November 1917, the White Paper laid plans for a binational Palestinian state with a permanent Arab majority. Future Jewish immigration to Palestine—without Arab consent, which was unlikely—would end after seventy-five thousand were admitted between 1939 and 1944. (Ten thousand would be admitted annually between 1940 and 1944, but, owing to the immediate Jewish plight in 1939, the allotment for that year was increased to twenty-five thousand.)

Once war began, the possibility of legal immigration constricted even more. Jewish emigration to Palestine—much of it "illegal"—did continue. Even when it could be arranged, however, the price of passage on ramshackle vessels was extremely high. Once afloat, passengers had no assurance of a successful arrival. Clandestine night landings along the Mediterranean coast were frequent but increasingly difficult, as British patrols tightened a net that either took Jewish refugees into custody or simply turned them back to sea. The British government did not directly murder Jews in the Holocaust, but its actions in the late 1930s and afterward further clarified the Jews' status as a largely unwanted people. The British government did not want to be inconvenienced by an influx of Jews into the *Yishuv*, the one community where they could have been welcomed unconditionally. Britain's power to back up that attitude militarily and politically helped to convince Hitler that the Jews were indeed unwanted refuse. Left in his hands, they were crushed.

The situation in other parts of the world was not much different, as the tragic case of the *St. Louis* illustrates.[59] On 13 May 1939, this German ship left Hamburg for Havana, Cuba, with 937 passengers aboard, nearly all Jewish refugees who planned to stay in Cuba only until visas to the United States could be obtained. The Jews had purchased Cuban landing permits, but they did not know that the Cuban president Federico Laredo Bru had invalidated such certificates earlier in the month. When the *St. Louis* reached Havana on 27 May, only twenty-eight passengers, including twenty-two Jews, were granted entry. Cuba did not want the refugees. In fact, five days before the *St. Louis* departed Germany, Cuba's largest antisemitic rally—forty thousand people gathered in Havana—had taken place. On 2 June Bru ordered the *St. Louis* to leave Cuban waters. The ship headed for Miami, Florida, but the U.S. government denied its passengers a haven. On 6 June, the *St. Louis* sailed back to Europe. Finally Great

Britain, the Netherlands, France, and Belgium agreed to take the refugees, but with the understanding, supported by the League of Nations, that their actions must not be viewed as setting precedents. Those who found refuge on the European continent were soon under the swastika again.

As autumn 1939 approached, pressures within Germany and around the globe increasingly turned the Jews into an unwanted people. These people did not lack ability, intelligence, or social utility. Their gifts and talents were abundant and their culture immensely rich, but Nazi Germany weighed those assets and found them wanting in comparison to the gain that would accrue if the Jewish presence disappeared. That step would be a major stride toward fulfillment of the National Socialists' dream of a *Volksgemeinschaft*. If actions speak louder than words, other nations in the world were not opposed to this Nazi sentiment. Implicit though the conclusion may have been, the plight of the Jews supported a proposition—reiterated again and again of other groups in our recent post-Holocaust world—that "here are people we can best afford to do without."

Implied or stated in enough times and places, that feeling fueled Nazi yearnings for some lasting solution to the Jewish problem and even gave Joseph Goebbels reason to think that he discerned what Hitler's professed opponents would never openly admit. "I believe," Goebbels wrote in his diary entry for 13 December 1942, "that both the English and the Americans are happy that we are exterminating the Jewish riffraff."[60] Goebbels's reasoning cannot have been off the mark entirely. Faced with the prospect that Hitler might flood them with unwanted Jewish refugees, governments around the world were not in a position to criticize the Nazis for their internal handling of the Jewish question. In effect, Hitler could and did say, "If you don't like the way we treat our minorities, take them yourselves." Few were ready to do so; most kept quiet and let Hitler proceed with the dirty work. Lacking a safety valve, pressure was building to move outright extermination of Jews to the top of the Nazi agenda. The cover of war would make that Final Solution possible; the outbreak of war would make it necessary. As Hitler and his armies prepared to invade Poland in 1939, the road to Auschwitz, paved with twists though it still continued to be, had its end in view.

# Chapter 6

# War and the Final Solution

*Without the war the Holocaust would not—and could not—have happened.*
Doris Bergen, *War and Genocide: A Concise History of the Holocaust*

On the anniversary of Hitler's coming to power, 30 January 1933, it was his custom to address the Reichstag. We have noted earlier the speech he gave on that occasion in 1939, but the words of his infamous "prophecy" bear repeating in this chapter, which begins an exploration of what Doris Bergen calls "the related goals of race and space: so-called 'racial purification' and territorial expansion."[1] Those goals provoked World War II, which, in turn, was a fundamentally necessary condition for the Holocaust. Hitler's prophecy said,

> If the international Jewish financiers in and outside Europe should succeed in plunging the nations once more into a world war, then the result will not be the Bolshevization of the earth, and thus the victory of Jewry, but the annihilation [*Vernichtung*] of the Jewish race in Europe.[2]

Hitler repeated this "prophecy" numerous times during the war. He even did so in the political testament he composed hours before committing suicide in the Führer bunker in Berlin on 29 April 1945. There, with the Third Reich in ruins, he still boasted of the prophecy's fulfillment and used it as moral justification for the destruction of European Jewry.[3] His speech of 30 January 1939, whose anti-Jewish themes he frequently repeated, is crucial for understanding why so many Germans followed him to the bitter end and why Jews continued unrelentingly to be murdered in large numbers until the very last days of the war. To see why that was the case, we need to see how the coming of war decisively affected the predicament of Jews under the swastika.

## A WAR LIKE NO OTHER

Prior to the outbreak of World War II the Nazi handling of "the Jewish question" drew heavily on precedents developed throughout the centuries by church authorities and secular governments. Precedent was insufficient, however, when the world war that began with Nazi Germany's invasion of Poland on 1 September 1939 presented the opportunity and, from the Nazi perspective, the necessity for a radically different approach. The Germans would call it *die Endlösung der Judenfrage* (the Final Solution of the Jewish question), an idea that early on was an invitation for invention because its meaning was neither crystal clear nor unchanging for everyone concerned. As Raul Hilberg has explained, the Nazi bureaucracy faced an unprecedented challenge when the end in view became doing away with the Jews of Europe altogether.[4] How should the Jews be eliminated? What would be done with their property and their corpses? How should the whole process be coordinated and, critically important, how could it be kept secret as far as possible? No blueprints existed to solve these problems, for no one had faced them before. The Final Solution required innovation. Every aspect of the operation required invention, and under the cover of war, invent and innovate the Nazis did.

During World War II Germany fought two wars: the first a relatively conventional war against France, Great Britain, and the United States; the other a war wholly unlike any other in modern history. The war against the West was frightful in the damage done and the lives lost, but the Geneva Convention concerning the humane treatment of prisoners of war was essentially observed by both sides, although toward the end of the war German General Alfred Jodl toyed with the idea of denouncing the convention and massacring all Allied prisoners of war as a way of "burning bridges" behind the Germans and spurring them on to desperate efforts in the face of defeat. Still, the basic norms of warfare were more or less observed in the West. The term *conventional*, however, could scarcely be applied to the war that Germany waged in the East. It was an uncompromising, racially motivated war of conquest, colonization, demographic revolution, and extermination. It was within the context of the war in the East that the Jews became targets for annihilation.

Prior to the German invasion of Poland on 1 September 1939, approximately 3.5 million Jews lived in Poland, whose total population was about thirty-five million. In the area of the Soviet Union conquered by Germany in the summer of 1941, more than 2.7 million Jews could be found. Although the fate of these Jews was unclear at the beginning of the war, Hitler's eventual plan was to murder every Jew that Nazi Germany could reach.[5] In the case of the Russians, Hitler regarded them not only as racially inferior but also as dominated by Jews, because he took the Russian Revolution to be a victory for Jewry, in spite of communism's profound antipathy toward Judaism. For Hitler, the defeat of Bolshevism and the destruction of the Jews were inseparable tasks.

## POSTWAR ANALYSIS

In the early years after World War II, there was little interest among German historians in studying the degree to which their nation as a whole was directly or indirectly involved in the Holocaust. In the 1950s it was often claimed that the majority of the German people had no knowledge of mass murder, let alone responsibility for it. The Germans were portrayed as the victims of a totalitarian tyranny that had imposed itself upon them. The SS was depicted as solely responsible for the Final Solution.[6] By fixing responsibility so narrowly, a convenient, if fictitious, explanation was offered for the absence of German popular resistance to the extermination of Europe's Jews.

The situation began to change in the 1960s. Interest in the Holocaust was aroused by the capture in Argentina on 13 May 1960 of Adolf Eichmann, one of the SS officers most directly involved in the implementation of the Final Solution, by agents of the Israeli secret service. Eichmann stood trial in Jerusalem 11 April–15 August 1961. The trial itself attracted worldwide attention and gave impetus to serious research on the Holocaust. Sixteen hundred documents and the testimony of 108 survivors provided the bulk of the evidence used to convict him. On 31 May 1962, Eichmann was executed, his body cremated, and his ashes cast into the Mediterranean. Meanwhile, the first comprehensive study of the Holocaust, *The Destruction of the European Jews*, was published in 1961 by an American scholar, Raul Hilberg.[7]

About the same time, two significant developments took place in Germany. First, a new generation arose that felt it had nothing to hide, and many of these people wanted to know the truth about the crimes of National Socialism. Second, several war crime trials of lesser Nazi officials and a series of highly-publicized scandals concerning the involvement of highly placed West German politicians in the Nazi regime broke what the German historian Ulrich Herbert has called a "conspiracy of silence."[8] The uncovering process was understandably slow and painful; it is still ongoing as of this writing. Nevertheless, by the 1990s a number of German historians had established themselves as among the most important and reliable scholars doing research on the Holocaust.[9]

Centrally related to the Holocaust's wartime context, one of the most important questions scholars have been probing is when and how the actual decision to exterminate the Jews of Europe took place. Initially, it was generally assumed that the Holocaust was the direct outcome of Hitler's long-term plans and his direct orders, although no document by Hitler explicitly authorizing the Final Solution has ever been found. The path to genocide, though not without twists and turns, was seen as one in which progressively harsher disabilities were imposed upon the Jews according to a preconceived plan that finally reached its intended culmination: extermination. Versions of that intentionalist view continue to be held by some highly respected and knowledgeable scholars.[10] Early on, it was challenged by Uwe Dietrich Adam, one of the first German historians to study in great detail the decision-making process leading up to the destruction of European Jewry.[11] Our view underscores the devastating intentions that Hitler and his followers consistently held about the Jews, but we also stress that these intentions developed over time and that they often entailed unintended implications and consequences, which required reconsideration and recalculation as well as invention and innovation.

## THE APPEARANCE OF MOBILE KILLING UNITS

As noted in chapters 4 and 5, during its early years the Nazi regime aimed at forcing the German Jews to emigrate. To achieve this goal the Nazis implemented a program of progressively intensifying economic and social strangulation to ensure the destruction of the Jews' civic existence. As the Nazis attempted to rid Germany of its Jews, they also discerned that the prospect of Jewish immigration would increase antisemitism outside of Germany. When the potential receiving nations balked at accepting more than a handful of Jews, the Germans were able to claim that the Jews were a universal problem and that no blame should accrue to them for their anti-Jewish policies.[12] For all practical purposes, the outbreak of war ended Jewish emigration options at the very time when Germany's rapid conquests added millions to the Jews already under Nazi control. By the autumn of 1940 Eichmann noted that there were 5.8 million Jews to be "evacuated from the *Lebensraum* of the German people."[13] Little more than a year later, he noted that eleven million Jews throughout all of Europe, including England, Switzerland, Sweden, Spain, and Turkey, were targeted for the "Final Solution."[14]

Although Germany had several million Jews under its control between September 1939 and June 1941, *no systematic program of overt and unremitting genocide was initiated until after the invasion of the Soviet Union on 22 June 1941.* Jews were subject to brutally sadistic treatment, sporadic killings, and catastrophic living conditions that guaranteed famine, sickness, and a high death toll, but overt mass murder had yet to be employed. Nevertheless, the first official, large-scale, murderous attacks on Jews actually came very soon after the invasion of Poland. Before analyzing those attacks in more detail, however, we should clarify the emergence of the German units that did the killing.

As previously noted, on 17 June 1936 Hitler appointed Himmler, who was already head of the SS, to be the chief of all the German police forces as well. Like many of the leading Nazis, Himmler was quite young—only in his mid-thirties—when he obtained immense power. He used his 1936 appointment to organize the police as follows: Kurt Daluege (1897–1946) headed the *Ordnungspolizei* (order police), the ordinary uniformed force that was responsible for law enforcement in Germany's cities, towns, and rural areas. Reinhard Heydrich, who already led both the *Sicherheitsdienst* (SD, the Nazi Party's intelligence and security service) and the Gestapo (secret police), received control of the *Sicherheitspolizei* (security police), which now brought the Gestapo and the Kripo (criminal police) together. This centralization—the *Ordnungspolizei* and *Sicherheitspolizei* both had main offices in Berlin—not only beefed up Himmler's political police force but also aligned the entire German police apparatus with Nazi aims and with the SS in particular. The latter reality became more apparent on 1 October 1939, when the headquarters of the SD and the *Sicherheitspolizei* were united under Heydrich's purview.[15] The new organization was called the *Reichssicherheitshauptamt* (Reich Security Main Office, or RSHA). (After Czech partisans assassinated Heydrich in June 1942, Ernst Kaltenbrunner [1903–46] succeeded him.)

Soon after Austria came under German control in March 1938, the security police organized special units to eliminate enemies of the state. By the autumn of that year, similar units were at work in the Nazi-occupied Sudetenland, where for the first time these assault squads were called *Einsatzgruppen*. The personnel for these *Einsatzgruppen* came from all the branches of Heydrich's security police. Thus, the SD, Gestapo, and Kripo were all represented in mobile units that came under the RSHA's jurisdiction. As for the 245,000 men who served in the Order Police by mid-1940, many of them were organized into battalions of approximately five hundred men. These battalions helped to maintain order behind the military lines in occupied Europe. Especially in Poland and other eastern territories, the Order Police also became heavily involved in killing Jews. Together the mass shootings carried out by the *Einsatzgruppen* and the Order Police accounted for about 1.3 million Jewish deaths.[16]

Now let us return to the early *Einsatzgruppen* killings that took place in Eastern Upper Silesia. This territory had been a part of Germany until the end of World War I, but after bitter fighting between Polish forces and German *Freikorps* units, it had been annexed to the newly independent Polish Republic.[17] An important German military and political objective at the beginning of the war was to expel the Poles and Jews from Eastern Upper Silesia and to reincorporate that region into the Reich. Thus on 3 September 1939 Himmler gave an assignment to *Obergruppenführer* (Lieutenant General) Udo von Woyrsch. As commander of the *Einsatzgruppe* that began operations in Poland, Woyrsch would be responsible for "ruthless suppression" of the "Polish uprising" in Eastern Upper Silesia, which is how the Germans described the Poles' resistance to the invasion of their native land.[18] In addition to "suppressing" Polish resistance, Woyrsch received instructions that the *Einsatzgruppe* was to use "extreme terror" to force the Jews to flee to the east.[19]

On 6 September 1939 troops under Woyrsch's subordinate, SS *Oberführer* (Senior Colonel) Dr. Emil Otto Rasch, carried out mass shootings of Jews in Katowice, a Polish industrial city in Silesia, while Order Police battalions beat unarmed Jewish civilians in the streets.[20] On 8 September in Bedzin, another Polish town, the Order Police humiliated Orthodox Jews by cutting off their beards and forelocks; army and *Einsatzgruppe* personnel used flamethrowers to set fire to the synagogue and several other buildings, shooting those who attempted to escape. Almost one hundred people, eighty Jews among them, were killed in this manner. Within the next two days several hundred Jews were publicly executed.[21]

Meanwhile, on 10 September the Germans ignited the synagogue in Katowice and moved eastward towards Cracow, killing unarmed civilians as they went. These incidents were among the earliest of many in which the Germans forced Jews into synagogues, schools, and other buildings and then burned them to death. At his trial in December 1967, Woyrsch did not deny that orders had been given to terrorize Jews into fleeing, but he claimed that Rasch, not he, had received them, an explanation that strains credulity.[22]

At first, German military authorities in the region were unaware of Himmler's orders to Woyrsch. On 11 September 1939, Lieutenant General Brandt recommended that Woyrsch be court-martialed because of the behavior of the troops under his command. Brandt received no direct response, but the next day Colonel Emil Zellner, quartermaster of the Fourteenth Army, informed the commanders in the area that Woyrsch's *Einsatzgruppe* was fully authorized to carry out "anti-insurgency" operations behind the advancing German lines.[23] The authorization gave Woyrsch carte blanche to continue the terror and the killings. Thereafter, his *Einsatzgruppe* proceeded to murder male Jews, plunder Jewish businesses, and publicly humiliate Jewish leaders in a number of towns. From 16 to 19 September, for example, *Einsatzgruppe* personnel collected between 500 and 600 Jewish men in the Polish city of Przemysl and took them to the city's outskirts, where they were forced to dig their own graves before being shot to death.[24] Once again the matter was brought to the attention of military authorities, and Colonel General Wilhelm List, commander of the Fourteenth Army, issued orders that officers were to prevent "illegal acts" by military and police personnel. There were even scuffles between SS personnel and German troops who were disgusted at the killing of unarmed civilians. Nevertheless, List was not prepared to interfere with Woyrsch's *Einsatzgruppe.* In an order of the day, List reminded his troops that Polish teachers, priests, urban intelligentsia, and Jews were *deutschfeindlich* (hostile to Germans). He also claimed that reports of brutality by Woyrsch's police were "exaggerated."[25]

Alexander Rossino has pointed out that, as brutal and sadistic as was Woyrsch's *Einsatzgruppe* in Poland in the fall of 1939, its behavior was radically different from that of the *Einsatzgruppen* that accompanied the *Wehrmacht* in the invasion of the Soviet Union in June 1941.[26] Although some scholars have interpreted the 1939 action in Eastern Upper Silesia as a direct anticipation of the genocide that was to follow, Rossino points out that the murder of Jews and the destruction of Jewish property in 1939 had as its objective the rapid expulsion of as many Jews as possible from those ethnically cleansed parts of Poland that were to be incorporated into or fall under the permanent control of the Reich. Presumably that expulsion would drive them into the eastern part of Poland, which had been seized by the Soviet Union in conjunction with a secret provision written into the German-Soviet nonaggression pact of 23 August 1939, an agreement that gave Hitler assurance that the Soviets would not interfere with his objectives in Poland. By the time Hitler broke his agreement with Stalin and invaded the USSR on 22 June 1941, the *Einsatzgruppen's* attacks soon made mass murder an end in itself. By contrast, in 1939 murder of civilians was a means, not an end. *At the beginning of the war the Nazi leadership in the field appeared to regard murderous expulsion rather than genocide as the preferred method of "solving" the so-called "Jewish problem."*

Woyrsch's method of dealing with the "Jewish problem" was harsh, but it continued policies in effect since Hitler had come to power. From 1933 on, the regime employed increasingly callous measures to encourage Jewish emigration. After the German takeover of Austria in 1938, the antisemitic measures became harsher, and within a brief period Eichmann could boast that 50,000 Jews had left. In October 1938, as noted above, 17,000 Polish Jews were forcibly expelled across the Polish border, a measure that led to *Kristallnacht*. With the massive pogrom that followed on 9–10 November 1938, it became obvious to almost all Jews that they had no future in Germany. In a speech on 6 December 1938, Hermann Göring made the same point as he emphasized the "good aspect" of *Kristallnacht*, that "the entire question of emigration has become acute, the other peoples realize: The Jew cannot live in Germany."[27]

Once the war started, voluntary departure was no longer an option, but *Hitler was determined that not a single Jew would remain within the borders of the Reich or the territories annexed to it.* The behavior of Woyrsch's *Einsatzgruppe* in Eastern Upper Silesia was thus part of a larger pattern. To the Germans, that territory was to be an integral part of the Reich. The Poles had wrongly taken it in 1918; now the Germans had rightfully taken it back. Having done so, they were determined to rid the territory of Jews.

## WHERE WERE THE JEWS TO GO?

By prior agreement between Germany and the Soviet Union, Poland was divided into two parts in September 1939. On 17 September, the Red Army occupied the eastern half, which they regarded as including parts of Belorussia and Ukraine. The German sector, which brought some two million Jews under Nazi jurisdiction, was subdivided. Much of western and northern Poland was annexed to the Reich; the annexed territory was known as the Warthegau. A large central region, which included the Polish capital, Warsaw, and the city of Cracow, became a German-occupied zone called the *Generalgouvernement* (general government). Hans Frank (1900–46), an early Nazi who had once been Hitler's personal lawyer, became its governor. His anti-Jewish policies were brutal.

On 28 September 1939, the Germans and the Russians finalized their Polish border terms. In exchange for the district of Lublin in southeastern Poland, the Germans agreed that the Baltic country of Lithuania belonged in the Soviet sphere of influence. In the summer of 1940 the USSR annexed the Baltic states of Estonia, Latvia, and Lithuania. That step had catastrophic consequences for the Jews in that region—approximately 250,000 in Lithuania, 95,000 in Latvia, and 4,500 in Estonia—when the Germans invaded those areas in the summer of 1941.

Meanwhile, as the historian Christopher Browning sums up the situation, "[b]y the end of September 1939 Himmler had proposed and Hitler had approved a grandiose program of demographic engineering based on racial principles that would involve the uprooting of millions of people."[28] The plan found expression in Hitler's Reichstag speech of 6 October 1939, which declared that "the most important task" facing the Reich was the creation of "a new order of ethnographic constellations, meaning a resettlement of nationalities." Specifically, Hitler asserted that there should be "an ordering and settlement of the Jewish problem."[29] In this speech as elsewhere, Hitler was advancing his military and political objectives and the place of the destruction of Jewish life within them. Hitler's fullest intentions have been succinctly stated by the American writer Richard Rhodes:

> The Final Solution—the systematic murder of the Jews of Europe and the Soviet Union—was intended to be *only the first phase* of a vast, megalo-maniacal project of privation, enslavement, mass murder and colonization modeled after the historic colonization of North and South America and on nineteenth-century imperialism but modernized with pseudoscientific theories of eugenic restoration. (italics added)[30]

Hitler's speech revealed intentions that went in two directions at once: Germans, including ethnic Germans, would occupy the newly acquired *Lebensraum*; concurrently, that territory would be ethnically cleansed. Poles and Jews would have to go. The program for the ethnic German resettlers came to be known as *Heim-ins-Reich* (home into the Reich). It envisioned the transfer of approximately 500,000 ethnic Germans from the Baltic and eastern European countries into the newly enlarged Reich and was tied in with the wholesale elimination of Jews from the same territory.[31] The formula was simple but deadly: *Germans in; Jews out.*

On 29 September 1939, about a week prior to Hitler's speech, Reinhard Heydrich had reported to leaders of the Reich Security Main Office (RSHA) that "in the area between Warsaw and Lublin a 'nature reserve' or 'Reich ghetto' is going to be established in which all the Polish and Jewish elements to be resettled from future German Gaus [districts] . . . will have to be accommodated."[32] This plan would be delayed, however, owing in part to the opposition of the *Wehrmacht* to the radical SS resettlement programs in Poland. At the time, Poland was still under German military government, and the SS and SD were not certain of the extent to which their radical measures would be tolerated by the military.

Unlike his colleagues, Adolf Eichmann was not inclined to accept a delay. When plans for a Jewish reservation were discussed in the RSHA, Eichmann decided to proceed to implement them on his own authority. On 18 October 1939, several trainloads of Jews were sent on his orders from Vienna, Katowice, and Ostrau to Nisko in the Lublin district, which had been ceded by Russia to Germany three weeks earlier. When the deportees arrived, the local German authorities were wholly unprepared to receive them. The chaotic conditions created by the muddled Nisko Plan and its sudden influx of Jews prompted local

German civil and military authorities to protest. On 26 October 1939 all further transports to Nisko were stopped by Himmler's orders. His first priority was to find "lodging and livelihood" in the Reich for incoming ethnic Germans.[33] Jewish deportations would have to wait. As for the several thousand Jews who had been deported to the Lublin district, many succumbed to hunger, cold, and disease. Others were shot. Several hundred escaped over the border to Russian-occupied Poland. Five hundred were detained in a local detention camp until they were returned to their original homes in April 1940, only to be transported back to the east for extermination later on. The Nisko operation, the first experiment in the mass deportation of Jews from the Reich, was clearly a failure. Nevertheless it provided the RSHA with useful experience for subsequent deportations.[34]

On 25 October 1939 Hitler terminated military government in Poland. For all practical purposes, his order left the country under the rule of the SS and, in the case of the General Government, German civil authorities. As noted, the deportation of the Jews from the Reich was directly coupled with the relocation of ethnic Germans into the enlarged Reich. Moreover, the same leaders were responsible for both operations.[35] On 7 October 1939, Hitler had appointed Himmler Reich Commissar for the Strengthening of the German Nation (*Reichskommissar für die Festigung des Deutschen Volkstums*, or RKF), in addition to his role as head of the SS and police. Himmler thus had a dual role. He was in overall command of the agencies responsible for the "solution" of the "Jewish problem" as well as for the "resettlement" of ethnic Germans.[36] Heydrich also had dual responsibilities. Under Himmler, his responsibilities were expanded to include directing both the Main Office for Immigrants (*Einwandererzentralstelle*) and the Main Office for Resettlers (*Umwandererzentralstelle*). Particularly with the latter task in mind, which entailed the removal of Poles, Jews, and other ethnic "inferiors," Heydrich created RSHA Section IV-D-4, to which Eichmann was assigned. In 1940, its area of competence was described in bland bureaucratic language as "matters of emigration and evacuation" (*Auswanderungs- und Räumungsangelegenheiten*). Little more than a year later, on 1 March 1941, Eichmann's office became Section IV-B-4, and its responsibilities were designated as "Jewish matters, evacuation matters."[37] From this office, Eichmann eventually coordinated the deportation of some three million Jews to Nazi death camps in Poland.

The aborted Nisko experiment had not helped to answer the question "Where are the Jews to go?" It was given that they had to be sent somewhere, but the destination remained uncertain as Himmler and Heydrich tried without decisive success to coordinate this part of their grandiose demographic engineering. In theory, two Jews or Poles were to be deported to make room for every German settler, but that was more easily said than done. To make matters worse, ethnic German resettlers were increasingly coming "home to the Reich." For example, between October and December 1939 sixty thousand Baltic Germans arrived in German port cities as part of the resettlement program. The Baltic Germans were followed in January and February 1940 by 120,000 ethnic Germans from central Poland.[38] A lack of "lodging and livelihood" threatened to send the resettlement program spiraling out of control, not least because the ethnic German resettlers included people who were physically disabled or mentally ill. To meet their housing needs, the Main Office for Immigrants took steps to evacuate hospitals and sanatoriums to make room for those in need. The displacements only added to a growing list of resettlement problems that had yet to be met. We will return to these aspects of what Doris Bergen calls "the related goals of race and space," but first it will be instructive to consider a third population initiative that became of decisive importance in Nazi Germany's ambitious demographic policies.

## A THIRD POPULATION INITIATIVE

The programs for the "resettlement" of ethnic Germans and the expulsion of Jews from Reich territory became linked, implicitly if not explicitly, to a third population initiative, the so-called "euthanasia program." Under this initiative, handicapped and mentally ill Germans of all ages were condemned as "life unworthy of life" (*lebensunwertes Leben*) and "useless eaters" (*unnütze Esser*).[39] They were murdered in hospitals and psychiatric institutions. This killing program had far-reaching effects. For example, one must not underestimate the importance of the fact that the first Nazi targets for mass destruction were not Jews but Germans who had been certified as "unfit" for life within Hitler's Reich.[40] They were gassed and cremated in special facilities by German doctors and nurses who were assisted by SS euthanasia "specialists." If the Nazis were prepared to eliminate Germans, they would be unlikely to cringe at the prospect of destroying those who belonged to "inferior" races. As we shall see, this program foreshadowed and contributed to the Holocaust in significant ways. Among other things, its existence shows that the Holocaust was neither instigated by the uneducated nor sustained by the ill-trained. On the contrary, the skilled and highly educated were at its core, and none more so than leaders from the medical profession and its allied fields. For in addition to being key leaders in the Nazi euthanasia program, which was part of the Nazis' demographic revolution, German medical personnel played important parts in the Final Solution. It evolved in part from what Robert Lifton has called a "biomedical vision." That "vision" produced a "therapeutic imperative" in which the health and "healing" of the German people entailed the killing of those who were deemed genetically defective and racially inferior.[41]

Ideologically, the euthanasia program's roots were deeply embedded in outlooks derived from Charles Darwin's theory that the human species has evolved through a process of natural selection involving the survival of the fittest. To that view was added the idea that human intervention could enhance that process and help to ensure that the fittest—the best—did survive and flourish. Among some social Darwinists, additional propositions supplemented the general perspective. For instance, the conviction arose among some British, French, Belgian, German, and American political leaders, scientists, physicians, and even numerous clergy

that the elimination of the "lower" (and colored) races was a desirable consequence of the evolutionary "progress" of the "higher" races. These sentiments
were especially strong among Western intellectual and political leaders in Europe
and America whose colonial and imperialist ventures in Africa, the New World,
and Australasia had genocidal consequences for the indigenous populations.[42]

Anxious to prevent "inferior" members of their own societies from dragging
their communities down to the level of the "inferior" races, a number of physicians, businesspeople, and corporate leaders—Americans prominent among
them—also embraced eugenics, an early form of genetic engineering that achieved
considerable popularity in the late nineteenth and early twentieth centuries.[43]
Not all social Darwinists were eugenicists. Nor were all eugenicists of one mind,
but they had social Darwinist inclinations. If their versions of social Darwinism
were more or less extreme, their outlook did emphasize that it would be unwise
to permit nature alone to determine the future character of the human species,
without the guiding control of scientific intelligence.[44] Specifically, the advocates
of eugenics sought to direct human breeding so that those afflicted with hereditary, debilitating physical or mental illness did not proliferate and enlarge the proportion of men and women in society with such disorders. Considerable racism
was involved in the eugenics movement's ideas concerning who would be prevented from breeding. For example, the high incidence of disease, mental disturbance, and asocial behavior among poverty-stricken African Americans,
Indians, and Mexican Americans was attributed to congenital defects in the way
these groups had evolved. White Anglo-Saxon Protestants and related Protestants
of northern European stock were said to be at the apex of the world's evolutionary hierarchy. Italians, Slavs, and Jews were regarded as considerably lower in evolutionary development. Not surprisingly, the proponents of this theory of
inherent, biologically determined WASP racial superiority were themselves of
white Anglo-Saxon Protestant background.[45]

Implicit in the theory of the inherited, biological basis of poverty, asocial
behavior, and susceptibility to debilitating disease was the conviction that neither education nor economic improvement of the allegedly inferior groups could
alter their defects. Moreover, the "inferior" groups were regarded as a long-term
danger to society. Offspring from unions of members of the "higher" and "lower"
groups were thought to inherit the undesirable qualities of the "lower" groups,
which tended to have far more children than, for instance, WASP high achiev-
ers. Above all, the dependent members of the "lower" groups were considered a
hopelessly nonproductive drain on society's economic and cultural resources.

The eugenics movement advocated a simple solution: compulsory sterilization. They proposed that population growth be "scientifically managed" so that
the "desirable" part of the population might increase as the unhealthy portion
disappeared. "Scientific selection" would improve on natural selection.[46] In
1904, with support from the eugenics movement, the Pennsylvania state legisla-
ture passed "An Act for the Prevention of Idiocy," which contained a compulsory
sterilization clause. That bill was vetoed by the governor. Nevertheless, between

1907 and 1928, more than twenty American states passed sterilization laws aimed at controlling the reproduction of socially deviant individuals. The United States was thus among the first countries to pass laws calling for compulsory sterilization in the name of racial purification.

As frequently happens when well-meaning individuals use government to "improve" society, the American eugenics laws were to have unintended consequences. One of them would be that the American attempt to unite science and law in the quest for a "healthy" society had a greater impact on Germany than the United States. As early as 1904 Ernst Haeckel (1834–1919), a German physician, zoologist, and philosopher who taught at the University of Jena, had called for the elimination by "mercy death" of Germany's "unfit" as a means of "saving useless expenses for family and state."[47] If such thinking did not make much headway at the time, it foreshadowed what would happen after Germany's defeat in World War I, when highly influential German scientists began to search for ways to restore the "healthy" portion of the German people. In 1920 Karl Binding, a jurist, and Alfred Hoche, a psychiatrist, published a book entitled *Die Freigabe der Vernichtung lebensunwerten Lebens* (Authorization for the destruction of life unworthy of life).[48] It argued for the state-sponsored killing of "worthless" people. Among the candidates proposed for elimination were the "mentally completely dead" and those who "represent a foreign body in human society," a concept with lethal implications once German eugenics and "scientific racial theory" united with Nazi ideology and its population policies. Furthermore, Hoche, who directed the psychiatric clinic at the University of Freiburg, cautioned against feeling any sympathy for "lives devoid of value."[49]

Binding and Hoche had planted seeds that would soon bear murderous fruit, but officials in the Weimar Republic were not fully prepared to act, although they were interested in compulsory sterilization of the hopelessly infirm, the feeble-minded, unwed mothers, and criminals eligible for parole. In August 1923, the director of health institutions in the district of Zwickau in Saxony wrote to the Ministry of the Interior that there was nothing especially radical about compulsory sterilization. "What we racial hygienists promote is not at all new or unheard of," he contended. "In a cultured nation of the first order, in the United States of America, that which we strive toward was introduced and tested long ago."[50] The ministry then sought the help of the Foreign Office to ascertain American practice in compulsory sterilization. After contacting American penal and mental institutions, the German embassy in Washington confirmed that more than twenty states had compulsory sterilization legislation on their books.[51] The example of the United States thus facilitated a favorable reception for compulsory sterilization in Germany. Under Hitler, compulsory sterilization would become one element in the Nazis' vast demographic agenda.

On 25 July 1933, less than six months after Hitler came to power, the new regime published its Law for the Prevention of Offspring with Hereditary Diseases, which required sterilization for men and women suffering from congenital illnesses.[52] The compulsory sterilization law was only a prelude. In 1935, according to the Nuremberg trial testimony of Dr. Karl Brandt, the National Socialist Reichskommissar for Health, Hitler told the Reich medical leader Gerhard Wagner that, if war came, he would initiate a program of euthanasia. As in so many of his promises to murder and destroy, Hitler proved true to his word.

Toward the end of October 1939, Hitler sent a letter—typed on his personal stationery and signed by him—to Philip Bouhler, who headed the Chancellery of the Führer of the NSDAP. Backdated to 1 September 1939, the day Nazi Germany had invaded Poland, it said, "Reich Leader Bouhler and Dr. med. Brandt are charged with the responsibility of enlarging the competence of certain physicians, designated by name, so that patients who, on the basis of human judgment, are considered incurable, can be granted mercy death after a discerning diagnosis."[53] The Führer Chancellery was a special department established by Hitler to handle his private affairs. It was ideally suited to administer a secret program, which this so-called "mercy death" initiative had to be.

Hitler's letter did not announce a new law, but it expressed his wishes, and thus this potent authorization set in motion a killing process that would destroy more than 140,000 lives, including at least 5,000 children.[54] In fact, with Bouhler's deputy, Viktor Brack, in charge, the euthanasia program began with disabled children who were selected for the killing program. Whether children or adults, most of the victims had been innocently entrusted by their families to Germany's health care institutions. The euthanasia program itself was the product of a vicious union of scientific arrogance and political power by men who were under no illusion concerning the negative public reaction that would ensue, were the program to become widely known. For that reason the killing institutions were camouflaged as healing agencies.[55]

The euthanasia program became known to insiders as Operation T4, or simply T4, because its Berlin headquarters were located at Tiergartenstrasse 4, the site of a confiscated Jewish villa. Along with younger physicians, T4's staff included a number of the Third Reich's more prominent medical doctors and psychiatrists, including Professor Werner Heyde, Dr. Friedrich Mennecke, and Dr. Hermann Pfannmüller. None of the approximately forty German physicians selected to work in Operation T4 was coerced.[56] Nor did they regard themselves as killers. Instead, they saw their actions as implementing a special therapy in a medical program that would benefit the German people. Everything about the project had the surface aura of medicine. Yet between January 1940 and August 1941 alone, when the program was officially terminated (it continued in even greater secrecy until the war's end), at least seventy thousand men, women, and children were killed. Moreover, while the program was under way, one prominent scientist, a Professor Kranz, wrote an article in the April 1940 issue of a National Socialist journal, *N.S. Volksdienst*, in which he estimated that there were one million Germans whose "removal" would be desirable.[57] In view of the fact that Kranz's opinion was published in an official Nazi publication during wartime, when censorship was at its most stringent, his views cannot be dismissed as the private excess of an idiosyncratic imagination. Clearly, if National Socialist ideologues were willing to contemplate the murder of one million of their fellow Germans, many of whom were merely handicapped, they would be entirely free of scruples when it came to murdering Jews and other "inferior" non-Germans.

When the euthanasia project was initiated, questionnaires for each patient were sent to all German mental hospitals and psychiatric clinics. The forms gathered basic information: the patient's name, age, illness, racial status, and prognosis. On the basis of the responses, two three-member committees of T4 medical experts —the first made up of junior physicians, the second consisting of more senior doctors—determined whether the patient should receive a "mercy death" (*Gnadentod*). They did so, not from an examination of the patient, but on the basis of the information forms alone. Each committee member used a red plus sign (+) to indicate death, a blue minus sign (-) to extend life. Senior officials had the final say; they were encouraged to select death for as many patients as their expert judgment would permit. Unanimity for a death decision was not required. In adult cases, economic calculations—could the patient do any productive work, or was he or she a "useless eater"?—were the most decisive in these life-and-death decisions.[58]

Once a decision for euthanasia was made, T4 ensured that the patient was delivered to the facility where the "mercy death" was administered. Early on, lethal injections were used, but the number of euthanasia candidates was too large to make that method efficient. Gassing became the procedure of choice. Installations for that purpose were developed at six code-lettered regional centers in Germany and Austria: Bernburg, Brandenburg, Grafeneck, Hadamar, Hartheim, and Sonnenstein. With the exception of Brandenburg, a former jail facility, these centers were housed in former hospitals. All used the euphemistic designation State Hospital and Nursing Home. In the years 1940 and 1941, each of these centers took the lives of thousands of people. Hartheim's tally, 18,269, was the largest.[59] On the occasion of the ten-thousandth "mercy killing" at Hadamar, the personnel celebrated with a party. As drinks were served, one staff member supplied the humor by dressing up and playing the part of a Roman Catholic priest.[60]

Some of these same facilities—particularly Bernberg, Hartheim, and Sonnenstein—were also used to kill prisoners selected from German concentration camps, which had expanding populations in 1940 but not yet the facilities to kill many inmates at once. This operation was code-named *Sonderbehandlung* (special treatment) 14f13—the number referring to a special file in a system that the Inspectorate of Concentration Camps used to record the deaths of prisoners and their cause. Between ten and twenty thousand persons were murdered in the 14f13 operation.[61]

Meanwhile, as T4's personnel and the SS became more closely connected in ways that would eventually link euthanasia and the Final Solution, thousands of patients were sent to the euthanasia centers. The decisions that condemned them to death were made without consulting either the victims or their families, who learned of the fate of their loved ones by a form letter of condolence. The letter informed the next of kin that the victim had died of heart attack, pneumonia, or some other fictitious ailment. Sometimes these letters underscored that the deceased had been released from incurable disabilities and that death was a deliv-

erance. It was also indicated that the police had ordered the immediate cremation of the body because of "danger of contagious disease" at the institution. The
letter further stated that visits to the institution were prohibited by the police for
the same reason.[62]

Although the killings were called "mercy deaths," they had nothing to do with
euthanasia as that term had previously been understood. Traditionally, euthanasia was the act of releasing a terminally ill patient from unbearable pain, usually
with consent. To the extent that it had ever been considered justified, euthanasia
had been an effort *on the patient's behalf*, not the state's. Nor was there any mercy
in the Nazi "mercy" killings. In the project's initial stages, there was uncertainty
about the best killing procedure. Since "useless eaters" were targeted, it should
not be surprising that calculated starvation was among the methods employed,
especially where children were concerned. Starvation, however, was not what
happened at the six major euthanasia facilities. At Brandenberg, the first T4
killing center to become operational, a remodeled room became a gas chamber,
which resembled a therapeutic "inhalation room" and later a shower. Carbon
monoxide gas was used for the killing. Crematorium ovens stood nearby for
corpse disposal. In the early stages, the gas chambers, which became standard in
all six of the centers, could kill between twenty and fifty persons at once, but in
some places the capacity became seventy-five, and at Hartheim as many as 150
people were gassed in a single operation.[63]

Each euthanasia center had two key administrators. One was the physician-
in-charge, who oversaw the gassings, handled the medical records, and ensured
that the facility had the appearance of a hospital. The other was a supervisor, usually a police officer, who was responsible for the nonmedical staff and site administration, including the security system that maintained secrecy. These officials
included doctors such as the psychiatrist Irmfried Eberl and policemen such as
Christian Wirth and Franz Stangl. Joined by Viktor Brack and other colleagues
from the euthanasia program, they would emerge as key administrators in the
Final Solution itself.

It was impossible to cover up the tens of thousands of murders carried out by
the euthanasia program, especially since the killing centers were located in Germany and Austria rather than in the conquered territories of the East. Effective
secrecy was dependent upon officially sanctioned duplicity, but some of the lying
was transparent. For example, one family was told that a victim had died as the
result of an infected appendix, but they knew that his appendix had been removed
ten years earlier. By 1941 protests were heard from some highly influential German church leaders. The most important of these protests was a sermon preached
on 3 August 1941 by Clemens August Graf von Galen, the Roman Catholic
bishop of Münster.[64] Another important opponent of the program was Theophil
Wurm, the Lutheran bishop of Württemberg. As we shall see, there were no such
overt protests by German church officials concerning the Final Solution.

The Vatican's response to the euthanasia program was more muted. The only
public protest to come from Rome was a brief statement by the Holy Office that
"the extinction of unworthy life by public mandate [is] incompatible with natural

and divine law." This statement was mentioned—both times in Latin only—on 2 December 1940 on Vatican radio and on 6 December 1940 in the official Vatican newspaper, *L'Osservatore Romano*. The bishop of Berlin, Konrad Preysing, read the Vatican text from the pulpit at St. Hedwig's Cathedral on 9 March 1941, as part of a sermon in which he protested against the Nazi state's violation of "the individual's right to life" and its use of "medical, economic, yes even eugenic grounds" for doing so. Beyond Preysing's action, very little was heard in Germany about the Vatican's reaction to the euthanasia program.[65]

Meanwhile, Gitta Sereny has shown that highly placed Roman Catholic leaders were aware, before World War II began, of Hitler's plan to initiate a euthanasia project.[66] In early 1939, Josef Mayer, a Catholic professor of moral theology at the University of Paderborn, was commissioned to write an opinion for Hitler on the subject of the church's attitude toward euthanasia. The substance of Mayer's one-hundred-page response was that, since there were reasonable grounds pro and con as well as Catholic authorities on both sides, euthanasia of the mentally incompetent could be considered "defensible." According to Sereny, the real purpose of commissioning Mayer's research was to determine how the church would respond to such a program. Hitler understood that the church would be opposed in principle to euthanasia. *The question that really interested him was whether the church would actively oppose the program.* When the text of Mayer's opinion was presented to Cesare Orsenigo, the papal nuncio (ambassador) to Germany, Orsenigo made no comments except to remark that he was taking "informal cognizance of the information." This was a diplomatic way to tell the Germans that he did not consider the matter sufficiently important to transmit to the Vatican. Without officially approving the killing operation, the nuncio signaled that there would be no serious Vatican opposition. He was correct.

In spite of the Vatican's passivity, Hitler could not ignore the growing discontent with the program in Germany, especially after von Galen's sermon. The sermon infuriated Hitler, but he decided that in wartime it was inopportune to begin a struggle with an important leader of Germany's Roman Catholic Church. Vowing to his inner circle that he would settle his score with von Galen after the expected German victory in the war, Hitler ordered the program "officially" terminated in August 1941. His stop order, however, pertained only to the major killing centers and their gas chambers. Euthanasia continued in other places and by other means throughout the war. Even after Germany's surrender in May 1945, euthanasia was still claiming the lives of handicapped children in the Bavarian state hospital at Kaufbeuren.[67]

## NO TERRITORIAL SOLUTION

Returning now to the territory that Nazi Germany annexed or occupied in the East, although T4's administration did not extend everywhere, its practice of murdering patients entrusted to health-care institutions was implemented concurrently by other agencies and even put to new uses. Götz Aly reports, for example, that "by autumn of 1939 and during the following winter, 10,000 to 15,000 mentally ill had already been murdered in Pomerania, West Prussia, and in occupied Poland."[68] In these cases, various killing methods were utilized. In addition to starvation and shooting, gassing was employed but in a novel way. For example, there were trucks—in some cases they were specially equipped in garages at the Sachsenhausen concentration camp in Germany—that were converted into portable gassing units. They were driven to the hospitals where patients were to be dispatched. Eventually gas vans would be used to murder Jews in the Final Solution, especially at the Chelmno death camp, which became operational on Polish soil in December 1941.

Meanwhile, the killings of the mentally ill were carried out as ethnic Germans were "brought home" to the Reich. The victims were not only non-German patients but also incapacitated ethnic Germans who were thinned out as the demographic shifts took place. Greater care was taken, however, when German lives were involved. Thus, according to the testimony of Vladimir Nikolayev, a Baltic German physician, about four hundred mentally ill German settlers from Latvia and Estonia were kept alive from 1939 until 1941. Then, on orders from Himmler, they were transferred to the psychiatric hospital at Tiegenhof, where "room was made for them" by doing away with the previous inmates. At Tiegenhof, the new arrivals were deliberately undernourished and, according to Nikolayev, "died like flies."[69] The fate of these unfortunates had been decided at an early stage of the Baltic Germans' resettlement. On 22 February 1940, the RKF office wrote, "There is no intention of giving pocket money to the mentally ill and infirm settlers housed in the hospital. Nor is there any intention of granting them Reich citizenship."[70] The leaders of the Baltic Germans did little to help their weaker comrades. For instance, Andreas von Koskull, one of the Baltic leaders, wrote a letter to German officials in which he expressed regret that the Baltic Germans had been unable to leave behind "the inferior portion" of their "national group."[71] For similar reasons, in January 1940 SS units murdered five hundred patients at an institution near the Soviet-Polish border to create a transit camp for ethnic Germans who were being resettled. About the same time, several hundred mentally ill patients at a psychiatric institution near the city of Gnesen were murdered in gas vans. By the fall of 1941, thirty thousand people had been murdered to make "space for ethnic German resettlers."[72]

The first systematic mass murders carried out by Nazi Germany under the cover of war were directly connected to demographic policies that both eliminated "defective" Germans and made room for ethnic Germans within the Reich. Jews were among the victims of these policies, but they were not the majority of those who were killed by them. That situation would soon change, but in the meantime the mammoth resettlement program and the murder of helpless, mentally ill patients were consistent with Hitler's Reichstag speech on 6 October 1939, when he said that Germany's most important task was to create "a new order of ethnographic constellations, meaning a resettlement of nationalities."[73]

When the decision to resettle ethnic Germans, Poles, and Jews was taken without adequate plans to provide "lodging and livelihood," the Nazis created a problem for themselves that could not be solved by humane means. Nevertheless, a solution for part of that problem was more and more at hand. Some lives were deemed unworthy of living. If the Nazis deemed a life "useless," they were prepared to eliminate that life with a good conscience. The Holocaust scholar Peter Haas has identified what he calls "the Nazi ethic," which allowed the perpetrators to engage in mass killings and to commit genocide while remaining convinced that they were moral, thoroughly decent Germans.[74] Moreover, if it was both right and moral to put to death physically handicapped and mentally ill Germans, there was little reason to spare hostile Poles, and even less to permit Jews to survive the war. There was no specific order to murder the mentally ill and infirm to make room for the ethnic Germans.[75] Nevertheless, there was a general attitude toward problem solving that did not preclude mass murder.

During the period from 1 September 1939 to 21 June 1941, Germany and Russia were nominally at peace and there were very few locations to which Germany could conveniently deport the Jews. As we have seen, the first area selected as a *Judenreservat* was located in the Lublin area at the easternmost part of the General Government. For reasons that we consider below, on 12 March 1940 Hitler declared that the region around Lublin could never be "a solution" to the Jewish problem.[76] However, Himmler and Heydrich were committed to clearing Jews out of the Reich, including the Warthegau. Poles who could not be absorbed into the Reich through Germanization or forced labor would have to go as well. The General Government appeared to be the only available dumping ground, but it was overpopulated and had neither the economic resources nor accommodations for the Jews and Poles whom Himmler and Heydrich proposed to expel from the Warthegau.

Initially Governor Hans Frank was willing to permit Jews, but not more Poles, to enter the General Government. In an address to German officials on 25 November 1939, he explained why:

> We won't waste much time on the Jews. It's great to get to grips with the Jewish race at last. The more that die the better; hitting them represents a victory for our Reich. The Jews should feel that we've arrived. We want to put 1/2 to 3/4 of all Jews east of the Vistula. We will crush these Jews wherever we can. Everything is at stake. Get the Jews out of the Reich, Vienna, everywhere. We have no use for Jews in the Reich. Probably the line of the Vistula, behind this line no more. We are the most important people here.[77]

Clearly Frank looked forward to inflicting abusive treatment upon the Jews in the hope that many, perhaps a majority, would perish. Nevertheless, it is important to reiterate that there was as yet no program of systematic mass murder specifically for Jews.

In spite of Frank's unwillingness to accept Poles, Himmler wanted to dump both Poles and Jews into the General Government. To counter Frank's refusal,

Himmler announced, imprudently as things turned out, that 1.5 million Jews would soon be deported from the General Government, thereby facilitating the expulsion of Polish farmers from western Poland and providing room for resettled ethnic Germans from southeastern Europe.[78] Himmler did not specify the location to which the deported Jews would be sent. In all probability, he was anticipating a forthcoming German invasion of the Soviet Union, as well as a speedy victory, after which the RSHA would be free to dump Jews somewhere in the vast reaches of that country.

In the meantime, the Jews had to be stored somewhere in the General Government. This meant compulsory ghettoization. As early as 21 September 1939 Heydrich had issued secret instructions to the leaders of the *Einsatzgruppen* concerning the fate of the Jews in occupied Poland. Heydrich made a distinction between the "final goal" (*Endziel*) of National Socialist Jewish policy, the attainment of which would require a lengthy period, and the stages towards its achievement, which could be carried out on a short-term basis.[79] Heydrich spelled out the short-term measures for dealing with the Jews. These included the concentration and ghettoization of the Jews in large cities that are "rail junctions or at least located on railroad lines" and the temporary use of Jewish labor and industry in the period between the unspecified "final goal" and the short-term measures to be taken to achieve that goal. Priority was to be given to deportations from the German territories of Danzig, West Prussia, and the newly annexed territories that were to be "cleared of Jews." Heydrich did include a cautionary note that a few "trade Jews" would have to remain behind temporarily to ensure "the provisioning of the troops," but he urged "the prompt aryanization of these enterprises" so that the remaining Jews could be deported.[80] All of this meant, of course, that ghettos were a temporary expedient.

Situated in western Poland, the city of Lodz—the Germans renamed it Litzmannstadt—became the site of Nazi Germany's first major Jewish ghetto.[81] A textile manufacturing center, Lodz was Poland's second largest city, its population of 665,000 more than a third Jewish. German forces occupied the city on 8 September 1939 and immediately began to persecute the Jews. By mid-November, the city's main synagogues had been destroyed, and Jews were required to wear a yellow armband. Later a yellow star was mandatory.

Initially, Lodz was not included in the Warthegau, but its industrial importance, its population of some sixty thousand ethnic Germans, and its desirability for the resettlement of Baltic Germans led to a reconsideration; Lodz became part of the Reich on 8 November 1939. About a month later, on 10 December 1939, Friedrich Übelhoer, the Nazi leader in the area, gave secret orders for the construction of a ghetto. Noting that immediate evacuation of Lodz's Jews was impossible, he specified that the ghetto was to be located in the city's Jewish slum quarter, which was already inhabited by some sixty thousand Jews. Jews from other parts of the city would be forcibly relocated to the ghetto, which was to be established suddenly and fenced off by "barbed wire barricades and other barriers." Übelhoer's directive concluded as follows:

> The creation of the ghetto is of course only a provisional measure. I reserve for myself the decision as to the point in time and the means by which the ghetto and the city of Lodz will be cleared of Jews. *The final goal, at any rate, must be to lance this festering boil.* (italics added)[82]

With Lodz's incorporation into the Reich, Himmler and Heydrich understood that the city's large Polish and Jewish population posed a serious problem for their demographic plans. The only available location to which they could be sent was the impoverished General Government, which would be further impoverished by the deportations. Undeterred by the expanded numbers or problematic conditions further east, Himmler and Heydrich planned to deport 600,000 Jews and 400,000 Poles from the Warthegau between November 1939 and the end of February 1940.[83] The illusion that such a project was feasible lasted less than two weeks. On 28 November 1939 Heydrich was compelled to fall back once again on the distinction between short- and long-term plans. Claiming that the long-term plan remained in place, he now asserted that the short-term plan would be to ensure that "enough Poles and Jews are to be deported so that the incoming Baltic Germans can be accommodated."[84] Rather than wait until plans for the larger deportation could be implemented, Heydrich's priority was to evict and deport a sufficient number of Poles and Jews so that the Baltic Germans could be decently resettled.

The material conditions of the Lodz Jews rapidly deteriorated. All of their assets, including household goods and clothes, were "expropriated," in reality stolen, by the *Haupttreuhandelstelle Ost* (Main Trust Company Office East). The stolen assets were then used to finance the ethnic German resettlement program. Deprived of their means of subsistence, the Jews were now declared to be a "superfluous" and "unproductive" population and, as such, a drain on the German economy. Not even taking into account the religious and racial hatred that isolated them, the economic disaster that had been inflicted upon the Jews of Lodz placed them in the same category as the "useless-eater" hospital patients who were being murdered to make room for the incoming ethnic Germans.

By the spring of 1940 it was obvious that there would be no *Judenreservat* in the Lublin region and that the Jews of Lodz would have to remain in their ghetto. On 30 April 1940 the Jews were prohibited from leaving it. Now containing approximately 160,000 Jews who were confined to an area of 1.54 square miles, a population density seven times greater than it had been before the war, the ghetto area was sealed during the night of 30 April–1 May.

At the Germans' behest, this beleaguered Jewish community was internally governed by a *Judenrat* (Jewish Council), which was headed by Chaim Rumkowski. There will be more to say about him in chapter 9, but for now it is important to observe that Rumkowski hoped to save at least a part of the ghetto population by utilizing its labor to produce war-related products for the Germans. For a time, Rumkowski's strategy worked. Empowered by the Germans to recruit a labor force, Rumkowski and the Jews of the Lodz ghetto made contributions that the Germans valued. The Lodz ghetto existed much longer than most of the ghettos established by Nazi Germany, but as the ghetto's malnutrition and disease-ridden conditions took hold, there were periodic selections of Jews for deportation to the nearby death camp at Chelmno, where some 55,000 Jews from Lodz where murdered in mobile gas vans. The Lodz ghetto was liquidated in August 1944. Rumkowski and the remaining 65,000 inhabitants were sent to Auschwitz. More than two hundred thousand Jews had lived in the Lodz ghetto during the war years. The survivors numbered between seven and ten thousand.[85]

When it became apparent that the Lublin area could not serve as the Jewish "reservation," the administrators of the resettlement program began to seek alternatives. With France's surrender to Germany on 22 June 1940, another solution seemed to present itself. On 3 July 1940 Franz Rademacher, the German Foreign Office's recently appointed "expert" on Jewish issues, produced a memorandum on "The Jewish Question in the Peace Treaty." Rademacher argued that "France must make the island of Madagascar available for the solution of the Jewish question."[86] Even before the war, there had been considerable discussion of Madagascar as the future dumping ground of Europe's Jews. For example, in December 1938 Georges Bonnet, the French foreign minister, informed Joachim von Ribbentrop, his German counterpart, that France planned to deport ten thousand Jews to its island colony.

As the so-called Madagascar Plan developed, overall governance of the island would be the responsibility of the SS in accordance with a scheme that would result in the resettlement of millions of European Jews. In Madagascar, the Jews would experience "natural decimation through resettlement."[87] In short, the Madagascar Plan was genocidal, but not in the same way that the Final Solution would be when it took hold in 1941. At this time *resettlement* denoted more than relocation; it meant "natural decimation." All too soon *resettlement* would be the euphemism for deportation to killing centers where the decimation was anything but "natural." It took place by mass gassings instead.

The SS was enthusiastic about the Madagascar Plan, as was Hitler, and Eichmann's office began to work out the steps necessary for the implementation of what Heydrich saw as "a territorial Final Solution."[88] As part of the plan, the Jews of Alsace and Lorraine, the northern French provinces newly annexed to Germany, were deported to southern France to await transfer to Madagascar.[89] More than six thousand Jews were forcibly deported to unoccupied France. The French were given no notice of their arrival. After being shuttled back and forth in sealed trains while French and German authorities haggled over their fate, the deportees were interned in a French concentration camp at Gurs near the Pyrenees.[90] Conditions were unspeakable and many of the Jews perished from the cold, disease, and malnutrition.[91]

Some scholars have argued that the Madagascar Plan served as a smoke screen for Hitler's real intentions, but that view has lost much of its credibility.[92] In the first flush of rapid victory over France, leading German authorities believed the plan was feasible. Much of the Mediterranean was controlled by Germany and Italy, and the Germans were making personnel plans for a "German East Africa." All that stood in the way of unfettered German control of the Mediterranean and the Suez Canal was the British Mediterranean Fleet, and Britain was not expected to remain long in the war. The British, however, refused to surrender, and by early autumn 1940, although the idea lingered for a while longer, it was clear that the Madagascar Plan would not work. Nevertheless, the plan had not been a cover; it was abandoned only when the military situation rendered it unworkable.[93]

As long as the Madagascar Plan had seemed feasible, Heinrich Himmler and Hans Frank could minimize their differences. Himmler, Heydrich, and the RSHA wanted the Jews deported from both the Reich and the newly annexed Warthegau. As head of the General Government in occupied Poland, Frank wanted to make his hard-pressed territory economically viable, but the territory had neither the financial resources nor the food supply to take in hundreds of thousands of Jews and Poles from the Warthegau. At a meeting of senior Warthegau and General Government officials held on 31 July 1940 to resolve their differences, Frank declared that the General Government could accept the deportees only "if all questions of food supply and economics are fully resolved."[94] Frank also cited the danger of epidemics, an inevitable consequence of ghetto incarceration under famine conditions, and the impending winter as reasons for his unwillingness to accept the deportees.

In the meantime, German resettlement officials had accelerated the rate at which they were bringing ethnic Germans "home to the Reich." Some two hundred thousand ethnic Germans had been resettled between October 1939 and February 1940. The euphoria of victory in Poland led the German government to promise the Soviet and Romanian governments to remove 250,000 ethnic Germans from their territory by the summer of 1940. That July, recognizing the pressure on the General Government that further deportations to that region would entail, and still hopeful that the Madagascar Plan would work, Hitler disapproved further deportations of Jews to that area.[95] Himmler's ability to deport Jews and to make room for the resettled ethnic Germans was thus made dependent on a speedy German victory over Britain and the subsequent implementation of the Madagascar Plan. By the winter of 1940–41 more than 200,000 ethnic Germans were living in 1,500 camps, where they lacked employment and were barely getting by on a subsistence diet. The situation was further complicated by Hitler's standing order of 17 October 1939, a year earlier, forbidding any normalization of the Polish economy.[96]

As Götz Aly and Susanne Heim have observed, by the autumn of 1940 the programs for the resettlement of ethnic Germans and for the deportation of Jews obstructed each other. It was impossible to proceed with resettlement, a fundamental imperative of National Socialist population policy, without deporting Jews to make room for the resettlers.[97] But the "system" was jammed. Moreover, the number of Jews Heydrich proposed to deport progressively increased. In the winter months of 1939–40, Heydrich had proposed the deportation of one million

Polish and "Greater German" Jews who were to be settled in the Lublin region. After the fall of France, he called for a "territorial final solution" for 3.25 million Polish, German, Bohemian, and Austrian Jews, a figure that was soon raised to 4 million to include the Jews of newly conquered France, Belgium, Holland, and Luxembourg. Nevertheless, as long as it was possible to believe in the feasibility of the Madagascar Plan, both Himmler and Heydrich on one side and Frank on the other were able to leave the deportation and resettlement issues unresolved. By September 1940 that hope proved illusory. Unable to achieve a quick victory over Britain, the German military leadership understood that the Reich lacked the capacity to take over Madagascar and transport Europe's Jews to the island.

Already in April 1940, SS authorities in Cracow, Hans Frank's headquarters for the General Government, had informed the Department for Resettlement in Warsaw that Lublin could not be used as a concentration site for deported Jews. Subsequently, steps were taken to prepare Jewish districts in the Warsaw area. They were to be ready before winter arrived. These plans, however, were halted for a time, owing to the possibility in the summer of 1940 that Poland's Jews might yet be destined for Madagascar. But almost as quickly, plans to establish a large ghetto in Warsaw were back on the table. Not only was the Madagascar Plan becoming a dubious solution, but also fear was growing that Warsaw's Jewish population—it had been harassed and impoverished since the German occupation began—would become a breeding ground for epidemics that could threaten the German army and other German personnel in the city. At the urging of German medical officials, it was important to quarantine Warsaw's Jews before winter, when the chances of lethal epidemics would be greatest.

On 12 October 1940—it was Yom Kippur, the most sacred day in Judaism's liturgical calendar—Warsaw's Jews were told that they would be ghettoized.[98] Little more than a month later they were confined in a 1.3 square mile area (about 2.4 percent of the area of the city). This cramped area, which was sealed on 15 November 1940 and enclosed by a high wall, would eventually imprison some 450,000 Jews. According to Hilberg, the scarcity of living space meant that 7.2 persons per room was the norm.[99]

The official food allocation for the Warsaw ghetto was 300 calories per person per day; the allocation was 634 calories for Poles and 2,310 for Germans. Almost all of the apartments in the ghetto lacked heat. Starvation, famine, and disease were rampant. Emaciated people dropped dead in the streets. German policies and the impossible conditions inside the ghetto restricted proper burial of the bodies. The hideous conditions were meant to kill the Jews with the least possible German effort. The conditions also provided the Germans with a rationale for more direct means of murdering them. Having manufactured a famine and destroyed the ghetto residents' resistance to disease, on the ironic pretext that ghettoization would forestall epidemics, the Germans in due course claimed that their emaciated victims had become all the more dangerous from a medical perspective and thus would have to be eliminated completely to reduce the health danger to the German and Polish populations.[100]

The ghetto made vivid impressions on the Germans who saw it firsthand. For those who could not do so, official German films brought the dismal scene into view. The following report by Alfred Rosenberg (1893–1946), the Nazi ideologue who authored *The Myth of the Twentieth Century* (1930), which promoted racism and antisemitism, is representative of the impact that the Warsaw ghetto had on German sensibilities. Noting that large ghettos "cannot represent the final solution of the Jewish question," he continued as follows in a report to the Reich press department:

> If there are any people left who still somehow have sympathy with the Jews then they ought to be recommended to have a look at such a ghetto. Seeing this race en masse, which is decaying, decomposing, and rotten to the core will banish any sentimental humanitarianism. . . . Seventy thousand Jews have been deported to Warsaw from the Warthegau. It is the "Reich rubbish dump" according to the desk officer responsible.[101]

Apparently it did not occur to Rosenberg that the ghetto Jews looked like emaciated corpses because of the Germans' deliberate wartime policy of inducing famine. Even if that thought had occurred to him, it would not have been likely to change his mind. Nazi propaganda relentlessly linked the Jews with typhus, a disease associated with malnutrition and unsanitary conditions. Rosenberg and his ilk regarded all Jews as dangerous bacilli against which one had to defend oneself. Implicit in the images is the idea that no territorial solution could be adequate for handling the Jewish menace. With war as the occasion and excuse, only the Jews' annihilation would suffice.

# Chapter 7

# "A Racial Struggle of Pitiless Severity"

*It is a question of existence, thus it will be a racial struggle of pitiless severity, in the course of which twenty to thirty million Slavs and Jews will perish through military actions and crises of food supply.*

Heinrich Himmler, June 1941

On 30 March 1941, two hundred fifty senior officers in the German military assembled at the Reich Chancellery in Berlin to hear Hitler spell out his intentions for war against the Soviet Union, a campaign that would be known as Operation Barbarossa. His two-and-a-half-hour talk stated that this war would be a struggle between two world outlooks (*Weltanschauungen*), National Socialism and Bolshevism. It would be, moreover, a "war of extermination" (*Vernichtungskrieg*) against Bolshevism and Judaism. The normal rules would not apply; there would be no mercy.[1]

Hitler's speech was an important indication that, while systematic extermination was not yet the norm in Poland, that policy would steer the Barbarossa campaign. Although the military leaders were asked to conduct an unprecedented war of annihilation against unarmed civilians, unlike any ever fought before on the European continent, they offered no protest.[2] On the contrary, they welcomed Hitler's views and, as Michael Burleigh observes, "hurried away to turn his words into legal forms, in so far as they had not independently initiated similar measures already."[3] Furthermore, Burleigh notes, in contrast to conflict that had appeared during the first weeks of the war in Poland, especially with regard to civilians, Operation Barbarossa would involve "early and harmonious cooperation between the military and the security forces."[4]

These developments were hardly surprising. Especially in eastern Europe, the German army became Hitler's army in every way, sharing his "values" and willingly

167

planning and participating in a *Vernichtungskrieg*. In the early postwar years, there was a strong tendency to distinguish between the SS and other organizations directly involved in the Final Solution, on the one hand, and the *Wehrmacht*, the regular German armed forces, on the other.[5] The latter allegedly fought a relatively honorable war. There were several motives for making this distinction: twenty million Germans had served in the armed forces, thirteen million of them in eastern Europe, where the worst atrocities were committed. The *Wehrmacht*, however, was not an organization separate from the German people; it was the German people in its most important wartime activity. Nevertheless, to indict the *Wehrmacht* as a criminal organization would have been tantamount to indicting the entire German people as criminal. This was impossible. There was no way both to punish the most populous nation in Europe apart from the USSR and at the same time to reintegrate it into the community of nations. While the International Military Tribunal (IMT) at Nuremberg was unwilling to condemn the *Wehrmacht* as a criminal organization, as it had the SS, the IMT did issue a scathing condemnation of the *Wehrmacht*'s officer corps:

> They have been responsible in large measure for the miseries and suffering that have fallen on millions of men, women and children. They have been a disgrace to the honorable profession of arms. Without their military guidance the aggressive ambitions of Hitler and his fellow Nazis would have been academic and sterile. . . .
> . . . When it suits their defence they say they had to obey; when confronted with Hitler's brutal crimes, which are said to have been within their general knowledge, they say they disobeyed. The truth is they actively participated in all these crimes, or sat silent and acquiescent, witnessing the commission of crimes on a scale larger and more shocking than the world has ever had the misfortune to know.[6]

A principal motive for exculpating the *Wehrmacht* was the growing conflict between the West and the Soviet Union and the Western powers' need to bring West Germany into the struggle against communism shortly after the end of World War II. Whatever their wartime misdeeds, former *Wehrmacht* officers were needed to establish what was now called the *Bundeswehr*. They were in a position to elicit from Chancellor Konrad Adenauer a statement insisting that the percentage of soldiers truly guilty of war crimes was so small that "the honor of the former German *Wehrmacht*" was untainted and that the "book must be closed once and for all on the issue of the collective guilt of former professional soldiers."[7]

Largely through the recent work of German scholars, a fuller picture has emerged. We know much more about the *Wehrmacht*'s extensive involvement in the mass murder of Jews and other unarmed civilians in the East who were regarded by the Germans as their racial inferiors.[8] Especially noteworthy has been the work of the *Militärgeschichtliches Forschungsamt* (Institute for Military History). Since 1979 leading scholars in the field have has been producing an extensive series of volumes on the Third Reich and World War II.[9] In addition, the

*Wehrmacht*'s murderous activity has been dramatically documented by an exhibition sponsored by the Hamburg (Germany) Institute for Social Research. Entitled "The German Army and Genocide: Crimes against War Prisoners, Jews, and Other Civilians, 1939–1944," this exhibit opened in Hamburg in March 1995 and traveled to more than thirty cities in Germany and Austria.[10] It consisted of more than a thousand photographs of torture, hangings, and mass shootings. Eighty percent of these photos were taken by German soldiers. The exhibit also contained letters and diary entries from soldiers who described matter-of-factly the mass murders they had committed. A typical example is the 5 October 1941 diary entry of army corporal Richard Heidenreich, who was stationed in Belorussia at the time:

> There were approximately 1,000 Jews in the village of Krupka and all of them had to be shot today. . . . After roll call, the column marched to the nearest swamp. The Jews had been told that they were all to be deported to Germany to work. But many of them guessed what was in store for them. . . . When we arrived at the swamp, they were ordered to sit down facing the direction from which they had come. 50 meters farther was a deep ditch full of water. The first ten had to undress to the waist. Then they had to climb down into the ditch and those of us who were to shoot them stood on the edge above them. . . . There were ten shots, ten Jews were mowed down. This went on until all were finished off. . . . The children clung to their mothers, wives to their husbands.[11]

The exhibition also gave evidence that German army units had been directed to destroy Jewish communities. Doubt concerning the *Wehrmacht*'s direct participation in the Holocaust was no longer possible. The exhibition was viewed by more than a million people. Understandably, it aroused bitter controversy. The facts concerning German army behavior had long been known to historians but not to the general public, which had believed that the *Wehrmacht*, with few exceptions, had behaved honorably during the war. Many Germans found it difficult to accept that what happened in the war was not only a military defeat but, much worse, a moral disaster.[12]

## THE *WEHRMACHT* IN SERBIA

The conduct of the *Wehrmacht* in Serbia provides an instructive example for our understanding of the war of annihilation that was rapidly approaching in 1941. On 6 April 1941, only a week after Hitler described the war that Germany would wage against the Soviet Union, the Germans—accompanied by Italian troops and then by Hungarian and Bulgarian units—invaded Yugoslavia, which was divided into two major areas.[13] On 10 April 1941 an "independent" Croatian state became Nazi Germany's ally.[14] By contrast, Serbia was occupied by the Germans and treated as an enemy state. In Serbia the *Wehrmacht*'s officers and enlisted men were predominantly Austrians. They were determined to punish the

Serbs, whom they blamed for having "started" World War I, which had ended with the destruction of the Austro-Hungarian empire.

Although the Germans controlled Serbia's urban areas, the German occupation was plagued persistently by partisan forces that controlled much of the countryside. The German response to partisan resistance was to kill hostages, especially Jews. During the summer of 1941, internment camps were set up in Belgrade and Sabac, and the military administration initiated a systematic roundup of all Jewish men as a preparatory step towards escalating the mass shooting.[15] Meanwhile, on 8 September 1941, the German Foreign Office Plenipotentiary in Belgrade, Felix Benzler, and Edmund Veesenmayer, a so-called "Jewish expert" attached to the Foreign Office, alleged that Jews had participated in sabotage and terrorism. They demanded that eight thousand Jews be removed from Serbia, perhaps placed on a barge and sent downstream on the Danube to the river delta in Romania. The proposal was rejected by Joachim von Ribbentrop, the German foreign minister, because of possible diplomatic problems with the Romanians.[16]

In mid-September 1941 Franz Böhme, an Austrian, arrived in Belgrade. Earlier that month he had been appointed commanding general, and all military and civilian organizations were placed under his command. To bring partisan resistance under control, he had been directed by Hitler to "restore order with the severest measures."[17] This directive was less than precise, but it gave Böhme leeway to proceed with no holds barred. Soon after he took command, a truck convoy from a German signal battalion was ambushed by Serb partisans on 2 October 1941. Twenty-one Germans were killed. Two days later Böhme ordered two *Wehrmacht* units to kill 2,100 men interned in the Sabac and Belgrade camps. Camp inmates were screened to make sure that only Jews and Gypsies were selected for execution. Böhme then ordered the "sudden" arrest of all Communists, suspected Communists, "all Jews," and some nationalist Serbs. They were to be held as additional hostages. In the event of further partisan actions that killed or wounded Germans, the hostages would be executed at the rate of one hundred for every German killed, fifty for every German wounded. Böhme specified that the *Wehrmacht was to be responsible for killing the hostages.* Preferably, the revenge would be taken by the unit that had suffered losses at the hands of the partisans. Böhme's detailed instructions, which differed only marginally from those given to the mobile killing squadrons (*Einsatzgruppen*) that would accompany the army's advance into Soviet territory, indicated that the shooting should be done at a range of eight to ten yards. To minimize "unnecessary touching of corpses," Böhme specified that the victims should kneel facing a previously prepared mass grave. As Hilberg puts the point, "[t]he army was now fully involved in the destruction process."[18] When asked whether women should be executed, Böhme said no, but, as we shall see, that reply did not mean that Jewish women and children were spared.

Partisan actions continued. The partisans were Serbs, but the selected hostages were Jews and Gypsies, who had not fought against the Germans. On 17 October 1941 Dr. Harald Turner, the head of the German military administration in Serbia and the official in charge of selecting the hostages and determining the time and place of execution, wrote privately to a friend, SS *Gruppenführer* Richard Hildenbrandt, laying out the real motives for the killings:

> I had 2,000 Jews and Gypsies shot during the last eight days in accordance with the quota 1:100 for bestially murdered German soldiers, and another 2,200, again almost exclusively Jews, will be shot in the next eight days. This is not a pretty business. At any rate, it has to be, if only to make clear to these people what it means to even attack a German soldier, and, for the rest, *the Jewish question solves itself most quickly this way.* (italics added)[19]

In July 1941 Hitler recognized that partisan warfare, troublesome though it was, had certain positive aspects. Addressing a conference of top leaders, he declared that partisan warfare "had its advantages: it gives us the opportunity to exterminate whatever stands in our way."[20] Over and over again, the *Wehrmacht* used the euphemism "antipartisan" to disguise its actions in the wholesale slaughter of innocent civilians. One army commander in Belorussia claimed to have shot 10,431 prisoners out of 10,940 taken in "battles with partisans" in the month of October 1941. The cost, he said, was only two German dead.[21]

Böhme's tour of duty in Serbia lasted from September to December 1941. During this period 160 *Wehrmacht* personnel were killed and 278 wounded. According to the official *Wehrmacht* count, there were 3,562 partisans killed in action and between 20,000 to 30,000 executed civilians, including nearly all adult male Jews and Gypsies.[22] This tally documented only one of many "antipartisan campaigns" that were in reality massacres of unarmed civilians.[23] Had the Germans engaged real partisans more extensively, their casualty rate would have been far higher.

Fifty years later some *Wehrmacht* veterans were still using the "antipartisan" excuse to justify their participation in the mass murder of unarmed civilians. As a young man, *Bundeswehr* General Jurgen Schreiber served as a *Luftwaffe* pilot in Serbia. When asked to comment on The German Army and Genocide exhibition shortly after its 1995 opening in Hamburg, Schreiber said, "That was a partisan war of particular ferocity, you know. It's a fact. You can't describe what we did as atrocities and ignore what the other side did to us."[24] Schreiber ignored the fact that the hostage killing was a cover for the extermination of Serbia's Jews and Gypsies, who had done nothing to the Germans.

At the beginning of 1942 Serbia's remaining Jewish population consisted of approximately seven thousand Jewish women, children, and old men. They were imprisoned in the Sajmište concentration camp. Guarded by men from an Order Police battalion (Reserve Police Battalion 64), the camp was situated in a former fairground across the Sava River from Belgrade. An additional five hundred younger Jewish men were also at Sajmište, having been spared from earlier executions and selected by the Germans to be part of the camp's "self-administration." The fate of these remaining Serbian Jews was sealed when

Turner requested that Berlin send a gas van to kill them. Except for Sundays, every day between March and May 1942 fifty to eighty women and children were told that they were being transported to a better camp. They were seated in the gas van and their baggage was placed in a separate truck. After a short drive the van stopped, and one of the two drivers pulled a switch that redirected exhaust fumes into the van's interior. As the van drove through the center of Belgrade to the Avala shooting range about nine miles south of the city, the Jews in the bus were asphyxiated. Work crews from a Belgrade prison, supervised by personnel from Reserve Police Battalion 64, buried the dead in pits that awaited them. When the killing operation was completed in the spring of 1942, the van was sent back to Berlin, where its killing efficiency was upgraded before it was sent to Belorussia for further killing actions against Jews, especially in the vicinity of Minsk.[25]

Meanwhile the *Wehrmacht*'s role in the coming war of extermination had been further amplified on 6 June 1941, sixteen days before the invasion of the Soviet Union, when the *Wehrmacht* High Command (*Oberkommando der Wehrmacht* [OKW]) issued special "guidelines for the treatment of political commissars," a decree that has come to be known as the infamous *Kommissarbefehl* (Commissar Order). Directly communicated in writing to a few senior army commanders and then passed orally down the chain of command, it included the following directions:

> In the struggle against Bolshevism, the enemy *cannot* be expected to behave according to the principles of humanity and international law. In particular, we can expect from the *political commissars of all types*—as actual bearers of resistance—hate-filled, cruel and inhuman treatment of our prisoners. . . . The initiators of barbaric, Asiatic methods of battle are the political commissars. . . . When captured in *battle* or *resistance*, therefore, they are to be shot at once. . . . Those taken prisoner will not be recognized as soldiers; the protection of POWs guaranteed by international war will not be accorded to them. After being separated from the others, they must be finished off.[26]

This order meant that the army would take on responsibilities akin to those of the *Einsatzgruppen*, especially when it became clear that *commissar* was a term whose meaning was scarcely different from *Jew*.

## OPERATION BARBAROSSA

Although the Germans had already ghettoized and killed tens of thousands of Jews in Poland after World War II began on 1 September 1939, the systematic annihilation of eastern European Jewry did not begin in earnest until the *Wehrmacht* attacked the Soviet Union on 22 June 1941. With an army of three million men and more than 3,500 tanks and assault weapons, the German drive to secure *Lebensraum* in the East rapidly took control of the Baltic states, Belorussia, and Ukraine. At first, German spirits and ambitions were high. By early autumn, Moscow itself seemed within reach, but already the earlier euphoria had diminished because the German offensive had been slowed by tough terrain, supply lines stretched thin, partisan raids behind the lines, and Soviet resistance. The Germans' situation would deteriorate further because in their confidence they had not prepared militarily to fight through a Russian winter.[27]

[*handwritten margin note: similar to WWI*]

In drawing up invasion and occupation plans for Operation Barbarossa, the German High Command knew that supply shortages would be a problem as the army moved into the vast territory of the USSR. Since Germany could not meet the food needs of its military forces during the Russian campaign, the planners decided that the Germans would confiscate the Russian food supply. On 23 May 1941 the economic policy guidelines of the Economic Organization in the East/Agricultural Group stated, "Many tens of millions of people will become superfluous in this region and will die or have to emigrate to Siberia." The guidelines rejected the idea that the conquered eastern regions could be fed with food from Ukraine, the Soviet breadbasket. Such food was to be used for the German army. Hermann Göring later explained the consequences of this policy: "This year, 20 to 30 million people in Russia will starve. Perhaps this is a good thing, as certain people must be decimated."[28] Vast population decimation—in this case by calculated starvation—had become an increasingly acceptable problem-solving tool not only for the SS but for the German military and civilian leadership as well.[29] Moreover, those who were prepared to initiate cold-blooded measures resulting in the death of twenty to thirty million people in the Soviet Union would have no reason to pause when it came to the mass murder of Jews.

As the German *Blitzkrieg* swept through Soviet territory during the early summer of 1941, it was accompanied by four relatively small, highly mobile *Einsatzgruppen* (attack or task groups). In Hitler's war of annihilation, their responsibility quickly escalated beyond seizing and killing the "Jewish-Bolshevik" leadership.[30] Heydrich's directives included instructions that "anti-Communist or anti-Jewish elements in the newly occupied territory" were to be "secretly encouraged" to instigate pogroms against local Jews.[31] Much more than that, within a few weeks Jews in general—women and children as well as men—had become the *Einsatzgruppen*'s targets in mass shootings. Before the *Einsatzgruppen* were disbanded in 1943 and steps were taken to obliterate the mass graves that marked their lethal work, these units—joined by native collaborators and local police in the occupied territories, as well as by units of the German Order Police—were the main perpetrators of the Holocaust prior to the establishment of major killing centers on Polish soil in 1942.

The personnel for each *Einsatzgruppe* numbered about 500 to 1000. Functioning under Heydrich's RSHA authority, and with clear understanding about their relation to and independence from the army, these battalion-sized task forces were subdivided into smaller operational units called *Einsatzkommando*s and *Sonderkommando*s and then strategically deployed from north to south on the eastern front—from the Baltic to the Caucasus. For example, *Einsatzgruppe* A, the largest of the four, led killing operations in the Baltic region. Its personnel consisted of an amalgam of the *Waffen*-SS (34 percent), Gestapo (9 percent), Criminal Police or "Kripo" (4.1 percent), Order Police (*Ordnungspolizei*) (13.4 percent), non-German auxiliaries such as Lithuanians, Latvians, and Ukrainians (8.8 percent), Security Police (*Sicherheitsdienst* or SD) (3.5 percent), and motorcycle, technical, and administrative personnel, including radio and teletype operators (27.2 percent).[32]

In addition to *Einsatzgruppe* A, which was led by SS-*Brigadeführer* (Brigadier General) Franz Walter Stahlecker, the basic deployment of these task forces was as follows: for White Russia or Belorussia, *Einsatzgruppe* B under SS-*Brigadeführer* Arthur Nebe; for the north and central Ukraine, *Einsatzgruppe* C under SS-*Brigadeführer* Dr. Otto Rasch; for the southern Ukraine, the Crimea, and the Caucusus, *Einsatzgruppe* D under SS-*Standartenführer* (Colonel) Otto Ohlendorf. The *Einsatzgruppen* had been assembled quickly, but decisions about the leadership had been taken deliberately. Most came from the SD and were predominantly respectable, well-educated, upper-middle-class professionals. They were not bloodthirsty killers, certainly not the scum of German society or even career SS men. Some were chosen by Heydrich because they had been members of SS auxiliaries who regarded their SS affiliation as an effortless, part-time avocation that could help them advance their civilian careers. Heydrich wanted to teach intellectuals such as Ohlendorf that membership in the SS was no "honorary" sideline. The commander of *Einsatzgruppe* D, Ohlendorf had studied at universities in Leipzig, Göttingen, and Pavia and held a doctorate in jurisprudence. In civilian life he had been research director of the Institute for World Economy and Maritime Transport in Kiel.[33] Several *Einsatzgruppe* leaders were lawyers. One, Ernst Biberstein, had been a Lutheran pastor. For the most part, these murderers were a representative cross section of well-educated, respectable Germans in the Third Reich.[34] Their superior educations did not prevent them from becoming mass murderers. After the war, they insisted that they were honorable citizens who had only done their duty when the order to exterminate the Jews was the law of the land. Recent research also shows that, distasteful though the bloody process may have been, there was considerable enthusiasm for the indiscriminate killing of Jews.[35]

It would have been impossible for the *Einsatzgruppen* to conduct so monumental a series of killing operations within a war zone without the wholehearted approval and cooperation of the military authorities, especially in the initial stages of a gargantuan, surprise invasion. When the Germans prepared to invade the Soviet Union, the *Wehrmacht* High Command agreed on the Army's close cooperation with the *Einsatzgruppen*. According to the agreement, "within the framework of their instructions" the *Einsatzgruppen* were "entitled to carry out executive measures against the civilian population."[36] The army would control the movement of the *Einsatzgruppen* as the front advanced. "Functional directives," what the units were actually ordered to do, would come from Heydrich, and the military agreed to provide the *Einsatzgruppen* with logistical support— food, quarters, fuel, communications—so that the work could be accomplished.

In addition to facilitating the efforts of the *Einsatzgruppen*, the *Wehrmacht* often went out of its way to turn over Jews to the *Einsatzgruppen* and to request their speedy dispatch. Moreover, the army frequently participated in the killing. German military leaders fully understood the *Einsatzgruppen*'s mission, agreed to it, and helped to move the process along. The extermination program was popular with the generals. When Heinrich Himmler addressed three hundred generals, admirals, and general staff officers in Posen, which was then part of the Reich, on 26 January 1944, he announced that the Führer's orders for the Final Solution to the Jewish problem had been carried out and "there no longer is a Jewish question." Save for five officers, all three hundred joined in applause.[37]

The *Einsatzgruppen* entered the Soviet Union on 23 June 1941, the day after the German invasion began. Some 500,000 Jews would be killed during the remainder of that year alone, but the death toll was limited to about 50,000 until a radical escalation took place in mid-August. Taking these facts into account, most contemporary scholars agree on two fundamental points: First, the mass murder of Soviet Jews in 1941 did not mean that the Final Solution for all European Jews was under way simultaneously. One step was leading to another, but the *Einsatzgruppen* were operating on a regional basis. Continental plans incorporating killing centers equipped with gas chambers had not yet been developed. Second, most, though not all, contemporary scholars believe that the decision to murder every last man, woman, and child among Soviet Jewry, with the temporary exception of skilled workers deemed indispensable, was not taken until some time after the initial German invasion. As Christopher Browning puts the point:

> On the empirical side, it is generally accepted that in the first weeks of Operation Barbarossa the Jewish victims were primarily adult male Jews, and that beginning in late July—at different times in different places at different rates—the killing was gradually expanded to encompass all Jews except indispensable workers—a process that was nearly complete in the Baltic by the end of the year but not yet elsewhere on occupied Soviet territory until 1942.[38]

There are, however, continuing debates concerning this murderous escalation. Did it result from the euphoria that attended early German victories, or did it reflect German frustration as Operation Barbarossa's logistical problems mounted? In addition, was the escalation clearly ordered from the top, did it evolve on a more decentralized basis, or does a credible account depend on some combination of those factors?

## THE ASSAULT ON THE JEWS OF LITHUANIA AND LATVIA

As one considers the annihilation of Jews in Soviet territory, what happened in Lithuania and Latvia is instructive. Lithuania, a Baltic country adjacent to both Germany and occupied Poland, had been part of the czarist empire until it was

occupied by Germany in 1915 during World War I. Proclaiming its independence in 1918, Lithuania remained independent until 1939. In accordance with
the secret agreement between Germany and the Soviet Union, Lithuania fell into
the Soviet sphere of influence. These dealings meant that Lithuania regained
some territory from Poland, including the city of Vilna and its surroundings. Vil-
nius, as the Lithuanians called it, had a long and rich Jewish tradition and was
called the Jerusalem of Lithuania. Its Jewish population of 75,000 raised the total
for Lithuanian Jewry to about 250,000. In October 1939 Soviet military bases
were established on Lithuanian soil. By mid-summer 1940 the USSR had annexed
the country. Kovno (Kaunas) had been the capital of independent Lithuania, but
now Vilna supplanted it. The German invasion of the Soviet Union included
Lithuania, which the Germans quickly occupied.

Attacking the Lithuanian town of Gargždai on 22 June 1941, the Germans
met resistance. Approximately one hundred German soldiers lost their lives. The
town had three thousand inhabitants, of whom one thousand were Jews. The
Germans accused the Jews of fighting for the Soviet Union. Subsequently, on 24
June, according to Christoph Dieckmann, the "first killings of Jews in the German-occupied Soviet Union took place" when two hundred men were killed
under the direction of German police with active Lithuanian cooperation.[39] Similar actions followed over the next four weeks. By 18 July 1941, the death toll had
risen to more than 3,300.

These initial killings were only the beginning. Kovno, for example, had forty
thousand Jews, about a quarter of the city's total population. The historian Ulrich
Herbert reports that when the Germans occupied Kovno on 24 June, "a dreadful bloodbath began that all but defies description."[40] Lithuanian nationalists
welcomed the Germans as liberators who were freeing them from Soviet oppression, which, the nationalists believed, had been supported by Lithuanian Jewry.
Thus the Lithuanian nationalists responded enthusiastically when the Germans
gave them carte blanche to chase Jews through the streets and slay hundreds of
their number while crowds, including children, gathered to enjoy the spectacle
and cheer on the perpetrators.[41] Shortly thereafter the Germans brought seven
thousand Jews to the Seventh Fort, one of a series of military installations constructed in the nineteenth century for the city's protection. On the pretext that
they were Jewish Bolsheviks, the Germans and their Lithuanian collaborators
killed most of the men in the next few days. The remaining Kovno Jews, some
thirty thousand, were ghettoized by mid-summer. With constraints on food supplies as a critical factor, the Germans decided in August 1941 that, with the exception of productive Jewish workers, it was better to kill the Lithuanian Jews than
to waste scarce resources by feeding them at even a meager level. By late October
1941 the Germans' *Einsatzgruppen* units, with help from local auxiliaries, had
killed more than ninety thousand Lithuanian Jews, including some twelve thousand from the Kovno ghetto.[42] About fifteen thousand Lithuanian Jews had fled
east to escape the German invasion in June 1941. Excluding that number, the

Germans and their local collaborators murdered almost 90 percent of Lithuanian Jewry during the Holocaust.

Situated north of Lithuania in the Baltic region, Latvia had also been an independent republic after World War I. Like Lithuania, it was annexed to the Soviet Union in the summer of 1940. When the Germans invaded on 22 June 1941, about seventy thousand Jews—living mainly in Riga, the country's capital—remained in Latvia.[43] Only about three thousand would survive the Holocaust.

Almost immediately after the German invasion, a Latvian *Sonderkommando* was organized to do much of the killing for the *Einsatzgruppe* in that country. The Latvians' motivation was analogous to the Lithuanians': Jews were suspect; their pro-Soviet leanings deserved retribution. On 2 July 1941 Stahlecker, the commander of *Einsatzgruppe* A, appointed a 31-year-old Latvian, Viktors Arajs, to head the indigenous *Sonderkommando*. Arajs recruited about three hundred men from the Latvian police and military. Under German supervision, they proceeded to shoot Jews at killing pits in the Bikernieki Forest, about four miles from the center of Riga. Twice a week the Latvian unit would depart from its headquarters about 3:00 A.M., seize victims at their homes, and take them to the killing pits. Alcohol was liberally distributed to the shooters when the day's killing was completed. Between July and September 1941 Arajs's Latvian killers accumulated a body count of about four thousand Jews and a thousand Communists.[44]

Arajs and his men also worked in outlying districts. When not occupied in Riga itself, they would board blue city buses, travel to Latvian villages, and murder Jewish men, women, and children. The killing was preceded by a census, usually ordered by the Latvian district police chief. Once the Jews were identified, they were methodically shot to death at the edge of burial pits throughout rural Latvia. The work done by the Latvians was important to the German effort to render Latvia *judenrein*, but by no means did it replace what was done by the German *Einsatzgruppen* units themselves. With help from their Latvian collaborators, the sweeps through the countryside conducted by Stahlecker's killing squadrons took the lives of more than twenty-three thousand Jews in outlying Latvian provinces in 1941 alone.

## KILLING PATTERNS

About four million Jews lived in the western Soviet Union when the Germans invaded in June 1941. Approximately 1.5 million of them escaped the German advance, leaving some 2.5 million to face the onslaught that followed. When the German army launched its surprise attack, the accompanying units of the *Einsatzgruppen* and Order Police rapidly rolled six hundred miles east. However, the farther into the interior the Germans penetrated, the fewer Jews they found. The majority of the Jews under Soviet control lived in the western regions of Belorussia, in Ukraine, and in the Baltic states. In the beginning, the *Einsatzgruppen* strategy had been to get to Jewish communities and seal their fate before the victims knew what was happening, but there was an unintended consequence of the speed of the German advance: the mobile killing squadrons inevitably bypassed many Jewish communities. Already in September 1941 the Germans realized that the Jews could not be killed in a single sweep. In spite of the huge number of Jews they had murdered thus far—some 500,000 by late 1941—hundreds of thousands remained alive in the newly conquered regions.

Following a pattern already in effect in Poland, the Germans decided that the surviving Jews would be concentrated in ghettos, where those capable of working for the *Wehrmacht* would be put to work, albeit under abusive conditions calculated to kill off as many as possible through starvation, cold, and disease. In the ghettos the Germans required the Jews to establish *Judenräte* (Jewish councils), to whom they gave the task of controlling the inner workings of the impoverished community. Ghettoization facilitated German control so that they could expropriate at will whatever property remained in Jewish hands and assure the Jews' availability when the decision to finish the killing was put into effect.

By the summer of 1942 a second sweep of killing in the eastern territories was under way, but it did not start concurrently in every region. To draw again on Browning's formulation, the second killing sweep began "at different times in different places at different rates" in late 1941 and early 1942. Once under way, it was more lethal than the first. Often through "ghetto clearing" operations, most of the Jews in German-occupied Soviet territory had been killed by the end of 1942. Adding together the body counts from the first and second sweeps, the total of Jewish deaths from these mass shootings exceeded 1.3 million.

During the second wave of killing, the *Einsatzgruppen's* role remained important, but the roles of the Order Police battalions expanded significantly. With German personnel stretched thin, essential contributions were also made by local collaborators. Having noted the *Einsatzgruppen's* success in obtaining local cooperation, Himmler gave orders on 25 July 1941 that reliable indigenous forces should be organized. During the next several months, with the Order Police facilitating the formation of such units from the Baltic states and Belorussia to Ukraine and the Crimea, the Germans had little difficulty obtaining the help they required from the collaborationist *Schutzmannschaft*. According to the historian Martin Dean, its strength "increased dramatically during the course of 1942 from 33,000 to some 300,000 men."[45] Under German supervision, the *Schutzmannschaft* had various branches—firefighters, for example—but its policing functions were of special importance. In that capacity, Dean has shown, the *Schutzmänner* played indispensable parts in the killing process. Motivated by opportunism and peer pressure as well as by antisemitism—the factors varying in importance from man to man—they rounded up Jews, served as guards at shootings, and engaged in killing outright.

From Riga and Kovno to Kiev and Odessa, all along the vast wartime front created by the German invasion, the sites of Jewish massacres in 1941–42 could be found. One of the worst of the mass killings took place on 29–30 September

1941 at a ravine called Babi Yar. Shortly after the Germans captured Kiev, the Ukrainian capital, units from *Einsatzgruppe* C slaughtered more than 33,000 Jews. The process employed there and elsewhere indicated that, early on, the killing operations were developing standardized patterns. With adaptations to fit local circumstances, they would repeat themselves again and again in the waves of killing in 1941 and 1942.[46]

Once the Jews had been identified, rounded up, and selected for killing, they were transported or marched to a ravine, antitank ditch, shell crater, or some other mass grave site, which sometimes was dug by the victims themselves. Attempts, not always successful, were made to close off the sites to outsiders. The victims were stripped of their valuables and clothes, lined up along the edge of the mass grave, and shot with submachine guns or other small weapons. *Genickschüssen* (neck shots) from behind at close range were preferred by some commanders, but others preferred massed fire from a greater distance. The dead or the nearly dead would fall into the graves.

In the western Ukraine, SS General Friedrich Jeckeln noticed that the haphazard arrangement of the corpses meant an inefficient use of burial space. More graves would have to be dug than absolutely necessary. Jeckeln solved the problem. He told a colleague at one of the Ukrainian killing sites, "Today we'll stack them like sardines."[47] Jeckeln called his solution *Sardinenpackung* (sardine packing). When this method was employed, the victims climbed into the grave and lay down on the bottom. Cross fire from above dispatched them. Then another batch of victims was ordered into the grave, positioning themselves on top of the corpses in a head-to-foot configuration. They too were killed by cross fire from above. The procedure continued until the grave was full. A variety of other methods took the lives of Jews in the eastern territories—Jews were killed in mobile gas vans, in buildings set ablaze, by drowning—but shooting procedures were the most widespread during the *Einsatzgruppen* and Order Police activities in 1941 and 1942.

There are many testimonies about these mass murders. We cite one from Latvia. It describes what happened on 30 November 1941 outside of Riga. Under the direction of Friedrich Jeckeln, whose killing achievements in the Ukraine led Himmler to transfer him to Latvia to speed up the elimination of Jews in that area, thirteen thousand Jews were murdered in a single day. Following that slaughter, another ten thousand Jews were cut down by Jeckeln and his men on 8 December. The "sardine packing" method used by Jeckeln in the Ukraine was equally efficient in these Latvian massacres. For his achievements, Himmler awarded Jeckeln a promotion on 11 December. The following account makes clear that the killing process, which proceeded without regard for the victims' age or gender, had a rationalized, assembly-line character.

> The columns of Jews advancing from Riga, comprising about one thousand persons each, were herded into the cordon, which was formed in such a way that it narrowed greatly as it continued into the woods, where the pits lay. The Jews first of all had to deposit their luggage before they entered the copse; permission to carry these articles had only been granted to give the Jews the

impression that they were taking part in a resettlement. As they progressed, they had to deposit their valuables in wooden boxes, and, little by little, their clothing—first overcoats, then suits, dresses, and shoes, down to their under-clothes, all placed in distinct piles according to the type of clothing.

On this particular day (30 November 1941), the air temperature in Riga, measured at two meters above ground, was −7.5°C at 7:00 A.M., −1.1°C at 1:00 P.M., and 1.9°C at 9:00 P.M. On the previous evening, 29 November 1941, there had been an average snowfall of seven centimeters. On 30 November between 7:00 A.M. and 9:00 P.M., it did not snow.

Stripped down to their underclothes, the Jews had to move forward along the narrow path in a steady flow toward the pits, which they entered by a ramp, in single file and in groups of ten. Occasionally the flow would come to a standstill when someone tarried at one of the undressing points; or else, if the undressing went faster than expected, or if the columns advanced too quickly from the city, too many Jews would arrive at the pits at once. In such cases, the supervisors stepped in to ensure a steady and mod-erate flow, since it was feared that the Jews would grow edgy if they had to linger in the immediate vicinity of the pits. . . . In the pits the Jews had to lie flat, side by side, face down. They were killed with a single bullet in the neck, the marksmen standing at close range—at the smaller pits, on the perimeter; at the large pit, inside the pit itself—their semi-automatic pistols set for single fire. To make the best of available space, and particularly of the gaps between bodies, the victims next in line had to lie down on top of those who had been shot immediately before them. The handicapped, the aged, and the young were helped into the pits by the sturdier Jews, laid by them on top of the bodies, and then shot by marksmen who in the large pit actu-ally stood on the dead. In this way the pits gradually filled.[48]

Earlier we noted that more than twenty-three thousand Jews were murdered in rural locations in Latvia.[49] Richard Rhodes argues that the subject of the sys-tematic killing of Jews in the rural areas of eastern Europe has "hardly been exam-ined in the literature of the Holocaust."[50] For decades, he suggests, the relevant material was to be found in Soviet archives that were unavailable to Western scholars during the Cold War. Nevertheless, Rhodes comments that "maps in Jewish museums from Riga to Odessa confirm that almost every village and town in the entire sweep of the Eastern territories had a killing site nearby." His obser-vation highlights an important issue concerning the way the Holocaust has been understood. For many years, scholars, including the authors of this volume, have tended to emphasize the depersonalized, rationalized, industrial character of the Holocaust with its death camps and their gas chambers. Even the title of this book, *Approaches to Auschwitz*, exemplifies that trend to some extent, for Auschwitz was the installation at which the greatest number of victims was mur-dered in large-scale gas chambers.

According to Michael Mann, the Nazi regime killed "approximately twenty million unarmed persons" during its twelve years in power, most during the last four years.[51] In many, if not most, cases this meant pointing a gun at an unarmed person who was often forced to disrobe completely and then stand on the edge of a pit into which he or she would fall when shot, or lie down in a pit, one body atop another, to await the final blow. Daniel Goldhagen's *Hitler's Willing Executioners* remains controversial because of his claims concerning the degree to which the vast majority of Germans welcomed the Nazis' genocidal project. Nevertheless, even if they do not agree with all of his depressing findings, many scholars share Steven Aschheim's view that Goldhagen deserves credit for reminding us "that millions of people were murdered outside of the death camps, and that the dominant image of depersonalized, bureaucratic industrial murder tends to underplay the importance of the perpetrators themselves."[52]

Rhodes argues that the "gas chambers and crematoria of the death camps have come to typify the Holocaust, but in fact they were exceptional. The primary means of mass murder the Nazis deployed during the Second World War was firearms and lethal deprivation."[53] At least in part, he overstates the case, but Rhodes's point is still on target. Shooting was no less lethal than gas, but it was less efficient in the sense that shooting was harder on the perpetrators' nerves. Gassing came to be preferred because it made it easier for the killers to kill. But here again, decisions were made in fits and starts; developments took place partly by trial and error. For example, in mid-August 1941 Heinrich Himmler visited Minsk, the Belorussian capital, where *Einsatzgruppe* B worked under the command of Arthur Nebe, who was responsible for more than forty-five thousand Jewish deaths in Belorussia.[54] Himmler asked to see a killing action. As *Einsatzkommando* 8 and Police Battalion 9 did the dirty work, the SS leader became increasingly uncomfortable. Noticing Himmler's distress, SS General Erich von dem Bach-Zelewski pointed out that the killing was devastating the killers. "These men," he said, "are finished (*fertig*) for the rest of their lives."[55] At the operation's conclusion, Himmler spoke to the men, stressing that the German cause required carrying out repulsive duties. Perhaps they had noticed his own revulsion, he said, but the important thing was to understand the necessity for the killing and to do one's duty. Meanwhile, Himmler assured them, their consciences could be relieved because he and Hitler took full responsibility for the necessary killing. Later, after visiting an asylum in Minsk where he ordered the patients' death, Himmler asked Nebe to consider killing methods that might be more humane for the killers. Nebe suggested that dynamite be used on the mental patients. Himmler agreed, but when this experiment was tried, the results were disastrous. Only somewhat more successful were the gas vans that by early 1942 had been sent to each of the *Einsatzgruppen*. Their reliability and capacity were too small for the expanding job of killing the Jews in the eastern territories. Even beyond the psychological disadvantages that Himmler had witnessed at Minsk, shootings carried out by mobile killing units had their limitations, for by 1942 the broadening scope of the killing project was assuming continental proportions that the mobile units could not handle. In addition to sending mobilized killing squadrons to the victims, Jews would be transported to stationary killing centers whose gas chambers—reflecting killing patterns from the Nazis' euthanasia program—could destroy Jews from all over the European continent and with less stress and strain on the killers in the process.

## "A QUESTION OF EXISTENCE"

Back in mid-June 1941, Heinrich Himmler had called his trusted SS and police leaders to a three-day meeting at Wewelsburg, a renovated castle that served as a conference and "spiritual" center for the SS elite. There he spoke about Operation Barbarossa. "It is a question of existence," he told his men, "thus it will be a racial struggle of pitiless severity, in the course of which 20 to 30 million Slavs and Jews will perish through military actions and crises of food supply."[56] Himmler's forecast was apt, not because events unfolded entirely as he envisioned them, but because the Germans' military plans for the invasion of the Soviet Union proved to be hopelessly unrealistic. For one thing, the Germans were so confident that the war would end speedily that they vastly underestimated the Red Army's equipment and its fighting ability. The German plans did not reckon on the possibility that the Red Army would be able to regroup and offer effective long-term resistance after the devastating initial attack.[57] When the war dragged on into the winter of 1941–42, the bitter cold of the Russian winter intensified the difficulties faced by the lightly clad German troops. In their arrogance, ignorance, and overconfidence, Hitler and the German military leaders had committed their nation to a monumental struggle that would prove disastrous. But the Jews especially would feel the ensuing fury.

The German invasion of the Soviet Union escalated Jewish death as, first, Jewish men were targeted and then—as summer passed and autumn arrived—all Jews in the eastern territories were increasingly decimated. Among the factors contributing to the escalation were military security and the issue of supplies.[58] As we have seen, the German planners expected to solve the army's shortages of grain, oil, and other supplies by requisitioning Soviet resources in the full knowledge that "many tens of millions of Soviet citizens would starve to death." Even before the invasion, those responsible for supplying the *Wehrmacht* knew that shortly after the invasion began, two-thirds of the entire invading force would no longer be able to rely on provisions from Germany.[59] The military situation was further complicated because the Germans could gain a decisive victory only by a *Blitzkrieg*, a lightning war, in which Panzer or attacking tank groups raced ahead of the main body of the army and inflicted crippling blows on the enemy. However, the rapidly advancing Panzer groups experienced far more serious supply problems than had been anticipated. Russian roads were in terrible shape, and it was impossible for the Panzer units to live off the land as planned, for hostile populations behind the German lines, as well as resistance ahead of the German advance, robbed the German troops of precious resources.

By the end of July, the entire German war effort appeared to be endangered by the supply problem. In some regions, famine was developing.[60] Although that outcome was intended by the Germans with their live-off-the-land policy, there were unintended consequences, because the supplies on which the Germans had counted were dwindling for them as well. By the end of July the Reich leadership recognized that Operation Barbarossa would not produce a quick victory. At the end of that month, about the time that he authorized Heydrich to explore possibilities for "the Final Solution of the Jewish question," Göring ordered that "agricultural products in the occupied regions of the East" be distributed solely to German troops, save for "those people performing important tasks for Germany."[61] As Christoph Dieckmann has pointed out, those unable to work for the German war industry were now subject to a merciless starvation policy. Even for those who could do the work that the German war machine required, Jews would be supplied only if there were sufficient stocks to meet the needs of the non-Jewish population.

Dieckmann argues persuasively that supply and security problems were central in decisions to kill all Jews in the eastern territories, a policy that was widely implemented by the late summer of 1941.[62] Such arguments, however, do not mean that there would have been no overall plan to kill the Soviet Jews—and, indeed, Jews everywhere—had the military and supply situation been more favorable to the Germans. Had Germany won the war, the Jews, if not killed outright, would have been deported to eastern regions of the former Soviet Union that would have assured their decimation and ultimate annihilation. The Nazis' racist antisemitism would have seen to that.

With increasingly difficult regional situations provoking it, the systematic mass murder of Soviet Jewry that was under way by mid-August 1941 was a process so vast in scope that, as Dieckmann also persuasively argues, Hitler's authorization for it would have been required. Under the circumstances, that authorization was to be expected. Although they would revive for a time in the autumn of 1941, military circumstances were calling Hitler's war aims into question. Instead of a quick victory in the East, which would give him control of the European continent, hopefully bringing the United Kingdom into Germany's orbit and preventing the United States from intervening, Hitler faced a war of attrition that could drag on and leave Germany disadvantaged, as it had been in World War I.

The mass killing of Soviet Jewry, save for those who could do productive work for the Third Reich, was regional policy in the summer of 1941 and not yet an aim whose scope was continental. But in the context of a brutal war, the killing of Jews had escalated and radicalized. In late 1941 and early 1942, those developments intensified. Nazi Germany's "Final Solution of the Jewish question" would soon be in full cry.

# Chapter 8

# "Priority over All Other Matters"

*The Jewish question takes priority over all other matters.*

Adolf Hitler

While the Germans continued their eastward advance into Soviet territory during October 1941, the appearance of a quick and decisive victory turned into reality of a different kind. Hitler confidently watched his armies draw closer to Moscow, but by 8 October, as *Wehrmacht* officer Siegfried Knappe sized up the situation, "the earth was simply a quagmire of mud."[1] Conditions deteriorated further for the Germans in the closing months of 1941. Moscow did not fall, and Nazi Germany's military plans were complicated by the Japanese, who attacked the American base at Pearl Harbor on 7 December. The Americans officially went to war with Japan one day later. Declaring war against the United States on 11 December, the Third Reich would face a life-or-death struggle on two fronts.

Although prospects for a bleaker 1942 loomed larger for Hitler as 1941 came to an end, his changing disposition did nothing to favor the Jews. Feasting on his success in the early weeks of Operation Barbarossa, an optimistic Hitler could authorize mass murder in the East but bide his time on the Jewish question overall, perhaps waiting even until complete military victory was his to answer it fully. But as circumstances literally and figuratively became "a quagmire of mud," a more paranoid mood came to the fore. With war bogging down and concurrently expanding in truly global proportions, Hitler found the Jews more threatening than ever. Unless he answered the Jewish question sooner rather than later, all might be lost.

During an October 1941 meeting, when he received complaints that Jewish deportations were interfering with military rail transport, Hitler replied that "the Jewish question takes priority over all other matters."[2] Whether that comment reflected Hitler's euphoria, his premonition that not everything was going his way, or some conflicted combination of the two remains a matter of scholarly debate and conjecture. In any case, "taking priority" awaited clarification. Why that was the case and how the major ambiguities were resolved are also among the matters on which scholars do not agree. Research on these issues is ongoing. Here we illustrate, sift, and sort some of the major evidence available at the time of this writing.

## FATEFUL DECISIONS: WHO TOOK THEM AND WHEN?

In the summer of 1941, when the Germans began to murder Jewish women and children as well as men in the occupied Soviet territories, no overall decision had yet been taken concerning the fate of the Jews in Germany and the other nations of western Europe. As noted earlier, several schemes had been put forth concerning where the Jews might be sent, including the Lublin region, Madagascar, and the farther reaches of the conquered Soviet Union. By the end of November 1941 mass killing in the East had been radicalized and extended by shooting squadrons and gas vans. Later there will be much more to say about Auschwitz, but in that place gassing experiments using a pesticide called Zyklon B had been carried out on Soviet prisoners of war in September 1941. Construction of killing centers on Polish soil at Belzec and Chelmno was under way. Whether those developments reflected regional or continental objectives remains an issue in discussion about the fateful decisions taken by Nazi leaders in 1941 and 1942.

In 1977 the prominent German scholar Martin Broszat took the functionalist position that "no comprehensive general order for extermination existed at all. Rather, the 'program' for Jewish extermination evolved gradually out of individual actions in the framework of institutions and realities until the spring of 1942 and obtained its determining character after the establishment of the extermination camps in Poland (between December 1941 and 1942)."[3] Agreeing with Broszat, Götz Aly holds that "the practice of extermination was applied experimentally" until April 1942.[4] Aly emphasizes that there were very real conflicts of interest between powerful Nazi figures and their respective institutions. Mass murder of the Jews became one way to solve them. The conflict between Heinrich Himmler and Hans Frank illustrates Aly's point. Himmler wanted Jews out of the Warthegau. After the war in the East began to go badly, the only place to which they could be deported was the General Government, but Frank did not want to accept them because of resource limitations and because he saw them as undesirables. Mass murder could relax the tension between the two Nazi leaders by satisfying them both. Aly further stresses that there was no explicit order from Hitler (*Führerbefehl*) concerning the extermination of the Jews. "The 'Final Solution,'" he writes, "was not ordered, it was not drawn up by this 'architect' or the other. What mattered was arriving at a consensus in the decision situation."[5] Hitler's role, concludes Aly, should not be regarded "as that of an unrelenting commander but rather that of a politician who left his followers considerable room, encouraged them to let their imagination roam in order to make the impossible possible—and who backed them unconditionally."[6]

Views such as Broszat's and Aly's rightly stress that plans for the "Final Solution" evolved over time and that competition among Hitler's followers played a key part in the unfolding of the destruction process. On the other hand, their outlooks downplay Hitler's role to such an extent that they do not concur with the scholarly currents that have become more dominant. Browning, for example, argues that the Final Solution decision arose out of "two peaks of victory euphoria" in the summer and autumn of 1941 that engendered in Hitler and his acolytes the conviction that nothing could prevent them from carrying out their most radical plans. According to Browning, "in mid-July 1941 Hitler instigated Himmler and Heydrich to undertake what amounted to a 'feasibility study' for the mass murder of European Jews and in early October 1941 he shared with Himmler and Heydrich his approval of their proposal to deport the Jews of Europe to killing centers in the east."[7]

Dated 31 July 1941 and signed by Göring, a written authorization prepared by Heydrich instructed him to send to Göring "in the near future, an overall plan covering the organizational, technical and material measures necessary for accomplishment of the final solution of the Jewish question which we desire."[8] This authorization was not yet a decision, let alone an order, to destroy all Europe's Jews, but Browning stresses that it did refer to what the Göring/Heydrich document called "a complete solution of the Jewish question within the German sphere of influence in Europe." That language made no distinction between Jews in Germany and western Europe and those in the East. By late August 1941, moreover, Heydrich's close associate Adolf Eichmann significantly changed the language he used to reject requests concerning Jewish emigration. Instead of referring simply to "the imminent Final Solution," Eichmann indicated that it was "now in preparation." Eichmann understood that the situation had become more ominous for all European Jews.

Previously, Hitler had rejected proposals to deport German Jews until "after the war," but, as Browning further underscores, on 16 and 17 September 1941 Hitler indicated to Himmler and other Nazi leaders that he wanted the Jews of Germany proper, the "Old Reich," as well as those in the protectorate of Bohemia-Moravia, to be removed as soon as possible.[9] After a month's delay, deportation of Reich Jews began on 15 October. Three days later, on 18 October, Himmler ordered an end to Jewish emigration. Meanwhile, at Chelmno, near Lodz, and Belzec in southeastern Poland, two sites had been selected for future killing centers. These developments took place, Browning argues, during Hitler's "mistaken victory euphoria" in October 1941.[10] Browning rightly calls Hitler's euphoria mistaken, for even when the Germans captured the Soviet Union's second largest city, Kiev, on 19 September and then encircled Soviet forces at Vyazma and Bryansk in early October, taking some 663,000 prisoners, Siegfried Knappe's "quagmire of mud" was about to make the road to Moscow less open than it seemed.

Meanwhile, although Browning thinks that neither specific plans nor explicit orders regarding all European Jews were given at this time, he also affirms that by mid-October 1941 "Hitler, Himmler, and Heydrich—and a widening circle of initiates thereafter—were aware that the ultimate goal or vision of Nazi Jewish policy was now the systematic destruction and no longer the decimation and expulsion of all European Jews."[11] Browning sums up his position as follows:

> Hitler solicited the preparation of a plan for the Final Solution in mid-July 1941 and approved the resulting outline in early October. In the following month initial steps were taken: the deportation of Reich Jews and death camp construction began, Jewish emigration came to an end, and various officials of the Foreign Office and Ostministerium joined a widening circle of initiates. Until late November the deported Reich Jews were interned in ghettos in Lodz and Minsk. Then, suddenly, on November 25 and 29, 1941, all five transports from Berlin, Munich, Frankfurt, Vienna, and Breslau to Kovno were massacred at Fort IX. Did this occur as the result of local initiative. . . ? Or was it the point at which the Nazi regime officially crossed the threshold between deporting and murdering Jews not just in conception but also in practice? I would suggest the latter interpretation.[12]

Browning acknowledges that the massacre of deported German Jews at Kovno produced "complications and complaints," which led Himmler to postpone further actions of that sort. The postponement did not mean that the overall plan for the Final Solution had changed, although the circumstances surrounding it had. With the United States entering the war, decisions were needed about how to proceed. Browning sees December 1941 and January 1942 as months in which Hitler affirmed that the Final Solution would go forward—"despite," as Browning says, "the changed military circumstances." Party leaders would need to be initiated "into a process already underway," and steps would have to be taken to ensure the "camouflage and rationalization" that would make the destruction process run as smoothly as possible.[13] Momentarily there will be more to say about some of the latter factors, but clearly Browning's outlook stresses Hitler's centrality far more than Brozsat's or Aly's. Furthermore, Browning connects the key decision points in July and October 1941 to moments when military victory euphoria engulfed Hitler.

Christian Gerlach, an important German scholar, contests Browning's interpretation of these events, including the view that Hitler's Final Solution decision arose out of victory euphoria. While there is little disagreement that the decision to murder Jewish men, women, and children in the occupied Soviet territories—save for a small number of skilled "work Jews"—took place in mid-summer 1941, debate continues concerning the Jews of Germany and western Europe. Gerlach's research has substantially influenced and complicated the analysis. His account of the decision for a continental Final Solution stresses the importance of events that took place in December 1941 and thereafter. A significant meeting known as the Wannsee Conference figures centrally in his account.[14]

In late November 1941 Reinhard Heydrich issued an invitation to a group of relatively high-level German officials. They represented government, party, and SS offices whose jurisdictions included racial policies and, in particular, issues pertaining to Jews. A follow-up message on 4 December clarified that the meeting scheduled for 9 December would take place at 56–58 Am Grossen Wannsee, the lakeside address of a comfortable SD guest house in an affluent Berlin suburb. Heydrich's invitation, which included a copy of Göring's 31 July 1941 authorization, indicated that the meeting's purpose would be to achieve "a common view among the central agencies involved in the relevant tasks" pertaining to "a comprehensive solution of the Jewish question."[15] Such an invitation was not to be refused, but if the invitees were not entirely sure what to make of it, their uncertainty would not be removed on 9 December. Prompted by the Japanese attack on the United States, but also by worsening conditions on the eastern front, instructions from Heydrich's staff on 8 December announced the meeting's indefinite postponement.

Heydrich convened his Wannsee Conference about six weeks later, on 20 January 1942, but, first, other events important for Gerlach's analysis must be noted. Most important among them is a meeting that Hitler himself convened after Nazi Germany's 11 December 1941 declaration of war on the United States, which eliminated any remaining hope that keeping some Jews alive might provide a bargaining chip to influence American behavior for the Germans' advantage. On the afternoon of 12 December Hitler spoke to some of the most important leaders of the Nazi Party. Göring and probably Heydrich were not in attendance, but the *Reichsleiter* and *Gauleiter* who assembled in Hitler's private quarters in the Reich Chancellery included Heinrich Himmler, Joseph Goebbels, Hans Frank, Martin Bormann, and Philipp Bouhler. These men were among Hitler's oldest and most trusted associates. Goebbels took notes on Hitler's key points:

> Regarding the Jewish question, the Führer is determined to clear the table. He warned the Jews that if they were to cause another world war, it would lead to their own destruction. Those were not empty words. Now the world war has come. The destruction of the Jews must be its necessary consequence. We cannot be sentimental about it. It is not for us to feel sympathy for the Jews. We should have sympathy rather with our own German people. If the German people have to sacrifice 160,000 victims in yet another campaign in the east, then those responsible for this bloody conflict will have to pay for it with their lives.[16]

According to Gerlach, the entry of the United States into the war created a new set of circumstances for Hitler. Not only did the altered military and political situation mean that he could no longer be certain that Germany would win the war, but also, with the United States now in the conflict, what had been for Hitler essentially a war between European powers became a *world war*, a war that in his Reichstag "prophecy" of 30 January 1939 he predicted would have the direst consequences for Europe's Jews:

> If the Jewish international financiers in and outside Europe should succeed in plunging the nations once more into a world war, then the result will not be the Bolshevization of the earth, and thus a victory of Jewry, but the annihilation of the Jewish race in Europe.[17]

Although it was the Japanese who had attacked the United States and Hitler who had declared war on the United States, Hitler's paranoid imagination led him to believe that the Jews were bringing about the "world war" to destroy Germany. The situation Hitler had anticipated in 1939 had arrived. With the Jewish threat looming larger than ever, Hitler decided to kill all Europe's Jews. Gerlach contends that Hitler took his "decision to liquidate European Jewry" after 7 December and "announced" it to "the party leadership on 12 December."[18] It is possible, although Gerlach thinks it "relatively improbable," that Hitler revealed his intention to Göring and Himmler between 7 and 12 December.[19] In any case, Hitler's announcement on 12 December was not an order, says Gerlach, but, given the setting and the personnel involved, it "had the effect of a directive."[20] The "directive," however, still left much detail unspecified. Hitler's "decision in principle," writes Gerlach, entailed that "the practical implementation, organization, and tempo of the extermination remained matters for the relevant local bodies to determine."[21]

At this point, the postponed Wannsee Conference comes back into view. For some time scholars have debated its timing and significance, especially if the decision to exterminate all European Jews was taken months instead of weeks before. On 8 January 1942, with a few changes in the original list, Heydrich contacted the invitees again. The delayed meeting would take place on 20 January 1942. If one accepts his December dating for Hitler's decision to destroy all European Jews, then, Gerlach argues, the meeting's purpose comes into bold relief: the Wannsee Conference was "closely connected" to Hitler's early December 1941 decision to destroy "*all*" Jews living in Europe," and it was "a precondition" for implementing that decision.[22] What, then, transpired at this gathering, which remains one of the most disturbing conferences in recorded history?

In addition to Heydrich and Adolf Eichmann, the SS officer who prepared the meeting records, thirteen men attended the Wannsee Conference.[23] All but two were in their thirties or forties. Representing the Reich Ministry for the Occupied Eastern Territories (primarily Lithuania, Latvia, and Estonia) were Dr. Alfred Meyer, who held a Ph.D. in political science, and Dr. Georg Leibbrandt, whose study of theology, philosophy, history, and economics had also given him a doctorate. Six others had advanced degrees in law. Coauthor of the 1935 Nuremberg Laws, Dr. Wilhelm Stuckart, represented the Ministry of the Interior. Dr. Roland Freisler, who later presided over the *Volksgerichtshof* (People's Court) whose show trials condemned nearly 1,200 German dissidents to death, came from the Ministry of Justice. Representing Hans Frank at the conference, Dr. Josef Bühler argued that the General Government in occupied Poland should be the Final Solution's priority target. Dr. Gerhard Klopfer worked under Martin Bormann as director of the Nazi Party Chancellery's legal division, where he was especially concerned with Nazi racial policies. Dr. Eberhard Schöngarth and Dr. Rudolf Lange—his killing squad had murdered some 60,000 Jews in Latvia by December 1941—served security and police interests in Poland and other Nazi-occupied territories in eastern Europe. The conference's other participants included Martin Luther (Foreign Office), Friedrich Kritzinger (Reich Chancellery), Otto Hofmann (SS Main Office for Race and Settlement), Erich Neumann (Four-Year Plan), and Heinrich Müller (Gestapo).

The men who planned, ate, and drank at the Wannsee villa on that snowy Tuesday in January 1942 were neither uneducated nor uninitiated as Heydrich asserted his mandate and put his outlines for the Final Solution on the table. If Lange and Schöngarth were the only ones who had led killing squadrons in eastern Europe, the others in attendance were deeply implicated, in one way or another, in making the Third Reich *judenrein*. Mark Roseman's assessment is accurate: "No one arrived at Wannsee with even the faintest intention of speaking up for the Jews."[24]

Our primary documentary sources concerning the conference consist of the Wannsee Protocol, a sanitized summary prepared by Adolf Eichmann—only one copy of thirty, the sixteenth, survived the war—and Eichmann's testimony at the time of his 1961 trial in Jerusalem. Neither source lacks problems: the first is by no means a transcript of the proceedings; the second contains testimony by a man on trial for his life. Nevertheless, taking those factors into account, the following picture emerges. Preceded and followed by socializing, the meeting was brief, probably taking no more than an hour and a half. Apparently Heydrich did most of the talking. He opened the meeting by making clear that Göring had "delegated to him the preparations for the final solution of the Jewish question in Europe."[25] He further emphasized that "overall control" of that initiative rested with Himmler and himself, "irrespective of geographical boundaries."[26] As Heydrich asserted these prerogatives, no dissent followed, thus helping to ensure success for what Mark Roseman calls "a concerted, coordinated campaign by Himmler and Heydrich to assert their supremacy," particularly over civilian offices such as those represented by Stuckart and Bühler.[27]

Next, after recalling the steps already taken to expel the Jews from the German people's life and living space, Heydrich cut to the chase. Estimating that eleven million European Jews would be involved, he referred to a "new solution," one that eclipsed emigration: namely, "evacuating Jews to the East."[28] Significantly, Richard Rhodes points out that Heydrich's country-by-country Jewish census was inaccurate twice over. Some of the population figures were hugely inflated; the Jewish population of France, for example, was much smaller than the 875,000 that Heydrich reported. Of greater interest, however, was the undercounting for some regions of eastern Europe, for it contained what Rhodes rightly calls an "explicit admission of 'killing, elimination and annihilation' hidden in plain sight."[29] The number of Jews listed for Estonia, Latvia, Lithuania, and Belorussia does not correspond to the much larger prewar population statistics but to their numbers *after* the *Einsatzgruppen* and police battalions had done much of their killing. Thus Estonia was listed as already free of Jews. Latvia's Jewish population was given as 3,500, roughly the number of men left alive for slave labor after most Latvian Jews had been murdered. The number listed for Lithuania was 34,000, which corresponded to the number of "work Jews" the Germans permitted to remain alive temporarily. It was no mystery that the euphemistic language attributed to Heydrich in the conference protocol did not mean resettlement. Or, to put the point differently, it was clear that "resettlement" meant death and murder.

Combing Europe from west to east, the protocol went on to specify, transports would send Jews to work. Those who were not "eliminated by natural causes" were to be "dealt with appropriately" lest their survival create "the germ cell of a new Jewish revival."[30] Masked though the protocol made it seem, this language left no doubt that every European Jew was sentenced to die, either by attrition, extermination through work, or outright murder. At his trial, Eichmann stated that on Heydrich's instructions he had edited the document to exclude overt references to killing and extermination.[31] When the presiding judge asked whether "the means of extermination, systems of killing" were discussed, Eichmann said, "I do know that these gentlemen were . . . discussing the subject quite bluntly, quite differently from the language I had to use later in the record. During the conversation they minced no words about it at all." When pressed further, Eichmann added, "I cannot remember it in detail, Your Honour, but they spoke about methods for killing, about liquidation, about extermination."[32] If Eichmann's testimony was vague on these points, it probably still hit the target, for one can scarcely imagine that the discussion remained as sanitary as the conference protocol suggests.

One more issue took time at the Wannsee Conference: the status of half and quarter Jews (*Mischlinge*) and mixed marriages. The 1935 Nuremberg Laws had given the *Mischlinge* some protection. Those same laws had forbidden future intermarriage, but existing intermarriages had been tolerated, and a decree by Göring on 28 December 1938 distinguished between those that were 'privileged' and "not privileged." Among other things, these classifications affected where the couples could live as the expropriation and relocation of Jews proceeded. According to the Wannsee Protocol, Heydrich acknowledged that the Nuremberg Laws would provide the Final Solution's "general framework" for defining Jewish racial classification, at least for Reich Jews, but he also mounted an assault on protections for "mixed marriages and persons of mixed blood."[33] With restricted exceptions, for example, he wanted half Jews to be treated as full Jews. Unless exempted, half Jews could be "evacuated"; those who were exempted would be sterilized. As for mixed marriages, Heydrich basically advocated that the Jewish spouse—or spouses in the case of marriages involving *Mischlinge*—should be evacuated or ghettoized.

No lasting policy decision on these matters emerged from Wannsee Conference. Nevertheless, Heydrich's views dominated sufficiently to reinforce the point that Himmler and Heydrich had extensive control over the handling of the Jewish question. Given the virulent antisemitism and the rationalizing bent of the SS, it is hardly surprising that Heydrich forced the definitional issues as much as he did at Wannsee. In a fully rational world, to paraphrase the seventeenth-century philosopher René Descartes, definitions would be "clear and distinct." The *Mischlinge* and mixed marriages impeded the finality that Heydrich wanted for the Final Solution. Issues about them resurfaced at Final Solution policy meetings subsequent to the Wannsee Conference. Differences of opinion persisted about the costs and benefits of reducing or cancelling exemptions for the *Mischlinge* and mixed marriages. Hilberg summarizes the outcome as follows:

> The *Mischling* controversy illustrates the bureaucracy's tremendous urge to make the "Final Solution" really final. The *Mischlinge* had not been bothered very much, but the mere fact that they existed was disturbing. They were living proof of a task unfinished, for they were carriers of "Jewish blood" and Jewish characteristics in the German community. . . . The *Mischlinge* and the Jews in mixed marriages were the only candidates for deportation who escaped the fate that Heydrich had chosen for them. The *Mischlinge* were saved because they were more German than Jewish. The Jews in mixed marriages were finally made exempt because, in the last analysis, it was felt that their deportation might jeopardize the whole destruction process.[34]

Heydrich had much reason to feel satisfied with the results of the conference. Although there were disagreements concerning some details, no serious objections or reservations, practical or moral, were expressed by any of the officials present. His satisfaction would have been enhanced by the fact that 20 January 1942 was also a day when he approved nominees for the War Service Cross Second Class. The list included Paul Blobel, who had been responsible for the massacres at Babi Yar; Dr. Albert Widmann, who had tried poison gas in mass murder at Mogilev in White Russia; and several others who had directed mass killing in the East.[35] Heydrich's satisfaction, however, was not destined to be long-lived. By 4 June 1942 Heydrich was dead, the victim of Czech partisans who shot him on 27 May as his open car drove through Prague. What, then, can be concluded about the Wannsee Conference and Christian Gerlach's argument about it?

The following points stand out: (1) The Wannsee Conference did not launch the Final Solution. According to Gerlach, however, it did provide what had not existed previously: namely, "the initial sketches of a comprehensive plan for total liquidation," including German Jews whose fate had been ambiguous.[36] (2) Just as prior decisions had led to the Wannsee Conference, the meeting on 20 January 1942 showed that many decisions were yet to be made. In particular, Himmler would have to drive the destruction process from the top in tandem with the local and regional underlings whose initiative did much to determine the details of implementation, precisely when and how the next lethal steps were taken. Nevertheless, the Wannsee Conference provided crucial, even essential, guidance that death for all of Europe's Jews was to be the goal for those initiatives to reach. (3) The Wannsee Conference could send its signals only because Hitler had first made his objectives clear. The timing and context of the meeting on 20 January 1942 strongly suggest to Gerlach that Hitler's decision and announcement to destroy all the European Jews came relatively close to the conference—in early December 1941, not two months earlier. (4) That timing, Gerlach believes, is consistent with developments in the East during the autumn of 1941 that escalated and radicalized mass murder but still largely on a regional basis. (5) It was not Hitler's victory euphoria, but his sense that all might be lost in an expanding and increasingly difficult war, that led to his late 1941 decision to destroy European Jewry entirely.

Who made the fateful decisions, and when were they made? Hitler was true to his word: in basic ways, he did give the Jewish question priority over all other matters. His role was central. Without Hitler, there would have been no Final Solution. By no means, however, did Hitler act alone. Himmler, Heydrich, Göring, Goebbels, Eichmann, and the Wannsee Conference participants—even if one mentions only a few names, the list quickly lengthens when the destruction process's key players alone are mentioned. Their parts—to say nothing of less known but not necessarily less important figures who operated at the periphery more than at the center of decision making—mean that many different decisions escalated and expanded the mass killing. Their exact timing remains contested, their precise relationship controversial. Aly, Browning, Gerlach, and others will continue to debate interpretations that are as important as they are different. All of them have weaknesses as well as strengths: Aly underplays Hitler's role. Arguably Browning's theses about Hitler's victory euphoria are oversimplified. Gerlach's case, like the others, rests on weaving together circumstantial evidence, particularly with reference to the fate of German Jews who were deported to the East in the late autumn of 1941.[37] If we take these accounts together, however, they help to show that the more we learn about the destruction process, the more incremental, protracted, and complicated it seems to have been. Given the Final Solution's scope, that outcome makes considerable sense, although it does not provide the simple explanations that one might prefer. Of this much, however, we can be sure: millions of Jews and other victims paid the ultimate price for deliberations of the kind that took place at the Wannsee villa on 20 January 1942; they did so because plans for genocide were not only laid but carried out. What that meant after the Wannsee Conference is the subject to which we now turn.

## EFFICIENT DEATH

Always wanting to work toward his Führer's wishes, Heinrich Himmler had a problem. How could he ensure that all of Europe's Jews would be destroyed without threatening the decency and civility of his SS men by ordering actions that would likely turn them into "neurotics or brutes"?[38] This problem was unsolvable, but not for Himmler's lack of trying. For example, on 12 December 1941, the date that Gerlach identifies as the one on which Hitler expanded his genocidal intentions, Himmler sent a secret order to his top SS and police leaders stating that these men had a "holy duty." They must "ensure that none of our men who have to fulfill this burdensome duty should ever be brutalized or suffer damage to their spirit and character in doing so." Referring to "the evenings of those days which have included such difficult tasks," he urged that there be "comradely" socializing. These evenings should include eating "in the best German domestic style, and music, and lectures and introductions to the beauties of German intellectual and emotional life." By no means, he cautioned, should the gatherings "end in the abuse of alcohol."[39] These expectations put Himmler out of touch with reality, but they did not exhaust his plans. Mass shootings would have to continue, but other forms of killing, more efficient ones, could get the job done with less stress and strain. The result was that six major killing centers, all of them situated on Polish soil, became operational in an eight-month period from December 1941 to July 1942.

As we shall see, two of these killing centers—Majdanek and Auschwitz-Birkenau—also served as concentration camps that contained prisoners from whom labor would be extracted before they perished. Nevertheless, it is important not to equate concentration camps and extermination camps. Although hundreds of thousands of concentration camp prisoners were tortured, forced to become subjects of mutilating medical experiments, and killed, the fundamental purpose of the concentration camps was different from that of the extermination camps. Originally concentration camps such as Dachau and Buchenwald were institutions of incarceration for opponents of the National Socialist regime who had committed no offense punishable in traditional German courts. Until November 1938 the camps contained few Jews. In the aftermath of *Kristallnacht*, 9–10 November 1938, thousands of Jews who had committed no crime were thrown into the camps. Most were released after paying a ransom or proving that they were about to emigrate. During the war the camp system was vastly expanded throughout all of German-occupied Europe. In addition to holding opponents of the regime, the concentration camps served as mammoth slave labor depots. Because the labor of non-German slaves was regarded as an expendable commodity, the death rate in the camps was extremely high. Nevertheless, incarceration in a concentration camp, unlike incarceration in an extermination camp, was not equivalent to a death sentence. However slim the odds, some wartime inmates could hope for eventual release, provided they were not Jewish.

Dante's *Inferno* suggests that the entrance to hell bears the inscription "Abandon all hope, ye who enter here." The same inscription would have been appropriate at the gateways to every Nazi death camp. These installations were situated in Poland near the largest concentrations of Jews in Europe, in close proximity to railroads and yet sufficiently remote from widespread public view so as to minimize publicity about them elsewhere, including Germany. Every human being condemned to a death camp was under an irrevocable sentence. These camps existed for a single reason: the extermination of Jews and Gypsies. Working in ways that resembled factory methods of mass production, the operations of these killing centers were unprecedented. Concentration camps and gas chambers had existed before, but innovative Nazi specialists brought the components together to do something novel: *kill unrelentingly, day after day, on an assembly-line basis.*

Located in the Warthegau, about forty miles west of Lodz, the first of these centers was at the village of Chelmno (Kulmhof in German). Following Hitler's mid-September 1941 decision to send Reich Jews eastward, Himmler directed the Warthegau's governor, Arthur Greiser, to take sixty thousand of the deportees into the Lodz ghetto. Governing an area that was supposed to become *judenrein*, Greiser did not want to accept the transports. Negotiations ensued: Greiser took twenty-five thousand deportees, apparently in exchange for Himmler's agreement that Greiser could liquidate one hundred thousand Polish Jews who were deemed unfit for work.[40] These arrangements were facilitated by SS Captain (*Hauptsturmführer*) Herbert Lange, who had used gas vans to murder handicapped patients in East Prussia and the Warthegau.

Situated near a small railroad station, the killing center developed at Chelmno consisted of two stationary parts. In the village an old, fenced-off manor house—the *Schlosslager*—became the camp's reception and extermination center. Camp personnel were also housed there. About 2.5 miles distant, a forest area—the *Waldlager*—provided a site for corpse disposal. Linking these two parts were the gas vans—eventually three of them—that Lange and his men began to operate on 8 December 1941, when the Holocaust's first large-scale gassing of Jews took place. Early versions of the gas vans employed tanks of carbon monoxide, but that procedure proved less efficient than the one that Albert Widmann developed in Belorussia. Recycled exhaust fumes became the killing agent of choice at Chelmno.

Chelmno operated from December 1941 to March 1943. It reopened in June and July 1944 during the liquidation of the Lodz ghetto. Like other aspects of the destruction process, the work at Chelmno became standardized. During the first weeks of the camp's operation, Jews in Chelmno's immediate vicinity were rounded up and trucked to the facility. By mid-January 1942 Jews and eventually five thousand Gypsies from the Lodz ghetto were the primary targets. They were crammed into train cars that went first to the junction at Kolo and then by a narrow-gauge track to the small station at Powiercie. Trucks took them from that station to the *Schlosslager*. The prisoners were told that they must bathe and that their clothes had to be disinfected prior to the prisoners' relocation to an eastern labor camp, where good conditions awaited them. After the Germans took any valuables, stripped groups of fifty to seventy men, women, and children were forced down a ramp, deceptively marked with signs "To the Washroom," and packed into one of the gas vans. The exhaust did its work in a few minutes. After or even during the killing, the vans drove to the *Waldlager*. Under German supervision, selected Jewish prisoners formed the *Sonderkommando* whose task it was to bury the bodies in mass graves and to clean the hideously soiled vans. Periodically the Jews forced to do this grisly work were executed so that they could never testify about the slaughter.

At Chelmno and throughout eastern Europe, the burial pits that contained the evidence of mass murder eventually made the Germans think twice. Should the war be lost, their murderous deeds might be discovered. Heaps of corpses could not be left behind with impunity. In June 1942 SS Colonel Paul Blobel was ordered to "erase the traces of *Einsatzgruppen* executions in the East."[41] As commander of *Einsatzkommando* 4a, a unit of *Einsatzgruppe* C, Blobel had carried out many mass executions, particularly at Babi Yar in late September 1941. He was among those recommended for the War Service Cross Second Class when Heydrich signed his list of nominees on 20 January 1942, the day on which the Wannsee Conference took place. Like Himmler's problem of ensuring the decency and civility of his SS killers, Blobel's dilemma was unsolvable. So much killing in so many places had already taken place, and much more was to come. Nevertheless Blobel tried his best. His work took him to Chelmno in the summer of 1942.[42] There his special unit, *Kommando* 1005, not only exhumed graves but also experimented with the best ways to burn large number of corpses at once. He even tried, unsuccessfully, to remove the traces by dynamiting the corpses. Although the crematoria built at Auschwitz-Birkenau were far more sophisticated than the pits, pyres, and primitive ovens that Blobel devised, his basic techniques for corpse disposal—including the crushing of bones—were widely used in the major German killing centers.

Only two Jews—Mordechaï Podchlebnik and Simon Srebnik—are known to have survived Chelmno. The Germans left the teen-aged Srebnik for dead when they fled what remained of the camp in January 1945 as the Soviet army approached. Srebnik survived. Years later he returned to Chelmno from Israel in the company of the film maker Claude Lanzmann. In *Shoah*, Lanzmann's 1985 epic about the Holocaust, Srebnik revisits the *Waldlager* and is heard to say, "It's hard to recognize, but it was here. They burned people here. A lot of people were burned here. Yes, this is the place. No one ever left here again."[43] Srebnik's words mourn the 150,000 Jews murdered at Chelmno.

Despite an efficient use of exhaust fumes, the capacity of Chelmno's gas vans was too small to handle the needs for death production that were developing in the East. Even as those trucks drove from the *Schlosslager* to the *Waldlager* and back during the winter of 1941–42, three sites in the General Government—Belzec, Sobibor, and Treblinka—were being developed as killing centers with larger and stationary gas chambers. At the Wannsee Conference, Hans Frank's representative, Josef Bühler, had urged that the Final Solution ought to begin in the General Government. He did not have long to wait. Entrusted by Heinrich Himmler to prepare the destruction of Jews in that area, SS and Police Major General Odilo Globocnik, whose offices were in the Lublin district, took over what would come to be known as Operation Reinhard, a huge killing program named in honor of Reinhard Heydrich after his death on 4 June 1942. Specifically, on or around 13 October 1941, Himmler directed Globocnik to develop a killing center at Belzec, where work was under way by early November. Globocnik's background as a construction engineer positioned him well to oversee the construction of Operation Reinhard camps, but he delegated much of the day-to-day responsibility for this part of the Final Solution to his subordinate SS Major Hermann Höfle. Under their direction, SS Lieutenant Richard Thomalla, who worked in the SS Central Building Administration in Lublin, led construction of the camps at Belzec, Sobibor, and Treblinka, all of them with a similar brick-and-lumber design.

At least four factors determined the location of these camps: Each was situated in a remote location, thus ensuring security and some secrecy. They were close to rail lines so that large numbers of people could be transported to these destinations. In addition, large Jewish populations were nearby, and the camps were at the eastern border of the General Government, which helped to maintain the deception that the arrivals were not being sent to their death but only to "resettlement" in the East. From camp to camp there was some variation in the layout, but Raul Hilberg succinctly describes the basic pattern as follows:

> The terrain of each camp was only a few hundred yards in length and width. . . . There were barracks for guard personnel, an area where the Jews were unloaded, an undressing station, and an S-shaped walkway, called the *Schlauch* (hose), two or three yards wide that was bordered by high barbed-wire fences covered with ivy. The *Schlauch* was traversed by the naked victims on their way to the gassing facilities. The entire arrangement was designed to convince the Jews that they were in a transit camp, where they would be required to clean themselves on the way to the "east." The gas chambers, disguised as showers, were not larger than medium-sized rooms, but during gassings they were filled to capacity. At the beginning, no camp had more than three of these chambers. The gas first used at Belzec was bottled, either the same preparation of carbon monoxide that had been shipped to the euthanasia stations or possibly hydrogen cyanide. Later, Belzec is reported to have been equipped with a diesel motor; Treblinka is said to have had one from the start; and Sobibor began with a heavy, eight-cylinder, 200+ horsepower, water-cooled Russian gasoline engine that released a mixture of carbon monoxide and carbon dioxide into the gas chambers. No crematoria were installed; the bodies were burned in mass graves.[44]

Globocnik did not have expertise in gassing operations, but personnel from the T4 euthanasia program did. They had acquired a considerable measure of experience in the efficient and economical extermination of any category of persons targeted for destruction by the German state. Although the euthanasia program had "officially" been put on hold, its staff was too valuable to disband. On the contrary, once the gassing of Jews became preferable to other methods of killing, it took on new life. Construction of the Belzec camp had begun in November 1941. By late December, SS Captain Christian Wirth had been appointed commandant. An experienced police officer, he had witnessed the first T4 gassing demonstration, which took place at the Brandenburg euthanasia center some time during the winter of 1939–40. Particularly at Hartheim but throughout the entire system of euthanasia centers, he had extensive administrative and supervisory authority. As the senior and most knowledgeable member of the euthanasia team that the T4 leader, Victor Brack, put at Globocnik's disposal, Wirth had considerable influence and authority in all of the Operation Reinhard camps.[45] He knew about the gas vans that operated at Chelmno. His contribution to the apparatus of mass murder was to combine a stationary chamber with motor-produced exhaust. With minor variations, Wirth's model became standard in all the Operation Reinhard camps. Wirth's experimentation at Belzec also helped to routinize the process that handled the Jews from their arrival in the killing center to the disposal of their corpses. As was the case at Chelmno, that process included the use of Jews who were selected for a time to work in the camp before they too were killed.

The year 1942 was the most lethal in Jewish history. During those twelve months, the killers who implemented Nazi Germany's Final Solution murdered 2.6 million Jews.[46] Few sites in the destruction process were more devastating than Belzec, the killing center situated in southeastern Poland near the railroad station at a village on the main line between the cities of Lublin and Lvov. A specially constructed railroad spur, less than a mile long, led directly to the camp. During Belzec's brief but deadly operations in a nine-month period from 17 March until mid-December 1942, trains with forty to sixty freight cars packed with Jews reached Belzec on a regular basis. Carried out by the German SS and their Ukrainian helpers, the gassings and shootings that followed accounted for at least 434,000 Jewish deaths.[47]

According to Margaret M. Rubel, a scholar whose work has focused on Belzec, a man named Rudolf Reder was one of only two known survivors from that death camp.[48] With thousands of other Jews from Lvov, Reder, 61, a former soap manufacturer, was deported to Belzec in mid-August 1942. All the Jews who entered Belzec were doomed, but Reder was one of the very few who were temporarily selected for work in the Jewish death brigade. The tasks of this unit—it numbered about five hundred brutalized and malnourished prisoners whose ranks were frequently thinned and replenished—involved digging mass burial pits, disposing of corpses, sorting loot (including baskets of gold teeth and vast amounts of women's shorn hair), and maintaining the camp's gas chambers, which used the carbon monoxide produced by a large engine. Reder would spend about three months in Belzec. Toward the end of November 1942 he managed to escape his guards during a trip to Lvov to obtain building materials for the camp. Remembering the address of his Polish housekeeper, Reder went to her flat, and she gave him refuge until the Red Army liberated the city in 1944.

Reder's compressed testimony about Belzec is among the most disturbing survivor narratives to emerge from the Holocaust. Assigned to a variety of jobs, he came to know the camp all too well. It was a place, he said, that "served no other purpose but that of murdering Jews."[49] Every transport—typically there were three a day—got the same treatment. The arriving Jews were ordered to undress and to set their belongings aside. They were told that a bath awaited them before they would be sent to work. Each time people heard that deceptive speech, Reder underscores, he could see "the spark of hope in their eyes." His account continues:

> But a minute later, and with extreme brutality, babies were torn from their mothers, old and sick were thrown on stretchers, while men and little girls were driven with rifle-butts further on to a fenced path leading directly to the gas chambers. At the same time, and with the same brutality, the already naked women were ordered to the barracks, where they had their hair shaved. I knew exactly the moment when they all suddenly realized what was in store. Cries of fear and anguish, terrible moans, mingled with the music played by the orchestra. . . . Before all six chambers were filled to capacity, those in the first had already been suffering for nearly two hours. It was only when all six chambers were packed with people, when the doors were locked into position, that the engine was set in motion.[50]

At Belzec, systematic murder combined with sadistic torture to produce circumstances in which the most one could really hope for was that death's arrival would come speedily and soon. After his liberation, Reder returned to Belzec to see what remained. His narrative ends by observing that the Germans had "covered this graveyard for millions of murdered Jews with fresh greenery. . . . The railway line was gone. Through a field I reached a young and sweet-smelling pine forest. It was very still. In the middle of it was a large sunny clearing."[51]

Few places revealed the Holocaust's essence more than Belzec, a camp, Reder said, that "heaved with mass murder."[52] Nevertheless, under Franz Stangl's administration, Sobibor and Treblinka competed for that dubious distinction. Like Globocnik and many other Operation Reinhard personnel, Stangl was an Austrian; he had been a T4 operative as well. Quickly built by Thomalla with conscripted Jewish labor in March and April 1942, Sobibor opened under Stangl's supervision in mid-May 1942. Located north of Belzec, close to the Bug River and the Chelm-Wlodawa rail line, Sobibor received transports that were, on average, smaller than Belzec's. Typically, only one transport with 2,000 to 2,500 Jews aboard its twenty freight cars arrived each day.[53] By the end of July, Sobibor's gas chambers had dispatched about one hundred thousand Jews. For the next two months, the gassing operations were sharply reduced because railroad repairs prevented trains from reaching the camp. The lull was not wasted, however, because when Sobibor resumed full operations in October, it did so with new gas chambers that featured enlarged capacity. After the Jewish prisoners revolted on 14 October 1943, the Germans liquidated the camp and shut it down. By that time, Sobibor had contributed about 250,000 Jewish deaths to the Final Solution's toll. Most were from the General Government, but as the Final Solution expanded, Jews from western Europe—the Netherlands, Belgium, and France—were also among Sobibor's victims. During the hiatus at Sobibor in the summer of 1942, Stangl, who had worked effectively at the camp, was reassigned to Treblinka, where the camp was running amok under the less than efficient direction of Irmfried Eberl, a Austrian psychiatrist who had been T4's physician-in-charge at Brandenburg and Bernburg. Stangl's arrival soon restored order.

Situated about fifty miles northeast of Warsaw, Treblinka became operational toward the end of July 1942. The camp took its name from a small Polish village and railroad station on the Malkinia-Siedlce line. About a year earlier, a labor camp—later called Treblinka I—had been developed to quarry gravel deposits. Relatively hidden in a wooded area, the extermination camp, which was called Treblinka II, was connected to the main rail line by a spur that brought the transports close to the gas chambers. The transports that reached Treblinka were huge. Typically, the loads of fifty to sixty cars were split so that more manageable convoys of twenty cars at a time were processed. Between late July and September 1942, some 300,000 Jews from the Warsaw ghetto were sent to their deaths in Treblinka's carbon monoxide gas chambers. At first the bodies were buried in mass graves, but by the autumn of 1942 those graves were being exhumed and huge burning pits were put to use. As in the other death camps, Jewish prisoners were forced to do much of the dirty work. A prisoner revolt took place on 2 August 1943. Although most of the three hundred escapees were caught and killed, the revolt did considerable damage to the camp. Within a few weeks the Germans dismantled the camp and tried to disguise what it had been.

A Czech Jew named Richard Glazar had been deported to Treblinka in early October 1942. He was among the very few on his transport who were selected for work—his tasks included sorting the loot that the Germans plundered from their victims. Glazar was also one of the approximately seventy Jews who survived the Treblinka uprising. He regularly saw the trains that delivered Jews by the thousands to Treblinka. By the spring of 1943 he knew how far Nazi mass murder had reached: convoys were arriving from distant Bulgaria and Greece. Glazar remembered Treblinka as "a huge junk store." Everything could be found there, he wrote, "except life."[54] Glazar was correct on both counts. Of the three Operation Reinhard camps, Treblinka's loot and death toll were the largest. Between 700,000 and 850,000 Jews were murdered there. In addition to those who were transported from nearby Warsaw, Treblinka's victims included Jews from many other European countries—Belgium and France, as well as Bulgaria and Greece, among them. Meanwhile, Franz Stangl, who administered Treblinka from September 1942 until August 1943, also "survived" Treblinka. After the war, he fled to Brazil, where he lived until he was arrested in 1967, deported to Germany, tried for his crimes, and sentenced to life imprisonment. His term had barely begun when he died of heart failure.

## DESTINATION AUSCHWITZ AND BEYOND

In its early stages, Raul Hilberg emphasizes, the Germans' destruction of the European Jews could rely on precedent. Eventually, however, the Final Solution created circumstances where "every problem was unprecedented." Chelmno and the Operation Reinhard camps showed how the Germans dealt with a multitude of new problems: "Not just how to kill the Jews," Hilberg notes, "but what to do with their property thereafter. And not only that, but how to deal with the problem of not letting the world know what had happened."[55] Invention and routinization went hand in hand. In varied ways that pattern pertained at two other camps, Majdanek and Auschwitz, which had functions both different from and related to those that characterized the four killing centers discussed thus far.

Established by SS chief Heinrich Himmler in July 1941 and under the juris-diction of Odilo Globocnik, the Lublin-Majdanek camp became operational under commandant Karl Koch that October.[56] In several ways, Majdanek dif-fered from Chelmno and the Operation Reinhard camps. First, Majdanek was situated not in a remote area but on the outskirts of Lublin, a major city in south-eastern Poland. Second, designed for a population of twenty-five to fifty thou-sand, this installation was a concentration camp where prisoners, housed in overcrowded barracks, were organized into forced labor gangs for German arma-ment industries and other enterprises. Thus Majdanek was one of hundreds of camps in the vast network that became administratively incorporated into the SS Economic-Administrative Main Office (*Wirtschafts-Verwaltungshauptamt*; WVHA), whose head was SS Lieutenant General Oswold Pohl. Third, although Majdanek's prisoners were primarily Polish Jews, including about 18,000 whom the Germans sent there after the Warsaw ghetto uprising in the spring of 1943, the 300,000 prisoners who passed through Majdanek were highly diverse. Some fifty nationalities could be found among them.

The conditions in Majdanek were brutal. Exposure, disease, and starvation took a heavy toll, especially during the winter of 1941–42. Increasingly, death from those causes was augmented by outright murder. Prisoners found unfit for work were regularly thinned out by shootings. In October 1942 gas chambers came on line as well. The precise number of people murdered in them is unknown, but reliable estimates suggest that tens of thousands met their fate in that way. Conservative death toll figures for Majdanek indicate that 170,000 to 235,000 people died or were murdered in that place.

One of the Holocaust's most lethal episodes is associated with Majdanek. In late October 1943 prisoners dug three huge trenches in the camp's southern sec-tor. On 2 November two trucks with loudspeakers appeared in the camp. These preparations were for *Erntefest* (Operation Harvest Festival), the Nazi code name for a massacre. At Majdanek's morning roll call on 3 November, Jews were sepa-rated from the other prisoners, sent to the trenches, and shot. Dance music blared from the camp's loudspeakers to drown out the screams and machine gun fire while the murder continued until nightfall. "Bloody Wednesday" left eighteen thousand Jews dead in Majdanek's pits. Intended to prevent repetition of Jewish prisoner revolts such as those at Treblinka and Sobibor earlier in 1943, *Erntefest* also went beyond Majdanek. Jewish prisoners at other camps in the Lublin dis-trict—eight to ten thousand at Trawniki and fifteen thousand at Poniatowa— were among those shot to death on November 3. It remained Majdanek's distinction, however, to be the most deadly site of the Germans' largest one-day killing operation against the Jews.[57]

"People lived and vanished overnight in this place," wrote Holocaust survivor Elie Wiesel.[58] Wiesel could have been referring to Chelmno, the Operation Rein-hard camps, or Majdanek, but he had another place in mind. The Polish people call it Oswiecim, but it is better known as Auschwitz, its German name. "The beginning, the end," Wiesel said, "all the world's roads, all the outcries of mankind, lead to this accursed place."[59] When he called Auschwitz an "accursed place," Wiesel knew whereof he spoke: He and his family were among the Hungarian Jews who were sent there in the spring of 1944. His mother and little sister were gassed on arrival. Wiesel and his father were selected for labor at Monowitz.

For some time, in one way or another, Nazi Germany had been approaching Auschwitz. The Holocaust's roads, figurative and literal, led to that place. At least two overarching factors make Auschwitz especially important. First, although history shows that the Holocaust was much too vast to be synonymous with one place alone, none comes closer than Auschwitz, for it was the most lethal of the Holocaust's multiple epicenters. More Jews were killed in this camp than at any other Holocaust site. Second, Auschwitz showed what Nazi Germany's genocidal intentions had come to mean: the development of massive factories of death designed to kill thousands of people a day and to dispose of their remains without a trace, but only after everything of value—labor from those who could work and property, including hair and gold teeth—was taken from them and used to support the Third Reich. As Michael Berenbaum has said, Auschwitz will always be the Holocaust's emblematic camp. Prison, slave labor installation, killing center—Auschwitz was three camps in one. It was the most extreme and intensified manifestation of Nazi evil. The importance of Auschwitz entails that the literature about it—in both historical and fictional forms—keeps growing.[60] It is far too large to cover comprehensively here, but for our purposes several key points need to be made.

The Polish town of Oswiecim, whose prewar population of 12,000 included 5,000 Jews, stands forty miles west of Cracow in Upper Silesia, a southwestern Polish province that the Nazis annexed to the Third Reich. Situated on major railroad lines and near the confluence of the Sola and Vistula rivers, Auschwitz, as the Germans called Oswiecim, was also the site of former Polish military barracks. They became the nucleus for the most notorious part of Nazi Germany's vast network of concentration, forced-labor, and death camps. Specifically, it was at Auschwitz that the largest number of Jews were gassed during the Final Solution.

In occupied Poland, the German army turned over the former Polish artillery base at Auschwitz to the SS Inspectorate of Concentration Camps, which later was incorporated into Pohl's WVHA. Initially it was thought that the red brick buildings would become a transit camp from which Poles would be sent to camps in the West to do forced labor. On 27 April 1940, however, SS leader Himmler decided to make Auschwitz a concentration camp. Instead of sending prisoner labor elsewhere, it would be based at Auschwitz and then used for various Germanizing construction and food production projects that Himmler envisioned for the surrounding part of Poland, which was now within the expanded Reich's territory. Himmler appointed SS Captain Rudolf Höss, later promoted to lieutenant colonel, to be the camp's commandant.

The early Auschwitz inmates were mostly Polish political prisoners, including numerous priests and nuns. During the camp's existence, about 215,000 Poles were imprisoned there, and almost 100,000 of them lost their lives. Auschwitz has become an immensely important memorial site for Poles as well as for Jews. Meanwhile, two 1941 developments advanced the growth of Auschwitz's territory and population, and soon Auschwitz became several camps in one. First, I. G. Farben, the huge German petrochemical company, sought a place to produce synthetic rubber and fuel. Raw materials, rail connections and facilities, plentiful water, tax advantages, and a potential source of cheap prisoner labor all made the Auschwitz region attractive. A factory site was selected to the east of the Auschwitz camp. To take advantage of I. G. Farben's growing labor requirements, which were lucrative for the SS because the company paid for the prisoner labor, the capacity of the Auschwitz camp was enlarged. Second, Germany's invasion of the USSR on 22 June 1941 meant imprisonment for hundreds of thousands of Soviet POWs. When Himmler successfully contended that Auschwitz would be a good place for many of them, another expansion took place, this time about a mile and half west of the main camp. Drainage would have to be engineered, but the SS planners thought that 125,000 prisoners could be interned on the swampy terrain at Birkenau, as the Germans called the nearby Polish village of Brzezinka.[61] As 1941 and 1942 progressed, Auschwitz itself became a large and multifaceted building site. The *Stammlager* (the main camp, Auschwitz I) remained at the center of the complex. Auschwitz II or Birkenau, it was initially hoped, would become the prisoner-of-war camp. Eventually, by late October 1942, a third installation became operational. Wanting to cut the time it took to get prisoner labor to its factory site each day, I. G. Farben arranged for an additional camp, Auschwitz III, close by the plant at Monowitz. This camp, which remained under the Auschwitz administration, was sometimes called Buna, taking that name from the synthetic rubber that I. G. Farben wanted to produce.

Thus far, our description of Auschwitz has scarcely mentioned Jews, but events soon developed in ways that require a focus in that direction. By mid-July 1941 some Soviet POWs were being sent to Auschwitz, where most were executed, some by shooting but others in September gassing experiments that employed Zyklon B. In late October, however, a large group of Soviet POWs—about ten thousand—reached Auschwitz. Himmler's expectations were frustrated when their devastated condition left them little life for work. Within a few months, fewer than one thousand remained alive. Even more serious for the construction projects that Himmler wanted to pursue, the military campaign on the eastern front had become problematic. Decisions were taken to use the Soviet POWs in work more closely related to the war effort than Himmler's building and agricultural projects in the Auschwitz area could claim to be.

Himmler's labor force seemed to be evaporating, but not entirely, because Jews could become the substitutes he needed, even as the Final Solution destined them to disappear. The labor distribution, however, underwent some changes as this shift took place, for bigger and better ways to dispose of Jewish lives and Jewish corpses were going to be needed. So it was that from the spring of 1942 and into the autumn of 1944 approximately 1.4 million Jews arrived at Auschwitz on trains from every part of Europe, many of them in 1944, when the war was lost to the Germans but Auschwitz-Birkenau, the single killing center that remained, was operating at full throttle.[62] About 300,000 of the Jews deported to Auschwitz from 1942 to 1944 were selected for slave labor; the rest were killed, most of them gassed on arrival.[63]

Auschwitz's death toll by gassing in 1942 could not compare with the combined figures from the Operation Reinhard camps, which dispatched more than a million Jews during that year alone, while the Jewish dead at Auschwitz numbered about 200,000.[64] Nevertheless, even as the Nazis suffered a crushing eastern front defeat at Stalingrad during the winter of 1942–43, the destructive potential at Auschwitz reached levels beyond anything that Belzec or Treblinka could offer. Between 31 March and 26 June 1943 four state-of-the-art crematoria came on line. Designed by German architects and fitted with specially crafted German equipment, these structures, which forced Jewish labor helped to build, included eight gas chambers, forty-six ovens, and the capacity to dispose of 4,416 corpses a day.[65] These facilities made possible the rapid annihilation of the Hungarian Jews when the Germans occupied Hungary, their faltering ally, on 19 March 1944. In less than three months during the spring and summer of 1944, approximately 435,000 of Hungary's 725,000 Jews were deported, almost all to Auschwitz, in 147 rail transports, which took advantage of a specially constructed rail spur that brought the trains to a ramp only a few minutes walk from the gas chambers.[66] German documentation indicates that 381,661 Hungarian Jews entered Auschwitz-Birkenau between 29 April and 30 June 1944. Dwork and van Pelt estimate that between 10 and 30 percent of those deportees were selected for labor, which suggests a death toll of more than 270,000 in a matter of weeks.[67] This onslaught necessitated the use of open-air burning pits to handle the excess bodies that could not be consumed by the overtaxed crematoria.

Subsequently there will be more to say about Auschwitz-Birkenau than this chapter can include, but two additional matters deserve attention. First, at frequent intervals, especially after a severe typhus epidemic broke out during the summer of 1942, an Auschwitz truck went to Dessau, Germany. It returned with large quantities of 200-gram, hermetically sealed tin canisters. They contained Zyklon-Blausäure, or Zyklon B, whose trade name—meaning "cyclone"—also referred to prussic acid, which in German is called *Blausäure* because it produces deep blue stains. In the gas chambers at Auschwitz-Birkenau the Zyklon B preferred by commandant Rudolf Höss took precedence over Christian Wirth's less reliable and more primitive motors that had generated carbon monoxide in the Operation Reinhard camps.[68]

A powerful pesticide developed during World War I, Zyklon B was used to combat contagious disease by fumigating lice-infested buildings. First used at Auschwitz in July 1940, it initially served those purposes there, especially as the camp's growth increasingly produced overcrowded barracks, malnutrition, and poor sanitation, all of which made dysentery, typhoid fever, and especially typhus constant threats. By the late summer of 1941, however, much more destructive uses for Zyklon B were found. Experiments on Soviet POWs confirmed that Zyklon B's vaporizing pellets offered a particularly efficient way to advance the Final Solution.

Several German companies—including Degesch, or the *Deutsche Gesellschaft für Schädlingsbekämpfung mbH* (German Vermin-Combating Corporation, a subsidiary of Degussa and I. G. Farben), and Tesch and Stabenow Verlag—profited by supplying Zyklon B to the SS. They even modified it for Auschwitz by removing the special odor that ordinarily warned people about their product's deadly presence. Auschwitz used tons of Zyklon B. Most of it went to conventional fumigation, but there was plenty left to pour into gas chambers packed with Jews. Once exposed to properly heated air—bodies tightly crammed into the gas chambers helped to ensure that the temperature was right—the crystals produced lethal gas. Death came minutes later.

Second, during the night of 2–3 August 1944 Zyklon B took the lives of nearly three thousand Roma and Sinti (Gypsies) at Auschwitz-Birkenau. In all likelihood, this destruction of the Gypsy "family camp" took place so that more room could be made for arriving transports of Hungarian Jews, some of whom were selected for labor. The "Night of the Gypsies," as that massacre came to be known, was symptomatic of two important realities that Auschwitz helps to underscore. First, during the Holocaust, Europe's Gypsy population was the one whose treatment by Nazi Germany most closely resembled the genocidal fate of Jews under the swastika. For example, when Nazi Germany enacted its Law for the Prevention of Hereditarily Diseased Offspring on 14 July 1933, that authorization for compulsory sterilization to prevent the "unfit" from breeding included Gypsies among its targets. Consisting of different "tribes" or "nations," this ethnic minority—called "Gypsies" because they were thought to have Egyptian origins—had been social outcasts since their arrival in Europe from India in the 1400s. The Sinti and Roma tribes were the most common in Germany and Austria, respectively.

Labeled "asocials" and racial "inferiors," Sinti and Roma were regarded as so "unfit" that Heinrich Himmler's circular of 8 December 1938, "Combating the Gypsy Nuisance," recommended "the final solution of the Gypsy question." Himmler spoke of "the physical separation of Gypsydom from the German nation," but such pronouncement did not mean that identical policies were developed and enforced for Jews and Gypsies alike. Anti-Gypsy ideology and propaganda never achieved the intensity of Nazi antisemitism. Gypsies were less tempting targets for expropriation of property. Hitler never gave priority to the "Gypsy question" in the same way that he concentrated on the "Jewish question." Although Himmler's orders of 16 December 1942 sent Germany's Gypsies to Auschwitz, he differentiated between "good" and "bad" Gypsies, significations that indicated racial purity or mixed-blood (*Mischling*) status, respectively. For Himmler, Gypsy *Mischlinge*, not racially "pure" Gypsies, were the primary concern. The latter, Himmler thought, should not be singled out for destruction because their Indian ancestry might trace back to an ancient Indo-Germanic people.[69] Nevertheless, although Gypsies were not targeted in the same way and despite the fact that, as Guenter Lewy argues, "no overall plan for the extermination of the Gypsy people was ever formulated,"[70] Nazi Germany's treatment of the European Gypsies was genocidal. Population data are insufficient to make precise judgments about the overall numbers and percentages of Gypsy death, but throughout Nazi-occupied Europe, tens of thousands of Gypsies were hunted down and shot or deported and killed in camps. Approximately 22,000 Roma and Sinti were sent to Auschwitz-Birkenau alone, where some 19,000 perished, including more than 5,600 who were gassed.[71] Even if the destruction of their life was not the Holocaust's centerpiece, Gypsies have good reason to speak of the *Porrajmos* ("the great devouring") when the genocide inflicted on their people is remembered.[72]

The use of Zyklon B at Auschwitz-Birkenau and the destruction of Gypsy as well as Jewish life in that place suggest that Nazi Germany's racist and antisemitic appetite for mass murder might have raged on and on, had it not been crushed, as at last it was, by superior military power. Jews were to be destroyed root and branch. But related fates were in store for countless other peoples. Steeped in visions of German superiority that made all "inferiors" threatening in one way or another, Nazi Germany's T4 program, its military campaigns of annihilation, its *Einsatzgruppen* and police squadrons, its inventiveness with gas vans, killing centers, and the most elaborate death camp of all, Auschwitz-Birkenau, reveal inclinations that would have produced killing without end. If Nazi Germany had gotten its way, the destruction of the European Jews would have been not only an end in itself but also a step in the direction of ever more thorough ethnic and racial cleansing. If Hitler and his followers had prevailed, Auschwitz-Birkenau would have been not only a singularly lethal place but a template for genocidal destinations beyond that accursed place.

## THE KILLING ENDS

Although the Third Reich was in retreat by the summer of 1944, it still held 750,000 persons in its huge but increasingly vulnerable concentration-camp network. Fierce fighting continued until Germany's surrender in May 1945, but in November 1944 Nazi Germany's deteriorating military circumstances led the Germans to stop the gassing operations at Auschwitz-Birkenau and to cover up the mass murder they had committed there. Before Soviet troops liberated the camp on 27 January 1945, the Germans ensured that the crematoria and their gas chambers were demolished; only their ruins remain. They also attempted to destroy as many documents and as much loot as possible, but the accumulations were too huge. When the Soviets arrived, for example, they founds hundreds of thousands of coats and suits and seven tons of human hair.[73] Also overlooked by the Germans were the blueprints for the camp's construction, including the crematoria. As the scholarship of Robert Jan van Pelt has shown, these documents have proved to be crucial in analyzing the devastating part that Auschwitz played in the Final Solution. As for the prisoners left in Auschwitz and other camps outside Nazi Germany's interior during the winter of 1944–45, the Germans knew that this labor source—including the incriminating testimony these men and women could deliver—would fall into the Allies' hands unless the prisoners were evacuated. Very little Jewish labor resulted from the evacuations that ensued, but immense brutality and suffering did.

Earlier the Germans had transported Jews and other prisoners in railroad cars and trucks, but forced marches also took place throughout the war. Especially during the winter of 1944–45, with other forms of transport scarcer than ever, the Germans ordered prisoner relocation marches over long distances. Starved, ill, wounded, and exposed to severe winter weather, the tormented prisoners were kept under guard, shot if they faltered, or left to die where they dropped from exhaustion. As the weeks and months passed, these *Todesmärsche*—death marches, as the prisoners called them—became increasingly brutal, deadly, and senseless. The term *death march*, however, understates the reality to which it refers. Daniel Goldhagen rightly speaks of *extermination* marches, for their routes were often circuitous and without clear destinations—except that they were intended to produce death.[74] The longer the marches lasted—and they lasted until the bitter end—the more Jews died. At least one began as late as 7 May 1945, the day before Germany officially surrendered.[75] In all, between 250,000 and 375,000 prisoners, most of them Jewish, perished during the extermination marches ordered by Nazi Germany during the throes of its defeat.[76]

Beginning in mid-January 1945, as the Soviet army liberated Warsaw and Cracow, about sixty thousand prisoners were evacuated on foot from the Auschwitz complex.[77] In hiding or too infirm to be moved, six to eight thousand prisoners were left behind in the Germans' haste to depart. More than fifteen thousand Jews died on the way to Gleiwitz and Wodzislaw, where those who remained alive were jammed into uncovered railroad cars. Without food or water, many more perished during the long and frigid journey that took the prisoners west to concentration camps such as Sachsenhausen, Gross-Rosen, Buchenwald, Dachau, and Mauthausen. In late January 1945 another fifty thousand Jews were evacuated on foot from the Stutthof camp system, which was situated on the Baltic coast in northern Poland. About five thousand of them trudged to the Baltic shore, where they were forced into the water and shot. The remainder headed for Lauenburg in eastern Germany, but when advancing Soviet units cut off the route, the prisoners were marched back to Stutthof. By late April 1945, Soviet ground forces surrounded Stutthof. Once again, the prisoners were marched to the sea, where hundreds were shot. Sea evacuation sent about four thousand prisoners to Germany. Many drownings on the way contributed to the estimated total of more than twenty-five thousand deaths that resulted from the Stutthof death marches.

In the final phase of the death marches, no one in Germany could believe in a German victory, but the cruelty inflicted on the Jews remained unrelenting. Goldhagen describes, for instance, the death march that followed the evacuation of 970 Jewish women from Schlesiersee, a satellite camp for women in the Gross-Rosen concentration camp complex.[78] This death march was not their first; already they had marched there from Auschwitz. In Schlesiersee's snow, their work consisted largely of digging antitank ditches. With nothing resembling adequate clothes and shoes, the women were beaten when they attempted to protect themselves from the frigid weather by wrapping themselves in their blankets. These beatings could only reduce the women's labor productivity but were inflicted nonetheless, which suggests that the "logic" in this case gave more priority to brutalizing Jews than to working them.

As Soviet forces approached, the SS guards evacuated Schlesiersee's prisoners and marched toward a camp for women slave workers at Grünberg near Breslau, now the Polish city of Wroclaw, which was still under German control. During this tortuous march, which took eight days to cover sixty miles, 150 of the 970 Jewish women died along the way.[79] About twenty perished because of exhaustion and starvation. Germans shot the others. The Schlesiersee women had barely arrived when the Germans decided that Grünberg must be evacuated too. On 29 January 1945 the new prisoners joined about 900 women from the Grünberg camp, and they were sent on their way in two groups, one headed for Helmbrechts, the other to Bergen-Belsen.

Consider what happened to the group of about one thousand women who were sent toward the Bavarian camp at Helmbrechts, which was a satellite of the Flossenbürg complex. Those who were unable to rise in the morning, or who dropped from exhaustion as they walked, were killed on the spot by the guards. Obviously weak prisoners were placed on a horse-drawn cart. When the cart was filled with the half-dead, they were taken into the woods and shot. In spite of the odds against them, 621 women in miserable health reached Helmbrechts after a month-long march of at least 250 miles during which they had to spend the nights outdoors in the snow, received little food or drink, and were subjected repeatedly to brutal beatings.

Commanded by Alois Dörr, who had joined the SS on 28 January 1933, the Helmbrechts camp stood at the edge of the German town from which it took its name. The town's residents could not have been ignorant about the camp, which supplied slave labor for German armaments industries. Given the harsh circumstances that prevailed in all of the German concentration camps, the living conditions of the non-Jewish prisoners were relatively good. Few of them died there. By contrast, the treatment the Jews received was extremely harsh. At night, for example, the Germans locked the barracks housing the Jewish women, making the latrines inaccessible. Suffering from dysentery, many of the Jewish women could not reach the barracks' buckets, which overflowed because they were insufficient to hold the bodily waste. The barracks stank terribly. In the morning, the camp guards would beat the Jewish women for soiling the barracks but refused to provide additional buckets to handle at least some of the problem.[80]

Although supplies of food and clothing were relatively plentiful at Helmbrechts, the Jews wore soiled rags and were fed only once a day. Their noontime soup was so meager that the other inmates disparagingly called it *Judensuppe* (Jew soup). Non-Jewish women at Helmbrechts did not die of hunger, but many Jewish women did. Photographs of the survivors, taken when the camp was liberated, show cadaverous human beings with a thin layer of discolored flesh covering their skeletal bodies.

On 13 April 1945, less than four weeks before Germany's surrender, Dörr ordered the evacuation of all Helmbrechts prisoners, including the very ill. He left the march's destination less than clear but indicated that the guards were free to dispose of the prisoners as they saw fit.[81] The march began with 580 Jewish women prisoners and 590 non-Jews, guarded by twenty-two men and twenty-five women. The female guards were as brutal as their male counterparts. On the march both food and clothing were available, but according to postwar testimony of both the German guards and the surviving Jews, none was given to the Jews. In a few towns German civilians attempted to give bread to the Jews but were forbidden to do so by the guards. The women were given no water; dehydration took its toll. In one town the mayor wanted to offer the women indoor accommodations, but Dörr refused the offer and compelled the Jews to sleep out of doors.[82] The Germans beat the Jews for any reason, including the "crime" of being sick. Jewish women were shot at will until the very end.

By early May, with the Allies closing in upon them, the Germans decided to abandon the Jewish women, but only after seeing them across the Czech border. As the march headed in that direction on 4 May 1945, an American plane strafed the German vehicles, killing a female guard who was pregnant. Some Jews fled in the chaos, but the attack drove the guards into a frenzy, and they fired into a group of defenseless, prostrate Jews. When American troops liberated the survivors two days later, only about half of the Jews remained alive among those who had started the utterly futile trek twenty-two days earlier.

The Helmbrechts march was one of many. All were marches to nowhere and served no military purpose. On the second day of the Helmbrechts march, moreover, a German lieutenant serving as a courier from Himmler found Dörr and conveyed Himmler's explicit orders not to kill any more Jews.[83] (At the time, Himmler was still under the impression that he could make a deal with the Allies and either succeed Hitler or be minister of police in a post-war German government.) Himmler's orders mattered not at all. The victims were helpless and totally unthreatening, but in the chaos that had descended on Germany, Dörr and his crew were free to torture and murder at will. Jews who perished during death marches were seldom buried. On at least one occasion, however, Dörr ordered burial, but in this case, a former German prisoner testified, one or more of the women being buried still "showed signs of life." She told Dörr that "he could not bury people who were still alive." Dörr replied, "They will perish anyhow. The more Jews perish, the better! They are anyhow about to die."[84]

Goldhagen was the first scholar to bring the death marches to the attention of a wider public audience. He notes that there were hundreds of similar marches from the end of 1944 to May 1945.[85] He also emphasizes that ordinary Germans contributed to their misery. In the final days of the Third Reich, the death marches' columns of walking skeletons were not hidden from the German public. As noted, at times some Germans acted out of pity. More often, they looked upon the predominantly Jewish prisoners as "subhumans" whom they jeered and at whom German children threw stones.[86] A survivor testified that on 13 April 1945 in the town of Gardelegen, Hitler Youth and the police chased between five and six thousand Jews into a barn, which they set afire after pouring gasoline on the structure and machine-gunning any who attempted to escape.[87] Corpses were still smouldering when American troops liberated Gardelegen the next day. Gardelegen was by no means the only site where victims were burned alive in Germany and eastern Europe.[88]

As we indicate above, in earlier studies on the Holocaust, scholars often tended to stress the cool, rational, bureaucratic character of the extermination process. The validity of that interpretation needs to be supplemented by the fact that, as Jewish survivors of the extermination marches and even their SS guards have testified, many Germans were also seething with hatred toward their victims.[89] At his postwar trial, one of the SS guards from the Helmbrechts death march made the following observation:

> If I were asked whether the purpose of the march was, more or less, that the Jewish prisoners should gradually be driven to death, I must say that one could indeed have this feeling. I have no proof of this, but the manner in which this transport was carried out speaks for it.[90]

When we ponder the possible motives for the seemingly purposeless German rage that could not be stilled as long as even one Jew remained alive in what was left of Nazi-controlled Europe, one explanation stands out as most plausible: starting in 1919, the steadily mounting propaganda of the German right held that the Jews had brought about Germany's downfall in World War I and were plotting to finish the job in World War II. This outlook had captured the minds and hearts of millions of Germans who should have known better. This was especially true of the SS and the military. As the war drew to a close, many Germans shared Hitler's view that the defeat of their country would be a victory for the Jews. In their minds, once again it was the Jews who had defeated their beloved land and had, this time, opened the gates to the conquest of their cherished *Heimat* (homeland) by the barbaric forces of Judeo-Bolshevism. If they could not defeat this enemy, they could at least vent their hatred and wreak their vengeance on the Jews under their control and do so in the cruelest possible way.

We cannot definitely prove that this mind-set could be found in millions of Germans, though not all, as the war came to an end. Nevertheless, this explanation is consistent with the following:

- Hitler's "prophecy" of 30 January 1939 and his subsequent repetitions of that prophecy both before and after the decision was taken to implement the Final Solution fully
- The summer 1941 decision, supported by the *Wehrmacht*, to murder Soviet Jewry, save for a small number of especially useful skilled workers and professionals
- Christian Gerlach's theory concerning the timing and the motivation for Hitler's decision to murder the Jews of Germany, which emphasizes Hitler's belief that, with America's entry into the war, the Jews had succeeded in bringing Germany into a world war
- The findings of Robert Gellately and others who reliably stress, in Gellately's words, that "the great majority of the German people [were] devoted to Hitler and they supported him to the bitter end in 1945"[91]
- Hitler's political testament composed in his Berlin bunker on 29 April 1945 a few hours before his suicide

Consider briefly this last point. Facing his own imminent death after launching the most destructive war in the history of humanity, a war that resulted in the death of over fifty million human beings, Hitler denied any and all responsibility for the war and blamed it on the Jews:

> It is untrue that I or anyone else in Germany wanted the war in 1939. It was wanted and provoked solely by international statesmen either of Jewish origin or working for Jewish interests. . . . Centuries will go by, but from the ruins of our towns and monuments the hatred of those ultimately responsible will always grow anew against the people whom we have to thank for all of this: international Jewry and its henchmen.

He then referred one last time to his infamous prophecy of 30 January 1939 and boasted of its fulfillment:

> I have left no one in doubt that if the people of Europe are once more treated as mere blocks of shares in the hands of these international money and finance conspirators, then the sole responsibility for the massacre must be borne by the true culprits: the Jews. Nor have I left anyone in doubt that this time millions of European children of Aryan descent will starve to death, millions of men will die in battle, and hundreds of thousands of women and children will be burned or bombed to death in our cities without the true culprits being held to account, albeit more humanely.[92]

At the very end of his life, with the country he led lying in ruins and occupied by its enemies, Hitler reaffirmed a view of reality that had proved to be as lethal as it was distorted: the Final Solution was the just deserts for those he called "the real criminals": the Jews. Responsible for the war, they had been "held to account," but "more humanely" than those "true culprits" had treated their German enemies.

These falsehoods were by no means embraced by Hitler alone. Hitler's lie that the Jews were responsible for all the ills that had befallen Germany served for him as moral justification to make exterminating them a top priority. It also permitted millions of Germans to believe that, although the annihilation of millions of unarmed men, women, and children was perhaps a dirty business, it was ethically justified. Moreover, the German people did not follow Hitler primarily because of coercion or fear. To a genocidal extent, they followed him as full partners until the killing ended.

Intentional starvation, forced labor, shooting, gassing, extermination marches—Nazi Germany destroyed the European Jews and millions of defenseless non-Jews in many ways, but they perished one by one. Each one, as Richard Rhodes says, was "a name, a person, a kin, a soul, a loss."[93] The Final Solution's immensity meant that there could be no precise quantification, let alone a qualitative assessment, as far as Jewish losses were concerned. Even the most reliable figures vary—but not flagrantly—depending on the years and geographical boundaries used to determine prewar census data, the margins of error in death reports from German and Jewish sources, and the difficulties of comparing prewar and postwar populations. One leading Holocaust scholar, Raul Hilberg, estimates that 5.1 million Jews were annihilated in the Holocaust. Most other scholars believe that the Jewish death total approaches the symbolic figure of six million. Yisrael Gutman and Robert Rozett, for example, put Jewish losses between 5,596,000 and 5,860,000. The German historian Wolfgang Benz raises the total of Jewish victims to more than 6.1 million.[94] Every reliable judgment asserts with confidence that between five and six million Jews—nearly two-thirds of European Jewry and one-third of the world's Jews—died in the Holocaust. With help from his allies, collaborators, and his German people, all of whom went far in making his wishes their own, Hitler remained true to his lethal claim. "The Jewish question" had taken "priority over all other matters."

# PART THREE
# RESPONSES TO
# THE HOLOCAUST

# Chapter 9

# Victims and Survivors

*In my opinion, there will always be more victims than perpetrators. In fact, all of humanity is likely to be a victim, given the current state of possibilities of destruction and unrest. Victims are not passive, except in their last moments. We must know how the Nazis' victims behaved, what cultural baggage they had to start with, and whether their behavior or their baggage was useful in any way. We must know what they thought, how they reacted, what they did. Therein lies a lesson, possibly, or a warning, possibly, or an encouragement, possibly.*

Yehuda Bauer, *Rethinking the Holocaust*

A prize-winning poet named Abba Kovner (1918–88) led one of the first Jewish resistance organizations in the ghettos of eastern Europe. About 57,000 Jews, approximately 30 percent of the population, lived in his home city, Vilna, often called the Jerusalem of Lithuania.[1] Engulfed by the German advance eastward in the summer of 1941, Vilna was occupied on 24 June and soon scourged by squads from *Einsatzgruppe* A. Assisted by Lithuanian police, the Nazis did away with twenty thousand Jews prior to ghettoizing the remainder on 6 September 1941. Most of the dead had been murdered at Ponary, a wooded area six miles from the city, but German precautions to make the mass killings inaccessible to public view did not prevent a few stunned survivors from returning to Vilna early that September. Their reports met disbelief. By the end of October another ten thousand Jews had vanished. Yet for those who remained behind, just as for those who did not envision their fate until too late, the picture remained unclear. As Kovner suggests, Vilna's survivors could see that "they were doomed to a life of suffering, trouble, and persecution. But that the slaughter of millions was a possibility—no;

that was something the darkest imagination could not conceive, something no one wanted to believe."[2]

Life seemed to hinge upon possession of a precious yellow work permit that entitled its holder "to protect his family, which, under German ground rules, was limited to husband, wife, and two children under sixteen."[3] There were never enough permits to go around. Moreover, the Germans intended that Jews themselves should have to make fateful decisions concerning which members of their own families would be most vulnerable. Those who lacked or could not be covered by these tickets for life continued to be prey for Ponary. The murderous roundups continued into December 1941. Thereafter the Vilna ghetto, reduced to some twenty thousand Jews—five thousand of them remaining there "illegally"—would continue struggling for life until it was liquidated in September 1943. Pivotal in that struggle were the 150 young Zionists who gathered in a soup kitchen at 2 Strashun Street on 1 January 1942 to hear Kovner read a call for resistance.[4] Adopting a biblical image (Ps. 44:11), it insisted, "We will not be led like sheep to the slaughter!"

Thanks to Kovner, there was armed resistance in the Vilna ghetto, but it is crucial to note his later testimony, namely, that his phrase "like sheep to the slaughter" continued to haunt him as long as he lived. What haunted Kovner was that his own words, ironically and inadvertently, were often stripped from their context and misused to undergird the impression that the Jews were ultimately the ideal victims for Hitler because they were so utterly passive in receiving the Germans' crushing blows. Kovner's point was not to say that Jewish behavior against Nazi Germany was characterized by armed resistance, nor to deny that there was Jewish passivity. But he was haunted by the fact that the phrase had become a code word. It designated a stereotype containing a lack of understanding no less real than that which prevented the Jews of Vilna from recognizing, as Kovner proclaimed in 1942, that "Hitler plans to destroy all the Jews of Europe, and the Jews of Lithuania have been chosen as the first in line."[5]

Kovner prefaced his first call for resistance by urging Jewish youth not to trust "those who are trying to deceive you." First and foremost, he had the Germans in mind. But the sources of deception were not restricted to them alone. They were present within the ghetto too. Disbelief and even hope could be deceptive, but beyond those personal and psychological dimensions, some interpreters have argued that a crucial source of deception could be found in much of the Jewish leadership during the Holocaust. Especially in the internal administration of the Jewish ghettos, it has been asserted, Jewish leaders themselves played vital if not collaborating roles in leading their own people to the slaughter by complying with the Germans.[6] For example, Hannah Arendt argued as follows in her 1963 book *Eichmann in Jerusalem*:

> Wherever Jews lived, there were recognized Jewish leaders, and this leadership, almost without exception, cooperated in one way or another, for one reason or another, with the Nazis. The whole truth was that if the Jewish people had really been unorganized and leaderless, there would have been

chaos and plenty of misery but the total number of victims would hardly have been between four and a half and six million people.[7]

Arendt's allegations might have taken the Vilna ghetto as a case in point. For example, when the Germans prepared the work permits that enabled some Jews to survive there, the distribution of those yellow tickets was handled not by the Germans themselves but by the Jewish council (*Judenrat*), which was charged with internal governance of the ghetto. Jewish leadership had to decide what to do with the work permits. The German instructions established quotas for skilled workers required by the wartime economy. Beyond those boundaries, the *Judenrat* had to handle the matter for itself, and this it did by distributing the tickets. As events unfolded, the distribution process involved the Vilna *Judenrat* in a selection process that determined who might live and who would die. If that fact was not apparent at first, it soon became unmistakable. For it was not long until the Jewish police, empowered to maintain law and order inside the ghetto, found themselves required, under SS supervision, to ferret out those without the work permits, who were subsequently killed at Ponary.

The man in charge of the Jewish police in Vilna was Jacob Gens. He not only participated in the roundups but gradually became the dominant Jewish leader inside the ghetto. One of Gens's biographers finds that "to the Germans he presented the image of a good and faithful servant." Some of Vilna's rabbis reminded Gens of Maimonides' teaching, namely, that even if only a single Jew's life were demanded, then all should be killed, rather than give up that person. Gens found a different justification more fitting for Vilna's circumstances: "I cast my accounts with Jewish blood and not with Jewish respect. If they ask me for a thousand Jews, I give them because if the Germans themselves came, they would take with violence not a thousand but thousands and thousands and the whole ghetto would be finished. With a hundred I save a thousand; with a thousand I save ten thousand." Gens believed that he would eventually stand vindicated "at the bar of judgment before Jews," though he also admitted that "many Jews regard me as a traitor."[8] Arendt found the latter part of Gens's self-estimate far more apt than the former.

Arendt's appraisal unleashed a storm of controversy, not least because this highly respected political philosopher happened to be Jewish. Although scarcely any scholar is prepared to follow her in thinking that an unorganized and leaderless Jewish people would have suffered less devastation during the Holocaust, there is little doubt that her proposition sparked a profound concern to determine in a systematic way how Jews had responded to Nazi persecution and the Holocaust. Personal testimonies and individual eyewitness accounts proved invaluable in this regard. In the process, as Hilberg points out, it also became clear that "not only was German destructive activity bureaucratic, but so also was Jewish dying. . . . There was a Jewish history which was not merely personal but also organizational, having to do not only with the way people felt, with their attitudes and reactions individual by individual, but also a very voluminous, complex and difficult subject matter, namely, the organization of Jewish life under the Nazis during the thirties and early forties."[9] These testimonies and documents, hundreds of thousands of them, are still being researched; interpretations are still being formed, debated, and tested.[10] When Hilberg calls that subject matter complex and difficult, he does not exaggerate. Situations and reactions were not identical, nor were the individuals involved. Enough exceptions are available to make almost every generalization questionable. All can agree that the victims as well as the killers had much to do with making the death count what it was. But how are the victims' roles to be described, and how are their responses to be appraised? Those unsettled questions must be addressed if we are not to be haunted by stereotypes or deceived by false impressions about the Holocaust.

## AN IMPULSE TOWARD COMMUNITY

Against Hannah Arendt's claim that an unorganized, leaderless band of Jews stood a better chance against the Nazis, it can be argued that her proposition is beside the point because such community dissolution was not more than remotely possible. Centuries of adversity had taught Jews to cope not by heading off in separate directions but by coming together to meet shared needs and to find ways to carry on their cultural, educational, economic, and religious lives. That same experience also vindicated the wisdom of developing leadership that could find favor with Gentile authority or at least ease the burdens that might be placed upon Jews. It was rarely the case, however, that widespread Jewish unity was easily achieved, as the situation in Germany during the 1930s illustrates.

About 550,000 Jews lived in Germany in 1933. Insofar as German Jews could be classified into coherent groups, their diversity and divisions—the latter partly caused by the increased immigration of eastern European Jews—were still considerable. There were, for instance, traditional Orthodox Jews who might see Hitler's oppression as a judgment or test befalling them as God's chosen people. At a distance from them were various Zionist factions, but their interests could also interpret Nazi oppression as instrumental in building Jewish nationalism and spurring emigration to Palestine. Still other Jews were members of internationally oriented Marxist organizations, Socialist or Communist. Their outlooks intensified opposition to Hitler but not necessarily along specifically Jewish lines. Perhaps the largest segment of German Jewry, however, was a highly assimilated middle- and upper-middle-class group. If not very religious, they still retained a primary identity as Jews but also thought of themselves very much as Germans. Their visibility was enhanced because they were concentrated in large cities and overrepresented in business, commerce, the professions, and university life. Though they were not captains of industry, their educational and entrepreneurial skills did give them a higher average income than non-Jewish Germans. All of these factors helped make them a target population.

When Hitler came to power in 1933, German Jews lacked an effectively unified organizational or ideological base for blunting—let alone physically resisting—the Nazis' antisemitic campaigns. Yet, as Hitler coalesced his power in 1933, many German Jews sensed that they must unify. Specifically it struck them that a single organization with a strong central leadership was needed. Enough consensus was achieved to launch the *Reichsvertretung der deutschen Juden* (Federal Representation of German Jews) on 17 September 1933, with Berlin's Rabbi Leo Baeck, one of Germany's most prestigious Jews, as its head.[11] The solidarity reflected by this organization, however, was fragile. For if German Jews talked about unity, their practices continued to be oriented toward factional differences. Simultaneously structured and fragmented by a multitude of diverse organizations, Germany's Jews were both more and less than a single community.

Raul Hilberg suggests that there are five main reactions that may be made to force of the kind that the Nazis brought to bear against German Jews in the 1930s: armed resistance, alleviation, evasion, paralysis, and compliance.[12] Armed resistance was not the *Reichsvertretung's* way, but neither was paralysis. Trying to represent all German Jews, it worked to expand economic possibilities, to facilitate emigration, and to defend Jews against defamation and violence. Early on, the *Reichsvertretung* frequently sent protesting memoranda to Nazi officials. As it petitioned the Nazi regime, it also advised German Jews about stances to take toward Nazi measures and worked to implement programs of education and culture, relief and welfare. Its tactics were primarily those of alleviation, predicated on the conviction that Jews could outlast and even discredit Hitler's antisemitism.

If alleviation tactics often led the *Reichsvertretung* to encourage evasion via emigration, on other occasions they required acts of compliance. One ironic example involved a plebiscite held on 12 November 1933. Hitler wanted a vote of approval for his domestic and foreign policies. Still possessing the right to vote, what were Jews to do? The *Reichsvertretung* petitioned the government for clarification, reminding the officials that the Jews would be suspect if they failed to vote and even more so if they voted no. Yet how could they possibly vote yes in their circumstances? Having to settle for explanations that an affirmative vote was needed to ensure Germany's international status and world peace, the *Reichsvertretung* counseled that "the vote of the German Jews can be only Yes."[13]

Tactics of alleviation and compliance perhaps helped to make Nazi oppression bearable. It could not be self-evident, moreover—except to those blessed with twenty-twenty hindsight—that a genocidal catastrophe was in store for German, let alone European, Jewry, for in the early months the restrictions placed on German Jews, oppressive though they were, did not stand out as unusually cruel in the light of previous history. But a catastrophe was in the making; nor would its course be reversed by alleviation or compliance. With the enactment of the Nuremberg Laws of 1935, any hint of Jewish criticism brought severe reprisals. In spite of the *Reichvertretung's* statement that the Nuremberg Laws "must create a basis on which a tolerable relationship becomes possible between the German and the Jewish people," hope that the Nazi dictatorship would be brief, or even that tolerable accommodations with it could be made, began to dwindle.[14] By 1938 even Heinrich Stahl, Baeck's deputy chair in the *Reichsvertretung,* would say that there was no future for Jews in Germany.[15] His forecast was grimly corroborated by *Kristallnacht.* In the wake of shattering glass, thousands of Jews were imprisoned in concentration camps. For several months suicides accounted for more than 50 percent of Germany's Jewish burials.

An event less spectacular but perhaps of even greater significance occurred a short while later. By a state decree of 4 July 1939 the *Reichsvertretung* became the *Reichsvereinigung der Juden in Deutschland.* Under this decree, relief efforts and the upkeep of Jewish schools remained within the purview of the organization, but other functions changed considerably. No longer was the emphasis to fall on the representation of Jewish interests, but rather the *Reichsvereinigung* would be an "association" including all persons classified as Jews by Nazi definitions. It would, moreover, be responsible for handling tasks assigned to it by the Interior Ministry, among them providing the Gestapo with information, communicating governmental decrees to the Jews, and helping to enforce those measures. Without changing personnel, the Jewish communal organization had been taken over by the Nazis. It would become instrumental in the forthcoming destruction process.

The Germans' experience with the *Reichsvertretung*-transformed-into-*Reichsvereinigung* provided a model that could be adapted to fit conditions created by the outbreak of war in September 1939. Hence, three weeks after the invasion of Poland, Reinhard Heydrich supplemented a crucial order. Not only would all Jewish communities of fewer than five hundred members be dissolved and transferred to concentration centers, but additionally "in each Jewish community, a Council of Jewish Elders is to be set up which, as far as possible, is to be composed of the remaining authoritative personalities and rabbis. . . . The council is to be made fully responsible, in the literal sense of the word, for the exact and prompt implementation of directives already issued or to be issued in the future."[16] Owing to their historic tradition of internal communal autonomy and responsibility, the beleaguered Jews initially regarded these Jewish councils (*Judenräte*) as legitimate mediating institutions between themselves and the German authorities. But the *Judenrat* was not the *Kehillah* (organized Jewish community) of old. It would become, however involuntarily, a functioning adjunct of the SS bureaucracy. Its responsibilities included the maintenance of tolerated social services, rationing and food distribution, the collection of demographic information, administration of labor permits, personnel allocation, and finally the rounding up of Jews to be sent to slave labor and extermination centers. Compliance with German orders did not cease even when the Germans demanded the rounding up of thousands of Jews daily for deportation. The success of the Germans in incorporating the *Judenräte* into the SS bureaucracy suggests that the capacities of a modern government include even the organization of an entire people to facilitate their own elimination.

Under German domination, the *Judenräte*'s first duty was to communicate or to carry out German orders, regulations, and wishes. Within those boundaries, they had to cope with Jewish communal needs as best they could. Increasingly these restrictions included the fences and walls of ghettos, especially in the East, where in 1941 for example, hundreds of thousands of Polish and Lithuanian Jews would be concentrated in Warsaw, Bialystok, Vilna, Cracow, and Lodz. From those locations, journeys to the death camps did not take long. The *Judenräte* would help see to that, just as the *Reichsvereinigung* did in Germany proper when deportations began there. By 10 June 1943 the Nazis could dissolve the *Reichsvereinigung*, for Germany was virtually *judenrein*.

Only two members of the *Reichsvereinigung* survived. One was Leo Baeck. Deported to Theresienstadt, he became an honorary member of the *Judenrat* in that ghetto. Even after he became convinced that rumors about gas chambers at Auschwitz were true, he decided to tell no one, reasoning that "living in the expectation of death by gassing would only be the harder."[17] Baeck spoke of his decision as grave. We can assume that he did what he thought was best, surmising that to publicize death by gassing would lower morale, increase despair, and make foregone a conclusion that might somehow be forestalled for those still in the ghetto. He continued to pursue tactics of alleviation until the end, thinking they were the best resistance against the Nazis. Inclinations to think that he was wrong, however well intentioned, should be held in abeyance until additional alternatives are considered.

## DILEMMAS AND ALTERNATIVES IN THE GHETTOS

Ghettoization of Jews was a crucial step in Nazi Germany's destruction process. It was in the ghettos, especially those in eastern Europe, that the Jews were concentrated, thus making other areas *judenrein*. When attrition from starvation and disease did not happen fast enough, Jews were then dispatched to die in the killing centers. Every ghetto was different, not only in terms of its leadership, inhabitants, and the precise policies dictated by the local German officials in charge, but also in physical location and design.[18] The largest, Warsaw, was eventually surrounded by a high brick wall.[19] Situated in the General Government, it still afforded more opportunity for Jewish escape than did the ghetto in Lodz. The latter appeared to be more open, surrounded only by barbed wire and a board fence, but it was situated in the Warthegau, a part of Poland annexed into the Reich and populated by ethnic Germans whose enthusiasm for Nazi antisemitism was strong. The smaller Vilna ghetto stood in the middle of the city. Access in and out was perhaps easier than in Lodz or Warsaw, and the surrounding territory afforded more options, owing to the forests nearby and to the diverse Gentile population in a domain that had once been Polish, then Lithuanian, and most recently a Soviet republic.

Variety in the ghettos spread across Europe from east to west, however, does not eliminate the fact that those places also had much in common. First, they were all political entities, characterized by enforced segregation of their inhabitants from the surrounding population. The Germans brought ghettos into existence to control and thin Jewish life, and the Germans required a Jewish leadership to implement their decrees. Second, each ghetto was a socioeconomic organization. Many inhabitants worked for the Germans. Indeed, most of the *Judenräte* perceived that only by maximizing those opportunities and by laboring diligently did their ghettos have a chance to survive. The ghettoized Jews often proved amazingly resourceful in making themselves economically valuable to the Germans. Makeshift factories purchased time for thousands of Jews. Smuggling, bribery, and other clandestine operations supplemented the precarious and ever-dwindling food supply. Yet the final outcome remained primarily under German control. That power dictated when Jews, working or not, were superfluous; it could also enlist the *Judenräte* and their Jewish police forces to curtail the illegal activities that became indispensable for sustaining ghetto life. Meanwhile the *Judenräte* and their offices were not the only centers of activity in a complicated community network of social-welfare organizations, cultural associations, religious and ideological collectives. With or without a *Judenrat's* blessing, these self-help institutions, voluntary and largely autonomous, did much to sustain the ghetto. Supplementing whatever a *Judenat* might do directly, they collected and distributed food, found people shelter, and organized other necessities. Under their encouragement, artists created, historians recorded, physicians practiced, and scientists did research as best they could. They were instrumental in seeing that outlawed schools functioned secretly. They supported theaters, orphanages, hospitals, and child-care centers. Without their auspices, banned religious observances could not have been so widely held.

Believing the Germans would lose the war, the *Judenräte* and the diverse self-help agencies acted as though the ghetto had a future. If they had no alternative, the fact remained that the ghetto was a German creation, which at best was a way station for Jews between prewar freedom and wartime annihilation. Ironically, by making life more bearable, even the best accomplishments of the *Judenräte* and other relief groups could be used to the Germans' own advantage, for every success encouraged the hope that things were not as bad as they always turned out to be. Signs that the vise was closing were available too. Preeminently, the ghetto economy, chronically wracked by unemployment and faced with constantly dwindling assets to procure the food needed for subsistence, was incompatible with long-term survival.[20] Yet strategies of physical resistance did not often meet with *Judenräte* approval. Instead the policy of rescue-through-work was upheld, and the meager resources available to the *Judenräte* were stretched to meet communal needs. Considering the duress, it is no surprise to learn that social equality and economic justice did not always prevail.[21] As in all other human societies, those with greater power, status, and needed skills commanded more of the scarce resources. The weak got less. In December 1941, for example, Warsaw's "Council functionaries were getting the largest food allocations, 1,665 calories a day, compared to an average of 1,125 calories allocated to the general population."[22] Even those who got more, however, were hardly immune to violent death.

The fundamental dilemma for the *Judenräte* was that "they could not serve the Jews indefinitely while simultaneously obeying the Germans."[23] That squeeze could be unbearable. Repeatedly it produced what the Holocaust scholar Lawrence Langer has called "choiceless choices."[24] To illustrate, consider the diary of Adam Czerniakow. Its entry for 29 April 1942 observes that the Nazis wanted ten maps and population figures for the Warsaw ghetto. That demand came to Czerniakow as chairman of that community's *Judenrat*. A balding engineer in his sixties, Czerniakow served in this position for nearly three years. Like the other statements in his diary, this one does not make forecasts or reflect on long-range plans. It records reports and rumors, many of them ominous, in subdued tones and without elaboration. If Czerniakow could sense that those orders to produce population data and maps might foreshadow deportations that would end in the gas chambers at Treblinka, those intuitions did not betray him.

Less than three months later his diary's last notation states, "It is 3 o'clock. So far 4,000 are ready to go. The orders are that there must be 9,000 by 4 o'clock."[25] The numbers cited by Czerniakow refer to the quota of Jews the Germans expected the Warsaw *Judenrat* to help them "resettle." By the end of World War II, 99 percent of the approximately half-million Jews who had occupied the Warsaw ghetto were dead, a majority of them slain at Treblinka after deportation. Czerniakow did not live to see this destruction process unfold to its bitter conclusion. Not long after finishing the last entry in his diary, he swallowed the cyanide tablet hidden in his desk.

Opinion about Czerniakow is divided. One Warsaw survivor, Alexander Donat, believes that if suicide bore witness to Czerniakow's personal integrity, it did not attest to his greatness, for he spread no alarm about the imminent deportations. Yet Czerniakow had worked day after day to alleviate Jewish need within the ghetto. Permitted to deal directly only with low-ranking Nazi officials, he nevertheless met with them time and again to solicit relief for his people. Unfortunately the results were paltry. Never could he obtain the food, space, or security the Jews so desperately needed. Periodically he might secure the release of a prisoner, get better conditions for Jewish children, or locate a little more to eat. What such victories meant, ironically, is part of Czerniakow's tragedy. They were seized upon as testimony that survival in the ghetto might be possible. In fact, the unrelenting German aim was to rid Warsaw of Jews completely and permanently.

*Judenräte* officials, however, were not privy to German plans. They did not know exactly what ultimate fate the Germans had in store for the Jewish ghettos. Nor did those officials ever volunteer to help deport Jews, even when German assurances about "resettlement" might have been tempting. To think that they *collaborated* with the Germans would be a perverse distortion, and even to say that they *cooperated* with them blurs the fact that these men were impelled by terror to comply. Noncompliance was an alternative, but it was a ticket for immediate deportation, if not summary execution. Czerniakow's path of suicide was another way out, one taken by several others in authority, but it offered little hope for the ghetto population as a whole, which the *Judenräte* were committed to save in the best ways they knew how. Hence, they tended to be leery of armed uprisings too, fearing these would bring severe German reprisals that would doom the entire community. In fact, the variety of *Judenräte* responses ranged widely. Jewish leaders in the Polish cities of Lublin and Cracow, for example, tended to obey every German order exactly and without diversionary tactics. Similar situations existed in Vienna and throughout the Netherlands. Even late in the war, when German intentions were at least an open secret, on the eve of the deportation of the Hungarian Jews, 3 May 1944, the *Judenrat* in Budapest petitioned the Hungarian interior minister: "We emphatically declare that we do not seek this audience to lodge complaints about the merit of the measures adopted, but merely ask that they be carried out in a humane spirit."[26] In places such as Minsk and Kovno, on the other hand, the *Judenräte* were actively involved in organizing or assisting armed resistance groups.[27] Similar situations existed in Slovakia and Belgium. Recalcitrance to compliance, it should be added, also tended to be greater during the period 1939–41 than afterward, owing to the fact that many of the early *Judenräte* members were experienced, responsible prewar leaders as well. Their stubbornness was thinned out by Nazi executions, and replacements less likely to frustrate German expectations were found.[28]

If a majority of *Judenräte* did not exhibit determined resistance to German orders, neither did most comply helplessly. In a broad middle range, where the strategy of rescue through work was the governing policy, there was still fairly often genuine *Judenräte* resistance to the German threat. At least that case can be made if the meaning of "resistance" encompasses "all active and conscious organized action against Nazi commands, policies, or wishes, by whatever means: social organization, morale-building operations, underground political work, active unarmed resistance or, finally, armed resistance."[29] In reckoning with the ghettos and camps, such a way of construing resistance is not out of place; for in any way that Jews refused to give up and disappear, it could be said that they thwarted the German aim. Hence when the *Judenräte* supported schools and cultural activities, when they worked to organize food supplies, when they tried to negotiate for Jewish lives or facilitate escape efforts, as some did from time to time, their resistance was real. In this light, even the strategy of rescue through work may be construed as a resistance tactic. And when Jewish leaders cautioned against armed uprisings or even took steps to quash them, which was not always the case, the line to draw is not necessarily one between resisters and nonresisters but rather between different philosophies of resistance. For not only was the possibility of armed resistance within the ghettos hamstrung by a lack of weapons, but resistance groups themselves also had to weigh if and when to strike. They could never be unaware of the devastating reprisals that the German policy of collective responsibility would visit on the entire community.

As head of the *Judenrat* in Lodz, Mordecai Chaim Rumkowski, a childless widower who had formerly been a businessman and the director of an orphanage, ruled that ghetto dictatorially "by force of personality, tenacity of purpose, organizational intelligence, and political shrewdness, even outwitting the SS in its attempt to displace him."[30] Mocked and despised both for his pretentious airs and his nearly fanatical belief that work would save the Jews of Lodz, he was nonetheless obeyed because his strategy seemed credible. By the summer of 1944, however, the snare and delusion were apparent. Indeed, as early as 16 December 1941 the Germans told Rumkowski that twenty thousand Jews must leave Lodz. When he announced this order to the ghetto four days later, Rumkowski claimed that he had persuaded the Germans to take only half that number.[31] The Jewish leadership itself, moreover, could determine those to be relocated. However inadvertently or unwillingly, Jews were taking an active role in the very process of population elimination that the National Socialists desired. The selectees, Rumkowski suggested, would probably move to smaller towns where food was more plentiful. The Resettlement Commission established by Rumkowski—it included representatives from the ghetto's police force, judicial and penal agencies, and office of vital statistics—determined that the first to go should be recent arrivals in the ghetto and persons convicted of crimes. The families of these "undesirables" were included. The Jewish bureaucracy in the ghetto did its work, enforcing the deportation orders by refusing fuel rations to those who declined to leave. Within a month, the first group went off, not to small towns but to the killing center at Chelmno. In a speech to vindicate his action, Rumkowski argued that he had received a ruthless order. He had carried it out to prevent the Germans from doing so even more violently, and he had also been able to reduce the numbers required. In fact, by removing part of the ghetto population, which he referred to as a "suppurating abscess," he implied that his action ensured safety for those who remained.

A lull of several weeks followed the last of the initial deportations. Then, in late February 1942, new orders resumed them. During the next six weeks, one thousand persons had to leave daily. The Resettlement Commission kept making the selections. When the supply of lawbreakers diminished, the unemployed and recipients of ghetto welfare came next. A strategy of thinning out first the harmful and then the unproductive elements in the ghetto repeated itself in numerous places. Through the spring and on into the summer, the Germans' calculated pattern of respite from and then resumption of the deportations continued too. Increasingly corroborated, rumors about Chelmno multiplied. Rumkowski had this information as new orders demanded deportation of the sick, adults over sixty-five, and children under ten. On 4 September 1942, ever hopeful that salvation might come through work, insisting that "the order could not be undone, it could only be reduced," Rumkowski cried, "Brothers and sisters, hand them over to me! Fathers and mothers, give me your children! . . . The part that can be saved is much larger than the part that must be given away."[32] Amidst escalating terror and panic, these orders were also carried out in Lodz by Rumkowski's forces and the Germans. Rumkowski had pleaded with the Germans to exempt the nine-year-olds. The petition refused, his conclusion was that "we can't go against the order, only lighten its execution. Do you think the Germans will be so gentle and kind if they carry out the order themselves?"[33]

In June 1940 about 160,000 thousand Jews lived in the Lodz ghetto. The unforgiving deportations left about 69,000 by August 1944. Now, under penalty of death, they were also ordered to the trains. The implications of deportation were no longer mysterious. Still, compliance followed initial refusal to obey, for there could be no doubt that the Germans would ravage the ghetto, but glimmers of hope remained that movement from Lodz would not be disastrous. Rumkowski urged the people to go peacefully. He could have stayed behind with the few hundred men and women assigned to clean out the ghetto, but he elected to join the last train with his brother and his family. When it departed on 30 August 1944, Chelmno was no longer operating, but Auschwitz was, and Rumkowski died there. The historian Michael Berenbaum reports that there are various accounts of his death, which may suggest more about the attitudes of Jews in the Lodz ghetto than about what actually happened:

> According to some eyewitness reports, Rumkowski was beaten to death by Jews. In another account, Rumkowski arrived at Auschwitz by train with a letter from Hans Biebow, the German overseer of the Lodz ghetto. He was "invited" to tour the camp by his "hosts." His wagon stopped at the crematorium, where he was burned alive without being gassed. In still another account, the aged Rumkowski, too old to work, was selected for the gas chamber upon his arrival.[34]

Unarmed, weak, and often starving, the Jews in Lodz lacked the resources to mount an effective resistance against the Germans or even against Rumkowski. But especially as the war dragged on, whatever inclination may have existed to do so was reduced by hope that Germany's defeat might come in time. Russian troops were not far away in the summer of 1944. Had they not stalled their own advance, tens of thousands of Jews might have survived, and Rumkowski's policy of salvation through work would have had a better outcome. That scenario did not unfold; work brought no salvation to Lodz. Rumkowski was no willful accomplice of the Germans. Nonetheless his ghetto remained so vulnerable to German domination that it became a self-destructive machine, even paying the one-way train fares charged by the German railways for transportation from Lodz to the death camps.

The tragedy is that, short of reversing and radically altering a two-thousand-year-old pattern of Jewish-Gentile relationships, it is hard to imagine that the Lodz ghetto, once established by the Germans, could realistically have been anything other than a death trap. The long-standing Jewish strategy of coping with Gentile threats had been that of alleviation and compliance, but the Germans were playing a new game with different rules. When their objective became a Final Solution, alleviation was at best momentary; compliance at worst meant self-destruction. To mount a more effective resistance would have taken years, even generations, of groundwork that reevaluated the basic assumptions of individual and communal Jewish life in Europe. Some movement in that direction had occurred—various Zionist impulses, for example, come to mind—but not even these envisioned what finally happened under Hitler. Until too late, there was simply no compelling logic to convince Europe's Jews that there would be a Holocaust. After it was too late, Jewish responses were characterized much less by violent resistance than by the rationalization that sacrifice of the few might save the many—especially if the latter worked hard. Where obedience to German orders could not be construed as a life-saving strategy, there were still Jewish arguments for compliance on the grounds that suffering could thereby be reduced.

The *Judenräte* lacked the knowledge and the power to compete with the Germans on anything approximating equal terms. Nor did the other people in the ghettos go like sheep to the slaughter. They did what they could and had to do to survive. No less than their leaders, however, they were simply unable to stem the tide that carried them away. No amount of new evidence, however, is likely to settle debate about the Jewish councils to everyone's satisfaction. The problem is that *intention, function,* and *result* in the cases of the *Judenräte* were intertwined and snarled with such complexity that it is extremely difficult to find precise language to describe the actions that the councils took. In order to save Jews, they had to participate in the destruction of Jews. If the emphasis falls on intention, the *Judenräte* appear in a more favorable light than if one stresses results. But evaluations that tip the scales by weighing one or the other of those elements must still reckon with the *Judenräte*'s functional status and its context of possibilities. The inescapable core of their function was to facilitate implementation of German decrees. The ways to avoid doing so were limited. Hence the intentions of the *Judenräte* might be good enough, in spite of the results, and yet the results, which make the functional status plain, show that even the best intentions may play into the hands of power that is utterly opposed to them. Success in showing that the *Judenräte*'s intentions were, generally speaking, not blameworthy makes the Holocaust less painful for Jews than it would be if the Jewish cause had been rife with overt collaboration.[35] But the most important outcome of that achievement may be to stress what powerlessness means. For whatever their intentions, the *Judenräte* were not effective life-saving agencies. They never could have been; they lacked the power requisite for such work. That condition was not their fault. Credit for it belongs to the Germans and to centuries of Gentile domination of a Jewish minority. Whether the *Judenräte* were blameworthy is much less important than the issue of who holds power and how a relatively powerless group can best defend its interests.

## FIGHTING RESISTANCE

German photographs of Jews confined in impoverished ghettos, lined up for the *Einsatzgruppen,* boarding Nazi transports, or filing toward the gas chambers may give the impression of obedient passivity. What those pictures do not show is that a lack of physical resistance at the time of imprisonment or mass murder is not something peculiar to Jews.[36] Faced with imminent execution by the Nazis,

French Maquisards, Russian prisoners of war, and Czechs at Lidice did not resist physically. Nor did the Poles deported from Warsaw after their abortive uprising in 1944, months after the Jewish ghetto fighters there had battled the forces of General Jürgen Stroop for weeks.

The pictures taken by German photographers, moreover, do not show the conditions prior to their being taken. Neither can they fully portray the experience of victims such as those described in Hermann Graebe's eyewitness account of what preceded one *Einsatzgruppe* action: "The father was holding the hand of a boy about ten years old and was speaking to him softly; the boy was fighting his tears. The father pointed to the sky, stroked his head, and seemed to explain something to him."[37] As for the prior conditions, Jews who had attempted to elude roundups usually paid with their lives. Once caught, those who did not remain calm could anticipate being shot summarily too. Families wanted to stay together as long as possible, and some individuals looked on their deaths as religious martyrdom. Nor, as Isaiah Trunk has argued, can the following be discounted:

> There is perhaps a further moral and psychological element explaining why most of the victims went quietly and passively to their death: a possible refusal to show the murderers any panic or hysteria that might have given additional pleasure to the sadists among them. The victims preferred dying with dignity and with scorn toward the killers. The Jews might also have actually wondered whether it was worth fighting for one's life in a world where the human beast could rule undisturbed amid the passive silence of the entire civilized world.[38]

Not all Jews, of course, shared this outlook concerning death with dignity. Caught in the Holocaust so that the question was no longer "How shall we live?" but "How shall we live before we die?" many Jews affirmed that a physically armed, fighting resistance was essential, not because it would save lives but because it would show a scorn toward the killers, a refusal to let Jewish life be taken with impunity.

Armed resistance during the Holocaust must be understood realistically. It neither did nor could materialize spontaneously, especially when Jews were weakened by hunger and disease and were woefully armed as well. Armed Jewish resistance was mustered only against great odds—internal as well as external—and the impetus behind it took time to develop just as the execution of anything approximating effective acts of armed resistance required careful preparation and judgment. The extent of armed resistance within Jewish ghettos, inside the Nazi concentration camps, among Jewish partisan units (it is estimated there were at least twenty-seven of them in Poland alone), and in underground groups across the European continent is now known to have been much greater than the stereotype of "sheep to the slaughter" implies. Insight about how this resistance emerged and what it accomplished is important for grasping further the odds that the Jews faced in combatting the German effort to annihilate them.

One can speak of *dissent* against a regime in situations where the possibility of significant legal opposition remains. For Jews, dissent against the Nazis was impossible; there were no significant legal channels within the German power structure that could be utilized. All opposition, therefore, was resistance, whose nucleus can be defined as "challenging the intrinsic right of authority to select and implement policy."[39] In varied forms, Jewish resistance to Nazism emerged early on and continued until the Third Reich was crushed. But this resistance was not primarily one of physical force. The realities of Jewish political status in Europe, the tradition of Jewish responses to adversity, and the lack of material support from other resistance groups during World War II kept from European Jewry the wherewithal to launch effective armed uprisings. A more compelling logic was that it was better not to take the risks of violent resistance, which might provoke even worse repression, than to endure existing conditions, however minimally bearable they might be.

Particularly in the ghettos and camps, hope for survival made it harder, not easier, to organize armed resistance. Moreover, as the hope for survival became sufficiently dimmed to remove it as an impediment to physical resistance, the odds made "victory" out of the question, although taking revenge on the Germans and bequeathing the example of armed resistance for future Jewish life provided key motivations. Even those motivations, however, might be insufficient to provoke armed rebellion, for one might feel that it is better to die with others than to resist absurdly, futilely, with no hope of winning, and with the very real possibility that one's agony might only increase. For others, however, it was precisely the hopelessness of their situations that led them to take action. They thought in terms neither of military victory nor of personal survival; they were determined to do what they could to stop the Germans. Particularly in the ghetto uprisings, a sense of Jewish honor and identity came to the fore along with ideological commitments—Zionism, socialism, and communism were the most typical—that emphasized a historical sense of struggle, group loyalty, and a cause that transcended personal survival.

Organized armed resistance by Jews occurred throughout Europe, although its presence in the West has been overlooked owing to the fact that it often functioned as "a kind of underground within the underground."[40] Jewish resistance in eastern Europe was at once more identifiable and more problematic, as some examples involving Jewish partisans illustrate. Unlike most partisan fighters, who can at least count on passive support in their locale, Jewish partisan units in eastern Europe often encountered as much hostility from local populations as they did from the Germans. In addition, although the Allied forces parachuted arms and material to Polish partisans, similar assistance was consistently withheld from Jewish resistance units, ostensibly because Jews were not a clearly defined national group. In eastern Europe, moreover, Jewish partisans had the best chance of survival if they were able to join a Soviet partisan group. Once accepted, however, they ceased to fight directly for their own people. Although Soviet policy opposed putting Jews in special jeopardy, some Soviet partisans were antisemitic. Under the best of circumstances, service in a Soviet unit involved subordinating direct action for one's fellow Jews to purely Russian war aims.

Within the ghettos, Jewish resistance had problematic aspects, not only because of extreme difficulties in obtaining arms, but even more fundamentally because Jewish opinion was divided religiously and politically. Even among the mostly young Zionist, Socialist, and Communist groups, who eventually sparked the armed fighting, there was early on no unanimity of opinion. Furthermore each group had its individual organizational problems, not the least of which was communication from place to place in areas under severe German restrictions. Prior to the first reports of mass murder, which began to circulate in the ghettos during the summer of 1941, the underground Zionist and left-wing political groups worked primarily to make ghetto life more bearable. Those concerns included clandestine journalism to expose *Judenräte* corruption. Although these groups were stunned by the incredible nature of the first reports, they responded differently from most—including many *Judenräte* officials—by investigating further. A majority of these leaders found their worst suspicions confirmed: Jews were facing an unprecedented annihilation. Diverse ideological views and local conditions, however, meant that even then there was no single, agreed-upon strategy but instead a series of quandaries to be faced. Even among those groups who agreed that it was essential to form combat groups and to accumulate an arsenal, there was a question whether to maintain their own cadre, escaping from the ghettos to fight with partisans in the forests, or to remain inside the ghetto walls to attempt protection of the entire community, a task that would entail a virtually suicidal encounter with German troops, even if it allowed release for feelings of hatred and revenge. These questions were answered differently, but in nearly all the large ghettos armed resistance developed, some of it as early as spring 1942. In Bialystok some fighters joined partisan groups; others stayed inside the ghetto to resist the German liquidation in August 1943. Urban guerrilla units hindered the deportation efforts in Cracow; some fought on until this ghetto succumbed in March 1943. The Germans met armed force in Vilna too. Even in Lodz, where German domination and *Judenrat* control were extremely strong, raids and sabotage operations occurred. None of the ghetto resistance efforts, though, is more celebrated than the one in Warsaw.

In the Warsaw ghetto, it is noteworthy that the first shots fired by the resistance movement were directed not at Germans but at Jews. The initial target was the chief of the Jewish police. Others belonging to the German-controlled Jewish bureaucracy were also assassinated, with the result that the Warsaw *Judenrat* lost much of its power. These events occurred in the late summer and early autumn of 1942. Only about seventy thousand Jews then remained in the ghetto, less than 20 percent of those who had once been there. Death in the gas at Treblinka had taken those who survived starvation and disease. Defense measures proceeded as the Jews awaited the next blow. Coming in January 1943, it caught the fighters by surprise, but the Germans drew fire, and Jews had the unaccustomed thrill of seeing them "retreat in fright from a handful of young Jews equipped only with a few pistols and hand grenades."[41]

Subsequently Himmler ordered the destruction of the ghetto. That task began on 19 April 1943. Under the leadership of Mordecai Anielewicz (1919–43), approximately 750–1,000 Jews armed with makeshift weapons sought to hold out as long as possible against a German force more than twice that size and vastly better armed. The Germans' assignment was to clear the ghetto in three days. It took four weeks instead. The first Jewish counterattack drove the Germans out of the ghetto. The result, however, was never in doubt. In a matter of days, Jews were caught and killed increasingly. The ghetto was in flames when May arrived. Some fighters, Anielewicz among them, took their own lives rather than fall into German hands. A few escaped through the sewers. Thousands of unarmed Jews perished in the fighting; more than fifty thousand others were captured and dispatched to killing centers and labor camps. Perhaps another five or six thousand got out of the ghetto during the confusion of the fighting, but most of them were tracked down later, thanks to Polish gangs who abetted the German search. German casualties, on the other hand, amounted to a few hundred. Armed resistance in the ghettos was no more effective as a life-saving device than the accommodating policies of the *Judenräte*, but the difference was that the resistance groups never rationalized their existence along those lines. For them, resistance was more an end in itself. Their model was the Zealot defense of Masada during the ancient Judeo-Roman war. These Jewish resisters had no illusions about their situation during World War II. Nevertheless, they were determined to fight to the bitter end.

Jewish partisan activity was a thorn in the Germans' flesh, no doubt winning life for numerous Jews, but the ghetto fighter, the partisan, and the Jewish member of other underground networks were never positioned to determine decisively the fate of their fellow Jews, let alone the destruction of the Third Reich. Even less could those Jews do so who mustered armed resistance in the camps. Besides small-scale fighting escapes from various labor camps and brigades, there were armed uprisings in Treblinka, Sobibor, and Auschwitz. Resources to carry out such activity were so scant, the odds against its accomplishing anything of material importance so great, that armed resistance in these places was rare. The astonishing thing is that it happened at all.

Armed revolts in the death camps were instigated primarily by veteran prisoners, who, in adapting to the most extreme conditions, had moved beyond confusion or despair but still recognized that they were as good as dead. If they no longer had the ideological zeal of some of the ghetto fighters, their experience taught them the ways of conspiracy and deception. Violence was not ruled out when rebellion became literally their only alternative. In Auschwitz, for example, it was chiefly Greek Jews assigned to work in the crematoria who succeeded in destroying one installation on 7 October 1944. Knowing that SS policy would consign them to death in a matter of months, these men, some of them formerly resistance and army personnel, worked with determination and with the cooperation of resistance movements all through the Auschwitz camp to accumulate the material needed for their sabotage.[42] Interestingly enough, at the last minute the resistance leadership in Auschwitz, echoing arguments used by the *Judenräte* in some ghettos, urged the *Sonderkommando*s not to proceed because doing so might result in the murder of the entire camp population. The revolt was not aborted, but the SS did crush it and eventually killed nearly all the crematoria workers involved. Earlier, about one hundred prisoners had managed to elude capture after escaping from Treblinka in the 2 August 1943 uprising in that camp. In the Sobibor revolt on 14 October 1943, about three hundred Jews escaped; two hundred avoided capture.[43]

The known samples suggest that many other acts of violent Jewish resistance occurred during the Holocaust, many of them motivated by a desire to get word to other Jews and to the outside world about what the Germans were doing. Although individual initiative and determination were important, these efforts were not usually the work of individuals acting in isolation. Friendship and cooperation were essential. So was commitment to a cause, or at least the willingness to risk everything rather than to accept defenselessly an inevitable death. Given the odds, the importance of such actions lies less in their objective success than in what they reveal about the range of human responses to extreme conditions of domination and about the costs of powerlessness. Far from being nonexistent, Jewish armed resistance was remarkable during the Holocaust. But its impressive quality derives largely from the fact that it came from a people facing hopeless odds. Whatever glory it contains, the price for it was too high. Not that the cost would have been reduced if the armed resistance had failed to materialize—that argument by some of the *Judenräte* lost its compelling power after 1943, and it will not convert many now. What remains persuasive, though, is that the tribute paid to a tragic Jewish resistance would be unnecessary if Europe's Jews had not been so defenseless in the first place.

## WOMEN AND CHILDREN

The Holocaust took an immense toll on Jewish children. From the Nazi perspective, their die was cast by the faith of their great-grandparents. No mercy could be shown to boys and girls thus targeted; they were the next generation of the racially threatening population that must be eliminated. Thus, "Jewish children had to fend for themselves in a world so base no prior experience could have prepared them for it. . . . The percentage of Jewish children who survived this German infanticide is the lowest of any age group to have come out of the Holocaust alive."[44] One and a half million Jewish children, most of them under the age of fifteen, lost their lives to the Germans and their collaborators in the major killing centers at Chelmno, Belzec, Sobibor, Treblinka, Majdanek, and Auschwitz, and in the ghettos, camps, and shooting sites that pocked the Nazi map of Europe. What about their mothers and grandmothers, their aunts and older sisters. What happened to women during the Holocaust?

Although many Holocaust memoirs written by women have existed for a long time, questions specifically about women, or about gender differences in any respect, got relatively little attention in Holocaust scholarship until the 1990s. In the most basic way, of course, the Holocaust's killing drew no distinctions among Jews: Hitler and his followers intended oblivion for them all—every man, woman, and child. Nevertheless, as pioneering efforts by scholars such as Myrna Goldenberg, Marion Kaplan, Dalia Ofer, Joan Ringelheim, Carol Rittner, Lenore Weitzman, and others have shown, the hell was the same for Jewish women and men during the Holocaust, but the horrors were frequently different.[45]

Women's experiences during the Holocaust varied immensely. While German women, for instance, were expected to bear children for the Third Reich (and they were decorated for doing so abundantly), Jewish women had to be prevented from becoming mothers. The Nazis invested considerable time and energy to find the most effective ways to sterilize them, but the "final solution" for this "problem" was death. Of course, if they were healthy and neither too old nor too young, Jewish women could be used before they were used up or killed. At Auschwitz, for example, some were "selected" for slave labor; at Ravensbrück, a concentration camp established especially for women, others became objects for the "scientific" experiments that were intended to advance Nazi programs of racial hygiene and purity.[46]

Women could be found among other victim groups during the Holocaust—Roma and Sinti, political prisoners, Jehovah's Witnesses, and the so-called "asocials," to name a few. In addition, women were among the neighbors who stood by while Jews were rounded up and deported all over Europe. They were among those who rescued Jews as well. Women could be found in virtually every intersection and intricacy of the Holocaust's web.

Some of the victims trapped in the Holocaust's web were non-Jewish German women, but German women, in particular, had other parts to play in the Final Solution.[47] Organized by Adolf Hitler and Heinrich Himmler, Reinhard Heydrich, and Adolf Eichmann, the Final Solution was instigated and dominated by men. The same can be said of virtually all modern genocides. In the case of Nazi Germany, however, some women held positions of responsibility in the Third Reich's concentration camps and killing centers.[48] Others were officials in the Nazi Party. Still others aided and abetted the destruction process as medical personnel, civil servants, secretaries, and members of other sectors of the home front's personnel-depleted workforce. Some German women stood trial and were convicted by postwar tribunals that judged war crimes and crimes against humanity.[49] Nevertheless, German women were not the primary perpetrators of the Holocaust. In general, their role was different: they worked in the German economy, and they were the sympathetic mothers, sisters, and daughters, the reassuring wives, friends, and lovers, of the German men who were usually more directly implicated in that disaster.

In general, one could scarcely say that German women were defenders of Jews or protesters against the Nazi regime, although significant exceptions to that rule could be found. Depending on the extent of their knowledge about the destruction of the European Jews, awareness that could have been greater or smaller depending on individual circumstances, many German women occupied for the most part a position between those of *perpetrator* and *bystander*—two of the categories that are often used to classify the various parts that people played during the Holocaust. We might speak of them as *partners*, for in multiple ways that is what they were in relationship to the German men who launched and carried out the Holocaust.

Nazi antisemitism meant that race—specifically the "purity" of German blood and culture—counted for everything. Nothing could be tolerated that might pollute the racial strength on which the Third Reich depended. According to Nazi theory, Jewish life posed this threat to a degree that surpassed every other; Germans could not afford to let Jews remain in their midst. As the history of Nazi Germany emphatically shows, racism's "logic" ultimately entails genocide, for if you take seriously the idea that one race endangers the well-being of another, the only way to remove that menace completely is to do away, once and for all, with everyone and everything that embodies it. The racism of Nazi ideology ultimately implied that the existence of Jewish families, and especially the Jewish women who mothered them, constituted a deadly obstacle to the racial purity and cultural superiority that Germany "deserved." Jewish women constituted that threat fundamentally because they could bear children.

Precisely because the Nazis targeted Jews and others in racial and biological terms, they had to see those victims in their male and female particularity. To destroy Jews in general—and forever—they had to override any protection that cultural convention afforded even Jewish women and girls; they had to destroy in particular those potential mothers who might bear the next Jewish generation. Heinrich Himmler, head of the SS, clearly understood this point. "We had to answer the question: What about the women and children?" Himmler remembered in one of his speeches. "Here, too, I had made up my mind. . . . I did not feel that I had the right to exterminate the men and then allow their children to grow into avengers, threatening our sons and grandchildren. A fateful decision had to be made: This people had to vanish from the earth."[50] It took the targeting of Jewish women as women to implement that decision.

Similar experiences are not identical. In the Holocaust, differences between men and women made a vital difference. That difference reflected the fact that human experience, suffering included, is usually gendered experience as well. The Holocaust helps to show that reality. The goal should *not* be to argue that what happened to women during the Holocaust was worse than what happened to men, that one gender's endurance and survival skills were necessarily superior to the other's, or that one gender's reflections and memories are clearer, more truthful, or more important than the other's. Nevertheless, it is a legitimate and important aspect of Holocaust studies to advance the growing realization that the history of the Holocaust is incomplete without responses to questions that focus explicitly on what women did and on what happened to them during those dark years.

To obtain a glimpse of what happened to Jewish women during the Holocaust, consider a line from a poem entitled "The Woman Poet": "You hear me speak. But do you hear me feel?"[51] Those words were written by Gertrud Kolmar (1894–1943), one of the most promising writers of her generation. Like so many in her time and place, however, her talent and her life were taken from her by anti-semitism, racism, and genocide. Gertrud Kolmar was a German, but she was also a Jew and a woman. She managed to survive in Berlin until the winter of 1943. In February of that year the Germans made a special drive to deport the last Jews from that city, even those who worked in war-essential industries. The last writing we have from Kolmar is a letter dated 20–21 February 1943. She was most likely caught in the roundup of Jewish workers that took place a few days later.

Camp records indicate that from late February until mid-March 1943 numerous transports brought several thousand Jews from Berlin to Auschwitz-Birkenau. Most of the women and children were gassed on arrival. The circumstances of Kolmar's death are uncertain, but she was probably among those who were immediately killed by Zyklon B. Berlin was declared *judenfrei* in June. The liquidation of German Jewry was officially completed in July. "You hear me speak. But do you hear me feel?" Gertrud Kolmar wrote those words some time before she entered Auschwitz, but especially after Auschwitz her words speak even more poignantly than before.

Much of the detail we possess about transports to Auschwitz comes from the careful work of Danuta Czech, a woman who painstakingly collated the data that forms the *Auschwitz Chronicle*, a day-by-day, night-by-night record of what transpired there. Drawing on documents that the Germans left behind or that the camp resistance kept, she lists how transport after transport arrived, and she indicates how many men and women were selected for immediate death or for slave labor. Gertrud Kolmar's name does not appear in that book of more than eight hundred pages, but again and again its entries remind us that Jewish women were targeted for destruction. Where women in the Holocaust are concerned, one event in Czech's book is particularly poignant. It happened on 25 June 1944. In a two-sentence paragraph, awesome not only for what it says but also for the questions its silence contains, Czech describes it this way: "Empty children's strollers are taken away from the storerooms of the personal effects camp, known as 'Canada,' which is located behind Camp B-IIf between Crematoriums III and IV. The strollers are pushed in rows of five along the path from the crematoriums to the train station; the removal takes an hour."[52]

Although Czech states the facts without embellishment or commentary, one may surmise what went on. Probably some of those baby carriages had arrived with Hungarian Jewish mothers. Perhaps they had been permitted to bring that equipment along—all the way to the gas chambers—to prolong the deception that made murder simpler. True, sometimes children were born in Auschwitz-Birkenau; some even lived long enough to have numbers tattooed on their frail bodies. But most mothers and children, especially Jewish ones, could not keep their lives, let alone their strollers, in that place. Having no utility, mothers and children usually disappeared in fire and smoke. German efficiency, however, could not let their empty prams be wasted. They had value. So off the carriages went, first to "Canada," and then to the train station in the camp's official five-row formation. Probably they were headed to Germany, where there still were mothers, raising children for the Reich, who could use them.

Czech says simply that the strollers were pushed to the train station. The removal, she adds, took about an hour. Testimony from another source, an Italian Jewish woman named Giuliana Tedeschi, brings to life the stark brevity of Czech's account. Part of a transport of 935 Italian Jews who reached Auschwitz-Birkenau on 10 April 1944, she was one of the 80 women and 154 men who did not go directly to the gas.[53] Those women were tattooed with numbers ranging from 76776 to 76855. Tedeschi's was 76847.

Tedeschi was the wife of an architect and the mother of two children, but as a woman in Birkenau she was alone, at least until she made friends with some of the other prisoners. Her moving memoir, *There Is a Place on Earth: A Woman in Birkenau*, not only recalls and records the horrors that surrounded her but also repeatedly draws attention to those human relationships that helped her to survive. There were moments of reprieve, but in Birkenau friendship meant sharing and resisting the limits that were imposed by what Tedeschi called "human bestiality."[54] As she would learn, that bestiality involved children's strollers.

There had been times in the camp when, at least comparatively speaking, Sundays were days of rest. During Tedeschi's time, however, that tradition had been abolished and special Sunday tasks were assigned. Sometimes she had to work along the railroad tracks that brought the Hungarian Jews to Birkenau during those late spring and summer days of 1944, when the Third Reich was collapsing but the gas chambers were operating at full and frenetic capacity. Close up, she saw the transports unload. She knew what the new arrivals did not, that death was imminent for all but a few. She also associates those Sundays with a smell:

> The whole camp was gradually pervaded by a smell that only we old hands could recognize, the smell that haunted our nostrils, that impregnated our clothing, a smell we tried in vain to escape by hiding away inside our bunks, that destroyed any hope of return, of seeing our countries and children again—the smell of burning human flesh.[55]

Sundays could make Tedeschi feel "morally destroyed, physically exhausted; the awareness of our impotence humiliated us, the instinct to rebel choked us."[56]

On Sunday, 25 June 1944, Tedeschi was one of fifty women who turned right when she went through the gate from her part of the camp. Ordinarily her work column went left, toward Birkenau's main gate and the road that led beyond. But on this particular Sunday the route was different. It led in the direction that most of the Hungarian Jews took only once. Up ahead, at the end of the rail spur, were Crematoriums II and III. It might be their turn, some of the women thought, but they were directed on, turned right again, and followed a path through the birch trees from which Birkenau took its name.

The path led to another crematorium. "The women went in through the big door," Tedeschi recalls, "and stood in the hall."[57] There death met them—not directly but in the form of fifty empty baby carriages. The Germans ordered them to push these strollers to safekeeping. Tedeschi says the distance was two miles; Czech says the removal took about an hour. That was neither far nor long—even to push a child's stroller—on any normal Sunday, but for Giuliana Tedeschi, 25 June 1944 was a Sunday she would never forget, nor in all likelihood could any woman who experienced it as she did.

Fear for their own lives "drained away," Tedeschi writes, "yet each face was stamped with a grimace of pain." And here is how her description of "this place on earth" continues:

> The strange procession moved forward: the mothers who had left children behind rested their hands on the push bars, instinctively feeling for the most natural position, promptly lifting the front wheels whenever they came to a bump. They saw gardens, avenues, rosy infants asleep in their carriages under vaporous pink and pale blue covers. The women who had lost children in the crematorium felt a physical longing to have a child at their breast, while seeing nothing but a long plume of smoke that drifted away to infinity. Those who hadn't had children pushed their carriages along clumsily and thought they would never have any, and thanked God. And all the empty baby carriages screeched, bounced, and banged into each other with the tired and desolate air of persecuted exiles.[58]

The accounts of Danuta Czech and Giuliana Tedeschi are close but not identical. Czech does not say who pushed the children's strollers. Tedeschi says that women were assigned the task and that her company's strollers came directly from a crematorium. Neither report mentions that men got stroller duty, but perhaps they did, for the fifty carriages mentioned in Tedeschi's report were by no means the only ones that reached Birkenau. More of them can be seen in Lili Meier's photographic *Auschwitz Album*, and there is at least one woman survivor who testified at the Nuremberg trials that sometimes hundreds of children's carriages arrived during a day's work in Birkenau.[59] If men got such assignments, their feelings would be no less important than those of Tedeschi and the other women she describes. But Tedeschi's report, a woman's testimony, is certainly one that needs to be heard and felt.

Was it an accident that women in Birkenau were assigned to move those baby carriages, a journey whose yearning and pain, grief and hopelessness, so far exceeded the hour and two miles that it took? It is hard to think so. Far more likely, the mentality that created Birkenau would have reasoned precisely: who better than women—Jewish especially, mothers even—to move empty baby carriages from a crematorium to safekeeping for the Reich? The Holocaust leaves behind heartbreaking memories and images, so many they cannot be counted. But none better epitomizes the plight of women during the Holocaust than the one offered by Giuliana Tedeschi: a Jewish woman prisoner pushing an empty baby carriage in Birkenau.

## THE SURVIVOR AS WITNESS

"There is a place on earth," Tedeschi's memoir begins, "a desolate heath, where the shadows of the dead are multitudes, where the living are dead, where there is only death, hate, and pain."[60] Birkenau stood in the very heart of Western civilization, within easy reach of the great universities, cathedrals, and institutions of European culture. In that "place on earth," so many of Western culture's humanizing promises failed. "Birkenau," says Tedeschi, "existed to suffocate hope and annihilate logic, to provoke madness and death."[61]

Hitler succeeded in destroying prewar Jewish life in Europe. His killers laid their hands on Jewish men and women, girls and boys, of every type and from every region. They included unskilled laborers from Lithuania and craftspeople from Greece; doctors from Paris, lawyers from Berlin, writers from Vienna; shopkeepers from Holland and farmers from Poland; Jewish families from Hungary and Romania; Jews of all ages, of diverse political outlooks and religious persuasions. Well after Hitler's suicide in April 1945 and Nazi Germany's surrender that May, the Holocaust's devastation continued, for liberation left the Jewish survivors less than free.[62] Most were in poor health and plagued by horrific memories. They found some relatives and friends alive, but more often than not they were struck with the news that loved ones had perished. The survivors usually could not return to their former homes, because those homes no longer existed. The few eastern European Jews who went home often experienced renewed antisemitism and found their property in the unfriendly hands of former neighbors. Most Jews who wanted to escape postwar Europe completely were unable to do so. Britain allowed merely a trickle of legal Jewish immigration to Palestine; illegal immigration was vigorously checked. Jewish refugees hoping to reach other countries, including the United States, often found restrictions rather than open doors. In 1945 most Jewish survivors had little choice but to stay in the DP ("displaced persons") camps that had been quickly established at such sites as former German army barracks, POW camps, and even concentration camps such as Bergen-Belsen and Dachau.

While no "official" definition of "Holocaust survivor" exists and not every victim or survivor of the Holocaust was Jewish, Holocaust survivors are primarily those children, women, and men who were identified as Jews by Nazi Germany, lived under the rule or occupation of Nazi Germany and its allies, and yet eluded the total annihilation that German policy eventually intended for the Jews of Europe and even worldwide. Every Holocaust survivor's experience is distinctive because survival involved different circumstances, times, and places. Some escaped Nazi persecution before World War II began in 1939 or before the Final Solution became Nazi Germany's official policy in 1941–42. Others endured the war years and the Final Solution itself, somehow making their way through impoverished ghettos, labor brigades, deportations, lethal camps, and death marches. Still others managed to survive by disguising themselves, hiding, or working in resistance groups. At the time of this writing, Michael Berenbaum,

former director of the Survivors of the Shoah Visual History Foundation, estimated that no more than 300,000 Jews who lived under the rule or occupation
of Nazi Germany and its collaborators after June 1941 were still alive. This aging
population is rapidly disappearing. By the middle of this century, it will no longer
exist. In recent years, survivor testimony has taken on a greater urgency, not only
because the time approaches when the last eyewitness of the Holocaust will be a
survivor no longer, but also because organized campaigns continue to deny that
the Holocaust ever happened.[63] Painful though it may be to dignify such charges
by responding to them, perceptive survivors have long known that they could not
allow denials of the Holocaust to be uttered without rebuttal.

The testimony of many Holocaust survivors may include narratives that reveal
an amazing resilience to begin again and to renew life—not least by giving birth
to children. After Auschwitz such testimony is welcomed, because the yearning
runs deep for wholeness to be restored and for the human spirit to be triumphant.
In jarring juxtaposition to those hopes, the testimony of those who survived the
Holocaust also testifies that the Holocaust remains at the depths of personal experience a disaster as inescapable as it is indescribable. When survivors bear witness,
their testimonies explore what the Holocaust survivor Ida Fink called "the ruins
of memory."[64] Speaking not about time "measured in months and years," as Fink
put it, but about time measured by devastating scraps—separations, selections,
silences—that forever fragment life and thwart its wholeness, survivor testimonies mute hope and leave credible optimism in short supply.[65]

The Fortunoff Video Archive for Holocaust Testimonies was established at
Yale University in 1982. Its holdings contain hundreds of testimonies that range
in length from thirty minutes to over four hours. Lawrence Langer, a leading
interpreter of literature and art about the Holocaust, conducted many of the
archive's interviews with Holocaust survivors or "former victims," as he prefers
to call them.[66] No one has studied these testimonies more thoughtfully. Published in his important book *Holocaust Testimonies*, Langer's findings provide
insightful guidance whenever survivor testimony is heard or read.

A governing theme in Langer's findings comes from Maurice Blanchot, the
French author of *The Writing of the Disaster*, a study that helped to inform Langer's
listening. "The disaster ruins everything," Blanchot's first sentence says, "all the
while leaving everything intact."[67] Like nature's changing seasons, the rising and
setting of the sun, apparently life goes on for the Holocaust's former victims.
Many testify, for example, how they married after liberation from the German
camps, built homes in new surroundings, raised children, and advanced careers.
Apparently their survival led to living lives that left everything intact. Only apparently, however, because the disaster leaves everything intact in another, far more
devastating, sense. Leaving the survivors alone, it removes—takes the former victims away from—the stability and coherence that normal life assumes. Thus, for
those who stayed alive after Auschwitz, life does anything but just go on. Such
living faces unhealing wounds, unending death, and unrelenting losses. For the
Holocaust's former victims, the disaster that came upon them so often pivoted

around disorienting/orienting scraps of time, crucial moments involving what Blanchot calls the "sovereignty of the accidental," a tyranny that ruled and destroyed life with systematic capriciousness.[68] Its disruptive impact makes the Holocaust a past ever present and always to be reencountered in the future.

Only one of the many testimonies that Langer sensitively weaves into his account, Philip K.'s epitomizes how "the disaster ruins everything." Resisting the reassurance of people "who pretend or seem to be marveling at the fact that I seem to be so normal, so unperturbed and so capable of functioning," Philip K. concludes *Holocaust Testimonies* by denying that "the Holocaust passed over and it's done with." No, he stresses, "it's my *skin*. This is not a coat. You can't take it off. And it's there, and it will be there until I die. . . ."[69]

Ghettoized, starved, deported, tattooed, beaten, raped, gassed, burned, callously scattered to the winds, but some of it left permanently scarred to live— Holocaust skin both covers and recovers what Langer calls "an anatomy of melancholy."[70] Physically rooted in the disaster, that anatomy is much more than skin-deep. Above all it probes memory. Often buried deeply but incompletely by an impossible necessity to forget, the memory resurrected—but not triumphantly—by the anatomy of melancholy is laden with what another former victim, Charlotte Delbo, calls "useless knowledge." Dissenting from the conventional wisdom that knowledge is always useful, Delbo's phrase is another that echoes in Langer's listening, for *Holocaust Testimonies* shows how survival in Auschwitz did little to unify, edify, or dignify the lives of former victims. It divided, besieged, and diminished them instead.

Langer's account, it must be emphasized, protests against any impulse that would judge and find wanting what the former victims did in their conditions of Holocaust extremity. On the contrary, he expresses esteem and admiration "to all the hundreds of men and women who told their stories before the camera."[71] Langer's judgment does seethe in quiet rage between the lines as one hears silently his writing of the disaster, but that judgment is properly reserved for the German policies that systematized the Holocaust's choiceless choices and the perpetrators who administered them. The disaster that came upon the Holocaust's victims was designed to make evident what Nazi ideology proclaimed, namely, that Jews were subhuman or even nonhuman, and its plan for doing so was to create conditions of domination so extreme that normal human life could not go on within them. That plan did not succeed entirely, but in the Nazi camps, as Leon H. puts it, "human life was like a fly."[72] Hunger, to mention but one of the Holocaust's hells, was not only "devastating to the human body," as George S. testifies, but also it was "devastating to the human spirit, . . . and you didn't know how to function."[73]

The victims did what they had to do—"This wasn't good and that wasn't good," remembers Hannah F., "so what choice did we have?"[74] Sidney L. adds to that realization when his testimony begins with the fact that he was one of nine children. The Holocaust's desolation left him as his family's lone survivor. One glimpses how far life under German domination was removed from usual human expectations about choice and responsibility when, with disarming simplicity, he recalls, "I was never asked 'Do you want to do such and such?'"[75] The glimpse, however, remains incomplete—"Well, how shall I describe to you how Auschwitz was?" puzzles Edith P.[76] Her question, which was asked in one way or another by many of the Holocaust witnesses Langer heard, seems addressed to herself as much as to her audience.

Speaking from his own experience, Langer rightly insists that listening to these testimonies requires extraordinary effort. So easily they can be distorted and falsified by the imposition of moral, philosophical, psychological, or religious categories. Part of what Langer calls "the grammar of heroism and martyrdom," the imposition of those categories can be singularly inappropriate, because they belong to a universe of normal discourse that the Holocaust eclipsed.[77] In the ruins of memory, expectation diminishes and yearning intensifies at once. The resulting tension remains, as it must, unreconciled and unreconciling.

The stark bleakness of Langer's anatomy of melancholy calls for coming to terms, if one can, with a condition that recalls Blanchot once more. As though he had heard Helen K. lament ("I can't believe what my eyes have seen") and pondered the question posed by Edith P. and so many others ("Do you understand what I'm trying to tell you?"), Blanchot invites meditation on circumstances in which "there is a question and yet no doubt; there is a question, but no desire for an answer; there is a question, and nothing that can be said, but just this nothing, to say. This is a query, a probe that surpasses the very possibility of questions."[78]

Optimism is scarce in the ruins of memory, but what Langer does find is "unshielded truth," an honesty that underscores what must be faced: "How overwhelming, and perhaps insurmountable," as he puts it, "is the task of reversing [the Holocaust's] legacy."[79] That legacy dwells in memory that is deep, anguished, humiliated, tainted, and unheroic. Correspondingly, that memory disturbingly uncovers selves who are buried, divided, besieged, impromptu, and diminished. Such is the taxonomy that Langer's anatomy of melancholy requires.

Often with greater penetration than written narratives by former victims, Langer is convinced, their oral testimony divulges the disruptions within these dimensions of the Holocaust's legacy. Written words can be polished, edited, and revised; they can become art in ways that oral testimonies cannot. Both oral and written testimony should have the respect each kind deserves. So Langer stresses that written accounts by former victims typically have a narrative quality—beginning, middle, and end—that eludes their oral counterparts even when the latter move from pre-Holocaust events to those that occurred after liberation. Importantly, thanks to the camera's eye, the oral testimonies that Langer heard are also visual. Spoken and unspoken, they communicate significantly through body language. In them hands and faces, especially eyes, have much to say. Such expressions, like the spoken thoughts they help to convey, are less controlled and controllable than written words.

Thus, even oral testimonies that start as chronological narratives are usually interrupted and disrupted by memories buried deep within—like the one that

constrains Edith P. to wonder, "Is there such a thing as love?" So harshly different from the world outside the ghettos and camps, such deep remembrances
expose selves divided by the anguish they contain. "I talk to you," Isabella L. tells
her interviewer, "and I am not only here, but I see Mengele [she lived in a barrack
from which he chose women, including her sister, for his experiments] and I see
the crematorium and I see all of that. . . . I am not like you. You have one vision
of life and I have two. I—you know—I lived on two planets. . . . We have these . . .
these double lives. We can't cancel out. It just won't go away. . . . It's very hard."[80]

Within such anguish may be recollections of humiliation that besiege—"I left
[my brother] there," laments Viktor C., "and I survived [prolonged weeping]. If
I forget anything, this I will never forget."[81] Even the present's recovered moral
sensibility can taint memory by disapproving the impromptu acts one had to
improvise—or failed to improvise—in the past: "How can you, how can you
*enjoy* yourself?" Leo G. questions himself.[82] The vulnerability that remains is
intensified by recognition that Holocaust survival is less a heroic triumph than a
matter of chance. At times, Helen K. grieves, "I don't know if it was worth it."

These strains are not the only ones Langer heard. Some of the former victims
tell about their determination to survive; they "knew" they would come out alive.
Others accent their defiance against German brutality. There are also many who
emphasize how important it has been for them to make their lives worthwhile
and to retain some hope after Auschwitz. Philip K. speaks for many of his fellow
survivors when he affirms, "We lost. . . . And yet we won, we're going on. . . ."[83]
Langer concludes that "several currents flow at differing depths in Holocaust testimonies." All of them, he adds, are "telling a version of the truth."[84] The truth
they tell, however, resists interpretations that console. Instead, its "disruption,
absence, and irreversible loss" are a reminder and a warning. The reminder is that
Holocaust testimonies need not have existed if the power of Nazi Germany had
been checked in time and if Europe's Jews had not been so defenseless. The warning is related: Although safety and security are never guaranteed, they do depend
on the strength and the commitments of the communities in which one dwells.
So in concluding this chapter's reflections about the Holocaust's victims and survivors, let us think further about power and powerlessness.


## THE VICTIM AS NONPERSON

World War II destroyed the National Socialist state. Survivors of a very different
kind, many of those directly involved in subjecting the Jews and other victims to
abusive slave labor and extermination were captured and brought to trial. It is
not surprising that former SS officers expressed no remorse. In general, they
claimed that they had merely obeyed orders. The only crime they could envisage
would have been disobedience, not mass murder. However, in addition to SS personnel, some of the most important and respected German industrial leaders
were brought to trial for knowingly and voluntarily employing slave labor under

conditions so abusive that the average victim died within three months. Utilization of slave labor was no isolated phenomenon. It was exploited by most of Germany's corporations, among them Siemens, Allianz, Volkswagen, Krupp, Bayer, and BMW.[85] After the war, some of the business leaders were sentenced to long prison terms for "crimes against humanity." Nevertheless, within five years not a single convicted industrialist remained in prison. Even after their restoration to positions of leadership and prosperity, the German industrialists expressed little regret for what they had done, although they were directly and knowingly involved in the deaths of tens of thousands of forced workers. In their attitudes, if not in their party affiliations, these men proved themselves to be unrepentant National Socialists.

How shall we understand these men, who in their daily lives were not sadistic brutes but respected business leaders in their community during the period of National Socialism and afterward? There is no evidence that in their personal lives they were men of exceptional evil. On the contrary, within their own community they were obviously capable of winning enduring respect and loyalty. Arguably these men felt no remorse because they regarded their victims as wholly outside their "universe of obligation—that circle of people with reciprocal obligations to protect each other."[86] Such was the condition of all of Germany's wartime enemies to some degree, but no group was more remote from any conceivable German universe of obligation than the Jews. Whatever residual sense of shared humanity linked the Jews to their neighbors before World War II tended to disappear under the murderous pressures of that war. Europe's Jews were considered alien to the universe of obligation not only of the National Socialists but of almost all peoples of the earth. This was evident in the refusal of countries to give even temporary shelter to more than a token number of those whom Hitler had condemned to death.

During the Holocaust, Europe's Jewish victims became *nonpersons*.[87] Originally, the *persona* was the mask worn by actors in the ancient theater. Without a *persona* one could not play a part. Eventually, the *persona* took on political meaning. A person was a being possessed of legal rights. Slaves and women were not regarded as full persons, because they had little or no right to a voice in the life of the community. It was, of course, clearly understood that slaves were biologically human, a fact dramatized in the frequent sexual encounters between masters and slaves. Nevertheless, as history continues to make clear, whether human beings are regarded fully as persons has less to do with biological than with political and legal conditions. Individuals who belong to no community willing or able to protect their rights may be biologically human, but politically they are nonpersons. Similarly, members of every group that has endured genocide were effectively stigmatized as nonpersons before their destruction. Before or concurrent with their travail, they were deprived of their political and legal status as members of the community in which they lived.[88]

The insightful testimony of Primo Levi (1919–87), an Italian Jewish chemist who survived Auschwitz after being deported to that place in 1944, recounts an episode that goes far to illustrate what follows when one becomes a nonperson. Not long after his arrival at Auschwitz, Levi reached out a window to quench his painful thirst with an icicle. When a guard "brutally snatched" the icicle, Levi dared to ask him "*Warum?*" (Why). Shoving the prisoner aside, the guard replied, "*Hier ist kein warum*" (Here there is no why).[89] Nonpersons are owed no explanations. They live or die at the pleasure of their masters. More than two decades earlier, well before the National Socialists came to power and that icicle was snatched from Levi's hand, the Czech Jewish author Franz Kafka prophetically dramatized the predicament of the nonperson. In his great novel *The Trial*, the protagonist, "K," is arrested without cause, accused of an unspecified crime by unknown accusers, and judged guilty by an unseen judge. When executed, his last words are "Like a dog," signifying his total loss of human status and the meaninglessness of his death. During the Holocaust, Kafka's fiction became reality.

Religion has attempted to overcome the contradiction between the biological and political definitions of being human by asserting that all human beings are equally beloved by their Creator. While in theory all persons are regarded by the biblical religions as children of a divine Creator, in reality no religion has been effectively capable of extending its universe of obligation beyond its own believers, at least not in times of extreme stress. Jews were never full persons in pre-Holocaust Christian Europe, and their post-Holocaust status remains an issue. Baptism was Christendom's ritual of entry into full personhood. The literature of Christianity vacillated between seeing the Jews as destined to become full persons when they finally converted and seeing them as incarnations of the devil. Christianity, however, was not alone in this denial. To the extent that Jews ascribed to themselves the role of an elect nation, chosen by God for a biblically certified eschatological mission, rejected intermarriage with those among whom they lived, and refused to share common food at a common table, they could not play equal political parts in Christendom. Again, what is at issue in our discussion is not biological but political status. Unless one has the good fortune to live in a state that is tolerant, pluralistic, and democratic—which has definitely not been the typical state of affairs in human history—one cannot, after all, be a full participant in the political life of a community while refusing to partake of a common table or to offer one's sons and daughters in marital union with one's fellow citizens. Moreover, the Jewish liturgy contained a profound rejection of political community. One cannot fully participate in the life of a community while praying that the time may come when God will take one to one's proper home elsewhere.

The above is said without any ascription of blame to either Judaism or Christianity. In particular, the Jewish yearning to return to an ancestral homeland, expressed throughout the prayer book, and the doctrine of *Galut*, which held that Israel was in exile among the nations, probably constituted the only appropriate response to a situation in which Jews could cease to be alien only by ceasing to be Jews. Nevertheless, the doctrines of both Judaism and Christianity had the practical effect of denying to Jews the status of full persons in political life. What was not understood until World War II was that the price of this denial could be mass extermination.

Confronted with the threat of extermination, the most fortunate potential victims are those with the material and psychological resources to become full persons somewhere else. Status can be changed by flight to another community in which the potential victims have the possibility of being treated politically as persons. This option was successfully taken by those German Jewish refugees who emigrated to the United States in the 1930s and eventually became American citizens. People can also become full persons by the intelligent and successful use of political and military force. Apart from those who are able to emigrate to a community in which they can become citizens, only those nonpersons who have the power to create a political community in which they can effectively define and defend themselves as persons can hope to overcome their negative status.

The sociologist Max Weber argued that a state is, above all, that institution which possesses a monopoly of force within a given territory.[90] If Weber is correct, and his understanding is ignored at one's peril, then membership in a political community implies having a share in that force, either by directly wielding it or by having an undoubted claim on protection from it. Lacking such shares of power, people easily become vulnerable targets; they can and often do become, in effect, nonpersons. It is a melancholy fact of human existence that personhood cannot be divorced from considerations of power. In the final analysis, human beings are reduced to the status of nonpersons by a want of power. The lack of remorse on the part of Germany's business leaders and many other Germans and Austrians after World War II can thus be seen as part of a larger phenomenon. Feelings of guilt and remorse are as much political and social as they are psychological. Especially in times of threat and danger, they are likely to be experienced only if one harms those who are part of one's own universe of obligation. No such feelings are likely to arise if one harms those for whom one feels no obligation. On the contrary, one is more likely to feel gratification for damage done to an enemy.

The late Benjamin Nelson succinctly described the evolution of civilization as a journey from "tribal brotherhood to universal otherhood."[91] Inherent in this predicament is the attrition of a sense of mutual obligation even among members of the same community.[92] Insofar as the religions of the West have taught that all men and women are the children of one sovereign Creator, they have sought to reverse the process of depersonalization and to enlarge the human universe of moral obligation so that it includes all of humanity. As the Holocaust's victims and survivors testify, that ideal is far from realized. The Holocaust and the other manifestations of large-scale demographic violence in our time make realization of that ideal more urgent and more problematic.

# Chapter 10

# Their Brothers' Keepers?
# Christians, Churches, and Jews

*Cain said to his brother Abel, "Let us go out to the field." And when they were in the field, Cain rose up against his brother Abel, and killed him. Then the Lord said to Cain, "Where is your brother Abel?" He said, "I do not know; am I my brother's keeper?" And the Lord said, "What have you done? Listen; your brother's blood is crying out to me from the ground!"*

Genesis 4:8–10

Since the Holocaust, informed laypersons, clergy, and scholars have asked the question, Did the Christian churches do all they could to prevent or, at least, to impede the so-called Final Solution? Because of the size, influence, and international character of the Roman Catholic Church, the question has been asked more often concerning Roman Catholic than Protestant leadership and institutions. The issue first attracted international attention in 1963 as a result of a sensational play, *Der Stellvertreter* (The deputy), by Rolf Hochhuth, a German Protestant. He portrayed Pope Pius XII as a heartless cynic who sought to act as mediator between the western Allies and Germany, thereby preserving the balance of power in Europe and preventing a Stalinist victory in the heart of Europe.[1] If the controversy had begun to fade in the 1990s, it was revived with the publication of *Hitler's Pope: The Secret History of Pius XII,* by John Cornwell, a former Roman Catholic seminarian.[2] In addition, the debate about Pope Pius XII and related issues has been complicated because, at the time of this writing, the pertinent Vatican archives have not been fully accessible to scholars, an issue that has caused great controversy in its own right. Many Vatican documents from the wartime period have appeared in the multi-volume *Actes et Documents du Saint-Siège relatifs à la Seconde Guerre mondiale* (1965–81), and in early 2003 scholars obtained access to newly opened Vatican archives that pertain to the prewar years of 1922 to 1939. A more complete picture of Pius XII's record during and after World War II, however, awaits the full opening of the Vatican's archives.

As a result of the renewed controversy, some scholars have raised a related issue. Perhaps, they ask, the real question is not whether the churches did all they could to help Jews during the war, but did a majority of European Christian leaders regard the elimination of Europe's Jews to be a benefit for European Christendom?[3] This perspective does not mean that such leaders approved of outright extermination. For many, Jewish emigration would have sufficed. Unfortunately, in the 1920s and 1930s, mass Jewish emigration from Europe was not feasible. To understand why some scholars now ask this question, it will be helpful to recall briefly our earlier discussions of the French and Russian Revolutions and also to consider the impact of defeat in World War I on Germany's religious leaders.

Before the French Revolution, the Roman Catholic Church considered Jews nonbelievers rather than heretics.[4] Judaism was the only non-Christian religion permitted to survive within European Christendom. The fundamental reason was theological. Under the influence of the apostle Paul and Augustine, the Church allowed Jews to *survive but not thrive,* in full confidence that God would eventually lead a remnant of Israel to accept Christ. It followed that the Jews were segregated, compelled to wear distinctive dress, and limited to occupations such as commerce and finance where they were least likely to influence Christians religiously. As an added assurance that Jews could not challenge the Church's cognitive monopoly, by which we mean the exclusive power to define true religious belief within a given territory, they were maligned as "deicides" or "murderers of God" in league with Satan. Under no circumstances were Jews permitted to lead the faithful astray. At stake was the credibility of the religious foundations of Christian civilization.

*All this changed with the French Revolution.* By granting full political and civic rights to the Jews and Protestants, the French Revolution destroyed the Church's cognitive monopoly in matters religious. The Roman Catholic Church saw the Jews not only as the chief beneficiaries of the new, hated world of modernity but also as its instigators. Hence, it was determined to restore, if possible, the old order. Moreover, there was one corner of Europe where the Church was free to set policy for the Jews without hindrance, namely, the band of Papal States in Italy in which the pope reigned as absolute sovereign until 1870. Within the Papal States, Jews were confined to ghettos whose gates were locked every evening, compelled to wear Jew badges on their clothing, and forbidden to have normal social relations with Christians. They were also forbidden to own property, practice the professions, attend university, or travel freely. After 1850, Pope Pius IX reestablished the Inquisition and gave the inquisitors direct authority over the Jews in his realm, an authority that was discontinued only when the secular kingdom of Italy was established in 1870.

The treatment of the Jews in the Papal States helps to explain the Church's silence, and in some cases outright approval, with regard to the discriminatory legislation introduced by the Nazis in 1933. Taking its cue from precedents previously established by the Church, the German government barred Jews from the professions and limited their contacts with non-Jews. There was little difference between these discriminatory laws and those of the Papal States. In Hungary, both the Catholic and Protestant churches made no secret of their approval of the discriminatory laws enacted by the Horthy regime in 1938.[5] Such laws also received the editorial approval of *La Civiltà Cattolica*, the highly influential Vatican-based Jesuit journal.

As we note below, there was widespread adherence to Nazi Germany's racial laws among mainstream German Protestants and even among some members of the Confessing Church (*Bekennende Kirche*), the German church most resistant to Nazi attempts to Aryanize Christianity. Insofar as there was Catholic opposition to anti-Jewish laws during the interwar period, it came largely from the United States and Great Britain, where Catholics were themselves in the minority and where the Church had learned that it could thrive without enjoying a cognitive monopoly.

Meanwhile, *race* was the sole domain in which the Roman Catholic Church could never accept National Socialist or Fascist anti-Jewish legislation. According to the Nazis, Jewishness was an indelible stain. For the Church, the "stain" could be washed away by baptism. Moreover, although the Church clearly favored a policy of segregation, it never advocated a policy of extermination.

## RED UPHEAVALS AND GERMAN DEFEAT

The Russian Revolution of 1917 and the subsequent Russian civil war sent shock waves throughout Europe and North America. Europe's most populous nation had fallen under the control of a militantly anti-Christian revolutionary movement. The Bolsheviks, moreover, were initially interested in *world* revolution, not just revolution in the former czarist empire. As the historian Richard Pipes has written, "the Bolsheviks seized power in Russia not to change Russia but to use her as a springboard to change the world."[6] They failed, but not for lack of trying. In the aftermath of World War I, radical left-wing regimes achieved temporary success in Bavaria and Hungary, in addition to Russia.[7] Although only a small minority of Europe's Jews were sympathetic to communism, Jews were visible in Russia's Communist leadership and in radical left-wing movements elsewhere in Europe. In addition, although baptized and hostile to Judaism, Karl Marx was of Jewish parentage. In the eyes of most conservative Europeans, communism was Jewish in both origin and spirit.

The revolutions in Bavaria and Hungary ended in right-wing victories. A violent wave of antisemitism followed in Munich, the birthplace and spiritual capital of National Socialism. During this turbulent period *The Protocols of the Elders of Zion*, which depicted an alleged Jewish conspiracy for world dominion, appeared in Munich. For Europe's conservatives, the *Protocols* "proved" that the Bolshevik revolution had been the result of a Jewish conspiracy to dominate the world and destroy Christianity.[8]

Never happy with Jewish emancipation, conservative Christian leaders throughout Europe saw in the antireligious Bolshevik movement proof positive of the utter folly of bestowing equal rights upon the Jews and of the urgent necessity to find a "solution" to the *Judenfrage*, the "Jewish question," a solution that might well include removing the Jews from the European continent. Emancipation had allowed Jews to become intellectuals, teachers, writers, politicians, financiers, and revolutionaries. As a result, the European churches had reason, for the first time in their history, to regard the Jews as *internal enemies within Christendom*. When Jews had been confined to the ghetto, their power was limited. Emancipation had given them an unprecedented ability to harm Christianity.

The attitudes of Germany's Christian leaders were shaped decisively by their nation's defeat in World War I. The victorious Allies saw the Germans as guilty of launching the bloodiest war in history.[9] Germany's religious leaders had a very different view. According to Klaus Scholder, a preeminent German Protestant church historian, "during the war the identification of the German cause with the will of God had reached such a height in German Protestantism that a German victory was made to seem virtually the fulfillment of divine righteousness."[10] Such sentiments were pervasive. The war had a special meaning for Germany's Protestants. They proudly called it "the German war," a war they saw as a continuation of the struggle of the Teutonic tribes against the Roman world in ancient times and Luther's revolt against Rome in the Reformation.[11]

Most German Protestants resented the demise of the monarchy. One of the Kaiser's official titles was *Summus Episcopus*, Supreme Bishop, of the German Evangelical Church. However, the old Protestant tradition of unquestioned loyalty to the state did not apply to the Weimar Republic. Protestant leaders were moved by strong feelings of nostalgia for the old imperial Reich. Thus Protestant nationalism and antisemitism were greatly strengthened during the Weimar years. The old world had been smashed by foreign enemies, and postwar unrest was ramped up by the extreme right, which claimed that the real damage had been done by the internal enemies who had signed the hated Versailles *Diktat*. Increasingly Jews were identified as the internal enemy.[12] The myth was taking hold that Germany had lost the war because of Judas-like betrayal. As a result, many Protestant pastors welcomed the rise of the Nazi Party. Even when hesitant about formal membership, they were definitely not repelled by Nazi antisemitism. In an interview with Victoria Barnett, Helmut Gollwitzer, an eminent Protestant theologian, recalled the atmosphere:

> Just as the average Protestant was middle class and "national," he was also anti-Semitic. . . . I was raised to believe that, until the Jews rejected Jesus, they were a loyal people . . . farmers and shepherds. Then God rejected them, and since that time they have been merchants, good for nothing, and they infiltrate everything, everywhere they go. And against that you had to defend yourself. In the Nazi party program it said that Jews should not be

permitted to be citizens. Most Germans held that to be a matter worth consideration. . . . Certain kinds of restrictions on their civil rights—that was
generally talked about and sympathized with.[13]

Gollwitzer's description suggests the degree to which both highly educated
German religious leaders and their followers were incapable of seeing loyalty to
Judaism as other than an enduring punishable offense against God. In the early
post-Holocaust years church leaders, in a number of church conferences, attempted
to distance themselves from the heritage of antisemitism that had proved so
destructive. Nevertheless, on 8 April 1948, when the Reich Council of Brethren
of the Evangelical Church of Germany finally issued a statement on the Jewish
question *after* the Holocaust, it was characteristically formulated in terms of
divine judgment for which there could be only one cure: "That God does not let
Himself be mocked is the mute sermon of the Jewish fate, for us a warning and
for the Jews an admonition as to whether they ought to turn to the One in whom
alone they, too, have their salvation."[14] The German church historian Wolfgang
Gerlach has identified the fundamental flaw of such efforts: "The church had not
yet acknowledged the idea that the original roots of anti-Semitism were theological not psychological or social."[15]

## THE PROTESTANT CHURCHES
## AND THE BIRTH OF THE THIRD REICH

Conditions in Weimar Germany did not stabilize until the hyperinflation of
1923 was brought under control. Unfortunately, after the Wall Street crash of 29
October 1929 the value of German equities collapsed. On 28 March 1930 President Paul von Hindenburg called on Heinrich Brüning, a financial expert and
leader of the Catholic Center Party, to become chancellor. Fearing a repetition of
the 1923 inflation, Brüning pursued a deflationary strategy that made a bad situation worse. Unemployment and business bankruptcies rapidly increased. By
the winter of 1932, Germany's industrial output had fallen by more than 50 percent. Brüning was derided as the "hunger chancellor."

Adolf Hitler became chancellor of the German Reich on 30 January 1933, not
as a result of popular acclaim, but through intrigue by members of the conservative elite. They regarded him as inexperienced and lacking the credentials needed
to run a complex modern state, but they also saw that he had one crucial asset:
an instinctive ability to express both the resentments and the political aspirations
of the nationalistic masses. Recklessly, they believed they could control him,
despite the fact that Hitler made no secret of his ambitious intentions.[16] As Ian
Kershaw has commented, "His intentions had scarcely been kept secret over the
years . . . heads would roll, he had said. Marxism would be eradicated . . . Jews
would be 'removed.' . . . Germany would rebuild the strength of its armed forces,
destroy the shackles of Versailles, conquer 'by the sword' the land it needed for its
'living-space.'"[17] Had the elites taken him at his word, they might have realized

that he was offering Germany—and the world—a recipe for catastrophe. Or did they at some level take him seriously, without envisioning the price that Germany would ultimately pay? They shared his detestation of the republic, much of his antisemitism, his determination to undo Versailles, and a determination to take whatever territory the nation required for its "living space." Within six months Hitler was well on his way to controlling the entire German state apparatus.

How did German Protestants react to the new regime? In the early post-World War II years, the predominant view of the Third Reich was that a small, ruthless group of fanatics had seized control and compelled the nation to obey its orders for war and extermination. Now contradicted by contemporary scholarship, the dubious myth arose that apart from the pro-Nazi "German Christians" the Protestant churches in Germany were persecuted "victims" of National Socialism.[18] The victorious Allies did little to question this view.

In fact German Protestants, especially Lutherans, shared a large measure of agreement with the Nazis. Both agreed that the "Jewish question" was among Germany's most pressing problems.[19] According to Daniel Goldhagen, it was "assumed as a matter of course that a 'Jewish Problem' did indeed exist, that the Jews were an evildoing tribe that had harmed Germany, and that a 'solution' must be found whereby their corrosive presence would be greatly reduced and their influence eliminated."[20]

Important exceptions existed. In 1928 a group of German Protestant leaders expressed their opposition to the rapidly growing antisemitism.[21] Two of the twentieth century's greatest theologians, Karl Barth (1886–1968) and Paul Tillich (1886–1965), were among them. Unfortunately, such voices were all too few.[22] Dismissed from the University of Frankfurt am Main in 1933 for opposing Nazi regulations, Tillich emigrated to the United States, where he taught at Union Theological Seminary, Harvard University, and the University of Chicago. Two years later, Barth returned to his native Switzerland.

In the first weeks of the Nazi regime, the fundamental attitude of most Protestant leaders was one of caution. They welcomed the defeat of the left-wing parties and the victory of militant German nationalism, but they insisted on church independence in religious matters. On 2 March 1933 Bishop Theophil Wurm of Württemberg praised the National Socialist movement, referring to the "great sacrifice" that had "broken the back of terror." He meant left-wing, not Nazi, terror. The Nazi cause, he affirmed, had taken up "the struggle against the influences destructive of our cultural life." At the same time, he insisted upon the churches' freedom to "proclaim the whole word of God" independent of state pressure.[23]

According to Scholder, Baron Wilhelm von Pechmann was one of the first of the leading Protestants to see the situation in its "true light." At a crucial meeting of Protestant church leaders in Berlin on 2–3 March 1933, Pechmann insisted that the German Protestant churches had to speak out against "the sea of hatred and lies."[24] His voice was largely unheeded. By 21 March 1933 most Protestant leaders had overcome their reservations and were expressing their enthusiasm for the so-called "national revolution." On that date the opening ceremony of the new Nazi-dominated Reichstag was held at the Garrison Church in Potsdam, where traditionally household guards of the Hohenzollern dynasty had dedicated themselves to the service of God and their king. Presiding over the event was the aging German president Paul von Hindenburg, who, dressed in his Prussian field marshal's uniform, raised his baton in respect to the empty throne of the exiled Kaiser Wilhelm II.[25] Hitler conducted himself with deference toward the old man, signaling the union of the old Protestant Prussia with the new National Socialism of the Third Reich. Bishop Otto Dibelius, a major church leader from the 1920s to the 1960s, delivered the sermon, preaching on the text "If God be for us, who can be against us?" (Rom. 8:31).

Dibelius was not opposed to the regime's antisemitism. In his 1928 Easter greeting to the clergy, he had declared, "I have always regarded myself as an anti-Semite. . . . The Jews have played a leading part in all the symptoms of disintegration in modern civilization. . . . May God bless our Easter and our Easter message."[26] Dibelius's views were typical of German Protestant attitudes. Wurm expressed similar sentiments both before and after the Holocaust.[27] Like that of so many of his colleagues, Wurm's antisemitism could coexist with strong opposition to National Socialism's neopaganism. In 1937 the Nazis almost sent him to a concentration camp.[28]

Meanwhile the German churches—Protestant and Catholic—helped to encourage antisemitism and eventually to facilitate the Final Solution by opening their baptismal registers to meet Nazi demands for proof of Aryan descent (*Ariernachweis*). By participating in the crucial step of defining who was or was not an Aryan, the churches facilitated the work of Nazi Germany's bureaucracy in identifying and ultimately destroying the Jews and those whose partial Jewish descent made them targets. The churches continued to supply such information even when they knew what was happening to the Jews.[29]

## THE GERMAN CHRISTIANS

Hitler's principal Protestant support came from the mainstream. The pacifist Jehovah's Witnesses refused to bow to Hitler and were mercilessly persecuted as a result, but the mainline Protestant churches sympathized with Hitler's political aims and at times even rewrote church doctrines to benefit Hitler still more.[30] Hitler's most fervent Protestant disciples came from a powerful minority known as the "German Christians," who in 1932 saw the Nazi agenda as the political expression of "true German Christianity."[31] To create a racially pure Aryan church, they sought to eliminate "non-Aryan" pastors and laypersons. The most radical German Christians also sought to eliminate the Old Testament and the letters of the apostle Paul from the church's canon.

Bolstered by the frequently repeated Nazi assurances of identification with and support of "positive Christianity," many—perhaps most—German Protestants and Catholics saw no obstacle to wholehearted commitment to the ideals of National Socialism in the early months of 1933. Just as Hitler wanted every other important organization under Nazi control, he wanted the Lutheran and Reformed regional churches united in a single *Reichskirche* (Reich Church), under a Reich Bishop. His preferred candidate was Ludwig Müller, a military chaplain and an *alte Kämpfer*, an old Nazi warrior from the early 1920s. Müller was not acceptable to the Protestant majority, but with Hitler's open support he was formally acclaimed as Reich Bishop at the synod of the Evangelical Church of the Old Prussian Union meeting in Berlin 5–6 September 1933.[32] The synod came to be known as the "Brown Synod" because many of the German Christian delegates came in the SA's brown, storm trooper uniforms.

On 7 April 1933 Hitler's regime had enacted a law that "retired . . . civil servants who are not of Aryan descent."[33] As Wolfgang Gerlach points out, this "Reich Law for the Restoration of the Professional Civil Service did not affect the clergy, religious teachers, or theological faculty," but in the autumn of 1933 the German Christians imposed their own "Aryan paragraph" on the Reich Church. Intended to eliminate "Jewish influences" on the church, this paragraph meant, in the words of Shelley Baranowski, that "baptized Jews, Protestants with Jewish ancestry, and Protestants married to 'non-Aryans' were forbidden to hold church office or serve as pastors."[34]

According to Victoria Barnett, the Protestant church's Aryan paragraph met immediate opposition, not because of its racist antisemitism, but because it raised the question of the church's subordination to the state.[35] In 1933 there were only thirty-seven "full Jews" among the eighteen thousand pastors in the German Evangelical Church; thus the issue of "non-Aryan" pastors did not seem very important initially. A major turning point came with the German Christian Sportspalast rally of 13 November 1933. With twenty thousand in attendance, Reinhold Krause, the movement's leader in Berlin, spoke about the new German *Volkskirche* as a first step in the "liberation from everything un-German in worship and confession; liberation from the Old Testament with its Jewish morality of rewards, these tales of cattle-traders and pimps."[36] Referring to Paul as "Rabbi Paul," he urged rejection of Paul's New Testament writings and even the symbol of the cross. He also called for "rapid, unqualified implementation of the Aryan Paragraph." Meanwhile, a journalist from Sweden, a Lutheran country, had reported his astonishment at an earlier meeting of the Brandenberg Synod in Berlin at which two hundred of the three hundred clergy were dressed in "brown uniforms, riding boots, waist and shoulder straps, with swastikas, badges of rank."[37]

Although he backed Müller, the German Christian who was elected Reich Bishop in September 1933, Hitler did not support the German Christians unequivocably. On 13 October 1933, Hitler's deputy Rudolf Hess announced the Nazi Party's neutrality in church affairs, for Hitler understood that some of the German Christians' positions were unacceptable to many Germans. Extreme views of the kind expressed a month later by Krause at the Berlin Sportspalast were a case in point. After that mid-November rally, the German Christian movement fragmented; even Reich Bishop Müller withdrew from it. These outcomes, however, did little to diminish Protestant support for Hitler or, in particular, to dampen the German Christians' enthusiasm for the Nazi program.

The German Christian movement reached its peak in 1939 with the establishment of the Institute for the Study and Eradication of Jewish Influence in German Church/Religious Life.[38] A large number of Germany's most important theologians and biblical scholars were affiliated with the Institute. Many of them had studied with Gerhard Kittel, professor at the prestigious Tübingen University and editor of *The Theological Dictionary of the New Testament*.[39] Prior to joining the Nazi Party in 1933, Kittel had an international reputation. His Nazi affiliation was based on conviction, not career opportunism. From 1933 to 1944 his writings emphasized the alleged menace of Jews and Judaism. As late as 1943 he wrote an article for Joseph Goebbels in which he accused Judaism of permitting Jews "full freedom to murder" non-Jews against whom they held "a deep-seated hatred."[40] When he wrote those words, Kittel could not claim ignorance of the extermination of the Jews. In his defense statement before a French military tribunal in June 1945, Kittel admitted that he learned of the Holocaust from his son, who was home on leave from the eastern front. Robert Ericksen reasons that Kittel wrote the article for Goebbels "to justify German murder of Jews as a necessary preemptive strike."[41]

From the Institute's inception, Walter Grundmann, professor of New Testament and *Völkisch* Theology at the nearby University of Jena, was its academic director. Grundmann had joined the Nazi Party in December 1930. Only Nazi supporters were appointed professors at Jena, whose theological faculty sought to be "a stronghold of National Socialism."[42] Grundmann and his colleagues attempted to prove that Christianity was the implacable enemy of Judaism and that Jesus was an Aryan at war with the Jews.[43] Nor did knowledge of the ongoing extermination of the Jews give them pause. On the contrary, in March 1944, with most of Europe's remaining Jews awaiting death in German captivity, Georg Bertram, Grundmann's successor, reported to the Institute's members that the war was "the fight of the Jews against Europe" and called for an even more radical dejudaization of Christian theology.

Grundmann was drafted in 1943 to fight on the eastern front, where he had ample opportunity to see how the war against Judaism was going. That war included about one thousand clergymen serving as chaplains in the German armed forces.[44] Because they served as both a morale-building resource and a source of moral authority, their presence was required in the most brutal German killing fields. If they did not preach Hitler's war against the Jews, they were assuredly its witnesses. Moreover, as Doris Bergen points out, the moral prestige of the chaplains' office was such that "their presence helped legitimize the Nazi war of annihilation and propagate among its warriors the comforting illusion that despite the blood on their hands, they remained decent people, part of a venerable religious tradition.[45]

Bergen recounts an incident in Ukraine in which SS and German soldiers left about ninety Jewish children, including babies, locked in a room in the August heat after massacring their parents.[46] Hearing the babies crying, some German soldiers were disturbed and turned to their chaplains, Pastor Wilczek and Father Tewes, for guidance. The chaplains' appeal for mercy was ultimately rejected by Field Marshal Walter von Reichenau, a convinced Nazi, who ordered the children killed.

According to Bergen, this case is the *only* fully corroborated account of a chaplain's attempt to intervene to prevent murder during the Holocaust. The chaplains were appalled by the children's misery but expressed no surprise at the mass murder of adults by *Einsatzgruppen* and regular army units. Moreover, according to his own account, Tewes's protest was limited to this single incident. Transferred to Russia, he witnessed greater brutality. Whenever German soldiers were troubled by the slaughter of Jews and other civilians, Tewes would tell them, "They were partisans." In reality, few Jews were partisans. Tewes thus assured troubled soldiers that they could participate in the Final Solution with a good conscience. Bergen concludes that "chaplains witnessed German atrocities and brought spiritual relief to those who perpetrated them."[47]

Among the chaplains, Nazi objectives, including genocide, were widely approved. This result was partly due to the way chaplains were selected. Candidates required approval by the Gestapo, church officials, and military authorities. "Insufficient antisemitism" was cause for rejection; there were few rejections. On the contrary, Bergen's research shows that the candidates' agreement with Nazi objectives was quite accurately taken for granted.[48] Whatever their motives, the desire of the chaplains, both Protestant and Catholic, to conform had the practical effect of supporting Nazi genocide by assuring the perpetrators that they could with good conscience do their "duty."

At war's end, the German Christians played a convenient role for the Protestant mainstream, including the Confessing Church. If their identification with the Nazi Party had been close, pastors and members of theological faculties could be deprived of their livelihood by the Allies' denazification tribunals.[49] Hence, German church authorities had a very strong postwar interest in playing down the churches' widespread complicity with Hitler's regime. Church leaders preferred to do their own purging and did so by moving against German Christians while leaving the mainstream untouched. Save for the German Christians, no serious attempt was made to investigate the clergy's support of Hitler's war aims.

An eminent American Protestant scholar has argued that "*apostasy* not *persecution* is the key word" in assessing why German Protestants and Catholics did not resist Hitler more effectively.[50] Today, there is a consensus that apostasy was rife among baptized Christians in Germany and elsewhere during the Nazi era, when millions of Christians did too little to thwart and too much to support a regime that would have sent Mary, Peter, Paul, and even Jesus to the gas chambers. This post-Holocaust evaluation, however, must be carefully construed, for given the unfolding of the history of Christianity, it is arguable whether anti-Judaism or Christian antisemitism did constitute apostasy according to the normative Christian interpretations of the time. Insofar as there was apostasy among

Germany's Christians in the Third Reich, it most clearly lay in racism and in the willingness of Christians in Germany to exclude from their fellowship baptized Jews and men and women whose parents or grandparents had been baptized. Ironically, anti-Judaism per se has not been traditionally regarded as apostasy by most Christians, but after the Holocaust, many leaders and thinkers in both Roman Catholicism and Protestantism have reevaluated Christianity's historic position on Jews and Judaism. Without compromising Christianity's fundamental affirmation that Christ is Lord and Redeemer, they have acknowledged a legitimacy to Judaism and Jews that their predecessors before and during the Holocaust were far less willing to grant.

## THE CONFESSING CHURCH IN NAZI GERMANY

As the German Christian movement gained strength, a Pastors' Emergency League (PEL), the precursor of the Confessing Church, was founded to help pastors who had been dismissed because of their ancestral background or arrested by the regime. By the end of 1933, the Confessing Church consisted of six thousand pastors.[51] In its founding statement the PEL explicitly opposed the Aryan paragraph, but the Confessing Church signaled little opposition to Nazi antisemitism save on the issue of baptized "non-Aryans."[52] Moreover, although they insisted upon the churches' freedom from state control in religious matters, Confessing Church members did not contest Hitler's legitimacy as head of the German state.[53]

The Confessing Church's best-known public document was the Barmen Declaration (May 1934), which condemned "the false doctrine that the State, over and above its special commission, should and could become the single and totalitarian order of human life." Nor, the Declaration added, could the church become "an organ of the State."[54] However, the Jewish question was not addressed. Barmen was one of the few attempts at criticism of the regime, but it also signaled the limits of that criticism.[55]

A thorough and consistent opponent of National Socialism, Karl Barth was the major author of the Barmen Declaration. He later regretted the document's silence on the persecution of the Jews. In May 1967, Barth wrote to Eberhard Bethge, a German clergyman and the authoritative biographer of Dietrich Bonhoeffer:

> I myself have long felt guilty that I did not make [the Jewish] problem central, at least public, in the two Barmen declarations of 1934, which I had composed. In 1934, certainly, a text in which I said a word to that effect would not have found agreement either in the Reformed Synod of January 1934 or in the General Synod of May at Barmen—if one considers the state of mind of the confessors of faith in those days. But that I was caught up in my own affairs somewhere else is no excuse for my not having properly fought for this cause.[56]

A Swiss national, Barth served as a professor in Germany from 1921 to 1935. He had no illusions about the pagan, anti-Christian nature of National Socialism. Hitler had said privately, "One is either a Christian or a German. You can't be both."[57] Most Germans deluded themselves that they could be both, but not Barth. With great prescience, Barth predicted that National Socialism would aim at the complete eradication of Christian belief and expression, but that "it could only move towards this goal . . . step by step, indirectly and in a variety of guises."[58]

Barth was also unlike the vast majority of his theological colleagues in publicly opposing the persecution of the Jews. On 10 December 1933, five months before Barmen, he had preached a sermon on the subject "Jesus Christ Was a Jew." In the hate-ridden atmosphere of the time, Barth's simple act showed great courage. Some members left the church in protest. Shortly thereafter, Barth wrote to a woman church member that "anyone who believes in Christ, who was himself a Jew, and died for Gentiles and Jews; *simply cannot* be involved in the contempt for Jews and ill-treatment of them which is now the order of the day."[59]

With the Nazis in power, all professors at German universities were required to open their lectures with the Nazi salute. Barth refused. After the death of Paul von Hindenburg on 2 August 1934, university professors were required to take an unconditional oath of loyalty to the Führer. Barth stipulated that he could be loyal only within the limits of his responsibilities as a Christian. The Nazi state rejected any limitation on the oath. Rudolf Bultmann, a world-class Christian scholar, urged Barth to take it. Barth refused. His action was unique. On 26 November 1934, he was suddenly suspended from his university duties. The reason given was that "by his behavior in office he has shown himself unworthy of the recognition, the respect and the trust which his calling requires."[60] The following year he accepted the position at the University of Basel in his native Switzerland that he held for the rest of his professional career. In Basel, Barth became the chair of the Basel Committee of Swiss Aid for [Exiled] German Scholars. He endeavored to facilitate the reception of anti-Nazi scholars, including Jews, in other countries.

Unlike so many others, this Christian's record remained resistant. On 5 December 1938, for example, he responded to *Kristallnacht* by declaring that "anyone who is in principle hostile to the Jews must also be seen as in principle an enemy of Jesus Christ. Antisemitism is a sin against the Holy Spirit."[61] During World War II Barth protested the German campaign against the Jews. On one occasion in Bern he visited Heinrich Rothmund, chief of the foreign division of the Swiss police, to appeal on behalf of a number of immigrant Jews. Later Barth organized a petition to the federal councilor Ernst Nobs, pleading that the Swiss government take prompt action on behalf of Hungarian Jews, who were in immediate danger of extermination.

Barth's courageous stand is noteworthy because he was arguably the greatest Christian theologian of the twentieth century. From start to finish he understood the real nature of National Socialism and tolerated no compromise with it. Ironically, his passionate opposition to National Socialism and his profound anti-

Judaism were of a piece. He believed with unshakable faith that "Christ is Lord." This meant that no human being could claim his unconditional loyalty and obedience, as Hitler demanded. Nevertheless, Barth held that Jews were not only in error but also *sinfully* in error for their inability to believe in Christ as Lord. As noted, after the Holocaust, many influential Protestant and Catholic religious thinkers were able to affirm their faith in Christ as Lord without regarding Jews as sinners for their inability to believe, but such insights had to await another generation. In 1942 Barth reproved a stricken Jewish community for failing to understand the Holocaust as divine punishment for its *willful* refusal to believe in the lordship of Christ. "There is no doubt," he wrote, "that Israel hears; now less than ever, can it shelter behind the pretext of ignorance and inability to understand. But Israel hears—and does not believe." In 1949, four years after Nazi Germany's surrender, Barth continued to suggest that the evil that came to the Jewish people was "a result of their unfaithfulness," that the Jew "pays for the fact that he is the elect of God," and that the Jewish people are "no more than the shadow of a nation, the reluctant witnesses of the Son of God and the Son of Man."[62]

Although he courageously opposed Hitler and helped to rescue his victims, Barth was a part of the problem, not the solution. Beliefs about the Holocaust as divine punishment were to be found even among German religious leaders who opposed Hitler most decisively. This situation indicates that within Germany Christian accommodation to Hitler was no weird, isolated aberration. It was ultimately rooted in beliefs about covenant and which community was truly chosen by God. Those beliefs had made Jews vulnerable for centuries.

A few members of the Confessing Church attempted to emulate Barth's opposition. Berlin's Dean Heinrich Grüber, with whom Richard Rubenstein had a crucial theological encounter in 1961, was one of their number. In September 1938 the Berlin Confessing Church set up the "Grüber office." Initially this office helped Jewish Christians to emigrate while emigration was possible, but Grüber later expanded his work to assist nonconverted Jews as well.[63] Before the Gestapo closed the office in December 1940, between seventeen hundred and two thousand Jews were helped to emigrate. Grüber was willing to help any Jew who approached him. Moreover, as emigration became more difficult, the office turned to formally "illegal" activities such as providing false ration cards, passports, and identity cards. Eventually, the office tried to find hiding places for Jews who could not get out in time. Grüber was arrested in December 1940 and sent to Sachsenhausen and then to Dachau concentration camps. Of the thirty-five workers in the office, only twelve, including Grüber, survived the war.[64]

On 4 June 1936 the ten members of the provisional board and council of the Confessing Church, Martin Niemöller among them, addressed a lengthy memorandum to Hitler.[65] The document went beyond the Barmen Declaration, stating that "when, within the compass of the National Socialist view of life, an antisemitism is forced on the Christian that binds him to hatred of the Jew, the Christian injunction to love one's neighbor still stands, for him."[66] It also protested against concentration camps, secret police methods, and other Nazi abuses but stopped short of disavowing antisemitism altogether. Only three copies of the final version were made as the memorandum was not intended to be made public. One was kept by Friedrich Weissler, a Jewish convert and a legal adviser to the Confessing Church, who gave his copy to Ernst Tillich to read. Meaning well, Tillich copied it and, with Werner Koch, shared it with the foreign press. The Confessing Church then publicly embraced the memorandum's contents and about a million copies of a pulpit declaration summarizing the memorandum were circulated. Shortly thereafter, Tillich, Koch, and Weissler were arrested and sent to concentration camps. Tillich and Koch were eventually freed, but Weissler's brutal treatment led to his death at Sachsenhausen on 19 February 1937. The Jewish convert had become the Confessing Church's first martyr.

## THE SPECIAL PLACE OF DIETRICH BONHOEFFER

Of all the Christian opponents of National Socialism, none has deservedly received more attention than Dietrich Bonhoeffer (1906–45). Implicated in the 20 July 1944 assassination plot against Hitler, Bonhoeffer was hanged by the SS at Flossenbürg on 9 April 1945. He is frequently cited to show that within Germany there was both individual and institutional Christian resistance against the Third Reich. "If we claim to be Christians," Bonhoeffer wrote, "there is no room for expediency. Hitler is the Anti-Christ. Therefore we must go on with our work and eliminate him whether he is successful or not."[67]

Bonhoeffer's path to martyrdom was anything but simple. From the outset the Bonhoeffer family had few illusions about Hitler.[68] Bonhoeffer grew up in a family environment of social tolerance and liberal ideas.[69] Stephen Haynes also points out that Bonhoeffer's "extended family brought him both specific *knowledge* of Nazi anti-Jewish measures and the opportunity to combat them through his family's contacts with the German resistance."[70] Undoubtedly his family provided much of the support that enabled him to do what only a handful of his fellow Germans were prepared to do: risk and finally sacrifice his life in the struggle to bring to an end the terrible evil that had overtaken his people.

From the beginning of the Hitler regime, the issue of political legitimacy was crucial for Bonhoeffer. It was one thing to disapprove of Hitler's tactics; it was quite another to regard the government as illegitimate and unworthy of obedience. Taking that step went counter to everything his Lutheran tradition taught about the individual's obligation to the state. Moreover, the Jewish question was of crucial importance to Bonhoeffer, both as a theologian and because his twin sister Sabine was married to Gerhard Liebhold, a professor at Göttingen University who, although Christian, was of Jewish origin. On 15 April 1933, just as the new regime initiated its laws effectively removing Jews and persons of Jewish descent from public employment, Bonhoeffer completed his essay "The Church and the Jewish Question." The essay is difficult and controversial and exhibits the extent to which Bonhoeffer's views of Jews were consistent with older, hostile, supersessionary Christian stereotypes.

The essay begins with a quotation from Martin Luther concerning the Jews in which he advises his followers to "Ask them to turn and accept the Lord. . . . Where they repent, leave their usury, and accept Christ, we would gladly accept them as our brothers."[71] In effect, Bonhoeffer repeats Luther's demand that Jews "repent" of their "*sin*" of fidelity to their own tradition. Nevertheless, something else may have been at work. A movement had already begun for the exclusion of non-Aryan Christians from religious fellowship in Protestant churches.[72] Bonhoeffer was skillfully using the words of the founder of German Protestantism to argue that the German Christian attempt to exclude baptized Jews from Christian fellowship had no theological support.

Bonhoeffer also discusses the significance of the fact that the state has imposed special laws upon the Jews solely because of race: "Without doubt the Jewish question is one of the historical problems which our state must deal with, and *without doubt the state is justified in adopting new methods here.*"[73] Nevertheless, Bonhoeffer also maintains that there is a way in which the church can legitimately criticize the state. When the state's actions foster lawlessness and disorder instead of order, the church can ask the state whether its actions are legitimate and in accordance with the legitimate state's character. The church can also aid the "victims of any ordering of society, even if they do not belong to the Christian community."[74] Bonhoeffer also cites a more drastic possibility, one that he was eventually driven to choose, "not just to bandage the victims under the wheel, but to put a spoke in the wheel." Such direct political action would be justified only if the state were to fail in its function of creating law and order. Several years were to pass before Bonhoeffer would completely despair of the church taking such a step and would take it by himself.

Meanwhile, Bonhoeffer also insisted that the church alone had the right to determine who belonged to its fellowship and who could serve as a pastor.[75] However, although he never wavered from this position, he still saw Jews largely through the prism of a conservative Lutheran interpretation. Thus Bonhoeffer also offers what appears to be a theological legitimation of the Nazi state's new anti-Jewish laws, as long as they did not apply to baptized Jews:

> Now the measures of the state towards Judaism in addition stand in a quite special context for the church. The church of Christ has never lost sight of the thought that the 'chosen people,' who nailed the redeemer of the world to the cross, must bear the curse for its action through a long history of suffering.[76]

Bonhoeffer continues with his own view of how Jews can bring their suffering to an end:

> But the history of the suffering of this people, loved and punished by God, is under the sign of the final home-coming of the people of Israel to its God.

And this home-coming happens in the conversion of Israel to Christ. . . .
The conversion of Israel, that is to be the end of the people's period of
suffering.[77]

Passages such as these are part of the reason that one Jewish critic characterized
Bonhoeffer as the best of a bad lot. Nevertheless, Bonhoeffer pulls back from
using his theological antisemitism to accord legitimacy to the Nazi persecution
of the Jews. "No nation," Bonhoeffer declares, "can ever be commissioned to
avenge on the Jews the murder at Golgotha."[78]

Clearly Bonhoeffer was theologically a child of his time and place. If even he
could not see the Jews in any other light, it is hardly likely that any other Christian leader in Germany, Protestant or Catholic, had an alternative view at the
time, at least not until the worst had happened. Like Barth, Bonhoeffer was part
of the problem. *At the same time, as objectionable as many today find Bonhoeffer's*
*supersessionist reading of his theological inheritance, without it he would have had*
*no Archimedean point with which to transcend his culture and oppose Hitler and*
*National Socialism.* Bonhoeffer and Barth shared an unshakable faith in Christ as
Lord that enabled them to reject as idolatrous National Socialism's claim to
unconditional loyalty.

During the academic year 1930–31, Bonhoeffer had been a postdoctoral fellow at Union Theological Seminary in New York City. He returned to Union in
June 1939 for a one-year program. Almost immediately, he realized that he
belonged in Germany. As he wrote to Reinhold Niebuhr,

> I have made a mistake. . . . I must live through this difficult period . . . with
> the Christian people of Germany. . . . Christians in Germany will face the
> terrible alternative of either willing the defeat of their nation in order that
> Christian civilization may survive, or willing the victory of their nation and
> thereby destroying our civilization. I know which of these alternatives I must
> choose; but I cannot make that choice in security.[79]

It is an understatement to say that Bonhoeffer's decision to will his own nation's
defeat and to work to bring it about was a difficult one.

By 1939 Bonhoeffer's brother-in-law Hans von Dohnanyi was an officer in
the *Abwehr*, the counterintelligence agency of Germany's armed forces and one
of the principal centers of the anti-Nazi resistance movement. As an official in
the Ministry of Justice, Dohnanyi had privately kept a "Chronicle of Shame," a
daily account of Nazi crimes and policies from 1933. Bonhoeffer thus knew far
more than most Germans about the misdeeds of the Hitler regime.[80] When Bonhoeffer returned to Germany, Dohnanyi secured an appointment for him in the
*Abwehr*, keeping him out of the *Wehrmacht* and giving him the cover to maintain communication with church contacts in Britain, Switzerland, and Sweden.

In April 1943 the Gestapo arrested Bonhoeffer and Dohnanyi for their part
in "Operation 7," a successful attempt to smuggle into Switzerland fourteen Jews,
eleven of whom were baptized. *Abwehr* funds were used and, of necessity, their
use disguised. When the Gestapo discovered the irregularity in the *Abwehr's*

books, Bonhoeffer and Dohnanyi were arrested. Although Operation 7 has sometimes been cited as evidence that Bonhoeffer was intentionally involved in the rescue of unbaptized Jews, other scholars find no supporting evidence.[81] The Gestapo did not learn that both men were deeply implicated in the plot to overthrow Hitler until after the attempt on Hitler's life on 20 July 1944. Bonhoeffer and Dohnanyi were executed on 9 April 1945.

Stephen Haynes argues that there is a "profound need for a hero of Christian conscience in the post-Holocaust world" and that the image of Bonhoeffer's risking his life to save German Jews is sustained by that need.[82] The evidence, however, is complex. Clearly Bonhoeffer knowingly chose a path that included opposition to some, if not all, of Nazism's anti-Jewish measures and did so in ways that entailed the possibility of martyrdom. Yet there is no evidence that he ever divested himself of the "witness-people myth," which sees Jews as a divinely chosen people whose sufferings are ultimately divinely inflicted. Haynes also argues that the above-cited passages from Bonhoeffer's essay "The Church and the Jewish Question" cannot be "improved by scholarly spin-control" and are in fact "compelling evidence of Bonhoeffer's brief role as theological bystander and unwitting collaborator with Nazi *Judenhass*."[83] Nevertheless, Haynes concludes, and we concur, that "by the time of his imprisonment he had achieved an exemplary solidarity with suffering Jews" and that he richly deserves the designation "Righteous Gentile."

## THE ROMAN CATHOLIC CHURCH

Concentrated in Bavaria and the Rhineland, Roman Catholics comprised one third of the German population during the years of World War I. In their own way they were as troubled by the lost war as were the Protestants.[84] Yet, in a land in which German nationalism emerged from Luther's Reformation, this minority found themselves suspect. Catholics never forgot Chancellor Otto von Bismarck's *Kulturkampf* (1871–87), in which he characterized Catholics loyal to Rome as *Reichsfeinde*, enemies of the Reich, a label that German Catholics sought to live down by embracing German nationalism and eventually Hitler's war aims.

In the 1920s and 1930s, far from being more loyal to Rome than to Germany, German Catholicism and Rome were at odds on the subject of National Socialism. According to Klaus Scholder, "whereas German Catholicism openly fought against National Socialism and rejected any compromise with Hitler," the issue was assessed very differently in Rome.[85] The Catholic Center Party was a force for moderation and democracy in Germany; it entered into parliamentary coalitions with the Social Democrats, a step Protestants were seldom willing to take.[86] Early on, most German Catholic bishops had mixed feelings about National Socialism. They disapproved of Hitler's violent racism and his espousal of "positive Christianity," a Nazi term that distorted the content of Christian faith. In most dioceses bishops banned membership by Catholics in the Nazi Party although they shared Hitler's anticommunism and his nationalism. Consequently, in August 1932 the Bishops Conference meeting in Fulda went so far as to declare, "If the [Nazi] party achieves the monopoly of power in Germany which it so ardently desires, the church interests of the Catholics will prove extremely bleak."[87]

The attitude of the Vatican could scarcely have been more different.[88] From 1930 to 1939 Eugenio Pacelli (1876–1958), later Pope Pius XII (reigned 1939–58), was Cardinal Secretary of State after serving as papal ambassador in Germany from 1917 to 1929. He was well acquainted with the German political scene. He was also prepared to enter into relations with any government that might come to power in Germany, and the likelihood that Hitler would come to power did not abate.

Pacelli was born in Rome on 2 March 1876. His father, Filippo, and his grandfather, Marcantonio Pacelli, were lay canon lawyers and intensely loyal to the institution of the papacy. Marcantonio was close to Pope Pius IX and was one of the founders of *L'Osservatore Romano*, which came to be the Vatican's official newspaper. Like the pope, Marcantonio and Filippo regarded the Roman Catholic Church as dangerously threatened by the destructive forces of modernity. In 1870 the Kingdom of Italy took over Rome, depriving the pope of his temporal power, a move the Vatican regarded as illegitimate. In the same year Pope Pius IX proclaimed the dogma of papal infallibility: when the pope speaks as supreme teacher of the Church, in matters of faith or morals, he is said to be infallible. The dogma was an important indication of the Church's determination to tolerate no compromise with modernity.

Ordained in 1896, Pacelli began his studies in canon law. As a brilliant Vatican insider, his career was on a fast track from the start. In 1901 Monsignor Pietro Gaspari, the Vatican equivalent of foreign minister, invited Pacelli to join him in the Secretariat of State. When Pacelli completed his doctoral dissertation, he was appointed secretary to Gaspari, who also served as president of the Papal Commission on Codification. In 1917 the commission brought forth the monumental *Corpus iuris canonici*, the Code of Canon Law, a comprehensive law book that exhaustively regulated conditions within the Church. A singularly important objective of the Codex, as it came to be known, was to strengthen papal power through stipulating that the pope alone had the right to name bishops. In many dioceses this provision was contrary to tradition, but papal appointment of bishops provided assurance that the dogma of papal infallibility would be strictly adhered to.

Upon completion of the Codex, Pacelli, now an archbishop, was appointed papal nuncio to Bavaria. (A nuncio represents the pope to a local government and to the bishops of a national church.)[89] The relation between the Vatican and another government was normally regulated by a concordat, a formalized relationship similar to a treaty. As World War I came to an end, all concordats required revision. Pacelli's appointment to Roman Catholic Bavaria was critical, because that German state would present the fewest obstacles to the signing of a new concordat tailored to the Vatican's satisfaction. Pacelli's appointment was critical for another, unanticipated reason. He was in Munich on 8 November 1918, when the royal house of Bavaria was overthrown and temporarily supplanted by three revolutionary socialist regimes whose leadership included a number of Jewish intellectuals and revolutionaries. The revolution ended in a right-wing bloodbath in April 1919, but not before the Reds entered Pacelli's compound, pointed a gun at him, demanded his limousine, and threatened to kill him. In later life Pacelli often alluded to this incident.

The European right took the Munich rebellion as "proof" that the Bolshevik revolution was the result of a Jewish conspiracy to dominate the world and destroy Christianity. If Pacelli had any doubts concerning the destabilizing consequences of Jewish emancipation before Munich 1918–19, he had none thereafter. His experience added credibility in his eyes—if indeed he needed any—to *La Civiltà Cattolica*'s oft-repeated insistence that the emancipation of the Jews had proved to be a disaster.

Nor was Pacelli the only future pope with firsthand experience of Bolshevism. Achille Ratti (1857–1939), a brilliant scholar who became Pope Pius XI (reigned 1922–39), was papal nuncio to Poland when Poland became an independent nation after World War I. Military conflict broke out between Catholic Poland and Bolshevik Russia in 1919. In June 1920, the Red Army advanced as far as Warsaw's suburbs. As the Polish army retreated, Poland's military and Catholic Church leaders claimed that Bolshevism was part of a Jewish plot to destroy Christianity and achieve world domination. There were large-scale pogroms, and Jews in the Polish army, even volunteers, were suspected of being traitors. Unfortunately, Communists of Jewish background were highly visible in both the officer corps and the lower ranks of the Red Army.[90] While Ratti was papal nuncio, Poland's bishops wrote to their fellow bishops outside of Poland, "The real goal of bolshevism is the conquest of the whole world. The race that directs it came to dominate it through their gold and their banks. Today the ancestral imperialist impulse that flows through its veins drives it to crush the people under the yoke of its domination."[91] It was not necessary to use the word "Jew." The accusation was clearly understood by Christians in Poland and elsewhere.

Ratti's experience in Poland was to influence his attitude toward Jews for the rest of his life. In 1932, he told Benito Mussolini, Italy's Fascist dictator, that the Church's problems in Russia were partly caused by "Judaism's antipathy for Christianity." "When I was in Warsaw," the pope said, "I saw that the [Bolshevik] Commissars . . . were all Jews." The pope did allow that most of Italy's Jews were "basically good," but insisted that the "hordes of Jews" living in central and eastern Europe were a threat to healthy Christian society, a lesson he said "he learned in Poland."[92]

Ratti returned to Italy convinced, with considerable justice, that communism was Christianity's gravest threat and, with far less justice, that the Jews were largely responsible. In 1922 Count John de Salis, the British minister to the Holy See, reported to the Foreign Office in London, "Everything in the Vatican is dominated by the pope's fear of Russian Communism, that the Soviets may reach Western Europe."[93] The Vatican's apprehension, it must be added, was not entirely misplaced.

The idea that Jews could be free and equal citizens was deeply offensive to the leaders of the Roman Catholic Church at the time. As a result, there was an intensification of strident anti-Jewish verbal violence in the Catholic press throughout Europe. It reflected themes, many of them especially strong in the late nineteenth and early twentieth centuries, that David Kertzer has summarized as follows:

> We told you to keep the Jews in the ghettoes, to prevent them from coming into contact with Christians, and yet you ignored our warnings and gave them equal rights. Now look what's happened! Thanks to the Jews, religion is everywhere threatened and social disorder spreads. Our only hope of restoring social harmony and economic security is to bring back the special laws that kept them in their place.[94]

Such thinking had long been evident in the influential Jesuit journal, *La Civiltà Cattolica*.[95] By 1880 *La Civiltà Cattolica* had embarked on an active antisemitic campaign that included the revival of accusations that Jews periodically murdered young Christian boys to use their blood in the making of Passover matzoh. A number of such ritual murder accusations were leveled against local Jews in eastern Europe. One of the worst occurred in Kishinev, Moldavia, during the Easter season in April 1903. A Christian boy had been murdered, and Jews were accused of the crime. It was later proved that the child was murdered by relatives, but not before forty-nine Jews lost their lives and more than five hundred others were injured, some seriously. In addition, seven hundred houses were looted and destroyed, and six hundred businesses and shops were pillaged in the pogrom that followed the accusation.[96]

In 1881 *La Civiltà Cattolica* launched a campaign to spread the ritual murder accusation throughout the Catholic world. That June Father Giuseppe Oreglia di San Stephano began the assault by asserting that the Talmud commanded the "Jewish race" to kill Christians. In a continuing series of articles, he gave examples of the alleged Jewish practice of ritual murder.[97] Oreglia's work was taken up by Father Saverio Rodina, S.J. In 1893, he published two articles reiterating the ritual murder charge and accusing the Jews of devising the capitalistic system to enslave and grow rich on the labor of Christians.[98] The ritual murder accusation was endorsed by *L'Osservatore Romano*. In an article entitled "Jewish Ritual Murder," that influential newspaper warned, "We think it is our duty to give a fraternal Christian bit of advice not to all Jews, but to certain Jews in particular: Don't throw oil on the fire. . . . Content yourselves . . . with the Christians' money, but stop shedding and sucking their blood."[99] According to Kertzer, in March and April 1892 alone, forty-four articles accusing Jews of ritual murder appeared in *L'Osservatore Cattolico*, a Catholic newspaper published in Milan, extracts of which were widely reprinted in Catholic newspapers in Italy, France, Austria, and Germany.[100]

The hostility fed on itself. Although the Jews were numerically insignificant, save in parts of eastern Europe, allegations of deicide, ritual murder, and desecration of the host rendered plausible the belief that Jews were involved in "the performance of magic aimed at undermining and ultimately destroying Christendom."[101] Such was the atmosphere in which both Achille Ratti, Pius XI, and Eugenio Pacelli, Pius XII, were bred. No policies of annihilation were advocated, but, short of that, the antisemitism in the Church's hierarchy and membership was widespread, deep-seated, and intense.

On 6 February 1922 Achille Ratti became Pope Pius XI. Ten months later Benito Mussolini became Italy's prime minister. The Vatican found Mussolini's strong anticommunism to its liking.[102] With Mussolini in power and parliamentary democracy effectively thwarted, the pope believed it was time for a concordat with Italy. The Lateran Treaty of 1929 with Fascist Italy was the Vatican's most important concordat in the 1920s. The Vatican recognized Rome as the capital of the Kingdom of Italy, and Italy recognized the pope's full sovereignty over the 109-acre Vatican City. Italy acknowledged the unhindered right of the Church to impose the Code of Canon Law within the country, and the Holy See agreed to prohibit the clergy and members of religious orders from being active in any political party.[103] In the ensuing Italian elections, the Vatican encouraged priests to support Mussolini, whom Pope Pius XI characterized as "a man sent by Providence."[104]

By July 1930 the Nazi Party was Germany's second largest. In August 1931 Heinrich Brüning, Germany's chancellor and a Roman Catholic leader, met with Pacelli in Rome. To foster opportunity for a Vatican-German concordat, Pacelli advised Brüning to form a right-wing government and indicated his willingness to see Hitler in the German cabinet. Brüning did not act on these initiatives, but Pius XI and Pacelli urged other Catholic Center Party leaders to explore cooperation with the Nazis. In December 1931 the pope told the Bavarian ambassador to the Vatican that cooperation between the Church and the Nazis could prevent "a still greater evil."[105]

With Hitler in power after 30 January 1933 Pacelli knew that he had a German politician with the power and inclination to sign a concordat agreeable to the Vatican. Such a concordat had been blocked by Protestants and Social Democrats, who were unwilling to cede greater control over German Catholics to the Vatican. Hitler was willing to agree to the Holy See's terms on papal appointment of bishops and the imposition of Canon Law on the German Church. His price was the complete withdrawal of Catholics from social and political action. The German bishops were opposed to the deal, but not the Vatican. The concordat, known as the *Reichskonkordat*, was signed in Rome on 20 July 1933. The document stipulated that only purely "religious, cultural and charitable" Catholic organizations were entitled to the protection of the Reich. All others were to be abandoned or merged with Nazi organizations. The concordat also had a depolitization clause that Hitler interpreted to mean that "the Holy See will ensure a ban on all clergy and members of religious congregations from party political activity."[106] The Vatican of Pius XI had become the first foreign power to sign a bilateral treaty with Nazi Germany. The action was widely interpreted as the Church's endorsement of National Socialism. At best, the endorsement was partial. The Church was not prepared to accept Hitler's racism, but apart from racism, there was very little, if anything, in the early anti-Jewish measures about which the Church disapproved.[107] On the contrary, there is much evidence that the Church *approved* Hitler's discriminatory measures, save as they applied to baptized Jews.

In spite of the Church's honest commitment to end all Catholic political activity, Nazi harassment of the Church continued unabated. Catholic officials were dismissed from their posts and arrested. Churches were desecrated. Catholic schools were closed. Priests were arrested. Members of religious orders were accused of sexual perversions. Nuns responsible for children in orphanages and schools were arrested for the alleged sexual abuse of their charges. Officials responsible for the finances of foreign missions were accused of currency fraud and other financial crimes.

By January 1937 Pius XI had had enough. On 14 March he issued an encyclical, *Mit brennender Sorge* (With burning anxiety), which condemned Nazi Germany's treatment of the Church. The pope characterized as idolatrous those who take "race, or the Volk, or the State" as absolute.[108] He warned the faithful to avoid "the seduction of a national German Church," insisting that there was one and only one path to salvation, faith in the Church and the primacy of the bishop of Rome.[109] The encyclical was not an outright condemnation of National Socialism, which the pope never named, nor did it express any sympathy for the plight of Germany's Jews. The encyclical did criticize those in Germany who wanted to ban the teaching and use of the Old Testament. However, Pius XI's defense of Scripture was coupled with the assertion that the Old Testament is "the story of the chosen people . . . repeatedly straying from God . . . who were to crucify Him."[110] The repetition of the deicide accusation undoubtedly reinforced the belief that Jewish suffering under Hitler was a continuation of their punishment for the crucifixion.

Concerned that the pope might jeopardize relations with Germany, Pacelli wrote to Diego von Bergen, the German ambassador to the Holy See, assuring him that *Mit brennender Sorge* contained no condemnation of the Nazi system of government.[111] Still, the encyclical was a straw in the wind. In June 1938 the pope took a further step. He charged Father John LaFarge, S.J., an American scholar, with the responsibility of preparing a preliminary draft of a major papal encyclical, *Humani Generis Unitas* (The unity of the human race), which would condemn racism *and* antisemitism. Pius XI died on 10 February 1939, perhaps without seeing the draft.[112] As the title suggests, the document condemns racism, but a distinction between legitimate and illegitimate antisemitism permeates the document. Racism is depicted as illegitimate, anti-Judaism as legitimate. Moreover, the document asserts that the European states were right to take measures to "defend" society against the "dangers" of contact with Jews, as long as the measures were "compatible with justice." [113]

One of the most intriguing indications of a change of heart had been Pius XI's meeting with Belgium pilgrims on 6 September 1938. The pope was not well, but he told the pilgrims, "Anti-Semitism is . . . a hateful movement, a movement that we cannot, we Christians, take any part in. . . . Anti-Semitism is inadmissible. We are all spiritually Semites."[114] As limited as was his attempt to undo its harm, *no other world leader was as outspoken in condemning racial antisemitism.* There was, however, one crucial step that he could not take: At the time, his religious tradition could see Judaism only as a failed, aborted, incomplete form of Christianity, rather than a religion with its own autonomous integrity. Neither he nor any other Catholic teacher could see both Judaism and Christianity as legitimate ways of worshiping God. Nor could they recognize that Jews were not rebelling against God in their fidelity to their own tradition. This outcome left Catholics and other Christians, moved by a spirit of goodwill and charity though they might be, with the problem of explaining *in terms of their own tradition* why Jews could not accept Jesus as their Messiah. They largely ignored Paul's answer, which was that God wills it so for God's own mysterious purposes. Instead, they ascribed Jewish unbelief to willful ignorance, spiritual blindness, hardness of heart, or partnership with Satan, reasons that were hardly likely to engender a willingness openly to defend Jews or protest their ill-treatment in the face of the Nazi juggernaut.

On 2 March 1939, three weeks after the death of Pius XI, Pacelli was elevated to the papacy, taking the name Pius XII. Immediately he began to mend relations with Germany.[115] Three days after the papal coronation he told the German cardinals that he intended to take personal charge of Church relations with Germany.[116] He received Diego von Bergen, Germany's ambassador to the Holy See, before any other diplomat and told him that Hitler's regime was as acceptable to him as any other government.[117] As Hitler prepared for war, he knew that a far more sympathetic pope than Pius XI sat on the throne of Peter.

When Pius XII notified Hitler of his election, the Nazi regime had already launched *Kristallnacht*, central Europe's worst pogrom in five hundred years.[118] The violence and terror were not hidden away in some remote part of eastern Europe; unleashed in every German city, they were highly visible and publicized throughout the world. Nazi Germany's massive November pogrom was a watershed. After 10 November 1938 it was impossible to retain any hopeful illusions concerning Hitler's Jewish policy. The Jews of Germany and Austria were confronted with the most implacably hostile regime in all of Jewish history. The new pope knew the facts.

Pius XII's response was understandably complex. Given the Church's diverse constituencies, he was not an entirely free agent even when the SS murdered more than two hundred Polish priests and imprisoned a thousand more between 1 September and 31 December 1939. When the war began, the pope attempted to maintain the appearance of strict neutrality. On 27 October 1939 his encyclical *Summi Pontificatus* expressed sympathy for the Poles, who were already suffering under a brutal German occupation. However, while the encyclical criticized "unilateral denunciation of treaties and the recourse to arms," it did so without explicitly naming Germany.[119] After Poland's Cardinal August Hlond submitted reports in the autumn and early winter of 1939–40, Pius XII directed Vatican Radio to denounce, in German as well as in other languages, Nazi Germany's policies against the Polish people. The plight of Polish Jewry, however, did not get specific attention.[120] When the Germans invaded Holland, Belgium, and Luxemburg in May 1940, the pope sent telegrams to their monarchs declaring that he would pray for the reestablishment of their "full liberty and independence." Pius XII's messages pleased neither the Germans nor the Western Allies. The French ambassador to the Vatican pointed out that it was one thing to express sympathy for victims of aggression, another to condemn the aggressor.[121] Poles living in exile had a similar reaction.

Meanwhile, as the pope penned these facile messages, the Jews' condition deteriorated. Extermination became Hitler's policy in the Soviet Union in the summer and fall of 1941, and in the rest of Europe early in 1942. The invasion of the Soviet Union also marked a definite shift in the Vatican's attitude toward Germany. At the Vatican, unhappy about Hitler's 1939 pact with Stalin, neutrality gave way to hope for a German victory over communism, but a victory in which Nazi Germany would exhaust itself. While the Vatican wanted a victory over communism, neither the pope nor his subordinates looked with favor on the prospect of a Nazi Europe.[122] One result was that the Vatican was confronted with an unprecedented situation when the government of Germany, a country with more than thirty million Catholics, decided to "solve" the Jewish problem by mass murder. Further complicating the situation was the fact that the extermination project could not be carried out without the active cooperation of governments the Vatican regarded as Christian and with which it enjoyed cordial relations, such as Vichy France, Lithuania, Slovakia, Croatia, and Hungary.

In the France of Marshal Henri Philippe Pétain, the Paris police, not the Germans, systematically arrested thousands of Jews and took them to transit camps near Paris for deportation in freight cars to Auschwitz.[123] Although the French Catholic bishops agreed in principle with discriminatory legislation, extermination was another matter. They designated Cardinal Célestin Suhard, archbishop of Paris, to protest the deportations to Pétain.[124] When the deportations began in the unoccupied zone of France in 1942, a joint commission of Catholics and Protestants expressed their "great sorrow" to Pétain, who evaded responsibility by blaming the Germans.[125] At first the deportees consisted almost solely of foreign Jews, primarily from Poland and eastern Europe. Apart from the Church's protest, there was little French resistance to these deportations, although resistance increased, even among some French antisemites, when deportations of French citizens began. It should be noted too that a number of French priests were arrested for sheltering Jews.

On 8 August 1942 Gerhardt Riegner, the representative of the World Jewish Congress in Bern, Switzerland, sent a brief, prophetic message reporting that plans had been discussed in the Führer's headquarters to concentrate the Jews of

Europe in the East and then to exterminate them "to resolve once and for all the Jewish Question in Europe."[126] On 26 September 1942 Myron C. Taylor, President Roosevelt's special representative to the Holy See, presented a similar report to Cardinal Luigi Maglione, the Vatican's secretary of state, detailing the full scope of the Nazi extermination program.[127] Despite comprehensive information from Catholic sources, Maglione was consistently evasive and asked Taylor for corroboration.[128] When diplomats, religious leaders, and representatives of Jewish organizations pleaded for the Vatican to take a stand against the slaughter, the secretary of state would almost invariably conclude his response with the statement *The Holy See has done and is doing all that which is in its power on behalf of the Jews.*

It is unlikely that Maglione would have taken strong actions on behalf of the Jews without explicit instructions to do so from his superior, Pius XII, and there is no evidence that such instructions were given. Nor did papal silence trouble his secretary of state. To illustrate, in the late summer of 1943, Maglione declared that the fate of Christian Europe hung in the balance of the struggle the Nazis were waging against Communists in the east. Receiving the German ambassador a few weeks later, at the very time when the Jews of Rome were being rounded up for deportation to Auschwitz, Maglione said that the Vatican had acted "so as not to give to the German people the impression that it has done or wished to do the least thing against Germany during this terrible war."[129]

In reality, the information about the Holocaust that Maglione received was trustworthy. It came from the papal nuncios to Hungary and Romania and the papal chargé d'affaires in Slovakia, Msgr. Giusseppe Burzio. Slovakia was one of the most Catholic countries in Europe. Its president was a priest, Msgr. Josef Tiso, as were many of the leaders of his Slovak People's Party. Immediately after separating from Czechoslovakia in April 1939, Slovakia enacted its own anti-Jewish legislation. Marriages between Christians and Jews were forbidden, and all Jews, including baptized Jews, were expelled from the general schools. Both Burzio and Maglione registered strong protests concerning the disabilities imposed upon Jewish Christians.[130]

On 27 October 1941 Burzio reported to the Vatican that Slovak army chaplains returning from the war in the East informed him that the Germans were systematically annihilating Jews of all ages.[131] This information was the first that the Vatican received about the massacre of the Jews from one of its own diplomats.[132] On 9 March 1942 Burzio sent a cable to Maglione describing the planned deportations of Slovakia's Jews. The Vatican received similar reports from its nuncios in Hungary and Romania. On 14 March Maglione handed a strongly worded protest on the deportations to Charles Sidor, the Slovak ambassador to the Holy See, expressing special concern that a country "inspired by Catholic principles" should adopt regulations with such painful consequences "for so many families." For the first time, Maglione did not differentiate between baptized and other Jews.

Ten days later the Vatican learned that the Germans were planning to force several thousand Jewish girls from Slovakia, some of whom were baptized, to act as prostitutes for troops on the Russian front. More than any other measure to date, this one aroused the indignation of both Maglione and Pius XII. The pope was especially offended that this could happen in a Catholic country and instructed Maglione to do whatever he could to get the government to stop. Nevertheless 52,000 Slovakian Jews were deported between 26 March and 30 June 1942.

Meanwhile, as the deportations continued, the Slovak bishops issued a pastoral letter describing the Jews as an accursed people for failing to recognize the Redeemer and for "having prepared a terrible and ignominious death for him on the cross." The letter concluded, "The Church cannot be opposed, therefore, if the state with legal regulations hinders the dangerous influence of the Jews."[133] In spirit and content the letter was like many others penned by Church leaders throughout Europe before and during the war.

There was some dissent in the Vatican. "The misfortune," lamented Msgr. Dominico Tardini, the Vatican's under secretary of state for extraordinary ecclesiastical affairs, "is that the President of Slovakia is a priest. That the Holy See cannot bring Hitler in line all can understand. But that [the Pope] cannot curb a priest, who can understand that?"[134] Like most of their superiors in the Vatican, however, the Slovak bishops saw the hand of God in Jewish misfortune. The Church's doctrine was twofold: Catholics are not permitted to employ violence against the Jews, but Jewish suffering is the just consequence of their rejection of Christ and their alleged deicide. Both doctrines were powerfully operative before post-Holocaust reform took place in the early 1960s Church council known as Vatican II. Those long-held doctrines help to explain why the Vatican was interested in protecting baptized Jews and why it was more concerned with the deportations in Slovakia than in most other countries. Once baptized, Jews were no longer under the deicide curse, and it was especially important that Jews be protected from unmerited violence in a Catholic country with a priest as president. Whereas discriminatory measures limiting Jewish influence and even expulsion were acceptable, a Christian state's active complicity in compulsory prostitution and mass murder was not. Nevertheless, no sanctions were threatened against Slovakia's priestly leadership. Nor did Pius XII ever make explicit that it was a sin for a Catholic priest to cooperate in delivering Jews to the Nazis.

A further religious impediment to rescue arose in March 1943, when Archbishop Angelo Roncalli, the apostolic delegate to Turkey and later Pope John XXIII, transmitted a request from the Jewish Agency for Palestine that the Vatican intervene with the Slovak government to permit a thousand Jewish children to emigrate to Palestine. Roncalli indicated that the British were willing to let the children enter. Archbishop William Godfrey, the apostolic delegate to the United Kingdom, sent a similar message the same day but referred to the settlement of Jewish children from all of Europe. The requests were handled by Tardini, who exhibited some interest in the proposal to rescue the Jewish children from Slovakia, but the idea of endorsing the settlement of Jews in Palestine gave him pause. "The Holy See," wrote Tardini, "has never approved the project of making Palestine a Jewish home. But unfortunately England does not yield. . . . And the question of the Holy Places? Palestine is by this time more sacred for Catholics than . . . for Jews."[135] This response and others of a similar kind indicate that, at the time, the Vatican took a political stand on Palestine on the basis of a religious position at least as old as the First Crusade, namely, the idea that Palestine was Christ's patrimony.

When the Vatican became convinced that Germany would lose the war, it began to adjust to the new reality. There was more activity on behalf of the Jews *after* the Vatican's views had changed than before. Pius XII met Myron C. Taylor, President Roosevelt's envoy, for three successive days starting on 20 September 1942. Taylor told the pontiff that Roosevelt rejected all peace negotiations, a deliberate reference to Vatican peace feelers, and declared that "the world has never seen such an avalanche of war weapons . . . as we shall launch in 1943 and 1944."[136] Undoubtedly the most threatening part of Roosevelt's message was the statement that the United States and Great Britain had excellent relations with the Soviet Union.[137] The United States thus put the Vatican on notice that, far from joining an anti-Communist crusade, it was planning to cooperate with the Soviet Union in dominating Europe and utterly destroying the governments of Germany and Italy.

From the pope's point of view, Roosevelt's war aims were disastrous. The Vatican saw Christian Europe as facing an even greater threat than it once faced from the conquering Muslims, who at least tolerated the practice of Christianity. Although Pius XII still hoped for a German victory over Bolshevism, a hint of something new began to appear in his messages. In his 1942 Christmas broadcast Pius XII called upon all people to dedicate themselves to the service of the human person and a divinely ennobled human society. Humanity, the pontiff briefly declared, owed such a vow "to the innumerable dead . . . to the suffering groups of mothers, widows, and orphans . . . to the innumerable exiles . . . to the hundreds of thousands who, without personal guilt, are doomed to death or to a progressive deterioration of their condition, sometimes for no other reason than their nationality or descent [*stirpe*] . . . to the many thousands of non-combatants whom the air war has [harmed]."[138] This statement was the most explicit public comment on the extermination of the Jews that Pope Pius XII made during the war. Unfortunately, there is no way to read the message other than as *a statement of what the living owe the dead.* The pope criticized totalitarianism without identifying any totalitarian country. He neither condemned the Germans for what they were doing nor did he call for a halt to the slaughter. In 1942 alone 2.7 million Jews, not "hundreds of thousands," had already been killed, and thousands more were being slaughtered every day.[139]

Finally, the Church offered some help to the Jews of Italy and Hungary. On 26 October 1943 SS Major Herbert Kappler demanded that the Jews of German-occupied Rome surrender fifty kilograms of gold within thirty-six hours. Fearful that it could not collect the sum, the Jewish community turned to the Vatican for help. The pope agreed to lend the community whatever amount it was unable to raise.[140] However, as Susan Zuccotti has observed, there is no evidence that when the Vatican learned in October 1943 that the Germans planned to deport Rome's 8,000 Jews, the pope acted on this knowledge. He neither spoke out before the deportations began nor did he protest publicly after they had taken place.[141]

The last mass deportation of the war took place in Hungary and was well under way by mid-May 1944. Adolf Eichmann had a force of eight SS officers and forty enlisted men to implement the deportation, but he had the cooperation of the pro-Nazi Hungarian government, which supplied twenty thousand men.[142] The Hungarian Cardinal Justinian Seredi actively sought to protect baptized Jews and Jews married to Catholics, but no others. He was urged to take a stand against the deportations by Msgr. Angello Rotta, the papal nuncio, but to no avail. Instead, the cardinal published a letter on 29 June 1944 defending the legal measures taken by the puppet Hungarian Nazi regime to eliminate "the noxious influence of the Jews." Any lay Hungarian reading the letter would rightly understand it as a defense of the Final Solution.[143] The Catholic historian Michael Phayer characterizes Seredi as "callously anti-Semitic."[144] Between 15 May and 9 July 1944 more than 437,000 Hungarian Jews were sent to Auschwitz.[145]

There was nothing secret about the deportations from Hungary. The Spanish, Swiss, and Swedish governments, all at least technically neutral, appealed for an end to them. In the early spring of 1944 the American War Refugee Board sent a request to the pope to intervene. The appeal was repeated by Harold Tittman, Myron Taylor's deputy, on 26 May. Finally, on 25 June the pope sent a telegram to Regent Horthy in Hungary, requesting that he stop the deportations. It came two months after the first American request and three weeks after the Allies had captured Rome.

Why was Pius XII willing—largely silently—to tolerate Hitler's program of mass extermination of every single Jew on the face of the earth? There have been many attempts to explain his posture, some offered by the pope himself. As we have seen, historians often cite the pope's unwillingness to do anything that might weaken what he regarded as the Third Reich's defense of Europe against Bolshevism. Pius XII is also reported to have told the Italian ambassador to the Vatican in 1940 that he was afraid of "making the plight of the victims even worse," a justification that his defenders continue to offer.[146] If that defense strains credibility, there is greater credibility in explaining the pope's considerable silence as partly motivated by his hope to play an important role in the peace negotiations at the end of the war. The pope sought the defeat of *both* National Socialism and communism but not of Germany, an outcome that would have required extraordinarily difficult diplomacy.[147] He is also depicted as assigning a very high priority to the safety and security of the Vatican itself from German bombing, as well as hostile incursion by Mussolini's Fascist regime and later by German occupation forces.[148] The pope was also fearful that the Germans might bomb Rome, were he to voice public objections to the Holocaust.

There is some merit to these explanations, but we believe that religion played a far greater part in the pope's wartime decisions and that *he was acting sincerely but mistakenly in what he regarded as the best interests of an endangered Christianity.* The Bolshevik Revolution and the Red uprisings in Bavaria and Hungary at the end of World War I served to confirm in Pacelli and his colleagues the conviction they already held, namely, that Jewish emancipation had unleashed upon Europe a force potentially capable of bringing about the moral and spiritual destruction of Christendom.

Pope Pius XII believed that the Church and National Socialism shared two common enemies, Bolshevism and Judaism. Ultimately, he saw Bolshevism as a bastardized form of Judaism. In effect, the Nazis were implementing a long cherished Vatican goal, the disenfranchisement of nonbelieving Jews in Christian Europe. Violence and extermination were another matter. Or were they? The Inquisition or the Congregation of the Holy Office never executed condemned heretics, those regarded by the Church as its internal enemies. It handed the condemned over to the secular arm that alone was authorized to impose the death penalty. Moreover, the Inquisition was alive and well in the Papal States in Italy until 1870. The Inquisition's responsibilities included oversight of the Jews in the Papal States, who were forbidden to provide Christians with food and lodging, own land, spend the night outside the ghetto, or have "friendly relations with Christians."[149] That was the state whose passing in 1870 was mourned by the entire Pacelli family and whose restoration they sought.

We began this chapter by asking whether Pope Pius XII and other significant European Christian leaders, plus many if not most of their followers, regarded the elimination of Europe's Jews as a benefit for European Christendom. The evidence suggests an affirmative answer. Unlike the Inquisition, Pius XII was not required to turn the internal enemy over to the secular arm. All that was required of him was to do nothing and to say as little as possible. The secular arm did the rest.

## THE BOUNDARIES OF OBLIGATION

When Germany attacked Poland, Germany's Catholic bishops asked the faithful "to join in ardent prayers that God's providence may lead this war to blessed success and peace for fatherland and people."[150] One exception to the rule was Bishop, later Cardinal, Konrad Preysing of Berlin, who had been a consistent opponent of the Nazi regime from its inception.[151] Another, and arguably the most notable of the Catholic clergy who spoke out in protest, was Msgr. Bernard Lichtenberg, *Domprobst* (Provost) of St. Hedwig's Cathedral in Berlin. He first spoke out on 10 November 1938, the day after *Kristallnacht*, when he prayed publicly "for the persecuted 'non-Aryan' Christians and Jews." He continued to utter the prayer publicly every day until arrested on 23 October 1941. On 22 May 1942 Lichtenberg was tried and sentenced.[152] He died on the way to the Dachau concentration camp in November 1943.[153] He received no support from Cesare Orsenigo, Pius XII's nuncio to Germany.

A small but morally significant number of Catholics attempted to rescue Jews. In addition to Bishop Preysing of Berlin, there was a group of anti-Nazi Munich Jesuits active in the resistance and laypersons such as Margarete Sommer and Gertrud Luckner. Preysing and Sommer rescued baptized and nonbaptized Jews alike and vainly attempted to get Pius XII and the German bishops to speak out against extermination.[154] Preysing wrote to the pope thirteen times in fifteen months during 1943 and 1944, imploring him to intervene, but to no avail.[155] Luckner was arrested on 24 March 1943 for her work with Caritas, an organization that helped Jews in many countries. She was brutally treated in Ravensbrück concentration camp and placed on a "death transport" to Bergen-Belsen in July 1944. She survived and after the war played an effective leadership role in Jewish-Christian reconciliation.[156] About 750 Jews were hidden in convents in Poland and 2,000 in Hungary, thanks to the courageous leadership of Matylda Getter in Poland and Margit Schlachta in Hungary.[157] Jews were also hidden in convents and monasteries in Italy and elsewhere in Europe.

One of religion's most important functions is to define a community's universe of moral obligation, that is, the circle in which people honor reciprocal obligations to protect each other.[158] At times, the universe of moral obligation has been broadly defined to include all of humanity. That message is the one implied by the parable of the Good Samaritan, in which Jesus illustrates the twin injunctions "You shall love the Lord your God . . . and your neighbor as yourself" (Luke 10:27). When a skeptical questioner asks him, "*And who is my neighbor?*" Jesus responds by telling of a Samaritan who, unlike two previous passersby, saw a grievously wounded man lying on the road and undertook to bind up his wounds and take care of him. For Jesus, it was the Good Samaritan who had properly defined the boundaries of obligation by proving "neighbor to the man who fell into the hands of the robbers" (Luke 10:36). The Good Samaritan met that standard because *he let need—not race, nationality, class, or creed—define his universe of obligation*. There is, however, another tradition in which Jesus is depicted as defining the boundaries of obligation far more narrowly. As we noted earlier, when questioned harshly by some Pharisees, Jesus tells them, "You are from your father the devil, and you choose to do your father's desires. He was a murderer from the beginning and does not stand the truth, because there is no truth in him" (John 8:44). Here the Pharisees and implicitly their followers and heirs are utterly cast out of the circle of moral obligation by Jesus. And the spiritual heirs of the Pharisees were the rabbis, the leaders of the Jewish religious mainstream from the first Christian century until today.

Historically, these definitions of the boundaries of obligation have coexisted in Christianity. In times when political and social stress can be maintained within tolerable limits, the more inclusive definition tends to predominate. Unfortunately, in times of disorienting social and political stress, especially defeat in revolution or war, the narrower definition can appear the more credible.

When, as we have seen, the Jews were incessantly assaulted in pulpit, press, and other propaganda sources with the accusation that they were eternally responsible for the excruciatingly painful murder of the Christian Savior, that they had regularly murdered young Christian boys for the ritual use of their blood, that Judas-like they sought to destroy on behalf of their "father the devil" the Christian nations that had granted them citizenship, it is hardly surprising that many Christians felt no sense of moral obligation when the German government launched a campaign of mass annihilation against the Jews. The plain fact is that verbal assault and aggression, especially when expressed by those acting in the name of God, can be deadly weapons because they so easily invite the use of the knife, gun, or gas chamber. Verbal aggression expressed by those with religious authority can stir up murderous emotions while stilling any sense of sin or guilt. Nor was the message altered after the war, when religious leaders in Germany and the Vatican urged their followers to refuse to cooperate with the war crime trials and actively sought to facilitate the escape of the worst of the practitioners of genocide through institutions such as Operation Ratline. The message was clear. If the murderers were guilty—and clearly many religious leaders saw no guilt—their alleged crimes were pardonable because they had acted as defenders of Christian civilization.

What is surprising is that some Christians included Jews within their circle of moral obligation. For example, Denmark's eight thousand Jews were less than 1 percent of the total population, but they were well integrated into that nation's life. Unlike the German Lutheran Church, the predominant Danish Lutheran Church made it clear that Christians were obliged to include Jews in their universe of moral obligation. Danish Christians helped ferry Jews to Sweden to escape Nazi deportation to Auschwitz. Demography and geography aided the Danes in their resistance. Their performance is undimmed by this fact, but it is highly unlikely that such large-scale rescue actions could have happened as easily and successfully elsewhere.

With fifty thousand Jews in a population of more than six million within its immediate prewar border, Bulgaria had been relatively free of anti-Jewish discrimination during the early decades of the twentieth century. Neutral at first, this Balkan state became a Nazi satellite primarily to regain territory lost after World War I. Soon the Germans began to pressure the Bulgarians to legislate against and then deport its Jews. In response, the head of the dominant Bulgarian Orthodox Church rejected Nazi racism, claiming that God alone had the right to "punish" the Jews, and he intervened personally to bolster Bulgarian reluctance to deport them. His action came too late to save fourteen thousand Jews living in the territory newly annexed by Bulgaria, but most of the Jews in "Old Bulgaria" survived.[159] Unlike those in Denmark, the Bulgarian Jews were not highly assimilated. Yet in both cases cultural, religious, and political solidarity existed between Christians and Jews. Resistance to deportation worked. That it did so in Bulgaria's case, however, cannot be divorced from recognition that the Nazis never took full control of their government as they did in Hungary, where 70 percent of a large Jewish population was destroyed in less than twelve months.

Denmark and Bulgaria were the brightest spots. The Dutch Reformed Church as a whole remained passive while the Germans deported 75 percent of Holland's

Jews. In Norway the Lutheran Church refused to pledge loyalty to the Nazi puppet, Vidkun Quisling. Although unable to stop deportation of Norwegian Jews to Auschwitz, it issued an open protest against that action. Those steps may have alerted some Jews and encouraged the Norwegian resistance to aid them, but only half of Norway's eighteen hundred Jews escaped death in the Holocaust. The Germans were less successful percentagewise in France and Italy, but in France the Roman Catholic hierarchy was certainly not unified in opposition to the elimination of Jews, while in Italy a more consistent Catholic distaste for Hitler's genocidal campaign probably reflected anti-German cultural convictions more than pro-Jewish religious ones.

Further east, the archbishop of the Greek Orthodox Church supplemented his petitionary appeals with liberal distributions of baptismal certificates to fleeing Jews and with instructions to priests and people to assist Jews when the German's hit Athens. Such measures were impotent to save even one-quarter of the Greek Jews. The head of the Romanian Orthodox Church spoke out against deportation in a country riddled with antisemitism, but if that effort helped to arrest the death rate, still three hundred thousand Jews perished, mainly at the hands of the Germans' Romanian allies. If many Hungarian Jews remained alive as late as 1944, that outcome was due less to actions of the dominant Roman Catholic Church than to Hungarian officials' calculation that the outright annihilation of their Jews would bring no appreciable gain. From distant Turkey, apostolic delegate Angelo Roncalli provided baptismal certificates to rescue some Hungarian Jews, but when the Germans occupied Hungary, the hierarchy under Cardinal Seredi said even less than the Vatican instructed in protesting the ensuing deportations. With few exceptions, the record was hardly better elsewhere; in some cases, such as Slovakia, where less than 20 percent of the Jews survived, it was much worse.

Antisemitism abounded. Nevertheless, some correlations still hold. Where the churches resisted, there were usually fewer Jewish victims. Where church officials spoke out against Nazi policies, Jews had more success in evading their enemies. Where significant church protest was found, state collaboration with the Nazis was checked at least to some extent. Likewise, when church protests were minimal or absent, such collaboration was unimpeded. When both church and state maintained some degree of solidarity with Jews, the yield of victims was lowest of all. Had these correlations been more widespread, Nazi success would have been far less. Realistically, however, there is not much reason to think that the churches involved were likely to act differently than they did.

## THE UNITED STATES

Thus far, our analysis of Christian responses to the Holocaust has focused on Europe; but what was the reaction of churches in the United States? We have strongly suggested that a majority of European Christian leaders regarded the elimination of Europe's Jews to be a benefit. The same can be said of some very important Americans and British officials. American officials were primarily interested in preventing a large-scale postwar Jewish immigration. The British were primarily interested in preventing Jews from immigrating to Palestine, then under British control.

On 23 March 1943 William Temple, archbishop of Canterbury, pleaded in the House of Lords for immediate steps to rescue the Jews. To quiet the public outcry, the Foreign Office proposed to the U.S. Department of State that "an informal United Nations Conference" be held to consider what steps could be taken for refugees from Nazi terror, but suggested that *no special preference be given to Jewish refugees*. The Foreign Office candidly informed the State Department of the reasons why it did not want to pressure the Germans to stop the slaughter: "There is the possibility that the Germans or their satellites may change over from the policy of extermination to one of extrusion, and aim as they did before the war at embarrassing other countries by flooding them with alien immigrants."[160] An international conference on refugees met on the Atlantic island of Bermuda on 19 April 1943. The conveners confidently expected the conference to be a failure. It was. When George Backer, a technical expert on refugees, was asked for his views during a meeting of the full American delegation, he said that the decision to give no special consideration to the Jewish problem was motivated by a desire to avoid the issue of extermination. For the conference to be a success, he argued, at least 125,000 Jews would have to be taken out of eastern Europe. Senator Scott Lucas of Illinois told the delegates that the British were fearful that if Germany were approached to release Jews, "that is exactly what might happen."[161] One delegate told reporters, "Suppose he [Hitler] did let 2,000,000 or so Jews out of Europe, what would we do with them?"[162] The conference ended with no public statement after deciding to do nothing of substance.

Important studies done by Robert W. Ross and David S. Wyman use the activity of the Protestant press as another point of reference.[163] By November 1942 and regularly thereafter authenticated information about the Nazi extermination of the Jews was made public in the United States. Nevertheless, although the religious press, both Protestant and Catholic, covered this news, and its readers were not uninformed about Jewish plight under the Nazis, it can scarcely be said that a meaningful response on behalf of the beleaguered Jews was aroused. One possible reason for the inaction was an unwillingness to do anything that would open American doors to more than a small number of Jewish refugees, even if that restrictive policy meant averting American eyes from the ongoing slaughter. Some 2,378,000 Jews immigrated to the United States between 1881 and 1925. The immigration was the largest in all of Jewish history. As has so often been the case, the new immigrants were met by hostility exacerbated by religious difference.[164] In 1924 membership in the Ku Klux Klan reached an all-time high and Congress passed the Johnson Act, which established scant immigrant quotas from eastern European areas such as Poland, Russia, and Romania and thereby effectively stopped Jewish immigration to the United States between the two world wars.[165]

The years leading up to World War II were also the years of the Great Depression. With the exception of very talented Jews such as Albert Einstein, Jewish immigration met opposition from American Christians of virtually every denomination, even when it became known that extermination awaited every Jew who came into Hitler's orbit. On 9 February 1939, after *Kristallnacht,* Senator Robert Wagner of New York and Representative Edith Rogers of Massachusetts introduced legislation in the United States Congress. The Wagner-Rogers Child Refugee Bill would grant entry to 10,000 refugee children under the age of fourteen in each of two years, 1939 and 1940. These girls and boys, primarily Jewish, would be beyond the number of immigrants allowed under the German quota. However, the often-amended bill became bogged down in committee. Lacking support from President Franklin D. Roosevelt, the Wagner-Rogers Bill was put aside early that summer. The legislation was opposed by the *Christian Century*, a leading journal of mainstream Protestant opinion, which argued that "admitting Jewish immigrants would only exacerbate America's Jewish problem."[166] Although Roosevelt's New Deal was often criticized by his opponents as the "Jew Deal," the American president during the Third Reich's existence could count the votes, and his administration's policy toward Jewish immigration was as stringent as any conservative could wish.[167]

Hitler's anti-Jewish measures and his wartime Final Solution never became even a third or fourth order of business for most American Christians. Some relief funds were raised and aid dispensed. Rallies were held, petitions signed, statements issued, and committees formed, some bringing Christians and Jews together. Mounting revelations of the Holocaust's full horror in 1942 and thereafter made little difference. Again, this reality is evident in the tone of the leading Protestant journal, the *Christian Century*. Its accounts of the Holocaust often included insinuations that reports of extermination were either exaggerated or outright fabrications.[168] Only on 9 May 1945 did the editors finally report on the Holocaust without such insinuations. In contrast to the vigorous reaction of the American Protestant press to the atomic bombing of Hiroshima and Nagasaki, the Holocaust's greater devastation elicited little more than stunned silence.

There were highly significant American exceptions among prominent Protestant leaders, who worked hard, frequently in cooperation with American Jewish agencies, to provoke a meaningful response. The most influential leader was Reinhold Niebuhr, one of the greatest American Protestant theologians of the twentieth century. Writing in the *Nation* in early 1942, Niebuhr stated bluntly that the Nazis were determined to exterminate the Jews and offered a far more sympathetic understanding of Zionism as a necessary response to the Holocaust than was forthcoming from the Vatican.[169]

## THE AVENUE OF THE RIGHTEOUS

In the spring of 1942 SS officer Ernst Biberstein went east. He had already been involved in deporting Jews to killing centers, but his new assignment would take him from an administrative post into the field to relieve an officer in *Einsatz-gruppe* C. One of four squadrons charged with eliminating Jews behind the lines of the German advance into Russia, *Einsatzgruppe* C policed Ukraine. Among its credits was the murder of more than thirty-three thousand Jews at Babi Yar the previous September, a task accomplished in only two days. Biberstein missed Babi Yar, but he did nothing to diminish the record of his unit once he assumed command. It was unnecessary to deport thousands of Jews, because Biberstein and his men worked efficiently. Before joining the SS in 1936, Biberstein had been a Protestant pastor. He was not bloodthirsty. No evidence shows that he sought to lead a crew of killers. Yet when one speaks about the murder of six million Jews by baptized Christians, Biberstein's case makes a point. His is only one example, admittedly extreme, within a spectrum of activity that included not only direct participation in murder but also the many sorts of complicity required to make a process of destruction happen.

As Biberstein moved from killing by administrative decision to killing by ordering executioners to fire machine guns, a young German soldier reached Munich, following orders that transferred him to the university there for training as a medic. Earlier his letters alluded to events that had shaken him to the core. "I can't begin to give you the details," he wrote. "It is simply unthinkable that such things exist. . . . The war here in the East leads to things so terrible I would never have thought them possible."[170] Willi Graf referred not to combat against Russian troops but to slaughter by the *Einsatzgruppen*. In Munich two of Graf's closest friends were Hans and Sophie Scholl, both in their early twenties. Motivated by an understanding of Christianity and a love for Germany that were at odds with Hitler's, the Scholls were determined to do more than ask haplessly, "What can we do?" With Hans in charge, their public dissent began. Together with their philosophy professor, Kurt Huber, 51, and some fellow students, they attacked Nazism by distributing leaflets from The White Rose, their resistance movement. Their group operated for less than a year, its output restricted to several thousand copies of seven different flyers. The war was still in Hitler's favor when the protest began in 1942. By the time the Scholls were caught, the tide had turned at Stalingrad. The White Rose could assume no credit for the reversal, but the Nazis took its activity seriously, all the more so as Hitler's war plans collapsed. On 22 February 1943, four days after their arrest, the Scholls and Christoph Probst stood trial. Eight hours later they were beheaded.

"Somebody, after all," testified Sophie Scholl, "had to make a start."[171] Some Christians did rescue Jews. When the documentation demonstrates that Christians and other Gentiles saved Jewish lives for altruistic reasons, they are celebrated as "Righteous among the Nations" at Yad Vashem, the Israeli Holocaust memorial in Jerusalem. At the time of this writing, about twenty thousand men and women have received this honor. Although most of these "Righteous Gentiles" were baptized Christians, not all were practicing believers. Fewer were church leaders. Still, the number of Christian rescuers recognized at Yad Vashem continues to grow. Until the 1990s, the "Righteous among the Nations" were identified by commemorative trees, the first ones planted in the 1950s.[172] Forming the Avenue of the Righteous, they stand in double rows along the walk that slopes upward to the memorial buildings. Too numerous to be placed along the original route, later additions make a grove on a scenic knoll nearby. When the number of trees, some two thousand of them, became too large for the space available, a decision was taken to inscribe the names of the rescuers, by country, on a wall that surrounds the park commemorating these special people. As the Yad Vashem memorial testifies, some Christians did what they could, often at grave risk to their own lives, to diminish the Holocaust's devastation.

Approximately one-third of Europe's Jews survived the war. Jewish endurance, ingenuity, and resistance alone account for much of that fact. Yet survivors often stress that they would not have lived unless non-Jews helped them. For example, a Lithuanian librarian, Anna Shimaite, delivered dozens of Jewish children from the Vilna ghetto. A Czech-German industrialist, Oskar Schindler, along with his wife, Emily, spent a fortune to rescue from SS selections some twelve hundred Jews working under his supervision in Poland. Swedish diplomat Raoul Wallenberg used his political authority, plus financial support from the American War Refugee Board, to shelter thousands of Hungarian Jews before disappearing inside the Soviet Union. Beyond the publicized cases there were many other acts of courage, mercy, and resistance.[173] Rescue depended not only on individuals but on groups of people working together. Networks of assistance, which involved communities and institutions at least to some extent, were critical.

Magda Trocmé was invited to plant a tree at Yad Vashem in 1972. Dedicated to her late husband, André, it branches out to remember more than a solitary Protestant pastor. Along with a more recent tree in her honor, its roots and foliage represent their children, the members of their church, and nearly all the citizens of Le Chambon-sur-Lignon.[174] The Trocmés began their work in September 1934 in the small Protestant church at Le Chambon, in the mountains of southeastern France. Descendants of a Huguenot religious minority violently persecuted in earlier French history, the congregation gradually responded to the new pastor and his wife.

During World War I André Trocmé lived in a part of France occupied by the Germans. As he saw the devastation of war, he made friends with a German medic who believed that Christians ought not to kill. Influenced by the medic's example, Trocmé gradually forged a theology that stressed nonviolent resistance to evil, which he defined as doing harm to human life. André's emphasis was on resistance to evil as much as on nonviolence. He came to believe the negative injunction "Do not kill" was insufficient; it had to be supplemented by positive action to relieve suffering and to block harm's way. It was the Christian's responsibility to be vigilant for ways to move against destructiveness. Such was André Trocmé's interpretation of Jesus' commandments to love God and one's neighbor as oneself. The Chambonnais would practice remarkably well what their Protestant preacher urged them to do.

The quality of life in Le Chambon had been rejuvenated by the Cévenol School, a private academy envisioned by Trocmé and administered by Edouard

Theis, who also served as André's assistant, and Roger Darcissac, another close friend. Along with Magda Trocmé, they led Le Chambon to seize the special opportunity to resist that came their way after France fell to Hitler on 22 June 1940. Geography placed Le Chambon in Vichy, the unoccupied region south of the Loire River where the Germans permitted their puppet, Marshal Henri Philippe Pétain, to govern. Within four months of the fall of France on 22 June 1940, the Vichy regime enacted its own harsh anti-Jewish legislation and authorized the internment of foreign Jews. Measures in the occupied zone were even more punitive and swiftly applied. On 27 March 1942 the first deportation to Auschwitz left the Drancy transit camp. In Paris that July, another roundup netted thirteen thousand non-French Jews. Awaiting deportation, nine thousand of these victims were hideously imprisoned in a sports stadium, the Velodrome d'Hiver. Half were children under sixteen. None of them survived the Holocaust. Pétain's government prepared to follow suit. Fifteen thousand foreign Jews were handed over to the Germans for deportation in August 1942, and three months later, when the Germans occupied Vichy, there were few havens of any kind for Jews on French soil. Le Chambon remained one of them.

During the winter of 1940–41 Magda Trocmé had answered an evening knock at her door. A frightened woman identified herself as a German Jew. She had heard that there might be help in Le Chambon. Could she come in? Magda Trocmé's answer was, "Naturally." That single word says a lot. From then on Jewish refugees arrived almost daily. None was turned away. They were fed, hidden, and whenever possible spirited across the Swiss border by cooperating Christians, some devout and some not, who were convinced that it is simply wrong to leave anyone in harm's way. Why these acts did not bring full German retribution to Le Chambon has not been fully explained, for the activities were never completely secret. One crucial reason has been identified: Major Julius Schmäling, a German who had governmental responsibilities for two years when the Germans occupied this region of France. He knew what the people of Le Chambon were doing and let it happen. Likewise, André Trocmé and his followers knew that they had some protection, and they did not let their opportunity slip away.

Aiding endangered Jews was not something the unpretentious Chambonnais Christians regarded as heroic or as unusually good. It was only the natural fulfillment of their commitment. Not that they overlooked the danger or the need for care. Organization, trust, and planning were essential to their success, as was a tradition of teaching and learning that had rooted their commitment in solid ground. The Chambonnais did not save everyone. They were not, after all, professional rescue specialists but only ordinary folk who had to improvise their resistance against trained killers.

Ninety thousand Jews in France lost their lives to those professionals. The amateur lifeguards of Le Chambon rescued about five thousand Jews. If that contrast does not overwhelm their achievement, then one might point out that their relative isolation in an inconsequential town may have kept them out of the spotlight because the French police and the Gestapo had more important prey to nab.

The Chambonnais had the luxury of room to maneuver, moreover, because they lived at first in Vichy France and because during the German occupation they got help from Major Schmäling. But the key point remains: they did not miss the rescue opportunities that were theirs.

Rescue was especially costly for Daniel Trocmé, André's young cousin. He had been asked by André to come to Le Chambon to help coordinate rescue efforts on behalf of refugee children. When the police raided Le Chambon looking for Jews, which they did with increasing frequency as the war continued, warnings usually came in time to allow the refugees to hide in the surrounding countryside. Once the warning came too late. The Germans caught Daniel and his children. Although he could have saved himself, he refused to leave the girls and boys. He died at Majdanek. Even after his death the Germans kept trying to find out whether, as they suspected, Daniel Trocmé was Jewish. A tree in his honor lives at Yad Vashem.

How goodness happened at Le Chambon suggests why it did not happen in many other communities of baptized Christians. Le Chambon had leaders who self-critically evaluated what it means to follow Jesus. They took the parable of the Good Samaritan as normative. Their universe of obligation broke the boundaries of racism, nationalism, and antisemitism. This leadership prepared its followers to look for opportunities to resist harmdoing. The preparation included awareness that it is critical to act in time. The Chambonnais were receptive. Without that disposition on their part, André Trocmé would have been a forgotten voice in the wilderness. It is possible that these men and women were responsive because, as French Protestants, they were the heirs of a minority status that had brought persecution and suffering to their ancestors. Outsiders, they may have been inclined to help others in similar positions. Or because they encountered refugees not en masse but as individuals, the Chambonnais may have recognized human hurt in ways that touched their better natures and did not overwhelm them with the hopelessness of meeting a need so vast that nothing one could do would make much difference. At one level the Chambonnais could have done otherwise, yet at a deeper level, had they turned away, they would have done violence to everything that made them the kind of people they were. Whatever the factors that moved the Chambonnais, they unhesitatingly chose to help when needy Jews stood before them. They knew how to answer well the question "Am I my brother's keeper?"

## SOME CONCLUDING REFLECTIONS

After the intense campaign carried out for decades before World War II in both the Catholic and Protestant pulpit and press of Europe concerning the allegedly nefarious Jewish menace, it is hard to believe that most churches would not have welcomed a very significant reduction in the number of European Jews. Moreover, when Holocaust survivors attempted to return to their original homes after the war, they were often met by open hostility and violence. In the eyes of far too many Europeans who otherwise welcomed the Third Reich's demise, Hitler did help to "solve" the Jewish problem. Few church officials wanted to be associated with death camps and genocide, although, as we have seen, very many of the best and most charitable did see the hand of God in such programs and institutions. In addition, after the war both the Vatican and the German Protestant leadership did their utmost to undermine the war crimes trials of high-ranking Nazis, and the Vatican established an escape system, Operation Ratline, that enabled some of the most vicious mass murderers to escape justice.[175]

With the onset of the Cold War, there was a certain advantage to having been an active participant in the worst war crimes of the Nazis and their Croatian allies, the Ustasa. Such activities were seen less as criminal than as attestation that the individual in question was an active anti-Communist who might be helpful in the coming struggle to defeat communism. In 1945 and 1946 Soviet armed forces controlled all of eastern Europe, and it was by no means certain that western Europe could remain free. Even before the end of the war a campaign to rescue the most vicious Nazi mass murderers and their collaborators began in Rome. Bishop Alois Hudal, rector of the ecclesiastical college at the Church of Santa Maria dell' Anima, one of the three seminaries for German priests in Rome, was a leading figure in this effort. According to Vatican historian Father Robert Graham, S.J., Hudal was "notorious in Rome for being openly philo-Nazi."[176] That judgment could help to explain why Hudal was the Catholic official who delivered a letter to the German army commander in Rome on 16 October 1944, which contained a Vatican request to suspend immediately the arrests of Jews in Rome and its vicinity.[177] Some time before, in August 1944, following the collapse of the German army in Italy, the Vatican Secretariat of State requested that the Allies permit the pope to send his personal representatives to visit the camps where the Allies held tens of thousands of Axis prisoners of war and civilian internees. These representatives would "assure normal religious assistance to Catholic prisoners."[178] After the request was granted, the Vatican requested that their representative be permitted to visit German-speaking internees in Italy and chose Hudal, the most openly pro-Nazi cleric of standing, as its representative. In fairness, it should be noted that American intelligence had a complete dossier on Hudal's writings and activities but offered no objections.[179]

The interned Nazis found a friend in Hudal. In 1962 Hudal, by then an archbishop, wrote that when he visited the camps, his first concern was to help former members of the Nazi Party, especially "so-called war criminals." Hudal claimed that many of these people were either innocent or had only followed orders. He contrasted his work of Christian love with "Talmudic hatred" of those who sought to punish alleged war criminals.[180] Among the war criminals whom Hudal eventually helped to escape were Franz Stangl, formerly commandant of the death camps at Sobibor and Treblinka; Walter Rauff, who organized gas-van murders; Gustav Wagner, another former commandant at Sobibor; Adolf Eichmann, deportation chief of the Reich Security Main Office (RSHA); and Alois Brunner, former commandant of Drancy and one of Eichmann's most notorious henchmen in the Final Solution.[181]

After the war, the Vatican appointed Hudal "Spiritual Head of the German People Resident in Italy." Historian Michael Phayer asks, "From among the many German-speaking priests residing in Rome, why did the Vatican choose the most notorious pro-Nazi for this position?"[182] According to Phayer, Pius XII and the postwar Vatican did not necessarily regard Nazi identity as a negative factor, and "the evidence unquestionably points to the Holy See's assistance to fleeing Nazis."[183] Germany's Cardinal von Galen was by no means alone when he wrote a diatribe against the trial of leading Nazi war criminals, which was published in Rome.[184] Between 1948 and 1952 Pius XII was involved in a major effort to pressure American authorities to commute the death sentences of major Nazi war criminals, including Otto Ohlendorf, the commander of *Einsatzgruppe* D, which had been responsible for the mass killings in Ukraine, and Oswald Pohl, the head of the SS Economic and Administration Main Office, which was in charge of concentration camp slave labor. At one point the Vatican sought from General Lucius B. Clay, the American military commander in occupied Germany, a blanket pardon for all Nazi war criminals who had received a death sentence. Clay refused, arguing that the individuals had been found guilty of very specific heinous crimes.[185] Already in August 1945 the pope had publicly defended Germany and called its citizens heroes and martyrs. Later that year he asserted inaccurately that most Germans had opposed Nazism with their whole heart.[186] Since the pope's reputation at the time was beyond reproach, his assertion of their innocence had an enormous impact on Germans, who were thereby able to disassociate themselves from the Nazi crimes. It was not until the early 1960s that Germans were able honestly to begin to face the truth about themselves.

If the Vatican under Pius XII regarded the Holocaust as a crime, it was very obviously a pardonable crime. However, for those Catholics and Protestants who continued to see the Jews as enemies determined to destroy Christian civilization—and there were many—the Holocaust was no crime at all. Even those perpetrators who shared Hitler's contempt for Christianity could be regarded as unwitting defenders of Christian civilization. Moreover, while the pope and his ecclesiastical subordinates were very largely silent about the Holocaust, they were by no means silent about their opposition to the system of justice the Allies employed to demonstrate that the worst perpetrators of Nazi war crimes could expect no future in a reconstituted Germany. Those who had cooperated in any degree with Hitler in the work of destruction found self-exculpatory rationalizations of their behavior preferable to critical self-reflection. It took another generation before the critical process could begin in earnest.

Far too many leaders of church and state saw in the Final Solution precisely what the Nazi leadership saw, a problem-solving exercise in which an unwanted population was conveniently eliminated. During the war, neither the pope nor other church leaders had to do anything physically to harm Jews. This was also true of those British and American leaders who feared that the German policy might change from the policy of extermination to one of extrusion. To repeat, all that was required was to do nothing and say as little as possible. The Germans under Hitler did the rest.

In fairness to the Roman Catholic Church, it must be stated that there is a vast difference between the way the Church has dealt with religious pluralism before and after Vatican II and most especially its relations with Judaism.[187] The same can be said of the mainline Protestant churches. Nevertheless, what Daniel Goldhagen has referred to as a moral reckoning is far from complete as far as post-Holocaust Christianity is concerned. We close this chapter by pointing out a few of his observations and recommendations. His controversial ideas will strike some readers as extreme, but they deserve attention nonetheless.

Although Goldhagen speaks specifically about the Roman Catholic Church, his reckoning has implications for all Christian communities. The most basic task of moral restitution sounds simple—eradicate antisemitism from Christianity—but it is not. In Goldhagen's view, conciliatory language, goodwill, apologies, even the most heartfelt expressions of sorrow, regret, and contrition are not enough. Nothing less than fundamental reform will do. The changes must go deep down, because antisemitism lies at the very roots of Christianity.

Specifically, then, what should the Roman Catholic Church do? How must it, and by implication other Christian churches, change? For starters, Goldhagen prods the Catholic Church to name names. It should identify the individual leaders who came up short during the Holocaust and repudiate them, including "all relevant Popes, bishops, and priests."[188] It should halt immediately the canonization of any person—read Pius XII specifically—who aided and abetted the persecution of Jews. The Church should develop memorials that bear witness to the Holocaust-related suffering and death in which it is implicated. A lengthy papal encyclical should be forthcoming; it should detail the history of the Church's antisemitism, denouncing that history, and any perpetuation of it, as sinful. These steps, however, only begin to deal with Goldhagen's list.

Antisemitism, Goldhagen believes, is inseparable from the Church's authoritarian and imperialistic pretensions. Therefore, the Church must abandon papal infallibility, dissolve the Vatican as a political state, embrace religious pluralism to make clear that salvation does not come through the Church alone, and revise its official *Catechism* to make unmistakable that any teaching smacking of antisemitism is "wrong, null, and void."[189] The biggest issue, however, involves the Bible itself. That problem, he argues, belongs to all Christianity, not just the Roman Catholic Church.

Goldhagen's reading of the New Testament leaves him with two striking impressions: First, Christianity is "a religion of love that teaches its members the highest moral principles for acting well. Love your neighbor. Seek peace. Help those in need. Sympathize with and raise up the oppressed. Do to others as you would have them do to you."[190] Second, the New Testament's "relentless and withering assault on Jews and Judaism" is not incidental because it portrays the Jews as "the ontological enemy" of Jesus, goodness, and God.[191]

The "Bible problem," moreover, is not just that two apparently contradictory perspectives collide, but that the collision takes place in texts that are regarded as sacred and divinely inspired. The need, Goldhagen contends, is for Christians to rewrite the New Testament, to expunge antisemitism from it; but he recognizes how difficult, perhaps insurmountable, that task may be. Nevertheless, Goldhagen does not despair. He thinks that the Christian tradition can be self-corrective, resilient, and revitalized if Christians find the will to be true to their tradition's best teachings about love and justice.

Wisely, Goldhagen does not presume to rewrite the New Testament. Nor does he venture to define everything that a truly post-Holocaust Christianity should be. Meanwhile, he seems to be betting that Christianity can gain new life by letting its old one die. How many Christians will welcome such prospects remains to be seen.

# Chapter 11

# What Can—and Cannot— Be Said? Artistic and Literary Responses to the Holocaust

*If the Lagers had lasted longer a new, harsh language would have been born; and only this language could express what it means to toil the whole day in the wind, with the temperature below freezing, wearing only a shirt, underpants, cloth jacket and trousers, and in one's body nothing but weakness, hunger and knowledge of the end drawing nearer.*

Primo Levi, *Survival in Auschwitz*

This chapter's epigraph comes from "October 1944," a portion of Primo Levi's classic memoir, *Survival in Auschwitz*. The Germans sent Levi to Auschwitz from his native Italy in late February 1944. He called his deportation "a journey toward nothingness."[1] Eight months later, Levi knew that autumn's receding light and retreating warmth meant that the devastation of another Auschwitz winter was at hand. "From October to April," he understood, "seven out of ten of us will die. Whoever does not die will suffer minute by minute, all day, every day."[2] *Winter*, Levi insisted, was not the right word for that dreadful season. Nor could *hunger* and *pain* capture the realities of Auschwitz. Such words, he thought, were "free words, created and used by free men who lived in comfort and suffering in their homes."[3]

If the Holocaust did not last long enough to produce in full the "new, harsh language" of which Levi spoke, that event continues to leave survivors, historians, philosophers, theologians, novelists, and poets groping for words. Related experiences confront filmmakers, musicians, and artists who try to use their gifts to ensure that the Holocaust will not be forgotten. Out of those struggles have come remarkable and instructive responses to the Holocaust. The philosopher Theodor Adorno argued that it would be barbaric to write poetry after the Holocaust.[4] The literary critic George Steiner had similar feelings when he wondered whether there has been too much writing after Auschwitz, much of it rendered insignificant by the Holocaust.[5] Their claims rightly condemn artistic and literary responses that trivialize the Holocaust, but those judgments should not be applied to all the literature and art that the Holocaust has evoked. On the contrary, not only have artistic and literary responses done much to keep memory of the Holocaust alive, but also the most powerful and authentic expressions of that kind help to drive home a deepened sense of the losses that the Holocaust produced, the warnings that reverberate from them, and the questions that remain. Just as no one history book can fully contain the Holocaust, let alone completely explain it, no film, musical score, painting, memoir, essay, novel, or poem can provide access to more than a sliver of that disaster. Yet when such contributions are well done, memory can be sharpened, feeling sensitized, understanding increased, and memorialization enhanced in ways that we can ill afford to be without. As preludes to this chapter's discussion of Holocaust-related art and literature, consider first some illustrations from film and music.

## STILL PHOTOS, MOVING PICTURES, POIGNANT NOTES

No medium has done more than film—both still photos and moving pictures— to spread awareness of the Holocaust.[6] Early on, military photographers and film crews—Russian, British, American—recorded what they found in the desolation of the camps that were liberated in 1945. Now the sources for stock images and footage used in museums, books, and latter-day documentaries, these photos and films provided the first images of the Holocaust, and they were also used in postwar judicial proceedings.[7] Before film was used to remember the Holocaust, however, it had played a key role in supporting Nazi Germany's racism and antisemitism. Approaches to Auschwitz went through cameras, film studios, and movie houses. With Leni Riefenstahl's *Triumph of the Will*, a documentary of the Nazi Party rally at Nuremburg in 1934, and Veit Harlan's *Jud Süss* (1940) as only two salient examples, film advanced Hitler's charismatic mystique and his virulent antisemitism at once. As war raged, German photos and films both captured and masked the *Wehrmacht*'s onslaughts while the same media were used to intensify Nazi propaganda about the racial inferiority of Jews and Gypsies and the necessity to rid Germany of "useless eaters," even if they happened to be German. Such examples show that artistic talent can serve many interests, including genocide. Nazi Germany's use of photography and film to glorify its lethal intentions came to an end, but memory of those offenses continues to challenge not only those who want to use these media for better purposes but also those who watch the results. On both counts—the impressions created and the impressions received—problems are not far to find.

Alain Resnais's *Night and Fog* (1955), an early documentary about the Holocaust, is as deceptive as it is captivating, for it so universalizes the Holocaust that the Jewish and German particularity of the event is unidentified. Similar criticism can be brought against Alan J. Pakula's *Sophie's Choice* (1982), an adaptation of William Styron's controversial novel, which focuses attention primarily on a fictional Polish woman, Sophie Zawistowska, who is deported to Auschwitz and then given the "choiceless choice" to pick one of her two children to be spared from the gas. (To mixed reviews, an operatic version of *Sophie's Choice* debuted in London in early December 2002.) Problems of a different kind plagued the NBC miniseries *Holocaust* (1978). The American audience was approximately 120 million, half of the nation's population at the time. When *Holocaust* aired in Germany the next year, it became, in Judith Doneson's words, "a political happening" that broke "a thirty-five-year taboo on discussing Nazi atrocities."[8] The film's focus on the Dorf and Weiss families left no doubt about the Holocaust's German and Jewish particularity, but the omnipresence of these families in every aspect of the Holocaust turned them into symbolic types that lent a melodramatic, soap-opera quality to the production, straining credibility even as the film domesticated the Holocaust and turned it into entertainment. More than that, *Holocaust* raised the insurmountable dilemma that stalks every attempt to make a movie out of the Holocaust: To what extent can and should a motion picture—documentary, fictional, or somewhere in between—reflect what happened in that event? *Holocaust* tried to cover the event's full scope in a four-part series. The project was bound to fail, and yet in significant ways it succeeded—at least in the sense that it made vast numbers of people more aware of the Holocaust's moral significance. It was not accidental that shortly after *Holocaust*'s airing in the United States in 1978, an executive order of President Jimmy Carter established the President's Commission on the Holocaust, whose duties included recommending appropriate ways to remember the Holocaust's victims. Chaired by Holocaust survivor Elie Wiesel, who was highly critical of the television production *Holocaust*, the commission recommended in 1979 that the United States Holocaust Memorial Museum should be created in the nation's capital.

The Washington museum opened its doors in 1993. That same year the masterful Steven Spielberg produced *Schindler's List*.[9] When television aired it several times since 1993, the audiences for this Oscar-winning film surpassed those for *Holocaust*. Based on Thomas Keneally's historical novel, the film made such a widespread and deep-felt impression that problems lurk in its very success. Oskar Schindler, the opportunistic German industrialist turned savior of Jews in occupied Poland, becomes the problematic "good Nazi" centerpiece in a narrative of rescue and redemption that overwhelms the fact that this story, remarkable as it may be, is scarcely representative of the Holocaust's vast destruction and darkness. Yet *Schindler's List* epitomizes the Holocaust for many of its viewers. The film becomes Holocaust history, despite the fact that no film can be Holocaust history.

No film grasps and wrestles with the latter dilemma better than Claude Lanzmann's epic *Shoah* (1985). Running almost ten hours in length, the film includes only a small fraction of the footage taken by the French filmmaker, who conducted interviews—many of them at Holocaust sites—with survivors, perpetrators, bystanders, and the Holocaust scholar Raul Hilberg. Not so paradoxically, Lanzmann's epic gains in intensity and credibility because its approach is indirect in comparison to many other Holocaust-related films. He does not attempt to recreate episodes, places, or people. Sensing correctly that the past can neither be recovered nor remembered in that way, he revisits the places where the worst took place. Today those areas are quiet and for that reason the screams they contain may be sensed better than any soundtrack could recreate them. As Lanzmann's cameras focus on pits or ovens where bodies burned, the Holocaust smells are absent—a telltale indication that all Holocaust representation, including historical analysis, is many steps removed from the reality it tries to grasp. Even when he documents resistance during the Holocaust, as Lanzmann does in his 2002 film *Sobibor, October 14, 1943, 4 p.m.,* which explores the prisoner revolt that took place at that killing center, he tells the story without attempting to recreate the rebellion visually. Yet awareness that the Holocaust cannot be separated from the stench of overcrowded ghettos and barracks or the pall of smoke from burning flesh penetrates consciousness, not in spite of, but because of Lanzmann's cinematic distance from the events themselves.

Something similar takes place in the collaboration of Mark Jonathan Harris and Deborah Oppenheimer, which led to *Into the Arms of Strangers* (2000), their Academy Award winner for best documentary feature.[10] Drawing on oral history and evocative film footage, it tells the bittersweet story of the *Kindertransport,* the rescue effort that brought about ten thousand Jewish children to the United Kingdom from Germany, Austria, and Czechoslovakia between November 1938 and the outbreak of war in September 1939. As it anticipates the closing of doors for refugees and the worst that was to follow, this film drives home in understated ways what the Holocaust entailed: namely, the separation—one by one—of Jewish parents and children and the intended total destruction of Jewish family life. Parents and children—Jewish and non-Jewish—can identify with anguish of that kind. Few films match the power of *Into the Arms of Strangers* to use history's particularity to communicate key aspects of the Holocaust's universal significance.[11]

Many more Holocaust-related films deserve commentary that space does not permit. They include Pierre Sauvage's *Weapons of the Spirit* (1988), which sensitively documents the people of Le Chambon-sur-Lignon, who hid some five thousand Jews in their French village and its surrounding countryside, and *Conspiracy* (2001), an instructive recreation of the Wannsee Conference on 20 January 1942. In the latter, historical authenticity and creative imagination blend to reproduce an important meeting. It is not known exactly what the participants said, but existing documents and historical research allow us to know a great deal about the persons, circumstances, and problems that governed those fateful winter minutes. Constructed though it has to be, the sound track's conversation does not strain credibility. On the contrary, it reveals how routine and ordinary the discussions and deliberations that doom millions to death can be. In its quiet, understated ways, *Conspiracy* puts Holocaust-related ethical questions in especially bold relief.

In distinctive ways, the same can be said of three films that received widespread attention at the time of this writing. Taking its title from Primo Levi's classic chapter in *The Drowned and the Saved,* Tim Blake Nelson's *The Grey Zone* concentrates on the *Sonderkommando* units at Auschwitz-Birkenau, the groups of Jewish men who were forced to work in the gas chambers and crematoria. To date no Holocaust-related film provides a more graphic depiction of the mass murder committed by the Germans in that place and the desperate plight of the Jewish victims, which included the *Sonderkommando* personnel. In *The Pianist,* Roman Polanski's treatment of Wladyslaw Szpilman's memoir, the setting is German-occupied Warsaw, where the dilemmas focus on the struggles for survival that confronted the ghettoized Jews in Poland's capital. In *Max,* the Dutch writer and director Menno Meyjes explores Hitler, but not as the German Führer who took the world to the Warsaw ghetto and the ovens of Auschwitz. Meyjes ponders the young Hitler, the frustrated artist and wounded veteran of World War I. Each film in this trio sparks debate. Is *The Grey Zone* too graphic and therefore, paradoxically, not able to capture what it purports to portray, because the realities and the dilemmas facing the *Sonderkommando* elude comprehension, cinematic or otherwise? Is *The Pianist* too entertaining and so well done aesthetically that it inadvertently masks the Holocaust's horror? As for *Max,* does its portrayal of Hitler make him too ordinary, too much a person with whom one might empathize as he struggles with his experiences of disappointment and adversity? To the extent that these films provoke thoughtful inquiry and discussion, their importance can be substantial. Time will tell how much that will be the case. Meanwhile, it seems certain that the Holocaust will continue to call forth films about it.

One thing more about most Holocaust films deserves notice: music plays an important part in them. The power of *Into the Arms of Strangers,* for example, is amplified by its sound track, which features children's songs from the period. "Give us, God, the evening," one of them asks, "the evening, the good evening, [and] thus a cheerful morning." For Jewish parents and children during the Holocaust, good evenings and cheerful mornings were few and far between. Like still photographs and moving pictures, music helped to make that so. Arguably no artistic influence on Hitler was greater than Richard Wagner's. Dedicated German nationalist and antisemite, Wagner (1813–88) was Hitler's favorite composer, and the staging of the composer's operas informed Hitler's ideology and inspired the emotional pageantry at Nazi rallies. Wagner's family contained fervent Nazi supporters, and his art supported the Third Reich's genocidal campaign against the Jews.[12]

Few artistic expressions stir human feeling more than music. Its presence in ceremonial occasions, political and religious ones especially, testifies to that. So it is not surprising that music played key parts in the Holocaust.[13] Nor was the role of music restricted to the influence of Wagner's operas on Hitler. Many classical works, such as those by Felix Mendelssohn and Gustav Mahler, were suppressed by the Nazis because of their composers' Jewish origins. Shortly after the Nazis took power in 1933, the Reich Music Office dismissed Jewish professional musicians. In Nazi culture, moreover, jazz, as well as much modern art, was labeled degenerate. As illustrated in Fania Fenelon's *Playing for Time*, orchestras composed of Jewish prisoners were formed in some concentration and death camps by Nazi decree. Meanwhile in Terezín and several other ghettos concerts were given, operas staged, and musical works were written by Jewish musicians such as Viktor Ullman, Gideon Klein, and Pavel Haas. As the "Partisans' Song" illustrates, music was important in Jewish resistance as well.

In the Holocaust's aftermath, music continues to have an important role. Lanzmann begins *Shoah* with Simon Srebnik, one of the very few survivors of Chelmno, who years later sings again the songs he sang for the Germans as a boy in the *Sonderkommando* of that death camp. Music also can heard in the many Holocaust commemorations that now take place. Sometimes they include compositions and songs from the ghettos, camps, and partisan groups. Other examples include Max Bruch's *Kol Nidre*, a haunting interpretation of the moving Jewish prayer that opens the evening service on Yom Kippur, and Leonard Bernstein's *Kaddish*, a poignant setting of the Jewish prayer for the dead. Still others are provided by Arnold Schoenberg's *A Survivor from Warsaw*, Henryk Gorecki's *Third Symphony*, Dmitry Shostakovich's meditation on Babi Yar in his *Thirteenth Symphony*, and Steve Reich's documentary music in *Different Trains*, a string quartet that includes the voices of Holocaust survivors and the sounds of trains that are so emblematic of the transports to Treblinka, Auschwitz-Birkenau, and other death-ridden Holocaust destinations. Arguably music is the art that stands at the greatest distance when representation of the Holocaust is concerned, but memory of the Holocaust can scarcely come without yearnings that music can express and amplify as no other artistic response can do.

## ART AND THE HOLOCAUST

Music can evoke images, but painting and sculpture create them. From the chilling drawings made by the victims themselves while they awaited death in the concentration and death camps to the contemporary work of Shimon Attie, who has projected photographic scenes of destroyed Jewish properties onto the walls of their present-day Berlin building sites, imagery dealing with the Holocaust has developed in challenging and provocative ways. Consideration of some important examples can illustrate how questions about context, authenticity, and appropriate imagery continue to inform the complex and varied field of artistic responses to the Holocaust.[14]

"Open Ends," an early twenty-first-century exhibit at New York's Museum of Modern Art (MOMA), indicated how modern art has responded to the violence of the twentieth century. Of the more than 550 artists whose work was represented, six addressed the Holocaust.[15] Born in 1927, Claude Lanzmann lived through the Nazi era. In the exhibit only his film-clip photograph of railroad tracks leading to the entrance of Auschwitz-Birkenau directly recalled the Holocaust.[16] Now functioning as an icon, Lanzmann's image calls up the Holocaust's devastation even for those who have only slight acquaintance with the history of that event.

The five other artists chosen for the exhibit were born in the 1940s and 1950s, which made them too young to have been drenched in the horrors of the camps by the first devastating revelations of the liberators. Sigmar Polke's *Watchtower*, a large (9′ 10″ x 7′ 4″), aesthetically elegant oil painting, includes menacing areas of black and suggestions of electrified wires, but it makes one wonder what viewers will see if they are unfamiliar with Holocaust history. Unless the viewer already understands that Polke's painting depicts one of the horrific images of the camps—the watchtowers that guarded the inmates night and day and the electrified fences that meant certain death for any prisoner who tried to cross their lines—the painting's message is likely to be lost. Polke's arrangement of brilliant white light, colorful flowers, and black shadows can become a metaphor for life and death, but contemplation of the beautifully painted canvas raises the question, How, if at all, can the enormity of the Holocaust be represented? To represent the Holocaust beautifully seems to be an aesthetic oxymoron.

The MOMA exhibit raised many questions regarding the effects of the Holocaust on the psyche of contemporary artists and viewers. What, for example, does Anselm Kiefer mean by his painting *Departing from Egypt*, a large scene of a desert landscape with an amorphous gray cloud hovering over it?[17] Would a better choice for this exhibit have been R. B. Kitaj's earlier painting *If Not, Not* (1975–76)? With its clear depiction of a concentration camp gate, the reference to himself holding a child, and the painting's various wounded figures tossed in a complex landscape, this work is a clear example of the complexities of memory after the Holocaust.[18] The same can be said of Arie Galles's *Fourteen Stations*, which could have made a most effective contribution to the MOMA exhibition. Working with wartime *Luftwaffe* and Allied aerial reconnaissance photographs that show Nazi concentration and death camps, his suite of fifteen large-format charcoal drawings—each one embedded with the Kaddish, the Jewish prayer for the dead—show how a collapse of time and space reflect the artist's lingering trauma of the Holocaust.[19]

Sometimes criticized but more often praised, *Maus: A Survivor's Tale*, Art Spiegelman's widely noted two-volume response to the Holocaust, uses comicbook styles and animal characters (Jews as mice, Germans as cats) to tell the story of his father's Holocaust experiences as he relates them to his son.[20] As the son reacts, Spiegelman illustrates how complicated memories of the Holocaust can be and shows their profound effects on succeeding generations. As a work of art in a museum, however, Spiegelman's piece in the MOMA exhibit becomes inert. It becomes an object, not a narrative, and thus its effectiveness, its ability to communicate, is lost. "Artworks," said Theodor Adorno, "may be all the more truly experienced the more their historical substance is that of the one who experienced it." When read, Spiegelman's *Maus* creates historical awareness as its rich and complex drawings are combined with text to teach those who encounter his art. But in art-exhibit format, *Maus* does not, cannot, do that work.

In contrast to MOMA's attempt to include the Holocaust in the history of contemporary art, two exhibits curated by Stephen Feinstein provide a better context for Holocaust art. Both *Witness and Legacy* (1995) and *Absence/Presence* (1999) were presented at the Center for Holocaust and Genocide Studies at the University of Minnesota. Among the forty-three artists included in these shows were famous names such as Ben Shahn, Larry Rivers, Jerome Witkin, and Samuel Bak. Each artist is either a refugee, the child of a survivor, or, as in the case of Jerome Witkin, someone who has been profoundly moved by the Holocaust.[21]

*Life? or Theater? A Play with Music,* the moving memoir by Charlotte Salomon, a young German Jewish woman who met her death in Auschwitz, has taken a rightful place as an art document. Discovered by Mary Lowenthal Felstiner, who selected 769 paintings out of more than a thousand that Salomon created between 1940 and 1942, this tragic autobiography in paint mirrors the emotional turmoil of a woman just before the curtain came down on her life.[22] When Salomon's paintings were exhibited at the Jewish Museum in New York, they met a serious, somber audience. The same can be said of the 2002 exhibit at the United States Holocaust Memorial Museum, which featured the work of Arthur Szyk (1894–1951), whose wartime cartoons and caricatures—frequently featured in American magazines and newspapers—rallied resistance against Hitler and urged rescue for Europe's Jews.

In contrast to Salomon's subtle work and Szyk's public art-as-protest, the controversial exhibit *Mirroring Evil, Nazi Imagery/Recent Art,* which appeared at the Jewish Museum in New York in 2002, brought forth howls of dismay from many Holocaust survivors.[23] Only time will tell what place the combination of erotic art with Nazi images and pretty cans of Zyklon B gas will have in post-Holocaust culture. These questions are raised succinctly in an introductory catalogue essay by James Young. Together with Saul Friedländer, Young asks whether Nazi images remain an important part of the story or whether they stir up unhealthy emotions.[24]

Not only does the context affect the display of Holocaust-related art, but also the background of the artists has an effect on their art. In *The Claims of Memory,* Caroline Wiedmer points out that, according to Friedländer and Dominick LaCapra, "the background of the person who analyses and represents the history of the Holocaust has far-reaching effects on the way that history is perceived, told and received."[25] This important distinction, as well as questions of context, is also important in considering the venues in which Holocaust-related art is shown.

Perhaps the most suitable context for art related to the Holocaust can be found in Osnabrück, Germany, where the distinguished architect Daniel Libeskind built a museum to house paintings by Felix Nussbaum (1904–44). Libeskind designed the museum to mirror the desperate career of the painter, who was hunted by the Nazis, escaped to Brussels only to be arrested, and was killed in Auschwitz. The space Libeskind created signifies the void left by Nussbaum's interrupted career.[26] Like the Jewish Museum in Berlin discussed below, Libeskind designed a complicated entrance to the building: dark, narrow corridors

and small windows slashed into slanted walls that create an ambiance of disloca-
tion and anxiety. This setting frames Nussbaum's self-portrait, which shows him
clutching his passport clearly labeled "JUIF-JOO." Set against a dark, cloudy
background, his face is frozen in terror, and fear lurks in his eyes. The visitor to
this museum space leaves with a chill.

Moving from the contemporary effects of the Holocaust and turning to the
foundational imagery that informs Holocaust-related art, one must start with the
art produced in the camps themselves, putting away all questions of style and
form.[27] The aesthetic questions, if they can be asked of these works, are hardly
relevant in this case, for truth telling motivated the artists, and the making of art
often functioned just to keep spirits alive. Hundreds of sketches, watercolors, and
drawings of life and death in the Nazi camps have been collected, and many of
them have been exhibited. They offer firsthand insight into the horror of those
places. Many of the camps themselves now have archives of prisoner art. Many
of the realities depicted by this art—starvation, inhuman work conditions, piles
of corpses—were photographed both by the Germans themselves and the Allies
who liberated the camps. However, the secret art produced by the inmates, on
pain of death if caught, contains imagery and emotion that photographs cannot
match. These drawings reach into the horror in a way that the Germans would
never have permitted, had they known about them.

Only after liberation could some truths be revealed.[28] For example, an already
established painter, David Olère, was arrested in 1943 by the French police, sent
to the Drancy transit camp and then to Auschwitz. There his assignment to a
*Sonderkommando* required him to work in the crematoria. One of the few who
emerged alive from that dreaded work, he endured death-march evacuation from
Auschwitz before his liberation by the Americans at Ebensee in May 1945. Following his release, Olère portrayed what he had witnessed. His art details the
destruction process: the gassing, the corpses, the ovens.[29] A related example can
be found in a charcoal drawing by Leon Delarbre. This work depicts six or seven
hanged men who provide a backdrop for the Nazis who chat casually in the fore-
ground. Delarbre endured multiple German camps: Auschwitz, Buchenwald,
Bergen-Belsen, and Dora.[30] Their clear and devastating content makes contemplation of Olère's and Delarbre's Holocaust art all but unbearable.

At Auschwitz commandant Rudolf Höss set up a small art studio, which was
soon expanded to accommodate more artists.[31] Among the tasks the prisoner-
artists had to perform was the copying of masterpieces stolen from museums, private collections, and Jewish homes. German power over the Bialystok ghetto led
to the establishment of a similar "Copies Workshop," where Jewish artists had to
copy masterpieces for resale.[32] At Terezín, where most of the artists were eventually killed, resistance against their German captors was evident.[33] In every ghetto
or camp where the work of resistance-through-art was done, it had to be hidden
to survive. Some artists buried their pictures in jugs, bricked them into walls, even
taped them to their bodies during forced marches. If materials were easier to get
in Theresienstadt than in many other places, bread often remained the price for

pencils and paints. Paper might be scrounged from any scraps that came to hand. Flour sacks and burlap bags became improvised canvases. All across Europe artist-victims created. Putting art in the service of history, they left behind glimpses of the Final Solution. Perhaps even more importantly, these works themselves are documents whose sheer existence tells what no words could ever say. Art historians and critics discern differences in the training, technique, and talent of these artists, but few will deny that the mixture of passion and detachment reflected in their works, individually and collectively, has exceptional power to transmute aesthetic debates and disagreements into respectful appreciation.

In Terezín, Fritz Taussig, who used the pseudonym Fritta, drew with an ironic, angry pen that seems to have been influenced by German expressionism. One of his images, *The Shops of Theresienstadt*, shows the Potemkin (false front) village that the Germans constructed and the artists painted. Among other things, this work was a German attempt to fool Red Cross visitors into thinking that life for the inmates was pleasant. Fritta painted the roofs of the shops with eyes peeking out. Just in front of the (false) *Parfumerie*, he drew a cart full of jumbled corpses.[34] At the time such works had to be hidden, but their truth has been revealed.

Leo Haas was another of the Terezín artists who were co-opted by the Germans to copy stolen masterpieces, to make portraits for the officers, and even to fresco an officer's living quarters. Even though being caught making their own drawings was a sure death sentence, Haas managed to conceal some five hundred drawings by hiding them in his barrack's wall. After liberation, he went back to Terezín and retrieved this precious stash.[35] Like Olère, Haas was one of the few artist-survivors, and he went on to a productive career. When the witnesses themselves have disappeared, the drawings and sketches produced under horrifying circumstances will remain, but this art is not for the big modern museums. This art is for quiet, meditative spaces protected from the analytic stares of those who look for style and formal qualities.

The artists were either under orders from their captors, or they were risking their lives to document their frightful reality. Art in the camps was no place for elaborate metaphor. That came later—for example, with the paintings of Henry Koerner (1915–91), a Viennese refugee who lost both parents, a brother, and all his family. He said of a painting of his parents: "And so I painted this scene in the Wiener Wald. I helped my parents to walk once more in their beloved Vienna Woods, and I hung the locket with its photo of their children on a tree where their ways parted."[36]

Samuel Bak (b. 1933) escaped with his mother from the Vilna ghetto, but not before an exhibition of the nine-year-old's art work had taken place.[37] Deeply embedded in the classical and biblical traditions, his art is profoundly governed by the Holocaust. Its overtones of Massacio, Michelangelo, and Dürer are combined, for example, with Hebrew letters and shattered tablets of the Ten Commandments. Amidst ravaged landscapes—and one might say mindscapes—his paintings sometimes contain angels who cannot fly and machines that will not work. Bak has painted a haunting essay on Michelangelo's great Sistine Chapel image of the creation of Adam and Eve: with a background of smoking chimneys that recall the Holocaust, the traditional shape of God is rendered only as an empty space, divinity's pointing finger paralyzed.

Koerner, Bak, and Jerome Witkin are unabashed by figurative compositions, transpositions of time and place, and canvases rich with allusions to the Holocaust. By contrast, one must ask what sociological phenomenon was operating in the American art scene in the late 1940s and in the 1950s when abstract expressionism ruled over Jewish artists such as Barnett Newman, Marc Rothko, and Larry Rivers. This movement was promoted by Jewish art critic Clement Greenburg. Even though at that time New York was a way station for artists escaping from the war in Europe, the revelations of the camps, with few exceptions, did not seem to penetrate the artistic or critical consciousness. In 1948, during the period that Koerner and Bak were struggling to find a way to tell their devastating stories, their loss of family, language and birthplace, Newman wrote, "We are freeing ourselves of the impediments of memory, association, nostalgia, legend, myth, or what have you, that have been the devices of Western European painting. The image we produce is the self-evident one of revelation, real and concrete that could be understood by anyone who will look at it without the nostalgic glasses of history."[38] But could this "freedom" have been a way to avoid the Holocaust's trauma? The fertile period of abstract expressionism promoted so strenuously by Greenberg might have had its roots in the impossibility at that time of dealing with the historical trauma that meant the end of eastern European Jewry. The artistic silence would seem to parallel the silence from Jewish philosophers and theologians of the time.

Rejecting the abstract mode, the American sculptor George Segal (1924–2000) had developed a type of molded plaster figures suggesting real-life experience. Having lost many relatives in the Holocaust, he was willing to compete for the design of a Holocaust memorial sculpture for the San Francisco Jewish community. In 1983 his sculpture was dedicated. On a cliff overlooking San Francisco Bay, Segal arranged his human figures—first cast in bronze and then painted white—in a star pattern on a platform surrounded by a barbed wire fence. One lone figure peers out over the fence into the distance.[39]

Since the early 1980s, the world's interest in memorializing the Holocaust has grown exponentially; most large American cities have a Holocaust center, archive, or memorial. Expecially noteworthy architecturally are the United States Holocaust Memorial Museum in Washington, D.C., and the Jewish Museum in Berlin.[40] Designed by James Ingo Freed, the Washington museum opened its doors on 23 April 1993, fifty years after the Warsaw ghetto uprising. It was built with private contributions on federally donated land near America's most prized public monuments. President Bill Clinton presided over the dedication, an occasion when Holocaust survivor and Nobel laureate Elie Wiesel spoke of his mother, who was murdered at Auschwitz-Birkenau: "To forget would mean to kill the victims a second time. We could not prevent their first death; we must not allow them to be killed again."[41] Each year millions of Americans and foreign tourists

visit this museum. High schools usually include a visit in the Washington itiner-
ary for their students.

Freed, born in 1930 in Essen, Germany, was evacuated at the age of nine to
Chicago, where he was later joined by his parents.[42] Freed escaped Germany's
devastation, but there is a hint of the camps integrated into Freed's building. The
light fixtures, the cramped darkened spaces, can create a shudder in the visitor
who may know the sites and recognize these details. As George Will wrote, "architecture is a high art when it compels a frame of mind."[43] The museum and its
exhibits do just that. Artifacts, films, photographs, texts, voices all provide sober
reminders of the Nazi period, the campaign of antisemitism, the Final Solution,
and the liberation of the camps by the American army in April and May 1945.
Young children are protected by barriers from the often shocking images of mass
murder. One the most moving among many heart-wrenching exhibits is the
atrium covered with hundreds of photographs of men, women, and children
from Eishyshok, a Lithuanian village whose Jewish population was virtually
destroyed in September 1941 by the Germans and their local collaborators.[44]

While Freed's architecture for the U.S. Holocaust Memorial Museum is a
sober, solid, and subtle structure, suitable for its place among U.S. government
buildings, Daniel Libeskind's design for the Berlin Jewish Museum is planned in
the form of a jagged and broken six-pointed star.[45] Noting that the design resembles "an architectural dagger plunged into the heart of complacency," James S.
Russell goes on to ask, "Can architecture and art help us to come to terms with
the enormous accomplishments and unfathomable evil experienced by a culture?"[46] Libeskind has a mystical answer to that question: "The Jewish Museum
is conceived as an emblem in which the Invisible and Visible are the structural
features which have been gathered in this space of Berlin and laid bare in an architecture where the unnamed remains the name which keeps still."[47] Presumably
Libeskind is referring to the fact that before World War II there were 160,000
Jews in Berlin. After the war, only 5,000 remained. Designed to show the history
of the Jewish people in Berlin since Roman times, the building itself is so dramatic that more than 400,000 people paid to walk through its rooms before any
exhibits had been displayed. The museum is now filled with years of memora-
bilia, and there remains a question whether the exhibits can match the architecture's power.[48]

The major drama of the building lies in its zinc-clad, zigzag shape. The zigzag
interior evokes disorientation and anxiety. By angling the walls, narrowing the
spaces, changing the heights of the rooms and manipulating the lighting, Libeskind succeeded in developing a high-tension atmosphere. In addition, he has
attached a tower to the dark, claustrophobic space; it admits only a tiny light at
the top. The building's voidlike quality recalls the nothingness that awaited not
only Primo Levi but Berlin's Jews as well. Light penetrates the building through
narrow, jagged windows, purposely placed at irregular heights that make it difficult to see outdoors. Successfully, even awesomely, architectural design and content are intertwined in Libeskind's building.[49]

While Libeskind may have stretched the bounds of expressive architecture, contemporary artists and photographers have also made imaginative leaps to express the continuing trauma of the Holocaust. Dora Apel writes, "Many contemporary artists engaged by the memory effects of the Holocaust have made clear their rejection of redemptive myths and archaic forms of commemoration. . . . They have largely rejected the iconic forms of barbed wire, corpses, guard towers, train tracks and smoke stacks as clichéd images whose power has been vitiated through overuse."[50] In her chapter "Picturing The Vanished/Transgressing the Present" she describes Shimon Attie's project *The Writing on the Wall.*[51] Attie combed the records of the Jewish quarter in Berlin, which was known as the *Scheunenviertel* (barn quarter). After unearthing the ravaged history of the neighborhood, which was once made up mainly of east European Jews who perished in the Holocaust, Attie found old photographs of the neighborhood and projected them on the original or nearby buildings. "By attempting to renegotiate the relationship between past and present events," he observed, "the aim of the project was to interrupt the collective processes of denial and forgetting."[52] Apel explains that Attie's use of documentary realism points to questions about the place of imagination in the hierarchy of archive, history, and witness testimony.[53]

Perhaps the most extreme post-Holocaust attempt to merge Jewish identity with history is, quite literally, embodied in a Russian-Jewish lesbian, Marina Vainshtein, who has tattooed her whole body with Holocaust imagery.[54] Born in Ukraine in 1973, Vainshtein fled Soviet antisemitism with her parents, came to Los Angeles, and settled in a neighborhood of mostly Hasidic Jews. Upon entering high school, she realized that she knew nothing about being Jewish; a severe identity crisis ensued. Vainshtein became obsessed with the Holocaust after meeting Nina Schulkind, a survivor of seven concentration camps. Despite Jewish tradition that forbids body mutilation, Vainshtein asks, "Why not have external scars to represent the internal scars?"[55] Her body is covered with images of the Holocaust, from ghetto scenes to cattle cars, shaved heads, barbed wire, and smoking chimneys.

It is a long way from the secret sketches by the doomed Jews of the concentration camps to the tattooed Jewish woman. But at the time of this writing Jews again feel threatened by war in Israel and antisemitism in Europe. That fear is felt even by fourth-generation American Jews who were stunned by the very first films from Europe showing Jews forced to clean streets with toothbrushes. Events in the twenty-first century are sharpening memory of the Holocaust for Jews who have been scarred by history. Many artists will not forget either; nor will they produce an easy art. Only time will tell what shapes their post-Holocaust work will take.[56]

## WHEN ONLY WORDS REMAIN

A teacher of Hebrew, Chaim Kaplan, kept a journal in the Warsaw ghetto. Dated 4 August 1942, the final line in its last entry asks a question: "If my life ends—what will become of my diary?"[57] Kaplan sensed there was nothing hypo-thetical about the first part of his uncertainty. No "if" existed; it was only a mat-ter of "when." And "when" was soon. By the end of that month, Kaplan had perished in the gas chambers at Treblinka. The only open part of his question was "what will become of my diary?" That issue was not on Kaplan's mind alone. Diaries—thousands of them—were kept by men, women, and children wherever the Nazi scourge targeted Jews.[58] It is likely that some version of Kaplan's ques-tion was asked by all of those writers.

A picture, it is often said, is worth a thousand words. Yet neither the haunt-ing silence of melodies that have disappeared nor the speechless power of line and color can substitute for words. Especially during the Holocaust, words were the most available resources for recording what had to be remembered. Whether spo-ken or written, they could give the dying a lasting voice.[59] Focusing on the writ-ten testimony, we cannot know how many eyewitness accounts have been lost forever. Those that survived make one wonder how they did. Smuggled, buried, occasionally just left behind—some of these scrolls of agony resurfaced, many of them from people who did not survive the Holocaust. These include the testi-monies of Janusz Korczak, who accompanied the children of his orphanage to their deaths at Treblinka, and Emmanuel Ringelblum, who coordinated *Oneg Shabbat*, the historical archive in Warsaw, as well as the tragic witness borne by *Sonderkommandos* who had to burn the bodies of their fellow Jews before their own lives were consumed. Linked with that company are survivors such as Primo Levy and Jean Améry, Isabella Leitner and Heda Margolius Kovály, to mention only a few, who have groped for words to write memoirs that might tell as directly as possible what happened, disappeared, and remained.

In addition, there are other writers—some of them survivors, others who were not in the Holocaust, still others who were and did not survive—who have enlisted the characters of fiction and the cadences of verse to reveal and to respond to the catastrophe that engulfed European Jewry. A representative sample of these authors and their works by no means exhausts what has come to be known as Holocaust literature. That category includes essays—historical, philosophical, and religious—as well as diaries and autobiographical accounts of eyewitnesses, in addition to those works of poetry and prose fiction that are substantively gov-erned by the Jewish plight under Hitler.[60] As the examples below illustrate, Holo-caust literature at its best underscores especially well the major implications and lingering questions that are fundamental for anyone who studies the Holocaust with the respect and concern that its history deserves.

Just as Holocaust literature includes diverse genres, its authors represent var-ied nationalities and write in different languages. Most, though not all, are Jew-ish, but even that shared identity promotes a broad stylistic spectrum. Permeating the diversity, however, are issues that these writers confront in common. They invite their readers to wrestle with them too. Despite their remarkable literary gifts, nearly all of these authors feel a profound ambivalence, one that is shared by the best Holocaust historians as well: it is impossible to write adequately about the Holocaust; yet that task must be attempted. They regard themselves as less than fully equipped to do such work; yet they are compelled to try. The corresponding tension for a reader—at least for one who was not "there"—is between an effort to understand and an awareness that the Holocaust eludes representation, let alone full comprehension.[61] These dilemmas have multiple dimensions. The Holocaust, for example, outstrips imagination. It is one thing to be creative when the possibilities open to imagination exceed what has become real. It is quite another to find that reality has already given birth to persons, places, and events that defy imagining. "Normal men," observed one survivor, "do not know that everything is possible."[62]

Perhaps history prepares post-Holocaust minds to be more accepting of the idea that "everything is possible." Nonetheless, how is one to comprehend that the Nazi way included "idealism" that did not merely permit torture and murder but commanded that they occur day and night? So a problem remains: can poetry and prose—in essay or fictional forms—help one to know what happened and to cope with its impact? There are no metaphors or adequate analogies for the Holocaust. Nor can Auschwitz be a metaphor or an analogy for anything else. If those realizations inform the ambivalence of those who write poetry or reflective prose about the Holocaust, still they must feel that their expressions are at least potentially capable of communicating something urgent that can be said in no other way. But that conviction makes their task no easier, and when a reader works to grasp what the best of the Holocaust writers say, he or she will sense how the Holocaust makes those writers struggle with words. How can words tell the truth, describe what must be portrayed, convey and yet control emotion so that clear insights will emerge? Every imaginative author faces such questions, but they become unusually demanding when one encounters the Holocaust. Now words and art forms must be used against themselves, since they are unable to say all that is required, and yet no other resources are available.

When writers emphasize the impossibility of communicating the realities of the Holocaust via words, they are sometimes accused of mystifying that event. They either make the Holocaust so exceptional that it loses contact with the rest of human history, the argument goes, or they obscure and becloud it in rhetoric that invests the Holocaust with a mythical or mystical aura that opposes lucid, rational analysis. Critical opinion may reach varied verdicts on those charges where different authors and works are concerned, but the representatives examined here—all of whom do see the Holocaust as unprecedented and fraught with dimensions and implications that go beyond the realms of politics, economics, and history—are not guilty of culling the Holocaust out of worldly reality. Nor have they obscured or beclouded the past. On the contrary, their efforts complement, and are complemented by, all sound historical analysis. They are rooted both in the enormity of human loss brought about by the Holocaust and in the need to retrieve whatever can be left of a human future after Auschwitz has exposed the illusory quality of so many cherished assumptions. Consider, then, the efforts of Victor Klemperer, Charlotte Delbo, Tadeusz Borowski, and Elie

Wiesel. The themes they emphasize—bearing witness, survival, honesty, and protest—help to reveal what can be communicated about the Holocaust and its reverberations when only words remain.

## BEARING WITNESS

No Holocaust diary more fully bears witness to Jewish plight in Nazi Germany than Victor Klemperer's.[63] Jewish by birth—his father was a rabbi—and therefore a Jew by Nazi definition despite the fact that he had converted to Christianity, Klemperer (1881–1960), a veteran of World War I and a distinguished scholar of the Enlightenment and French literature, lived in Dresden, where he escaped the fate of most Jews in that city, largely because his wife, Eva, was an "Aryan." From 1933 to 1945, Klemperer chronicled everyday life in the Third Reich. He wrote not only about events but also about his reactions and those of family, friends, and acquaintances around him. His scholarly interest in language intensified his awareness of the ways in which the Nazi state used words as political tools to advance antisemitism, racism, war, and the destruction of Jewish life. After the war, using notes from his diaries, he published *LTI—Notizbuch eines Philologen* (LTI—Notebook of a philologist) in which he showed how the Nazis had turned German into a language of euphemism and bureaucracy that led to Auschwitz.[64]

Having recounted the early years of Hitler's regime, including the escalating anti-Jewish legislation, the November pogrom *(Kristallnacht)* of 1938, and the German invasion of Poland, the first volume of *I Will Bear Witness* ends with the New Year's Eve observation that 1941 was the most dreadful year that he and Eva had experienced. On Klemperer's mind were the ever more constrained and dangerous conditions that the intensification of war and Nazi antisemitism inflicted upon them. In late June the Germans had invaded the Soviet Union. That autumn, German Jews were ordered to wear the "yellow star, " and the Nazis halted all Jewish emigration from Germany and German-occupied territory. Klemperer was among the 163,000 remaining German Jews who were trapped in a regime that was rapidly moving to implement its murderous Final Solution.

At the time, dependent as he was on rumors and secondhand reports from foreign news broadcasts, Klemperer could not have known the details of those developments. They included Chelmno, the Nazi death camp that became operational on 8 December, and construction projects at Belzec and Auschwitz-Birkenau, two other Polish sites where millions of Jews would be gassed to death. Klemperer's last words for 1941 refer to murder and deportations—often he speaks of "evacuation" instead—but as his diary's second volume reveals, it took time for Klemperer to realize that the worst was yet to come.

The Holocaust destroyed about 2.7 million Jews in 1942, making that year the most lethal in Jewish history. Primarily because of his "mixed" marriage, which gave him fragile privileges as the Jewish spouse of an "Aryan" woman,

Klemperer remained alive. Unbeknownst to him, while Klemperer dealt with his personal dilemmas in Dresden's severe winter cold, the fate of Jews in such marriages had been discussed during an important meeting in the Berlin suburb of Wannsee on 20 January 1942. There, under the leadership of Reinhard Heydrich, the SS lieutenant general who was also chief of the Reich Security Main Office, fifteen government and SS officials, many with doctorates from German universities, convened at a comfortable lakeside villa to coordinate the Final Solution. One proposal at the Wannsee Conference was to dissolve mixed marriages so that the Jewish spouses could be targeted more easily, but at that time no further action was taken on the matter.

While the Wannsee Conference took place, Klemperer's diary entry indicates that he was spending time with Paul Kreidl, a Jewish resident in the special Dresden Jews' House where the Klemperers also were forced to live. A week earlier Kreidl had shared a disturbing rumor: Jews sent from Germany to Riga, Latvia, had been shot. The rumor was true. On 21 January Kreidl was one of 224 Dresden Jews deported to the Riga ghetto, a victim caught in a power struggle between those Nazis who were willing to postpone Jewish death while Jews did labor in key wartime industries and those who wanted to make Germany *judenrein* (free of Jews) immediately.

Klemperer's reflections reveal the forlorn mixture of anxiety and ambiguity, gossiped information and nonsensical incongruity, immediate need and tentative hope that make his diary compelling because of the desperate plight it conveys. On 16 March 1942 he writes about the Hitler jokes he heard during a morning work break, the hearsay about the military situation on the eastern front, a report about lenient anti-Jewish policies in Hungary, a new ban in Germany that prohibited Jews from buying flowers, and the growing scarcity of food and fuel. In his eclectic list of experiences mentioned on this date, Klemperer writes that he has also heard of a place called Auschwitz, which was described to him as "the most dreadful concentration camp."[65] How dreadful Auschwitz was he could not know, but within days of his Auschwitz reference, while he notes the latest rations reductions in Dresden, gas chambers were put into operation in a renovated farm house at Auschwitz-Birkenau, the main killing center in the Auschwitz complex, with Polish Jews as the victims.

Six months later, on September 19, Klemperer observes that the decree requiring German Jews to wear the yellow star is one year old. "What indescribable misery has descended upon us during this year," he writes. "Everything that preceded it appears petty by comparison."[66] Two days later, on Yom Kippur, the sacred Day of Atonement, he describes visits to the Pinkowitzes and Neumanns, who will soon be deported. "Going into a beyond," as Klemperer puts it, his friends' situation is grim, and yet the diarist resists the most dire conclusion, for the available reports have been "no more than supposition."[67] By this time, however, with the turning-point battle of Stalingrad under way but far from decided against Nazi Germany, more than 250,000 Jews from the Warsaw ghetto had been murdered in the gas chambers at Treblinka.

On New Year's Eve Klemperer again takes stock. He says that 1942 has been the worst of the ten years he has experienced under Nazi rule. Apart from some reading, he has not been able to do any of the scholarly work that means so much to him. The people with whom the Klemperers spent last New Year's Eve have all been "blotted out by murder, suicide, and evacuation."[68] With no end in sight, he constantly feels in "mortal danger." As the year draws to its close, Klemperer can only conclude that 1942 has been the worst year "thus far." For him and many other European Jews, he expects that the terror will increase, and it does. Consider, for example, what took place on 27 February 1943.

That morning, Jews remaining in Germany, even those in armaments industries, were rounded up at their workplaces and assembled for deportation. Even mixed marriages seemed to provide protection no longer, but then something remarkable happened in Berlin. At the Rosenstrasse Jewish community center, where several hundred Jewish men were interned, their non-Jewish wives appeared and protested publicly against the impending deportation. Ordered to disperse, threatened with violence if they did not, the women persisted. Uneasy about the unrest that might spread, the Nazi officials relented and released the Jewish men in mixed marriages. The next day Klemperer makes no comment about the Rosenstrasse protest—probably no news of it reached him—but he does record that "the current action did *not* concern the mixed marriages."[69]

Although no further action against Jews in mixed marriages would be taken until the war's final months, Klemperer saw that his safety was ever more precarious. On 28 February 1943 he recalls that his wife has recently heard a German woman's account of a postcard message sent by her son from the eastern front. "I'm still alive"—repeated three times—is all it said. "That is also how far my feelings go," writes Klemperer. "Depending on my mood, and changing from hour to hour, the emphasis is now on 'alive,' now on 'still.'"[70] About four months later, on 12 June, Klemperer estimates that only a handful of Jews remain in Dresden. He hears contradictory rumors: mixed marriages will be broken up; mixed marriages will still be safe havens. His mood, he says, keeps shifting "between fear, hope, indifference."[71] Still, as the Klemperers hold out, the reader becomes increasingly aware that, despite the threats of despair and death, Victor and Eva are expanding and deepening the meaning of *resistance*.

Back on 27 May 1942—the same day that Czech resistance fighters fatally wounded Reinhard Heydrich in Prague—Klemperer noted once again how hunger exhausted him. Although he had fought for Germany during the World War I, armed resistance against the Third Reich was scarcely a wartime option for a Jew in Dresden. Writing would be Klemperer's chosen form of resistance instead. "I will bear witness," he vowed, "precise witness!"[72] Although he could not know that his diary would achieve best-seller status more than fifty years later, there are moments when he senses that he may be writing for history, that it is crucial to record his everyday existence because that detail will be essential to document what Nazi Germany did to the world and to the Jews in particular.

On 8 June 1942 Klemperer mentions that he has heard about Heydrich's death, but the diarist's personal situation remains the focus. The result is that his diary becomes an extended lamentation for the Jews of Dresden, an anguished indictment of the Germany he still loves in spite of its Nazi ways, and a sustained record of the efforts that he and his wife make to endure, to preserve the semblance of a decent life in inhuman circumstances, and to survive for better times. Whether those times will be theirs remains unclear, for in addition to his jeopardized existence as a Jew under Nazi rule, German civilians are endangered as the war is brought close to home by the Allies' air raids, which intensify in 1942 and reach devastating proportions by the end of 1943. The end of that year finds Klemperer observing that Dresden has not yet been hit, but nevertheless it is a place of fear—for all the city's inhabitants, not only its very few Jews.

Six months later Klemperer's wife brings him news that the Allies' D day invasion at Normandy is under way, but on that day, 6 June 1944, he is "no longer or not yet able to hope."[73] His ambivalence was not misplaced, for even though the war had definitely turned against Nazi Germany, the Holocaust still raged in 1944. On 19 March, for example, while Klemperer did air raid duty, German troops occupied the territory of their faltering Hungarian ally and the last large group of European Jews came under the Nazis' genocidal control. By 9 July, when Klemperer wrote that he could "no longer imagine myself transformed back into a human being," some 437,000 Hungarian Jews had been deported to Auschwitz, where most of them were gassed.[74] On 3 September, as Klemperer reports that Dresden's Hitler Youth are marching and singing, another diarist, a young Jewish woman named Anne Frank, is deported to Auschwitz from the Netherlands with her family and hundreds of other Dutch Jews. Klemperer knows nothing of her, but his 1 September judgment—written on the fifth anniversary of the Second World War's beginning—sums up the situation: "No safety anywhere."[75] The year ends with air-raid alerts in Dresden, with the numbed feeling that the war will end "perhaps in a couple of months, perhaps in a couple of years."[76]

On 12 February 1945 the last of the Dresden Jews learn that they must report for special labor duty. No illusions remain; the orders are a death sentence. Klemperer is not included in the first groups, but he carries the orders to others and expects no mixed-marriage reprieve. Then, on the night of 13 February the situation changes. The Allied air raids begin. The resulting firestorm reduces Dresden to rubble, enabling the city's surviving Jews to destroy the documents and yellow stars that identify them and perhaps eventually to rebuild their lives in the Third Reich's ruins. The Klemperers managed to do so.

Of all the documents from the Second World War and the Holocaust, Klemperer's diary is among the most unusual. Few of them chart day-to-day life in Nazi Germany from the Third Reich's start to finish. From a German Jew's perspective, none does so as thoroughly. Bearing precise witness, Klemperer not only recalls how much was lost but also warns that we forget at our peril.

## AFTERWORDS

*Useless knowledge*: that is what Charlotte Delbo (1913–85) said her experience in Auschwitz and Ravensbrück gave her.[77] She was not Jewish. Nevertheless Delbo was sent to Auschwitz in 1943. Of the 230 Frenchwomen in her convoy, she was one of forty-nine who survived. Delbo saw what happened to the Jews, her French comrades, and herself. An Auschwitz fate, however, did not have to be hers. When the Germans occupied her native France in June 1940, Delbo was on tour in South America with a theater company. Against the advice of friends, she returned to France in 1941, rejoining her husband, Georges Dudach, and working with him in the resistance.

Arrested by collaborating French police on 2 March 1942, the couple was handed over to the Germans, who imprisoned the two separately. Delbo got a brief visit with her husband just before a firing squad executed him on 23 May. A prisoner in France until her deportation, Delbo describes her arrival in January 1943 as follows: "The doors of the cattle cars were pushed open, revealing the edge of an icy plain. It was a place from before geography. Where were we? We were to find out—later, at least two months hence; we, that is, those of us who were still alive two months later—that this place was called Auschwitz. We couldn't have given it a name."[78]

Those words come from Delbo's superb trilogy, *Auschwitz et après* (Auschwitz and after), whose anguished visual descriptions and profound reflections on memory make it an immensely powerful Holocaust testimony. Its three parts begin with *Aucun de nous ne reviendra* (None of us will return), which she wrote in 1946 after she had been released to the Red Cross from Ravensbrück, a Nazi concentration camp for women. She recuperated in Sweden and then returned to France. Delbo waited nearly twenty years, however, before she allowed *None of Us Will Return* to be published in 1965. Parts of *Une connaissance inutile* (Useless knowledge) were also written shortly after Delbo's return to France, but this second volume in the trilogy did not appear until 1970. Its sequel, *Mesure de nos jours* (The measure of our days), soon followed.

"Auschwitz," Delbo said in *La mémoire et les jours* (Days and memory), "is so deeply etched in my memory that I cannot forget one moment of it."[79] In the months and years *after* Auschwitz, she relearned what she had forgotten from *before* her ordeal. *Here* in the France to which she returned, she could do what was never possible *there*—simple things, such as using a toothbrush. *Now* she could do what was unthinkable *then*—such as calmly eating with a knife and fork. And yet, as she apparently became the person she had been before her intervening imprisonment in Auschwitz—charming, cultivated, civilized—she could hardly experience the smell of rain without recalling that "in Birkenau, rain heightened the odor of diarrhea."[80] What happened in Auschwitz did nothing, *then* or *now*, she testified, to dignify life. What happened in Auschwitz forever diminished life instead.

Delbo's ongoing relationship with mass death made her dwell on what, if anything, it could mean to survive. The first volume of Delbo's trilogy suggests that survival is impossible, for it is titled *None of Us Will Return*. At Auschwitz, she wrote, "the station is not a railroad station. It is the end of the line." She remembered those who had arrived at "a station that will remain nameless for them," recalling, too, how they expected "the worst—not the unthinkable."[81] The unthinkable, which Delbo never mystifies, the sheer unending grind of death— unredeeming and unredeemable—became so pervasive that it was beyond transfiguration. If gas, disease, starvation did not waste one away, survival after Auschwitz did not mean a return to life but only, in Lawrence Langer's words, *death-with-life* or "dying living." What that condition entails, why it is a factor to be contended with, not only by literal survivors, but also in some sense by all who live after Auschwitz—those are two of the questions that govern Delbo's Holocaust literature.

Disjunction characterizes death-with-life just as memory produces "dying living." As her mind returns her to Auschwitz, Delbo recalls a dying woman whose face reflected "naked despair." She cannot forget the soon-dead "living skeletons" who were everywhere in Auschwitz, and then Delbo breaks off, for "now I am sitting in a café, writing this text."[82] What her mind's eye sees did happen, but when a woman is reduced to the mechanical movements of a skeleton, mere narrative cannot describe such horror, and the search for terms graphic enough to depict the reality turns what happened into a story. So the words must be broken off. Only then is it possible that they may succeed in coming close to saying what needs to be said. Yet the disjunction is more than that, for there sits Delbo in the café, writing, while her life is with the death of a naked skeleton. The disjunction is not limited to the breaking off of words or to the chasm between "then" and "now," "here" and "there," which are, after all, disjunctions bridged by a single person's experience. A more radical disjunction is that between those who think they know and those who really do. This is a gap that words reveal more than bridge. For example, living can be so reduced to a bodily endurance that "you can see your mother dead and not shed a tear."[83] And then the disjunction doubles back again: a writer sitting in a café, perhaps able to cry again, must reckon with a knowledge that makes her wonder whether, or at least in what sense, she is the same person "before" and "after."

Delbo wants her readers to see bodies. That is what survivors, direct and indirect, must contend with. Unmistakably the bodies are human, and yet in what sense? Beautiful, resilient, and strong—these are not apt terms to describe the last vestiges of a human being, whose existence is better portrayed by focusing on a hand, an elbow, a neck, whose life has been reduced to physical exertion, and even that energy is so drained and waning that when "the dog leaps on the woman, sinks its teeth in her neck . . . we do not stir, stuck in some kind of viscous substance which keeps us from making the slightest gesture—as in a dream."[84]

In Auschwitz, writes Delbo, "Not one of us utters, 'I'm hungry, I'm thirsty, I'm cold.'" There such things go without saying. Indeed to mention them would be absurd. To contend with death-in-life is to recognize that one group of human beings can create an environment, not just for scattered individuals here and there, but for masses of men and women, calculated to induce hunger, thirst, and cold so that the most common expressions of need are reduced to silence. Sound does break the silence in Auschwitz, however, often in howls and screams. They reached the blue of an indifferent sky more than responsive ears. And so little remains: a discarded wooden leg survives its owner, reappearing out of mud and snow long after the flesh it supported has rotted. There is no reverence for life, nor for death, though to die might bring a moment in which one knows "no more suffering and struggling, . . . a bliss one did not know existed." The very lack of reverence for death, however, brings Delbo back to life: "I wish to die but not to be carried out on the small stretcher. Not to be carried by on the small stretcher with hanging legs and head, naked under a tattered blanket. I do not want to be carried on the small stretcher." But if Auschwitz reduces the reasons for living to that extent, Delbo concluded that "it is far better to know nothing if you wish to go on living."[85]

Part II of *Auschwitz and After* is *Une connaissance inutile*, which can mean either a knowledge or an acquaintance, both useless. Once more a firsthand acquaintance with and a knowledge about the human body loom large, and the issue is what to do with the awareness that Auschwitz creates. For example, Delbo describes a thirst-quenching drink. So deprived that she plunged her face horse-like into a water bucket, she realized, "Saliva was returning to my mouth. The burning feeling round my eyelids was fading. Your eyes burn when the lacrymal glands dry up. My ears could hear again. I was living." She experienced some physical restoration and learned how much one can stand. The chance to bathe in a stream prompted her to observe that "I removed my panties, stiff with dry diarrhea . . . yet the smell didn't nauseate me." But what is such knowledge worth? As Delbo reflects, survival confers little dignity or pride. Instead particular memories may be degradingly useless, partly because meaningful communication about them is so nearly impossible. In a post-Holocaust world, when most people say, "I am thirsty," they just "step into a café and order a beer."[86]

As for love, it is no longer so tragically triumphant as conventional wisdom— better to have loved and lost than never to have loved at all—would have it. To an overwhelming degree, Delbo suggests, the Holocaust defeated love. Her own husband was executed by the Gestapo before she was transported to Auschwitz. Granted a last meeting, they found their impending separation compounded by the only act of love that seemed possible: mutual deception, men and women pretending to each other not to know the fate awaiting them. Ending that way, love is not triumphal. In Auschwitz love could not even be remembered well. Memory itself was a luxury that energy did not permit. It added pain too great for those already living beyond their means.

Auschwitz did not exist without respite. Some camp jobs were better than others, transfers to less lethal sites sometimes occurred, and liberation eventually beckoned for some. Delbo went through those phases. As she did so, other forms of useless knowledge became apparent. They involved things known "before": the taste of a cup of coffee, sleeping late, doing what one pleases. Such things, once taken for granted, were so well known that they ought to come back quickly. But they did not. They must be relearned, but even then, none was possible as before, at least not unless one becomes oblivious. Liberation pushes one toward oblivion, even in terms of memory, but whatever consolation that might contain was mocked by the fact that compounded the uselessness of being there. If Charlotte Delbo is correct, survival after Auschwitz brings with it alienation and sadness more than a return of normality, especially for those who were "there," but also in part for any who will open themselves to the "useless knowledge" of that experience.

For centuries philosophers and poets have urged, "Know thyself." Delbo is ambivalent: "I've spoken with death / and so / I know / the futility of things we learn / a discovery I made at the cost / of a suffering / so intense / I keep on wondering / whether it was worth it." Experience broadened her horizons only to shrink her sense of wonder and possibility. She does not feel herself to be a better person for what she has endured, though some effort to justify living seems imperative: otherwise "it would be too senseless/ after all / for so many to have died / while you live / doing nothing with your life." To survive in that way, however, she "must unlearn / for otherwise I clearly see / I can no longer live." And the poet's voice even cautions that for those who were not there perhaps it is "better not to believe / these ghostly tales."[87]

*Mesure de nos jours* (Measure of our days), the trilogy's final volume, utilizes a series of monologues by Delbo's narrator and some of her friends to underscore how reentry into "normal" life is fraught with difficulties. As for herself, the narrator says, "I was no longer open to imagination, or explanation. This is the part of me that died in Auschwitz." That adds up to death-in-life, but this transformation has not changed very much. The world remains full of imagination and explanation. Mounette, who did not return, had thought that "if we return, nothing will be the same." But Mado, who did return, finds that Mounette was wrong. In so many ways, the world goes on as if the Holocaust never happened. Yet Mado finds that "I'm living without being alive. . . . I do what one does in life, but I know very well that this isn't life, because I know the difference between before and after."[88] How, then, is one to respond to simple, perennial questions, such as "Where are you from?" "Auschwitz" is not the answer expected, but "Bordeaux" does not say what must be said. Mounette was not wrong, at least not entirely: nothing is the same after Auschwitz. Yet that truth is allowed to slip away, and not without reason, for "to live in the past is not to live." But Mado adds that she has "no way of grasping the present. I try at times to imagine what I'd be like were I like everyone else, that is, if I had not been taken over there. I don't succeed in doing so. I am other."[89]

Other of Delbo's women do "return." For Poupette, who wanted so much to survive, sadness continues to accumulate as a present and a future shadowed by an Auschwitz past lead to a marriage that does not work, problems over children, and other tribulations for which there might be consolation if one had not already suffered too much. Marie-Louise apparently has done much better. Now a wife and a mother, well situated in a country estate, she talks freely about the camp, reads about the Holocaust extensively, and has even returned to visit Auschwitz. "As you can see," she explains, "I've got everything I need. I'm happy."[90] If things are that simple, Delbo suggests, then Marie-Louise's reentry is as truncated as that of the others. For if they cannot master the unlearning required for happiness, Marie-Louise's achievements in that regard have reduced the past to a superficiality that betrays it. Marceline's problem is different. Her husband offers encouragement: you cannot let bad memories crush you; human nature has uncanny ways of adapting and readapting. Nonetheless, about the same time each year, Marceline falls sick. The cause of her illness is medically unclear, but she calls it "the anniversary of my typhus."[91] Auschwitz is in her blood. Adaptability has limits more severe than her husband's optimism knows.

Near the end of the book, several of the surviving women attend the funeral of a comrade. One remarks that she never weeps at funerals now, because a person is lucky to have one. None of them could even dream of a funeral in Auschwitz, but now they have other dreams about that place. The narrator reports hers, a recurrent one, "inexplicable" like Marceline's fever. It is the nightmare of being paroled from prison, trying hard to run away or to forget the way back, but then returning as she had promised to do. As she returns, her cries awaken her at the moment of seeing the barbed wire and chimneys. "I always cry out," she says, "before I might see more."[92] Fevers and nightmares reveal the "dying living" of dislocated selves. "Do I have several faces?" asks Delbo's narrator. She envisions three: one intelligent and mobile; a second covering the first, "weary, worn down, frozen"; and a third, "covering both of these, a latchkey mask, the one we put on to go out, move through life."[93]

The chapter fades before the funeral. Instead of ending *Measure of Our Days* with a ceremony for a single death, a gesture singularly inappropriate for a reflection on the unnoticed slaughter of millions, Delbo focuses on Françoise, another woman who saw her husband before he was shot and she was deported. "To start life over again," she sighs, "what an expression. . . . If there is a thing you can't do over again, a thing you can't start over again, it is your life."[94] Looking back on all that has been lost, on the many invisible dimensions of history, the issue remains: how to live with what one knows, including its uselessness. Remaking life, renewing it—those concepts are too optimistic for survivors like Delbo. The response cannot be any message that simply says, "Put the past behind," or "Good triumphs over evil," or "There's a good reason for everything." Not only would such facile chatter trivialize, falsify, and deny the Holocaust, but, as Delbo indicates, at least for herself, forgetting is out of the question. Her austere trilogy ends with no chorus of hope, without moral exhortation. Yet grief or rage is not its final mood. Instead she asks for acceptance, understanding, and help: "I do not know / if you can still / make something of me / If you have the courage to try. . . ."[95] The question lingers with its challenge: Can survival be found that refuses to let desolation be the only measure of our days?

# HONESTY

Charlotte Delbo's arm had an Auschwitz tattoo. So did Tadeusz Borowski's. Like Delbo, Borowski (1922–51) was not Jewish, but he was sent to Auschwitz in late April 1943. He had finished his university degree "underground," because the Germans prohibited such training for Poles. Completing his last examinations just as major roundups began in Warsaw during the spring of 1940, Borowski found work that kept him from being conscripted for labor in Germany. He wrote too, his poetry and prose appearing in Warsaw's clandestine press. Eventually arrested and jailed for his resistance activities, he spent two months in Pawiak, the notorious prison that stood adjacent to the Warsaw ghetto. From his cell he saw the Jewish uprising and the German retaliation. At Auschwitz he nearly died from pneumonia, but luck was with him, and he found himself assigned to relatively light work, ultimately serving as a medic. Evacuated from Auschwitz in the late summer of 1944, Borowski was liberated at Dachau the next May. In time he returned to Poland. He seemed destined to be an important voice in the Communist press. This future, however, was cut short on 1 July 1951, when Borowski opened a gas valve and took his own life.

Published posthumously, *This Way for the Gas, Ladies and Gentlemen* contains the remarkable short stories that Borowski left behind. They are all about Auschwitz and about Borowski as well. Written shortly after his release, authored in the first person, the narrator in several of the stories is one Vorarbeiter Tadeusz, a deputy kapo. This perspective gives Borowski's stories uncompromising realism, bitter irony, and humane feeling all at once, each of these qualities complicated by Borowski's experience—involving what Primo Levi would call the "gray zone"—so that some boundaries between victim and executioner are blurred.[96]

Toward the end of Borowski's compact volume there is a brief meditation, less than a thousand words long, called "A Visit." The narrator sits at a writing desk after Auschwitz. He looks out a window. He sees and recollects: men working, weeping, gathering fortunes, killing; women doing the same. He also recalls those on their way to the gas who "begged the orderlies loading them into the crematorium trucks to remember what they saw. And to tell the truth about mankind to those who do not know it."[97] The author ponders the many men and women he saw in Auschwitz. He will write about them, but he wonders "which one of them I should visit today." His selection is complicated, he notes, because "I am troubled by one persistent thought—that I have never been able to look also at myself." In his stories, Borowski did look at himself, perhaps so much so that the looking drove him to the gas. "I do not know," he wrote, "whether we shall survive, but I like to think that one day we shall have the courage to tell the world the whole truth and call it by its proper name."[98] Borowski's "whole truth" fosters disillusionment. No less than his stories, the outcome of his life enjoins Borowski's readers to be troubled, persistently, about what to make of the disillusionment that an honest encounter with the Holocaust unavoidably creates.

In *This Way for the Gas, Ladies and Gentlemen* disillusionment begins with the statement that "all of us walk around naked." While waiting for a new transport to arrive, Vorarbeiter Tadeusz and his fellow inmates are deloused. Their nakedness, however, turns out to be more than physical. In this Auschwitz block dwell prisoners with privileges: they have enough to eat. Though "a bit coarse to the taste," their bread is "crisp, crunchy." There is bacon, milk, even French wine, because after these laborers unload the trains of people destined for death, they can take some of the food left behind. Other items required to enhance life in Auschwitz can be "organized" later from the huge storage area known as "Canada." Concern mounts when transports do not arrive. Work is hard when the cars roll in, but as Henri says, "They can't run out of people, or we'll starve to death in this blasted camp. All of us live on what they bring."[99]

Henri's friend, the narrator of this story, does other work. He has not been on the ramp before, that place where the new arrivals undergo selection. Having cleared things with the kapo, Henri invites him along. Off they go to meet Polish Jews from Sosnowiec-Będzin. On this bright, hot day, the first cars reach Auschwitz shortly after noon. The unloading begins. Ironically, "a Red Cross van drives back and forth, back and forth, incessantly: it transports the gas that will kill these people." Darkness brings no relief—until the last of the thousands have been dispatched. Even Henri, who claims that "since Christmas, at least a million people have passed through my hands," is exhausted. He and his comrades, however, have their reward. For several days the entire camp will be sustained by the Sosnowiec-Będzin Jews, who are already burning. Everyone will agree that "Sosnowiec-Będzin was a good, rich transport."[100]

The Auschwitz described in Borowski's stories is filled with reports of filth, disease, starvation, sadistic violence, and mass murder. His point is that in this world of human domination and destruction such happenings have been so commonplace that it is possible to add, "Work is not unpleasant when one has eaten a breakfast of smoked bacon with bread and garlic and washed it down with a tin of evaporated milk." He suggests that Auschwitz is a new form of human society where living depends on dying; living well depends on access to power that condemns others. Not that the appalling quality of such relationships goes unnoticed—the brutality is not disguised or rationalized—but Borowski's narrator frames matter-of-factly events that seem poles apart and yet are part of the same time and space at Auschwitz. In the spring of 1943, for example, the medical orderlies get to build a soccer field near the hospital barracks. One Sunday, as the narrator reports in "The People Who Walked On," "I was goalkeeper." Although the selection ramp could be viewed from the playing field, the goalkeeper's back was to it when a train arrived. Retrieving a ball that had gone out of bounds, he noticed the arrivals. A short while later, the ball again went astray. A second time the goalkeeper's attention was drawn to the ramp. It stood empty; the train was gone, too. Virtually unnoticed—perhaps because the process was so routine, or because the goalkeeper's attention was so much on the game, or both—"between two throw-ins in a soccer game, right behind my back, three thousand people had been put to death."[101]

Borowski's narrator is no unfeeling brute. If he smiles "condescendingly when people speak to me of morality, of law, of tradition, of obligation," he also feels revulsion and outrage over the cruel juxtaposition of events and believes that evil "'ought to be punished. No question about it.'" Witnessing the incongruity of an infant in Auschwitz, he feels that he would also "like to have a child with rose-colored cheeks and light blond hair."[102] And though he would dismiss that vision as a "ridiculous notion," he also has written love letters to his fiancée, an inmate in Auschwitz's FKL *(Frauen Konzentration Lager)*. *This Way for the Gas* collects them in a segment called "Auschwitz, Our Home."

These letters speak honestly, without illusion and yet not without tenderness. There is nothing cloying or sentimental when Borowski writes, "One human being must always be discovering another—through love. . . . This is the most important thing on earth, and the most lasting." The reasons those words ring true is that they are uttered against a backdrop of lucidity about the propensities men and women have to dehumanize each other and themselves as well. He ascribes no heroism to his remaining alive. He is only one of the ten lucky souls plucked from labor in the killing center at Birkenau and assigned to the Auschwitz hospital for medical training. His absurd "mission" will be "to lower the camp's mortality rate and to raise the prisoners' morale," but he does not deny that it may keep him alive, and he can even speak of certain days as "delightful." Life in these quarters, with its library, museum, its view "almost pastoral—not one cremo in sight"—seems almost to have found a haven.[103]

No "philosophic formula" can grasp all that happens at Auschwitz, partly because what seems inexplicable and abnormal has become totally familiar. Without "hocus pocus" or "hypnosis," mass murder happens, and "we have now become a part of it." This, too, is reported matter-of-factly, without self-loathing or righteous indignation. Yet the letter writer quietly urges an outlook less resigned: "Look carefully at everything around you, and conserve your strength. For a day may come when it will be up to us to give an account of the fraud and mockery to the living—to speak up for the dead."[104]

When it comes to revealing how the Holocaust mocked human life, nothing is more important than to testify that human domination can become so oppressive that it turns hope, that most natural and irrepressible emotion, into a trap. "We were never taught how to give up hope," Borowski says, "and this is why today we perish in gas chambers." He means that, apart from our own power, there is nothing to guarantee that human domination will not reduce a person's life to "a body that has been exploited to the utmost: with a number tattooed on it to save on dog tags, with just enough sleep at night to work during the day, and just enough time to eat. And just enough food so it will not die wastefully. . . . If you die—your gold teeth, already recorded in the camp inventory are extracted. Your body is burned and your ashes are used to fertilize the fields or fill in the ponds." Borowski's disillusionment does not stop with the realization that victims fitting those descriptions are real. It also announces honestly how widespread the complicity can be. Disillusionments about safety and immunity must be accompanied by those that unmask pretense about virtue and innocence. Borowski said of the camp, indeed of the whole world, "this is a monstrous lie, a grotesque lie."[105] Hope, too, is deceptively false unless it can be forged out of disillusionment's truth.

Where disillusionment's truth will lead, especially when hope is involved, is uncertain, as a few final glimpses of Borowski's work make clear. In "Silence," a group of released prisoners are about to lynch an SS guard. Unwittingly a young American officer intervenes when he enters the newly liberated barracks to urge respect for law and to assure the men that the guilty will be brought to justice. Feigning approval, waiting until the officer had stopped at all the blocks and returned to his headquarters, the ex-prisoners drag the SS man to the floor, "where the entire block, grunting and growling with hatred, trampled him to death." In "The January Offensive," Borowski recounts a postwar discussion in which some former inmates of concentration camps insist that "morality, national solidarity, patriotism and the ideals of freedom, justice and human dignity had all slid off man like a rotten rag." Listening to them was a Polish poet who responded with an incident that reputedly occurred in January 1945. After fierce fighting, Russian troops had freed a Polish city from German control and were advancing west. Among the Russian soldiers was a young woman who needed attention at the hospital in that place. Though unwounded, she was pregnant and in labor. Her healthy child born, the mother stayed at the hospital only a single day. Baby tied to her back, automatic rifle in hand, she resumed her way to Berlin. The former inmates were skeptical. If the poet's story was not made up, it certainly suggested that the Russian woman had not been humane, for she had needlessly endangered the life of her own child. The discussion ended, but in a postscript Borowski adds that one of the Auschwitz comrades eventually received a letter from a woman "whom he had left pregnant in the gypsy camp when in October '44 he was taken in a transport from Birkenau to Gross-Rosen, Flossenbürg and Dachau."[106] Along with hundreds of other sick and pregnant women, that mother and her child had been liberated by the Russians' January offensive.

Back in Warsaw, Borowski's narrating writer notes that the world has for some time seemed to be "inflating at incredible speed, like some ridiculous soap bubble" which "will dissolve forever into emptiness, as though it were made not of solid matter but only of fleeting sounds." He describes his feelings in his new-old postwar city, noting the crumb-dry dust of the ruins, the newly installed windows and freshly painted walls of restored buildings, whose rooms are occupied by people of importance. He goes there to ask "perhaps a trifle too politely, for things that are perhaps too trivial, but to which nevertheless I am entitled—but which, of course, cannot keep the world from swelling and bursting like an overripe pomegranate, leaving behind but a handful of grey, dry ashes." The crowds of people he sees on the streets during the day seem to him to make a weird snarl, a gigantic stew, flowing "along the streets, down the gutter," and seeping "into space with a loud gurgle, like water into a sewer."[107]

As darkness falls, he looks out a window, then pushes himself away and heads for his writing desk, engulfed by a feeling that he has lost valuable time. The world still exists. He will try to muster "a tender feeling" for those who remain in it, and "attempt to grasp the true significance of the events, things and people I have seen. For I intend to write a great, immortal epic, worthy of this unchanging, difficult world chiseled out of stone."[108]

Is this ending ironic, perhaps made all the more so by Borowski's suicide, or did he accomplish what he intended to do? The answer depends on what can—and cannot—be said. It also depends on how one answers this question: where does the disillusionment of Holocaust literature lead? In Borowski's case the answer remains ambiguous and ambivalent, because the truth he could discern did not point in a single, clear-cut direction, least of all to optimism. Unmistakably, though, Borowski placed a premium on exposing illusion. In that respect the words of his living and the silence of his dying are of one piece. Both resound with the insistence we have heard from him before: "It will be up to us to give an account of the fraud and mockery to the living—to speak up for the dead."[109]

## PROTEST

A transport arrives at Birkenau. Bewildered Jews from Sighet and other Hungarian towns emerge from train-car prisons into midnight air fouled by burning flesh. Elie Wiesel, his father, mother, and little sister are among them. Separated by the SS, the boy loses sight of his mother and sister, not fully aware that the parting is forever. Father and son stick together. In the commotion, they hear one of the kapos exclaim, "What have you come here for, you sons of bitches? What are you doing here? . . . You'd have done better to have hanged yourselves where you were than to come here. Didn't you know what was in store for you at Auschwitz? Haven't you heard about it? In 1944?"[110]

Wiesel and his father learned soon enough what awaited them. They were sent "left" by the SS doctor whose baton determined life and death. Their line marched directly toward a pit of flaming bodies. Steps from the edge, they were ordered toward the barracks. The fire, however, had left its mark: "Never shall I forget those flames which consumed my faith forever." Wiesel's father perished, but the son survived. For more than ten years he published nothing, and then *Night* appeared. This memoir, lean and spare, describes his death camp experiences in 1944–45. It begins with a boy who "believed profoundly." It ends with a reflection: "From the depths of the mirror, a corpse gazed back at me. The look in his eyes, as they stared into mine, has never left me."[111]

Since the publication of *Night*, Wiesel has authored more than forty books—novels, plays, dialogues, reflections on biblical characters, meditations on contemporary Jewish life, interviews, and reflections that include a two-volume autobiography entitled *All Rivers Run to the Sea* and *The Sea Is Never Full*. Rarely do these works speak so explicitly about Auschwitz as *Night* does, but never is the Holocaust absent from his writings. Arguably Wiesel's collective works form the most impressive contribution to Holocaust literature made by any single author.[112] "I knew the story had to be told. Not to transmit an experience is to betray it. . . . But how to do this?"[113] Words, Wiesel reports, had to be searing, but they all seemed "inadequate, worn, foolish, lifeless." The effort to transform them had to be made—perhaps so he would not go mad, but certainly because writing might wrench the victims from oblivion and keep death from having the final say. In Wiesel's view, writing is a way to remain faithful, provided a Holocaust author writes "certain things rather than others" and takes responsibility "not only for what he says, but also for what he does not say."[114] The words needed to tell the story faithfully would have to share Klemperer's sense of bearing witness, Delbo's grappling with survival, and Borowski's disillusioning honesty. But those qualities would need to be supplemented by protest against despair. In Wiesel's writings, that characteristic has been salient.

"At Auschwitz," Wiesel declares, "not only man died, but also the idea of man. . . . It was its own heart the world incinerated at Auschwitz."[115] Along with his sense that God needlessly permitted the Holocaust, an event that no good-to-come could possibly justify, these experiences of loss produce despair, which means to lose or to give up hope. Nonetheless, Wiesel asserts, to be Jewish is "never to give up—never to yield to despair."[116] This is more easily said than done, as Wiesel shows in some of the masterful dialogues, simple and complex at once, that appear in his works from time to time. Most of these dialogues make no explicit reference to the Holocaust, yet that catastrophe is their setting. One in *A Jew Today* is between "A Father and His Son."

The father, who perished in the Holocaust, is concerned. "How," he asks his survivor-son, "are you able to resist despair?" Not so difficult, comes the reply, because memory puts things in perspective. If something seems good now, admittedly it turns out to be less so against the backdrop of what happened then. But when things seem terrible in the present, they are also less terrible by contrast. This answer is not convincing. It shows, in fact, that resistance to despair is exceedingly difficult, for what happened *then* shrouds all remaining life. What he feels, the son goes on to tell his father, is "sadness, Father. Nothing but sadness." He confesses not to be seeking happiness; it is too simple to be real in a survivor's history. Nor is love what he looks for; it is a gift bestowed and received, not something one can go out and find. Power is not the goal either. Neither is knowledge; it is to be feared, not because it is inessential to keep learning about what happened but because such awareness may be taken as a substitute for understanding. The two—knowing and understanding—are not identical where Auschwitz is concerned, at least not for Wiesel, and indeed the father's son wants "only one thing: to understand, that is all."[117] The problem is that understanding is even more difficult to obtain than happiness, love, power, or knowledge. In fact, Wiesel suggests, it is impossible to understand the Holocaust; it must be impossible to understand it, for to understand it would be to have an acceptable answer to why it happened. Answers of that kind do not, must not, exist. But if that outcome is not the worst one imaginable, it still does little to drive despair away.

Before he died, the father asked his son to remember and to tell everything. The son said he would, then qualified his answer honestly: he would try his best. The father believed him then and still does now, and yet the father is concerned. The dead have heard the son's testimony, but what about the living? "If we have not succeeded in changing mankind," the father wonders, "who can ever succeed? Tell me, son: Who will change man? Who will save him from himself? Tell me, son: Who will speak on his behalf? Who will speak for me?"[118] Committed to say what the dead cannot, survivors have often tried. But, the son admits, they are weary. No, despair does not give up easily.

This dialogue never happened. It could not have happened. And yet it did. Wiesel tells a tale about meeting an old teacher who had known Wiesel's grandfather. The teacher wanted to know what his friend's grandson was doing. When Wiesel answered that he was a writer of stories, the teacher asked, "What kind?" Specifically, he wanted to know, were these stories about things that happened or could have happened? Yes, replied Wiesel, his stories were of that kind, but the old teacher, sensing ambiguity in the response, pressed on: well, did the stories happen or didn't they? No, Wiesel admitted, not all of the things in his stories did happen; in fact, some of them were invented from start to finish. Disappointment came over the old man. That means, he said, that you are writing lies. Taken aback, Wiesel paused, then responded, "Things are not that simple, Rebbe. Some events do take place but are not true; others are—although they never occurred."[119] Wiesel adds that he does not know whether his answer was sufficient, but he has not stopped telling and writing "legends of our time."

Separated from husband and son, father and brother, a mother and her daughter walk together, and they too have a dialogue.[120] The little girl, eight years old, wonders where they are going. Their destination, says the mother, is "the end of the world." Her daughter asks if that stopping point is far, for she is tired. So is everyone, her mother replies, and the little girl responds, "Even God?" Her mother does not know, but she adds, "You will ask Him yourself." What might God say to an eight-year-old girl who would like to see "the peddlers, the acrobats, the tame bears," but who instead sees the chimneys and names of a factory that makes and destroys history by consuming "the innocence of the world"?[121] Perhaps nothing at all, which would not be good, even though silence might be better than some of the words that God could speak or that human voices have offered apologetically on God's behalf.

Arguably one reason why despair is not easy to dispel is that the Holocaust is inexplicable with God but also cannot be understood without God. In *Night* Wiesel spoke of the flames that destroyed his faith forever. That assertion is not inconsistent with his continuing dialogue with God. For if Auschwitz made it no longer possible to trust God's goodness simply, it made questions about God and wrestling with God all the more important. Wiesel has been heard to say, "If I told you I believed in God, I would be lying; if I told you I did not believe in God, I would be lying." This survivor refuses to let God go, because that act may be one way to testify that the human heart was not completely incinerated at Auschwitz. Yet Wiesel remains at odds with God, because the only way he can be for God after Auschwitz is by being against God too. To accept God without protest would both vindicate God and legitimize evil too much. Nowhere does Wiesel argue for that point more effectively than in his drama *The Trial of God*, whose stage instructions indicate that it should be played as a tragic farce.

The play is set in the seventeenth-century village of Shamgorod at the season of Purim, a joyous festival replete with masks and reenactments that celebrate a moment in Jewish history when oppressors were outmaneuvered and Jews were saved. Three Jewish actors have lost their way, and they arrive at the village. Here they discover that Shamgorod is hardly a place for festivity. Two years before, a murderous pogrom ravaged this town. Only two Jews survived. Berish the inn-keeper escaped, but he had to watch while his daughter was unspeakably abused on her wedding night. She now lives mercifully out of touch with the world.

In the region of Shamgorod anti-Jewish hatred festers once again, and it is not unthinkable that a new pogrom may break out and finish the work left undone. Purim, however, cannot be Purim without a play, and so a *Purimspiel* will be given, but with a difference urged by Berish. This time the play will enact a trial of God. As the characters in Wiesel's drama begin to organize their play within a play, one problem looms large. The Defendant, God, is silent, and on this Purim night no one in Shamgorod wants to speak for God. Unnoticed, however, a stranger has entered the inn, and just when it seems that the defense attorney's role will go unfilled, the newcomer—his name is Sam—volunteers to act the part. Apparently Berish's Gentile housekeeper Maria has seen this man before. Have nothing to do with him, she warns, but the show begins.

Berish prosecutes. God, he contends, "could use His might to save the victims, but He doesn't! So—on whose side is He? Could the killer kill without His blessing—without His complicity?"[122] Apologies for God do not sit well with this Jewish patriarch. "If I am given the choice of feeling sorry for Him or for human beings," he exclaims, "I choose the latter anytime. He is big enough, strong enough to take care of Himself; man is not."[123] Still, Berish will not let God go. His protest is as real as his despair. Neither denies God's reality; both affirm it by calling God to account.

Sam's style is different. He has an answer for every charge, and he cautions that emotion is no substitute for evidence. In short, he defends God brilliantly. Sam's performance dazzles the visiting actors who have formed the court. Who is he? they wonder. Sam will not say, but his identity and the verdict implicit in *The Trial of God* do not remain moot. As the play's final scene unfolds, a mob approaches to pillage the inn at Shamgorod once more. Sensing that the end is near, the Jewish actors choose to die with their Purim masks in place. Sam dons one too, and as he does so, Maria's premonitions are corroborated. Sam's mask is worthy of his namesake, Samael, whose name, like Sam's mask, signifies Satan. As a final candle is extinguished and the inn's door opens to the sound of deaf-ening and murderous roars, Satan's laughter is among them.

Set three centuries before, this play is not about the Holocaust. Yet it is, because Wiesel introduces the script by reporting that he witnessed a trial of God in Auschwitz. What he does not mention in that foreword, but has indicated on another occasion, is that when the three rabbis who conducted the Auschwitz trial had finished and found God guilty, those men noted that it was time for their customary religious observances, and so they bowed their heads and prayed.[124] Why they did so may be related to a story Wiesel tells about a Jewish family long ago expelled from Spain. Plagued at every turn, they could find no refuge, except that sleep turned into death for them, one by one. At last only the father was left, and he spoke to God:

> "Master of the Universe, I know what You want—I understand what You are doing. You want despair to overwhelm me. You want me to cease believing in You, to cease praying to You, to cease invoking Your name to glorify and sanctify it. Well, I tell you: No, no—a thousand times no! You shall not succeed! In spite of me and in spite of You, I shall shout the Kaddish, which is a song of faith, for You and against You. This song You shall not still, God of Israel."[125]

The little girl who asked a question about God as she moved toward the end of the world also had one for her older brother: "Will you remember me too?" He tells her that he has "forgotten nothing." He will tell that she was only eight, that she had never seen the sea or been to a real wedding, and that she never hurt anyone. She wants him to remember how she loved her new winter coat, Shabbat, and God. He shall; he will speak too. The little sister worries about her brother, now a man so alone and cold. She grieves for herself, for him, for them all. She also asks two more questions and her brother answers.

> "When you speak of your little sister leaving you like that, without a hug, without a goodbye, without wishing you a good journey, will you say that it was not her fault?"
> *"It was not your fault."*
> "Then whose fault was it?"
> *"I shall find out. And I shall tell. I swear it to you, little sister. I shall."*[126]

The Nazis found Jews guilty of being Jewish and sentenced them to death. Some interpreters have argued that various Jewish failures contributed to their own demise. But the Holocaust was not the fault of eight-year-old sisters, nor of any of the victims or survivors—at least not first and foremost. On the contrary, Wiesel stresses that, at first, many of those freed from the Nazi camps believed that the world must not have known about their fate. Disabused of that naïveté, they still clung to the idea that if they told what had happened to them, the effect would be sobering and transforming.

That hope too proved illusory, for the story has been told, responsibility has been assessed, and if anything, the Holocaust is more widely a part of human memory today than at any time before. The labor, however, has not been sufficient to check the violence, suffering, and indifference that waste life away. Instead we see the threats of terrorism, weapons of mass destruction, and genocide. Not even antisemitism has been eclipsed. Perhaps eventual self-destruction is the price humankind must pay for Auschwitz, but that counsel of despair is not Wiesel's last word. In stating his case for and against God, against and for humanity, he identifies more with the movement of another ageless dialogue. God's creation is at stake. It is far from perfect, and thus this dialogue has God speak first:

> "Could you have done better?"
> *"Yes, I think so."*
> "You could have done better? Then what are you waiting for? You don't have a minute to waste, go ahead, start working."[127]

Those lines are unambiguous, predicated on an undeniable truth rooted in the Holocaust, namely, that unless people take a stand against mass death, its toll will be taken more easily. Yet a question remains: have things gone so far that memory and protest rooted in the Holocaust are essentially futile?

In 1981 Wiesel published a novel entitled *The Testament*. It traces the odyssey of Paltiel Kossover, a character who represents hundreds of Jewish intellectuals condemned to death in 1952 by Stalin, a man whose contributions to mass death exceed Hitler's by millions. In this novel the Holocaust stands not center stage but, as usual in Wiesel's works, casts its shadows before and after all the action. Moreover, this book contains Wiesel's most fundamental answer to the question about futility. Arrested, interrogated, Kossover expects to disappear without a trace. Encouraged by his interrogator to write an autobiography—in it, the official hopes, the prisoner will confess more than he does by direct questioning—Kossover has no reason to think that it will ever reach anyone he loves. Even less can he assume that by telling the tale of his own experience he will in any way influence history. Still, he tries his best, and what his best amounts to is summarized in an ancient story—often repeated by Wiesel—that serves as *The Testament's* prologue.

It speaks of a Just Man who came to Sodom to save that place from sin and destruction. Observing the Just Man's care, a child approached him compassionately:

> "Poor stranger, you shout, you scream, don't you see it's hopeless."
> "Yes, I see."
> "Then why do you go on?"
> "I'll tell you why. In the beginning I thought I could change man. Today, I know I cannot. If I still shout today, if I still scream, it is to prevent man for ultimately changing me."[128]

The stranger did everything he could—to no avail except that he remained faithful.

The Holocaust changed the world. Just as Holocaust-related art affects those who create and those who appreciate it, Holocaust literature changes those who write and those who read it. The artists and writers we have encountered in this chapter have shared Wiesel's aim that their struggles with images, sounds, and words can help to make just men and women who will keep the hunger and thirst for righteousness alive. In Wiesel's novel, Kossover's testament does find its way out of a Soviet prison. It reaches and touches the poet's son. Stranger things have happened in our day, and there are testaments aplenty. If they reach and touch us, then a chance remains that protest will survive to keep despair at bay. If that happens, the enormous loss signified by the Holocaust is not all that remains. A future, stripped of illusions, still awaits determination.

# Chapter 12

# God and History: Philosophical and Religious Responses to the Holocaust

*You will sooner or later be confronted by the enigma of God's action in history.*

Elie Wiesel, *One Generation After*

Religion was not a sufficient condition for the Holocaust, but it was a necessary one. What happened at Auschwitz is inconceivable without beliefs about God first held by Jews and then by Christians. Historians have noted similarities between the Holocaust, on the one hand, and the massacre of the Armenians in World War I, Stalin's mass destruction of classes and groups, the Pol Pot regime's genocide of Kampuchea's urban population, and the recent genocide in Rwanda, on the other.[1] There is, however, one aspect of the Holocaust that is qualitatively different from all other programs of extermination and mass destruction in the modern period: no instance of mass murder other than the Holocaust has raised so directly or so insistently the question of whether it was an expression of *Heilsgeschichte*, that is, God's providential involvement in history. More than any other disaster in modern times, the Holocaust resonates with the religiomythic traditions of biblical religion, the dominant religious tradition of Western civilization. Given the classical theological positions of both Judaism and Christianity, the fundamental question posed by the Holocaust is not whether the existence of a just, omnipotent God can be reconciled with radical evil. That is a philosophical question. The religious question is the following: *Did God use Adolf Hitler and the Nazis as his agents to inflict terrible sufferings and death upon six million Jews, including more than one million children?*

In the Holocaust's aftermath the question of whether God, as traditionally understood in biblical and rabbinic Judaism, was the ultimate Author of the catastrophic events is inescapable for religious Jews and, perhaps, for religious

Christians as well. Religious thought addresses this issue in a multitude of ways. The approach in this chapter will not be to provide a survey of that field.[2] Instead, it will illustrate what is at stake in the dilemmas surrounding God and the Holocaust by concentrating primarily on the Christian theologian Paul van Buren and three Jewish thinkers, Ignaz Maybaum, Emil Fackenheim, and this book's coauthor, Richard Rubenstein. In particular, the discussion in this chapter concentrates on the place of the state of Israel in post-Holocaust reflection, a topic that brings many key issues into bold relief.

To start with the perspective of biblical and rabbinic Judaism, the justice and the power of God can be denied only with great difficulty, if at all. Within the normative Jewish mainstream, God has been traditionally understood to be the infinitely righteous, radically transcendent, and absolutely omnipotent Creator of all things. At a very early stage in its development Judaism rejected moral and theological dualism as a way of solving the problem of theodicy, that is, the problem of divine justice. Deutero-Isaiah rejected the Persian idea that there are two equally potent divine powers in the cosmos, one good and the other evil, insisting that God alone is the creator of both good and evil.[3] Insofar as God is regarded as uniquely involved in the history and destiny of Israel, there may be no way of avoiding the exceedingly painful conclusion that God is the ultimate Author of all that has happened to the people of Israel, including the Holocaust.

Although people have found it difficult to accept so harsh and uncompromising a view of the divine-human relationship, one of the most influential philosophical attempts to resolve the apparent contradiction between God's justice and power has been to interpret particular suffering as indispensable to the fulfillment of universal ends. According to the German philosopher G. W. F. Hegel, who is among the most influential philosophers of modern times, particular evil can be said to be overcome in the life of the Absolute. In contemplating the course of world history, with its record of crime, suffering, and slaughter, Hegel was able to write in utter calm and philosophical detachment:

> In order to justify the course of history, we must try to understand the role of evil in the light of the absolute sovereignty of reason. We are dealing here with the category of the negative . . . and we cannot fail to notice how all that is finest and noblest in history is immolated on its altar. Reason cannot stoop to consider the injuries sustained by *single individuals, for particular ends are submerged in the universal ends.*[4]

For Hegel individual injury is overcome in universal ends. However, Hegel never faced a situation of universal injury such as the Holocaust, or the threat of universal extinction in a nuclear disaster. When the universal order is itself threatened with extinction, the idea that a particular misfortune can be overcome in the universal loses its credibility. There is a profound difference between a situation in which some persons suffer and perish unjustly but the group survives and one in which an entire group or even all of humanity is obliterated.

The inappropriateness of the Hegelian reconciliation to the human condition after Auschwitz has been expressed by another philosopher, Theodore Adorno:

> We cannot say any more that the immutable is truth, and that the mobile, transitory is appearance. The mutual indifference of temporality and eternal ideas is no longer tenable even with the bold Hegelian explanation that temporal existence, by virtue of the destruction inherent in its concept, serves the eternal represented by the eternity of destruction . . . [Auschwitz made] a mockery of the construction of immanence as endowed with a meaning radiated by an affirmatively posited transcendence. . . . The administrative murder of millions made of death a thing one had never yet to fear in just this fashion. There is no chance any more for death to come into the individuals' empirical life as somehow conformable with the course of that life. The last, the poorest possession left to the individual is expropriated. That in the concentration camps it was no longer an individual who died, but a specimen—this is a fact bound to affect the dying of those who escaped the administrative measure.[5]

Many modern philosophers did not regard the *Shoah* as presenting a problem worthy of their reflection.[6] For example, Francois Fedier, a French disciple of the influential twentieth-century philosopher Martin Heidegger, reports that he did not regard Auschwitz as important enough to discuss with his mentor. Fedier has been quoted as saying, "I never thought of posing questions except those about philosophy."[7] Nor did Heidegger believe that the Holocaust merited reflection or explanation. In response to a letter from his former student Herbert Marcuse, asking why he had remained silent concerning the extermination of six million Jews, Heidegger equated post-war Soviet treatment of East Germans with the Nazi treatment of the Jews. Heidegger implied that the Soviet treatment was worse since it was done openly, whereas "the bloody terror of the Nazis was in fact kept secret from the German people."[8] In spite of Heidegger's extraordinary talent as a thinker, he was apparently unable to distinguish between a Communist regime that sought to dominate but not eliminate East Germans and a Nazi regime that actively sought to exterminate every single Jew it could find. Moreover, the great philosopher was either uninformed or less than forthcoming in claiming that the truth of the Holocaust was unknown to the German people.[9]

The question of God and the Holocaust has been of far greater interest to religious thinkers and theologians than to philosophers. It is our view that a principal function of theology is to foster *dissonance reduction* where significant items of information are perceived to be inconsistent with established beliefs, values, and collectively sanctioned modes of behavior.[10] At first glance, the Holocaust would appear to be such an item of information inconsistent with established beliefs in divine justice and would naturally concern religious thinkers. Nevertheless, as we shall see, many important Jewish religious authorities have emphatically rejected the idea that the Holocaust is in any way inconsistent with the traditional Jewish conception of divinity. In spite of the fact that the Shoah has been characterized by Rabbi Irving Greenberg, a leading Jewish Holocaust theologian, as "the most radical counter-testimony to religious faith, both Jewish and Christian," some of the most faithful and observant Jewish religious leaders have offered a contrary opinion.[11] These leaders have asserted that their faith in God has been confirmed by the catastrophe.

## TRADITIONAL RELIGIOUS THOUGHT AND THE HOLOCAUST

We take the views of Rabbi Elchonon Wassermann of Baranovitch (1875–1941) as representative of much of Orthodox Jewish thought during the Holocaust years.[12] Writing between *Kristallnacht* and the beginning of the war, Wassermann interpreted the Nazi onslaught as due to three Jewish "evils": secular nationalism; assimilation, especially through Reform Judaism; and the contempt for the Torah allegedly present in the scientific study of Judaism. For Wassermann, the Nazi assault was ultimately God's appropriate response against those who had proven unfaithful to God's Torah. Wassermann also saw the promise of redemption in the misfortunes. Indeed, he argued that the more intense the suffering of the people, the closer the advent of the Messiah, a theme which has been taken up once again in contemporary Israel.

Wassermann's life was fully consistent with his faith. When his murderers took him from the Kovno ghetto in July 1941, he spoke of his own death, as well as the death of others like him, as a *Korban*, a sacrificial offering, for the Jewish people:

> Let us go with raised heads. God forbid, that any thought should enter anybody's mind which makes the sacrifice (*Korban*) unfit. We now carry out the greatest *Mitzvah, Kiddush Hashem* (sanctification of God's name). The fire which will burn our bodies is the fire which will resurrect the Jewish people.[13]

Wassermann's response to the Holocaust was typical of many Orthodox rabbis of the period in both eastern Europe and North America. Far from being a "radical counter-testimony to religious faith," the events were widely regarded as confirming the tradition and the fulfillment of God's plan. After the Holocaust, the opinions of Rabbi Joseph Isaac Schneersohn, the late Lubavitcher Rebbe, provided another example of the same tendency. According to Schneersohn, Hitler was but God's instrument for chastising the Jews who had abandoned the ways of Torah; Nazism was divine punishment visited upon the Jews for rejecting the Torah and choosing assimilation.[14]

The Orthodox interpretation of the Holocaust as divinely inflicted punishment and/or the sacrificial precondition for the coming of the Messiah rests upon the biblical doctrines of covenant and election. As noted, whenever Israel experienced radical communal misfortune, her religious teachers almost always interpreted the event as did Wassermann and Schneersohn, that is, as divine punishment. This was the case in 586 B.C.E. when Jeremiah prophesied concerning the impending fate of Jerusalem then threatened by Nebuchadnezzar, king of Babylon:

> The word of the LORD came to Jeremiah: See, I am the LORD, the God of all flesh; is anything too hard for me? Therefore, thus says the LORD: I am going to give this city into the hands of the Chaldeans and into the hands of King Nebuchadrezzar of Babylon, and he shall take it. The Chaldeans who are fighting against this city shall come, set it on fire, and burn it, with the houses on whose roofs offerings have been made to Baal and libations have been poured out to other gods, to provoke me to anger. For the people of Israel and the people of Judah have done nothing but evil in my sight from their youth; the people of Israel have done nothing but provoke me to anger by the work of their hands, says the LORD. (Jer. 32:26–30)

The translators of the New Revised Standard Version of the Bible, the text cited in this book's scriptural citations, employ especially harsh language when they indicate that the people of Israel "have done nothing but evil" in God's sight and "nothing but provoke [God] to anger." (Jer. 26:30) A more accurate rendering of the Hebrew would be as follows: "For the children of Israel and the children of Judah have done only that which was evil in my sight from their youth; for the children of Israel have only provoked me by the work of their hands, says the Lord." In a more accurate way the translation we propose still makes clear that, given Jeremiah's belief in the election of Israel, it was impossible for him to view the fall of Jerusalem as an event devoid of profound religious significance. The prophet understood that divine election placed an awesome responsibility on Israel, one that entailed God's judgment, which could be severe.

Jerusalem fell again at the end of the Judeo-Roman War of 66–70 C.E. At the time the rabbis, who succeeded the prophets and the priests as the religious authorities within Judaism, interpreted their people's misfortunes as had their predecessors. A characteristic example of the rabbinic response is to be found in the liturgy for the Holy Days and Festivals still used by traditional Jews:

> Thou hast chosen us from among all peoples; thou hast loved us and taken pleasure in us, and hast exalted us above all tongues; thou hast hallowed us by thy commandments, and brought us near unto thy service, O our King, and thou hast called us by thy great and holy Name. . . . But on account of our sins we were exiled from our land and removed far from our country.[15]

To the extent that Judaism and Christianity affirm the election of Israel, both traditions must consider the Holocaust as more than a random occurrence. Unable to accept the Holocaust as a purely punitive event, some Orthodox Jews have interpreted it as the catastrophic precondition for the final messianic redemption of Jewish and world history, the "birth pangs of the Messiah." In the aftermath of World War II, Rabbi Jehiel Jacob Weinberg (1884–1966), a Holocaust survivor and one of the most important authorities on Jewish law of his time, held that the creation of the state of Israel had inaugurated the messianic process that would lead to the complete redemption of Israel and humanity. Shifting his focus from the utter destructiveness of the war to what he regarded as the providential birth of the state of Israel, he held that creation of the state inaugurated a messianic process leading to complete redemption. He saw the messianic era as the "hope for a bright future full of miracles of a worldwide revolution" and wrote of the state of Israel as "the joy of my life."[16] Similarly, contemporary Orthodox Jews in Israel affiliated with Gush Emunim (the Bloc of the Faithful) consider the Holocaust to be an indispensable event in God's redemptive plan for human history.

## A CHRISTIAN RESPONSE

Slowly and painfully, many Christians have discovered the impact of the Holocaust on their own tradition. Awareness that Christian antisemitism contributed much to the destruction of European Jewry requires Christians, no less than Jews, to reconsider the most fundamental aspects of their faith.[17] Although Christian theology in America has usually played a secondary and derivative role to European and specifically German theological work, American religious thinkers have been in the vanguard in the field of Holocaust theology. Significantly, there are more Jews in the United States than in any other country, and this has made reflection on the Holocaust by American Christians all the more important.

Initially, American Christian responses to the Holocaust concentrated on two main areas: appraisal of church life in the Third Reich and inquiry about the Christian roots of antisemitism. These analyses were largely historical and were followed by a movement that has gone beyond historical scholarship toward substantial rethinking of Christian-Jewish relations in the light of the Holocaust. Seriously studying what Jewish thinkers have to say, Christian writers such as Robert McAfee Brown, Harry James Cargas, A. Roy and Alice Eckardt, Darrell Fasching, Eva Fleischner, Stephen Haynes, Franklin Littell, John T. Pawlikowski,, and John K. Roth have contributed to this process. A most significant example has been provided by the late Paul M. van Buren, who worked out a systematic Christian theological response to the Holocaust. In a multivolume work that assesses Christian thought in light of the Holocaust—including the sensitive question of how Christians should regard Jesus after Auschwitz, the vigor of Jewish religious life throughout the centuries, and the reemergence of the state of Israel—van Buren did much to overcome Christian triumphalism and the notion that Christianity has superseded or negated Jewish faith.[18] Regrettably, his suggestions about God's relation to Auschwitz are less credible than his estimates about how to reconceive the relations between Christians and Jews so that anti-Jewish sentiment in Christianity can be laid to rest.

Van Buren's theology stresses that Christians worship the God of the Jews. Although he underscores the difficulties of speaking about God at all after

Auschwitz, van Buren stresses that God has created human beings free and responsible. To bestow us with those qualities, he believes, is a loving thing for God to do. It also entails that God has "to sit still and to suffer in agony as His children move so slowly to exercise in a personal and loving way the freedom which He has willed for them to have and exercise."[19] Confronted by the question "Where was God at Auschwitz?" van Buren believes that God was in the midst of that destruction, suffering "in solidarity with His people." The objectives of this suffering God, he surmises, might have included "trying to awaken His creatures to their irresponsibility. Perhaps He was trying, by simply suffering with His people, to awaken His church to a new understanding of love and respect for them." Obviously uneasy about those answers, van Buren adds, "The cost seems out of all proportion to the possible gain, so silence may be the wiser choice."[20] Nevertheless, van Buren eschews this choice and goes on to elaborate his views about God's suffering.

These views amount to a conventional apologetic defense of God predicated on the principle that God's creation of human freedom "constitutes a divine self-determination. . . . Having made this decision and taken this step, there are some things which God cannot be and some choices that are no longer open to Him."[21] Specifically, according to van Buren, God could not intervene to stop the Holocaust "without ceasing to be the God of love and freedom who has . . . conferred responsibility and free creative power on His creatures."[22] Here van Buren begs the question twice over. Responsibility and free creative power are not incompatible with Holocaust interventions by God unless God or van Buren defines them that way. Moreover, if van Buren or God does define them that way, then one might wonder how that decision is supposed to embody love, seeing that its outworkings in history led to unremitting slaughter in the Holocaust. Van Buren pleads that, if we are to think of God as a parental figure—the imagery is common to both Judaism and Christianity—"then this must surely be an agonizing period in God's life."[23] Well it might be, though less because of van Buren's emphasis that God is so explicitly bound by the existence of human freedom and more by second thoughts about what God did in creating a world of freedom in which irresponsible destructiveness destroys more than love appears to save.

About one matter van Buren is perfectly credible: "God is not a God who does it all for His creatures." He may even be correct that if more Christians had acknowledged that fact earlier, millions murdered by Hitler might have been rescued. But if we are to go on to suggest, as van Buren does, that the Holocaust becomes divine revelation, informing us "that God requires that we take unqualified responsibility before Him for His history with us,"[24] then at the very least, common decency would seem to enjoin us to ask God—or at least van Buren—whether there was not a more effective, less wasteful, way for God to get that message across. Van Buren reads the emergence of the state of Israel in a similar light. That development did occur because of human initiative, but to speak of such effort as containing a revelation from God concerning human responsibility should raise still more questions about what God is doing. For however wonderful van Buren may have thought the state of Israel to be, even Holocaust sur-vivors emphasize that it was in no way worth the price of the Holocaust. More-over, rightly or wrongly, the Palestinians and the overwhelming majority of Muslims throughout the world regard the founding of the state of Israel as a cat-astrophic event that is clearly contrary to the will of Allah. Van Buren is on highly problematic grounds when he attempts to read divine intent into so conflict-ridden an event, but in taking that step he is by no means alone.

Van Buren's Christian theology tries to retain a view in which God's goodness is as great as God's suffering and God's love is as vast as God's freedom. As far as history is concerned, however, his account suggests that God's power recedes as humanity's emerges. Van Buren believes that Christians take "the crucifixion to be God's greatest act," the very essence of suffering love.[25] But van Buren's per-spective underplays the fact that the crucifixion would have been just another Roman execution, had it not been succeeded by what certain Jews took to be a substantial intervention in human affairs, namely, the resurrection of Jesus from death itself. At the very core of Christianity—and this poses a serious inconve-nience for van Buren's Holocaust theology—is the assertion that God's divine power far exceeds anything that human beings can do. Arguably God is not bound by human freedom unless God chooses to be. And if God wants to be, so that the divine presence at Auschwitz is that of suffering with the victims and not interceding on their behalf, then that is a problem for us all—God, Christians, Jews, and everybody else.

A credible Christian theology in a post-Holocaust world neither can nor will want to take God off the hook, so to speak, quite as easily as does van Buren, unless it is true that Christians are simply unwilling to confront the awesome and dreadful possibility that their God of love is at times needlessly and even wan-tonly involved with evil that did not have to be. "If we are to speak of ourselves as being responsible for history, " writes van Buren, "then we shall have to find a way to speak of God that corresponds."[26] True, people are responsible for history, but humanity's responsibility cannot be the whole story. It is irresponsible, not to say unchristian, to assign responsibility inequitably. If God exists, God must bear a fair share. God's responsibility would be located in the fact that God is the One who ultimately sets the boundaries in which we live and move and have our being. Granted, since we are thrown into history at our birth, we appear in social settings made by human hands. But ultimately those hands cannot account for themselves. To the extent that they were born with the potential and the power to be dirty, credit for the fact belongs elsewhere. "Elsewhere" is God's address. God's only excuse may be that God does not exist. To use human freedom and responsibility as a defense for God simply does not ring true, at least not com-pletely. God's establishment of that very freedom and responsibility, given the precise forms it has taken in history, rightly puts God on trial.

Van Buren remains hopeful about human existence after the Holocaust. Hav-ing stressed God's limited intervening role in history, he asserts that history shall be redeemed. To transform history into something very different from the slaughter bench Hegel envisioned it to be, radical changes are required. The issue is who will carry them out? By van Buren's reckoning, the burden of freedom places overwhelming responsibility on human shoulders, unless God changes and suddenly falls back on a more dramatic divine intervention within history than van Buren's theory suggests. But where is the evidence to suggest that, in the world since the Holocaust, human beings have made or are likely to make substantial progress in redeeming history? Who, in short, is going to do the redeeming? Van Buren holds little stock in secular humanity; its ways did too much to pave the way to Auschwitz. Christians, he believes, are declining in absolute numbers in the world. Perhaps, then, the task falls to the Jews, a singularly questionable idea in view of the enduring conflict in the Middle East. If lions and lambs are to lie down together in peace on this earth, nothing less than a massive intervention in history by God appears to be necessary. Given what appears to be God's continued policy of nonintervention, the historical order will probably remain less than redeemed. Meanwhile, Jews and Christians alike are left to await the fulfillment of God's promises, even as some may try themselves to make the world less destructive.

## COVENANT AND ELECTION

Given the central role of the doctrines of covenant and election in Jewish religious belief, it has been impossible for Jewish thinkers to ignore the Holocaust's religious implications. No subject has so dominated the concerns of Jewish thinkers, at least since the mid-1960s when two radically different theological interpretations of the Holocaust first appeared: *The Face of God after Auschwitz* by Ignaz Maybaum and *After Auschwitz* by Richard Rubenstein.[27] Rubenstein's volume has received far more attention from both scholars and the media. There is general agreement that the Holocaust became a predominant subject within Jewish theology after its publication. Although Maybaum's book was written in English, it was published in the Netherlands and for many years remained almost totally unknown in the United States. No two Holocaust theologians are in such total disagreement. Precisely for that reason, they ought to be considered together. Their disagreement illuminates many of the crucial issues confronting religious faith after Auschwitz.

Maybaum, a Viennese-born Reform rabbi, served congregations in Germany until 1939, when he immigrated to England and served for many years as a liberal rabbi and theologian. In *The Face of God after Auschwitz* Maybaum affirmed the continuing validity of God's covenant with Israel and insisted without qualification that God continues to intervene in history, especially the history of the chosen people, *the Holocaust being one of God's most important interventions.* Maybaum also held that Israel has a divinely ordained mission to bring knowledge of the true God and divine law to the nations of the world. That idea was strongly affirmed in the nineteenth century by Reform Jewish thinkers in both Germany and the United States. Although it never met with favor among traditional Jews or Zionists, the idea of the "mission of Israel" is important for Maybaum's understanding of the Holocaust.

While Maybaum saw the Holocaust as God's deliberate intervention, he categorically rejected the idea that it was in any sense a divine punishment. Instead, in what some would take to be an exceedingly strange interpretation, Maybaum actually held that the Holocaust was a supreme instance of providential divine intervention. Having rejected the punitive interpretation, Maybaum offered a sacrificial interpretation of the *Shoah*, using the crucifixion as his model. Maybaum asserted that just as Jesus was the innocent victim whose death made possible the salvation of humanity, so too the millions of Holocaust victims must be seen as divinely chosen sacrificial offerings.

A rabbi's use of the crucifixion as a theological model may seem strange, but Maybaum argued that God's purposes can be understood only if God addresses the nations of the world in the language they understand. Maybaum held that the nations of the world can hear and respond to God's call only when it is expressed in the language of death and destruction. Hence the importance of the crucifixion, which is a key image through which the Christian world can comprehend God's activity. According to Maybaum, it was the awesome fate of six million Jews, *precisely because they were God's chosen people*, to become sacrificial victims in the death camps so that God's purposes for the modern world might be understood and fulfilled: "The Golgotha of modern mankind is Auschwitz. The cross, the Roman gallows, was replaced by the gas chamber."[28]

Maybaum regarded the Holocaust as God's terrible means of bringing the world fully into the modern age. He argued that this transition could not have occurred without the destruction of all that was medieval in Europe. Maybaum pointed out that the vast majority of Jewish victims were eastern Europeans who, he argued, still lived in a medieval, feudal way, more or less as their ancestors had, ritually and culturally isolated from their neighbors. In spite of the fact that it took a Hitler to destroy this allegedly outmoded way of life, Maybaum interpreted the extermination of eastern European Jews as an ultimately beneficent act of creative destruction. Unfortunately, so too did the National Socialists, though for very different reasons. With the passing of the eastern European Jewish community, which had been the most faithful to the ancient beliefs and traditions of rabbinic Judaism, the world's Jews were concentrated in countries such as the United States, western Europe, Russia, and Israel, in which, according to Maybaum, they were free to participate fully in an era of Enlightenment, progress, rationality, and modernity.

Maybaum also expressed a quasi-messianic enthusiasm for the place and role of the Jews in the post-Holocaust world. Maybaum's enthusiasm for the destruction of the allegedly medieval elements in traditional Jewish life was such that he could equate the modernized, post-Holocaust Judaism of the "enlightened" Western world with the "first fruits" of redemption: "The Jewish people is, here and now, mankind at its goal. We have arrived. We are the first fruits of God's harvest."[29] Maybaum was not alone in his messianic enthusiasm. The messianic theme has also had a powerful, if controversial, hold over many Orthodox Jews in contemporary Israel, especially among those settlers on the West Bank who see the Holocaust as the "birth pangs of the Messiah" and a prelude to the return of the Jewish people to the "whole land of Israel."[30]

There are obviously enormous problems with Maybaum's defense of the biblical God of history and the election of Israel. No matter what "higher" purposes were, in Maybaum's view, served by the Holocaust, Maybaum's image of God was that of One who was quite willing to subject millions of innocent people to suffering and death that were unprecedented for any human collectivity. In fairness, it must be said that Maybaum's interpretation of the Holocaust was motivated by a desire to defend the doctrine of covenant and election as that doctrine was understood in classical Reform Judaism. Maybaum understood the nature of the theological vocation and was prepared to fulfill it on behalf of the community he served. He grasped the logical entailments of the faith he defended. Most non-Orthodox religious thinkers affirm the God-who-acts-in-history but deny that God acted in history at Auschwitz. By asserting that God's ways are "mysterious," such thinkers seek to affirm traditional faith while avoiding the negative consequences of so doing. What distinguished thinkers like Elchonon Wassermann, Joseph Schneersohn, and Ignaz Maybaum was their refusal to take the easy escape route of liberal evasion. They understood that, absent the affirmation of some version of the traditional biblical view of God, Torah, and covenant, Judaism's status is reduced to that of a particular community's socially constructed religion.

Rubenstein had not heard of Maybaum until some time after the 1966 publication of the first edition of *After Auschwitz*. Had he read Maybaum before writing *After Auschwitz*, Rubenstein would certainly have referred to him in explaining his reasons for rejecting the traditional biblical theology of covenant and election. He did so in the second edition.[31] Meanwhile Rubenstein's theologically controversial position had not been triggered initially by intellectual speculation but by his crucial encounter on 17 August 1961 with Dean Heinrich Grüber, dean of the Evangelical Church in East and West Berlin. Rubenstein was spending that summer in the Netherlands and had scheduled a research trip to West Germany to begin on Sunday, 13 August. On that day, the infamous Berlin Wall was hastily erected by the East German regime to separate East and West Berlin, thereby creating a major international crisis. Rubenstein postponed his trip until Tuesday, 15 August when, at the invitation of his hosts, the *Bundespresseamt* (the Press and Information Office of the Federal Republic of Germany), he flew to Berlin to view the situation firsthand.

On arrival in Berlin, Rubenstein found an atmosphere of extreme crisis. Many Berliners were fearful that the Third World War was about to start. Wherever he went, the atmosphere was apocalyptic in the true sense of the word. People were afraid that nuclear war might break out, bringing the world to an end. In that atmosphere, Rubenstein was invited to meet with Grüber at his home in the West Berlin suburb of Dahlem. The meeting was set for 4:30 P.M. on Thursday,

17 August. As Rubenstein entered Grüber's home, a column of American tanks rumbled by noisily on the street outside. Rubenstein and Grüber discussed many issues; inevitably the conversation turned to the Holocaust. During World War II, Grüber headed the "Grüber office," set up by the Berlin Confessing Church to help baptized Jews whose treatment by the Nazis was no different than that meted out to other Jews. He also helped Jews faithful to their own tradition, working to send Jewish children to British families and setting up "family schools" for them in some churches when they were barred from attending German schools. According to Helen Jacobs, a member of the Confessing Church group that aided Jews, Grüber was arrested in December 1940 and sent to Sachsenhausen concentration camp for three years because he had spoken "in outrage" against the first Jewish deportations in Stettin.[32] In the 1961 Jerusalem trial of Adolf Eichmann, Grüber was the only German to testify against that Holocaust perpetrator.

In his conversation with Rubenstein, Grüber affirmed a biblical faith in the God-who-acts-in-history and in the covenant between God and Israel. Like Maybaum, Grüber believed that the Holocaust was God's doing. He too likened Hitler to Nebuchadnezzar as one of the "rods of God's anger." When Grüber asserted that Israel was God's chosen people and that nothing could happen to the Jews save that which God intended, Rubenstein asked him: "Was it God's will that Hitler destroyed the Jews?" Grüber replied by quoting from the Psalms: "For thy sake are we slain all the day long" (Ps. 44:22). He then continued: "For some reason, it was part of God's plan that the Jews died. God demands our death daily. He is the Lord. He is the Master; all is in his keeping and ordering."

Grüber had no doubt that Hitler's actions were immoral and that Hitler would be punished. Rescue activity on behalf of Jews and testimony against Eichmann bear witness to that part of Grüber's thinking. Theologically, however, Grüber apparently believed that Hitler's actions were not simply immoral when God was their ultimate perpetrator: "At different times God uses different people as His whip against His own people, the Jews, but those whom He uses will be punished far worse than the people of the Lord."[33] Rubenstein did not have time to ask Grüber to specify why the Jews were being punished, but despite Grüber's assistance to beleaguered Jews there is no reason to doubt that he placed Jewish misfortune in the theological framework that has characterized most of Christian history.

In fact, Grüber's colleagues in the German Evangelical Church, meeting in Darmstadt in 1948, asserted that the Holocaust was a divine punishment visited upon the Jews. In a problematic spirit of brotherhood they called upon the Jews to cease their rejection and continuing crucifixion of Jesus Christ.[34] Such pronouncements are seldom heard any more, but it remains significant that three years after the end of World War II the leaders of the Evangelical Church were telling Jews that they had nobody to blame but themselves for the Holocaust and their only possible hope was to cease to be Jews and become Christians. While some of the document's signatories may have been motivated by malice, it is very likely that others were genuinely moved by the Jewish tragedy. Given their view of the role of the Jews in *Heilsgeschichte*, they were incapable of seeing any other way for Jews to escape the continuing wrath of God.

Grüber, like Maybaum, took his faith in the God-who-acts-in-history with the utmost seriousness, knowing full well what such a faith entailed. He did not attempt to avoid its painful, logical consequences. If God acts in history, it was clear to Grüber that God was the ultimate Author of the Holocaust. Grüber had the courage of his convictions, whether he was expressing his opposition to National Socialism during the Third Reich or affirming his belief in the God of the Bible to a visiting Jewish theologian in 1961. There was, however, an important difference between Grüber and Maybaum. Ironically, the rabbi had used the crucifixion as his model for understanding the Holocaust, whereas Grüber used the prophetic-Deuteronomic model of the God of the covenant as his model. Grüber saw the Jews as guilty offenders against God's law. In fairness to the dean, he had a similar view of his own people. Maybaum could neither challenge God's sovereignty nor imagine any crime that would justify extermination at the hands of the Nazis. He had no doubt about the innocence of the victims. That conviction compelled him to turn either to the model of the Suffering Servant or to the crucifixion. Given his commitment to faith in the God of covenant and election, Maybaum had no option save to regard the Jews as innocent sacrificial victims.

When Rubenstein left Grüber's home, something within him had changed irrevocably. The change had been gestating for a long time. Rubenstein's years of study for the Reform rabbinate (1942–45) coincided almost exactly with the period when Hitler's Final Solution was carried out. Initially, Rubenstein accepted Reform Judaism's optimistic faith in enlightenment and progress, a position Reform has since modified. Specifically, Rubenstein's liberal faith in progress began to change during the High Holy Days in 1944, soon after the advancing Russian armies in eastern Poland discovered the Nazi concentration and death camp at Majdanek. The reports about Majdanek were the first of many that were to come. The worst fears about wartime Germany's treatment of the Jews had proven overly optimistic.

Rubenstein could no longer accept Reform Judaism's optimistic faith in progress and human perfectibility. Nor could he find credible the biblical doctrine that God had chosen Israel. As he put it, "Chosen for what?—for Majdanek and Auschwitz?"[35] Disenchanted with liberal religion's naïve optimism about human nature, Rubenstein began a spiritual journey that led him to more traditional forms of Judaism—absent the doctrine that God had chosen Israel—in the belief that their understanding of human nature was fundamentally more realistic. His journey remained a personal quest until he worked through the impact of his crucial meeting with Dean Grüber in Berlin.

There was little that Grüber said about Jewish misfortune that had not been spoken by the prophets and the rabbis in the past. Rubenstein understood that Grüber was a man of courage and good will who, because of his beliefs, could not have offered any other opinion. Grüber's position was essentially in harmony with Scripture, but Rubenstein was convinced that an inescapable difficulty was involved in the position of both Grüber and traditional Judaism. In summary form, these new convictions were expressed in *Commentary* magazine's August 1966 symposium on "The Conditions of Jewish Belief" as follows:

> I believe the greatest single challenge to modern Judaism arises out of the question of God and the death camps. I am amazed at the silence of contemporary Jewish theologians on this most crucial and agonizing of all Jewish issues. How can Jews believe in an omnipotent, beneficent God after Auschwitz? Traditional Jewish theology maintains that God is the ultimate, omnipotent actor in the historical drama. It has interpreted every major catastrophe in Jewish history as God's punishment of a sinful Israel. I fail to see how this position can be maintained without regarding Hitler and the SS as instruments of God's will. The agony of European Jewry cannot be likened to the testing of Job. To see any purpose in the death camps, the traditional believer is forced to regard the most demonic, anti-human explosion of all history as a meaningful expression of God's purposes. The idea is simply too obscene for me to accept. I do not think that the full impact of Auschwitz has yet been felt in Jewish theology or Jewish life. Great religious revolutions have their own period of gestation. No man knows when the full impact of Auschwitz will be felt, but no religious community can endure so hideous a wounding without undergoing vast inner disorders.[36]

It may still be the case that "the full impact of Auschwitz" has yet to be felt in Jewish theology. Meanwhile, in the *Commentary* statement Rubenstein had attacked the views of the great Jewish thinkers of the period without naming those leaders. They included Martin Buber, Abraham Joshua Heschel, Gershom Scholem, Joseph B. Soloveitchik, and Mordecai M. Kaplan, all of whom had little to say about the Holocaust.[37] The attack was both unavoidable and foolhardy. Both Heschel and Kaplan had been Rubenstein's teachers.[38] He had been Heschel's student at both the Hebrew Union College, the seminary for the training of Reform rabbis, during the wartime years of 1942–45 and the Jewish Theological Seminary from 1948 to 1952. Nevertheless, their views on God and the Holocaust were very different.[39]

Both Heschel and Kaplan had affixed their signatures to Rubenstein's rabbinic diploma. Although an ordained rabbi with a Harvard Ph.D. in the history of religion, Rubenstein knew that he would never have the depth of knowledge of Judaism possessed by Heschel, Kaplan, and the other great Jewish thinkers of the period, all of whom had been born in Europe and, save for Kaplan, received their education there in biblical and rabbinic studies, as well as in Hebrew language and literature. Without exception, Jewish knowledge was second nature to them. By contrast, Rubenstein was the son of American-born parents who were not religious. He did not have the customary Bar Mitzvah and did not begin to study Hebrew seriously until age seventeen. He possessed none of the authority of the great thinkers, and he could point to no precedents in Jewish tradition to validate the radical positions he found himself compelled to take. There appeared to be no reason to take Rubenstein's thinking seriously, save for the fact that the question of God and the Holocaust was unavoidable and the great thinkers had little or nothing to say about it.

For example, when publication of Martin Buber's book *Eclipse of God* was announced in 1952, there was some expectation that he would deal with the problem.[40] This was not to be. While the book expresses concern for the collapse of faith in a transcendent deity in modern philosophy, the Holocaust is nowhere discussed as relevant to that issue.[41] As Zachary Braiterman has pointed out, Buber did discuss God and Auschwitz explicitly in an essay entitled "The Dialogue between Heaven and Earth," in which he asked, "How is life with God still possible in a time in which there is an Auschwitz? . . . Dare we recommend to the survivors of Auschwitz and the Job of the gas chambers: 'Give thanks to the Lord, for He is good; for His mercy endureth forever'"?[42] In the essay Buber saw in God a harsh and capricious cruelty that he refused to justify. Buber nevertheless concluded on an affirmative note, claiming that God appears to human beings through the catharsis that evil engenders. He expressed the conviction that, radically destructive as the "catharsis" of Auschwitz might have been, it would ultimately be followed by a redeemed humanity's return to God.[43] Implicitly, for Buber the Holocaust had a felicitous ending.

Like Buber, Abraham Joshua Heschel (1907–92) was profoundly anguished by the destruction of European Jewry. The world of European Jewry had been his, and its destruction had taken many members of his immediate and extended family. Nevertheless, although he criticized God, especially in his posthumous work *A Passion for Truth*, Heschel could not sustain this position.[44] He held that modern humanity in its amorality and viciousness, rather than the God of history, was to be faulted for the devastation he and his fellow Jews had endured. After the birth of the state of Israel and Israel's victory in the Six Day War of 1967, Heschel's faith in divine providence was reinforced: In *Israel: An Echo in Eternity* he stated that "History is a nightmare. . . . [But] the end of days will be the end of war; idolatry will disappear, knowledge of God will prevail."[45] The theme of despair is a discernible subtext even in Heschel's most affirmative work, but it is never the last word. For Heschel, dread and despair, even after Auschwitz, are ultimately the prelude and necessary gateway to standing in God's redemptive presence.[46]

Rubenstein never met Rabbi Joseph B. Soloveitchik (1903–93) although he was fully cognizant of his importance as the preeminent American Orthodox intellectual leader of his time. Moreover, Soloveitchik's son-in-law, Professor Isadore Twersky, was a member of Rubenstein's thesis committee at Harvard. Born in Poland, Soloveitchik stemmed from one of the most important and enduring rabbinic families in Lithuania, the world center of Talmudic studies before the Holocaust. He received a classical Lithuanian Talmudic education that laid the foundation of his later preeminent authority in Jewish law, philosophy, and theology. He entered the University of Berlin in 1925 and received his doctorate in philosophy in 1931. In 1941 Soloveitchik succeeded his father as professor of Talmud at the Rabbi Isaac Elchanan Theological Seminary of Yeshiva

University in New York, the most important post in a traditional seminary. Among his disciples he was known popularly as "the Rav," an elevated designation for rabbi and teacher of other rabbis. Given his authority as an Orthodox leader, he could hardly ignore the issue of God and the Holocaust. Unflinchingly he asserted the justice and omnipotence of God in the face of any and all human suffering. Soloveitchik wrote, "When the impulse of intellectual curiosity seizes hold of a person, he ought to do nought but find strength and encouragement in his faith in the creator, vindicate God's judgment, and acknowledge the perfection of his work. 'The Rock His work is perfect; for all His ways are just.'"[47]

Apparently, Soloveitchik saw no problem in acknowledging "the perfection of [God's] work" after Auschwitz. Moreover, his affirmation of the absolute justice of God was given an even more radical formulation in his reflections on the Akedah, Abraham's aborted sacrifice of Isaac on Mt. Moriah.[48] Soloveitchik argued that we belong unconditionally to God, our Creator, as do all our possessions and family members. Consequently, humanity "has no choice when the Voice of God calls out to him, as it did to Abraham, to 'take now thy son, thine only son and sacrifice him' but to arise and unquestioningly obey the command." Were God to call for human sacrifices, according to Soloveitchik, we would be unconditionally obliged to obey. Fortunately, God in God's graciousness does not make such a demand, but the decision is God's, not ours. Admittedly, such obedience involves profound pain and suffering. For Soloveitchik, it is through such sacrifices or through the bitter suffering that is often its surrogate that "we feel ourselves 'in the presence of God.'" There is no word about the Holocaust in this meditation, but it is difficult to believe that the Holocaust was far from his mind or from that of his readers. Soloveitchik saw even the Holocaust as the mysterious handiwork of the just and righteous God of Judaism.

As a result of the *Commentary* statement and its expansion in his latter writings, Rubenstein has often been accused of atheism, a charge rejected by some of the most informed students of Holocaust theology.[49] On the contrary, Rubenstein's writings contain no denial of the existence of God, although the biblical image of the God who elected Israel is explicitly rejected. As Rubenstein came to understand, there are alternatives. Apart from thinkers like Maybaum, Soloveitchik, Wassermann, and Schneersohn, one can affirm with Jewish messianists that the Holocaust was an indispensable aspect of the "birthpangs of the Messiah" that leads to the reestablishment of the Holy Temple and the possession of "the whole land of Israel" by the Jewish people. Alternatively, one can also affirm with American Christians who are premillennial dispensationalists or "end-timers" that the Holocaust was part of the divine timetable leading up to Armageddon and Christ's second coming. Nevertheless, Jewish messianists can scarcely avoid the fact that millions of innocent victims died horribly for the sake of the Lord's plan. For Christian end-timers there is no problem, because God's redemptive plan for humanity's redemption trumps all other considerations. Nevertheless, apart from the question of whether *any* utopia is worth the bloody price of a Holocaust, the messianic views justify the *real* death of millions for the sake of an *imaginary* glorious future. Moreover, both Jewish and Christian messianists ultimately transform a bitter conflict over the control of territory between Israelis and Arabs into a holy war in which non-Jews or non-Christians, depending on one's version of messianism, have no rights in the land. For their part, adherents of radical Islam make a comparable claim concerning the exclusive rights of Muslims to the Holy Land.

Although not an atheist, Rubenstein did assert that "we live in the time of the death of God." The meaning of that statement is summarized in the following passage:

> No man can really say that God is dead. How can we know that? Nevertheless, I am compelled to say that we live in the time of the "death of God." This is more a statement about man and his culture than about God. The death of God is a cultural fact. Buber felt this. He spoke of the eclipse of God. I can understand his reluctance to use the more explicitly Christian terminology. . . . Had I lived in another time or another culture, I might have found some other vocabulary to express my meanings. I am, however, a religious existentialist after Nietzsche and after Auschwitz. When I say we live in the time of the death of God, I mean that the thread uniting God and man, heaven and earth, has been broken. We stand in a cold, silent, unfeeling cosmos, unaided by any purposeful power beyond our own resources. After Auschwitz, what else can a Jew say about God?[50]

Moreover, in the second edition of *After Auschwitz* Rubenstein stated that he no longer regarded the cosmos as "cold, silent, unfeeling." At the very least, insofar as humanity is a part of the cosmos and is capable of love as well as hate, the cosmos itself cannot be said to be entirely cold and silent. Nor can a cosmos that is replete with life and sentient beings be regarded as unfeeling, save in its ultimate indifference to the fate of humanity and nations. Rubenstein also holds that the source of the life of the cosmos is the Divine Life. As the ultimate unity of all things, the Divine Life is the Absolute and, as such, always the same. Paradoxically, as the life of the cosmos, it is forever mobile, never static. Ever changing, it is, as life, perpetually feeding on itself. Hence, Rubenstein can speak of Divinity's creative destructiveness without assigning it a providential meaning.

Rubenstein's highly publicized rejection of the biblical God and the doctrine of the chosen people would have been a matter of little consequence, had Rubenstein been a professor of philosophy, sociology, or psychology.[51] As a rabbi, Rubenstein is what rabbi and psychotherapist Dr. Jack H. Bloom has identified as a "symbolic exemplar," that is "the symbol of something other than himself," namely, the religious beliefs and values of the community.[52] Moreover, no matter what profession a rabbi might elect instead of the rabbinate, in the eyes of the community, once a rabbi, always a rabbi.[53] The publication of Rubenstein's views as a rabbi was a step of extraordinary seriousness, especially when it put him wholly at odds with the renowned teachers who had trained him, certified his fitness to be a rabbi, and unquestionably knew more about the Jewish tradition than he. His opinions understandably elicited the question whether anyone who accepted such views had any reason for remaining Jewish. For millennia the literature and liturgy of normative Judaism have been saturated with the idea that God chose Israel and that the obligation to obey the laws and traditions of the Torah is divinely legitimated. Why, it was asked, should anyone keep the Sabbath, circumcise male offspring, marry within the Jewish community, or obey the dietary laws if the God depicted in the Bible as the Lord of history does not exist?

From one point of view, there is merit to these questions. From another, there is little or none. Without a credible affirmation of the existence of the God of the prophets and the rabbis, Judaism may become a voluntary matter of personal preference, a preference some may be tempted to abandon. Immediately after World War II, the argument was advanced that racism prevents any escape from Jewish identity. In reality intermarriage provides an escape route for the grandchildren, if not the children, of mixed marriages. While relatively few Jews join the Christian world through baptism, many facilitate their children's entry into the Christian world by marrying Christian partners. Those who desire to abandon Jewish identity can begin the process even if they cannot complete it. Moreover, the very high percentage of Jews who marry non-Jews in North America and elsewhere may itself be an unspoken response to the Holocaust. For some, Judaism may no longer be worth dying for. In any event, awareness of the negative practical consequences of unbelief can hardly be used as an argument to enhance the credibility of a belief system.

Rubenstein responded to the question of whether Judaism can be maintained without traditional faith by arguing that the demise of theological legitimations did not entail an end to the psychological and sociological functions all religions fulfill. Save for the infrequent case of conversion, entrance into Judaism is a matter of birth rather than choice. Even conversion to Christianity does not entirely cancel out Jewish identity. There is an ethnic component to Jewish identity, intensified by recent historical experience, which persists long after the loss of faith. Every Jew can say of the *Shoah*, "It happened to *us*." For non-Jews, the *Shoah* is something that happened to *them*. Just as no Armenian can ever entirely forget the Armenian genocide, Holocaust consciousness has become an ineradicable component of the Jewish psyche.[54] Some Jews have attempted to minimize or blot out awareness of the Holocaust, but all it takes is a swastika painted on a synagogue or another Jewish institution to recall them to awareness.[55] Rubenstein argued that religion is more than a system of beliefs; it is also a system of historical memories, shared rituals, and customs by which members of a community cope with or celebrate crucial moments in their own lives and the life of their inherited community. He thus maintained that religion is not so much dependent upon belief as upon practices related to the life cycle and a sense of shared history and culture. No matter how tenuous the faith of the average Jew or Christian, he or she would normally find his or her inherited tradition the most suitable vehicle for consecrating such events as the birth of a child or a marriage. In a crisis such as the death of a parent, spouse, or child, the need to turn to the rituals of one's inherited tradition would be even more urgent.

In the aftermath of the *Shoah*, with the rebirth of an independent Jewish state for the first time since antiquity, there was a certain plausibility to the argument that a people that is at home on its own land lives a very different kind of life than a band of nomadic wanderers. During the whole period of their wanderings, the vast majority of the Jewish people prayed that they might be restored to the land of their origin. Wherever they dwelt in the Diaspora, their lives and their safety were wholly dependent upon the tolerance of others. During the two thousand years of the Diaspora, Jewish history always had a goal, namely, return to the homeland. That goal was given expression in prayers, originally written in the aftermath of the Judeo-Roman War, that are still recited three times daily in the traditional liturgy.[56]

If the goal of Jewish history was return to the land of Israel, there could be a sense, at least in principle, in which Jewish history came to an end when that goal was attained and a Jewish state was established in Israel. It may have made sense, Rubenstein argued, to worship a God of history while Jewish history was unfulfilled, that is, while Jews still envisioned the goal of their history as a return to Israel in the distant future. The Jewish situation changed radically when that goal appeared to have been attained. In recent years, however, Rubenstein has recognized a fundamental problem in the claim that Jewish history had come to an end, if only in principle, with the return of the Jewish people to the land of Israel.

In one sense, the notion that the return constituted the end in principle to Jewish history can be validated by both the traditional prayer book and rabbinic literature. The theme of exile and return permeates Jewish religious thought. Nevertheless, any claim that the state of Israel constitutes *in actuality* the end of Jewish history must confront the obvious fact that the "end" has been followed by a cycle of wars and violence between the returnees and the Arab communities domiciled in the region. From the Arab perspective, the Jewish "return" constitutes a wholly unacceptable colonialist intrusion into their historic lands. The "return" could only be regarded as having succeeded if a viable and realistic peace settlement were achieved between Israel and its neighbors. Unfortunately, the prospects for such a peace are slight at best. It seems more likely that Israel and her neighbors will be locked in a painfully long period of conflict for the foreseeable future, and that is hardly an end to history.[57] At the time of this writing, moreover, there appears to be a critical mass of radical Muslims who will *never* accept the existence of the state of Israel in any form. Calling for unremitting *jihad* against Israel, the Muslim extremist groups, which have mobilized a steady stream of suicide bombers, proclaim in Arabic, if not in English, the destruction of the Israeli state and its people as their ultimate goal.[58] The conflict has been exacerbated by the deep wound to Muslim pride involved in the Israeli military victories since the 1948 war of independence. As a result, Nazi propaganda radically demonizing the Jews has found renewed life in Muslim countries. Denials of the Holocaust, coupled with regret that Hitler did not finish the job, have been expressed in *Al-Akhbar,* the Egyptian government's daily newspaper.[59] Antisemitic allegations of a Jewish world conspiracy and radical Jewish evil had been largely absent from the Islamic world before the current conflict. They are now widely circulated in the media of that world.[60] Both *The Protocols of the Elders of Zion* and Hitler's *Mein Kampf* have been translated into Arabic and are widely disseminated.[61] With the proliferation of weapons of mass destruction, Israelis must reckon with the possibility that their attempted return could end in a nuclear or biochemical holocaust.[62] Clearly the "goal" of Jewish history has not been reached. By no means is Jewish history at an end.

Rubenstein's view of the human condition has a strongly Hobbesian component. The English philosopher Thomas Hobbes (1588–1679) had postulated that originally men and women lived in a "state of nature," an original human condition of war of "every man against every man" that preceded the founding of civil society.[63] Hobbes understood that human beings cannot long tolerate such a condition of moral and social chaos. In Hobbes's version of the social contract, human beings surrender their liberty to a sovereign to whom they pledge their unconditional obedience in the expectation that the sovereign will use his or her power to enable subjects to live in civil society in security and felicity. In describing the state of nature, Hobbes did not intend to depict actual historical origins. His purpose was to demonstrate the necessity of entering into a covenant with a ruling authority if people were to enjoy *limited* liberty compatible with a peaceful and felicitous existence. Nevertheless, Hobbes denied that the state of nature was altogether mythical or hypothetical. On the contrary, all sovereigns and, in modern times, all sovereign states are in the state of nature vis-à-vis their peers. Normally prudence dictates that sovereigns find means other than war to settle their disputes. However, when words and persuasion fail, resort to war always remains an option. Unfortunately it is problematic to think that the conflict between radical Muslims and Israel will be resolved by words and persuasion. That reality has meant that Israel remains in a continual state of war—at times high intensity, at times low intensity—with neighbors who, to say the least, would not mourn its destruction.

Just as Rubenstein had insisted in 1966 that Jewish theology could not ignore the question of God and the death camps, today he insists that Jewish theology, especially in its view of God, cannot ignore the current realities of post-Holocaust Jewish history, especially in Israel. That reality must include the potentially devastating consequences of the conflict between Israel and its neighbors. For the traditionally minded, there is no problem. The God of the Bible has promised God's people "the whole land of Israel" and in God's own time God will be faithful to this promise. Similarly, Christian end-timers have no problem. They consider the return of the Jews to the Holy Land to be the prelude to Armageddon and the final return of Christ in glory. Even a nuclear Armageddon would not be regarded as disconfirmation of that belief.

On the other hand, nontraditional Jews may have a problem. The fundamental issue between Judaism and Christianity, namely, whether Jesus of Nazareth is the Messiah, need not require immediate resolution. The situation between Judaism and radical Islam is altogether different. That conflict concerns claims to the possession of territory that some on both sides regard as religiously legitimated and therefore as nonnegotiable. For millennia human beings have gone to war over this kind of disagreement. Not only is Israel the Holy Land for Jews; in Muslim tradition Jerusalem is *al-Quds*, the Holy City, and the *al-Aqsa* mosque on the Temple Mount is the site of Muhammad's ascent to heaven (*Mi'raj*) after his miraculous journey in a single night from Mecca to Jerusalem (*Qur'an* 17:1). Moreover, Muslims divide the world into the *dar al-Islam*, the abode of Islam, and the *dar al-harb*, the abode of war, the domain into which Muslims could and should expand.[64] For centuries all of the land of Israel was effectively under Muslim control and, as such, *dar al-Islam*. This dominion ended with the conquest of Jerusalem by armed forces under British command on 9 December 1917. Legitimate Muslim leaders have been traditionally obligated to wage *jihad* to return it to *dar al-Islam*. This is especially compelling when a territory was forcibly removed from the abode of Islam, as, in the minds of most Muslims, was the territory of Israel.[65] From a radical Muslim perspective, contemporary Israel cannot be regarded as other than *dar al-harb*.

Since Rubenstein has rejected the God of History, he cannot argue that God favors Israel in the current conflict. Nor does he hold that Muslims who seek to destroy the state of Israel are villains. He has long argued that one must distinguish between *villains* and *enemies*. Villains gratuitously harm their neighbors. Enemies make war when disputes with their neighbors cannot be resolved by peaceful means. Seeing radical Muslims as *enemies* rather than *villains* may be difficult for Israelis because radical Muslim propaganda has recycled Nazi propaganda to depict Jews as the most despicable of villains. Nevertheless, Rubenstein's views concerning Israel's historical vicissitudes are consistent with his ideas about God after Auschwitz. Understandably, his personal sympathies and commitments are with the Israelis, especially after the Holocaust, but he has consistently excluded providential intent from his idea of God and has regarded both creation and destruction transcending the human categories of good and evil as inherent in the life of Divinity.

But if the life of Divinity transcends the categories of good and evil, where would the order, stability, and justice required by the human community come from? Rubenstein holds that they can only come from men and women who take seriously Thomas Hobbes's admonition concerning the consequences of disorder inherent in the war of all against all that characterizes the state of nature: "In such condition," writes Hobbes, "there is no place for industry, because the fruit thereof is uncertain: and consequently no culture of the earth; no navigation . . . ; no arts; no letters; no society; and which is worst of all, continual fear and danger of violent death; and the life of man, solitary, poor, nasty, brutish, and short."[66] Rubenstein's outlook sees turbulence and conflict as endemic to the human condition. The turbulence can be held in check only for a time by those possessing superior power and, we hope, wisdom. If the rise and fall of empires are an expression of the turbulence and conflict within the Ground of Being, then it is, as Hobbes maintained, the force and power of the sovereign or the sovereign community that is the guarantor of peace, order, and stability.

Zachary Braiterman, one of Rubenstein's insightful critics, states that "the problem of evil and suffering ultimately threatens to scuttle Rubenstein's Dionysian faith, just as it threatens traditional faith in the God of History." Braiterman argues that "a God so involved in the world and its attendant suffering becomes deeply complicit and can only invite the wrath and enmity of her aggrieved children."[67] Rubenstein's rejoinder emphasizes that turbulence and conflict are the more or less inescapable prices we pay for life. No person, community, or nation is assured of tranquility, felicity, and security. Men and women must work hard for such good fortune, knowing that it may not be of long duration. For Rubenstein, there is absolutely nothing for which God could be held blameworthy. One could only express "wrath and enmity" toward a God who set conditions for God's favor in a covenant and then failed to deliver. The whole thrust of Rubenstein's theology has been to reject such a God. It follows that religion is not about the expectation of personal and communal reward for good conduct. It is about *identity, historical memory, and the familial and communal sharing and commemoration of sacred times and seasons in the life of the individual and the community.*

## MENDING THE WORLD

One of the most powerful religious responses to the Holocaust has come from the philosopher Emil Fackenheim, who left his native Germany in 1939 after imprisonment in the Nazi concentration camp at Sachsenhausen, taught for many years at the University of Toronto, and then immigrated to Israel. According to Fackenheim, the Holocaust was the most radically disorienting "epoch making event" in all of Jewish history.[68] Fackenheim insisted that the Jewish people must respond to this shattering challenge with a reaffirmation of God's presence in history. Although he acknowledged that it is impossible to affirm God's saving presence at Auschwitz, Fackenheim insisted that a "commanding Voice" spoke at Auschwitz, and that it enunciated a "614th commandment" to supplement the 613 commandments of traditional Judaism. The new commandment was said to be that "the authentic Jew of today is forbidden to hand Hitler yet another, posthumous victory." Fackenheim spelled out the 614th commandment as follows:

> We are, first, commanded to survive as Jews, lest the Jewish people perish. We are commanded, second, to remember in our very guts and bones the martyrs of the Holocaust, lest their memory perish. We are forbidden, thirdly, to deny or despair of God, however much we may have to contend with him or with belief in him, lest Judaism perish. We are forbidden, finally, to despair of the world as the place which is to become the kingdom of God, lest we help make it a meaningless place in which God is dead or irrelevant and everything is permitted. To abandon any of these imperatives, in response to Hitler's victory at Auschwitz, would be to hand him yet other, posthumous victories.[69]

Few, if any, post-Holocaust religious statements by a Jewish thinker were better known as the twentieth century drew to its close.[70] For some time Fackenheim's 614th commandment struck a deep chord in Jews of every social level and religious commitment. Much, but by no means all, of Fackenheim's writing is on a philosophic and theological level beyond the competence of the ordinary layperson. Not so this passage, which is largely responsible for the fact that Fackenheim's interpretation of the Holocaust became for a time the most influential within the Jewish community. A people that has endured catastrophic defeat is likely to see the survival of their community and its traditions as a supreme imperative. By referring to a divine command, Fackenheim gave potent expression to this aspiration. Instead of questioning whether the traditional Jewish understanding of God could be maintained after Auschwitz, he insisted that those who questioned God's presence to Israel, *even in the death camps*, were accomplices of the worst destroyer the Jews have ever known. The passion and the psychological power of this position are undeniable.

Nevertheless, Fackenheim's position can have unfortunate consequences. Those Jews "who denied or despaired" of the scriptural God have been cast in the role of accomplices of Hitler. Given the influence of Fackenheim's ideas within the Jewish community, that is a matter of considerable seriousness. Moreover, Fackenheim went so far as to suggest that those who did not hear the "commanding Voice" at Auschwitz were *willfully* rejecting God: "In my view, nothing less will do than to say that a commanding Voice speaks from Auschwitz, and that there are Jews who hear it and Jews who *stop their ears*."[71] Fackenheim seems to have either excluded or ignored the possibility that some Jews might honestly be unable to believe that God was in any way present at Auschwitz, no matter how metaphorically the idea was presented. To stop one's ears is, after all, a voluntary act. The practical consequence of Fackenheim's insistence that the "commanding Voice" had prohibited Jews to deny or despair of God was to limit for a time meaningful theological debate on the Holocaust *within* the Jewish community to those who could affirm, as did Fackenheim, that the God of Israel was somehow present at Auschwitz. Instead of seeing the Holocaust as the shared trauma that had shaken every Jew—and certainly every Jewish theologian—to the core of his or her being, the Jewish community has, following Fackenheim's lead, often treated theological dissenters as if they were "accomplices" who handed Hitler "yet other, posthumous victories." Fackenheim is not responsible for this development. But even as his description of the commanding Voice gave expression to a deep-seated Jewish response to the Holocaust, it also defined the limits beyond which the Jewish community was apparently unwilling to tolerate theological debate.

In spite of its power, Fackenheim's position was not without difficulty even for the tradition he sought to defend. Given Fackenheim's conviction that revelation is inseparable from interpretation, it was not clear whether the commanding Voice was to be taken as real or metaphorical. There is now reason to believe that Fackenheim would reject both alternatives and would hold that the commandment would have been unreal absent an affirmative Jewish response. Taken literally, there does not appear to be any credible evidence that anybody heard the 614th commandment, as indeed Fackenheim's later description of how he came to write the passage indicates. In *To Mend the World* (1982), Fackenheim told his readers that after he had come to the conclusion that the Holocaust was a radical challenge to Jewish faith, "my first response was to formulate a '614th commandment.'"[72] Clearly, as understood in traditional Judaism, one does not formulate a commandment. It derives from a divine source. In any event, whatever the psychological power of the 614th commandment, its status as commandment remains—perhaps unavoidably—ambiguous.

Fackenheim's critics also found considerable difficulty with his assertion that the commanding Voice had enjoined Jews to "survive as Jews." In the case of traditional Jews, no such commandment was necessary. They have always believed that Jewish religious survival was a divine imperative. They had no need of an Auschwitz to receive such an injunction. In the case of secularized Jews, the commandment appeared to be a case of pedagogic overkill. It hardly seemed likely that even a jealous God would require the annihilation of six million Jews as the occasion for a commandment forbidding Jews to permit the demise of their tradition.

Perhaps the most important aspect of the 614th commandment was the injunction not to deny or despair of God, lest Hitler be given "yet other, posthumous victories." Here Fackenheim confronted the fundamental issue of Holocaust theology. Fackenheim told his readers what God has commanded. Does this mean that Fackenheim perpetrated a fiction in order to maintain the theological integrity of his reading of Judaism? Given Fackenheim's faith in some sense of a Divine Presence, it was hardly likely that he could have thought of God as absent from Auschwitz. As Fackenheim came to realize that the real difficulty lay in formulating a view of God that took the Holocaust into account, he understood that one could no longer speak of a *saving* presence at Auschwitz. Yet utter defeat and annihilation could not be the last word. A way out of the ashes had to be found. The 614th commandment expressed what most religious Jews regard as their sacred obligation in response to the Holocaust. In the language of Jewish faith, that response could most appropriately be communicated in the imagery of the commandments. Fackenheim's 614th commandment is religiously and existentially problematic. That, however, is beside the point. *It is perhaps best to see Fackenheim's 614th commandment as a cri de coeur, a cry of the heart, transmuted into the language of the sacred.* That would at least help to explain why it has touched so many Jews so deeply.

In *To Mend the World*, Fackenheim revisited the Holocaust as a radical "counter-testimony" to religious faith.[73] Specifically, he turned his attention to the question of how the process of mending and healing after the catastrophe could begin. He used a term taken from the tradition of Jewish mysticism, *Tikkun*, "to mend or restore," to denote the process. In the case of Jews and Judaism, Fackenheim regarded the creation of the state of Israel "on the heels of the Holocaust" as the most authentic response to the National Socialist "logic of destruction" that came to full expression in the Holocaust. Incomplete and endangered though it might be, Fackenheim urged, the establishment of the state of Israel would be the fundamental Jewish act of *Tikkun*. It constitutes a profound attempt to overcome the Holocaust, not in theory or by a return to the grudging sufferance of the Christian world, but by the creation of conditions in which, for the first time in two thousand years, Jews have assumed responsibility for their own future, both biologically and spiritually. "The state of Israel," Fackenheim has written, "is collectively what the [Holocaust] survivor is individually—testimony on behalf of all mankind to life against death, to sanity against madness, to Jewish self-affirmation against every form of flight from it."[74]

According to Fackenheim, if the broken threads of Judaism are to be mended—and at this writing it is not clear that they can be—the mending can take place only in Israel, if for no other reason than the fact that in the Diaspora Jews remain dependent upon others for their survival. For Fackenheim, this *Tikkun* will involve both religious and secular Jews, who are bound together by a common inheritance that includes not only the Holocaust but the Bible. Neither the secular nor the religious Jew would have found a home in Israel, were it not for the Bible. The Holocaust may have driven them to the eastern shores of the Mediterranean. Only the Bible has the power to keep them there.

Fackenheim may have overloaded the significance of the state of Israel. He recalls, for example, that "the poet Yehuda Halevi wrote that Jerusalem would not be rebuilt until Jews yearned for her very dust and stones. Today one travels through the replanted valleys of Galilee and is lost in *wonder*. And one walks through the Jewish Quarter of the Old City, ravaged by the Jordanians a generation ago, and is filled with a strange *serenity*."[75] As Braiterman points out, "the very words *wonder* and *serenity* automatically ascribe a superordinate theological and philosophical significance to the State."[76] The language overheats even more when Fackenheim argues that the split between religious and secular Jews and their very different cultures is being overcome in Israel "with world-historical consequences as yet unknown."[77] If anything, the tensions between extreme Orthodox Jews and non-Orthodox Jews have intensified since Fackenheim made that judgment. Moreover, the conflict in the Middle East may have "world-historical consequences," but they are more likely to result from what the Harvard political scientist Samuel Huntington calls the "clash of civilizations" than from an overcoming of the split between religious and secular Jews in Israel.[78]

Having experienced Jewish powerlessness as a young man in Nazi Germany, Fackenheim is understandably appreciative of the society Jews have been able to create in Israel, a society in which Jews can defend themselves. Fackenheim has characterized the state of Israel as "a moral necessity."[79] He rested that claim on the basis of the Holocaust and the fact that in its aftermath the great majority of the surviving Jews neither wanted to return to, nor were wanted by, the countries of their origin. However, like North America when the first white settlers arrived, Palestine was not an empty country when Jews went there after the Holocaust. It was part of the predominantly Muslim Middle East in which the Palestinians, both Muslim and Christian, saw Jewish immigration as a settler-colonialist movement similar to that undertaken by Europeans in the earlier age of imperialism. Palestinians were determined to resist the movement by whatever means they could. Moreover, while the Jewish entry into Palestine solved one refugee problem, it created another, one that increased greatly with the passage of time and the inability of any of the nations in the region to accept and integrate the Palestinians into their midst. What for Fackenheim was the supreme Jewish act of *Tikkun* was for the Palestinians the intrusion into their region of a group alien in both religion and culture. It was also the beginning of the monstrous problem of men, women, and children in refugee camps yearning to return to homes and villages in an Israel that could neither trust them nor integrate them.

In a series of wars, starting with Israel's 1948 war of independence and continuing until the period in which we write, the Israelis demonstrated that they had learned two fundamental lessons from of the Holocaust: first, that threats against one's existence must be taken with the utmost seriousness; second, that "human rights" are functionally meaningless unless one is a member of a community that has the power and the resolve to defend its members' rights. In the Holocaust no community was willing or able to defend the Jews. In this book's epilogue we will return to this point in greater detail, but whatever meaning one ascribes to the concept of human rights, they were of little consequence to the Nazis' victims. In the final analysis, a community must rely upon its military and diplomatic capabilities if it is to survive.

"The heart of every *authentic* response to the Holocaust," asserted Fackenheim, "is a commitment to the autonomy and security of the state of Israel."[80] Although Rubenstein is as committed to the security of the state of Israel as Fackenheim, he took a bleakly Hobbesian view of the enduring Arab-Israeli conflict. Since its inception, he contended, Israel bore more than a little resemblance to Hobbes's depiction of "persons of sovereign authority" in *Leviathan*. Like them Israel would remain in an unending "posture of war," sometimes hot, sometimes cold, sometimes punctuated by truce with its neighbors. Moreover, the strife would be exacerbated by profound religious and cultural differences and conflicting territorial claims. This analysis did not mean that Rubenstein assessed the enterprise as without great merit. He agreed with Fackenheim that creation of the state was the authentic Jewish response to the Holocaust and the risks involved were both necessary and unavoidable. Nevertheless, just as he refused to see God's involvement in the Holocaust, so too he saw no such involvement in the continuing conflict. In spite of the Holocaust, God was on the side of neither the Israelis nor the Arabs. Insofar as a resolution of the conflict was possible, it would be determined by the relative strength and determination of the warring parties. In the worst case scenario, there is a vast difference between being led before a firing squad at a mass grave pit or into a mass gas chamber and dying in combat in defense of one's home and family.

## WHITHER POST-HOLOCAUST THEOLOGY?

After Auschwitz, does the ancient and hallowed faith in the biblical God of covenant and election have a future among religious Jews and religious Christians as well? Undoubtedly it does. Indeed, despite the problems that continue to haunt it, that theological option is probably the one most likely to have a future. Whatever doubts secularized Jews or Christians may currently entertain, faith in the God of covenant and election has been the hallowed, authoritative faith of these communities for millennia. In its multiple versions, that faith has given Jews and Christians two supremely important gifts, the gifts of meaning and hope. In particular, instead of viewing experience as a series of unfortunate and essentially meaningless events, biblical-rabbinic faith has enabled the Jewish people to see their history as a meaningful expression of their relations with their God. Moreover, no matter how desperate their situation became, their faith enabled them to hope that, sooner or later, "those who sow in tears will reap in joy." In different but related ways, believing Christians have made similar affirmations.

The traditional biblical-rabbinic view that God is the ultimate Actor in history and that the Jewish people are bound to God by an eternal covenant remains the most coherent, logically consistent way of understanding Jewish experience and history that is acceptable to the Jewish people. Rubenstein has pointed out the bitter, yet inescapable, consequences of holding this faith after Auschwitz. Nevertheless, no credible theological alternative to some form of the theology of covenant and election, however interpreted, has emerged that does not deny key foundations of normative Judaism. Even Rubenstein insists on retaining the language of covenant and election in the liturgy, leaving each individual to interpret its meaning in accordance with his or her insights and experience.

Some form of faith in covenant and election appears to be indispensable to the Jewish and Christian religious mainstreams. One does not have to be a Jew or a Christian to be a monotheist. What distinguishes Judaism is the faith that God has chosen the Jewish people to serve and obey God by fulfilling the commandments revealed in Scripture and authoritatively interpreted by the rabbis. Moreover, it can be argued that the Christian world *expects* Jews to affirm faith in the biblical God of covenant and election for a simple but compelling reason: from Christianity's perspective, the Jews were the chosen people to whom God sent God's Son as humanity's Redeemer. In the Christian narrative, of course, the Jews failed to recognize the true nature of Jesus Christ. Hence, in that narrative, God's election passed from the Israel "according to the flesh" to the Israel "according to the spirit," namely, to all those who have recognized Christ's true nature. Nevertheless, most believing Christians still have no doubt that, sooner or later, at least a "saving remnant" of Israel will finally see the light.[81] Like Judaism, Christianity cannot abandon the doctrines of covenant and election.

Christian influence on Jews and Judaism is far greater than is commonly recognized. By virtue of the fact that both Christians and Jews regard the Bible as of divine inspiration, Christians give Jews a context of plausibility for their most deeply held beliefs. If Jews lived in a culture in which the majority accorded the Bible no greater respect than we accord the Greek myths, Jews might still hold fast to their beliefs but they would receive no external reinforcement. Even the fact that Jews and Christians disagree about the true nature of Jesus reinforces the context of plausibility, for the disagreement is about the true meaning of the Book both regard as divinely inspired.

The profound influence of American Christianity on American Judaism, even on Orthodox Judaism, ought not to be underestimated. The world's largest Jewish community lives in the United States, which remains decisively Christian. To a considerable degree that community's security, along with that of the state of Israel, depends on the behavior of American Christians. The state of Israel's strongest American Christian supporters are conservative Christians who believe in the inerrancy of scriptural revelation, especially end-timers or premillennial dispensationalists. As conservative Christian influence continues to grow within the United States, it will encourage Jews to affirm a faith rooted in biblical revelation.

Thus both external and internal influences foster a renewed Jewish affirmation of covenant and election. Even many Jews whose reasons for remaining in the synagogue are primarily cultural and psychological rather than religious are likely to convince themselves that the principal beliefs of the Jewish mainstream are true. To do otherwise would be to create too great a dissonance between belief and practice. If the survival of the Jews as a group outside of Israel is perceived to depend upon religious affiliation and some measure of Jewish religious practice—which in turn are thought to be legitimated by faith in the God of covenant and election—even those whose basic commitment is cultural are likely to find some way to affirm the *only system of religious belief that legitimates Jewish survival.* The alternative is to abandon Jewish identification altogether.

For those who question traditional belief after Auschwitz yet continue to participate in Jewish religious life, including regular attendance at synagogue worship, their beliefs and their practice will be in tension as long as they cannot affirm the traditional foundations of Jewish religious life. During the synagogue service, for example, when they are called to read the Torah, they are obliged to recite the blessing "Praised be Thou, O Lord our God who has *chosen us from among all peoples* and given us the Torah" (italics added). Traditionally, the entire body of Jewish religious practice was founded upon belief in God's revelation to Moses, the patriarchs, and the prophets and its authoritative interpretation by the rabbis. Those Jews who cannot affirm this fundamental body of belief will experience a painful dissonance between their beliefs and their religious practices. As the horror of the Holocaust recedes in time, religious Jews may once again find themselves reducing the dissonance by declaring with the traditional prayer book that "because of our sins all this has come upon us." That time has not yet come, but it may be on its way.

# Epilogue

# Business as Usual?
# Ethics after the Holocaust

*In many ways, the post-Holocaust world is a broken world. . . . We now know that ordinary human beings are capable of doing and tolerating terrible things. We cannot rule out the possibility that other societies in the future will build concentration camps, gas chambers, and crematoria. Nor do we have any guarantees that the world will react any differently than it did in the past.*

Victoria J. Barnett, *Bystanders: Conscience and Complicity during the Holocaust*

*Arbeit macht frei.* Work makes one free. That slogan arched the entry to Nazi concentration and death camps. Attention usually focuses on the principal extermination centers—Auschwitz-Birkenau, Belzec, Chelmno, Majdanek, Sobibor, and Treblinka—where millions of Jews were dispatched on arrival. The Germans and their collaborators also managed thousands of forced-labor camps. According to the historian Shmuel Krakowski, "more than 8.4 million foreign workers were employed in Germany at the end of 1944. Among them were about 2 million prisoners of war, some 5.7 million so-called civilian workers, and 700,000 concentration camp prisoners."[1] Especially the Jews among the slave laborers knew the irony in the Nazi slogan, for *Vernichtung durch Arbeit*—annihilation by work—was the reality for them and many others as well.

During the scarcities of wartime, Jewish labor was useful, even essential. Nevertheless, periodic economically motivated exemptions from death did not last for Europe's Jews. Once the Final Solution began, if Jews were spared at all, they would be worked to death. Nazi Germany's policies led to a crushing defeat. Does it follow, then, that genocide serves nobody well and that the Nazis would have advanced even their self-interest, had they made more sensible use of the Jews?

355

To say yes takes too lightly the fact that relatively few Germans, civilian or military, judged any cost sufficiently compelling to make them intervene decisively against the destruction process.

Within the Third Reich, ridding German culture of Jews was a fixed, predetermined end that governed other policies. The issue was not this aim's validity but how the goal could most practically be attained. The drive behind this objective, however, did not rest solely on ideological or patriotic beliefs. Beyond concerns about security and survival, there were careers to advance, honors to win, and profits to extract. In such circumstances, it was business as usual and then some. For example, some German corporations invested huge sums to construct factories that could capitalize on slaves provided by the SS. Already intertwined extensively, the private and governmental sectors found such arrangements more than acceptable.[2] By consuming Jewish labor, German industry got cheap energy. The by-products partly assuaged Heinrich Himmler's insatiable hunger for Jewish corpses. Genocide had its benefits. Thus rationalized, Nazi slavery created nothing less than a new form of human society, one predicated—neither figuratively nor randomly but literally and systematically—on working certain people to death for political gain and economic profit. The care with which estimates were made is documented by records from the SS Business Administration Main Office (*Wirtschaftsverwaltungshauptamt* or WVHA). Calculating that a concentration camp inmate could be expected to work for nine months—a figure that turned out to be too high— SS economists reckoned that a total profit of 1631 reichsmarks could be forecast for an inmate's labor. This calculation figured the cost precisely: food, clothing, and RM2 for burning the corpse. Included on the profit side of the ledger were the benefits of an efficient use of the inmate's effects: gold from teeth, clothes, valuables, money. Though no cash figure was mentioned, this report noted that additional income could be realized from utilization of the corpse's bones and ashes.[3]

Other illustrations from medicine, law, education, science, and the civil service clarify another crucial point: the Holocaust could not have occurred without help from countless professionally skilled civilians and the institutions they represented. As the implications of that claim are drawn out, the most important one will not be that Germans of the Hitler era were a special breed, a people unnaturally irresponsible and cruel. On the contrary, this German case is better regarded as symptomatic of potentialities that are widespread in modern civilization. With that proposition in mind, one more fact with ominous possibilities for the future bears underscoring. Typically, the professions and their institutions, at least as they existed in Germany during the 1930s and 1940s, proved incapable of stopping mass murder. Quite to the contrary, those professions and their institutions moved genocide along until it could be stopped only by superior military force from the outside. That fact indicates that civilization's ethical traditions and moral sensibilities were inadequate too, which prompts Victoria Barnett to state correctly that "the post-Holocaust world is a broken world."[4] Therefore, as this book draws to its close, attention to the professions and to ethics after the Holocaust seems fitting.

## ORDINARY OFFICIALS, EXTRAORDINARY TASKS

People often assume that a society's well-educated elite will not lead a nation into temptation but deliver it from evil. The case under scrutiny here unfortunately does not validate that assumption.[5] German doctors and lawyers, for instance, were quite prepared to advance Hitler's agenda. The same holds for German educators from the kindergarten to the university. As for scientists and bureaucrats, they may not have been so ideologically committed as many German teachers or as financially motivated as the captains of German industry, but these professionals also joined their peers in medicine and law to salute the Führer. They did not always flock eagerly to the swastika—indeed they sometimes resented and even resisted attempts to Nazify their professions—yet by sticking to the practical, problem-solving rationality that their professional training emphasized, they remained both sufficiently apolitical and nationalistic to suit Hitler's purposes. The following question, therefore, suggests itself: are professional elites more likely to side with or against the reigning political establishment? The German case is instructive, not merely because it helps to corroborate the former position, but also because it makes clear that the genocidal intentions of an established regime, far from having to beg or coerce support from the professions, may prove so attractive that an elite will support murderous regimes. With those possibilities in mind, let us look more closely at some details.

In the Holocaust's lore, few names are more infamous than Josef Mengele's. Long thought to be hiding somewhere in South America, this man was the target of an extensive international manhunt. Acting on a tip on 31 May 1985, West German police raided the home of Hans Sedlmeier, an employee of the Mengele family business. Letters were discovered, some of them apparently written by Mengele himself. Their trail led to São Paulo, Brazil. The ensuing investigation revealed that Mengele had lived in the vicinity for some thirteen years until he drowned in 1979. Early in the summer of 1985 forensic experts testified that the remains of a man thought to be Wolfgang Gerhard were actually Mengele's. In March 1986 Mengele's death was corroborated further when X-rays of his teeth were shown to match those of the skeleton experts had previously identified as that of Mengele.

Born in 1911, the "Angel of Death," as he came to be known, was especially loathsome because he was a doctor, a healer turned exterminator. Son of a prominent German family, handsome and elegant, Mengele was bright and studied hard. He enjoyed philosophy and earned two doctorates, a Ph.D. in anthropology as well as an M.D. He was a competent, qualified researcher with a special interest in genetics. Before arriving at Auschwitz by choice on 30 May 1943, SS-*Hauptsturmführer* (Captain) Mengele had served three years with a Waffen-SS unit in the East. There he had been wounded and declared unfit for combat. His numerous military decorations included the Iron Cross First and Second Class. As an SS doctor at Auschwitz, he would send some tens of thousands of Jews to their deaths.

Mengele met the transports arriving at Auschwitz. Directing a cacophony of life and death, his baton pointed left or right, selecting who should go directly to the gas and who should be saved for work. Meeting trains, however, was not the only activity to fill the time of Dr. Mengele and his medical associates at Auschwitz.[6] For example, Mengele specialized in experiments on Jewish children—twins whenever possible—to find ways to increase the birthrate of German women. He experimented by surgery or syringe on several hundred pairs of children. Very few of these girls and boys survived.[7] Other physicians also certified prisoners to be fit for torture, injected drugs to obtain confessions, and practiced surgery on death camp inmates. They regularly monitored the gas chambers as well. Ostensibly acting as scientists, Nazi doctors also joined Mengele in research.[8]

Human beings are often the most suitable subjects for medical experiments. Nazi doctors did not have to settle for dogs or monkeys. Their guinea pigs were human, although Nazi research aimed to exclude Jews from that species. In Auschwitz's society of total domination, the experimentation process could be streamlined. No informed consent from the subjects was necessary, nor was any compensation owed them. Inhibiting moral restraints took a back seat to practical and ideological passions for knowledge. In the name of Nazi science and cost-effective rationality, anything and everything could be done to these prisoners—and was. Nor was the work done solely by individual researchers. German pharmaceutical firms took advantage of opportunities to test their new products on prisoners. Except as data to be studied, no one had much regard for the victims of these experiments. Exposure to low pressure, cold, and sea water; deliberate infection of specifically inflicted wounds to produce gangrene; injection of caustic chemicals into women's uteri; mutilation and grafting of limbs; detailed study of skulls removed from Jewish bodies with scientific care—extraordinary research of this kind was done by respectable professionals who reported their findings at scientific meetings where no protests were recorded. Although some of the research, had it involved the willing participation of the subjects, might have constituted normal attempts to extend medical knowledge, most was scientifically useless. The point, however, is not that only German doctors under a dictator like Hitler are capable of utilizing defenseless human beings as the unwilling or unwitting subjects in problematic projects of demographic and genetic engineering. That potential knows no national boundaries.[9] Medicine, no less than war, can be politics carried out by other means.

Germany's medicine had long been preeminent in the world, and by no means were all German doctors like Mengele. Most accepted only fragments of the Nazi ideology or were simply professionally indifferent to it. Probably fewer than four hundred of the ninety thousand German doctors actively took part in experiments such as those conducted at Auschwitz. Yet the medical profession as a whole did practically nothing to call such activity into question. Nor had it raised any protest in 1933 when Jewish doctors were restricted from practicing. Silence obtained in the latter case partly because Gentile physicians benefited economically from a reduction of competition for positions and patients. Throughout the Nazi era, the potential for dissent was also minimized because the German medical profession had no tradition of overt political involvement.

If German doctors typically regarded themselves as apolitical, it is also noteworthy that between 1933 and 1945 more than 30 percent were members of the Reich's Physicians' League, an adjunct to the Nazi Party. They were well-represented in the SS as well. Patterns in other German professions were not much different. If the majority of German lawyers, for example, neither held Nazi beliefs before Hitler took power nor were converted wholeheartedly to them afterward, most were civil servants, including judges, whose actions corroborated the thesis that modern bureaucracies will serve any master with the power to control them.[10] Long accustomed to an authoritarian jurisprudence, the bench and the bar found the Weimar Republic more anomalous than the Third Reich, largely because so little in the German legal profession changed during that democratic interlude. Nor were Hitler's nationalism and antisemitism a liability, as far as most lawyers were concerned. On the contrary, German lawyers overwhelmingly backed the revitalization of Germany that Hitler promised, and the Gentile majority welcomed ways to curtail the competition brought about by the disproportionate number of Jews in this profession. Thus laws, decrees, decisions, and sentences were handed down in accord with Hitler's wishes by persons disciplined in German legal training. Add to these considerations the fact that German lawyers never had the social status enjoyed by leaders in business or the military, and the following conclusion rings true: if one were seeking effective opposition to Hitler within the professions, the bench and the bar would have been nearly the last places to look. Risking their careers, if not their families and their lives, heroic individual exceptions could be found in this case, as in all the others discussed in this epilogue, but more than anything else they would only prove the rule that professional expertise in Germany sided far more with Hitler than against him. In the lawyers' case, moreover, that rule contains a telling reminder: a society's legal experts may not outlaw genocide but legitimate and even legalize it instead.

For the most part, German school teachers and university professors were not Hitler's adversaries either. Quite the opposite, the teaching profession proved one of the most reliable segments of the population as far as National Socialism was concerned. Throughout the Weimar period, Germany's educational establishment, continuing its long authoritarian tradition, remained unreconciled to democracy.[11] Once in power, the Nazis expunged dissenting instructors, but there were not many. On the other hand, at least two leading Nazis, the rabid antisemites Heinrich Himmler and Julius Streicher, had formerly been teachers. Eventually more than 30 percent of the top Nazi Party leadership came from that background. Teachers, especially from elementary schools, were by far the largest professional group represented in the party. Altogether almost 97 percent of them belonged to the Nazi Teachers' Association, and more than 30 percent of that number were members of the Nazi Party itself. From such instructors, German boys and girls learned what the Nazis wanted them to know. Hatred of Jews was central in that curriculum.[12]

If Hitler's German contemporaries gave him strong support, even more loyal were the children of that generation, the young men and women born during or shortly after World War I. Indeed, to a large degree the Nazi effort was a youth movement, led mainly by men in their forties to early fifties who could count on the young people who had grown up deprived in defeated Germany and thus wanted something more. In 1931 antisemitic riots broke out in universities throughout Germany and Austria. They were inspired by the Nazi Student Organization, which counted some 60 percent of all German undergraduates in its ranks, about twice the level of Nazi support at that time among the population as a whole.[13] Far from decrying their students' pro-Nazi actions, many German professors moved into Hitler's orbit. Some three hundred of the nation's most illustrious scholars, for example, signed a declaration urging votes for Hitler just before the decisive election in March 1933.

On the eve of Hitler's rise to power, more than ten percent of Germany's professors were Jewish, as were a quarter of the nation's Nobel laureates. German intellectual and scientific life was drastically diminished as most of them fled the country. Among the remaining professors disillusionment with Nazi ways became increasingly common, stimulated partly by an anti-intellectual streak among Nazi leaders, who always considered this university elite suspect. Nonetheless, whether through a widespread disdain for politics in general, or from a mixture of sympathy, indifference, and fear—if not outright backing—generated by the Third Reich in particular, the German academic community continued to teach and to do research in ways that made it much more Hitler's friend than foe. Educational institutions and leaders are rightly regarded as bulwarks against prejudice, totalitarianism, and mass death, but the Holocaust counsels that educational professions can serve very different ends. Education is not automatically good; everything depends on its quality. The teaching and scholarship done ordinarily in Nazi Germany's schools and universities helped to transmute Auschwitz from an extraordinary possibility into an acceptable routine.

Professions define people. One tragic legacy of the Holocaust is that there can no longer be total innocence in such identifications. For what profession was not implicated in making the Holocaust happen? Attempts to displace Albert Einstein's "Jewish" physics with a superior "Aryan" version constituted utter folly; nevertheless Germany's professional scientific societies allowed themselves to be Nazified.[14] That step helped to make it impossible for many of the nation's best scientists to work there, because they were Jewish. Through 1935, nearly 20 percent of the natural science faculties in Germany were dismissed for that reason. Some twenty contemporary or future Nobel prize winners were among them. This lost scientific expertise returned to haunt Hitler with a vengeance, but the Holocaust shows again that no profession is intrinsically safe from culpability in mass death.

Engineering reveals a similar story.[15] Like the German scientific community, these technocrats were content to leave the affairs of state to Nazi politicians, as long as their own departments and careers advanced. By rising to the challenge of an abundance of Nazi projects, the engineers served themselves on both counts, while meeting Hitler's aims as well. German engineers posed few questions about the ends their efforts achieved, particularly insofar as the Holocaust was concerned, but they handled with distinction their job of calculating precisely the most efficient ways to reach the goals set by their Führer.

An army of professional civil servants expedited the Final Solution too.[16] Conveniently Hitler found at his disposal the expertise of an already existing bureaucracy, which for the most part consisted of hard-working, incorruptible people. Typically, they issued no protests as restrictions against Jewish civil servants were implemented in April 1933. Expressing little dissent at that time, they were not inclined to do so as conditions for the Jews went from bad to worse. New offices such as Göring's Air Ministry and Goebbels's Ministry of Propaganda had to be established after the Nazi victory. Nazis especially committed to handling the Jewish question were put into influential new slots. Yet the Nazi Party never had to restructure or permeate extensively a civil service that would do its bidding without protest. Some officials were dismissed; others were pressured to conform. But most German civil servants toed the line without dissent, and many joined the Nazi Party eagerly. Sincerely believing that carrying out their state duties was the right thing to do, they would help to annihilate millions of human beings with an undisturbed conscience. Related activities, unfortunately, have not been absent from modern bureaucracies before or since.

As Hitler came to power, the established state secretaries and their longtime subordinates were motivated primarily by yearnings for a national revival. Antisemitism was strong among them too, and while these older bureaucrats may have initiated relatively little in the way of anti-Jewish campaigns, they hardly flinched when the Nazis put such plans into motion. Those directives made the German bureaucracy grow, for nearly every branch of the civil service soon needed its so-called "Jewish experts" and the personnel to administer the laws that Nazi racism and antisemitism decreed. Mostly these desks were filled by ordinary, if ambitious, university graduates who had specialized in law and were intent on successful administrative careers. Personally these younger men may not have been zealously antisemitic, but they understood that power and influence were at stake in managing well the Jewish affairs that fell to them. They did not run the Final Solution, but often they worked hard to please their superiors, the party members who infiltrated the civil service at higher levels and made sure the bureaucracy facilitated the evolving stages of expropriation and population elimination that hit the Jews. Antisemitism, nationalism, political calculation, personal ambition: those factors were enough to ensure that, with few individual exceptions, the German civil service—old guard, young men on the rise, or party infiltrators—would make the Final Solution work. Granted, there were rivalries among these offices. The spoils went to those who could extend furthest their offices' influence in deciding the Jewish question. Yet even if competition often exceeded cooperation, the new results still meant death for the Jews.

The destruction of the European Jews—indeed any state-sponsored program of population elimination—required attention to a multitude of details. Among the most important were those involving the *Deutsche Reichsbahn* (German National Railway, or DRB).[17] As Alfred Mierzejewski indicates, the *Reichsbahn* played three crucial parts in the destruction of European Jewry: "It provided logistical support for the construction and operation of the camps; it brought the victims to their deaths; and it carried the booty looted from them to enterprises and agencies in the Reich that exploited that property for the German war effort."[18] Absent the role played by the DRB, European Jewry could not have been destroyed. Operating within the German bureaucracy as a part of the Transportation Ministry, the *Reichsbahn* was one of the largest organizations in the Third Reich, including in 1942 about half a million civil servants and nine hundred thousand workers. German military conquests, not to mention the demands of war itself, enlarged and complicated the rail system, but the people who ordinarily staffed it proved capable of handling the extraordinary tasks assigned them. Essentially the same personnel who ran the *Reichsbahn* before the war did so between 1939 and 1945 and afterward as well. During the war they simply adjusted to the needs at hand. These included moving troops, industrial cargo, and Jews from all over Europe.

The destruction of the European Jews was not supported by a special budget. The *Reichsbahn* had bills to pay; it could not transport Jews for free. In this case, its paying customer was the SS, which used the proceeds from confiscated Jewish property to make many of the payments. The SS also had to compete with other agencies for allocation of rail space. According to Mierzejewski, the Jewish transports, euphemistically called *Sonderzüge* (special trains) had "low priority for movement. . . . The result was that they were allowed onto the main line only after all other traffic had passed. Wehrmacht trains, military supply trains, trains carrying armaments, and coal trains all moved before the Sonderzüge."[19] Nevertheless, no European Jew was left alive for lack of transportation. Although the Jewish transports amounted to only a small fraction of the DRB's total traffic volume, the number of Jews who were packed aboard justified discounted rates for the approximately two thousand trains that rolled to shooting sites and killing centers strategically located near heavily traveled trunk lines. Hilberg sums up the basic procedure as follows:

> Even though Jews were carried in freight cars, they were booked by the Reichsbahn's financial specialists as passengers. In principle, any group of travelers was accepted for payment. The basic charge was the third-class fare: 4 pfennig per track kilometer. Children under ten were transported for half this amount; those under four went free. Group fare (half of the third-class rate) was available if at least 400 persons were transported.[20]

These fares were all one-way.

The *Reichsbahn*'s personnel were respectable citizens. No experts in Jewish affairs, they were merely people doing their jobs. Yet what they did could have been neither a mystery nor a secret to most of them. The German railroads delivered about three million Jews to their deaths. That death traffic, Mierzejewski notes, constituted "approximately half of all the Jews who lost their lives under the Nazi regime."[21] Whether in headquarters or in the field, the professionals who kept the trains chugging came to know that they managed death trains.[22] Railroad personnel did not protest what was going on. In only a few cases did any of them request a transfer. When transfers were requested, they were granted without prejudice to the individual's career.[23] Meanwhile the death trains rolled on. Business went forward as usual, showing how easily even the most common enterprises can and do turn out to be vital elements in destroying the defenseless.

## CRIMES AGAINST HUMANITY

The Universal Declaration of Human Rights adopted by the General Assembly of the United Nations on 10 December 1948 proclaimed that "recognition of the inherent dignity and of the equal and inalienable rights of all members of the human family is the foundation of freedom, justice and peace in the world."[24] Such language has a long history, but it is not accidental that the United Nations spoke out in the aftermath of Holocaust. Postwar judicial proceedings against captured Nazi leaders helped to provide the context for the UN Declaration. The best known trials included those held in Nuremberg between 1945 and 1949. Conducted by the International Military Tribunal (IMT), which included judges from the United States, Great Britain, France, and Russia, the first Nuremburg trial lasted from November 1945 until October 1946.[25] Twenty-four of Nazi Germany's leaders had been indicted by the IMT on 6 October 1945, including Hermann Göring, Ernst Kaltenbrunner, and Albert Speer, but when the trial began in Nuremberg's Palace of Justice on 20 November 1945, three defendants were missing: Robert Ley had committed suicide, Gustav Krupp's ill health made him unfit to stand trial, and Martin Bormann, whereabouts unknown, had to be tried in absentia.

At Nuremberg the IMT brought four charges against the defendants: (1) crimes against peace, (2) war crimes, (3) crimes against humanity, and (4) conspiracy to commit any of the aforementioned crimes.[26] Making no mention of the Holocaust or the *Shoah*—such terms were not yet widespread—these indictments did not identify specifically what had happened to the Jews or to other civilian populations targeted by Nazi Germany and its collaborators. Yet Article 6 of the IMT's charter did define crimes against humanity to include "murder, extermination, enslavement, deportation, and other inhumane acts committed against any civilian population, before or during the war, or persecutions on political, racial or religious grounds." Those charges were repeatedly brought against defendants in other courtrooms too. Most of the German actions against the Jews were punishable under the traditional laws of war. Such laws, however, did not automatically pertain to anti-Jewish measures executed entirely within

Axis territory. Nor were the Nazis' prewar anti-Jewish actions covered under that jurisdiction. "Crimes against humanity" was conceived to handle "murder, extermination, and 'persecution on political, racial or religious grounds,' whether committed 'before or during the war,' just so long as such acts were undertaken or executed in connection with other acts 'under the jurisdiction of the Tribunal.'"[27] The prosecution of prewar and wartime acts under this count, however, never entirely lost an ex post facto quality, for the defendants were not obviously subject to any "international agreement in existence in 1933, 1939, or even 1944 that made it illegal to persecute religions or to exterminate populations."[28]

When the IMT's verdicts were announced on 1 October 1946, nineteen of the Nuremberg defendants—including Martin Bormann, head of the Nazi Party Chancellery—were found guilty. Three men were acquitted: Hjalmar Schacht, former minister of economics; Franz von Papen, first vice-chancellor of the Nazi government; and Hans Fritzsche, chief of the Propaganda Ministry's Radio Division. Seven defendants received prison sentences that ranged from ten years to life. Twelve defendants, including Nazi military leaders Wilhelm Keitel, chief of staff of the *Wehrmacht* High Command, and Alfred Jodl, chief of the *Wehrmacht* Operations Staff, were condemned to death by hanging. Ten executions took place in the early hours of 16 October. Bormann was missing from the group condemned to death. Shortly before Hermann Göring was to be hanged, he escaped the gallows by swallowing cyanide.

In addition to the proceedings carried out by the IMT, subsequent trials were held in the occupation zones of the four Allied powers. In the American zone, German industrialists were prosecuted in three additional trials at Nuremberg. Understandably necessary though such postwar trials were from psychological, political, and moral points of view, no legal structures were adequate to handle the Holocaust's injustice. Arguably modest prison sentences were handed down to German industrialists who had exploited Jewish slave laborers and other forced workers: Alfried Krupp, twelve years; Walter Dürrfeld and Otto Ambros of I. G. Auschwitz, a corporate subsidiary of I. G. Farben, eight years; and Carl Krauch, six years. No defendants related to I. G. Farben were found guilty for supplying poisonous gas to Auschwitz.[29] Nor were any of these civilian industrialists in prison for long. By the end of the 1950s, the Western Allies had released those for whom they were responsible. For the most part, a similar pattern held in the Soviet Union and other eastern European countries formerly occupied by Nazi Germany.

The cases of two industrialists are especially instructive. First, conviction at Nuremberg for the enslavement and mass murder of two hundred thousand inmates at Auschwitz did not bar Otto Ambros from later employment as a high-level technical advisor to a major American corporation. He was only one of thousands of Nazi war criminals who found a haven in the United States after World War II.[30] Second, Friedrich Flick received a Nuremberg sentence of seven years in prison for his support of the SS and for the use of slave labor in his vast industrial empire, Mitteldeutsche Stahlwerke, which "controlled over three hundred companies . . . [and] manufactured everything from toilet paper to dynamite."[31] Many of Flick's colleagues were acquitted altogether, but some of them joined their leader in jail. By January 1951, however, the American official in charge of such matters, John J. McCloy, had released them all. Good behavior figured into that decision, but of greater importance was the Cold War. American political policy needed German industrial leadership. Quickly German industry was back at work rebuilding its forces and its bank accounts. When Friedrich Flick died in 1972, he was the richest man in Germany and among the wealthiest in the world. He paid nothing at all to his former Jewish slaves in spite of persistent efforts on their behalf. A fitting epitaph might be the pronouncement he made in self-defense at Nuremberg: "Nothing will convince us that we are war criminals."[32] Flick's fate and disposition are not an isolated case, thus leading one to ask, What happened to justice? What does the term *human rights* mean? If people search for "some credible set of theonomous or autonomous moral norms governing the conduct of men and nations," where are they left?[33]

The Holocaust scholar Raul Hilberg might have had versions of such questions in mind when he spoke at a conference on ethics after the Holocaust at the University of Oregon in 1996. Explaining that he did not consider himself a philosopher or theologian, Hilberg asserted that ethics is the same today as it was yesterday and even the day before yesterday; it is the same after Auschwitz as it was before and during the lethal operations at that place. Especially with regard to needless and wanton killing, he emphasized, ethics is the same for everyone, everywhere. Hilberg left no unclarity. Such killing is wrong. We know that "in our bones," he said, for such knowledge is the heritage of many years.

Senses of right and wrong are real. The Holocaust helps to focus them. Even Heinrich Himmler knew as much. He and the other perpetrators of the Holocaust were aware of the psychological and even ethical turmoil created by their orders to kill. They did their best to make those tasks easier, more "humane," by distancing the killers from their victims. Thus, they substituted mass gassings for the shootings of the *Einsatzgruppen*. But did Himmler and the other perpetrators know "in their bones" that what they were doing was wrong? In some cases, there is evidence that says so. The perpetrators covered their tracks as best they could. Many of the killers numbed themselves with alcohol. Some Germans refused orders to kill Jews, especially when children were the targets. On the other hand, such evidence is mostly circumstantial. It was not very often enhanced by admissions of guilt or expressions of remorse. Far more common were excuses that referred to orders that must be obeyed or to fears of punishment if obedience was not forthcoming, despite the fact that no documented case has been found to indicate that dire punishment resulted when a German refused orders to kill unarmed civilians. For the most part, Nazi leaders and Holocaust perpetrators remained unrepentant. At the end of the day, their behavior does not show that they knew that their killing of the Jews was wanton, needless, and wrong. On the contrary, their behavior suggests that they believed their killing to be right and good, albeit extremely difficult, even loathsome, to do. It would be comforting if Hilberg's convictions were true, but the Holocaust does not inspire confidence that all human beings know—in their bones or in any other way—that mass killing and genocide are wrong.

To the extent that knowledge of wrongdoing complicated the killing that the perpetrators carried out month after month, year after year, that moral sensitivity did have to be overridden. Himmler and his henchmen could rely on an ally of vast authority to accomplish that task: human consciousness itself.[34] Humanity's capacity to think is amazingly pliable, especially so in its ability to justify whatever the powers that be want done. The explanations offered by German industrialists to warrant their use of slave labor—for example, Germany was fighting for its life, what else could one do?—were only one strand in a web of rationalization and repression that did much to ensure that dissenting moral scruples would be subordinated to "higher necessities" or even that the dictates of morality and mass murder would coincide.[35] The Nazis were not totally successful in this regard. But when one remembers that the persons responsible for the Holocaust were a cross-section from virtually every profession, skill, and social class, then the persistence with which the Final Solution went forward without effective moral dissent is the more striking.

One effective way for the Nazi machine to bridge the gap between possible moral inhibitions and the destruction of so many human lives was to mask what was going on. Thus, instead of parading Auschwitz openly, steps were taken to shut off information from those who did not have to know. On the other hand, it was important to be sure that people who did know were involved in making the Final Solution happen. Within this circle, discussion of the killing was discouraged; criticism of it was taboo. Repeated use of euphemisms in memos and reports made everything easier as well. Where conscience still created dissonance, other remedies were available. Nazi propaganda never relented in its insistence that Germany must be rid of the Jews. They were portrayed simultaneously as conspirators who would destroy the nation, as criminals who would greedily seize what was not theirs, as vermin who plagued superior human life. In short, their elimination was promoted at once as a preventative war, a meting out of economic and social justice, and a health-restoring purge. This persuasion, however, still might not dispel entirely an individual's uneasiness about his or her involvement in the anti-Jewish campaigns.

Whether a person was part of the relatively small cadre who killed firsthand or one of the huge network of desk-bound personnel who destroyed people by composing memoranda, drafting blueprints, signing correspondence, and making telephone calls, he or she frequently took comfort from referring to orders from superiors and the necessity to obey. Indeed, at times orders were created after the fact to help people reconcile what had already taken place without explicit directives. Separation of duty from personal feeling was also important; life was compartmentalized into public affairs and private relations. One could organize transports to Auschwitz during the day and then embrace spouse and children in the evening. Denial of personal vindictiveness or pleasure in doing one's duty was essential too. Recognizing the unpleasantness of certain tasks, far from making them impossible, could support the conviction that they must, after all, be done. Transfer possibilities also alleviated pressure. Provided they were pursued without protest or criticism, new assignments could be arranged, for other personnel could be found to fill the needed roles, and it was more efficient to rotate people than to court disruption.

Still other defense mechanisms included role distinctions. A Friedrich Flick, for example, might employ slaves, but he could tell himself that he would never administer a killing center as Franz Stangl did at Treblinka and Rudolf Höss at Auschwitz. Perhaps even a Stangl or a Höss could compare himself favorably to persons with hands more overtly bloody than his and be convinced that he would never go that far. Such boundaries were frequently crossed, of course, but even if they were not, such comparative thinking enabled people to keep doing the jobs that were already theirs. That outcome was sufficient to keep the Holocaust going. Emphasis on group responsibility could also neutralize individual pangs of conscience. Since so many were involved in carrying out the Final Solution, one could argue that no individual's part could be too reprehensible. Furthermore, no matter how much one might wish or try to make things different, the vastness of the operation seemed to render one powerless to intervene effectively. That line of thought probably did as much as anything to ensure that the Holocaust could be stopped only by superior military force from the outside. Prevalent especially in the upper echelons of power, one more justification is worth noting: the view that life unfolds in a jungle of power struggles. If one does not keep winning, which to the Nazis entailed killing, then one loses; this can be a fate worse than death. That vision energized Hitler and his key aides. It ensnared a group of people who worked until most of European Jewry perished, Germany lay in ruins, and much of Western civilization became a wasteland.

"The owl of Minerva," wrote the philosopher Hegel, "spreads its wings only with the falling of the dusk." He meant that human reason and philosophy in particular achieve understanding only in retrospect; they are hard pressed to give "instruction as to what the world ought to be."[36] If Hegel is correct, the tools of moral philosophy and religious ethics are meager. Still, they have a role to play that nothing else can duplicate. Moral reflection, for example, can clarify and intensify feelings of wrong. Such thinking can show the importance of those feelings by revealing what happens when they fail to work their way into practice. Yet that understanding alone does little to change the world as long as societies concretely reward activities that kill and take punitive action toward those who refuse to cooperate. If one wants to affirm the United Nations' declaration that "everyone has the right to life, liberty, and security of person," one must realize that such claims are as frail as they are abstract. The same is true of the United Nations Convention on the Prevention and Punishment of the Crime of Genocide, which was submitted to the UN's membership in December 1948. The United States became the ninety-seventh nation to approve the treaty when the

Senate ratified the pact on 19 February 1986. The long delay was occasioned by fears that if the United States agreed to the treaty that makes genocide a crime, the nation might be indicted by its adversaries. At the time of this writing, related fears persist as the United States carefully negotiates its relationship to the International Criminal Court that became a reality in 2002. Meanwhile, history continues to testify that it is power, not pacts, that breaks or makes mass killing. Rights, liberty, and security of person are real only in specific times and places, only in actual political circumstances. Apart from such concrete settings, those ideals are only that. Granted, they are ideals that attract. They can bring out the best in people. They can even rally powerful forces behind them. They may even have a transcendent status ordained by God. To assume, however, that they are more than ideals until men and women take responsibility to make them a concrete reality may well be an illusion.

## A NEGATIVE ABSOLUTE?

In our pluralistic world, where cultural, religious, and philosophical perspectives vary considerably, many people believe that values are so relative to one's time and place that the "truth" of moral claims is much more a result of subjective preference and political power than a function of objective reality and universal reason. That relativistic outlook meets resistance in the Holocaust, for there is a widely shared conviction that the Holocaust was *wrong*, or nothing could be. It was something that did not have to happen, should not have happened, and nothing akin to it ought to happen again. Michael Berenbaum puts the point effectively when he emphasizes that the Holocaust has become a "negative absolute." Even if people remain skeptical that rational agreement can be obtained about what is right, just, and good, the Holocaust seems to reestablish conviction that what happened at Auschwitz and Treblinka was wrong, unjust, and evil—period. More than that, the scale of the wrongdoing, the magnitude of the injustice, and the devastation of the Holocaust's evil are so radical that we can ill afford not to have our ethical sensibilities informed by them. As another Holocaust scholar, Franklin Littell, has stressed, "study of the Holocaust is like pathology in medicine."[37] Pathology seeks to understand the origins and characteristics of disease and the conditions in which it thrives. If such understanding can be obtained, the prospects for resistance against disease, and perhaps even a cure, may be increased.

Unfortunately, to identify the Holocaust as a negative absolute that reinstates confidence in moral absolutes is a step that cannot be taken easily, and no one is advised to rush to judgment that study of the Holocaust can obtain the hopeful results of medical pathology at its best. The fact is that the Holocaust signified an immense human failure. It did harm to ethics by showing how ethical teachings could be overridden or even subverted to serve the interests of genocide.[38] When Berenbaum calls the Holocaust a "negative absolute," the absoluteness involved means that not even ethics itself was immune from failure and, at times, complicity in the pathological conditions and characteristics that nearly destroyed Jewish life and left the world morally scarred forever. The status of ethics after the Holocaust is far from settled. One way to focus that fact further involves two of the Holocaust's perpetrators, Kurt Prüfer and Fritz Sander, and two of the Holocaust's victims, Calel Perechodnik, who did not survive, and Jean Améry, who did.

On 20 August 1942, Calel Perechodnik, a Polish Jew, returned home. This fact is known because Perechodnik recorded it in writing that he began on 7 May 1943. Sheltered at that time by a Polish woman in Warsaw, the 26-year-old engineer would spend the next 105 days producing a remarkable document that is at once a diary, memoir, and confession rooted in the Holocaust.

Shortly before Perechodnik died in 1944, he entrusted his reflections to a Polish friend. The manuscript survived, but it was forgotten and virtually unknown in the English-speaking world until Frank Fox's translation appeared in 1996.[39] Charged with ethical issues, Perechodnik's testament is of special significance because he was a Jewish ghetto policeman in Otwock, a small Polish town near Warsaw. While that role was not his chosen profession, it was a part that he decided to play in February 1941—not knowing all that would soon be required of him.

Already the German occupiers of his native Poland had forced Perechodnik, his family, and millions of other Polish Jews into wretched ghettos. "Seeing that the war was not coming to an end and in order to be free from the roundup for labor camps," Perechodnik wrote, "I entered the ranks of the Ghetto Polizei."[40] When Perechodnik returned home on 20 August 1942, he knew in ways that can scarcely be imagined how optimistic, mistaken, fateful, and deadly even his most realistic assumptions had been. His decision to join what the Germans called the *Ordnungsdienst* (Order Service) had not only required Perechodnik to assist them in the destruction of the European Jews but also implicated him, however unintentionally, in the deportation of his own wife and child to the gas chambers at Treblinka on 19 August 1942. Perechodnik's testament says that he returned home on 20 August, but his words indicate that a genocidal Nazi Germany meant that "home" could never be a reality for him again. That reality challenges some of humanity's fondest assumptions about moral judgments and ethical norms.

In *The Cunning of History* Richard Rubenstein underscored some of the challenges when he contended that "the Holocaust bears witness to *the advance of civilization*."[41] To see how that proposition bears on Calel Perechodnik's case and how it is charged with ominous portents for the future, note that in 1933, the year when Hitler took power in Germany, the Chicago World's Fair celebrated what its promoters optimistically acclaimed as "A Century of Progress." As *The Cunning of History* points out, the fair's theme was expressed in a slogan: "Science Explores; Technology Executes; Mankind Conforms."[42] Cast in those terms, the Holocaust not only bears witness to the tragically cunning and ironic elements of "progress" but also delivers a warning about what could—but ought not to—lie ahead for humanity.

The Final Solution was symptomatic of the modern state's perennial tempta-tion to destroy people who are regarded as undesirable, superfluous, or unwanted because of their religion, race, politics, ethnicity, or economic redundancy. The Nazis identified what they took to be a practical problem—the need to eliminate the Jews and other so-called racial inferiors from their midst—and they moved to solve it. The Holocaust did not result from spontaneous, irrational outbursts of random violence, nor was the Final Solution a historical anomaly. It was instead a state-sponsored program of population riddance made possible by mod-ern planning and the best technology available at the time.

When we think of the dilemmas that Calel Perechodnik and his family con-fronted in wartime Poland, it is crucial to understand that the Nazis' racist anti-semitism eventually entailed a destruction process that required and received cooperation from every sector of German society. On the whole, moreover, the Nazi killers and those Germans who aided and abetted them directly—or indi-rectly as bystanders—were civilized people from a society that was scientifically advanced, technologically competent, culturally sophisticated, efficiently orga-nized, and even religiously devout.[43] Those people were, as Michael Berenbaum has cogently observed, "both ordinary and extraordinary, a cross section of the men and women of Germany, its allies, and their collaborators as well as the best and the brightest."[44]

Some Germans and members of states allied with Nazi Germany resisted Hitler and would not belong in the following catalog, but they were still excep-tions to prove the rule.[45] There were, for example, pastors and priests who led their churches in welcoming nazification and the segregation of Jews it entailed. In addition, teachers and writers helped to till the soil where Hitler's racist anti-semitism took root; their students and readers reaped the wasteful harvest. Lawyers drafted and judges enforced the laws that isolated Jews and set them up for the kill. Government and church personnel provided birth and baptismal records that helped to document who was Jewish and who was not. Other work-ers entered such information into state-of-the-art data processing machines. Uni-versity administrators curtailed admissions for Jewish students and dismissed Jewish faculty members. Bureaucrats in the Finance Ministry handled confisca-tions of Jewish wealth and property. Postal officials delivered mail about defini-tion and expropriation, denaturalization and deportation.

Driven by their biomedical visions, physicians were among the first to exper-iment with the gassing of "lives unworthy of life." Scientists performed research and tested their racial theories on those branded subhuman or nonhuman by Nazi science. Business executives found that Nazi concentration camps could provide cheap labor; they worked people to death, turning the motto *Arbeit macht frei* (Work makes one free) into a mocking truth. Radio performers were joined by artists such as the gifted film director Leni Riefenstahl to broadcast and screen the polished propaganda that made Hitler's policies persuasive to so many. Railroad personnel drove the trains that transported Jews to death, while other officials took charge of the billing arrangements for this service. Factory workers modified trucks so that they became deadly gas vans; policemen became members of squadrons that made mass murder of Jews their specialty. Meanwhile, stockholders made profits from firms that supplied Zyklon B to gas people and that built crematoriums to burn the corpses.

Rubenstein's argument that the Holocaust is symptomatic of an ironic advance of civilization gets telling support from the historian Gerald Fleming, whose research led him to archives in Moscow that became available in the early 1990s after the Cold War's end. For some time, Fleming had been studying the Auschwitz Central Building Authority records that were captured by Soviet troops and stored in Soviet archives. In May 1993 his searching led him to File 17/9 of the Red Army's intelligence branch. Previously off limits to historians from the West, this file contained information about four senior engineers who had worked for a German firm named Topf und Söhne. It was known that these men had been arrested by the Soviets in 1946, but Western intelligence lost track of them after that.

Topf had been manufacturing cremation furnaces for civilian use since 1912. That fact was less than noteworthy, but the puzzle that eventually took Fleming to File 17/9 involved another piece of information that was much more significant. Nameplates on the crematorium furnaces in Nazi concentration camps at Buchenwald, Dachau, Mauthausen, Gross-Rosen, and Birkenau (the main killing center at Auschwitz) showed that they too were Topf products.

At the war's end, Kurt Prüfer, a specialist in furnace construction and one of Topf's senior engineers, had been interrogated by the American Third Army. He persuaded his interrogators that the concentration camp crematoriums had existed for health reasons only. The Americans released him. The Red Army, however, could document another story. Although German orders in late November 1944 called for the destruction of equipment and records that would implicate Auschwitz-Birkenau as a death factory, the enterprise was simply too vast to cover up. When the Red Army liberated that place two months later, the massive evidence included, in Fleming's words, details about "the construction of the technology of mass death, complete with the precise costs of crematoriums and calculations of the number of corpses each could incinerate in a day."[46] Well beyond documenting the Red Army's arrest of Prüfer and three of his colleagues in Erfurt, Germany, on 4 March 1946, File 17/9 contained transcripts of the revealing interviews that interrogators had conducted with Prüfer and his associates.

At Auschwitz-Birkenau the *Krema*, as they were sometimes called in German, became full-fledged installations of mass death.[47] Especially given the constraints on wartime building projects, the construction of the four carefully planned units at Birkenau took time. Topf was only one of eleven civilian companies needed to produce them. Utilizing prisoner labor as much as possible, the building began in the summer of 1942, but it was nearly a year before the last facility was operational. Each included an undressing room, a gas chamber, and a room containing Topf's incineration ovens. These lethal places were designed to dispatch thousands of people per day. Even so, Prüfer told his Red Army interrogators, "the [crematorium] bricks were damaged after six months because the strain on the furnaces was colossal." Periodic malfunctions notwithstanding, the gassing and burning went on and on.

"From 1940 to 1944," Prüfer went on to tell his captors, "twenty crematoriums for concentration camps were built under my direction." His work took him to Auschwitz five times; he knew that "innocent human beings were being liquidated" there. In addition to excerpts from the Red Army's interviews with Prüfer, Fleming's article contains parts of the depositions taken from one of Prüfer's superiors, chief engineer Fritz Sander, whose approval at Topf headquarters was necessary for Prüfer's projects. In late 1942 Sander himself developed plans to "improve" what was happening at Auschwitz-Birkenau. He envisioned crematoriums with even higher capacity than those already planned for installation there. To Sander's dismay, his project was not accepted. It would have used "the conveyer belt principle," he explained. "That is to say, the corpses must be brought to the incineration furnaces without interruption."

Apparently without remorse or apology, Sander admitted his knowledge of the mass murder at Auschwitz. "I was a German engineer and key member of the Topf works," he reasoned on 7 March 1946. "I saw it as my duty to apply my specialist knowledge in this way in order to help Germany win the war, just as an aircraft construction engineer builds airplanes in wartime, which are also connected with the destruction of human beings." Less than three weeks later, Sander died in Red Army custody, the victim of a heart attack. Having been sentenced to "25 years deprivation of liberty," Prüfer died of a brain hemorrhage on 24 October 1952.

## RIGHT AND WRONG

The Holocaust's evil appears to be so overwhelming that it forms an ultimate refutation of moral relativism. No one, it seems, could encounter Auschwitz and deny that there is a fundamental and objective difference between right and wrong. Nevertheless, as Fleming's "Engineers of Death" suggests, short of Germany's military defeat by the Allies, no constraints—social or political, moral or religious—were sufficient to stop the Final Solution. One might argue that Nazi Germany's defeat shows that right defeated wrong and that goodness subdued evil, thus showing that reality has a fundamentally moral underpinning. The Holocaust, however, is far too awesome for such facile triumphalism.

The Nazis did not win, but they came too close for comfort. Even though the Third Reich was destroyed, it is not so easy to say that its defeat was a clear and decisive triumph for goodness, truth, and justice over evil, falsehood, and corruption. Add to those realizations the fact that the Nazis themselves were idealists. They had positive beliefs about right and wrong, good and evil, duty and irresponsibility. We can even identify something that can be called "the Nazi ethic." The Final Solution was a key part, perhaps the essence, of its practice, which took place with a zealous, even apocalyptic, vengeance.[48] It would be too convenient to assume that the Nazi ethic's characteristic blending of loyalty, faith, heroism, and even love for country and cause was simply a passive, mindless obedience. True though the judgment would be, it remains too soothing to say only that the Nazi ethic was really no ethic at all but a deadly perversion of what is truly moral. Most people are unlikely to serve a cause unless that cause makes convincing moral appeals about what is good and worthy of loyalty. Those appeals, of course, can be blind, false, even sinful; and the Nazis' were. Nevertheless the perceived and persuasive "goodness" of the beliefs that constituted the Nazi ethic—the dedicated SS man embodied them most thoroughly—is essential to acknowledge if we are to understand why so many Germans willfully followed Hitler into genocidal warfare.

Paradoxically the Final Solution threatens the status, practical and theoretical, of moral norms that are contrary to those that characterized the Nazi ethic, whose deadly way failed but still prevailed long enough to call into question many of Western civilization's moral assumptions and religious hopes.[49] This dilemma is underscored by statements from *The Cunning of History* that bring Calel Perechodnik's case to mind again: "there are absolutely no limits to the degradation and assault the managers and technicians of violence can inflict upon men and women who lack the power of effective resistance."[50]

Hans Maier, a contemporary of Perechodnik, would concur with Rubenstein's appraisal, which includes the debatable claim that "*rights do not belong to men by nature*. To the extent that men have rights, they have them only as members of the polis, the political community. . . . Outside of the polis there are no inborn restraints on the human exercise of destructive power."[51] Born on 31 October 1912, the only child of a Catholic mother and a Jewish father, more than anything else Maier thought of himself as Austrian, not least because his father's family had lived in that land since the seventeenth century. Hans Maier, however, lived in the twentieth century, and thus it was that in September 1935 he studied a newspaper in a Viennese coffeehouse. The Nuremberg Laws had just been promulgated in Nazi Germany. Maier's reading made him see unmistakably that, even if he did not think of himself primarily as Jewish, the Nazis' policies meant that the cunning of history had nonetheless given him that identity.

Maier lacked the authority to define social reality in the mid-1930s. Increasingly, however, Nazi Germany did possess such power. Its laws made him Jewish even if his consciousness did not. As he confronted that reality, the unavoidability of his being Jewish took on another dimension. By identifying him as a Jew, Maier would write later on, Nazi power made him "a dead man on leave, someone to be murdered, who only by chance was not yet where he properly belonged."[52]

When Nazi Germany annexed Austria in March 1938, Maier drew his conclusions. He fled his native land for Belgium and joined the resistance after Belgium was occupied by the Germans in 1940. Captured by the Gestapo in 1943, Maier was sent to Auschwitz and Bergen-Belsen, where he was liberated in 1945.

Eventually taking the name Jean Améry, by which he is remembered, this philosopher waited twenty years before breaking his silence about the Holocaust. When Améry did decide to write, the result was a series of remarkable essays about his experience. One is simply entitled "Torture." Torture drove Améry to the following observation: "The experience of help, the certainty of help," he wrote, "is indeed one of the fundamental experiences of human beings." Thus the gravest loss produced by the Holocaust, Améry went on to suggest, was that it destroyed what he called "trust in the world, . . . the certainty that by reason of written or unwritten social contracts the other person will spare me—more precisely stated, that he will respect my physical, and with it also my metaphysical being."[53]

Améry doubted that rights belong to people by nature. "Every morning when I get up," he tells his reader, "I can read the Auschwitz number on my forearm. . . . Every day anew I lose my trust in the world. . . . Declarations of human rights, democratic constitutions, the free world and the free press, nothing can lull me into the slumber of security from which I awoke in 1935."[54] Far from scorning the human dignity that those institutions emphasize, Améry yearned for the right to live, which he equated with dignity itself. His experience, however, taught him that "it is certainly true that dignity can be bestowed only by society, whether it be the dignity of some office, a professional or, very generally speaking, civil dignity; and the merely individual, subjective claim ('I am a human being and as such I have my dignity, no matter what you may do or say!') is an empty academic game, or madness."[55] Lucidity, believed Améry, demanded the recognition of this reality, but lucidity did not end there. He thought it also entailed rebellion against power that would make anyone a "dead man on leave." Unfortunately, it must also be acknowledged that Améry's hopes for such protest were less than optimistic. On 17 October 1978 he took leave and became a dead man by his own hand.

Adolf Hitler and his Nazi regime intended the annihilation of Jewish life to signify the destruction of the very idea of a common humanity that all people share. Jean Améry, who saw that the Nazis "hated the word 'humanity,'" had amplified that point when he said, "Torture was no invention of National Socialism. But it was its apotheosis."[56] Améry meant that the Third Reich aimed to produce men, women, and children whose hardness would transcend humanity in favor of a so-called racially pure and culturally superior form of life that could still appropriately be called Aryan or German but not merely "human." Insofar as *humanity* referred to universal equality, suggested a shared and even divine source of life, or implied any of the other trappings of weakness and sentimentality that Hitler and his most dedicated followers attributed to such concepts, National Socialism intentionally tried to go beyond humanity. Such steps entailed more than killing allegedly inferior forms of life that were thought to threaten German superiority. Moving beyond humanity made it essential to inflict torture—not only to show that "humanity" or "sub-humanity" deserved no respect in and of itself, but also to ensure that those who had moved beyond humanity, and thus were recognizing the respect deserved only by Germans or

Aryans, had really done so. Hitler and his Nazi followers did not succeed completely in implementing their antisemitism, but they went far enough in establishing what Améry aptly called "the rule of the antiman" that none of our fondest hopes about humanity can be taken for granted.[57]

## PRESENT CIRCUMSTANCES

The writings that Calel Perechodnik left behind include a poignant and disturbing document composed in Warsaw, Poland, on 23 October 1943. Almost apologetically, Perechodnik states, "I am not a lawyer by profession, and so I cannot write a will that would be entirely in order, and I cannot in the present circumstances ask for help from the outside."[58] Explaining his "present circumstances," Perechodnik observes that, "as a result of the order of German authorities, I and my entire family, as well as all the Jews of Poland, have been sentenced to death."[59] This death sentence, he notes, has claimed almost all of his family, and thus Perechodnik's formal, documentary language is also an understated lamentation that records their fate as best he knows it. He has no personal property, Perechodnik goes on to say, but he is the legal heir to property left by his wife, Chana, and his father, Ussher. He makes clear what should be done with it. His last testament is a real will, prepared as carefully and executed as properly as Perechodnik knew how.

Nobody can say how much Perechodnik believed that anybody—let alone any legal system, government, or state—would care about his will. Nevertheless— perhaps with irony and protest as much as hope, perhaps to resist despair by asserting his human dignity, or perhaps with none of those feelings—Perechodnik writes respectfully and specifically asks "the Polish court to make possible the execution of this will according to both the spirit of my wishes as well as the law involved."[60] Perechodnik lists the property to which he is heir and designates those to whom he wants to leave it. Giving addresses and exact locations, he carefully explains that the property exists in Otwock, his hometown. There is the movie house called "Oasis." There are two lots and two villas. The latter contain apartments.

The apartments were homes. Not just people but families—Jewish and Polish, members of Perechodnik's family, Perechodnik himself—returned to those family homes after work, school, or shopping, and after journeys that took them away but brought them back home again. After Perechodnik saw his wife and child deported to Treblinka in August 1942, he said that he returned home, but he did not return there—could not do so—because the Holocaust destroyed not only Perechodnik's physical home, leaving him ghettoized, but senses of home that are even more precious and profound than the specific places and times without which those deeper senses of home cannot exist.

If we think about the most fundamental human needs and about the most important human values, *home* looms large. Home means shelter and safety, care and love. It has much to do with the senses of identity, meaning, and purpose that govern our lives, because home involves our closest relationships with other people and provides key motivations and reasons for the work we do. Not all particular homes fit that description, which sometimes leads us to speak of "broken homes," a condition that no one chooses as good. Unfortunately, the Holocaust and the devastating world war that provided "cover" for it did more than break homes. It ruined them—physically and metaphysically—because the Nazi assault, driven by a debased yearning for an exclusively German homeland, was so successful in destroying the *trust* on which home depends.

The senses of home that we identify most with goodness depend on stability, fidelity, communal ties, law, government that encourages mutual respect, a shared ethical responsibility, and, for some but not all persons, religious faith. Phrases about home—for example, "going home" or "being at home" or even "leaving home"—reflect those elements. The Holocaust, as the philosopher Jean Améry said, destroyed trust in the world. It showed that without sufficient defense, violent powers can leave people bereft of home, if those powers leave their victims alive at all. True, human resilience may act remarkably to rebuild senses of home in the ruins but never without a residue of distrust that is metaphysical and perhaps religious as well as political.

One of this book's arguments is that remembering the Holocaust confers obligations in the present and for the future. Moral indignation, of course, can be largely irrelevant when the powers that be determine that the disappearance of defenseless persons and the prosperity of their persecutors constitute business as usual. After Auschwitz ethics must be concerned with outcomes. Seeking ways to "return home," it must emphasize not only good intentions that persist *in spite of* history but also how to achieve results that increase the trust on which our best senses of home depend. So much depends on the human will. That fact means that the relationship between *might* and *right* is crucial. Although might does not make right, relationships between right and might still remain, and they are as important as they are complex.

Consider why Calel Perechodnik was unable to return home. He could not do so because Nazi power prevented him from doing so. No ultimately sustainable reasons—judgments that could stand full critical scrutiny—could be found to justify that Nazi power, but nevertheless Perechodnik could not return home. Might did not make right in that case, but might had much to do with the functional status of right. The same point can be seen in relationships such as the following: A law that is not obeyed may still be a law, but its functional status depends on obedience and credible sanctions against disobedience. An injunction that is not heeded lacks credibility. When Nazi Germany unleashed the Holocaust, the force of the injunction "Thou shalt not murder" was impugned to the degree that millions of Jews were slaughtered before the violence of a world war crushed the Third Reich. Similarly, if God is not acknowledged, God's existence is not necessarily eliminated, but God's authority is curtailed. And if God's authority lacks credibility, then the nature of God's existence is affected too.

Our senses of moral and religious authority have been weakened by the accumulated ruins of history and the depersonalized advances of "civilization" that have taken us from a bloody twentieth century into an even more problematic twenty-first. A moral spirit and religious commitment that have the courage to persist *in spite of* humankind's self-inflicted destructiveness are essential, but the question remains how effective those dispositions can be in a world where power, and especially the power of governments, stands at the heart of that matter. To find ways to affect "the powers that be" so that their tendencies to lay waste to human life are checked, ethics after Auschwitz will need to draw on every resource it can find: appeals to human rights, calls for renewed religious sensitivity, respect and honor for people who save lives and resist tyranny, and attention to the Holocaust's warnings, to name only a few. Those efforts will need to be accompanied by efforts that build these concerns into our educational, religious, business, and political institutions. Moves in those directions can be steps toward home.

If one considers human rights after the Holocaust, it is unlikely that humankind will ever reach full agreement on a single worldview that will ground belief in such rights. But it does not follow that appeals to human rights are dashed as well. If people feel the need to ground appeals to human rights, a variety of options—philosophical and religious—may remain credible, even if they will not be universally accepted. More importantly, there may be considerable agreement—especially after the Holocaust—about what the functional interpretation of human rights ought to be. Here too there will not be universal agreement, but the Holocaust itself has had an important impact in helping to clarify what ought not to happen to human beings. If we think about what ought not to happen to human beings, moreover, we may find considerable agreement about what should happen. At least after the Holocaust, most people will agree that Calel Perechodnik ought not to have been prevented from returning home—in all the best senses of *home*—and if that is true, then what ought to have happened (again in all the best senses of that phrase) is not so far to find.

In her afterword to *Nightfather*, a remarkable novel about a young daughter's poignant attempts to understand her Holocaust-survivor father, the Dutch writer Carl Friedman—whose father was a Holocaust survivor—quotes the poet Remco Campert, another author from the Netherlands. "Resistance does not start with big words," Campert says, "it starts with small deeds. Asking yourself a question / that is how resistance starts / then putting that question to somebody else."[61] Nazism and the Holocaust assaulted the values that human beings hold most dear when we are at our best. Resistance to protect them came too late then; hence resistance continues to be urgent now, and it begins perpetually with small deeds, the raising of critical questions among them. Approaches to Auschwitz show that nothing human, natural, or divine guarantees respect for those values, but nothing is more important than our commitment to defend them, for they remain as fundamental as they are fragile, as precious as they are endangered.

# Notes

## Preface and Acknowledgments

1. Peretz's testimony is quoted in Dan Cohn-Sherbok, ed., *Holocaust Theology: A Reader* (New York: New York University Press, 2002), 35.
2. Charlotte Delbo, *Auschwitz and After*, trans. Rosette C. Lamont (New Haven, Conn.: Yale University Press, 1995), 138.
3. Raul Hilberg, *Sources of Holocaust Research: An Analysis* (Chicago: Ivan R. Dee, 2001), 204.
4. Halter's stained-glass window can be found at Beth Shalom, Nottinghamshire, the first Holocaust center in the United Kingdom. Beth Shalom, where thousands of British students annually receive education about the Holocaust, was founded and developed by Stephen and James Smith, who have also helped us immensely. We also express gratitude to Glen Powell, a member of the Beth Shalom staff, who helped us obtain the version of Roman Halter's art needed by the design team at Westminster John Knox Press.

   The story behind the photograph that led to Halter's art provides an important glimpse into some of the Holocaust's detail. On the night of 24 May 1944, a transport of 3,500 Hungarian Jews departed the Carpathian city of Berehovo for Auschwitz-Birkenau. Arriving two days later, this transport rolled directly through the camp's gates, taking advantage of a special spur added to the rail network earlier that year. The ensuing "selection" left the new arrivals just steps away from the barracks where some of them would live and from the gas chambers where most of them, especially the women and children, would die.

   The handling of the Berehovo transport was routine—with one significant exception. Usually photography was strictly forbidden at Auschwitz, but on this occasion two SS cameramen were on the ramp where the cattle cars unloaded. They took nearly two hundred pictures of the Jews from Berehovo, documenting the selection process thoroughly. Lili Jacob, eighteen, was one of those selected to work. After being quarantined for several weeks, she was tattooed on her left arm with number A-10862 on 25 July 1944. The eldest of six children and the only daughter, she would be the sole survivor of her family. In December 1944 she was evacuated from Auschwitz-Birkenau and sent to Dora, a missile plant located underground near Nordhausen, Germany. Gravely ill from typhus and malnutrition as that labor camp was being evacuated in April 1945, Jacob was carried into a recently vacated SS barrack by some fellow prisoners. There she not only began to recover but also discovered a brown clothbound album containing photographs. To her amazement, she recognized people in them. She recognized the place where the photographs had been taken, too. Lili Jacob Meier, her married name, possessed what has come to be known as *The*

*Auschwitz Album*, the series of pictures taken by the SS cameramen who recorded the arrival and decimation of the Berehovo transport that had taken her to Auschwitz along with the grandmother with children portrayed in Halter's stained-glass window at Beth Shalom. For the photographic source of Halter's "The Last Journey," see Peter Hellman, *The Auschwitz Album: A Book Based upon an Album Discovered by a Concentration Camp Survivor, Lili Meier* (New York: Random House, 1981), 96.

## Prologue

1. For further detail about this episode, see Michael Burleigh, *The Third Reich: A New History* (New York: Hill and Wang, 2000), 118–20.
2. Sigmund Freud, *Civilization and Its Discontents*, trans. James Strachey (New York: W. W. Norton, 1961), 112.
3. At the outset, three points about terminology are important. First, an important issue can be focused by the following question: When one speaks about the Holocaust's perpetrators, should the primary designation be *Nazis* or *Germans*? The answer is neither straightforward nor easy. The former category is too narrow, the latter too broad. Without Nazis—a designation that, strictly speaking, entailed membership in the Nazi Party—the Holocaust would not have happened. On the other hand, arguably not every member of the Nazi Party was a Holocaust perpetrator, but large numbers of Germans who were not party members did become perpetrators. In fact, the Holocaust's scope was so vast that party members alone would have been insufficient to enact the destruction that took place. It would be a serious misjudgment, however, to make *Germans* and *perpetrators* equivalent categories. Not only were non-German collaborators essential for the Third Reich's onslaught against European Jewry, but also there were German bystanders, resisters, and rescuers who were not directly implicated in mass murder. When we are discussing the development of the Third Reich's anti-Jewish policies, it will make sense to speak of Nazis in some places, Germans in others. Context—historical and interpretive—will determine the choice of terminology in our analysis.

   Second, it is important to clarify how the adjectival terms *Nazi* and *German* will be used in our discussion. Our basic rule will be to use *Nazi* when we refer to the ideology and actions of the Nazi party. *German* will refer to the acts, institutions, and laws of the state of Nazi Germany or of the Third Reich. Hence, we will speak of Nazi antisemitism and Nazi racism, for example, but of German laws and German military occupation. Again, context—historical and interpretive—will be important in determining the particular choice of terminology.

   Third, as we discuss the content of Nazi ideology, how Jews were regarded in the Third Reich, and what the German objectives in World War II entailed, one can scarcely avoid describing Nazi racial stereotypes, allegations, and slurs about Jews and other people whom the Nazis despised (the misconception, for example, that Jews are a race). Nor can one escape using terms from the Nazi vocabulary—for example, *Aryan* (a problematic racial synonym for Nordic or German) or *judenfrei* (meaning "Jew-free")—that express the genocidal antisemitism and racism that characterized the Third Reich. As this book tries hard to make clear, the Nazi worldview and vocabulary—from start to finish—were based on distortions, inaccuracies, and falsehoods. Nevertheless, it is important to grasp that most Germans during the Third Reich took that worldview and vocabulary to be clear, accurate, and true. When they acted accordingly, the consequences were so catastrophic that humanity will be dealing with them for a long time to come.
4. Anne Frank, *The Diary of a Young Girl*, ed. Otto H. Frank and Mirjam Pressler, trans. Susan Massotty (New York: Doubleday, 1995), 332.

5. For an overview of World War II's death statistics, see J. M. Winter, "Demography of the War," in *The Oxford Companion to World War II*, ed. I. C. B. Dear (Oxford: Oxford University Press, 1995), 289–92.

6. The Holocaust scholar Raul Hilberg estimates that 5.1 million Jews perished in the Holocaust. Israel Gutman and Robert Rozett put Jewish losses between 5.5 and 5.8 million. More recently, the German historian Wolfgang Benz contends that the number of Jewish deaths exceeded 6.2 million. The figures remain imprecise for several reasons, including the years and geographical boundaries used to determine prewar census data; the margins of error in death reports from German and Jewish sources; the difficulties of comparing prewar and postwar populations; and the fact that the Germans and their collaborators did not record the death of every victim.

   The information in this note is cited from John Roth's contributions to John K. Roth et al., *The Holocaust Chronicle* (Lincolnwood, Ill.: Publications International, 2000). See also Raul Hilberg, *The Destruction of the European Jews*, 3 vols., revised and definitive edition (New York: Holmes & Meier, 1985), 3:1219 and *The Destruction of the European Jews*, 3rd ed. (New Haven, Conn: Yale University Press, 2003), 3:1320; Israel Gutman, ed., *Encyclopedia of the Holocaust*, 4 vols. (New York: Macmillan, 1990), 1797–1802; Wolfgang Benz, *The Holocaust*, trans. Jane Sydenham-Kwiet (New York: Columbia University Press, 1999), 152–53.

   The 2003 edition of Hilberg's comprehensive *The Destruction of the European Jews* appeared as this revised edition of *Approaches to Auschwitz* went to press. Although Hilberg's 2003 edition came too late for us to take full account of his latest findings, our references to *The Destruction of the European Jews* cite the pages for both the 1985 and the 2003 editions. The first page reference will be for the 1985 edition; the second for the 2003 edition.

7. Further information about many of these people—especially the handicapped and homosexuals—can be found in the insightful essays contained in Robert Gellately and Nathan Stoltzfus, eds., *Social Outsiders in Nazi Germany* (Princeton: Princeton University Press, 2001). For coverage of Nazi policy toward Gypsies, see Guenter Lewy, *The Nazi Persecution of the Gypsies* (New York: Oxford University Press, 2000).

8. For further information about the Soviet POWs, see Christian Streit, "The Fate of Soviet Prisoners of War," in *A Mosaic of Victims: Non-Jews Persecuted and Murdered by the Nazis*, ed. Michael Berenbaum (New York: New York University Press, 1990), 142–49.

9. See Karl A. Schleunes, *The Twisted Road to Auschwitz: Nazi Policy toward German Jews, 1933–1939* (Urbana: University of Illinois Press, 1970).

10. Uriel Tal, "Excursus on the Term: *Shoah*," *Shoah* 1 (1979): 10–11.

11. Sigmund Freud, *The Future of an Illusion*, trans. W. D. Robson-Scott (New York: Doubleday, 1957), 98, 74, 66.

12. Walter Laqueur, *The Terrible Secret: Suppression of the Truth about Hitler's "Final Solution"* (Boston: Little, Brown & Co., 1980), 7. For different views about the appropriateness of the term *Holocaust*, see the remarks made by the German historian Eberhard Jäckel in *Remembering for the Future: The Holocaust in an Age of Genocide*, 3 vols., ed. John K. Roth and Elisabeth Maxwell (New York: Palgrave, 2001), 1:12–13; and Jon Petrie, "The Secular Word HOLOCAUST: Scholarly Myths, History, and Twentieth Century Meanings," *Journal of Genocide Research* 2 (2000): 31–63.

13. See Laqueur's "In Place of a Preface," in *The Holocaust Encyclopedia*, ed. Walter Laqueur (New Haven, Conn.: Yale University Press, 2001), xiii.

14. We shall use the terms *antisemitism* and *antisemitic* instead of *anti-Semitism* and *anti-Semitic*. Particularly in the later decades of nineteenth-century German

politics, the term *Semite* was exploited to set Jews apart from non-Jews, including even from other so-called Semitic peoples—Arabs, for example—and particularly to reinforce a negative, race-based perception of Jews and Judaism. The hyphenated and capitalized form *anti-Semitism* and its variations honor, however inadvertently, distinctions that are erroneous and misleading. Jews are not a race, nor is the category "Semite" a clear one. The forms *antisemitism* and *antisemitic* retain the prejudicial, anti-Jewish meaning, but they also protest the harmful confusions that attend the hyphenated and capitalized forms of those terms.

15. See Franklin H. Littell, *The Crucifixion of the Jews* (New York: Harper & Row, 1975).
16. See Emil L. Fackenheim, *God's Presence in History: Jewish Affirmations and Philosophical Reflections* (1970; Northvale, N.J.: Jason Avonson, 1997).
17. Hilberg, *The Destruction of the European Jews*, 1:8–9 and 1:4–5.
18. Many of the following themes are set forth in two previous books by Richard L. Rubenstein. See *The Cunning of History: Mass Death and the American Future* (New York: Harper & Row, 1975) and *The Age of Triage: Fear and Hope in an Overcrowded World* (Boston: Beacon Press, 1983).
19. See Hannah Arendt, *The Origins of Totalitarianism* (New York: Harcourt Brace Jovanovich, 1973) and *The Jew as Pariah: Jewish Identity and Politics in the Modern Age*, ed. Ron H. Feldman (New York: Grove Press, 1978). For an instructive account of how people in the twentieth century were increasingly pushed into refugee and "unwanted" status, see Michael R. Marrus, *The Unwanted: European Refugees in the Twentieth Century* (New York: Oxford University Press, 1985); pages 27–39, 51–68, 141–45, and 208–95 are especially relevant for our concerns.
20. In the historiography of the Holocaust, arguments between *intentionalists* and *functionalists* have received much attention. The issue is how best to understand the motivations and decisions that produced the Holocaust. Intentionalists—Lucy Dawidowicz and Gerald Fleming among them—contend that from the mid-1930s, if not earlier, Hitler's antisemitism and Nazi policy pointed toward the outright destruction of Jewish life. War provided the cover to realize long-considered murderous intentions. In his variation on this theme, which emphasizes what he calls "eliminationist antisemitism," the controversial Daniel Goldhagen argues that these intentions expressed desires that were deep-seated and widespread among most of the German population when the Nazis came to power.

Functionalists—Christopher Browning and Philippe Burrin are two of many examples—see the situation differently. Emphasizing that early Nazi policy toward the Jews was not murderous, they find the Nazi leaders trying various options for solving the "Jewish problem"—forced emigration and resettlement—before unyielding anti-Jewish policy and wartime circumstance in the summer of 1941 made mass killing an alternative that was both preferred and unavoidable. Neither the intentionalists nor the functionalists have been of one mind, but in general the latter find the Nazis groping their way toward what became the Final Solution, while the former think that Hitler had plans of that sort in mind well before World War II began.

Most Holocaust scholars now incline toward a functionalist interpretation, but not without giving aspects of the intentionalist perspective due respect. At the very least, it is recognized, the immense destruction process that was eventually unleashed against European Jewry could scarcely have taken place without Hitler's authorization. One result is the emergence of what has been called *moderate functionalism*, which is the position that we take in this book. Moderate functionalism still leaves room for varied interpretations. Our version emphasizes two basic points: (1) the Final Solution, far from being envisioned in detail before 1941, evolved over time, and (2) Hitler's authority, as well as Nazi ideology, was a necessary condition for the mass murder that eventually took place. For a succinct summary of Holocaust historiography, including further commentary on the intentionalist-functionalist debate, see Michael R. Marrus, "Historiography," in *The Holocaust Encyclopedia*, ed. Laqueur, 279–85.

21. With specific reference to the town of Auschwitz itself, Debórah Dwork and Robert Jan van Pelt have identified it to be part of the territory that Nazi demographers took to be essential for German *Lebensraum* (living space) in eastern Europe. In this region of Nazi-occupied Poland and in many other parts of eastern Europe, Nazi plans—driven largely by the SS leader Heinrich Himmler—called for massive population movements that would resettle ethnic Germans into colonized territory, forcibly relocate the local inhabitants, and, one way or another, eliminate the Jews. See Dwork and van Pelt's *Auschwitz: 1270 to the Present* (New York: W. W. Norton, 1996). Also relevant in this context is the work of Götz Aly, especially his *"Final Solution": Nazi Population Policy and the Murder of the European Jews*, trans. Belinda Cooper and Allison Brown (London: Arnold, 1999).

22. Rubenstein, *The Cunning of History*, 72.

23. While the Holocaust is the quintessential instance of genocide in human history, the hope that genocide would happen "Never again!" after the Holocaust has been dashed again and again—in Cambodia, Bosnia, and Rwanda, to name the sites of three post-Holocaust genocides. For further insight about the nature, causes, and mechanisms of genocide, plus consideration of the steps that effective genocide prevention requires, see the contributions by leading genocide scholars in Carol Rittner, John K. Roth, and James M. Smith, eds., *Will Genocide Ever End?* (St. Paul, Minn.: Paragon House, 2002). A revealing analysis of American policies and responses to genocide in the twentieth century, including the Holocaust, can be found in Samantha Power, *"A Problem from Hell": America and the Age of Genocide* (New York: Basic Books, 2002).

24. Raphael Lemkin, *Axis Rule in Occupied Europe: Laws of Occupation, Analysis of Government, Proposals for Redress* (Washington: Carnegie Endowment for International Peace, 1944), 79. For more detail on Lemkin's life and contributions, see Power, *"A Problem from Hell,"* 17–85. See also Steven L. Jacobs, ed., *Raphael Lemkin's Thoughts on Genocide: Not Guilty* (Lewiston, N.Y.: Edwin Mellen Press, 1992), which is the posthumous publication of a manuscript by Lemkin.

25. See, for example, Alan S. Rosenbaum, ed., *Is the Holocaust Unique? Perspectives on Comparative Genocide*, 2d ed. (Boulder, Colo.: Westview Press, 2001).

26. Helen Fein, *Accounting for Genocide: National Responses and Jewish Victimization during the Holocaust* (New York: Free Press, 1979), 3.

27. Steven T. Katz, "The Uniqueness of the Holocaust: The Historical Dimension," in *Is the Holocaust Unique?* Rosenbaum, ed., 49–50.

28. Yehuda Bauer, *A History of the Holocaust*, rev. ed. (New York: Franklin Watts, 2001), 364.

29. Yehuda Bauer, *Rethinking the Holocaust* (New Haven, Conn.: Yale University Press, 2001), 74.

30. Cited by Yehuda Bauer, *The Holocaust in Historical Perspective* (Seattle: University of Washington Press, 1978), 37, 160 n.16. See also Bauer, *Rethinking the Holocaust*, esp. 20–21, 74, 265–67, and 278 n.6. Jonathan Glover agrees that the Holocaust has "a terrible darkness all its own," which he defines by citing the German historian Eberhard Jäckel, who states that "the National-Socialist murder of the Jews was unique because never before had a nation with the authority of its leader decided and announced that it would kill off as completely as possible a particular group of humans, including old people, women, children, and infants, and actually put this decision into practice, using all the means of governmental

power at its disposal." See Jonathan Glover, *Humanity: A Moral History of the Twentieth Century* (New Haven, Conn.: Yale University Press, 2000), 396.

31. For the U.S. census figures, see Frank Chalk and Kurt Jonassohn, *The History and Sociology of Genocide: Analyses and Case Studies* (New Haven, Conn.: Yale University Press, 1990), 202. For accounts that stress the extreme decimation of the native North American population, see David E. Stannard, "Uniqueness as Denial: The Politics of Genocide Scholarship," in *Is the Holocaust Unique?* ed. Rosenbaum, 245–90, esp. 266, 287 n.51, and Ward Churchill, "Genocide of Native Populations in the United States," in *Encyclopedia of Genocide*, 2 vols., ed. Israel W. Charny (Santa Barbara, Calif.: ABC-Clio, 1999), 434–37.

32. Chalk and Jonassohn, *The History and Sociology of Genocide*, 249.

33. Cited in Fein, *Accounting for Genocide*, 15.

34. See ibid., 17.

35. Rouben Paul Adalian, "Armenian Genocide," in *Encyclopedia of Genocide*, ed. Charny, 61.

36. Fein, *Accounting for Genocide*, 4.

37. See Stephen R. Haynes, *Reluctant Witnesses: Jews and the Christian Imagination* (Louisville, Ky.: Westminster John Knox Press, 1995), 7.

38. Ibid., 7–8.

## Chapter 1

1. Albert Camus, *The Rebel: An Essay on Man in Revolt*, trans. Anthony Bower (New York: Vintage Books, 1956), 297.

2. For a comprehensive treatment, see H. H. Ben-Sasson, ed., *A History of the Jewish People* (Cambridge, Mass.: Harvard University Press, 1976).

3. A helpful resource for biblical history is provided by Howard Clark Kee, Eric M. Meyers, John Rogerson, and Anthony J. Saldarini, *The Cambridge Companion to the Bible* (Cambridge: Cambridge University Press, 1997).

4. One might also speak of these people as "proto-Israelites" to indicate that they were precursors of the Jewish people but not yet fully formed into that identity or conscious of it.

5. For more detail on Marr, see Moshe Zimmerman, *Wilhelm Marr: The Patriarch of Anti-Semitism* (Oxford: Oxford University Press, 1986).

6. An authoritative source on the subject is Robert Wistrich, *Antisemitism: The Longest Hatred* (New York: Schocken Books, 1992). See also Jocelyn Hellig, *The Holocaust and Antisemitism: A Short History* (Oxford: Oneworld Publications, 2003).

7. For more on this point, see John Dominic Crossan, *Who Killed Jesus? Exposing the Roots of Anti-Semitism in the Gospel Story of the Death of Jesus* (San Francisco: HarperSanFrancisco, 1995), esp. 147–59.

8. Some scholars argue that Jesus is best regarded not only as a rabbi but as a Pharisee as well. Only apparently at odds with the New Testament, this revisionist view has much to commend it. See, for example, Clark M. Williamson, *Has God Rejected His People? Anti-Judaism in the Christian Church* (Nashville: Abingdon, 1982), 11–29. This book also provides a reliable overview of the development of anti-Jewish teaching within the Christian tradition. For more in this vein about Jesus, see Harvey Falk, *Jesus the Pharisee* (Ramsey, N.J.: Paulist Press, 1985) and Leonard C. Yaseen, *The Jesus Connection: To Triumph over Anti-Semitism* (New York: Crossroad, 1985).

9. The New Testament letters by and attributed to Paul have often been read as expressing anti-Jewish outlooks, including the idea that God has rejected the Jews because they failed to accept Jesus as the Messiah. Important current scholarship questions and revises this interpretation, which would seem to make Paul an early

proponent of Christian hostility toward Jews. The work of Krister Stendahl, Lloyd Gaston, Stanley Stowers, and John Gager, for example, finds Paul preaching the redemption of the Gentiles through faith in Jesus but also emphatically maintaining God's faithfulness to the covenant with the Jews and affirming the validity and holiness of the law set forth in the Torah. For informative analyses, see John G. Gager, *Reinventing Paul* (New York: Oxford University Press, 2000) and Sidney G. Hall III, *Christian Anti-Semitism and Paul's Theology* (Minneapolis: Fortress Press, 1993).

10. Josephus, *The Jewish War*, trans. H. St. J. Thackeray (Cambridge, Mass.: Harvard University Press, 1968), 6.3.420.

11. On the Pharisees, see Jacob Neusner, *From Politics to Piety: The Emergence of Pharisaic Judaism* (Englewood Cliffs, N.J.: Prentice-Hall, 1973).

12. On Rabbi Yochanan, see Jacob Neusner, *First-Century Judaism in Crisis* (Nashville: Abingdon, 1975).

13. See ibid., 145–47.

14. Judah Goldin, ed., *The Fathers According to Rabbi Nathan* (New Haven, Conn.: Yale University Press, 1955), 36. Cited in Neusner, *First-Century Judaism in Crisis*, 147.

15. See Josephus's account in *The Jewish War*, 7.331–94.

16. Norman Perrin, *The New Testament: An Introduction* (New York: Harcourt Brace Jovanovich, 1974), 40–41.

17. These include W. D. Davies, *The Setting of the Sermon on the Mount* (Cambridge: Cambridge University Press, 1964) and S. G. F. Brandon, *The Fall of Jerusalem and the Christian Church* (London: S.P.C.K., 1968).

18. See, for example, Norman Perrin, *Rediscovering the Teaching of Jesus* (New York: Harper & Row, 1967).

19. See Brandon, *The Fall of Jerusalem and the Christian Church*, 185–205.

20. Cited in Neusner, *First-Century Judaism in Crisis*, 167.

21. See Leon Festinger, Henry W. Riecken, and Stanley Schachter, *When Prophecy Fails* (Minneapolis: University of Minnesota Press, 1956); Leon Festinger, "Cognitive Dissonance," *Scientific American* 207 (Oct. 1962): 93–102; and Elliot Aronson, "The Rationalizing Animal," *Psychology Today* (May 1973): 46–52.

22. Reliable sources for more information on these topics include Norman A. Beck, *Mature Christianity in the Twenty-first Century: The Recognition and Repudiation of the Anti-Jewish Polemic in the New Testament*, rev. ed. (New York: Crossroad, 1994), 285–312; James H. Charlesworth, ed., *Jesus Two Thousand Years Later* (Harrisburg, Pa.: Trinity Press International, 2000); Reimund Bieringer, Didier Pollefeyt, and Frederique Vandecasteele-Vanneuville, eds., *Anti-Judaism and the Fourth Gospel* (Louisville, Ky.: Westminster John Knox Press, 2001); Paula Fredriksen and Adele Reinhartz, eds., *Jesus, Judaism, and Christian Anti-Judaism: Reading the New Testament after the Holocaust* (Louisville, Ky.: Westminster John Knox Press, 2002).

23. See Richard L. Rubenstein, "The Dean and the Chosen People," in *After Auschwitz: History, Theology, and Contemporary Judaism*, 2d ed. (Baltimore: Johns Hopkins University Press, 1992), 3–13. Unless otherwise indicated our subsequent citations from *After Auschwitz* are to the second edition noted here.

## Chapter 2

1. The term is Jules Isaac's. See his books *The Teaching of Contempt: Christian Roots of Anti-Semitism*, ed. Claire Huchet-Bishop and trans. Helen Weaver (New York: Holt, Rinehart & Winston, 1964) and *Jesus and Israel*, trans. Sally Gran (New York: Holt, Rinehart & Winston, 1971). A Jewish historian who lived in France,

Isaac lost most of his family in the Holocaust. Subsequently, he turned his attention to the Christian roots of antisemitism and the links between the Holocaust and long-standing Christian hostility toward Jews. Among those who felt the impact of Isaac's work was Pope John XXIII, who began important post-Holocaust revisions that have helped to eliminate much of the "teaching of contempt" from Christian theology. For more detail on the entire history of the relationships between Roman Catholic Christianity and the Jewish tradition, see James Carroll, *Constantine's Sword: The Church and the Jews* (Boston: Houghton Mifflin, 2001) and David I. Kertzer, *The Popes against the Jews: The Vatican's Role in the Rise of Modern Anti-Semitism* (New York: Alfred A. Knopf, 2001).

2. Because the term *antisemitism* and its variations are relatively recent, having appeared first in the second half of the nineteenth century, a distinction is sometimes made between *antisemitism* and Christian *anti-Judaism*, which might be regarded as earlier than and different from *antisemitism*. Briefly and broadly, we take *antisemitism* to refer to negative emotions, beliefs, and practices focused on Jews as Jews. Common usage, we believe, now follows that broad definition of the term. In our view, Christian anti-Judaism, which is a highly theological concept, is best interpreted as a foundational form, but not the entirety, of Christian antisemitism, for Christian animosity has been directed at Jews as Jews, not just at Judaism or at Jews as religious practitioners. Christian animosity toward Jews is not restricted to religious considerations alone. The religious aspects mix and mingle with a wide variety of other prejudicial ingredients that are social, political, and economic. While recognizing the particular and foundational reality of Christian anti-Judaism, we also refer to Christian antisemitism because, in addition to fitting better with common usage, the concept's scope reaches further and deeper than that of Christian anti-Judaism alone.

3. In making these points, we are indebted to Carroll, *Constantine's Sword*, 58, 633 n.1 and to Padraic O'Hare, *The Enduring Covenant: The Education of Christians and the End of Antisemitism* (Valley Forge, Pa.: Trinity Press International, 1997), 7.

4. The quotations in this paragraph are from Léon Poliakov, *The History of Anti-Semitism*, vol. 1: *From the Time of Christ to the Court Jews*, trans. Richard Howard (New York: Schocken Books, 1974), 25. For more on the subject of Christian-Jewish relations during this period, see John Gager, *The Origins of Anti-Semitism: Attitudes toward Judaism in Pagan and Christian Antiquity* (New York: Oxford University Press, 1983); Robert L. Wilkin, *John Chrysostom and the Jews: Rhetoric and Reality in the Late Fourth Century* (Berkeley: University of California Press, 1983); and Wistrich, *Antisemitism*.

5. For more information on these points, see Haynes, *Reluctant Witnesses*, 25–63.

6. Bauer, *A History of the Holocaust*, 34. For more detail on antisemitism in Poland during this period, see Hillel Levine, *Economic Origins of Antisemitism: Poland and Its Jews in the Early Modern Period* (New Haven, Conn.: Yale University Press, 1991).

7. Poliakov, *History of Antisemitism*, 1:123.

8. Cited in ibid., 1:122.

9. For more detail on Luther and the Jews, see Mark U. Edwards Jr., *Luther's Last Battles: A Study of the Polemics of the Older Luther, 1531–1546* (Ithaca, N.Y.: Cornell University Press, 1983) and Richard Marius, *Martin Luther: The Christian between God and Death* (Cambridge, Mass.: Harvard University Press, 1999). See also Carroll, *Constantine's Sword*, 365–68, 426–28; Haynes, *Reluctant Witnesses*, 45–50; Heiko A. Oberman, *The Origins of Anti-Semitism in the Age of Renaissance and Reformation*, trans. James I. Porter (Philadelphia: Fortress Press, 1984); and Wistrich, *Antisemitism*, 38–42.

10. Ernst Troeltsch, *The Social Teachings of the Christian Churches*, 2 vols., trans. Olive Wyon (New York: Harper & Row, 1960), 2:468.

11. Ibid., 2:468–69.

12. Martin Luther, *On the Jews and Their Lies*, trans. Martin H. Bertram, in *Luther's Works*, ed. Franklin Sherman and Helmut T. Lehman (Philadelphia: Fortress Press, 1971), 47:192.

13. Troeltsch, *The Social Teachings of the Christian Churches*, 2:470.

14. See Walter Bienert, *Martin Luther und die Juden: Ein Quellenbuch mit zeitgenössischen Illustrationen, mit Einführungen und Erlauterungen* (Frankfurt am Main: Evangelisches Verlagswerk, 1982), 130–32.

15. Ibid., 130.

16. Luther, *On the Jews and Their Lies*, 47:137.

17. Ibid., 47:138.

18. Ibid., 47:138–39.

19. "Ein Wort zur Judenfrage, der Reichsbruderrat der Evangelische Kirche in Deutschland" (8 April 1948), in *Der Ungekündigte Bund: Neue Begegnung von Juden und Christlicher*, ed. Dietrich Goldschmidt and Hans-Joachim Kraus (Stuttgart: Gemeinde Kreuz Verlag, 1962), 251–54.

20. The "Declaration of the Evangelical Lutheran Church in America to the Jewish Community," dated 18 April 1994, officially rejects what it calls Martin Luther's "anti-Judaic diatribes and the violent recommendations of his later writings against the Jews." Calling Luther's rhetoric "violent invective," the declaration expresses "deep and abiding sorrow over its tragic effects on subsequent generations. . . . including the Holocaust of the twentieth century." This declaration further states that "we recognize in anti-Semitism a contradiction and an affront to the Gospel, a violation of our hope and calling, and we pledge this church to oppose the deadly working of such bigotry, both within our own circles and in the society around us."

21. Luther, *On the Jews and Their Lies*, 47:139.

22. Ibid., 47:154.

23. Ibid., 47:172.

24. Ibid., 47:156–57. For the biblical reference to the Persians, see Esther 9:5ff.

25. See Norman Cohn, *Warrant for Genocide: The Myth of the Jewish World Conspiracy and the Protocols of the Elders of Zion* (New York: Harper & Row, 1967).

26. For more on Henry Ford's antisemitism, see Neil Baldwin, *Henry Ford and the Jews* (New York: Public Affairs, 2001).

27. Bienert, *Martin Luther*, 174–77.

28. Luther, *On the Jews and Their Lies*, 47:267–69.

29. Ibid., 47:268 n. 173.

30. H. H. Borchert and George Merz, eds., *Martin Luther: Ausgewählte Werke* (Munich, 1936), 3:61ff. See also Aarne Siirala, "Reflections from a Lutheran Perspective," in *Auschwitz: Beginning of a New Era?* ed. Eva Fleischner (New York: KTAV, 1977), 135–48.

31. See John S. Conway, *The Nazi Persecution of the Churches, 1933–45* (New York: Basic Books, 1968), 1–44, 261–67, and esp. 411 for Dibelius. For further information about other leading German theologians and their roles during the Nazi period, consult Robert P. Ericksen, *Theologians under Hitler: Gerhard Kittel, Paul Althaus, and Emmanuel Hirsch* (New Haven, Conn.: Yale University Press, 1985).

32. For more information about the role of German Lutheranism in the Third Reich, see Doris L. Bergen, *Twisted Cross: The German Christian Movement in the Third Reich* (Chapel Hill: University of North Carolina Press, 1996) and Robert P. Ericksen and Susannah Heschel, eds., *Betrayal: German Churches and the Holocaust* (Minneapolis: Fortress Press, 1999).

33. While the topic reaches beyond the scope of this book, the upsurge of religiously inspired violence in the late twentieth and early twenty-first centuries, seen especially but not exclusively in Islamic fundamentalism, is related to these factors. Significant studies in this field include Mark Juergensmeyer, *Terror in the Mind of God: The Global Rise of Religious Violence*, updated ed. (Berkeley: University of California Press, 2001) and Gilles Kepel, *The Revenge of God: The Resurgence of Islam, Christianity, and Judaism in the Modern World*, trans. Alan Braley (University Park, Pa.: Pennsylvania State University Press, 1994).

34. Quoted from Michael Berenbaum, ed., *Witness to the Holocaust* (New York: HarperCollins, 1997), 161.

35. Our discussion of Pope Paul IV is indebted to Carroll, *Constantine's Sword*, 371–84. For further discussion of the *limpieza de sangre* doctrine and racism, see George M. Fredrickson, *Racism: A Short History* (Princeton: Princeton University Press, 2002).

36. Carroll, *Constantine's Sword*, 376.

37. Ibid.

38. Important arguments in support of this thesis are offered by Zygmunt Bauman, *Modernity and the Holocaust* (Ithaca, N.Y.: Cornell University Press, 1991).

39. The passages quoted from Voltaire (1694–1778) are taken from Paul Mendes-Flohr and Jehuda Reinharz, eds., *The Jew in the Modern World: A Documentary History*, 2d ed. (New York: Oxford University Press, 1995), 305. This volume is an excellent resource for modern Jewish history.

40. Quoted from ibid., 115.

41. Additional views about the Enlightenment's impact on Jewish life can be found in Jacob Katz, *From Prejudice to Destruction: Anti-Semitism, 1700–1933* (Cambridge, Mass.: Harvard University Press, 1980).

42. See, for example, Bauer, *A History of the Holocaust*, 23–35.

43. Ibid., 38–42.

## Chapter 3

1. See Mendes-Flohr and Reinharz, eds., *The Jew in the Modern World*, 343–46.

2. Daniel Jonah Goldhagen, *Hitler's Willing Executioners: Ordinary Germans and the Holocaust* (New York: Alfred A. Knopf, 1996), 428, 591 n. 26. The cover of Goldhagen's book features a photograph of a Nazi rally at which Treitschke's slogan was prominently displayed. A useful and more moderate perspective than Goldhagen's is provided by another book that appeared in the same year. See John Weiss, *Ideology of Death: Why the Holocaust Happened in Germany* (Chicago: Ivan R. Dee, 1996). For criticism of Goldhagen, see Franklin H. Littell, ed., *Hyping the Holocaust: Scholars Answer Goldhagen* (East Rockaway, N.Y.: Cummings & Hathaway, 1997) and Robert R. Shandley, ed., *Unwilling Germans? The Goldhagen Debate*, trans. Jeremiah Riemer (Minneapolis: University of Minnesota Press, 1998). Another important perspective on German antisemitism—one that also dissents from Goldhagen—is provided by Helmut Walser Smith, *The Butcher's Tale: Murder and Anti-Semitism in a German Town* (New York: W. W. Norton, 2002). Smith's focus on the town of Konitz in 1900 shows in detail how anti-Jewish sentiment worked and was inflamed in a particular place. Less interested in generality than in particularity, Smith seeks to understand the process that made "latent anti-Semitism manifest" in Konitz (22).

3. George L. Mosse, *Toward the Final Solution: A History of European Racism* (New York: Howard Fertig, 1978), 168.

4. For a good overview of this French background, see Robert Wistrich's chapter "France: From Dreyfus to Le Pen" is his *Antisemitism*, 126–44. When the Ger-

mans occupied France in June 1940, about 350,000 Jews lived there. Less than half were French citizens. Jewish refugees from Germany, the Netherlands, Belgium, and Luxembourg numbered in the tens of thousands.

5. Robert S. Wistrich, *Hitler and the Holocaust* (New York: Modern Library, 2001), 16.

6. See Katz, *From Prejudice to Destruction*, 108, 119–120. For further background on related topics, see Jacob Katz, *Out of the Ghetto: The Social Background of Jewish Emancipation, 1770–1870* (Cambridge, Mass.: Harvard University Press, 1973).

7. For more detail about this thesis, see Rubenstein, *The Age of Triage*, 128–67.

8. See Arthur Hertzberg, *The French Enlightenment and the Jews* (New York: Columbia University Press, 1968), 280–313. See also Katz, *From Prejudice to Destruction*, 34–47.

9. Hertzberg, *The French Enlightenment and the Jews*, 365–66.

10. We take this term from C. B. MacPherson, *The Political Theory of Possessive Individualism: Hobbes to Locke* (Oxford: Clarendon Press, 1962).

11. On socialist antisemitism, see Edmund Silberner, *Sozialisten zur Judenfrage* (Berlin: Colloquium Verlag, 1962) and George Lichtheim, "Socialism and the Jews," *Dissent* 15 (July–Aug. 1968): 314–42.

12. On Fourier, see Silberner, *Sozialisten zur Judenfrage*, 16–27; Lichtheim, "Socialism and the Jews," 316–24; and Katz, *From Prejudice to Destruction*, 120–22.

13. See Karl Marx, "On the Jewish Question," in *Karl Marx: Selected Writings*, ed. David McLellan (Oxford: Oxford University Press, 1977), 39–62. See also Robert F. Byrnes, *Antisemitism in France*, vol. 1, *The Prologue to the Dreyfus Affair* (New Brunswick, N.J.: Rutgers University Press, 1950).

14. Pierre Haubtmann, ed., *Carnet de P. J. Proudhon: Text inédit et intégral* (Paris: M. Rivière, 1961), 2:337–38. Quoted in Lichtheim, "Socialism and the Jews," 322.

15. Lichtheim, "Socialism and the Jews," 323.

16. *Encyclopedia Judaica*, s.v. "Paris."

17. See Byrnes, *Antisemitism in Modern France*, 41, 96–97.

18. Ibid., 41.

19. A. M. Carr-Saunders, *World Population* (Oxford: Clarendon Press, 1936), 49, 56.

20. Byrnes, *Antisemitism in Modern France*, 126.

21. Quoted in ibid., 127.

22. On this topic and related issues see Kertzer, *The Popes against the Jews*, esp. 166–85. Also relevant are Carroll, *Constantine's Sword*, 439–49 and David I. Kertzer, *The Kidnapping of Edgardo Mortara* (New York: Alfred A. Knopf, 1997).

23. Our interpretation of the Dreyfus affair is informed by scholarly works such as Hannah Arendt, *The Origins of Totalitarianism*, rev. ed. (New York: Harcourt Brace Jovanovich, 1973), 89–120; Jean-Denis Bredin, *The Affair: The Case of Alfred Dreyfus*, trans. Jeffrey Mehlman (New York: George Braziller, 1986); Michael Burns, *Dreyfus: A Family Affair, 1789–1945* (New York: HarperCollins, 1991) and *France and the Dreyfus Affair: A Documentary History* (New York: St. Martin's, 1999); Carroll, *Constantine's Sword*, esp. 450–71; Guy Chapman, *The Dreyfus Case: A Reassessment* (New York: Reynal & Co., 1955); Leslie Derfler, *The Dreyfus Affair* (Westport, Conn.: Greenwood Press, 2002); Nicholas Halasz, *Captain Dreyfus: The Story of a Mass Hysteria* (New York: Simon & Schuster, 1955); Robert L. Hoffman, *More Than a Trial: The Struggle over Captain Dreyfus* (New York: Free Press, 1980); Michael R. Marrus, *The Politics of Assimilation: The French Jewish Community at the Time of the Dreyfus Affair* (Oxford: Clarendon Press, 1971); and Ivan Strenski, *Contesting Sacrifice: Religion, Nationalism, and Social Thought in France* (Chicago: University of Chicago Press, 2002).

24. Halasz, *Captain Dreyfus*, 20–21.

25. For a reproduction of this front page of *La Libre Parole*, see Burns, *France and the Dreyfus Affair*, 35.
26. See ibid., 50, and Halasz, *Captain Dreyfus*, 56.
27. Quoted in Halasz, *Captain Dreyfus*, 57.
28. See Maurice Paléologue, *An Intimate Journal of the Dreyfus Case*, trans. Eric Mosbacher (New York: Criterion Books, 1957), 53.
29. On the identification of the Jews with Judas, see Rubenstein, *After Auschwitz*, 21–22 and 50–51.
30. This conversation is discussed and quoted in Carl Schorske, *Fin-de-Siècle Vienna: Politics and Culture* (New York: Alfred A. Knopf, 1980), 162.
31. For biographical information on Esterhazy, see Chapman, *The Dreyfus Case*, 119–21.
32. See Burns, *France and the Dreyfus Affair*, 65.
33. For details on this matter, see ibid., 39, 68.
34. See ibid., 88.
35. See, for example, Max Weber, "Bureaucracy," in *From Max Weber: Essays in Sociology*, ed. H. H. Gerth and C. Wright Mills (New York: Oxford University Press, 1976), 196–244.
36. The text of Zola's letter, with a copy of the famous front page from *L'Aurore*, can be found in Burns, *France and the Dreyfus Affair*, 93–103.
37. Quoted in Chapman, *The Dreyfus Case*, 199.
38. Quoted in Halasz, *Captain Dreyfus*, 123. For background about the anti-Jewish role of *La Civiltà Cattolica*, see Kertzer, *The Popes against the Jews*, 133–51.
39. Quoted in Halasz, *Captain Dreyfus*, 123.
40. Burns, *France and the Dreyfus Affair*, 120. Burns adds that "the assembly ordered that the speech and the incriminating letter be posted in every one of France's thirty-six thousand town halls."
41. Maurrus's defense appeared in *Gazette de France*, 6–7 Sept. 1898. The text is reproduced in Burns, *France and the Dreyfus Affair*, 122–23.
42. See Eugen J. Weber, *Action Française: Royalism and Reaction in Twentieth-Century France* (Stanford, Calif.: Stanford University Press, 1962).
43. The English leaders included Cardinal Henry Manning, Archbishop of Westminster, and the Duke of Norfolk. See Kertzer, *The Popes against the Jews*, 176, 184, 214–22.
44. Weber, *Action Française*, 445.
45. Quoted in Burns, *France and the Dreyfus Affair*, 53.
46. *The Jewish Chronicle*, London, 17 Jan. 1896. Herzl's text, which anticipated his plan for the establishment of a Jewish state, is reproduced and helpfully annotated in Mendes-Flohr and Reinharz, eds., *The Jew in the Modern World*, 533–38.
47. For these details about the Dreyfus family, we are indebted to Burns, *Dreyfus: A Family Affair*, especially 467–87, and Carroll, *Constantine's Sword*, 467–71.

## Chapter 4

1. Peter the Great mandated the European calendar for Russia in 1700, but he retained the Julian version, not the Gregorian style initiated by Pope Gregory XIII in 1582. After the Russian revolution, in 1918, the "new calendar"—the Gregorian version—went into effect. The dates in our account of Russian history refer to the new calendar.
2. Quoted in Howard Morley Sachar, *The Course of Modern Jewish History* (New York: Dell Publishing Co., 1977), 246. The discussion in the first two sections of this chapter is indebted to Rubenstein, *The Age of Triage*. For more detail, see especially 135–64.

3. For more detail on Pobedonostsev, see Robert F. Byrnes, *Pobedonostsev: His Life and Thought* (Bloomington: Indiana University Press, 1968).

4. The most authoritative Hitler biography is Ian Kershaw's two-volume study, *Hitler, 1889–1936: Hubris* (New York: W. W. Norton, 1999) and *Hitler, 1936–1945: Nemesis* (New York: W. W. Norton, 2000). Other recent works of importance include Brigitte Hamann, *Hitler's Vienna: A Dictator's Apprenticeship*, trans. Thomas Thornton (New York: Oxford University Press, 1999) and Fritz Redlich, *Hitler: Diagnosis of a Destructive Prophet* (New York: Oxford University Press, 1999). Among older studies that remain influential, see Karl Dietrich Bracher, *The German Dictatorship: The Origins, Structures, and Effects of National Socialism*, trans. Jean Steinberg (New York: Praeger Publishers, 1970); Alan Bullock, *Hitler: A Study in Tyranny* (New York: Harper & Row, 1962); Joachim Fest, *Hitler*, trans. Richard and Clara Winston (New York: Harcourt Brace, 1974); Sebastian Hafner, *The Meaning of Hitler*, trans. Edwald Osers (Cambridge: Harvard University Press, 1983); and Eberhard Jäckel, *Hitler's Weltanschauung* (Middletown, Conn.: Wesleyan University Press, 1972). For worthwhile overviews of the themes, issues, and problems that confront Hitler's biographers, see John Lukacs, *The Hitler of History* (New York: Alfred A. Knopf, 1997) and Ron Rosenbaum, *Explaining Hitler: The Search for the Origins of His Evil* (New York: Random House, 1998). Also significant for our purposes are Gerald Fleming, *Hitler and the Final Solution* (Berkeley: University of California Press, 1984) and Sarah Gordon, *Hitler, Germans, and the "Jewish Question"* (Princeton: Princeton University Press, 1984). The latter volume has especially influenced our interpretations.

5. Quoted in A. J. Ryder, *Twentieth-Century Germany from Bismarck to Brandt* (New York: Columbia University Press, 1973), 40.

6. Oscar Handlin, *The Uprooted*, 2d ed. (Boston: Atlantic, Little, Brown, 1973), 32.

7. Carr-Saunders, *World Population*, 49ff.

8. See, for example, R. J. Rummel, *Death by Government* (New Brunswick, N.J.: Transaction Publishers, 1994), 13. Also relevant are Gil Eliot, *The Twentieth-Century Book of the Dead* (New York: Charles Scribner's Sons, 1972), 41, 94, 124 and Jonathan Glover, *Humanity*, 315–97. The twentieth-century's toll of human-inflicted death includes some sixty-five thousand Hereros, who were killed in what is arguably the first genocide of that century. In the German colony of Southwest Africa—today Namibia—the indigenous Hereros rebelled in 1904 when they learned of German plans to confine them to reservations. The German response to make the colony Herero-free was swift and lethal. By mid-August 1904, most of the Hereros' military force was destroyed. When they had offered to surrender, Lieutenant General Lothar von Trotha, with authorization from the kaiser, gave what came to be known as the *Vernichtungsbefehl* (extermination order). The remaining Hereros, women and children included, were driven into the Omaheke Desert, where the Germans had made water holes inaccessible and let the Hereros die of thirst. Among the German colonists at the time was the father of the key Nazi leader Hermann Göring.

In the aftermath of the genocide, the German scientist Eugen Fischer did racialist research on miscegenation. "Without exception," he concluded, "every European nation that has accepted the blood of inferior races—and only romantics can deny that Negroes, Hottentots, and many others are inferior—has paid for its acceptance of inferior elements with spiritual and cultural degeneration." Fischer proposed that "one should grant them the amount of protection that an inferior race confronting us requires to survive, no more and no less and only for so long as they are of use to us—otherwise free competition, that is, in my opinion, destruction." When Hitler wrote *Mein Kampf,* some of Fischer's racial writings were in his possession. Fischer joined the Nazi Party in 1932, occupied influential academic and research posts, and became a leading player in the so-called "race hygiene" and eugenics movement, which figured centrally in the mass murder and genocide that characterized the Nazi regime.

Another German writer who influenced Hitler was the geographer Friedrich Ratzel, his nation's leading authority on colonization in the late nineteenth and early twentieth centuries and the author of an 1897 book on political geography, which Hitler consulted while writing *Mein Kampf.* Ratzel also published a 1904 book, *Der Lebensraum,* in which he coined the term *Lebensraum* (living space) and elaborated the importance of territorial expansion as essential for the well-being of the German people. The term and its expansionist concept would both play a large part in Nazi objectives, which required not only the gaining of new territory but also its depopulation so that "inferior" groups would not threaten German racial purity. For more information on these points, see Henry Friedlander, *The Origins of Nazi Genocide: From Euthanasia to the Final Solution* (Chapel Hill: University of North Carolina Press, 1995), 11–14; Ben Kiernan, "Studying the Roots of Genocide," in *Will Genocide Ever End?* ed. Rittner, Roth, and Smith, 142; and Richard Rhodes, *Masters of Death: The SS Einsatzgruppen and the Invention of the Holocaust* (New York: Alfred A. Knopf, 2002), 92–95.

9. See *Encyclopedia Britannica* (2002), s.v. "World War I" and also Eliot, *The Twentieth-Century Book of the Dead,* 23, 218.

10. For an account of Verdun, see Alistair Horne, *The Price of Glory: Verdun, 1916* (New York: Harper & Row, 1967), 36. Of particular interest is a memorandum by Falkenhayn to the kaiser written in December 1915. There Falkenhayn argues for a strategy by which "the forces of France will bleed to death." For a bitter account of the slaughter by a German soldier, see William Hermanns, *The Holocaust: From a Survivor of Verdun* (New York: Harper & Row, 1972). Young Germans marched off to war singing, *"Siegreich wollen wir Frankreich schlagen, sterben als ein tapferer Held"* [Victoriously we will crush France and die as brave heroes].

11. As noted in the previous chapter, Daniel Goldhagen believes that, well before Hitler, the overwhelming majority of Germans were imbued with an "eliminationist" antisemitism that ultimately became "exterminationist." Goldhagen's thesis has been attacked as overly simplistic largely because of his insistence that *only* German antisemitism could yield so genocidal an outcome. His insistence on the complicity of ordinary Germans has been less criticized for good reasons. See Goldhagen, *Hitler's Willing Executioners.*

Goldhagen's book was followed by the publication of an extraordinary wartime diary by Victor Klemperer, a converted Jew who was dismissed from his academic position but was permitted to survive in Dresden because of his German spouse. Later, there will be more to say about Klemperer's diary, but in this context it is significant to note that his two volumes provide a day by day account of his experiences as a Jew in Nazi Germany. Although he registers acts of kindness and sympathy on the part of a few Germans, his diaries record with painstaking clarity the humiliations and indignities to which he was subjected daily. The diaries also make abundantly clear how deeply Nazi values had penetrated the beliefs and behavior of the overwhelming majority of Germans in all walks of life. See Victor Klemperer, *I Will Bear Witness: A Diary of the Nazi Years,* trans. Martin Chalmers, vol. 1 (New York: Random House, 1998); vol. 2 (New York: Random House, 2000). See also Robert Gellately, *Backing Hitler: Consent and Coercion in Nazi Germany* (New York: Oxford University Press, 2001). Gellately's detailed analysis of public opinion in Nazi Germany shows that "from the beginning of the new Reich in 1933, into the war years, and down to its last desperate months . . . Hitler was largely successful in getting the backing, one way or another, of the great majority of citizens" (vii–viii). For further discussion of related points see Eric A. Johnson, *Nazi Terror: The Gestapo, Jews, and Ordinary Germans* (New York: Basic Books, 1999).

12. *Encyclopedia Britannica* (2002), s.v. "Somme, First Battle of." For a more detailed account of the battle, see Martin Middlebrook, *The First Day on the Somme* (New York: W. W. Norton, 1972). Middlebrook numbers the casualties of both sides as 1,300,000. He is less critical of Haig than many of the general's detractors. Those who defend Haig tend to assert that the British offensive at the Somme relieved pressure on the French at Verdun and thus made it possible for the French to remain in the war. See also Major General Sir John Davidson, K.C.M.G., C.B., D.S.O., director of operations in France, 1916–18, *Haig: Master of the Field* (London: P. Nevill, 1953) for a spirited defense of Haig. One of Haig's most unremitting critics was Winston Churchill. See Churchill, *The World Crisis*, rev. ed. (London: Odhams, 1938), 950–73, 1070–93. Haig was promoted to the rank of field marshal after the battle.

13. See Robin Prior and Trevor Wilson, *Passchendaele: The Untold Story* (New Haven, Conn.: Yale University Press, 1996).

14. On the casualties, see ibid., 185–87, 194–95. For a brief summary of the battle, see the edited text of Geoffrey Miller, "The Battle of 3rd Ypres (Passchendaele)" at http://www.ukans.edu/~kansite/ww_one/comment/ypres3.html.

15. The subculture and its long-term political consequences are graphically yet succinctly described in Omer Bartov, *Mirrors of Destruction: War, Genocide, and Modern Identity* (New York: Oxford University Press, 2000), 10–43.

16. See Robert Blake, ed., *The Private Papers of Douglas Haig 1914–1918* (London: Eyre & Spottiswoode, 1952), 9.

17. For examples of this fraternization, see Glover, *Humanity*, 156–64.

18. See Bartov, *Mirrors of Destruction*, 12–14. Especially for the defeated Germans, the war also produced its harvest of bitterness and despair. Disillusionment and discontent mixed and mingled with a glorification of sacrifice and war to provide a deep reservoir of emotion on which Hitler and the Nazis could draw. A helpful discussion of related themes is found in Robert Weldon Whalen, *Bitter Wounds: German Victims of the Great War, 1914–1939* (Ithaca, N.Y.: Cornell University Press, 1984).

19. Bartov, *Mirrors of Destruction*, 13.

20. Ibid., 18.

21. Ibid., 14–22.

22. Ibid., 99–104. Bartov points out that the French, although victors in the Great War, felt that they were among its victims. Furthermore, French concerns about national unity and identity after the war led to a resurgence of antisemitism, especially in the 1930s. When France fell to Germany in 1940, there was a widespread perception that a Jewish presence, increased by a considerable refugee population, was not advantageous to France. That outlook facilitated the willing cooperation of Pétain's collaborationist government in the deportation of tens of thousands of Jews to certain death in Auschwitz. For the intensification of French antisemitism in the 1930s, see Michael R. Marrus and Robert O. Paxton, *Vichy France and the Jews* (New York: Basic Books, 1981); Eugen Joseph Weber, *The Hollow Years: France in the 1930s* (New York: W. W. Norton, 1994); and Susan Zuccotti, *The Holocaust, The French, and the Jews* (New York: Basic Books, 1993).

23. See Bartov, *Mirrors of Destruction*, 25. Also relevant are Fest, *Hitler*, 67–86, 511–38, and Robert G. L. Waite, "Adolf Hitler: A Life Sketch," in *Hitler and Nazi Germany*, ed. Robert G. L. Waite (New York: Holt, Rinehart & Winston, 1969).

24. Contrary to Hitler's oft-repeated claim, no "stab in the back" had defeated Germany. Instead, superior Allied resources and German exhaustion eventually

brought the war to an end. Some eleven million men, almost 20 percent of the German population, had been mobilized. About 1.7 million of them were killed, another 4.2 million wounded. Furthermore, from March to July 1918 alone, 750,000 German soldiers were wounded and about 1.75 million more were incapacitated by one of the world's worst influenza epidemics.

25. Bauer, *A History of the Holocaust*, 63.
26. As the Jew became seen increasingly as a betrayer, that image was reinforced by the New Testament's narratives about Judas's betrayal of Jesus (see Mark 14:10–21; Matthew 26:14–25). In its portrayal of Jesus' disciples, the Christian imagination traditionally regarded Judas as definitively Jewish. The other disciples were seen, anachronistically, as Christians or at least as faithful to their leader. Throughout much of Christian history, the Jews were identified with Judas. Since Judas alone among those present at the Last Supper was traditionally so identified, the implied moral of the Judas story was that one can never trust a Jew. The Judas story, which is part and parcel of the passion drama, would be heard and relived by Christians in Germany during Holy Week as well as in the passion plays that were highly popular in Germany and Austria. Few stereotypical images have been as consistently reinforced in the most emotionally potent environments as the one that equates Jews with Judas. In Nazi Germany the image of Jew as Judas supported the belief that Jews would have to be eliminated, lest they attempt again to betray and destroy Germany. So intense was this belief among some Germans that, even when they knew that all was lost, they continued to kill the Jewish "enemy" until the very end of the war in 1945.
27. In this paragraph and subsequent ones dealing with Hitler's rise to power, we draw on material that John Roth prepared for Roth et al., *The Holocaust Chronicle*.
28. Our discussion of *Mein Kampf* is indebted to Michael D. Ryan, "Hitler's Challenge to the Churches: A Theological Political Analysis of *Mein Kampf*," in *The German Church Struggle and the Holocaust*, ed. Franklin H. Littell and Hubert G. Locke (Detroit: Wayne State University Press, 1974), 148–64.
29. The concept of *Lebensraum* also figures prominently in Hitler's so-called *Zweites Buch*, which he wrote in the late 1920s but did not publish. See Adolf Hitler, *Hitler's Secret Book*, trans. Salvator Attanasio (New York: Grove Press, 1983).
30. Saul Friedländer, *Nazi Germany and the Jews*, vol. 1, *The Years of Persecution, 1933–1939* (New York: HarperCollins, 1997), 73–112.
31. Yehuda Bauer, *Rethinking the Holocaust*, 92.
32. Goldhagen, *Hitler's Willing Executioners*, 454.
33. For statistical data on the Nazis, consult Tim Kirk, *The Longman Companion to Nazi Germany* (New York: Longman, 1995).
34. Gordon, *Hitler, Germans and the Jewish Question*, 83–84.
35. Congressional Committee on Immigration, *Temporary Suspension of Immigration*, Sixty-fifth Congress, Third Session, House of Representatives, Report no. 1109, 6 December 1920.
36. Celia S. Heller, *On the Edge of Destruction: Jews of Poland between the Two World Wars* (New York: Columbia University Press, 1977), 101–7. For more on Poland, see Richard C. Lukas, *The Forgotten Holocaust: The Poles under German Occupation 1939–1944* (Lexington: University Press of Kentucky, 1986); Antony Polonsky, ed., *"My Brother's Keeper?": Recent Polish Debates on the Holocaust* (London: Routledge, 1990); Yisrael Gutman and Shmuel Krakowski, *Poles and Jews between the Wars* (New York: Schocken Books, 1986); and Jan Karski, *The Great Powers and Poland 1919–1945: From Versailles to Yalta* (Lanham, Md.: University Press of America, 1985). Karski is one of the heroes of the Polish resistance. His eyewitness accounts of the Holocaust in Poland were communicated in person to Western leaders, including Franklin D. Roosevelt, in November 1942. A tree at

Yad Vashem, Israel's Holocaust memorial in Jerusalem, honors him as a "Righteous Gentile."

37. Here it is relevant to note that Polish-Jewish relations still show Holocaust-related stresses and strains. Debates about these tensions flashed in 2001 when Jan T. Gross, a Polish-born New York University political scientist published *Neighbors: The Destruction of the Jewish Community in Jedwabne, Poland* (Princeton, N.J.: Princeton University Press, 2001). Gross documents what happened in Jedwabne, a village about 120 miles northeast of Warsaw, the Polish capital, on 10 July 1941, a few weeks after the Nazi invasion of Soviet-held territory put the town under German occupation. On that day, 1,600 of Jedwabne's Jews were beaten and brutally murdered by their non-Jewish neighbors. A postwar monument falsely attributed the slaughter to the Germans. They undoubtedly approved it, but Poles did the killing, which may have been motivated by the perception that Jedwabne's Jews had cooperated with the Soviets. On the sixtieth anniversary of the massacre a new memorial was installed, but it did not state explicitly that Poles killed the town's Jews. Controversy about the complex relations between Jews and Poles in a country where Nazi Germany's Final Solution annihilated about 90 percent of Poland's nearly 3.5 million Jews is not likely to go away anytime soon. Meanwhile, at the time of this writing an estimated twenty thousand Jews continue to live in Poland.

38. Quoted in John Toland, *Adolf Hitler* (New York: Ballantine Books, 1977), 384. Further background on the German situation during this period is available in Burleigh, *The Third Reich*, especially 27–145, and Harold James, *The German Slump: Politics and Economics 1924–1936* (Oxford: Clarendon Press, 1986).

39. See Klaus Scholder, *The Churches and the Third Reich,* trans. John Bowden (Philadelphia: Fortress Press, 1987), 1:247.

40. Burleigh, *The Third Reich*, 155.

41. See Toland, *Adolf Hitler*, 439.

42. Adolf Hitler, *Mein Kampf,* trans. Ralph Manheim (Boston: Houghton Mifflin, 1971), 398.

43. For more detail on these matters, particularly as they related to the broader history of economic and political modernization in the West, see Rubenstein, *The Age of Triage*, especially 146–50.

44. For example, on 7 April 1933, the Law for the Restoration of the Professional Civil Service, which will be discussed in greater detail below, went into effect. It drove all Jewish professors of law from their positions in German universities. As a result, 120 of the 378 teaching positions at German law schools were available for new appointments, who were chosen on the basis of their commitment to National Socialism. See Ingo Müller, *Hitler's Justice: The Courts of the Third Reich,* trans. Deborah Lucas Schneider (Cambridge, Mass.: Harvard University Press, 1991), 69. On the displacement of Jewish physicians, see Michael H. Kater, *Doctors Under Hitler* (Chapel Hill: University of North Carolina Press, 1989), 177–221. As Kater shows, National Socialist doctors wanted the "complete riddance of the Jewish competition" (203). When Hitler came to power in 1933, there had been approximately 6,500 Jewish doctors in Germany. By late September 1938, Kater documents, they had "to all intents and purposes vanished from the German medical scene" (200).

45. Schleunes, *The Twisted Road to Auschwitz*, xiv. For later developments related to this point, see Christopher R. Browning, *Fateful Months: Essays on the Emergence of the Final Solution* (New York: Holmes & Meier, 1985) and *The Path to Genocide: Essays on Launching the Final Solution* (Cambridge: Cambridge University Press, 1992); and Peter Longerich, *The Unwritten Order: Hitler's Role in the Final Solution* (Charleston, S.C.: Tempus Publishing, 2001). Along with Browning,

Robert Jan van Pelt, and other leading Holocaust scholars, Longerich served as an expert witness for the defense in the 2000 libel trial before the British High Court, a proceeding in which David Irving sued Deborah Lipstadt, an American historian of the Holocaust, and Penguin Books, her British publisher, on the grounds that Lipstadt's book *Denying the Holocaust* had falsely labeled him a Holocaust denier. Since Lipstadt's defense never backed away from identifying Irving as a denier, it had to show that Irving persistently distorted historical evidence in writings and speeches that did deny the Holocaust. Thus, in a court of law the defense had to document in detail not only that the Holocaust happened but also how. The case was decided in favor of the defendants, Lipstadt and Penguin Books.

Longerich's task was to document Hitler's role in the Holocaust. His book is based partly on the extensive report that he prepared for the trial. At one point, he summarizes his findings as follows: "The murder of the European Jews was not the outcome of a single order but the result of a policy pursued by the regime over a relatively long period of time, which was time and time again driven forward decisively by Hitler himself" (120).

For more detail on the Irving-Lipstadt trial, see the transcript of Justice Charles Gray's deliberation and decision in the case, *The Irving Judgment: David Irving v. Penguin Books and Professor Deborah Lipstadt* (London: Penguin Books, 2000). Also significant in this regard is Robert Jan van Pelt, *The Case for Auschwitz: Evidence from the Irving Trial* (Bloomington: Indiana University Press, 2002). Van Pelt is a Holocaust historian who has specialized in the architecture of Auschwitz. His part in the Irving-Lipstadt trial was to demonstrate the existence of gas chambers at Auschwitz and to show that they were used to murder hundreds of thousands of Jews. Van Pelt's book is based largely on his testimony in the trial.

46. See Lucy S. Dawidowicz, *The War against the Jews 1933–1945* (1975; New York: Bantam Books, 1976), 21–23. For two views that take issue with Dawidowicz, see Yehuda Bauer, "Genocide: Was It the Nazis' Original Plan?" in *Reflections on the Holocaust*, ed. Irene G. Shur, Franklin H. Littell, and Marvin Wolfgang (Philadelphia: American Academy of Political and Social Science, 1980), 35–45; and John K. Roth "How to Make Hitler's Ideas Clear?" *Philosophical Forum* 16 (1984–85): 82–94.

47. Philippe Burrin, *Hitler and the Jews: The Genesis of the Holocaust,* trans. Patsy Southgate (London: Edward Arnold, 1994), 19. Even as Hitler waged war from September 1939 and on into 1941, Burrin believes both that Hitler's antisemitism gave him "less than a master plan" and that Hitler's anti-Jewish outlook had become much more than "a simple obsession" (150). Now he "harbored the intention of exterminating the Jews"; nevertheless, his intention was "not absolute but conditional" and would be carried out "only in the event of a well-defined situation" (23). Burrin thinks the crucial situation arose when Hitler feared, in the late summer and autumn of 1941, that Germany's military campaign against the Soviet Union might not be won. As we shall see, historians continue to debate the question of when the Final Solution became state policy.

48. For further excerpts from this speech, see Berenbaum, ed., *Witness to the Holocaust*, 160–62.

49. Gellately, *Backing Hitler*, 4.

50. Ibid.

51. Heinz Höhne, *The Order of the Death's Head: The Story of Hitler's SS*, trans. Richard Barry (1966; New York: Ballantine Books, 1971), 17. The subsequent discussion of the Röhm purge draws on John Roth's discussion of the topic in Roth et al., *The Holocaust Chronicle*.

52. See Klaus Fischer, *Nazi Germany: A New History* (New York: Continuum, 1995), 293, and Alan Bullock, *Hitler: A Study in Tyranny*, abr. ed. (New York: Harper & Row, 1971), 168–69.

## Chapter 5

1. Adolf Hitler, "Letter to Adolf Gemlich, September 16, 1919," in *A Holocaust Reader*, ed. Lucy S. Dawidowicz (New York: Behrman House, 1976), 30.
2. Hitler, *Mein Kampf*, 65. The emphasis is Hitler's.
3. Saul Friedländer refers to Hitler's addresses to the conservative-nationalist Hamburg National Club of 1919 on 28 February 1926 and the Düsseldorf Industry Club on 27 January 1932. See Friedländer, *Nazi Germany and the Jews*, 101–2. See also Kershaw, *Hitler, 1889–1936: Hubris*, 358–59.
4. See Ulrich Herbert, "Extermination Policy: New Answers and Questions about the History of the 'Holocaust' in German Historiography," in *National Socialist Extermination Policies: Contemporary German Perspectives and Controversies*, ed. Ulrich Herbert (New York: Berghahn Books, 2000), 19.
5. Ibid., 19–20.
6. Ibid., 20.
7. Ibid., 20–21. See also Scholder, *The Churches and the Third Reich*, 1:99–119 and 254–279; Victoria Barnett, *For the Soul of the People: Protestant Protest against Hitler* (New York: Oxford University Press, 1992), 14–17; Ericksen and Heschel, eds. *Betrayal*; and Werner Jochmann, "Die Ausbreitung des Antisemitismus in Deutschland," in *Gesellschaftskrise und Judenfeinschaft in Deutschland*, ed. Werner Jochmann (Hamburg: Christians, 1988), 99–170.
8. Herbert, "Extermination Policy," 24–25. See also Ulrich Herbert, *Best: Biographische Studien über Radikalismus, Weltanschauung, und Vernunft, 1903–1989* (Bonn: J. H. W. Dietz, 1996), 68ff.
9. Herbert, "Extermination Policy," 26.
10. Ibid.
11. Ibid. See also Ulrich Herbert, "Weltanschauungseliten: Ideologische Legitimation und politische Praxis der Führungsgruppe der nationalsocialistischen Sicherheitspolizei," *Potsdamer Bulletin für zeithistorische Studien* 9 (1997): 4–18, and Herbert, *Best*, 191ff.
12. Between 1933 and 1937 the SD grew from two hundred and fifty members to about five thousand. Michael Burleigh points out that "some 41 percent of the SD had higher education, at a time when the national average was 2 or 3 percent." See Burleigh, *The Third Reich*, 186.
13. Herbert, "Extermination Policy," 26.
14. See Edwin Black, *The Transfer Agreement: The Dramatic Story of the Pact between the Third Reich and Jewish Palestine* (New York: Carrol & Graf, 2001), 46–70.
15. Here we draw on material prepared by John Roth for Roth et al., *The Holocaust Chronicle*.
16. The Nazis' definitional scheme was based, of course, on a fundamentally false premise, that Jews are a race. Jews are not a race. In principle, any human being can be a Jew. The possibility of conversion testifies to that. For the Nazis, however, Jews were a race. In Germany, moreover, the Nazis had the power to define social reality. Their racial definition of Jews testified to that.
17. Burleigh, *The Third Reich*, 295–96.
18. Raul Hilberg, "The Nature of the Process," in *Survivors, Victims, and Perpetrators: Essays on the Nazi Holocaust*, ed. Joel E. Dimsdale (New York: Hemisphere Publishing Co., 1980), 5.

19. See Karl A. Schleunes, ed., *Legislating the Holocaust: The Bernhard Loesner Memoirs and Supporting Documents*, trans. Carol Scherer (Boulder, Colo.: Westview Press, 2001). Loesner (1890–1952), a lawyer, joined the Nazi Party in 1931 and served in the Third Reich's Ministry of the Interior from April 1933 to March 1943. His duties included the drafting and oversight of anti-Jewish legislation, including the Nuremberg Laws, but he advocated distinctions between full Jews and *Mischlinge* that put at least a partial break on that legislation's severity.

20. When the Nazis came to power in 1933, Germany's Jewish population, which never rose above approximately 1 percent, numbered about 550,000. According to Yehuda Bauer, in the period 1933–39, an estimated 232,000 emigrated, which amounted to about 6 percent of the 1933 Jewish population annually. The permanent emigration figures for 1933 were about 37,000 (some 53,000 left at first but 16,000 returned). For 1934 and 1935, the emigration totals were approximately 23,000 and 21,000, respectively. The highest number left in 1939, when about 68,000 Jews departed Germany. When Austria was added to the Reich in 1938, the Austrian Jewish population numbered about 200,000. About 117,000 of that number emigrated in 1938–39. Saul Friedländer reports that by May 1939 there were 213,000 full Jews remaining in the *Altreich* (Germany prior to the annexation of Austria). That population was elderly and increasingly poor. See Bauer, *A History of the Holocaust*, 117–18, 121, 131, and Friedländer, *Nazi Germany and the Jews: The Years of Persecution 1933–1939*, 316–17, 393 n.21.

21. For a discussion of the Nazis' use of the Olympic Games, see Duff Hart-Davis, *Hitler's Games: The 1936 Olympics* (New York: Harper & Row, 1986) and Richard D. Mandell, *The Nazi Olympics*, rev. ed. (Urbana: University of Illinois Press, 1987).

22. Martin Gilbert and Richard Gott, *The Appeasers* (Boston: Houghton Mifflin, 1963), 144ff.

23. Quoted in Leni Yahil, *The Holocaust: The Fate of European Jewry, 1932–1945*, trans. Ina Friedman and Haya Galai (New York: Oxford University Press, 1990), 106.

24. Schleunes, *The Twisted Road to Auschwitz*, 230.

25. Ibid., 237.

26. Otto Dov Kulka, "Public Opinion in Nazi Germany and the 'Jewish Question,'" *Jerusalem Quarterly* 25 (fall 1982).

27. Klaus Drobisch et al., *Juden unterm Hakenkreuz: Verfolgung und Ausrottung der deutschen Juden, 1933–1945* (Frankfurt am Main: Röderberg Verlag, 1973), 159–60.

28. See Benz, *The Holocaust*, 31–32.

29. For more detail on the Heydrich text, see Berenbaum, ed., *Witness to the Holocaust*, 45–46.

30. Benz sets the number at 30,000. See Benz, *The Holocaust*, 31. According to Ulrich Herbert, the number was 20,000. See Herbert, "Extermination Policy," 24. Karol Jonca agrees with Benz. See Jonca, "Kristallnacht" in *The Holocaust Encyclopedia*, ed. Walter Laqueur, 890.

31. Schleunes, *The Twisted Road to Auschwitz*, 241.

32. Friedländer, *Nazi Germany and the Jews: The Years of Persecution 1933–1939*, 281, 284–92. We draw on Friedländer's chronology for other anti-Jewish sanctions mentioned in this paragraph.

33. Ibid., 281. Benz reports that "the Jews were in fact forced to pay 1.12 billion." See Benz, *The Holocaust*, 33.

34. For more detail on this topic and related issues, see Jonathan Petropoulos, *The Faustian Bargain: The Art World in Nazi Germany* (New York: Oxford University Press, 2000).

35. Friedländer, *Nazi Germany and the Jews: The Years of Persecution 1933–1939*, 286–87.
36. Ibid., 291.
37. Quoted in ibid., 283.
38. Canon Bernhard Lichtenberg was a notable, if singular, exception. On 10 November 1938 he offered prayer for the Jews. See Michael Phayer, *The Catholic Church and the Holocaust, 1930–1965* (Bloomington: Indiana University Press, 2000), 16. He continued to recite a daily prayer for the Jews until arrested on 23 October 1941. When interrogated, he declared that deportation of the Jews was irreconcilable with Christian moral law. He asked to be permitted to accompany the deportees as their spiritual adviser. He died on 5 November 1943 while being transported to Dachau. See Guenter Lewy, *The Catholic Church and Nazi Germany* (New York: McGraw-Hill, 1964), 293.
39. See Herbert, "Extermination Policy," 24.
40. Debórah Dwork and Robert Jan van Pelt, *The Holocaust: A History* (New York: W. W. Norton, 2002), 102.
41. Höhne, *The Order of the Death's Head*, 17.
42. On Himmler, see Richard Breitman, *The Architect of Genocide: Himmler and the Final Solution* (New York: Alfred A. Knopf, 1992).
43. Schleunes, *The Twisted Road to Auschwitz*, 230.
44. Concentration camps have a late nineteenth- and early twentieth-century history. Nazi Germany did not invent them. For example, the term *reconcentrados* was used to refer to camps in Cuba that were established by the Spanish general Valeriano Weyler in his suppression of an 1895 rebellion. During the Boer War (1899–1902), the term *concentration camp* designated British internment centers in South Africa that were used to prevent Boer civilians from helping guerrillas. Anticipating the removal of this Boer population, these camps were established along railroad lines. The Boers called these camps *laagers*. In Nazi Germany, a concentration camp was a *Konzentrationslager*.
45. Gellately, *Backing Hitler*, 51–69.
46. For an outline of the SD's organization, see Friedländer, *Nazi Germany and the Jews: The Years of Persecution, 1933–1939*, 197–202. For more on Eichmann, see Jochen von Lang, ed., *Eichmann Interrogated: Transcripts from the Archives of the Israeli Police*, trans. Ralph Mannheim (New York: Vintage, 1984) and Hannah Arendt, *Eichmann in Jerusalem: A Report on the Banality of Evil* (New York: Viking Press, 1964).
47. The document is reprinted in English translation in J. Noakes and G. Pridham, eds., *Nazism 1919–1945: A Documentary Reader*, 2 vols. (New York: Schocken Books, 1990), 2:1104.
48. See Claude Lanzmann, *Shoah: An Oral History of the Holocaust* (New York: Pantheon Books, 1985), 72.
49. Hans-Günter Adler, *Der verwaltete Mensch: Studien zur Deportation der Juden aus Deutschland* (Tübingen: Mohr, 1974), 74. We are indebted for this citation to Götz Aly, *"Final Solution": Nazi Population Policy and the Murder of the European Jews*, trans. Belinda Cooper and Allison Brown (London: Arnold, 1999), 3. For a discussion of the evolving meaning of other terms in the Nazi vocabulary of ethnic cleansing and genocide, see Longerich, *The Unwritten Order*, 15–17.
50. The number included Germany and regions annexed to Germany (743,000), Poland (2,300,000), Bohemia and Moravia (77,000), Belgium (80,000), Holland (160,000), Luxemburg (2,500), Denmark (7,000), Norway (1,500), Slovakia (95,000), and France (270,000). See Adler, *Der verwaltete Mensch*, 75 ff., and Aly, *"Final Solution,"* 96–97.
51. On 31 July 1940, Hitler spoke of a "five-month campaign" against the Soviet Union to begin sometime in early 1941. See Andreas Hillgruber and Gerhard

Hümmelchen, *Chronik des Zweiten Weltkrieges: Calendarium militärischer und politischer Ereignisse 1939–1945*, rev. ed. (Düsseldorf: Droste, 1978), 40, and Aly, *"Final Solution,"* 95–96.

52. Schleunes, *The Twisted Road to Auschwitz*, 260. See also Aly, *"Final Solution,"* and Herbert, "Extermination Policy."

53. See Black, *The Transfer Agreement*, 166ff. For an account that debunks the claim that much more could have been done to rescue Jews from the Nazis, see William D. Rubinstein, *The Myth of Rescue: Why the Democracies Could Not Have Saved More Jews from the Nazis* (New York: Routledge, 1997).

54. On the Evian conference, see Henry L. Feingold, *The Politics of Rescue: The Roosevelt Administration and the Holocaust 1938–1945* (New York: Holocaust Library, n.d.), 22–24, and *Bearing Witness: How America and Its Jews Responded to the Holocaust* (Syracuse, N.Y.: Syracuse University Press, 1995); Michael R. Marrus, *The Unwanted: European Refugees in the Twentieth Century* (New York: Oxford University Press, 1985); and David Wyman, *Paper Walls: America and the Refugee Crisis, 1938–1941* (Amherst, Mass.: University of Massachusetts Press, 1968).

55. *Foreign Relations of the United States, 1938*, vol. 1 (Washington, D.C.: 1950), 740–41 (italics added). See also Feingold, *Bearing Witness*, 75, and Judith Tydor Baumel, "Evian Conference," in *The Holocaust Encyclopedia*, ed. Lacqueur, 172–74.

56. See Friedländer, *Nazi Germany and the Jews: The Years of Persecution 1933–1939*, 249.

57. For a detailed examination of the Haavara Agreement, see Black, *The Transfer Agreement*.

58. More detail on British policy toward the European Jews before and during the Holocaust can be found in Bernard Wasserstein, *Britain and the Jews of Europe, 1939–1945* (New York: Oxford University Press, 1979).

59. For more detail, see the website at the United States Holocaust Memorial Museum: *www.ushmm.org*. Its entry on "Voyage of the 'St. Louis'" informs our discussion. See also Arthur D. Morse, *While Six Million Died: A Chronicle of American Apathy* (New York: Hart Publishing Co., 1968), 270–88.

60. See Louis P. Lochner, ed., *The Goebbels Diaries 1942–43* (New York: Doubleday, 1948), 241.

## Chapter 6

1. Doris Bergen, *War and Genocide: A Concise History of the Holocaust* (Lanham, Md.: Rowman & Littlefield, 2002), 1.

2. Quoted in Berenbaum, ed., *Witness to the Holocaust*, 161. Berenbaum reproduces larger passages from the speech as well.

3. For key passages from Hitler's "political testament," dated 29 April 1945, see ibid., 163–65.

4. See, for example, Hilberg's comments in Lanzmann, *Shoah*, 70–73.

5. The historian Gerhard L. Weinberg makes an important point in this context. Acknowledging that "time and again, the German government postponed steps in the racial transformation that was a major purpose of the war," he adds that such postponements did not mean that the Nazis' ideological objectives changed. It is important to remember, says Weinberg, "that the Germans had expected to win, not lose, the war, and that therefore the leaders of the Third Reich always assumed they would have decades, even centuries, to carry out their plans." See Weinberg, "The Holocaust and World War II: A Dilemma in Teaching," in *Lessons and Legacies II: Teaching the Holocaust in a Changing World*, ed. Donald G. Schilling (Evanston, Ill.: Northwestern University Press, 1998), 29.

6. The question of who knew what and when is explored by Walter Laqueur, *The Terrible Secret*, 2nd ed. (New York: Henry Holt, 1998).

7. Raul Hilberg, *The Destruction of the European Jews* (Chicago: Quadrangle Books, 1961). As mentioned in our prologue (see note 6) this magisterial work was revised and reissued, first, as *The Destruction of the European Jews*, revised and definitive edition (New York: Holmes & Meier, 1986) and, more recently, as *The Destruction of the European Jews*, 3rd ed. (New Haven, Conn.: Yale University Press, 2003). We cite both of the revised editions, in each instance the 1985 edition first and the 2003 edition second.

8. Herbert, "Extermination Policy," 5.

9. This chapter and the two that follow are in considerable measure indebted to the efforts of these German scholars as well as to those of earlier American, British, and Israeli pathfinders.

10. For examples and further details on this point, see Richard Breitman, *Official Secrets: What the Nazis Planned, What the British and the Americans Knew* (New York: Hill & Wang, 1998); Fleming, *Hitler and the Final Solution*; and Marrus, "Historiography," in *The Holocaust Encyclopedia*, ed. Laqueur, 279–85.

11. Uwe Adam, *Judenpolitik in Dritten Reich* (Düsseldorf: Droste Verlag, 1972).

12. In his Reichstag speech of 30 January 1939, Hitler said, "It is a shameful spectacle to see how the whole democratic world is oozing sympathy for the poor tormented Jewish people but remains hard-hearted and obdurate when it comes to helping them—which is surely, in view of its attitude, an obvious duty. The arguments that are brought up as an excuse for not helping them actually speak for us Germans and Italians." See Berenbaum, ed., *Witness to the Holocaust*, 160.

13. Götz Aly, "'Jewish Resettlement': Reflections on the Political Prehistory of the Holocaust," in *National Socialist Extermination Policies*, ed. Herbert, 58.

14. This figure is found in the report prepared by Adolf Eichmann after the Wannsee Conference, 20 January 1942. See Berenbaum, ed., *Witness to the Holocaust*, 165–71. The Nazi calculation was too high. The European Jews actually numbered closer to nine million.

15. Himmler also controlled all armed SS units, which included personnel who ran the concentration camps. During the winter of 1939–40, these units became known as the *Waffen-SS*. By the end of 1942, the *Waffen-SS*, augmented by *Volksdeutsche* (ethnic Germans) and other recruits, had more than 900,000 men. The mobile killing squads that decimated eastern European Jewry included *Waffen-SS* personnel.

16. For more detail on these matters, see Christopher R. Browning, *Ordinary Men: Reserve Police Battalion 101 and the Final Solution in Poland* (New York: Harper-Collins, 1992); Peter Longerich, "SS and the Police," in *The Holocaust Encyclopedia*, ed. Laqueur, 603–13; and Rhodes, *Masters of Death*.

17. The *Freikorps* were private, right-wing paramilitary units. Formed in the aftermath of World War I, these private armies consisted primarily of war veterans and unemployed young people. Numbering in the hundreds of thousands, the *Freikorps* fighters crushed the attempts of leftists to gain control in Munich in 1919. They also fought to prevent Poland's control of former German territory. Officially dissolved in 1921, the *Freikorps* were an important source of support for the Nazi Party.

18. Alexander B. Rossino, "Nazi Anti-Jewish Policy during the Polish Campaign: The Case of Einsatzgruppe von Woyrsch," *German Studies Review* 24 (Feb. 2001): 37.

19. Ibid.

20. Ibid., 39.

21. Donald Grey Brownlow and John Eluthère Du Pont, *Hell Was My Home: Arnold Shay, Survivor of the Holocaust* (West Hanover, Mass.: Christopher Publishing

House, 1983), 45. We are indebted to Rossino, "Nazi Anti-Jewish Policy" for this reference.

22. Testimony of Udo von Woyrsch, *Zentrale Stelle der Landesjustizverwaltung zur Aufklärung nationalsozialistische Verbrechen, in Ludwigsburg* (Central Federal Justice Administrative Office Regarding Nazi Crimes, in Ludwigsburg), AR-Z 302/67, 1:238f. We are indebted to Rossino, "Nazi Anti-Jewish Policy" for this reference.

23. Rossino, "Nazi Anti-Jewish Policy," 40.

24. Ibid., 41–42.

25. Ibid., 43. The actions of the *Wehrmacht* (German army) reported here should not lead to the conclusion, which some have erroneously drawn, that the German military was opposed to the persecution and mass murder of the Jews. On the contrary, the German army was deeply implicated in the destruction process. See, for example, Ernst Klee, Willi Dressen, and Volker Riess, eds., *"The Good Old Days": The Holocaust as Seen by Its Perpetrators and Bystanders* (New York: Free Press, 1991) and Hamburg Institute for Social Research, *The German Army and Genocide: Crimes against War Prisoners, Jews, and Other Civilians in the East, 1939–1944*, trans. Scott Abbott (New York: New Press, 1999).

26. Rossino, "Nazi Anti-Jewish Policy," 44.

27. Quoted in Aly, "'Jewish Resettlement,'" 58.

28. Browning, *Nazi Policy, Jewish Workers, German Killers*, 5.

29. See Aly, *"Final Solution"*, 34; Aly, "'Jewish Resettlement'," 59.

30. Rhodes, *Masters of Death*, 240.

31. See Aly, "'Jewish Resettlement,'" 54–64.

32. Noakes and Pridham, eds., *Nazism 1919–1945*, 2:1053–54, and S. Goschen, "Eichmann und die Nisko-Aktion in Oktober 1939," in *Vierteljahrshefte für Zeitgeschichte* (29.1.1981), 80. For further information about the structure of the RSHA, see Hilberg, *The Destruction of the European Jews*, 1:274–90 and 1:276–94. Previously, on 21 September 1939 Heydrich had dispatched a confidential message to *Einsatzgruppen* leaders. Addressing the "Jewish Question in Occupied Territory," Heydrich distinguished between final and intermediate goals. His message did not define the *Endziel* (final goal), but it was clearer about the intermediate steps: Jews should be concentrated, that is, moved from the countryside and villages into city ghettos, where railroad transportation would be readily available. Certain parts of occupied Poland would become *judenrein* to facilitate the resettlement of ethic Germans. Jewish councils (*Judenräte*) were to be appointed and held responsible for carrying out "the exact and prompt implementation of directives." Heydrich's program could not be implemented immediately, but in due course it was. The text of Heydrich's message can be found in Berenbaum, ed., *Witness to the Holocaust*, 71–74.

33. Browning, *Nazi Policy, Jewish Workers, German Killers*, 7.

34. See Noakes and Pridham, eds., *Nazism 1919–1945*, 2:1053–55.

35. Aly, "'Jewish Resettlement,'" 58–61.

36. Ibid., 59–60.

37. For details on these points, see ibid., 60–61, and Aly, *"Final Solution,"* 63–65. On 1 October 1943 the tasks of Section IV-B-4 were more fully designated as follows: "Jewish Matters, Evacuation Matters, Seizure of Assets Hostile to *Volk* and State, Revocation of German Citizenship."

38. Aly, "'Jewish Resettlement,'" 67.

39. On the "euthanasia" program see Götz Aly, Peter Chroust, and Christian Pross, *Cleansing the Fatherland: Nazi Medicine and Racial Hygiene*, trans. Belinda Cooper (Baltimore: Johns Hopkins University Press, 1994); Friedlander, *The Origins of Nazi Genocide*; Robert J. Lifton, *The Nazi Doctors: Medical Killing and*

*the Psychology of Genocide* (New York: Basic Books, 1986); Kater, *Doctors under Hitler*; and Robert N. Proctor, *Racial Hygiene: Medicine under the Nazis* (Cambridge, Mass.: Harvard University Press, 1988).

40. As Henry Friedlander points out, Jews were by no means excluded from the Nazi euthanasia program. "Jews," he says, "were victims of the euthanasia killings from the very beginning. . . . One can estimate that about 4,000, perhaps even 5,000, Jews became victims of the euthanasia killings." Friedlander, *The Origins of Nazi Genocide*, 270–71.

41. See Lifton, *The Nazi Doctors*, 3–18. What Lifton calls "medicalized killing" fitted with Nazi propaganda that portrayed Jews and other unwanted groups as blood-sucking parasites, disease-causing bacteria, or deadly cancers. Programs of race hygiene, sterilization, euthanasia, ethnic cleansing, and genocide were all part of a Nazi war against racial pollution. This therapeutic imperative led to a complex but related set of health policies and programs. As Robert Procter has shown, Nazism was "a vast hygienic experiment designed to bring about an exclusionist utopia. That sanitary utopia was a vision not unconnected with fascism's more familiar genocidal aspects: asbestos and lead were to be cleansed from Germany's factory air and water, much as Jews were to be swept from the German body politic. Nazi ideology linked the purification of the German body politic from environmental toxins and the purification of the German body from 'racial aliens.' . . . The history of science under Nazism is a history of both forcible sterilization and herbal medicine, of both genocidal 'selection' and bans on public smoking." See Robert N. Proctor, *The Nazi War on Cancer* (Princeton: Princeton University Press, 1999), 7, 277.

42. For a succinct but devastating overview of the movement, see Sven Lindqvist, *"Exterminate All the Brutes,"* trans. Joan Tate (New York: New Press, 1996).

43. For a significant history of the eugenics movement and its implications, see Daniel J. Kevles, *In the Name of Eugenics: Genetics and the Uses of Human Heredity* (Cambridge, Mass.: Harvard University Press, 1995).

44. On these points and related topics, see Stephan L. Chorover, *From Genesis to Genocide: The Meaning of Human Nature and the Power of Behavior Control* (Cambridge, Mass: MIT Press, 1977), 30–55; Stefan Kühl, *The Nazi Connection: Eugenics, American Racism, and German National Socialism* (New York: Oxford University Press, 1994); and Lifton, *The Nazi Doctors*.

45. See Richard Hofstadter, *Social Darwinism in American Thought* (Boston: Beacon Press, 1955), 170–200.

46. In a parallel American development, a movement was started to restrict immigration to the United States, limiting entry primarily to the Protestant and Germanic countries of northern Europe. Its aims were largely achieved when the U.S. Congress passed its restrictive immigration bill in 1924.

47. Ernst Haeckel. *Die Lebenswunder* (Stuttgart: A. Kroner, 1904), 128.

48. Karl Binding and Alfred Hoche, *Die Freigabe der Vernichtung Lebensunwerten Lebens: Ihr Mass und Ihre Form* (Leipzig: Felix Meiner Verlag, 1920)

49. See Chorover, *From Genesis to Genocide*, 97–98.

50. Quoted in ibid., 98.

51. See ibid., 98–99.

52. The law took effect on 1 January 1934. Henry Friedlander notes that the law was established on 14 July 1933. On that date, the Third Reich signed an important treaty (concordat) with the Vatican. Not wanting to jeopardize their agreement with the Roman Catholic Church, the Nazis withheld publication of the sterilization law for several days. Exact statistics cannot be obtained, but Friedlander states that "it is generally agreed that at least 300,000 persons were sterilized during the years preceding World War II. During the war, when euthanasia largely

replaced sterilization as a means to control so-called inferiors (*Minderwertige*), sterilization was devalued; still, an estimated additional 75,000 persons were probably sterilized after 1939" (Friedlander, *The Origins of Nazi Genocide*, 30).

53. Quoted in Friedlander, *The Origins of Nazi Genocide*, 67.

54. Ibid., 61, 151.

55. Insofar as the public, or even other governmental agencies, had dealings with the staff and offices that ran the "euthanasia" program, they thought they were dealing with agencies such as the *Reichsarbeitsgemeinschaft Heil- and Pflegeanstalten* (Reich Cooperative for State Hospitals and Nursing Homes), the *Gemeinnützige Stiftung für Anstaltspflege* (Charitable Foundation for Institutional Care), the *Gemeinnützige Kranken-Transport G.m.b.H.* (Charitable Foundation for the Transport of Patients, Inc.), the *Zentralverrechnungsstelle Heil- und Pflegeanstalten* (Central Accounting Office for State Hospitals and Nursing Homes), or the *Reichsausschuss zu wissenschaftlichen Erfassung von erb- und anlagebedingten schweren Leiden* (Reich Committee for the Scientific Registration of Severe Hereditary Ailments). These front organizations masked the real activities hidden behind their euphemistic names, which included the overall administration of every phase—from finance to transportation—of adult and child euthanasia. See ibid., 68–74.

56. For information about key T4 personnel, see ibid., 216–45.

57. See Léon Poliakov, *Harvest of Hate: The Nazi Program for the Destruction of the Jews of Europe* (New York: Holocaust Library, 1979), 185, 321 n.4.

58. See Friedlander, *The Origins of Nazi Genocide*, 75–85. Economic arguments were used to support the euthanasia program. Especially in wartime, valuable resources could be saved for much more important purposes if care for "useless eaters" was no longer required. Cost-benefit analyses were part of the "scientific" nature of the enterprise.

59. Ibid., 109.

60. See Fleming, *Hitler and the Final Solution*, 27.

61. For further information on the 14f13 operation, see Friedlander, *The Origins of Nazi Genocide*, 142–50.

62. Ibid., 104–6. For a typical letter, see Joachim Remak, ed. *The Nazi Years: A Documentary History* (New York: Simon & Schuster, 1969), 138–39.

63. Friedlander, *The Origins of Nazi Genocide*, 96–97.

64. The substance of Bishop von Galen's sermon is reprinted in Remak, ed., *The Nazi Years*. 139–40. See also Beth A. Griech-Polelle, *Bishop von Galen: German Catholicism and National Socialism* (New Haven, Conn.: Yale University Press, 2002).

65. See Gitta Sereny, *Into That Darkness: An Examination of Conscience* (New York: Vintage Books, 1983), 74–75. Sereny points out that Preysing's sermon was preached at a mass celebrating the coronation of Pope Pius XII. The new pope subsequently wrote to Preysing, thanking him and indicating, in the pope's words, that he had taken "careful cognizance, especially too of your sermon on the occasion of the coronation mass at St. Hedwig's. We welcome every honest word with which you bishops defend the right of God and of the Holy Church in public." Pope Pius XII, however, issued no public protest about Hitler's euthanasia program.

66. Ibid., pp. 60–77.

67. Friedlander, *The Origins of Nazi Genocide*, 162–63.

68. Aly, "'Jewish Resettlement,'" 67.

69. See Aly, *"Final Solution,"* 74.

70. Ibid., 85 n.67.

71. See ibid., 85–86, n.67.

72. Aly, "'Jewish Resettlement,'" 69.

73. Quoted in ibid., 59.

74. See Peter J. Haas, *Morality after Auschwitz: The Radical Challenge of the Nazi Ethic* (Philadelphia: Fortress Press, 1988).

75. Aly, "'Jewish Resettlement,'" 69.

76. Aly, *"Final Solution,"* 70.

77. Noakes and Pridham, eds., *Nazism 1919–1945*, 2:1055.

78. Aly, "'Jewish Resettlement,'" 70, 81 n.60.

79. Heydrich estimated that the "long-term goal" would be achieved over "the next year." See Browning, *Nazi Policy, Jewish Workers, German Killers*, 3–5.

80. For further excerpts from Heydrich's text, see Berenbaum, ed., *Witness to the Holocaust*, 71–74.

81. In October 1939 at Piotrkow Tribunalski the Germans established the first ghetto in occupied Poland, but the size of the Lodz ghetto was far greater.

82. See Noakes and Pridham, eds., *Nazism 1919–1945*, 2:1061–63.

83. On 8 November 1939 Friedrich Wilhelm Krüger, the higher SS and police chief in Cracow in the General Government, remarked that "in daily transports of 10,000 people, 600,000 Jews and 400,000 Poles from the eastern Gaus, and later also all Jews and Gypsies from the Reich territory, would be sent to the General Government." See Aly, *"Final Solution,"* 77.

84. See ibid., 77, 86 n.81.

85. For a helpful overview of the Lodz ghetto, see Michael Unger, "Lodz," in *The Holocaust Encyclopedia*, ed. Laqueur, 398–404.

86. The text of the memorandum is reproduced in Noakes and Pridham, eds., *Nazism 1919–1945*, 2:1075–77. For more on this topic and on Rademacher, see Christopher R. Browning, *The Final Solution and the German Foreign Office* (New York: Holmes & Meier, 1978) and *Nazi Policy, Jewish Workers, German Killers*, 15–17. For an overview of the Madagascar Plan, see Browning's article on the subject in *The Holocaust Encyclopedia*, ed. Laqueur, 407–9.

87. Aly, *"Final Solution,"* 92, 173. Friedrich Schumacher, a geologist, prepared a report for the Foreign Office in which he concluded that "Madagascar has no valuable mineral resources, making it sufficiently worthless to be used for the Jews."

88. Noakes and Pridham, eds., *Nazism 1919–1945*, 2:1077. Learning of Rademacher's initiative, Heydrich was not pleased that the Foreign Office might compromise his power over Jewish affairs. He stepped in to assert his authority in matters pertaining to Jewish emigration. Thus Eichmann was called in to develop his version of a Madagascar Plan. During the summer of 1940, Eichmann and Rademacher laid rival plans for this territorial solution to the Jewish question. See Browning, "Madagascar Plan," in *The Holocaust Encyclopedia*, ed. Laqueur, 408.

89. The de facto annexation of Alsace and Lorraine took place 22 June 1940, the day of the French surrender to the Germans (Aly, *"Final Solution,"* 90).

90. See Marrus and Paxton, *Vichy France and the Jews*, 10–11. Situated about fifty miles from the Spanish border, the camp at Gurs, which was established in 1939, had once been used to house Spanish refugees who fled during their country's civil war. Under the control of Vichy France (1940–42), its prisoner population of Jews and unwanted refugees reached fifteen thousand in 1941. The Germans controlled the camp directly from 1942 to 1944. In 1942–43 some six thousand Jews were deported from Gurs to their deaths at Auschwitz-Birkenau and Sobibor, two of the Nazi killing centers in Poland. Many of the Jews were deported from Gurs while that camp was under French control.

91. A report about these deportees, written in Karlsruhe, Germany, on 30 October 1940 is reproduced in Noakes and Pridham, eds., *Nazism 1919–1945*, 2:1079–80.

92. According to Hannah Arendt, for example, the plan was "meant to serve as a cloak under which the preparations for the physical extermination of all the Jews of Western Europe could be carried forward." See her *Eichmann in Jerusalem*, 77.

93. Aly, "'Jewish Resettlement,'" 64; Browning, *Nazi Policy, Jewish Workers, German Killers*, 17.

94. Quoted in Aly, *"Final Solution,"* 107.

95. Ibid., 92, 115–16.

96. Ibid., 113–14.

97. See Götz Aly and Susanne Heim, *Architects of Annihilation: Auschwitz and the Logic of Destruction*, trans. A. G. Blunden (Princeton: Princeton University Press, 2002).

98. Plans for a Jewish ghetto in Warsaw had already been discussed in November 1939. A section in an old part of the city, largely inhabited by Jews, was made off-limits to German soldiers and designated as a *Seuchensperrgebiet* (quarantine). But this pre-ghetto development and the restrictions imposed on Warsaw's Jews did not yet amount to a closed ghetto. Over the course of the next year, various initiatives started and stopped as far as ghettoization was concerned. Medical concerns about epidemics, especially typhus, kept pressing the issue. German doctors not only wanted ghettoization; they wanted the Warsaw ghetto to be tightly closed as well. See Hilberg, *The Destruction of the European Jews*, 1:224–28 and 1:225–30.

99. Ibid., 1:227 and 1:230. See also the report on the history of the creation of the Warsaw ghetto by Waldemar Schön, director of the Department for Resettlement, to the governor of the Warsaw District, 20 January 1941, in Noakes and Pridham, eds., *Nazism 1919–1945*, 2:1063–67.

100. See Noakes and Pridham, eds., *Nazism 1919–1945*, 2:1067–68, including the harrowing description of conditions in the ghetto that are excerpted from the diary of Stanislav Rozycki, a Pole who managed to visit the ghetto.

101. Ibid., 2:1069–70. After the invasion of the Soviet Union, Rosenberg was appointed Reich Minister for the Occupied Eastern Territories. He was sentenced to death as a major war criminal and hanged by the International Military Tribunal at Nuremberg in 1946.

### Chapter 7

1. See the excerpt from the diary of General Franz Halder that is reproduced in Noakes and Pridham, eds., *Nazism 1919–1945*, 2:1086–87. See also Burleigh, *The Third Reich*, 517–21; Christian Streit, "The German Army and the Politics of Genocide," in *The Policies of Genocide: Jews and Soviet Prisoners of War in Nazi Germany*, ed. Gerhard Hirschfeld (London: Allen & Unwin, 1986), 3ff.; Jürgen Föster, "The German Army and the Ideological War against the Soviet Union," also in Hirschfeld, 17ff. German plans for war against the USSR had been under way well before the meeting in Berlin on 30 March 1941. According to Michael Burleigh, "planning for Barbarossa had commenced in June 1940," but "directives on the conduct of the war began to flow only after March 1941" (517).

2. Some *Wehrmacht* leaders had initially objected to the murder of unarmed Jews in Poland, but this opposition did not surface in Operation Barbarossa. In the German view, Poland was populated by racial inferiors, but Poland was also an essentially conservative, predominantly Roman Catholic, and anti-Communist country. The measures taken there were harsh, but the war against Poland was not the radicalized, ideological war of annihilation that Nazi Germany waged against the Soviet Union, which was regarded by the Nazis as the center of world revolution in which the Jews played decisive parts. Especially the destruction of

Jewish men, the Nazis believed, would enfeeble and bring about the collapse of the Soviet state.

3. Burleigh, *The Third Reich*, 519.
4. Ibid. The "war of annihilation" mentality also helps to account for the unprecedented brutality that Soviet prisoners of war experienced at the hands of the Germans. A few weeks after Operation Barbarossa began on 22 June 1941, General Herman Reinecke, chief of the General Armed Forces Office (*Allgemeines Wehrmachtsamt*), and Reinhard Heydrich, head of the Reich Security Main Office, concluded a partnership agreement whose principal purposes included the selection and murder of Jewish POWs from the Soviet ranks. The agreement stated that the *Wehrmacht* was to "free itself" from all Soviet prisoners of war who spread Bolshevism. It was also agreed that the situation required "special measures." The next day Heydrich ordered his regional leaders to cull from the Soviet POWs all "professional revolutionaries," political officers in the Red Army, "fanatical" Communists, and "all Jews." These actions began an unprecedented departure from the traditions of warfare in the Western world. Eventually hundreds of thousands of Soviet POWs would be murdered. Never before on such a scale had a military command agreed to participate in the killing of unarmed enemy soldiers *after* they had surrendered. See Hilberg, *The Destruction of the European Jews*, 1:334–41 and 1:346–53.
5. The *Wehrmacht* consisted of the German army, navy, and air force. Of these three branches, the German army was the most deeply implicated in the Holocaust.
6. International Military Tribunal, *Trial of the Major War Criminals before the International Military Tribunal, 14 November 1945–1 October 1946* (Nuremberg: International Military Tribunal, 1947), 1:278–79.
7. *Verhandlung des Deutschen Bundestages, Stenographischer Bericht, 1: Wahlperiode* (Bonn: Deutscher Bundestag, 1949),6:4983–84.
8. See Omer Bartov, *Hitler's Army: Soldiers, Nazis, and War in the Third Reich* ( New York: Oxford University Press, 1992); Hans-Adolf Jacobsen, "Kommissarbefehl und Massenexekutionen sowjetische Kriegsgefangener," in *Anatomie des SS-Staates*, ed. Hans Buchheim et. al. (Olten: Walter-Verlag, 1965); Mannfred Messerschmidt, "German Military Law in the Second World War," in *The German Military in the Second World War*, ed. Wilhelm Deist (Dover, N.H.: Berg Publishers, 1985); Wilhelm Deist, ed., *The Build-Up of German Military Aggression* (New York: Oxford University Press, 1990); Jurgen Förster, "The German Army and the Ideological War against the Soviet Union."
9. Militärgeschichtes Forschungsamt, ed., *Das Deutsche Reich und der Zweite Weltkrieg* (Stuttgart: Deutsche Verlags-Austalt, 1979). We are indebted for this reference to Omer Bartov, "Professional Soldiers," in *The German Army and Genocide: Crimes against War Prisoners, Jews, and Other Civilians, 1939–1944*, ed. Hamburg Institute for Social Research, 16 n.10.
10. The exhibition's explanatory text and photographs have been published in *The German Army and Genocide*.
11. *The German Army and Genocide*, 128.
12. See, for example, Lucian Kim, "German Photo Exhibit Prompts Thousands of Angry Words," *Christian Science Monitor*, 21 July 1997; Michael Z. Wise, "Bitterness Stalks Show on Role of the *Wehrmacht*," *New York Times*, 6 November 1999.
13. At the time of the German invasion, about 80,000 Jews lived in Yugoslavia. Approximately 55,000–60,000 of them were killed in the Holocaust. The percentage of Jews who perished in Yugoslavia during the Holocaust was among the highest in any European country. See Walter Manoshek, "The Extermination of the Jews in Serbia," in *National Socialist Extermination Policies*, ed. Herbert, 163.

14. Under the leadership of Ante Pavelić, this puppet regime was run by the Ustasha, a Croatian fascist movement that engaged in ethnic cleansing against Serbs and promoted severely antisemitic policies. At the Jasenovac camp complex, which was located about sixty miles from Zagreb, the Croatian capital, approximately 100,000 persons—primarily Serbs but also many Jews and Gypsies—were brutally killed through starvation, disease, beatings, and shootings. About forty thousand Jews lived in Croatia; approximately 80 percent of them were murdered. See Yeshayahu A. Jelnick, "Yugoslavia," in *The Holocaust Encyclopedia*, ed. Laqueur, 706–13.

15. *Befehlshaber in Serbien* Ia to *Wehrmachtbefehlshaber Südost* (12th Army), 17 September 1941, NOKW-1057. We are indebted to Hilberg, *The Destruction of the European Jews*, 2:684 and 2:729 for this reference. For an informed exposition of the conduct of the *Wehrmacht* in Serbia, see Manoschek, "The Extermination of the Jews in Serbia," 163–85.

16. See Hilberg, *The Destruction of the European Jews*, 2:684–85 and 2:729–30; Manoschek, "The Extermination of the Jews in Serbia," 172.

17. Quoted in Manoschek, "The Extermination of the Jews in Serbia," 171.

18. Hilberg, *The Destruction of the European Jews*, 2:687 and 2:732.

19. Quoted in ibid., 2:689 and 2:734.

20. Memorandum by Martin Bormann, 16 July 1941, ND 221-L, *IMG*, vol. 38, p. 88. This reference is cited in Streit, "The German Army and the Policies of Genocide," 9.

21. See Bartov, *Hitler's Army*, 83–84, 89, 92–93.

22. Manoschek, "The Extermination of the Jews in Serbia," 178.

23. Bartov, *Hitler's Army*, 84; see also Streit, "The German Army and the Policies of Genocide;" Christian Streit, *Keine Kameraden: die Wehrmacht und die sowjetischen Kriegsgefangenen 1941–1945* (Stuttgart: Deutsche Verlags-Anstalt, 1978); Alfred Streim, *Die Behandlung sowjetischer Kriegsgefangenen im "Fall Barbarossa,"* (Heidelberg: Müller, Juristicher Verlag, 1981).

24. Ian Traynor, "Hitler's Army Shares SS Guilt," *The Guardian* (London), 6 April 1995.

25. Manoschek, "The Extermination of the Jews in Serbia," 179–80.

26. See Aly, *"Final Solution,"* 187, and Noakes and Pridham, eds., *Nazism 1919–1945*, 2:1087 n.1.

27. For a more detailed discussion of the war on the eastern front, see Gerhard L. Weinberg, *A World at Arms: A Global History of World War II* (Cambridge: Cambridge University Press, 1994), 264–309.

28. See Aly, *"Final Solution,"* 186. Also relevant is Christian Gerlach, "German Economic Interests, Occupation Policy, and the Murder of the Jews in Belorussia, 1941/43," in *National Socialist Extermination Policies*, ed. Herbert, 210–39.

29. As Christopher Browning has suggested, it is useful to distinguish among three terms and policies: population decimation, genocide, and Final Solution. See Browning, *Nazi Policy, Jewish Workers, German Killers*, 29–30. Population decimation refers to large-scale elimination of people, usually in a targeted region, but without necessarily differentiating those people by ethnicity, nationality, race, or religion. Genocide is the intended destruction, in part or completely, of a group defined by ethnicity, nationality, race, or religion. "Final Solution" is an extreme case of genocide, one that refers to the utter annihilation, root and branch, of the Jews (and perhaps of other groups in the future). Operation Barbarossa entailed widespread population decimation. It became genocidal in its treatment of Soviet Jews. It went far in bringing about the Final Solution, but in and of themselves the German policies toward Jews during Operation Barbarossa were not the Final Solution.

30. Thus the war against the Soviet Union greatly increased the danger to the Jews. Germany was about to set out on a racial and ideological war to destroy forever the threat of Bolshevism. After more than two decades of right-wing propaganda, the view that Jews and Judaism were responsible for Bolshevism was widely prevalent among the leaders and the enlisted ranks of the *Wehrmacht*, as well as among many other Europeans. Hence the injunction to execute "commissars" immediately upon capture could and did become applicable to Jews from the very beginning. The equation of Judaism with Bolshevism in the mind of the Germans was one of the reasons why the *Wehrmacht*, fearful that Jews would be Bolshevik spies or saboteurs, sought the evacuation of 200,000 persons from the area of the General Government intended as a training ground for troops preparing for the invasion of Russia. That only a small but visible minority of Jews were actually Communists mattered not at all.

31. These pogroms, which took place in many cities and towns along the eastern front, could be ferocious in their brutality. Sometimes these actions—motivated by combinations of antisemitism, anticommunism, and the seizure of Jewish property—broke out even before the Germans arrived. From the German perspective, these "self-cleansing" actions served more than one purpose. In addition to terrorizing and murdering Jews, they implicated local populations in policies that the Nazis were implementing, and they identified people who could be useful to the Germans in carrying out further dirty work. See Martin Dean, *Collaboration in the Holocaust: Crimes of the Local Police in Belorussia and Ukraine, 1941–44* (New York: St. Martin's Press, 2000), 20–21.

32. See Hilberg, *The Destruction of the European Jews*, 1:286–90 and 1:289–92; Höhne, *Order of the Death's Head*, 405–6; Rhodes, *Masters of Death*, 12–14. For additional detail on German troops on the eastern front in World War II, see Omer Bartov, *The Eastern Front: 1941–45, German Troops and the Barbarization of Warfare*, 2d. ed. (New York: Palgrave Macmillan, 2001).

33. Hilberg, *The Destruction of the European Jews*, 1:287–88 and 1:289–90.

34. See ibid., 1:287–89 and 1:289–91.

35. See Klee, Dressen, and Riess, eds., *"The Good Old Days"*; Browning, *Ordinary Men*; Goldhagen, *Hitler's Willing Executioners*; and Bartov, *Hitler's Army*.

36. Text of draft agreement dated 26 March 1941 in letter by General Eduard Wagner, General Quartermaster of the Army, to Heydrich 4 April 1941, in Hilberg, *The Destruction of the European Jews*, 1:284 and 1:287.

37. See Fleming, *Hitler and the Final Solution*, 52–58.

38. Browning, *Nazi Policy, Jewish Workers, German Killers*, 30. For other views relevant to this point, see Aly, *"Final Solution,"* 214–30; Hans Mommsen, "The Realization of the Unthinkable," in *The Policies of Genocide*, ed Hirschfeld, 121–22; Konrad Kweit, "Rehearsing for Murder: the Beginning of the Final Solution in Lithuania in 1941," *Holocaust and Genocide Studies* 12 (spring 1998): 3–26; Michael MacQueen, "The Context of Mass Destruction: Agents and Prerequisites of the Holocaust in Lithuania," *Holocaust and Genocide Studies* 12 (spring 1998): 27–48; Christoph Dieckmann, "The War and the Killing of the Lithuanian Jews," in *National Socialist Extermination Policies*, ed. Herbert, 242–51.

39. Dieckmann, "The War and the Killing of the Lithuanian Jews," 240–45.

40. Herbert, "Extermination Policy," 30.

41. Accounts by the German participants of the slaughter in Kovno, including an official report by General Walter Stahlecker, head of *Einsatzgruppe* A, appear in Klee, Dressen, and Riess, eds., *"The Good Old Days,"* 23–58.

42. See Dieckmann, "The War and the Killing of Lithuanian Jews," 259–62. Lithuanians participated in many, if not most, of the subsequent killings. In addition to their deeply rooted antisemitism, Lithuanian nationalists in particular bitterly

resented the Soviet occupation of their country between 1939 and 1941 and identified the Jews as both agents of communism and the NKVD, the Soviet secret police and predecessor of the KGB. Overwhelmingly, they regarded the Germans as their natural allies and the German occupation as an opportunity to settle accounts with the Jewish minority.

43. The 1935 census counted about ninety-five thousand Latvian Jews. By the time the Germans occupied the country, about twenty-five thousand had left. Some had departed before the Soviet annexation. Others had been deported to Siberia. Still others—some fifteen thousand—fled to the Soviet interior as the Germans advanced.

44. See Rhodes, *Masters of Death*, 119–21. For more detail on Latvia, see Andrew Ezergailis, *The Holocaust in Latvia 1941–1944* (Riga: Historical Institute of Latvia, 1996).

45. Dean, *Collaboration in the Holocaust*, 60. Dean's book is an important source for this relatively new area of research. See also Hilberg, *The Destruction of the European Jews*, 1:368–70 and 1:382–85.

46. Our account is indebted to Hilberg, *The Destruction of the European Jews*, 1:317–21 and 1:327–30.

47. Rhodes, *Masters of Death*, 113–14. Jeckeln was the Higher SS and Police Leader for Ukraine. He began to supervise mass killings in that area on 28 July 1941. Over the course of the next month, he was responsible for the murder of at least forty-four thousand Jews. Wanting to speed up the process of making Latvia *judenrein*, Himmler ordered Jeckeln, one of the most ruthless and efficient of the German killers, to Latvia on 31 October 1941. He and his staff moved into Riga on 5 November. On 30 November he oversaw the murder of thirteen thousand Riga Jews. Another ten thousand were killed by Jeckeln's men on 8 December.

48. This account is from testimony at the Riga Trial (50) 9/72, verdict of 23 February 1973, 69–73, Staatsanwaltschaft Hamburg. For this text, we are indebted to Gerald Fleming, *Hitler and the Final Solution*, 78–79. For further information about these massacres, see Rhodes, *Masters of Death*, 206–14.

49. Ezergailis, *The Holocaust in Latvia*, 225.

50. Rhodes, *Masters of Death*, 121.

51. Michael Mann, "Were the Perpetrators of Genocide 'Ordinary Men' or 'Real Nazis'? Results from Fifteen Hundred Biographies," *Holocaust and Genocide Studies* 14 (winter 2000): 331.

52. Quoted in Dominick LaCapra, *Writing History, Writing Trauma* (Baltimore: Johns Hopkins University Press, 2001), 135. See also Steven Aschheim, "Reconceiving the Holocaust," *Tikkun* 11 (1996): 64.

53. Rhodes, *Masters of Death*, 156. Rhodes also stresses the gratuitous and sadistic violence that accompanied these killing operations. He describes as follows an episode that epitomizes such violence: "A woman in a small town near Minsk saw a young German soldier walking down the street with a year-old baby impaled on his bayonet. 'The baby was still crying weakly,' she would remember. 'And the German was singing. He was so engrossed in what he was doing that he did not notice me'" (140). Countless episodes of such violence are recorded in Ilya Ehrenburg and Vasily Grossman, *The Complete Black Book of Russian Jewry*, trans. and ed. David Patterson (New Brunswick, N.J.: Transaction Publishers, 2002).

54. Nebe had also been head of the German criminal police. His career remains as fascinating as it was lethal, because he was executed in Nazi Germany on 4 March 1945 for his part in the near-miss assassination attempt against Hitler on 20 July 1944.

55. See Hilberg, *The Destruction of the European Jews*, 1:331–34 and 1:341–46, and Breitman, *The Architect of Genocide*, 194–97.

56. Quoted in Browning, *Nazi Policy, Jewish Workers, German Killers*, 23.
57. Klaus Reinhardt, *Moscow—the Turning Point: The Failure of Hitler's Strategy in the Winter of 1941/42*, trans. Karl B. Keenan (Oxford: Berg, 1992), 35.
58. Dieckmann, "The War and the Killing of the Lithuanian Jews," 251.
59. Ibid., 253.
60. Ibid., 254–55.
61. Ibid., 257.
62. Ibid., 262.

### Chapter 8

1. Quoted in Rhodes, *Masters of Death*, 180.
2. Quoted in ibid., 183.
3. Quoted in Aly, "'Jewish Resettlement,'" 73.
4. Ibid., 73–75.
5. Ibid., 74.
6. Ibid., 73. For related but not identical views on the thesis that Hitler's underlings "worked towards" Hitler, "taking independent initiatives to promote what they surmised the Führer's wishes to be, even to anticipate them," see Dwork and van Pelt, *Holocaust*, especially 258.
7. Browning, *Nazi Policy, Jewish Workers, German Killers*, 33.
8. Ibid., 36. The text of Göring's authorization is reprinted in Noakes and Pridham, eds., *Nazism 1919–1945*, 2:1104.
9. Browning, *Nazi Policy, Jewish Workers, German Killers*, 37. See also Peter Witte, "Two Decisions Concerning the 'Final Solution' to the Jewish Question," *Holocaust and Genocide Studies* 9 (winter 1995): 318–45.
10. Browning, *Nazi Policy, Jewish Workers, German Killers*, 39.
11. Ibid., 39.
12. Ibid., 51–52.
13. Ibid., 53–54.
14. See, in particular, Christian Gerlach, "The Wannsee Conference, the Fate of German Jews, and Hitler's Decision in Principle to Exterminate All European Jews," *Journal of Modern History* 70 (Dec. 1998): 759–812. The essay is reprinted in Omer Bartov, ed., *The Holocaust: Origins, Implementation, Aftermath* (New York: Routledge, 2000), 106–61. Also important is Mark Roseman, *The Wannsee Conference and the Final Solution: A Reconsideration* (New York: Henry Holt, 2002).
15. Quoted in Roseman, *The Wannsee Conference*, 81.
16. Quoted in Gerlach, "The Wannsee Conference," 785. Roseman's translation differs slightly; see *The Wannsee Conference*, 87.
17. Quoted in Berenbaum, ed., *Witness to the Holocaust*, 161.
18. Gerlach, "The Wannsee Conference," 784, 792.
19. Ibid., 791.
20. Ibid., 788–89.
21. Ibid., 790.
22. Ibid., 760.
23. The following biographical material is taken from material prepared by John Roth for Roth et al., *The Holocaust Chronicle*.
24. Roseman, *The Wannsee Conference*, 139.
25. Quoted from the translation in ibid., 158.
26. Ibid., 159.
27. Ibid., 121–24.
28. Ibid., 161.

29. Rhodes, *Masters of Death*, 237.
30. Ibid., 164–65.
31. See Raul Hilberg, ed., *Documents of Destruction: Germany and Jewry 1933–1945* (Chicago: Quadrangle Books, 1971), 102–4.
32. See ibid., 103.
33. See the protocol text in Roseman, *The Wannsee Conference*, 167–71.
34. Hilberg, *The Destruction of the European Jews*, 2:426, 430 and 2:443, 447. The numbers of *Mischlinge* and mixed marriages at stake in these debates were relatively small. In 1939, Hilberg estimates, "there were 64,000 *Mischlinge* of the first degree and 43,000 *Mischlinge* of the second degree in the Old Reich, Austria, and the Sudeten area" (2:418 and 2:435). Approximately 30,000 intermarriages existed at the same time in this area, which meant that about one out of ten German Jews was married to a non-Jew (1:169 and 1:168).

   A striking example of the support given by German partners to their Jewish spouses took place during the winter of 1943. In the wake of the telling German defeat at Stalingrad, a rousing speech by Goebbels on 18 February savaged Jews and rallied German support for "total war." Nine days later, on 27 February, ten thousand Berlin Jews were arrested in a final push to make the city *judenrein*. About two thousand of these predominantly male Jews were intermarried. Prior to the deportation and certain death that awaited them, they were temporarily imprisoned in the former Jewish community facility on Rosenstrasse. Despite the Gestapo's attempts to break up their protest, courageous Germans, mostly women who shouted, "Give us our husbands back," mounted a weeklong demonstration against the arrest of their spouses.

   In the context of "total war," the German leadership decided not to endanger home-front morale by crushing the protest. The Rosenstrasse Protest, as it came to be known, achieved its goal: the imprisoned Jewish spouses and their children were released; most survived the Holocaust. Significantly, the heroism of the non-Jewish spouses began long before the Rosenstrasse demonstrations, when they resisted strong Nazi pressure to divorce or abandon their spouses. In addition, their action at Rosenstrasse reveals at least two other points that deserve underscoring. First, the spouses of the arrested Jews knew that deportation meant death. The mass murder of Jews was no secret in Germany at the time. Second, the protest provides evidence that, in the words of Nathan Stoltzfus, "the regime's policies on racial purification could be influenced by a credible threat of unrest." See Nathan Stoltzfus, "The Limits of Policy: Social Protection of Intermarried German Jews in Nazi Germany," in *Social Outsiders in Nazi Germany*, ed. Robert Gellately and Nathan Stoltzfus (Princeton: Princeton University Press, 2001), 138. For an extended treatment of the Rosenstrasse Protest and intermarriage in Nazi Germany generally, see also Nathan Stoltzfus, *Resistance of the Heart: Intermarriage and the Rosenstrasse Protest in Nazi Germany* (New Brunswick, N.J.: Rutgers University Press, 2001).
35. See Gerlach, "The Wannsee Conference," 797.
36. Ibid., 811.
37. Gerlach and Browning disagree about how to regard the transports of Reich Jews who were sent to Kovno and Riga in late November 1941. When the deportation of Reich Jews began on 15 October 1941, transports eventually went to Lodz, Minsk, Kovno, and Riga. At first, ghettoization but not execution took place. Then there was a change. The transports to Kovno between 25 and 29 November contained about five thousand Jews. They were not ghettoized but killed shortly after their arrival. At Riga on 30 November another transport of Reich Jews met the same fate. Then there was another change: The murder of the Reich Jews caused unrest. Himmler called a halt for the time being. Browning

thinks that Himmler's intervention implies that a decision to kill the Reich Jews had been made some time before, but that the complications produced by such action led to a pause. Gerlach thinks that as yet there was no clear policy about how the deported Reich Jews were to be handled. Local initiatives at the transports' destinations determined what took place. The two scholars agree that there was an intervention from higher up and that there was, more or less, a pause in the killing, but they do not agree about the clarity concerning the fate of the Reich Jews. The result is that they also conflict on the meaning of Heydrich's invitations to conferences at the Wannsee villa—the first involving the postponed meeting, the second involving the meeting that took place on 20 January 1942. At stake in their disputes is the timing of a decision—no doubt Hitler's—to destroy all the European Jews. As we have seen, Browning dates that decision two months earlier than Gerlach.

38. Rhodes, *Masters of Death*, 167. On the issue of the crucial relation between Hitler's wishes and the strategies of his henchmen and the power bases they held in the Third Reich, see Dwork and van Pelt, *Holocaust*, esp. 259–84. Noting Hitler's early interests in Wagnerian opera, the ceremonies and rallies of Mussolini's regime in Italy, and Hitler's ongoing engagement with the arts, they see him not only as a man who meant what he said but also as a leader who was concerned less with detail than with the broader picture. Accurately and succinctly Dwork and van Pelt describe the basic relationship between Hitler and other Nazi leaders as follows: "Hitler dealt with ideas, aims, goals. Precise instructions were superfluous. His underlings 'worked towards' these ideas, taking independent initiatives to promote what they surmised the Führer's wishes to be, even to anticipate them. This led to ferocious competition within the party. Hitler always endorsed the victorious person or faction and thus was never embarrassed. Ferocity drove the Nazi state hierarchy and policies emerged out of an institutional jungle of rivalry and conflict. Programs, laws, decrees, regulations, written and even specific oral directives were simply not needed. Broad authorization sufficed" (260). See also Frederic Spotts, *Hitler and the Power of Aesthetics* (New York: Overland Press, 2002).

39. Quoted in ibid., 168.

40. See Longerich, *The Unwritten Order*, 75–76, 83–84.

41. Affidavit by Blobel, 18 June 1947, NO-3947, cited in Hilberg, *The Destruction of the European Jews*, 1:389 and 1:406.

42. See Hilberg, *The Destruction of the European Jews*, 3:976–79 and 3:1042–44, and Rhodes, *Masters of Death*, 258–62.

43. Lanzmann, *Shoah*, 5.

44. Hilberg, *The Destruction of the European Jews*, 3:878 and 3:936–37.

45. See Friedlander, *The Origins of Nazi Genocide*, 203–4. According to Yitzhak Arad, "between twenty and thirty-five SS men served in each of the [Operation Reinhard] death camps, and, with few exceptions, they were from the euthanasia program." See Yitzhak Arad, *Belzec, Sobibor, Treblinka: The Operation Reinhard Death Camps* (Bloomington: Indiana University Press, 1987), 17–19.

46. Hilberg, *The Destruction of the European Jews*, 3:1220 and 3:1321.

47. Death estimates for Belzec often range as high as 600,000, but research by Peter Witte and Stephen Tyas indicates that a more conservative figure is appropriate. See Peter Witte and Stephen Tyas, "A New Document on the Deportation and Murder of Jews during 'Einsatz Reinhardt' 1942," *Holocaust and Genocide Studies* 15 (winter 2001): 468–86.

48. Rubel has translated and annotated Reder's eyewitness account of his time in Belzec, which was originally written with the help of a woman named Nella Rost. This unusually important Holocaust document was published by the Jewish Regional Historical Commission in Cracow, Poland in 1946, but it did not

appear in English until 2000. See Rudolf Reder, "Belzec," trans. Margaret M. Rubel, in *Polin: Studies in Polish Jewry*, vol. 13, *Focusing on the Holocaust and Its Aftermath*, ed. Antony Polonsky (London: Littman Library of Jewish Civilization, 2000), 268–89.

49. Ibid., 276.

50. Ibid., 276.

51. Ibid., 289. Reder's reference to "millions of murdered Jews" at Belzec should not be read as a factual statement but as his way of identifying the magnitude of what happened at that Holocaust site.

52. Ibid., 283.

53. Arad, *Belzec, Sobibor, Treblinka*, 79.

54. Richard Glazar, *Trap with a Green Fence: Survival in Treblinka*, trans. Roslyn Theobald (Evanston, Ill.: Northwestern University Press, 1995), 16. Our account of Treblinka draws on material prepared by John Roth for Roth et al., *The Holocaust Chronicle*.

55. See Lanzmann, *Shoah*, 73.

56. Koch had formerly been commandant at the Buchenwald concentration camp. In conjunction with Himmler's decree that SS men should be above reproach, an SS corruption investigation implicated him in embezzlement and unwarranted murder. Koch lost his post at Majdanek in August 1942 and later stood trial. Found guilty by an SS tribunal, he was executed. Koch's wife, Ilse, was an SS female overseer who, like her husband, developed a well-deserved reputation for sadism.

57. Browning, *Ordinary Men*, 135.

58. Elie Wiesel, "Listen to the Wind," in *Against Silence: The Voice and Vision of Elie Wiesel*, 3 vols., ed. Irving Abrahamson (New York: Holocaust Library, 1985), 1:167. Our account of Auschwitz relies on material prepared by John Roth for Roth et al., *The Holocaust Chronicle*. We are also indebted to Raul Hilberg, "Auschwitz," in *The Holocaust Encyclopedia*, ed. Laqueur, 32–44.

59. Elie Wiesel, *From the Kingdom of Memory* (New York: Summit Books, 1990), 105.

60. The most significant historical works on Auschwitz include the following: Danuta Czech, *Auschwitz Chronicle 1939–1945*, trans. Barbara Harshav, Martha Humphries, and Stephen Shearier (New York: Henry Holt, 1990); Dwork and van Pelt, *Auschwitz 1270 to the Present*; Yisrael Gutman and Michael Berenbaum, eds., *Anatomy of the Auschwitz Death Camp* (Bloomington: Indiana University Press, 1994); Hilberg, *The Destruction of the European Jews*; Rudolf Höss, Pery Broad, and Johann Paul Kremer, *KL Auschwitz Seen by the SS* (Oswiecim: Auschwitz-Birkenau State Museum, 1996); Franciszek Piper and Teresa Swiebocka, eds., *Auschwitz: Nazi Death Camp* (Oswiecim: Auschwitz-Birkenau State Museum, 1996); and van Pelt, *The Case for Auschwitz*.

61. Dwork and van Pelt, *Auschwitz: 1270 to the Present*, 263.

62. As Michael Berenbaum points out, the annihilation was facilitated by the fact that Auschwitz was a substantial rail hub. Lines connecting to many European cities were possible, thanks to "forty-four parallel tracks at the train station, more than twice the number of New York's Pennsylvania Station." See Michael Berenbaum, *The World Must Know: The History of the Holocaust as Told in the United States Holocaust Memorial Museum* (Boston: Little, Brown & Co., 1993), 115.

63. Dwork and van Pelt, *Holocaust*, 312, 361. Like many Holocaust statistics, the precise number of Jews who entered Auschwitz and who were killed on arrival or spared to work cannot be obtained. The numbers cited here are reliable estimates. Other careful scholars offer somewhat different data, but there is a consensus—many scholars prefer a conservative reckoning—that between 1.1 and 1.5 mil-

lion people were gassed to death at Auschwitz. About 90 percent were Jews. Other death tolls included approximately 90,000 Poles, 22,000 Gypsies, 15,000 Soviet POWs, and 10,000 to 15,000 people of other nationalities. See Gideon Greif, "Gas Chambers," and Hilberg, "Auschwitz," both in *The Holocaust Encyclopedia*, ed. Laqueur, 44, 236.

64. Dwork and van Pelt, *Auschwitz: 1270 to the Present*, 336. For a lower estimate, see Hilberg, "Auschwitz," 37.

65. Dwork and van Pelt, *Holocaust*, 305–6.

66. In addition, Hungary's population included a hundred thousand Christian converts of Jewish origin, who were classified as Jews under racial criteria.

67. Dwork and van Pelt, *Holocaust*, 311–12. These scholars sum up the situation at Auschwitz-Birkenau as follows: "Frenetic gassing and burning continued through July 1944. One-third of the total number of people murdered at Auschwitz were killed in two months. Or, to put it differently, Auschwitz had been in operation for thirty-months. In that period, March 1942 to November 1944, between 1 million and 1.1 million people were killed, on an average of 32,000 to 34,000 a month. During the Hungarian Action the Germans, with dispatch and efficiency, increased that average five- to six-fold, murdering 400,000" (ibid., 312).

68. Our discussion of Zyklon B is informed by Dwork and van Pelt, *Auschwitz: 1270 to the Present*, 218–21, 292–95; *The Irving Judgment: David Irving v. Penguin Books and Professor Deborah Lipstadt*, 195–206; Peter Hayes, *Industry and Ideology: I. G. Farben in the Nazi Era* (Cambridge: Cambridge University Press, 1993), 361–63; Hilberg, *The Destruction of the European Jews*, 3:885–92 and 3:951–60; and van Pelt, *The Case for Auschwitz*.

69. Guenter Lewy, *The Nazi Persecution of the Gypsies* (Oxford: Oxford University Press, 2000), 136.

70. Ibid., 225.

71. Michael Zimmerman, "The National Socialist 'Solution of the Gypsy Question,'" in *National Socialist Extermination Policies*, ed. Herbert, 203.

72. In addition to Lewy's book, helpful sources about the Gypsies include Michael Burleigh and Wolfgang Wipperman, *The Racial State: Germany 1933–1945* (Cambridge: Cambridge University Press, 1991), 113–35; David M. Crowe, *A History of the Gypsies of Eastern Europe and Russia* (New York: St. Martin's Press, 1996); Friedlander, *The Origins of Nazi Genocide*, 246–62, 290–96; Donald Kenrich and Grattan Puxon, *Gypsies under the Swastika* (Hatfield: University of Hertfordshire Press, 1995); Zimmermann, "The National Socialist 'Solution of the Gypsy Question,'" 186–209.

73. Berenbaum, *The World Must Know*, 184.

74. For route maps, see Goldhagen, *Hitler's Willing Executioners*, 347, 366–68.

75. Ibid., 369.

76. Ibid., 330, 354.

77. Hilberg, "Auschwitz," 44. See also Czech, *Auschwitz Chronicle 1939–1945*, 781–92.

78. See Goldhagen, *Hitler's Willing Executioners*, 332–54.

79. Ibid., 333.

80. Ibid., 340–41. These conditions illustrate was has been called "excremental assault," which was widespread throughout the Holocaust. Terrence Des Pres, who coined the term, notes that "prisoners were *systematically* subjected to filth." This condition was more than exacerbated by overcrowding and inadequate facilities. Serving to humiliate and debase the prisoners, Des Pres argued, "it made mass murder less terrible to the murderers because the victims appeared less than human. They *looked* inferior." See Terrence Des Pres, *The Survivor: An Anatomy of Life in the Death Camps* (New York: Oxford University Press, 1976), 57–61.

For a related but somewhat different view, see Dwork and van Pelt, *Auschwitz: 1270 to the Present*, 268. With particular reference to Auschwitz, Dwork and van Pelt state that "the design of the wash barracks and the privies was, in fact, lethal," but, they add, "Des Pres is incorrect that the defilement was the result of the SS's desire to exercise total power. Architects and bureaucrats are to blame: the design was inadequate, and not enough material and financial resources were allocated for the camp's construction." At the end of the day, however, Dwork and van Pelt concur with Des Pres to this extent: the facilities constructed to handle excrement at Auschwitz were "an assault and a biological disaster."

81. Goldhagen, *Hitler's Willing Executioners*, 344–45.
82. Ibid., 348–49.
83. Ibid., 356.
84. Ibid., 359–60.
85. Ibid., 364.
86. Ibid., 365.
87. Ibid., 367–68.
88. For photographs of the burned victims at Gardelegen, see ibid., 369–70. For related photographs of other German victims, see Robert H. Abzug, *Inside The Vicious Heart: Americans and the Liberation of Nazi Concentration Camps* (New York: Oxford University Press, 1985).
89. Goldhagen, *Hitler's Willing Executioners*, 369.
90. See ibid., 371.
91. Gellately, *Backing Hitler*, 1.
92. Quoted in Berenbaum, ed., *Witness to the Holocaust*, 163–65.
93. Rhodes, *Masters of Death*, 257.
94. Hilberg, *The Destruction of the European Jews*, 3:1219–20 and 3:1320–21; Israel Gutman and Robert Rozett, "Estimated Jewish Losses in the Holocaust," in *Encyclopedia of the Holocaust*, ed. Gutman, 4:1797–1802; Wolfgang Benz, "Death Toll," in *The Holocaust Encyclopedia*, ed. Laqueur, 137–45.

## Chapter 9

1. For further information see Herman Kruk, *The Last Days of the Jerusalem of Lithuania: Chronicles from the Vilna Ghetto and the Camps, 1939–1944*, ed. Benjamin Harshav and trans. Barbara Harshav (New Haven, Conn.: Yale University Press, 2002) and Dina Porat, "Vilna," in *The Holocaust Encyclopedia*, ed. Laqueur, 663–67.
2. Abba Kovner, "A First Attempt to Tell," in *The Holocaust as Historical Experience*, ed. Yehuda Bauer and Nathan Rotenstreich (New York: Holmes & Meier, 1981), 81. For more on Kovner, see Bauer, *A History of the Holocaust*, 271–73.
3. Dawidowicz, *The War against the Jews*, 387.
4. For the text of this "Proclamation of the Vilna Ghetto Resistance Organization," see Berenbaum, ed., *Witness to the Holocaust*, 154.
5. Kovner, "A First Attempt to Tell," 81, 252. See also the biblical roots of the reference: Psalms 44:11 and Isaiah 53:7.
6. A sensitive discussion of these controversial issues is provided by Hilberg, *The Destruction of the European Jews*, 3:1030–44 and 3:1104–18.
7. Hannah Arendt, *Eichmann in Jerusalem*, 111. Arendt covered the Eichmann trial in Jerusalem for the *New Yorker*; her book emerged from that experience. Eichmann fled to Argentina at the end of World War II. On 11 May 1960 the Israeli secret service captured him and took him to Israel. Charged with crimes against the Jewish people, crimes against humanity, and war crimes, he stood trial from 11 April to 14 August 1961. Found guilty as charged, he was hanged on 31 May

1962. The Eichmann trial aroused worldwide attention. Further insight about Arendt can be found in Richard J. Bernstein, *Hannah Arendt and the Jewish Question* (Cambridge, Mass.: MIT Press, 1996).

8. Leonard Tushnet, *The Pavement of Hell* (New York: St. Martin's Press, 1972), 162, 169, 170, 169.

9. Raul Hilberg, "Discussion: The *Judenrat* and the Jewish Response," in *The Holocaust as Historical Experience*, ed. Bauer and Rotenstreich, 231–32.

10. Based in Los Angeles, the Survivors of the Shoah Visual History Foundation, which opened in April 1994, has gathered testimony in some thirty languages from more than fifty thousand Holocaust survivors and witnesses. Similar collections exist at Yad Vashem in Israel, the United States Holocaust Memorial Museum in Washington, D.C., Yale University, and other venues. Research on Holocaust survivors and their testimonies has become a major scholarly field. Significant works include Joshua M. Greene and Shiva Kumar, eds., *Witness: Voices from the Holocaust* (New York: Free Press, 2000); Henry Greenspan, *On Listening to Holocaust Survivors: Recounting and Life History* (Westport, Conn.: Praeger, 1998); Lawrence L. Langer, *Holocaust Testimonies: The Ruins of Memory* (New Haven, Conn.: Yale University Press, 1991); and Donald Niewyk, ed., *Fresh Wounds: Early Narratives of Holocaust Survival* (Chapel Hill: University of North Carolina Press, 1998). Also helpful in this area of research is Eve Nussbaum Soumerai and Carol D. Schulz, *Daily Life during the Holocaust* (Westport, Conn.: Greenwood Press, 1998).

11. Helpful information about the *Reichsvertretung* is provided by Hilberg, *The Destruction of the European Jews*, 1:180–87 and 1:180–88.

12. Ibid., 3:1030 and 3:1104.

13. See Dawidowicz, *The War against the Jews*, 245–46.

14. For the *Reichsvertretung*'s response to the Nuremberg Laws, see Berenbaum, ed., *Witness to the Holocaust*, 28–30.

15. Dawidowicz, *The War against the Jews*, 263–64.

16. See Berenbaum, ed., *Witness to the Holocaust*, 72.

17. Quoted in Dawidowicz, *The War against the Jews*, 475.

18. See, for example, Bauer, *A History of the Holocaust*, 183–208, and Browning, *Nazi Policy, Jewish Workers, German Killers*, 58–115.

19. For a history of the Warsaw ghetto, see Yisrael Gutman, *The Jews of Warsaw, 1939–1943: Ghetto, Underground, Revolt*, trans. Ina Friedman (Bloomington: Indiana University Press, 1989). For an account about Jews who managed to hide in the city of Warsaw, see Gunnar S. Paulsson, *Secret City: The Hidden Jews of Warsaw, 1940–1945* (New Haven, Conn.: Yale University Press, 2003).

20. For more information on these topics, see Charles G. Roland, *Courage under Siege: Starvation, Disease, and Death in the Warsaw Ghetto* (New York: Oxford University Press, 1992).

21. Significant glimpses about these realities are provided by Wladyslaw Szpilman, *The Pianist: The Extraordinary True Story of One Man's Survival in Warsaw, 1939–1945*, trans. Anthea Bell (New York: Picador USA, 2000).

22. Isaiah Trunk, *Judenrat: The Jewish Councils in Eastern Europe under Nazi Occupation* (New York: Stein & Day, 1977), 356.

23. Raul Hilberg, "The Ghetto as a Form of Government: An Analysis of Isaiah Trunk's *Judenrat*," in *The Holocaust as Historical Experience*, ed. Bauer and Rotenstreich, 159.

24. A "choiceless choice," says Langer, is a critical decision that does not "reflect options between life and death, but between one form of 'abnormal' response and another, both imposed by a situation that was in no way of the victim's own choosing." See Lawrence L. Langer, "The Dilemma of Choice in the Deathcamps," in

*Holocaust: Religious and Philosophical Implications,* ed. John K. Roth and Michael Berenbaum (St. Paul, Minn.: Paragon House, 1989), 224. See also Lawerence L. Langer, *Versions of Survival: The Holocaust and the Human Spirit* (Albany: State University of New York Press, 1982), 72. Berenbaum adds that "in the universe of choiceless choices, one could not choose between good and bad or even a lesser of two evils, but between the impossible and the unacceptable." See Berenbaum, ed., *Witness to the Holocaust*, 202.

25. Adam Czerniakow, *The Warsaw Diary of Adam Czerniakow,* ed. Raul Hilberg, Stanislaw Staron, and Josef Kermisz and trans. Stanislaw Staron et al. (New York: Stein & Day, 1979), 385. Other important testimonies from the Warsaw ghetto include Chaim Kaplan, *Scroll of Agony: The Warsaw Diary of Chaim A. Kaplan*, ed. and trans. Abraham I. Katsh, rev. ed. (New York: Collier Books, 1973); Kazik (Simha Rotem), *Memoirs of a Warsaw Ghetto Fighter,* ed. and trans. Barbara Harshav (New Haven, Conn.: Yale University Press, 1994); Abraham Lewin, *A Cup of Tears: A Diary of the Warsaw Ghetto*, ed. Antony Polonsky and trans. Christopher Hutton (Oxford: Basil Blackwell, 1988); Vladka Meed, *On Both Sides of the Wall: Memoirs from the Warsaw Ghetto*, trans. Steven Meed (Washington, D.C.: Holocaust Library, 1993); Emmanuel Ringelblum, *Notes from the Warsaw Ghetto: The Journal of Emmanuel Ringelblum,* ed. and trans. Jacob Sloan (New York: Schocken Books, 1974); Yitzhak Zuckerman, *A Surplus of Memory: Chronicle of the Warsaw Ghetto Uprising,* ed. and trans. Barbara Harshav (Berkeley: University of California Press, 1993).

26. Quoted in Hilberg, *The Destruction of the European Jews*, 2:841 and 2:900.

27. In the Kovno ghetto, Dr. Elchanan Elkes, the highly respected head of the *Judenrat,* actively supported forest-based partisan units and anti-Nazi underground activity. For details on the Kovno ghetto, see Joel Elkes, *Values, Belief, and Survival: Dr. Elkhanan Elkes and the Kovno Ghetto, a Memoir* (London: Vale Publishing, 1997); Avraham Tory, *Surviving the Holocaust: The Kovno Ghetto Diary*, trans. Jerzy Michalowicz (Cambridge, Mass.: Harvard University Press, 1990); United States Holocaust Memorial Museum, *Hidden History of the Kovno Ghetto* (Boston: Little, Brown & Co., 1997). The last has an extensive bibliography regarding the Kovno ghetto.

28. Yehuda Bauer makes much of this latter point. See *A History of the Holocaust*, 171–82, and *Rewriting the Holocaust*, 129–30.

29. Yehuda Bauer, "Jewish Leadership Reactions to Nazi Policies," in *The Holocaust as Historical Experience*, ed. Bauer and Rotenstreich, 173–74. In *Rewriting the Holocaust*, Bauer emphasizes that "individual acts of resistance, armed or unarmed," not only the actions of groups, which might be implied by the term *organized*, need to be taken into account (119). Bauer writes at some length about resistance in *Rewriting the Holocaust*, 119–66.

30. Dawidowicz, *The War against the Jews*, 325. For more on Rumkowski and the Lodz ghetto in general, see Lucjan Dobroszycki, ed., *The Chronicle of the Lodz Ghetto, 1941–1944*, trans. Richard Lourie (New Haven, Conn.: Yale University Press, 1984).

31. See Dobroszycki, ed., *Chronicle of the Lodz Ghetto*, 96–97. Related to this point is the text of a speech by Rumkowski, dated 2 March 1942, which is reprinted in Berenbaum, ed., *Witness to the Holocaust*, 81–84. In this speech, Rumkowski emphasizes that "experience has made clear that the basic law of our times is: 'Work protects us from annihilation'" (81).

32. Quoted from a speech by Rumkowski, which is reprinted in Berenbaum, ed., *Witness to the Holocaust*, 84–86. See also Lawrence L. Langer's insightful essay, "Ghetto Chronicles: Life at the Brink," in his *Admitting the Holocaust: Collected Essays* (New York: Oxford University Press, 1995), 41–50.

33. Tushnet, *Pavement of Hell*, 53.
34. Berenbaum, *The World Must Know*, 82, 84.
35. Yehuda Bauer discusses Jewish collaboration in *Rewriting the Holocaust*, 143–48. Some individual Jews did act as "Gestapo spies and agents" (148). According to Bauer, "their numbers are unknown; they were not many, but they caused tremendous damage" (148). Jewish police, Bauer notes, are often singled out "because of their role in cooperating or collaborating with the Germans in delivering Jewish victims to the Nazi murder machine" (143). Although reliable research shows that "most police forces cooperated with the Germans," Bauer notes that "in fourteen ghettos . . . the police were a part of the Jewish resistance" (143–44). Jewish police who did cooperate with the Germans are best understood as "simply frightened people who served the Germans to save their own lives" (148). Finally, Bauer identifies at least one Jewish group that did collaborate overtly. Called the Trzynastka (The Thirteen) because its base was at 13 Leszno Street in the Warsaw ghetto, this group, which was headed by Abraham Gancwajch, apparently believed that the Germans would win the war and that Jewish survival depended on collaboration with them. According to Bauer, the Germans found the Trzynastka to be of limited use. Gancwajch's fate is undocumented, but rumor suggests that the Germans shot him in early spring 1943.
36. Bauer, *Rewriting the Holocaust*, 26–27.
37. From an affadavit by Hermann Friedrich Graebe (10 November 1945). Quoted in Hilberg, *The Destruction of the European Jews*, 3:1043–44 and 3:1118. Graebe, a German engineer, witnessed *Einsatzgruppe* massacres in Ukraine. He was one of only a few German civilian professionals who risked his own life to save Jews from the Nazis. His affidavit about the mass shootings provided crucial evidence in some of the postwar trials. For Graebe's biography, see Douglas K. Huneke, *The Moses of Rovno* (New York: Dodd, Mead, 1986).
38. Isaiah Trunk, *Jewish Responses to Nazi Persecution: Collective and Individual Behavior in Extremis*, trans. Joachim Neugroschel and Gabriel Trunk (New York: Stein & Day, 1979), 55. Emphasizing a different point, but one that supplements Trunk's observations, Richard Rhodes points out that mass murder was so incomprehensible that it created paralyzing shock in many of the Jewish victims. European Jews, Rhodes indicates, had been "socialized more to civil methods of settling disputes," and relatively few of them "were personally violent." Jewish civility, he believes, "left Jewish communities unprepared to resist concerted violent assault." That civility was a virtue, but not one that would be respected by Nazism's "violent socialization." Rhodes makes one additional point that is important in this context: "When there are (for whatever complex reasons of patriotism, military discipline or mortal threat) no other reasonable choices, people do what they are told. Did not Eichmann and Blobel walk unaided to the gallows when their time came? They at least deserved their deaths." See Rhodes, *Masters of Death*, 251–52, 279.
39. George M. Kren and Leon Rappoport, *The Holocaust and the Crisis of Human Behavior* (New York: Holmes & Meier, 1980), 100.
40. Ibid., 111.
41. Zivia Lubetkin, *In the Days of Destruction and Revolt*, trans. Ishai Tubbin (Tel Aviv: Hakibbutz Hameuchad Publishing House, 1981), 153. Zivia Lubetkin survived, reached Israel in 1946, and lived there until her death in 1979. Along with her husband, Itzhak Zuckermann, she was one of the leaders in the Jewish resistance movement in Warsaw. (Zuckermann also survived the Holocaust. Shortly before his death in 1981, Claude Lanzmann asked for his impression of the Holocaust. In one of the most trenchant summaries any survivor ever offered, Zuckermann replied, "If you could lick my heart, it would poison you." See Lanzmann, *Shoah*,

196.) Lubetkin's book is her memoir about life in the Warsaw ghetto and specifically about the ghetto uprising. For further detail on aspects of women's struggle for life in the ghettos, resistance movements, and the Holocaust generally, see Elizabeth R. Baer and Myrna Goldenberg, eds., *Experience and Expression: Women, the Nazis and the Holocaust* (Detroit: Wayne State University Press, 2003); Dalia Ofer and Lenore J. Weitzman, eds., *Women in the Holocaust* (New Haven, Conn.: Yale University Press, 1998); and Carol Rittner and John K. Roth, eds., *Different Voices: Women and the Holocaust* (St. Paul, Minn.: Paragon House, 1993).

42. Women played a key part in obtaining explosives that were used in the October uprising at Birkenau. For more detail, see Rittner and Roth, eds., *Different Voices*, 130–42.

43. Arad, *Belzec, Sobibor, Treblinka*, 298, 341.

44. Trunk, *Jewish Responses to Nazi Persecution*, 70–71. Children also participated in resistance activity. In the Warsaw ghetto, for example, several thousand of them smuggled food that was life-sustaining, at least temporarily, for their families. See Debórah Dwork, *Children with a Star: Jewish Youth in Nazi Europe* (New Haven, Conn.: Yale University Press, 1991), 199. Dwork's book provides a most helpful discussion about the plight of Jewish children and young people during the Holocaust. See also George Eisen, *Children and Play in the Holocaust: Games among the Shadows* (Amherst: University of Massachusetts Press, 1988) and Raul Hilberg, *Perpetrators Victims Bystanders: The Jewish Catastrophe 1933–1945* (New York: HarperCollins, 1992), 139–49.

45. See Myrna Goldenberg, "Different Horrors, Same Hell: Women Remembering the Holocaust," in *Thinking the Unthinkable: Meanings of the Holocaust*, ed. Roger S. Gottlieb (New York: Paulist Press, 1991), 150–66. Holocaust memoirs by women are more numerous than ever. Arguably none is more important than Charlotte Delbo's. As a non-Jew and a member of the French resistance, she survived both Auschwitz and Ravensbrück. See the trilogy contained in her *Auschwitz and After*, trans. Rosette C. Lamont (New Haven, Conn: Yale University Press, 1995). Among the most important scholarly books specifically about Jewish women in the Holocaust, the following are representative: Baer and Goldenberg, eds., *Experience and Expression;* Judith Tydor Baumel, *Double Jeopardy: Gender and the Holocaust* (London: Vallentine Mitchell, 1998); Brana Gurewitsch, ed., *Mothers, Sisters, Resisters: Oral Histories of Women Who Survived the Holocaust* (Tuscaloosa, Ala.: University of Alabama Press, 1998); Marion A. Kaplan, *Between Dignity and Despair: Jewish Life in Nazi Germany* (New York: Oxford University Press, 1998); S. Lillian Kremer, *Women's Holocaust Writing: Memory and Imagination* (Lincoln, Neb.: University of Nebraska Press, 1999; Mary Lagerwey, *Reading Auschwitz* (Walnut Creek, Calif.: AltaMira Press, 1998); Ofer and Weitzman, eds., *Women in the Holocaust;* Michael Phayer and Eva Fleischner, *Cries in the Night: Women Who Challenged the Holocaust* (Kansas City, Mo.: Sheed & Ward, 1997); Rittner and Roth, eds., *Different Voices;* Roger A. Ritvo and Diane M. Plotkin, *Sisters in Sorrow: Voices of Care in the Holocaust* (College Station: Texas A & M University Press, 1998); and Nechama Tec, *Resilience and Courage: Women, Men, and the Holocaust* (New Haven, Conn.: Yale University Press, 2003). As illustrated by these writings, major areas of current research interest about women in the Holocaust include the roles that Jewish and non-Jewish women played in resistance against the Holocaust, the responsibilities that Jewish women had for maintaining families and households that were increasingly savaged by Nazi policy, the distinctive ways in which women in the Nazi camps established and sustained relationships of caring with one another, and women's activities—both among the perpetrators and the victims—as nurses, physicians, and other health professionals.

46. For detail on Ravensbrück, see Jack G. Morrison, *Ravensbrück: Everyday Life in a Women's Concentration Camp 1939–1945* (Princeton, N.J.: Marcus Wiener Publishers, 2000) and Rittner and Roth, eds., *Different Voices*.

47. For discussions of issues that faced non-Jewish women in Nazi Germany see Renate Bridenthal, Atina Grossman, and Marion A. Kaplan, eds., *When Biology Became Destiny: Women in Weimar and Nazi Germany* (New York: Monthly Review Press, 1984); Gellately and Stoltzfus, eds., *Social Outsiders in Nazi Germany*; Elizabeth Heineman, "Sexuality and Nazism: The Doubly Unspeakable," forthcoming in *Journal of the History of Sexuality*; Claudia Koonz, *Mothers in the Fatherland: Women, the Family, and Nazi Politics* (New York: St. Martin's Press, 1987); Ofer and Weitzman, eds., *Women in the Holocaust*; Alison Owings, *Frauen: German Women Recall the Third Reich* (New Brunswick, N.J.: Rutgers University Press, 1993); Rittner and Roth, eds., *Different Voices*; Jill Stephenson, *Women in Nazi Germany* (London: Pearson Education Ltd., 2001); and Adelheid von Saldern, "Victims or Perpetrators: Controversies about the Role of Women in the Nazi State," in *Nazism and German Society, 1933–1945*, ed. David F. Crew (New York: Routledge, 1994): 141–65.

48. See Daniel Patrick Brown, *The Camp Women: The Female Auxiliaries Who Assisted the SS in Running the Nazi Concentration Camp System* (Atglen, Pa.: Schiffer Military History, 2002).

49. As illustrated by Bernhard Schlink, *The Reader*, trans. Carol Brown Janeway (New York: Pantheon, 1997), even Holocaust-related fiction can become involved in debates about women and the Holocaust. Schlink's widely read and controversial novel focuses on Hanna Schmitz, who is tried and convicted of wartime crimes against Jews. Partly because Schlink portrayed this fictional SS guard as illiterate, in fact an unlikely scenario, his novel created sympathy for Hanna but also provoked dissent about the legitimacy and authenticity of Schlink's interpretation of the Holocaust and the part of ordinary Germans in it.

50. The quotation is from a speech that Himmler gave to SS leaders in October 1943. See Mendes-Flohr and Reinharz, eds., *The Jew in the Modern World*, 685.

51. Gertrud Kolmar, *Dark Soliloquy: The Selected Poems of Gertrud Kolmar*, trans. Henry A. Smith (New York: Seabury Press, 1975), 55–57. For more information on Kolmar, see Gertrud Kolmar, *My Gaze Is Turned Inward: Letters, 1934–1943*, ed. Johanna Woltmann and trans. Brigitte Goldstein (Evanston, Ill.: Northwestern University Press, 2002); Langer, *Versions of Survival*, 191–250; and Rittner and Roth, eds., *Different Voices*, 1–19.

52. Danuta Czech, *The Auschwitz Chronicle 1939–1945*, 652.

53. Ibid., 608. Often Czech's data about the arriving transports at Auschwitz-Birkenau make clear that more women than men were immediately dispatched to the gas chambers and that fewer women than men were spared for slave labor and the survival chances, however remote, that such a fate might offer.

54. Giuliana Tedeschi, *There Is a Place on Earth: A Woman in Birkenau*, trans. Tim Parks (New York: Pantheon Books, 1992), 10.

55. Ibid., 90.

56. Ibid., 89.

57. Ibid., 94.

58. Ibid., 95.

59. See Hellman, *The Auschwitz Album*, 38–39. Although *The Auschwitz Album* identifies her only as S. Szmaglewska, it is likely that this woman is the Polish author of early memoirs about Birkenau, which unfortunately have long been out of print. See Seweryna Szmaglewska, *Smoke over Birkenau*, trans. Jadwiga Rynas (New York: Henry Holt, 1947) and *United in Wrath* (Warsaw: "Polonia" Foreign Languages Publishing House, 1955). Szmaglewska's testimony at the Nuremberg

Trials can be found in *Trial of the Major War Criminals before the International Military Tribunal* (Nuremberg: 1947), 8:317–23. In this testimony Szmaglewska, who says she was in Birkenau from 7 October 1942 until January 1945, is identified as Severina Shmaglevskaya. For another reference to the baby strollers in Auschwitz, see Rudolf Vrba and Alan Bestic, *I Cannot Forgive* (New York: Grove Press, 1964). With help from the camp resistance, Vrba, a Slovakian Jew, escaped from Auschwitz in the spring of 1944 and reported what was happening there. Before his escape he worked in "Canada," the storehouse area in Auschwitz-Birkenau.

60. Tedeschi, *There Is a Place on Earth*, 1.
61. Ibid., 138.
62. Our discussion of survivors in this paragraph and the next draws on material prepared by John Roth for Roth et al., *The Holocaust Chronicle*.
63. See Deborah Lipstadt, *Denying the Holocaust: The Growing Assault on Truth and Memory* (New York: Free Press, 1993).
64. Ida Fink, *A Scrap of Time and Other Stories*, trans. Madeline Levine and Francine Prose (New York: Schocken Books, 1987), 3.
65. Ibid., 3.
66. See L. Langer, *Holocaust Testimonies*, xii.
67. Maurice Blanchot, *The Writing of the Disaster*, trans. Ann Smock (Lincoln: University of Nebraska Press, 1986), 1.
68. Ibid., 3.
69. Langer, *Holocaust Testimonies*, 205. To respect the survivors' privacy, Langer abbreviates their names.
70. Ibid., 204.
71. Ibid., xviii.
72. Ibid., 93.
73. Ibid., 91.
74. Ibid., 26.
75. Ibid., 16.
76. Ibid., 105.
77. Ibid., 163.
78. Blanchot, *The Writing of the Disaster*, 9.
79. Langer, *Holocaust Testimonies*, 204, xv.
80. Ibid., 53–54.
81. Ibid., 98.
82. Ibid., 146.
83. Ibid., 205.
84. Ibid., xi.
85. In the late 1990s major efforts were launched to win reparations for Jewish survivors of the Holocaust and for other people who had been exploited as slave laborers in the Third Reich. These efforts included attempts to obtain restitution for immense amounts of property—bank accounts, stock holdings, insurance policies, land, houses, businesses, jewelry, and artworks—that had been stolen or otherwise made inaccessible to Holocaust victims. German firms and Swiss banks have been prominently involved in establishing multibillion-dollar funds to approximate justice. Unfortunately, the Holocaust continues to defeat justice. Reparations and restitutions are unavoidably destined to be woefully incomplete because the losses are so great and too much time has passed. The attempt to compensate victims of the Holocaust has tried to bring a modicum of closure to the Holocaust, but the Holocaust eludes closure, for the inventory of its damages shows that there are always more. For further discussion of related topics, see Michael Thad Allen, *The Business of Genocide: The SS, Slave Labor, and the Con-*

*centration Camps* (Chapel Hill: University of North Carolina Press, 2002); John Authers and Richard Wolffe, *The Victim's Fortune: Inside the Epic Battle over the Debts of the Holocaust* (New York: HarperCollins, 2002); Elazar Barkan, *The Guilt of Nations: Restitution and Negotiating Historical Injustices* (New York: W. W. Norton, 2000); Michael Bazyler, *Holocaust Justice: The Battle for Restitution in America's Courts* (New York: New York University Press, 2003); Stuart Eizenstat, *Imperfect Justice: Looted Assets, Slave Labor, and the Unfinished Business of World War II* (New York: Public Affairs, 2003); and Petropoulos, *The Faustian Bargain.* Petropoulos calls the Nazi regime a "kleptocracy" to signify that theft of Jewish property was not an accidental or trivial aspect of the Holocaust but a central feature of the destruction of European Jewry.

86. The quoted phrase is the sociologist Helen Fein's. See *Accounting for Genocide*, 4. According to Fein, a necessary though not a sufficient condition for genocide is the definition of the victim as outside of a dominant group's universe of obligation (9).

87. For the idea of the victim as "nonperson," see Kren and Rappoport, *The Holocaust and the Crisis of Human Behavior*, 73–98.

88. See Rubenstein, *The Cunning of History*, 31–35.

89. Primo Levi, *Survival in Auschwitz*, trans. Stuart Wolff (New York: Collier Books, 1976), 25.

90. See Max Weber, "Politics as a Vocation," in *From Max Weber*, ed. Gerth and Mills, 78.

91. We quote the phrase from the subtitle of Benjamin Nelson's *The Idea of Usury: From Tribal Brotherhood to Universal Otherhood*, 2d ed., enl. (Chicago: University of Chicago Press, 1969).

92. The political philosopher Norman Geras develops related points in *The Contract of Mutual Indifference: Political Philosophy after the Holocaust* (London: Verso, 1998), 25–48. "Here is the core idea," he writes. "If you do not come to the aid of others who are under grave assault, in acute danger or crying need, you cannot reasonably expect others to come to your aid in similar emergency; you cannot consider them obligated to you. Other people, equally unmoved by the emergencies of others, cannot reasonably expect to be helped in deep trouble themselves, or consider others obligated to help them. I call this *the contract of mutual indifference*" (28, Geras's italics).

## Chapter 10

1. Rolf Hochhuth, *Der Stellvertreter* (Reinbek bei Hamburg: Rowohlt Verlag GmbH, 1963); English translation, *The Deputy* (New York: Grove Press, 1964). *Amen,* a controversial film based on Hochhuth's play, was produced in 2002 by the noted director, Constantin Costa-Garvas. Much of his film focuses on Kurt Gerstein (1905–45), an enigmatic Holocaust figure. A mining engineer, Gerstein joined the Nazi Party in 1933 but remained in the Confessing Church, whose Protestant membership offered some resistance to Hitler, a topic that will be discussed at greater length as this chapter unfolds. Arrested for circulating religious tracts in 1936, he was confined to a concentration camp for a time, prohibited from working in state-owned mines, and expelled from the Nazi Party in 1938. He proceeded to study medicine, and then, after his sister-in-law was killed in the "euthanasia" program in early 1941, Gerstein became determined to find out, from the inside, what the Nazi regime was doing. He enlisted in the *Waffen-SS,* where his background in engineering and medicine placed him in its hygiene department. Largely owing to his reputation for expertise with prussic acid (Zyklon B) and other toxic gases, the young lieutenant soon became head of the

*Waffen-SS* disinfection services. In the summer of 1942 he was ordered to deliver a consignment of Zyklon B to the Lublin area in eastern Poland. (Apparently unbeknownst to Gerstein, that disinfectant had already been used as a killing agent at Auschwitz.) Gerstein's destination turned out to be Belzec, where it was hoped that his expertise with Zyklon B could help to enhance the killing operations that were based on less efficient carbon monoxide. That hope did not pan out, but while Gerstein was at Belzec, he witnessed the killing operations, which on that occasion included long delays because of malfunctioning engines. Deeply troubled, Gerstein resolved to expose Nazi Germany's mass murder. In addition to a Swedish diplomat, a Swiss journalist, and an agent of the Dutch underground, Gerstein approached church leaders, including the papal nuncio in Berlin. His interventions were largely futile, and, although he may have sabotaged some shipments of Zyklon B, he continued to be responsible for ordering that gas for the SS, who used it both for disinfection of buildings and for murdering Jews at Auschwitz. The French arrested Gerstein as a war crimes suspect at the end of World War II. In July 1945 he was found dead in his jail cell. It remains unclear whether he committed suicide or whether he was assassinated by other SS officers who feared his testimony. For more detail on Gerstein, see Saul Friedländer, *Kurt Gerstein: The Ambiguity of Good* (New York: Alfred A. Knopf, 1969).

2. John Cornwell, *Hitler's Pope: The Secret History of Pius XII* (New York: Viking Press, 1999).

3. See John K. Roth, "'High Ideals' and 'Innocuous Reaction': An American Protestant's Reflections on Pius XII and the Holocaust" and Richard L. Rubenstein, "Pope Pius XII and the Holocaust," both in *Pope Pius XII and the Holocaust,* ed. Carol Rittner and John K. Roth (New York: Continuum, 2002); Richard L. Rubenstein, "The Vatican Statement on the Shoah and the Vatican during World War II," in *Remembering for the Future,* ed. Roth and Maxwell, 2:455–80; and John Pollard, "Pacelli and the Jews: The Debate Rages On," *Tablet* (London), 15 June 2002. Also relevant in this regard is Daniel Jonah Goldhagen, *A Moral Reckoning: The Role of the Catholic Church in the Holocaust and Its Unfulfilled Duty of Repair* (New York: Alfred A. Knopf, 2002).

4. Here we use the term *Church* to refer to the Roman Catholic Church. When referring to Christian denominations in the plural, we use the term *churches*.

5. On Christian attitudes toward anti-Jewish laws in Hungary during the 1930s, see Moshe Y. Herczl, *Christianity and the Holocaust of Hungarian Jewry,* trans. Joel Lerner (New York: New York University Press, 1993), 81–169.

6. Richard Pipes, *A Concise History of the Russian Revolution* (New York: Vintage Books, 1995), 286.

7. On the Red revolution in Munich see Allan Mitchell, *Revolution in Bavaria, 1918–1919* (Princeton: Princeton University Press, 1965); Ruth Fischer, *Stalin and German Communism* (Cambridge, Mass.: Harvard University Press, 1948); Charles B. Maurer, *Call to Revolution: The Mystical Anarchism of Gustav Landauer* (Detroit: Wayne State University Press, 1971); Rosa Leviné-Meyer, *Leviné the Spartacist* (London: Gordon & Cremonesi, 1978); Richard Grunberger, *Red Rising in Bavaria* (New York: St. Martin's Press, 1973).

8. The *Protocols* had originally been prepared by the Russian police and given to Czar Nicholas II to influence policy. Although personally antisemitic, the czar detected the fraud and refused to use it. See Leon Poliakov, "Elders of Zion, Protocols of the Learned," in *Encyclopedia Judaica,* CD Rom edition (Jerusalem: Judaica Multimedia, 1997).

9. It is estimated that more than 8.5 million combatants were killed in the war, with some 21 million wounded and 7.7 million prisoners and missing. Among those

killed were 1.7 million German and 1.2 million Austro-Hungarian soldiers. The number of civilian deaths attributable to the war, the displacement of peoples, and death from blockade-induced starvation are estimated to have been no less than 13 million. The figures are those of the United States Department of War, February 1924. See "World War I: Killed, Wounded, and Missing," Table 4: Armed Forces Mobilized and Casualties in World War I, *Encyclopedia Britannica*, DVD edition, 2001.

10. Klaus Scholder, *The Churches and the Third Reich,* trans. John Bowden (London: SCM Press, 1988), 1:6.
11. Ibid. See also Thomas Mann, *Betrachtungen eines Unpolitischen* (Berlin: S. Fischer, 1956), 39f.
12. In 1920 the Association of Jewish Veterans felt compelled to publish a leaflet addressed to German mothers and informing them that 12,000 Jewish soldiers fell during the war. The leaflet testified accurately that the same percentage of Jews were killed as the percentage of fallen soldiers in the population at large, but to no avail. A reproduction of the leaflet is found in Hagen Schulze, *Germany: A New History*, trans. Deborah Lucas Schneider (Cambridge, Mass.: Harvard University Press, 1998), 206.
13. Quoted in Barnett, *For the Soul of the People,* 15.
14. See Wolfgang Gerlach, *And the Witnesses Were Silent: The Confessing Church and the Persecution of the Jews,* trans. and ed. Victoria Barnett (Lincoln: University of Nebraska Press, 2000), 228–29.
15. Ibid., 230.
16. The plotters included highly placed conservatives such as Franz von Papen, the Roman Catholic former chancellor, and Oskar von Hindenburg, the president's son. The best account of the intrigues that preceded Hitler's becoming chancellor is found in Kershaw, *Hitler, 1889–1936,* 377–427.
17. Ibid., 423–24.
18. See Kurt Meier, *Kreuz und Hakenkreuz im Dritten Reich* (Munich: Deutscher Taschenbuch Verlag, 1992) and Conway, *The Nazi Persecution of the Churches, 1933–1945.* For these references, we are indebted to Ericksen and Heschel, eds., *Betrayal,* esp. 70 and 202 n.6. Along with the work of many other scholars, the contributions by Gerlach, Ericksen, Heschel, Stephen Haynes, and Doris Bergen, referred to in this documentation, discredit the myth of the German churches as "persecuted victims."
19. Dietrich Bonhoeffer addressed himself to this issue in 1933. See "The Church and the Jewish Question," in *No Rusty Sword: Letters, Lectures, and Notes 1928–1933*, ed. Edwin H. Robertson and trans. John Bowden (London: Fontana, 1974), 217–25.
20. Goldhagen, *Hitler's Willing Executioners*, 432.
21. See John S. Conway, "The Churches," in *The Holocaust: Ideology, Bureaucracy, and Genocide,* ed. Henry Friedlander and Sybil Milton (Millwood, N.Y.: Kraus International Publications, 1980), 204.
22. For a study of some important German theologians who took positions altogether different from Barth and Tillich, see Ericksen, *Theologians under Hitler.* For an overview of Christian support for National Socialism, see Erickson and Heschel, eds., *Betrayal.*
23. See Scholder, *The Churches and the Third Reich*, 1:228–29.
24. Ibid., 1:229.
25. Kershaw, *Hitler, 1889–1936*, 464–65.
26. See Conway, *The Nazi Persecution of the Churches,* 410–11.
27. In 1949 Wurm wrote to a meeting of lay leaders meeting in Darmstadt, "Can anyone in Germany speak about the Jewish question without mentioning how

Jewish literature sinned against the German people through its mockery of all that is holy, since the days of Heinrich Heine? Or of the sufferings endured in numerous regions by German farmers at the hands of Jewish money-lenders?" Theophil Wurm, Letter to Bruderrat, 17 January 1949, cited in *Betrayal*, ed. Ericksen and Heschel, 19.

28. See Conway, *The Nazi Persecution of the Churches*, 208–12.

29. Barnett, *For the Soul of the People*, 201.

30. For further information on the Jehovah's Witnesses, see John K. Roth, *Holocaust Politics* (Louisville, Ky.: Westminster John Knox, 2001). In addition to the works already cited in this chapter, further insight about the German churches, Protestant and Catholic, can be found in Bergen, *Twisted Cross*; Arthur C. Cochrane, *The Church's Confession under Hitler*, 2nd ed. (Pittsburgh: The Pickwick Press, 1976); Richard Gutteridge, *Open Thy Mouth for the Dumb: The German Evangelical Church and the Jews 1879–1950* (Oxford: Basil Blackwell, 1976); Ernst Christian Helmreich, *The German Churches under Hitler: Background, Struggle, and Epilogue* (Detroit: Wayne State University Press, 1979); and Frederic Spotts, *The Churches and Politics in Germany* (Middletown, Conn.: Wesleyan University Press, 1973).

31. Barnett, *For the Soul of the People*, 27. See also Bergen, *Twisted Cross*, 5. Bergen's book is the most comprehensive and reliable treatment of the German Christians in English. See also Bergen, "Nazi-Christians and Christian Nazis: The 'German Christian' Movement in National Socialist Germany," in *What Kind of God? Essays in Honor of Richard L. Rubenstein,* ed. Betty Rogers Rubenstein and Michael Berenbaum (Lanham, Md.: University Press of America, 1995), 175–86.

32. Note that the term *evangelical* has different connotations when applied to German and American churches. The German Evangelical churches were much more akin to the mainline American Protestant denominations than to "born again" Christians, to whom the term is usually applied in the United States.

33. "Law for the Restoration of the Professional Civil Service," *Reichsgesetzblatt*, 1 (1933): 175, English translation in *Documents on the Holocaust: Selected Sources on the Destruction of the Jews of Germany and Austria, Poland and the Soviet Union* ed. Yitzhak Arad, Israel Gutman, and Abraham Margaliot, trans. Leah Bern Dor (Lincoln: University of Nebraska Press, 1999), 39–41.

34. See Gerlach, *And the Witnesses Were Silent*, 19; Shelley Baranowski, "The Confessing Church and Antisemitism: Protestant Identity, German Nationhood, and the Exclusion of the Jews," in *Betrayal*, ed. Ericksen and Heschel, 101; and Helmreich, *The German Churches under Hitler*, 144.

35. Barnett, *For the Soul of the People*, 35.

36. Scholder, *The Churches and the Third Reich*, 1:552–53.

37. Ibid., 1:469.

38. For an overview of the Institute and Walter Grundmann, its first director, see Susannah Heschel, "Making Nazism a Christian Movement: The Development of a Christian Theology of Antisemitism During the Third Reich," in *What Kind of God?* ed. Rubenstein and Berenbaum, 159–174. See also Susannah Heschel, "When Jesus Was an Aryan: The Protestant Church and Antisemitic Propaganda," in *Betrayal*, ed. Ericksen and Heschel, 68–89, and Bergen, *Twisted Cross*, 24.

39. See Robert P. Ericksen, "Genocide, Religion, and Gerhard Kittel," in *In God's Name: Genocide and Religion in the Twentieth Century*, ed. Omer Bartov and Phyllis Mack (New York: Berghahn Books, 2001), 67. This essay is an insightful introduction not only to the role of Kittel in fostering the objectives of Adolf Hitler, but also to that of a wider group of German theologians and scholars. For an earlier but more comprehensive analysis see Ericksen, *Theologians under Hitler*.

40. Gerhard Kittel, *Die Behandlung des Nichtjuden nach dem Talmud* (*Archiv für Judenfragen*) vol. 1, Group A (Berlin: P. Hochmuth, 1943), 7. See Ericksen, "Genocide, Religion, and Gerhard Kittel," 71.

41. Ericksen, "Genocide, Religion, and Gerhard Kittel," 71.

42. Heschel, "When Jesus Was an Aryan," 79 and 83.

43. Ibid., 74–77.

44. According to Doris Bergen, the best estimates are that 480 Protestants and an equal number of Catholics served throughout the war as chaplains. Bergen, "Between God and Hitler: German Military Chaplains and the Crimes of the Third Reich," in *In God's Name*, ed. Bartov and Mack, 123 and 136 n.7.

45. Ibid., 124.

46. Ibid., 125. Our discussion of this issue is indebted to Bergen's important insights about the role of the chaplains in the German armed forces.

47. Ibid., 127.

48. Ibid., 133.

49. For example, Gerhard Kittel spent a year and a half in prison. For aiding and abetting Nazi crimes against Jews, he also lost his professorship and his position as editor of the *Theological Dictionary of the New Testament*. See Ericksen, "Genocide, Holocaust, and Gerhard Kittel," 71.

50. Franklin H. Littell, "Church Struggle and the Holocaust," in *The German Church Struggle and the Holocaust,* ed. Littell and Locke, 16.

51. Barnett's *For the Soul of the People* presents an authoritative account of the Confessing Church.

52. See Baranowski, "The Confessing Church and Antisemitism," 90–109.

53. Ibid., 90.

54. Conway, *The Nazi Persecution of the Churches*, 84.

55. Barnett, *For the Soul of the People*, 55.

56. Cited in Eberhard Bethge, "Troubled Self-Interpretation and Uncertain Reception in the German Church Struggle," in *The German Church Struggle*, ed. Littell and Locke, 167. See also Robin W. Lovin, *Christian Faith and Public Choices: The Social Ethics of Barth, Brunner, and Bonhoeffer* (Philadelphia: Fortress Press, 1984).

57. Cited in Conway, *The Nazi Persecution of the Churches*, 15.

58. Eberhard Busch, *Karl Barth: His Life from Letters and Autobiographical Texts*, trans. John Bowden (Philadelphia: Fortress Press, 1976), 223.

59. Letter to E. Steffens, 10 January 1934, cited in Busch, *Karl Barth*, 235.

60. Busch, *Karl Barth*, 255–56.

61. Ibid., 290.

62. Karl Barth, *Church Dogmatics,* trans. G. Bromiley et al. (Edinburgh: T. & T. Clark, 1957), II, 2, 235. The 1949 quotations are from Karl Barth, "The Jewish Problem and the Christian Answer," in *Against the Stream* (London: SCM Press, 1954), 196, 198. We are indebted to Emil Fackenheim, *To Mend The World: Foundations of Future Jewish Thought* (New York: Schocken, 1982), 133. In that book, Fackenheim, one of the twentieth century's most important Jewish thinkers, describes Barth as "the last great Christian supersessionist thinker" (284).

63. On the "Grüber office," see Barnett, *For the Soul of the People*, 144–46.

64. For more on Grüber, see Rubenstein, "The Dean and the Chosen People," in Rubenstein, *After Auschwitz*, 3–13. Grüber was the only German to testify for the prosecution in the 1961 trial of Adolf Eichmann in Jerusalem.

65. Niemöller would later be imprisoned at the Sachsenhausen and Dachau concentration camps. After the war, it was Niemöller who wrote these often-cited lines: "First they came for the socialists, and I did not speak out—because I was not a

socialist. Then they came for the trade unionists, and I did not speak out—because I was not a trade unionist. Then they came for the Jews, and I did not speak out—because I was not a Jew. Then they came for me—and there was no one left to speak for me."

66. See Cochrane, *The Church's Confession*, 275, and Barnett, *For the Soul of the People*, 83–85.

67. Quoted in Littell, "Church Struggle and Holocaust," 15.

68. Fifteen years after the war's end, Dietrich's father, psychiatrist Karl Bonhoeffer, wrote, "From the start, we regarded the victory of National Socialism in 1933 . . . as a misfortune—the entire family agreed on this." See Eberhard Bethge, *Dietrich Bonhoeffer: A Biography*, rev. ed., ed. Victoria Barnett (Minneapolis: Fortress, 2000), 258.

69. See Stephen R. Haynes, "Bystander, Resister, Victim: Dietrich Bonhoeffer's Response to Nazism," forthcoming in *The Bonhoeffer Phenomenon: Portraits of a Protestant Saint*.

70. According to Renate Bonhoeffer, Bonhoeffer's niece, "the Jewish question was the dominant theme in family conversations and with it all other political questions were connected." Cited in Edwin H. Robertson, "A Study of Dietrich Bonhoeffer and the Jews Jan–April 1933," in *Remembering for the Future*, ed. Yehuda Bauer et al. (Oxford: Pergamon Press, 1988), 1:122. We are indebted to Haynes, "Bystander, Resister, Victim," for this citation.

71. Dietrich Bonhoeffer, "The Church and the Jewish Question," 217.

72. See Noakes and Pridham, eds., *Nazism, 1919–1945*, 1:224, and Bergen, *Twisted Cross*, 88ff.

73. Bonhoeffer, "The Church and the Jewish Question," 219 (italics added).

74. Ibid., 221.

75. Ibid., 223.

76. Ibid., 222.

77. Ibid., 222.

78. See Dietrich Bonhoeffer, "The Church and the Jews," in *No Rusty Swords*, 237.

79. Quoted in Bethge, *Dietrich Bonhoeffer*, 655.

80. F. Burton Nelson, "The Life of Dietrich Bonhoeffer," in *The Cambridge Companion to Dietrich Bonhoeffer*, ed. John W. de Gruchy (Cambridge: Cambridge University Press, 1999), 37–38.

81. In conjunction with Bonhoeffer's nomination to be named a "Righteous Gentile" at Yad Vashem, the following report is significant: "The material submitted for the Bonhoeffer nomination clearly establishes that he was instrumental in persuading his brother-in-law, Hans von Dohnanyi . . . to include Charlotte Friedenthal among a group of Jews (some of whom had converted to Christianity) which the *Abwehr* planned to move to Switzerland. . . . This rescue operation was planned and carried out by the *Abwehr*, with the full backing of Admiral Canaris, the *Abwehr* head, who himself added four Jewish persons to the group. In addition, Mrs. Friedenthal, a baptized Jewess, had until then occupied a responsible position in the Confessing Church. Bonhoeffer's role was in referring her to Dohnanyi, but he was not personally involved in this rescue operation. There is no other record of a direct involvement by Bonhoeffer in the rescue of Jews (baptized or not). In September 1943, five months after his arrest, the Gestapo drew up a large charge sheet against Bonhoeffer. The accusations relate to Bonhoeffer's evading the draft and his association with the *Abwehr*. The sole item with respect of the Jewish issue is Bonhoeffer's request to his brother-in-law, Dohnanyi, to assist a certain Jewish professor, the uncle of a Jewish Christian convert, who was incarcerated in the French camp of Gurs. It is not known whether such assistance was acted upon" (Personal communication, Mordecai Paldiel to Richard L.

Rubenstein, 18 October 2001). Paldiel is director of the Department for the Righteous of Yad Vashem, Israel's Holocaust Martyrs' and Heroes' Remembrance Authority.

82. Haynes, "Bystander, Resistor, Victim." See also Geffrey B. Kelly, F. Burton Nelson, and Renate Bethge, *The Cost of Moral Leadership: The Spirituality of Dietrich Bonhoeffer* (Grand Rapids, Mich.: Wm. B. Eerdmans, 2002).

83. Ibid.

84. See Guenter Lewy, *The Roman Catholic Church and the Third Reich* (Boulder, Colo.: Da Capo Press, 2000).

85. Scholder, *The German Churches*, 1:150–51.

86. See Guenter Lewy, *The Catholic Church and Nazi Germany* (New York: McGraw-Hill, 1964), 8–24.

87. Scholder, *The German Churches*, 1:157.

88. As a result of the controversy over the role of the Vatican during World War II, a very large body of scholarly literature has been devoted to the subject. The most comprehensive collection of Vatican documents pertaining to World War II is to be found in *Actes et Documents du Saint Siège relatifs à la Seconde Guerre mondiale*, ed. Pierre Blet, Robert A. Graham, Angelo Martini, and Burkhart Schneider (Vatican City: Libreria Editrice Vaticana, 1965–81). Henceforth we abbreviate *Actes et Documents* as *ADSS*. The additional works we have consulted include James Carroll, *Constantine's Sword*; Cornwell, *Hitler's Pope*; Saul Friedländer, *Pius XII and the Third Reich: A Documentation*, trans. Charles Fullman (New York: Alfred A. Knopf, 1966); Goldhagen, *A Moral Reckoning*; John F. Morley, *Vatican Diplomacy and the Jews during the Holocaust: 1939–1943* (New York: KTAV, 1980); Phayer, *The Catholic Church and the Holocaust, 1933–1965*; Rittner and Roth, eds., *Pope Pius XII and the Holocaust*; and Susan Zuccotti, *Under His Very Windows: The Vatican and the Holocaust in Italy* (New Haven, Conn.: Yale University Press, 2001).

89. Phayer, *The Catholic Church and the Holocaust*, 83.

90. Heller, *On the Edge of Destruction*, 51–52.

91. Pavel Korzec, *Juifs en Pologne: La question juive pendant l'entre-deux-guerres* (Paris: Presses de la Fondation Nationale des Sciences Politiques, 1980), 110 n.113. Cited in Kertzer, *The Popes against the Jews*, 247.

92. Kertzer, *The Popes against The Jews*, 263. Kertzer's source is Renato Moro, "Le premesse dell'atteggiamento cattolico di fronte alla legislazione razziale fascista. Cattolici ed ebrei nell'Italia degli anni venti (1919–1932)," *Storia Contemporanea* 19:1118.

93. See Anthony Rhodes, *The Vatican in the Age of Dictators 1922–1945* (London: Hodder & Stoughton, 1973), 18.

94. Kertzer, *The Popes against The Jews*, 134.

95. Until the mid-twentieth century, the director of the journal met with the papal secretary of state before the publication of each issue. Often the pope himself would review and approve the content of the forthcoming issue. See Kertzer, *The Popes against The Jews*, 135.

96. See "Kishinev," *Encyclopedia Judaica*, CD-ROM edition.

97. Kertzer, *The Popes against the Jews*, 159–60. See articles "Blood Libel" and "Tiszaeszlar" in *Encyclopaedia Judaica*, CD-ROM edition.

98. Father Saverio Rondina, "La morale giudaica," *La Civiltà Cattolica*, 1897, II, 257–71. We are indebted to Kertzer, *The Popes against the Jews*, 144–46.

99. "Omicidio rituale giudaico," *L'Osservatore Romano*, 23 Nov. 1899. We are indebted to Kertzer, *The Popes against The Jews*, 163.

100. See Kertzer, *The Popes against the Jews*, 163.

101. Cornwell, *Hitler's Pope*, 26; see also R. Po-chia Hsia, *The Myth of Ritual Murder: Jews and Magic in Reformation Germany* (New Haven, Conn.: Yale University Press, 1988).

102. Denis Mack Smith, *Mussolini* (New York: Alfred A. Knopf, 1982), 159–61.
103. Scholder, *The Churches and the Third Reich,* 1:163.
104. Cornwell, *Hitler's Pope,* 114.
105. Scholder, *The Churches and the Third Reich,* 1:154.
106. Cornwell, *Hitler's Pope,* 147.
107. Kertzer, *The Popes against the Jews,* 25–132; See also Kertzer, *The Kidnapping of Edgardo Mortara.*
108. *Mit brennender Sorge,* in *Actes de S. S. Pie XI* (Paris: Maison de la Bonne Press, 1937), 13–16. The text is also available online at *www.vatican.va/holy_father/ pius_xi/encyclicals/documents/hf_p-xi_enc_14031937_mit-brennender-sorge_en. html.*
109. Ibid., 22.
110. Ibid., 15–16.
111. Lewy, *The Catholic Church and Nazi Germany,* 283.
112. Decades later the draft text was discovered and became known as the "hidden encyclical." The subject is covered in Georges Passelecq and Bernard Suchecky, *The Hidden Encyclical of Pius XI,* trans. Steven Rendall (New York: Harcourt Brace, 1997).
113. The text *Humani Generis Unitas* is reprinted in Passelecq and Suchecky, *The Hidden Encyclical.* See esp. 246–59.
114. Cited in Kertzer, *The Popes against the Jews,* 280.
115. See Saul Friedländer, *Pius XII and the Third Reich* (New York: Alfred A. Knopf, 1966), 3–24.
116. *ADSS,* vol. 2. *Lettres aux Eveques Allemands.* See also Rhodes, *The Vatican in the Age of Dictators,* 226–28.
117. Friedländer, *Pius XII and the Third Reich,* 9–10.
118. Breitman, *The Architect of Genocide,* 53.
119. See Rhodes, *The Vatican in the Age of Dictators,* 237.
120. *ADSS: El Saint Siège El la Situation Religieuse en Pologne et dans les Pays Balts, 1939–1945,* vol. 3, no. 102, 19 January 1940.
121. Rhodes, *The Vatican in the Age of Dictators,* 243.
122. For the conversation in which the pope expressed concern about these matters, see Friedländer, *Pius XII and the Third Reich,* 74–75.
123. On the deportations from France, see Marrus and Paxton, *Vichy France and the Jews,* 241–80.
124. *ADSS: Le Saint Siège et la Guerre Mondiale, Novembre 1942–Décembre 1943,* vol. 7, no. 610.
125. Ibid.
126. For the text of the Riegner message, see Friedländer, *Pius XII and the Third Reich,* 117.
127. Letter from Myron C. Taylor to Cardinal Maglione, 26 September 1942, *Foreign Relations of the United States,* (Washington: United States Government Printing Office, 1961), 3:775–76.
128. Ibid., 3:775.
129. Morley, *Vatican Diplomacy and the Jews,* 206.
130. Letter of Luigi Cardinal Maglione, Secretary of State, to Charles Sidor, Minister of Slovakia to the Holy See, in Morley, *Vatican Diplomacy and the Jews,* 221–25.
131. *ADSS,* vol. 8, nos. 327–28.
132. See Morley, *Vatican Diplomacy and the Jews,* 78.
133. The date of the pastoral letter was 26 April 1942. See *ADSS,* vol. 8, no. 519.
134. Cited by Fein, *Accounting for Genocide,* 101–2. Together with Msgr. Giovanni Battista Montini (later Pope Paul VI), Tardini was one of the two principle assistants to the Vatican's secretary of state during the Holocaust.

135. *ADSS*, vol. 9, no. 272. See Morley, *Vatican Diplomacy and the Jews*, 92.
136. The Vatican's initial reaction to America's entry into the war was similar to Germany's. Both regarded the Americans as too undisciplined and militarily incompetent to present a threat for a very long time. This view was reflected in the Vatican's attempts to counter American diplomatic initiatives in Latin America in January 1942. When the United States attempted to get the nations of Latin America to break off diplomatic relations with Germany, Italy, and Japan, its efforts were largely thwarted by the Vatican. See Friedländer, *Pius XII and the Third Reich*, 90.
137. Roosevelt's message is to be found in *ADSS*, vol. V, no. 431. See also Rhodes, *The Vatican in the Age of Dictators*, 265–71.
138. We use Susan Zuccotti's translation in *Under His Very Windows*, 1. She notes that in this wartime speech, "Pius XII never used the words Jew, anti-Semitism, or race." Zuccotti notes further that the Italian *stirpe* is often translated—incorrectly, she argues—as *race*, and doing so ignores "subtle differences between the two terms." (See *Under His Very Windows*, 329 n3.) In Zuccotti's view, which we accept, *stirpe* is better translated as *descent*, a term whose meaning in the 1942 context only adds to the generality of the pope's language.
139. Nazi leaders were not pleased by Pius XII's Christmas oratory, but neither were those who were victimized by them. On 2 January 1943, for example, Wladislaw Raczkiewicz, the president of the Polish government in exile, protested to the pope, saying that his people "implore that a voice be raised to show clearly and plainly where the evil lies and to condemn those in the service of evil." The British, Belgian, and Brazilian governments also protested to the Vatican for having failed to name Germany. The protests pained the pope, who was convinced that he had spoken as plainly as he could. Pius XII and his subordinates were convinced that they could not explicitly denounce the German atrocities. That judgment remains among the most sharply criticized of the Vatican's wartime policies. See especially Goldhagen, *A Moral Reckoning*, and Friedländer, *Pius XII and the Third Reich*, 131–47.
140. Susan Zuccotti, *The Italians and the Holocaust: Persecution, Rescue, Survival* (New York: Basic Books, 1987), 109–13.
141. Ibid., 127.
142. See Fein, *Accounting for Genocide*, 106–10.
143. For a discussion of Seredi's letter, see Herczl, *Christianity and the Holocaust of Hungarian Jewry*, 205–15.
144. Seredi declared that he had kept silent in public because he was attempting to protect baptized Jews. Since that effort had failed, he rejected any responsibility for the ensuing events. The text of Seredi's letter is in Friedländer, *Pius XII and the Third Reich*, 220–21. Phayer's characterization is found in *The Catholic Church and the Holocaust*, 109.
145. Hilberg, *The Destruction of the European Jews*, 2:849 and 2:908.
146. On this point see Phayer, *The Catholic Church and the Holocaust*, 54.
147. Ibid., 54–61.
148. See Zuccotti, *Under His Very Windows*, 314–15, and Phayer, *The Catholic Church and the Holocaust*, 61–66.
149. "Editto della Santa Inquisizione contro gl'Israeliti degli Stati Pontifici," in Achille Gennarelli, *Il governo pontifico e lo stato romano, documenti preceduti da una esposizione storica* (Rome: 1860), part 1, 304–5, cited in Kertzer, *The Kidnapping of Edgardo Mortara*, 190.
150. "Gemeinsames Wort der deutschen Bishöfe," *Martinus-Blatt*, no. 38, 17 September 1939.
151. See Klaus Scholder, *A Requiem for Hitler and Other New Perspectives on the German Church Struggle* (Philadelphia: Trinity Press International, 1989), 157–67.

152. For a discussion of the significance of Lichtenberg's sacrificial behavior, see Fackenheim, *To Mend the World*, 289–90.
153. The Foreign Office expected Papal Nuncio Orsenigo to inquire about Lichtenberg's arrest and was prepared to tell him that he had been arrested for praying for the Jews. Apparently, the Foreign Office believed that the nuncio and the pope would find that reply satisfactory. See Friedländer, *Pius XII and the Third Reich* 100–101.
154. Phayer, *The Catholic Church and the Holocaust*, 73–77.
155. Ibid., 81.
156. On Gertrud Luckner, see ibid., 114–17.
157. See ibid., 117–22.
158. Fein, *Accounting for Genocide*, 33.
159. For more detail on the rescue of Jews in Bulgaria, see Tzvetan Toderov, *The Frailty of Goodness: Why Bulgaria's Jews Survived the Holocaust*, trans. Arthur Denner (Princeton: Princeton University Press, 2001).
160. David Wyman, *The Abandonment of the Jews: America and the Holocaust 1941–1945* (New York: Pantheon Books, 1984), 105.
161. Ibid., 341–43.
162. Ibid., 120.
163. In addition to Wyman, *The Abandonment of the Jews*, see Robert W. Ross, *So It Was True: The American Protestant Press and the Nazi Persecution of the Jews* (Minneapolis: University of Minnesota Press, 1980). Also relevant in this regard are Robert H. Abzug, *America Views the Holocaust 1933–1945: A Brief Documentary History* (New York: St. Martin's, 1999) and Deborah E. Lipstadt, *Beyond Belief: The American Press and the Coming of the Holocaust 1933–1945* (New York: Free Press, 1986).
164. See "United States of America: 1880–1929: The Great Immigration," *Encyclopedia Judaica*, CD Rom Edition, 1997.
165. Howard M. Sachar, *The Course of Modern Jewish History*, 313–14.
166. *Christian Century*, 30 November 1938, 1456–59. For this reference, we are indebted to Lipstadt, *Beyond Belief*, 114.
167. There is ongoing scholarly debate about the extent and adequacy of American responses to the Holocaust. Our perspective is that the plight of Europe's Jews was never a decisive reason for America's involvement in the war against Hitler. The American posture was that military power should be used only in direct efforts to defeat Nazi Germany. Special consideration for Jewish needs was regarded as contrary to the best national and military interests. The U.S. government did not make the saving of European Jewry a top priority, although the American record in rescuing Jews surpassed that of England, the Soviet Union, and the other Allies. That result depended largely on the War Refugee Board (WRB), established by President Roosevelt on 22 January 1944, which helped to save approximately two hundred thousand Jews. Earlier American efforts could have saved thousands more. During the three-and-a-half years that the United States waged war against Nazi Germany, State Department policies allowed only twenty-one thousand refugees—most of them Jewish—to enter the country, just 10 percent of those who could have been legally admitted under the already restrictive quotas. Better results were thwarted by widespread antisemitism and anti-immigration sentiment in American society, as well as by the indifference of political leaders and in particular the refusal of the president to speak out. Bowing to political pressures generated by goverment officials John W. Pehle, Raymond Paul, and Josiah E. DuBois Jr., who had documented a State Department record of distorted messages, sabotaged proposals, and general procrastination where Jewish plight was concerned, Roosevelt finally brought the WRB into exis-

tence. Even then, the board was underfinanced. Ninety percent of its costs had to be covered by Jewish contributions. Not until June 1944 did the United States make special provisions to bring Jewish refugees to America outside the existing immigration quotas. Under these provisions, fewer than a thousand Jewish refugees were brought to the United States, where they were long detained under less than desirable conditions at Fort Ontario, an obsolete army facility near Syracuse, New York.

Meanwhile, the first of several American air reconnaissance missions over the Auschwitz area occurred on 4 April 1944. Some of these aerial photographs showed lines of Auschwitz prisoners waiting their turn to enter the gas chambers, but military attention riveted on the more central points of interest: German industrial plants at Monowitz and surrounding areas. Later that year, air force bombing in this region was extensive. During the spring and summer of 1944, there had been Jewish pleas that the rail routes to Auschwitz and the gas chambers and crematoria themselves should be targeted. These pleas reached the Allied governments. Arguably the logistical problems in undertaking such missions were not insurmountable. The Allies had air supremacy over Europe. Hungary was being bombed almost daily. Although the Allies firebombed Dresden, annihilating more than one hundred thousand civilians to no military purpose, they decided to leave Auschwitz alone.

For more detail on these matters and the disputes about them, see Abzug, *America Views the Holocaust*; Feingold, *Bearing Witness*; Michael Neufeld and Michael Berenbaum, eds., *The Bombing of Auschwitz: Should the Allies Have Attempted It?* (New York: St. Martin's Press, 2000); Power, *"A Problem from Hell"*; William D. Rubinstein, *The Myth of Rescue*; Wyman, *The Abandonment of the Jews*; and David S. Wyman and Charles H. Rosenzveig, eds., *The World Reacts to the Holocaust* (Baltimore: Johns Hopkins University Press, 1996). Also significant is Michael Beschloss, *The Conquerors: Roosevelt, Truman, and the Destruction of Hitler's Germany 1941–1945* (New York: Simon & Schuster, 2002), which argues that Roosevelt himself was chiefly responsible for the decision not to bomb Auschwitz and that he also regarded the United States as a Protestant country where Catholics and Jews resided "under suffrance." See Beschloss, *The Conquerors*, 51, 63–69 and *Newsweek*, 14 Oct. 2002, 37–39.

168. See, for example, Charles Clayton Morrison, "Horror Stories From Poland," *Christian Century*, 9 Dec. 1942, 1518–19, and Morrison, "Polish Atrocities Are Entered in the Books," *Christian Century*, 30 Dec. 1942, 1611. These texts are found in Abzug, *America Views the Holocaust*, 136–37.

169. Reinhold Niebuhr, "Jews after the War," *Nation*, 21 and 28 Feb. 1942. Niebuhr's texts are reproduced in Abzug, *America Views the Holocaust*, 116–25.

170. Cited in Richard Hanser, *A Noble Treason: The Revolt of the Munich Students against Hitler* (New York: G. P. Putnam's Sons, 1979), 152–53. See also Annette E. Dumbach and Jud Newborn, *Shattering the German Night: The Story of the White Rose* (Boston: Little, Brown & Co., 1986) and Inge Scholl, *The White Rose: Munich 1942–1943*, trans. Arthur R. Schultz (Middletown, Conn.: Wesleyan University Press, 1983).

171. Hanser, *A Noble Treason*, 274.

172. The Bible likens righteous persons to "trees planted by streams of water, which yield their fruit in its season, and their leaves do not wither" (Psalm 1:3). At Yad Vashem, which means "place and name" (see Isa. 56:5 KJV), evergreen carob trees honor the "Righteous Gentiles." Durable in Israel's climate, this tree is also a Christian symbol. Tradition holds that John the Baptist came from a spring-fed valley nearby; the bean pods produced by the carob tree are probably the "locusts" that sustained him in the wilderness (See Mark 1:6).

173. For a sampling of people who rescued Jews, see Martin Gilbert, *The Righteous: The Unsung Heroes of the Holocaust* (New York: Henry Holt, 2003) and Carol Rittner and Sondra Myers, eds., *The Courage to Care* (New York: New York University Press, 1986). For an important analysis of rescuers, see Samuel P. Oliner and Pearl M. Oliner, *The Altruistic Personality: Rescuers of Jews in Nazi Europe* (New York: Free Press, 1988).

174. See Philip P. Hallie, *Lest Innocent Blood Be Shed: The Story of the Village of Le Chambon and How Goodness Happened There* (New York: Harper Perennial, 1994) and *In the Eye of the Hurricane: Tales of Good and Evil, Help and Harm* (Middletown, Conn.: Wesleyan University Press, 2001).

175. Some aspects of this story have been described by Katharina von Kellenbach in an as yet unpublished paper, "The German Churches and the Nuremberg Trials." See also Ronald Webster, "Opposing 'Victors' Justice': German Protestant Churchmen and Convicted Criminals in Western Europe after 1945," *Holocaust and Genocide Studies* 15 (spring 2001): 47–69, and Phayer, *The Catholic Church and the Holocaust*, 162–75.

176. Mark Aarons and John Loftus, *Unholy Trinity: The Vatican, the Nazis, and Soviet Intelligence* (New York: St. Martin's Press, 1992), 29.

177. For details, see Zuccotti, *Under His Very Windows*, 161–63. See also Friedländer, *Pius XII and the Third Reich*, 205–6. Zuccotti points out that, while its origins are less than clear, the letter expressed papal discomfiture about the German roundups of Jews in Rome. Hudal did not initiate it.

178. Aarons and Loftus, *Unholy Trinity*, 36.

179. Ibid., 22–23.

180. See Alois C. Hudal, *Römische Tagebücher* (Graz: Leopold Stocker Verlag, 1976), 21.

181. Aarons and Loftus, *Unholy Trinity*, 28. For an account of Hudal's activities on behalf of Stangl, see Sereny, *Into That Darkness,* 289ff. See also Phayer, *The Catholic Church and the Holocaust*, 166.

182. Phayer, *The Catholic Church and the Holocaust*, 167.

183. Ibid., 168.

184. Ibid., 162–63. On von Galen, see Beth Griech-Polelle, "A Pure Conscience Is Good Enough: Bishop von Galen and Resistance to Nazism," in *In God's Name*, ed. Bartov and Mack, 106–22.

185. Phayer, *The Catholic Church and the Holocaust*, 163.

186. Ibid., 161.

187. On 16 March 1998, the Holy See's Commission for Religious Relations with the Jews released the Church's most important statement on the Holocaust, *We Remember: A Reflection on the Shoah*. Although the statement's positive evaluation of Pius XII's wartime role remains divisive, the new spirit that animates the Church's attitude towards Judaism is expressed in *We Remember*'s hope for the future: "We wish to turn awareness of past sins into a firm resolve to build a new future in which there will be no more anti-Judaism among Christians or anti-Christian sentiment among Jews, but rather a shared mutual respect, as befits those who adore the one Creator and Lord and have a common father in faith, Abraham." For further detail on related topics, see *Catholic Teaching on the Shoah: Implementing the Holy See's "We Remember,"* which was published by the Secretariat for Ecumenical and Interreligious Affairs, National Conference of Catholic Bishops, Washington, D.C., in 2001. Also helpful in this regard are Rittner and Roth, eds., *Pope Pius XII and the Holocaust*; Carol Rittner and John Roth, eds., *"Good News" after Auschwitz? Christian Faith within a Post-Holocaust World* (Macon, Ga.: Mercer University Press, 2001); Carol Rittner, Stephen D. Smith, and Irena Steinfeldt, eds., *The Holocaust and the Christian World: Reflections on*

*the Past, Challenges for the Future* (New York: Continuum, 2000); and Michael A. Signer, ed., *Humanity at the Limit: The Impact of the Holocaust Experience on Jews and Christians* (Bloomington: Indiana University Press, 2000). For Jewish responses to developments in post-Holocaust Christianity, see Tivka Frymer-Kensky, David Novak, Peter Ochs, David Sandmel, and Michael Signer, eds., *Christianity in Jewish Terms* (Boulder, Colo.: Westview Press, 2000).

188. Goldhagen, *A Moral Reckoning*, 246.
189. Ibid., 259.
190. Ibid., 3.
191. Ibid., 262, 266.

## Chapter 11

1. Levi, *Survival in Auschwitz*, 13. Two detailed biographies of Levi's life, which ended—probably in suicide—in 1987, are provided by Carole Angier, *The Double Bond: Primo Levi, a Biography* (New York: Farrar, Straus & Giroux, 2002) and Myrian Anissimov, *Primo Levi: Tragedy of an Optimist*, trans. Steve Cox (Woodstock, N.Y.: Overlook Press, 2000).

2. Levi, *Survival in Auschwitz*, 112.

3. Ibid., 112–13.

4. See Theodor W. Adorno, "Cultural Criticism and Society," in *Prisms*, trans. Samuel and Shierry Weber (London: Neville Spearman, 1967), 34. This essay was originally published in 1951. See also Theodor W. Adorno, *Notes to Literature*, 2 vols., ed. Rolf Tiedemann and trans. Sherry Weber Nicholsen (New York: Columbia University Press, 1992), 2:87.

5. See George Steiner, *Language and Silence: Essays on Language, Literature, and the Inhuman* (New York: Atheneum, 1976), 53–54.

6. For studies of Holocaust-related still photography, see Bryan F. Lewis, "Documentation or Decoration? Uses and Misuses of Photographs in the Historiography of the Holocaust," in *Remembering for the Future*, ed. Roth and Maxwell, 3:341–57; Helmut Walser Smith, ed., *The Holocaust and Other Genocides: History, Representation, Ethics* (Nashville: Vanderbilt University Press, 2002), 131–36; and Barbie Zelizer, *Remembering to Forget: Holocaust Memory through the Camera's Eye* (Chicago: University of Chicago Press, 1998). Still photographs are important partly because they provide important perspectives on pre-Holocaust Jewish life in Europe. For significant examples of such photography, see Mara Vishniac Kohn, ed., *Children of a Vanished World*, trans. Miriam Hartman Flacks (Berkeley: University of California Press, 1999); Roman Vishniac and Elie Wiesel, *A Vanished World* (New York: Noonday Press, 1986); and Ann Weiss, ed., *The Last Album: Eyes from the Ashes of Auschwitz-Birkenau* (New York: W. W. Norton, 2001).

7. On these points see Robert H. Abzug, *Inside the Vicious Heart: Americans and the Liberation of Nazi Concentration Camps* (New York: Oxford University Press, 1985) and *America Views the Holocaust*; Jeffrey Shandler, *While America Watches: Televising the Holocaust* (New York: Oxford University Press, 1999); Larry D. Wilcox, "Shadows of a Distant Nightmare: Visualizing the Unimaginable Holocaust in Early Documentary Films," in *Remembering for the Future*, ed. Roth and Maxwell, 3:478–500.

8. Judith E. Doneson, *The Holocaust in American Film*, 2d ed. (Syracuse: Syracuse University Press, 2002), 189, 193. In addition to Doneson's book, other important studies of Holocaust-related film include Ilan Avisar, *Screening the Holocaust: Cinema's Images of the Unimaginable* (Bloomington: Indiana University Press, 1988) and Annette Insdorf, *Indelible Shadows: Film and the Holocaust*, 2d ed. (Cambridge: Cambridge University Press, 1989).

9. Scholarly analysis of *Schindler's List* is considerable and growing. The following works are among the most insightful commentaries: Doneson, *The Holocaust in American Film*; Thomas Fensch, ed., *Oskar Schindler and His List: The Man, the Book, the Film, the Holocaust, and Its Survivors* (New York: Paul S. Eriksson, 1995); Yosefa Loshitzky, ed., *Spielberg's Holocaust: Critical Perspectives on Schindler's List* (Bloomington: Indiana University Press, 1997); Alan Mintz, *Popular Culture and the Shaping of Holocaust Memory in America* (Seattle: University of Washington Press, 2001), 125–58; Michael Rothberg, *Traumatic Realism: The Demands of Holocaust Representation* (Minneapolis: University of Minnesota Press, 2000); and Barbie Zelizer, ed., *Visual Culture and the Holocaust* (New Brunswick, N.J.: Rutgers University Press, 2001). Also important is Jon Blair's excellent documentary *Schindler* (1992). Blair is an outstanding cinematic interpreter of the Holocaust, whose *Anne Frank Remembered* (1995) is arguably the best film made about that iconic Holocaust victim. For the perspective of Schindler's wife, Emilie, see Emilie Schindler, *Where Light and Shadow Meet: A Memoir,* trans. Dolores M. Koch (New York: W. W. Norton, 1996).

10. See also Mark Jonathan Harris and Deborah Oppenheimer, *Into the Arms of Strangers: Stories of the Kindertransport* (New York: Bloomsbury, 2000).

11. Its Academy Award notwithstanding, Robert Benigni's *Life Is Beautiful* (1997) is a much less credible attempt to use the parent-child motif in a Holocaust "comedy" that distorts the realities of the Nazi camps and magnifies beyond credibility the feel-good theme that the "human spirit" managed to triumph even in the Holocaust.

12. For more detail on the connections between the Wagner family and Nazi Germany, including Adolf Hitler in particular, see Gottfried Wagner, *Twilight of the Wagners: The Unveiling of a Family's Legacy* (New York: St. Martin's Press, 1999). Richard Wagner is Gottfried Wagner's great-grandfather.

13. A growing literature plays variations on this theme. See, for example, Martin Goldsmith, *The Inextinguishable Symphony: A True Story of Music and Love in Nazi Germany* (New York: John Wiley & Sons, 2000); Szymon Laks, *Music of Another World* (Evanston, Ill.: Northwestern University Press, 2000); Anita Lasker-Wallfisch, *Inherit the Truth: A Memoir of Survival and the Holocaust* (New York: St. Martin's Press, 2000); and Richard Newman, *Alma Rosé: Vienna to Auschwitz* (New York: Amadeus, 2000). The works by Laks, Lasker-Wallfisch, and Newman show how the Germans exploited the musical talents of camp inmates and also how that same talent may have helped a few Jews to survive. For accounts that analyze how the Third Reich both encouraged and suppressed musical expression, see the trilogy by Michael Kater: *Composers of the Nazi Era: Eight Portraits* (New York: Oxford University Press, 2000), *Different Drummers: Jazz in the Culture of Nazi Germany* (New York: Oxford University Press, 1992), and *The Twisted Muse: Musicians and Their Music in the Third Reich* (New York: Oxford University Press, 1997). Another helpful study is provided by Alan E. Steinweis, *Art, Ideology, and Economics in Nazi Germany: The Reich Chambers of Music, Theater, and the Visual Arts* (Chapel Hill: University of North Carolina Press, 1996).

14. For a helpful survey of current developments in Holocaust-related art, see Dora Apel, *Memory Effects: The Holocaust and the Art of Secondary Witnessing* (New Brunswick, N.J.: Rutgers University Press, 2002).

15. See the museum's catalog, *Modern Contemporary: Art at MOMA since 1980.* The exhibit ran from September 2000 to January 2001. The artists who focused on Holocaust representation were Claude Lanzmann, *La fin du voyage,* 1985, film; Anselm Kiefer, *Departing from Egypt,* 1984, drawing; Christian Boltanski, *The Storehouse (La Grande Reserve),* 1988, sculpture; Art Spiegelman, *Maus: A Sur-*

*vivor's Tale*, 1980–85, illustrated book; Sigmar Polke, *Watchtower*, 1984, oil painting; and Shimon Attie, *Almstadtstrasse 43*, photograph.

16. The clip was taken from Lanzmann's epic film, *Shoah* (1985).

17. For an excellent discussion of *Sulamith*, Kiefer's more famous Holocaust-related work, see Liza Saltzman, "Lost in Translation: Clement Greenberg, Anselm Kiefer, and the Subject of History," in *Visual Culture and the Holocaust*, ed. Barbie Zelitzer (New Brunswick, N.J.: Rutgers University Press, 2001), 74–88. For further information on Kiefer, see Matthew Biro, *Anselm Kiefer and the Philosophy of Martin Heidegger* (New York: Cambridge University Press, 1998) and Lisa Saltzman, *Anselm Kiefer and Art after Auschwitz* (New York: Cambridge University Press, 1999). Sara Rich provides an insightful discussion of Kiefer in her review of the books by Biro and Saltzman. See *The Art Bulletin* 82 (Sept. 2000): 595–609.

18. See James Aulich and John Lynch, eds., *Critical Kitaj* (New Brunswick, N.J.: Rutgers University Press, 2001), especially Aulich's essay "Kitaj, History, and Tradition," 153–58.

19. See *Fourteen Stations* (Morristown, N.J.: Morris Museum, 2002).

20. Art Spiegelman, *Maus: A Survivor's Tale*, 2 vols. (New York: Pantheon Books, 1986, 1991). For a helpful analysis of *Maus*, see Rothberg, *Traumatic Realism*, esp. 1–2, 202–19. See also Dominick La Capra, *History and Memory after Auschwitz* (Ithaca, N.Y.: Cornell University Press, 1998), 139–79.

21. See Stephen C. Feinstein, ed., *Witness and Legacy: Contemporary Art about the Holocaust* (Minneapolis: Lerner Publication Co., 1995) and *Absence/Presence: The Artistic Memory of the Holocaust and Genocide* (Minneapolis: University of Minnesota Press, 1999). The former includes a significant essay by Matthew Baigel, "The Persistence of Holocaust Imagery in American Art."

22. For an excellent background article on Charlotte Salomon and her work, see the following internet site: *http://www.remember.org/educate/sal.html.*

23. See the exhibition catalog, Norman L. Kleeblatt, ed., *Mirroring Evil, Nazi Imagery/Recent Art* (New Brunswick, N.J.: Rutgers University Press, 2002), especially James Young's preface, "Looking into the Mirrors of Evil," xv–xviii.

24. See especially Saul Friedländer, *When Memory Comes*, trans. Helen R. Lane (New York: Farrar, Straus & Giroux, 1979) and Friedländer, ed., *Probing the Limits of Representation: Nazism and the Final Solution* (Cambridge, Mass.: Harvard University Press, 1992).

25. Caroline Alice Wiedmer, *The Claims of Memory: Representations of the Holocaust in Contemporary Germany and France* (Ithaca, N.Y.: Cornell University Press), 138 and note 121.

26. For a description of this museum, see Victoria Newhouse, *Towards a New Museum* (New York: Monacelli Press, 1998), esp. 11, 96–98. Newhouse discusses Libeskind and other architects who are working to restore the historic connection between container and context in uniquely contemporary ways.

27. See, for example, Janet Blatter and Sybil Milton, *Art of the Holocaust* (New York: Rutledge Press, 1981). This book is a monumental collection of more than 350 reproductions of drawings and paintings, which are organized into art from the ghettos, the transit camps, and the concentration camps. With a preface by Irving Howe and an historical introduction by Henry Friedlander, this work is among the best introductions to its topic. For a perspective that focuses significantly on the ghetto and transit camp at Theresienstadt (Terezín), see Anne D. Dutlinger, ed., *Art, Music, and Education as Strategies for Survival: Theresienstadt 1941–45* (New York: Herodias, 2001).

28. On this point, see Ella Liebermann-Shiber, *On the Edge of the Abyss*, 2d ed. (New York: Sanford C. Bernstein, 1994). See also Nelly Toll, *Without Surrender: Art of the Holocaust* (Philadelphia: Running Press, 1978).

29. For more detail, see Serge Klarsfeld, *David Olère: L'Oeil du Témoin/The Eyes of a Witness* (New York: Beate Klarsfeld Foundation, 1989).

30. Mary S. Costanza, *The Living Witness: Art in the Concentration Camps and Ghettos* (New York: Free Press, 1982).

31. Ibid., 26.

32. Ibid., 24–25.

33. Leo Haas, "The Affair of the Painters of Terezín," in *Art from the Ashes: A Holocaust Anthology*, ed. Lawrence L. Langer (New Haven, Conn.: Yale University Press, 1995), 670–75.

34. See Blatter and Milton, *Art of the Holocaust*, plate 94.

35. Costanza, *The Living Witness*, 33.

36. Henry Koerner, *Unfinished Sentence* (unpublished manuscript, 1956). See also Feinstein, ed., *Absence/Presence*, whose cover reproduces Koerner's famous painting *My Parents II*, 1946.

37. For further detail on Bak's life and work, see the following: Samuel Bak, *Painted in Words: A Memoir* (Bloomington: Indiana University Press, 2002); Samuel Bak, Lawrence L. Langer, et al., *Between Worlds: The Paintings and Drawings of Samuel Bak, 1946–2001* (Boston: Pucker Gallery, 2002); Samuel Bak and Lawrence L. Langer, *Landscapes of Jewish Experience: Paintings* (Waltham, Mass.: Brandeis University Press, 1997); Lawrence L. Langer, *In a Different Light: The Book of Genesis in the Art of Samuel Bak* (Boston: Pucker Art Publications, 2001); and Lawrence L. Langer, *Preempting the Holocaust* (New Haven, Conn.: Yale University Press, 1998), 80–120.

38. See Herschel B. Chipp, *Theories of Modern Art* (Berkeley: University of California Press, 1968), 553.

39. For a full description of the Segal sculpture, see James E. Young, *The Texture of Memory: Holocaust Memorials and Meaning* (New Haven, Conn.: Yale University Press, 1993), 309–19.

40. For detail on the Washington museum's architecture and design, see Adrian Dannatt, *United States Holocaust Memorial Museum: James Ingo Freed* (London: Phaidon Press, 1995) and Jeshajahu Weinberg and Rina Elieli, *The Holocaust Museum in Washington* (New York: Rizzoli, 1995).

41. See the *New York Times*, 23 April 1993.

42. This information was retrieved from *http://www.artic.edu/aic/collections/dept_architecture/freed.html.*

43. George F. Will, "Telling Their Truth," *Washington Post*, 22 April 1993, A23.

44. See Yaffa Eliach, *There Once Was a World: A Nine-Hundred-Year Chronicle of the Shtetl of Eishyshok* (Boston: Little, Brown, 1999).

45. For an analysis of the Berlin museum, see James E. Young, *At Memory's Edge: After-Images of the Holocaust in Contemporary Art and Architecture* (New Haven, Conn.: Yale University Press, 2000), 152–83.

46. See *Architectural Record* 188 (January 1999): 76–91.

47. Quoted in the preface to *Daniel Libeskind: Jewish Museum in Berlin*, text by Bernard Schneider, photography by Stefan Müller (Munich: Prestel Verlag, 1999).

48. On this point, see Amos Elon, "A German Requiem," *New York Review of Books*, 15 November 2001, 40–44, and Julia M. Klein, "The Jewish Museum," *Chronicle of Higher Education*, 9 November 2001, B15–17.

49. Victoria Newhouse, "Designs That Reach Out and Grab," *New York Times*, 4 June 2000.

50. Apel, *Memory Effects*, 20.

51. Ibid., 43–56.

52. Ibid., 48.

53. Ibid., 56.
54. Ibid., 169–77.
55. See ibid., 173.
56. For additional and valuable information about art and the Holocaust, see the following internet site: *http://www.chgs.umn.edu/visual_artistic_resources.html.*
57. Chaim A. Kaplan, *Scroll of Agony: The Warsaw Diary of Chaim A. Kaplan,* rev. ed., ed. and trans. Abraham I. Katsh (New York: Collier Books, 1973), 400.
58. For more information on this topic, see Michal Grynberg, ed., *Words to Outlive Us: Eyewitness Accounts from the Warsaw Ghetto,* trans. Philip Boehm (New York: Metropolitan Books, 2002); David Patterson, *Along the Edge of Annihilation: The Collapse and Recovery of Life in the Holocaust Diary* (Seattle: University of Washington Press, 1999); and Alexandra Zapruder, ed., *Salvaged Pages: Young Writers' Diaries of the Holocaust* (New Haven, Conn.: Yale University Press, 2002).
59. Stories that emerged from the Holocaust, orally passed from one person to another and from one community to another, form a significant category in their own right. Yaffa Eliach has collected and traced to their origins almost ninety examples. See her *Hasidic Tales of the Holocaust: The First Original Hasidic Tales in a Century* (New York: Oxford University Press, 1982).
60. Especially when Holocaust literature focuses on memoirs, fiction, and poetry, the foremost interpreter is arguably Lawrence L. Langer. His numerous works on this topic include *Admitting the Holocaust, The Age of Atrocity: Death in Modern Literature* (Boston: Beacon Press, 1978), *The Holocaust and the Literary Imagination* (New Haven, Conn.: Yale University Press, 1975), *Preempting the Holocaust,* and *Versions of Survival* (Albany: State University of New York Press, 1982). See also Langer's useful edition, *Art from the Ashes.* For other noteworthy studies of Holocaust literature, see Alan L. Berger, *Crisis and Covenant: The Holocaust in American Jewish Fiction* (Albany: State University of New York Press, 1985); Sidra Dekoven Ezrahi, *By Words Alone: The Holocaust in Literature* (Chicago: University of Chicago Press, 1980); Sara R. Horowitz, *Voicing the Void: Muteness and Memory in Holocaust Fiction* (Albany: State University of New York Press, 1997); David Patterson, *The Shriek of Silence: A Phenomenology of the Holocaust Novel* (Lexington: University Press of Kentucky, 1992); Alvin H. Rosenfeld, *A Double Dying: Reflections on Holocaust Literature* (Bloomington: Indiana University Press, 1988); Robert Skloot, *The Darkness We Carry: The Drama of the Holocaust* (Madison: University of Wisconsin Press, 1988); and Sue Vice, *Holocaust Fiction: From William Styron to Binjamin Wilkomirski* (New York: Routledge, 2000). Helpful encyclopedias about Holocaust literature include Lillian Kremer, ed., *Holocaust Literature: An Encyclopedia of Writers and Their Works* (New York: Routledge, 2002); David Patterson, Alan L. Berger, and Sarita Cargas, eds., *Encyclopedia of Holocaust Literature* (Westport, Conn.: Oryx Press, 2002); and Thomas Riggs, ed., *Reference Guide to Holocaust Literature* (Farmington Hills, Mich.: St. James Press, 2002).
61. Virtually all the works referenced in this chapter wrestle with problems pertaining to representation of the Holocaust. For additional resources on this topic, see Inga Clendinnen, *Reading the Holocaust* (Cambridge: Cambridge University Press, 1999); Geoffrey H. Hartman, *The Longest Shadow: In the Aftermath of the Holocaust* (New York: Palgrave, 2002); Dominick LaCapra, *Writing History, Writing Trauma* (Baltimore: Johns Hopkins University Press, 2001); Berel Lang, *Holocaust Representation: Art within the Limits of History and Ethics* (Baltimore: Johns Hopkins University Press, 2000); Alvin H. Rosenfeld, ed., *Thinking about the Holocaust: After Half a Century* (Bloomington: Indiana University Press, 1997); and James E. Young, *Writing and Rewriting the Holocaust* (Bloomington: Indiana University Press, 1988).

62. David Rousett, *The Other Kingdom*, trans. Roman Gutherie (New York: Reynal & Hitchcock, 1947), 168.
63. Klemperer, *I Will Bear Witness: A Diary of the Nazi Years.*
64. Klemperer's study of Nazi language has been translated into English as *The Language of the Third Reich: LTI—Lingua Tertii Imperii: A Philologist's Notebook*, trans. Martin Brady (New York: Continuum, 2002).
65. Klemperer, *I Will Bear Witness*, 2:28.
66. Ibid, 2:147.
67. Ibid., 2:148.
68. Ibid., 2:181.
69. Ibid., 2:205.
70. Ibid., 2:205.
71. Ibid., 2:238.
72. Ibid., 2:61.
73. Ibid., 2:323.
74. Ibid., 2:332.
75. Ibid., 2:351.
76. Ibid., 2:386.
77. Our discussion of Delbo draws on material prepared by John Roth for Roth et al., *The Holocaust Chronicle.*
78. Charlotte Delbo, *Auschwitz and After*, trans. Rosette C. Lamont (New Haven, Conn.: Yale University Press, 1995), 167.
79. Charlotte Delbo, *Days and Memory*, trans. Rosette C. Lamont (Marlboro, Vt.: Marlboro Press, 1990), 2.
80. Ibid., 1.
81. Delbo, *Auschwitz and After*, 4–5. Our interpretation of Delbo is indebted to Langer, *The Age of Atrocity*, 201–44.
82. Delbo, *Auschwitz and After*, 28–29.
83. Ibid., 11.
84. Ibid., 28.
85. Ibid., 33, 64–65, 67, 225.
86. Ibid., 145, 151.
87. Ibid., 226, 230.
88. Ibid., 239, 258.
89. Ibid., 264.
90. Ibid., 279.
91. Ibid., 335.
92. Ibid., 345.
93. Ibid., 338.
94. Ibid., 348.
95. Ibid., 352.
96. See Primo Levi, *The Drowned and the Saved*, trans. Raymond Rosenthal (New York: Summit Books, 1986), 36–70.
97. Tadeusz Borowski, *This Way for the Gas, Ladies and Gentlemen*, trans. Barbara Vedder (New York: Penguin Books, 1967), 175.
98. Ibid., 176, 122.
99. Ibid., 29–31.
100. Ibid., 38, 46, 49.
101. Ibid., 58, 83, 84.
102. Ibid., 110, 90, 89.
103. Ibid., 110, 98, 100.
104. Ibid., 112–13, 115–16.
105. Ibid., 122, 131, 142.

106. Ibid., 163, 168, 166–67.
107. Ibid., 177, 179.
108. Ibid., 180.
109. Ibid., 115–16.
110. Elie Wiesel, *Night*, trans. Stella Rodway (New York: Bantam Books, 1982), 28. In his review of *Shoah*, Lanzmann's film (see *New York Times*, 3 November 1985), Wiesel notes that it took him a long time to understand the anger of the prisoners who met his transport at Auschwitz. Later he learned that this squad was the one to which Rudolf Vrba belonged. With Alfred Wetzler, he had escaped Auschwitz weeks earlier to warn the Hungarian Jews and to tell the world about Auschwitz. Apparently the effort had been in vain—hence the anger.
111. Ibid., 32, 1, 109.
112. For more detail on Wiesel's authorship, see *Against Silence*, ed. Irving Abrahamson; Michael Berenbaum, *God, the Holocaust, and the Children of Israel* (West Orange, N.J.: Behrman House, 1994); Robert McAfee Brown, *Elie Wiesel: Messenger to All Humanity*, rev. ed. (Notre Dame, Ind.: University of Notre Dame Press, 1989); Harry James Cargas, *Harry James Cargas in Conversation with Elie Wiesel* (New York: Paulist Press, 1976); Jack Kolbert, *The Worlds of Elie Wiesel: An Overview of His Career and Major Themes* (Selinsgrove, Penn.: Susquehanna University Press, 2001); Carol Rittner, ed., *Elie Wiesel: Between Memory and Hope* (New York: New York University Press, 1990); John K. Roth, *A Consuming Fire: Encounters with Elie Wiesel and the Holocaust* (Atlanta: John Knox Press, 1979); and Elie Wiesel and Richard D. Heffner, *Conversation with Elie Wiesel*, ed. Thomas J. Vinciguerra (New York: Schocken Books, 2001). For a specific emphasis on *Night*, see Harold Bloom, ed., *Elie Wiesel's Night* (Philadelphia: Chelsea House, 2001). For an extremely critical, and controversial, view about *Night*, see Naomi Seidman, "Elie Wiesel and the Scandal Rage," *Jewish Social Studies: History, Culture, and Society* 3 (fall 1996): 1–19.
113. Elie Wiesel, "Why I Write," trans. Rosette C. Lamont, in *Confronting the Holocaust: The Impact of Elie Wiesel*, ed. Alvin H. Rosenfeld and Irving Greenberg (Bloomington: Indiana University Press, 1978), 201.
114. Ibid., 201–2. See also Elie Wiesel, *The Oath*, trans. Marion Wiesel (New York: Random House, 1973), 154.
115. Elie Wiesel, *Legends of Our Time*, trans. Stephen Donadio (New York: Avon Books, 1970), 230.
116. Elie Wiesel, *A Jew Today*, trans. Marion Wiesel (New York: Random House, 1978), 164.
117. Ibid., 140–41.
118. Ibid., 143.
119. Wiesel, *Legends of Our Time*, viii.
120. Wiesel, *A Jew Today*, 144–45.
121. Ibid., 146–47.
122. Elie Wiesel, *The Trial of God*, trans. Marion Wiesel (New York: Random House, 1979), 129.
123. Ibid., 133.
124. Robert McAfee Brown notes this tale in "Wiesel's Case Against God," *Christian Century*, 30 January 1980, 109–12.
125. Wiesel, *A Jew Today*, 136.
126. Ibid., 149, 152.
127. Elie Wiesel, *Messengers of God*, trans. Marion Wiesel (New York: Random House, 1976), 35–36.
128. Elie Wiesel, *The Testament*, trans. Marion Wiesel (New York: Summit Books, 1981), 9.

## Chapter 12

1. On the elements of continuity and singularity between the Holocaust and other genocides, see Rubenstein, *The Age of Triage*. See also Chalk and Jonassohn, *The History and Sociology of Genocide*; Rittner, Roth, and Smith, eds., *Will Genocide Ever End?*; Rosenbaum, ed., *Is the Holocaust Unique?*; and Isidor Wallimann and Michael Dobkowski, eds., *Genocide and the Modern Age: Etiology and Studies of Mass Death* (Westport, Conn.: Greenwood Press, 1987). On Rwanda, see Linda R. Melvern, *A People Betrayed: The Role of the West in Rwanda's Genocide* (London: Zed Books, 2000) and Power, *"A Problem from Hell."*

2. Helpful overviews of post-Holocaust religious reflection include Cohn-Sherbok, ed., *Holocaust Theology*; Michael L. Morgan, *A Holocaust Reader: Responses to the Nazi Extermination* (New York: Oxford University Press, 2000); Roth and Berenbaum, eds., *Holocaust*; and David G. Roskies, *Against the Apocalypse: Responses to Catastrophe in Modern Jewish Culture* (Syracuse, N.Y.: Syracuse University Press, 1999).

3. Isaiah 45:7 is thought to be such a rejection: "I form light and create darkness; I make weal and create woe; I the LORD do all these things."

4. G. W. F. Hegel, "Introduction: Reason in History," in *Lectures on the Philosophy of World History*, ed. Johannes Hoffmeister, trans. H. B. Nisbet (Cambridge: Cambridge University Press, 1975), 43 (italics added). For further Holocaust-related discussion of Hegel and other philosophers who have dealt with radical evil— Immanuel Kant, Friedrich Nietzsche, Hannah Arendt, and Emmanuel Levinas among them—see Richard J. Bernstein, *Radical Evil: A Philosophical Interrogation* (Cambridge: Polity Press, 2002) and Susan Neiman, *Evil in Modern Thought: An Alternative History of Philosophy* (Princeton: Princeton University Press, 2002).

5. Theodore W. Adorno, *Negative Dialectics*, trans. E. B. Ashton (New York: Seabury Press, 1973), 361–62.

6. For further discussion on this theme, see Roth, *Holocaust Politics,* 27–32. See also Stephen T. Davis, ed., *Encountering Evil: Live Options in Theodicy*, 2d ed. (Louisville, Ky.: Westminster John Knox Press, 2001) and Glover, *Humanity.*

7. James H. Markham, "Over Philosophy's Temple, Shadow of a Swastika," *New York Times*, 4 February 1988.

8. Heidegger's letter to Marcuse, dated 28 January 1948, is found in the Marcuse archives in Frankfurt. See Thomas Sheehan, "Heidegger and the Nazis," *New York Review of Books*, 16 June 1988, 42.

9. See Laqueur, *The Terrible Secret*, 1–40, 196–208.

10. See Rubenstein, *The Age of Triage*, 132.

11. Irving Greenberg, "Cloud of Smoke, Pillar of Fire: Judaism, Christianity, and Modernity after the Holocaust," in *Auschwitz: Beginning of a New Era?* ed. Fleischner, 9–13.

12. Elchonon Wassermann, *Ma'amar Ikvossoh Demeshicho Vema'ma'amar al Ha'Emunah* (Treatise on the footsteps of the Messiah and on faith) (New York: 1939, in Yiddish), cited in Gershon Greenberg, "Orthodox Theological Responses to Kristallnacht: Chayyim Ozer Grodzensky ('Achiezer') and Elchonon Wassermann," *Holocaust and Genocide Studies* 3 (1988): 431–41. We are indebted to Greenberg for his authoritative and continuing help over the years on the subject of Orthodox responses to the Holocaust. See also Bauer, *Rethinking the Holocaust,* 186–212, and Greenberg, "Orthodox Religious Thought," in *The Holocaust Encyclopedia*, ed. Laqueur, 457–65.

13. Quoted in Greenberg, "Orthodox Theological Responses to Kristallnacht," 439.

14. Joseph Isaac Schneersohn, "Redemption Now," *Netzach Yisroel* III (1948): 6–7 [Hebrew], cited in Gershon Greenberg, "Reflections upon the Holocaust within American Orthodoxy, 1945–48," unpublished paper, 1988.

15. Joseph H. Hertz, ed., *The Authorized Daily Prayer Book* (Bloch Publishing Co., 1948), 820–21. See also Richard L. Rubenstein, *The Religious Imagination* (Indianapolis: Bobbs-Merrill, 1968), 127–30.

16. Marc B. Shapiro, *Between the Yeshiva World and Modern Orthodoxy: The Life and Works of Rabbi Jehiel Jacob Weinberg 1884–1966* (London: Littman Library of Jewish Civilization, 1999), 177–78.

17. See, for example, Rittner, Smith, and Steinfeldt, eds., *The Holocaust and the Christian World* and Rittner and Roth, eds., *"Good News" after Auschwitz?*

18. See Paul van Buren, *A Theology of the Jewish Christian Reality*, 3 vols. (New York: Seabury Press, 1980–88).

19. Van Buren, *Discerning the Way*, vol. 1 of *A Theology of the Jewish Christian Reality*, 116.

20. Ibid., 117.

21. Van Buren, *A Christian Theology of the Jewish People*, vol. 2 of *A Theology of the Jewish Christian Reality*, 62–63.

22. Van Buren, *Discerning the Way*, 119.

23. Ibid., 153.

24. Ibid., 151, 181.

25. Ibid., 115.

26. Ibid., 99.

27. A second, extensively revised edition of *After Auschwitz* appeared in 1992. See Rubenstein, *After Auschwitz: History, Theology, and Contemporary Judaism*. In revising this chapter, the authors had to omit material that remains pertinent for the issues under consideration. Interested readers can consult the first edition of *Approaches to Auschwitz* (Atlanta: John Knox Press, 1987), 290–336.

28. Ignaz Maybaum, *The Face of God after Auschwitz* (Amsterdam: Polak & Van Gennep, 1965), 36.

29. Ibid., 63. For this citation, we are indebted to Steven T. Katz, *Post-Holocaust Dialogues: Critical Studies in Modern Jewish Thought* (New York: New York University Press, 1983), 162.

30. See Rubenstein, *After Auschwitz*, 201–10.

31. Ibid., 162–67.

32. On the "Grüber office," see Barnett, *For the Soul of the People*, 144–46.

33. Cited in Rubenstein, *After Auschwitz*, 1st ed., 54–55.

34. "Ein Wort zur Judenfrage, der Reichsbruderrat der Evangelischen Kirche in Deutschland," 8 April 1948, in *Der Ungekündigte Bund*, ed. Goldschmidt and Kraus, 251–54.

35. Richard L. Rubenstein, *Power Struggle: An Autobiographical Confession* (New York: Charles Scribners' Sons, 1974), 66.

36. Rubenstein's statement in the *Commentary* symposium also appears in *After Auschwitz*, 1st ed., 144–53. The passage quoted here appears on 153.

37. See Zachary Braiterman, *(God) after Auschwitz: Tradition and Change in Post-Holocaust Jewish Thought* (Princeton: Princeton University Press, 1998), 62–84, 87.

38. Kaplan (1881–1983) was the founder of the Reconstructionist movement in Judaism. Rubenstein affiliated with the movement in the very early years of his rabbinate. Like Soloveitchik, Kaplan's roots were in Lithuania, from which his family immigrated to the United States when he was nine years old. Kaplan believed in human progress and held an optimistic view of the course of human history. Rejecting belief in an all-powerful Creator God of history, he held that God is the "power that makes for salvation in the world," a view he asserted before the Holocaust and continued to maintain thereafter.

39. Rubenstein has a brief discussion of Heschel's influence on him in *Power Struggle*, 62–63, 87–88, and 128–129.

40. Martin Buber, *Eclipse of God: Studies in the Relation between Philosophy and Religion* (New York: Harper & Row, 1952).

41. Buber's failure to deal with the theological implications of the Holocaust in *Eclipse of God* is discussed in Rubenstein, "Buber and the Holocaust: Some Considerations on the 100th Anniversary of His Birth," *Michigan Quarterly Review* 18 (summer 1979).

42. Braiterman, *(God) after Auschwitz*, 67; Martin Buber, "The Dialogue between Heaven and Earth," in his *At the Turning: Three Addresses on Judaism* (New York: Farrar, Strauss & Young, 1952), 61–62.

43. "Though His coming appearance resembles no earlier one, we shall recognize again our cruel and merciful Lord" (Buber, *At the Turning*, 62).

44. Abraham Joshua Heschel, *A Passion for Truth* (New York: Farrar, Straus & Giroux, 1973).

45. Abraham Joshua Heschel, *Israel: An Echo in Eternity* (New York: Farrar, Straus & Giroux, 1967), 113. We are indebted to Zachary Braiterman, *(God) after Auschwitz*, 70, for this citation.

46. Edward Kaplan, "Mysticism and Despair in Abraham J. Heschel's Religious Thought," *Journal of Religion* 57 (Jan. 1977): 33–47.

47. Joseph Soloveitchik, "Kol Dodi Dofek," (The voice of my beloved knocks) in *Theological and Halakhic Reflections on the Holocaust,* ed. Bernhard Rosenberg and Fred Heuman (Hoboken, N.J.: KTAV, 1992), 60.

48. Soloveitchik had studied and was clearly influenced by the works of the Danish Christian thinker, Søren Kierkegaard (1813–55), especially *Fear and Trembling,* trans. Alastair Hannay (New York: Viking Penguin, 1985), which contains a singularly influential meditation on the Akedah.

49. See Michael L. Morgan, *Beyond Auschwitz: Post-Holocaust Jewish Thought in America* (New York: Oxford University Press, 2001), 106–8, and Braiterman, *(God) after Auschwitz*, 94–95.

50. Rubenstein, *After Auschwitz*, 1st ed., 151–52.

51. Rubenstein was invited to participate in a *Playboy* interview and write about the "death of God" for that magazine at a time when the magazine was widely read by college students: "Religion and the New Morality: A Symposium," *Playboy*, June 1967 and "Judaism and the Death of God," *Playboy*, July 1967. His theology was also reported on extensively in the *New York Times* and in a *Time* profile. For further information on related topics, see Stephen R. Haynes and John K. Roth, eds., *The Death of God Movement and the Holocaust: Radical Theology Encounters the Shoah* (Westport, Conn.: Greenwood Press, 1999).

52. For an elaboration on the theme of the rabbi as symbolic exemplar, see Jack H. Bloom, *The Rabbi as Symbolic Exemplar* (Binghamton, N.Y.: Haworth Press, 2002), 137–153, esp. 142.

53. Ibid., 145.

54. On the Armenian genocide as cultural and psychic inheritance, see Michael Arlen, *Passage to Ararat* (New York: Farrar, Strauss & Giroux, 1975).

55. For Jewish attempts to downgrade the significance of the Holocaust, see Stephen Kepnes, Peter Ochs, and Robert Gibbs, *Reasoning after Revelation: Dialogues in Postmodern Jewish Philosophy* (Boulder, Colo: Westview Press, 1998), 40–42, 70–71, 84–86. For an account that minimizes the significance of both the Holocaust and the state of Israel, see Marc H. Ellis, *Ending Auschwitz: The Future of Jewish and Christian Life* (Louisville, Ky.: Westminster John Knox Press, 1994).

56. The prayers are "Sound the great horn for our freedom; raise the ensign to gather our exiles, and gather us from the four corners of the earth. Blessed art thou, O Lord, who gatherest the dispersed of thy people . . ." and "And unto Jerusalem, thy city, return in mercy, and dwell therein as thou hast spoken; rebuild it soon

in our days as an everlasting building, and speedily set up therein the throne of David. Blessed art thou, O Lord, who rebuildest Jerusalem" (Hertz, *Prayer Book,* 143).

57. The idea of "an end to history" has roots in both classical theology and Hegelian philosophy. The American political philosopher Francis Fukuyama made a somewhat similar point about the collapse of communism and the triumph of liberal democracy as the "end of history." Fukuyama did not foresee an end to conflict between groups, but he argued that liberal democracy constituted the "end point of mankind's ideological evolution" and the "final form of human government," and, as such, constituted the "end of history." He argued that "if we looked beyond liberal democracy and markets, there was nothing else towards which we could hope to evolve; hence the end of history" (Francis Fukuyama, "The West Has Won," *Guardian* [London], 11 October 2001). Fukuyama's ideas were first set forth in "The End of History?" *National Interest,* summer 1989. He expanded on his ideas in *The End of History and the Last Man* (New York: Free Press, 1992).

58. For a frank discussion by the leaders of Hamas of their long-range objectives, see Joel Brinkley, "Bombers Gloating in Gaza as They See Goal Within Reach: No More Israel," *New York Times,* 4 April 2002.

59. For example, Fatma Abdallaj Mahmoud, a regular columnist in *Al-Akhbar,* the official Egyptian state newspaper, has said, "With regard to the Holocaust . . . this is no more than a fabrication, a lie, and a fraud! . . . I, personally . . . complain to Hitler, 'If only you had done it, brother, if only it had really happened, so that the world could sigh in relief [without] their evil and sin'" (Fatma Abdallaj Mahmoud, "Accursed Forever and Ever," *Al-Akhbar,* [Cairo], 29 April 2002).

60. See Bernard Lewis, *What Went Wrong? Western Impact and Middle Eastern Response* (New York: Oxford University Press), 154–55.

61. The Egyptian weekly *Roz Al-Youssuf* reported on 17 November 2001 that the *Protocols* had been dramatized in a thirty-part series entitled "Horseman without a Horse" for broadcast by Arab Radio and Television (ART) to the Middle East, North America, Latin America, Australia, and Africa.

62. On 14 December 2001 Ali Akhbar Hashemi Rafsanjani, former president of the Islamic Republic of Iran, gave the *al-Quds* (Jerusalem) Day sermon at Tehran University. In the sermon he declared that use of a nuclear bomb against Israel will leave nothing on the ground, whereas it will only damage the world of Islam (*Iran News* [English], Teheran, 15 December 2001).

63. Thomas Hobbes, *Leviathan* (Indianapolis: Bobbs-Merrill, 1958), 16 (part 1, chap. 13).

64. Fred M. Donner, "The Sources of Islamic Conceptions of War," in John Kelsay and James Turner Johnson, *Just War and Jihad: Historical and Theoretical Perspectives on War and Peace in Western and Islamic Traditions,* (Westport, Conn.: Greenwood Press, 2001), 51.

65. Later, Islamic legal scholars added a third category, *dar al-sulh,* the "abode of treaty," that comprised those non-Muslim states with which it was deemed permissible temporarily to enter into treaties to avoid potentially harmful conflicts (Kelsay and Johnson, *Just War and Jihad,* 98–99).

66. Hobbes, *Leviathan,* 107 (part 1, chap. 13).

67. Braiterman, *(God) after Auschwitz,* 99–100.

68. See Fackenheim, *God's Presence in History,* 8–14, and Emil L. Fackenheim, *To Mend the World: Foundations of Future Jewish Thought* (New York: Schocken Books, 1982), 9–22.

69. In traditional Judaism, the number of commandments given by God to Israel is said to be 613. The passage originally appeared in *Judaism* 16 (summer 1967): 272–73. The text of Fackenheim's contribution to that journal's symposium on

"Jewish Values in the Post-Holocaust Future" is reprinted in Fackenheim, *The Jewish Return into History: Reflections in the Age of Auschwitz and a New Jerusalem* (New York: Schocken Books, 1978), 19–24. See also Fackenheim, *God's Presence in History*, 84–98. In the 1997 edition of the latter work, Fackenheim includes a new preface, "No Posthumous Victories for Hitler: After Thirty Years, the '614th Commandment' Reconsidered." Noting that the phrase "'no posthumous victories for Hitler' became a slogan, often poorly understood, and as such liked by some, disliked by others, mocked by a few," Fackenheim adds that "what 'no posthumous victories for Hitler' asked of Jews was, of course, not to spite Hitler, but to carry on *in spite of* him" (xii, Fackenheim's italics).

70. One of the most noteworthy competitors for that distinction would be Irving Greenberg's "working principle," namely, that "no statement, theological or otherwise, should be made that would not be credible in the presence of the burning children." See Greenberg, "Cloud of Smoke, Pillar of Fire: Judaism, Christianity, and Modernity after the Holocaust," 23.

71. Fackenheim, *The Jewish Return into History*, 31 (italics added).

72. Fackenheim, *To Mend the World*, 10.

73. Ibid., 13.

74. Fackenheim, *The Jewish Return into History*, 97.

75. Ibid., xiii. Italics added.

76. Braiterman, *(God) after Auschwitz*, 152.

77. Fackenheim, *Encounters between Judaism and Modern Philosophy* (New York: Basic Books, 1973), 167–68.

78. Samuel P. Huntington, *The Clash of Civilizations and the Remaking of World Order* (New York: Simon & Schuster, 1996).

79. Fackenheim, *The Jewish Return into History*, 197–98.

80. Ibid., 282. The quotation comes from a chapter in the *Encyclopedia Judaica Yearbook 1974* (Jerusalem: Keter, 1974) entitled "The Holocaust and the State of Israel: Their Relation," which Fackenheim published originally in 1974. Significantly, in the 1997 edition of *God's Presence in History*, Fackenheim chose to reprint this same chapter, along with his new preface. Commenting on his decision to reprint the chapter about the Holocaust and Israel, and referencing Saddam Hussein and Hamas explicitly, Fackenheim wrote the following, which remains as insightful as it was in 1997: "Currently, just one thing is certain: Only with true peace in Israel will the Jewish people be at peace. Only then will they be, at long last, rid of Hitler's shadow" (xvi).

81. For the views of Paul of Tarsus on Israel's "unbelief" and her ultimate conversion, see Romans 9–11.

## Epilogue

1. Shmuel Krakowski, "Forced Labor," in *Encyclopedia of the Holocaust*, ed. Laqueur, 210. See also Allen, *The Business of Genocide;* Joseph Borkin, *The Crime and Punishment of I. G. Farben* (New York: Free Press, 1978); and Benjamin B. Ferencz, *Less Than Slaves: Jewish Forced Labor and the Quest for Compensation* (Cambridge: Harvard University Press, 1979).

2. See, for example, two essays by Peter Hayes: "State Policy and Corporate Involvement in the Holocaust," in *The Holocaust and History: The Known, the Unknown, the Disputed, and the Reexamined,* ed. Michael Berenbaum and Abraham J. Peck (Bloomington: Indiana University Press, 1998), 197–218; and "The Degussa AG and the Holocaust," in *Lessons and Legacies V: The Holocaust and Justice,* ed. Ronald Smelser (Evanston, Ill.: Northwestern University Press, 2002), 140–77.

3. This SS document is cited in Jacob Robinson, *And the Crooked Shall Be Made Straight: The Eichmann Trial, the Jewish Catastrophe, and Hannah Arendt's Narrative* (New York: Macmillan, 1965), 285. Another telling example of efficiency calculations in the German destruction process is cited in Lanzmann, *Shoah*, 103–4. He quotes from a document dated 5 June 1942 and sent from the killing center at Chelmno to Berlin. The memorandum urges that trucks ordered from the Saurer Company and slated for delivery to Chelmno must meet the technical requirements "shown by use and experience to be necessary." The vans were slated for use as mobile gas chambers using carbon monoxide.

4. Victoria J. Barnett, *Bystanders: Conscience and Complicity during the Holocaust* (Westport, Conn.: Praeger, 2000), 149.

5. See, for example, Guy B. Adams and Danny L. Balfour, *Unmasking Administrative Evil* (Thousand Oaks, Calif.: Sage Publications, 1988); Götz Aly and Susanne Heim, *Architects of Annihilation: Auschwitz and the Logic of Destruction,* trans. A. G. Blunden (Princeton: Princeton University Press, 2003); Rainer C. Baum, *The Holocaust and the German Elite: Genocide and National Suicide in Germany 1975–1945* (Totowa, N.J.: Rowman & Littlefield, 1981); Bauman, *Modernity and the Holocaust*; Harold James, *The Deutsche Bank and the Nazi Economic War Against the Jews: The Expropriation of Jewish Owned Property* (Cambridge: Cambridge University Press, 2001); and Henry Ashby Turner Jr., *German Big Business and the Rise of Hitler* (New York: Oxford University Press, 1985).

6. For more on Mengele, see Gerald Astor, *The Last Nazi: The Life and Times of Dr. Joseph Mengele* (New York: Donald I. Fine, 1985); and Gerald L. Posner and John Ware, *Mengele: The Complete Story* (New York: McGraw-Hill, 1986). Further insights about the role of the German medical profession during the Hitler era can be found in Alexander Mitscherlich and Fred Mielke, *Doctors of Infamy: The Story of the Nazi Medical Crimes,* trans. Heinz Norden (New York: Henry Schuman, 1949); Richard Grunberger, *The 12-Year Reich: A Social History of Nazi Germany 1933–1945* (New York: Holt, Rinehart, & Winston, 1971); Hilberg, *The Destruction of the European Jews*, 3:936–47 and 3:1002–13; Helen Kubica, "The Crimes of Josef Mengele," in *Anatomy of the Auschwitz Death Camp,* ed. Gutman and Berenbaum, 317–37; Lifton, *The Nazi Doctors*; Robert Jay Lifton and Amy Hackett, "Nazi Doctors," in *Anatomy of the Auschwitz Death Camp,* ed. Gutman and Berenbaum, 301–16; Francis R. Nicosia and Jonathan Huener, eds., *Medicine and Medical Ethics in Nazi Germany: Origins, Practices, Legacies* (New York: Berghahn Books, 2002); and Rubenstein, *The Cunning of History,* 48–67.

7. See Lucette Matalon Lagnado and Sheila Cohn Dekel, *Children of the Flames: Dr. Josef Mengele and the Untold Story of the Twins of Auschwitz* (London: Pan Books, 1992).

8. For helpful detail, see George J. Annas and Michael A. Grodin, eds., *The Nazi Doctors and the Nuremberg Code: Human Rights in Human Experimentation* (New York: Oxford University Press, 1992) and Benno Müller-Hill, "Human Genetics and the Mass Murder of Jews, Gypsies, and Others," in Berenbaum and Peck, eds., *The Holocaust and History,* 103–14.

9. See, for example, Jonathan D. Moreno, *Under Risk: Secret State Experiments on Humans* (New York: Routledge, 2000) and Peter Williams and David Wallace, *Unit 731: Japan's Secret Biological Warfare in World War II* (New York: Free Press, 1989).

10. See Müller, *Hitler's Justice: The Courts of the Third Reich*. Also helpful are Grunberger, *The 12-Year Reich,* 285–323, and Telford Taylor, "The Legal Profession," in *The Holocaust: Ideology, Bureaucracy, and Genocide,* ed. Henry Friedlander and Sybil Milton (Millwood, N.Y.: Kraus International Publications, 1980).

11. See Grunberger, *The 12-Year Reich*, 285–323. For more information on education in Nazi Germany, see Gregory Paul Wegner, *Anti-Semitism and Schooling under the Third Reich* (New York: Routledge, 2002).

12. Two relevant discussions of these topics are Gilmer W. Blackburn, *Education in the Third Reich: A Study of Race and History in Nazi Textbooks* (Albany: State University of New York Press, 1984) and Christa Kemenetsky, *Children's Literature in Hitler's Germany* (Athens: Ohio University Press, 1984).

13. For more detail, see Geoffrey J. Giles, *Students and National Socialism in Germany* (Princeton: Princeton University Press, 1999) and Jacques R. Pauwels, *Women, Nazis, and Universities: Female University Students in the Third Reich, 1933–1945* (Westport, Conn.: Greenwood Press, 1984).

14. See Alan Beyerchen, "The Physical Sciences," in *The Holocaust*, ed. Friedlander and Milton, 151–63. For more detail, see Alan Beyerchen, *Scientists under Hitler: Politics and the Physics Community in the Third Reich* (New Haven, Conn.: Yale University Press, 1977).

15. See Thomas R. Hughes, "Technology," in *The Holocaust*, ed. Friedlander and Milton, 165–81.

16. See Christopher R. Browning, "The Government Experts," in *The Holocaust*, ed. Friedlander and Milton, 183–97, for a summary elaboration of some aspects of this dimension of the Holocaust. For more detail, see Christopher R. Browning, *The Final Solution and the German Foreign Office: A Study of Referat D III of Abteilung Deutschland 1940–43* (New York: Holmes & Meier, 1978).

17. A significant early study of the *Reichsbahn*'s activity in the Holocaust is available in Raul Hilberg, "German Railroads, Jewish Souls," *Society* 14 (Nov.–Dec. 1976): 60–74. See also Hilberg, *The Destruction of the European Jews*, 2:407–16, 486–88 and 2:424–33, 507–9.

18. Alfred C. Mierzejewski, "A Public Enterprise in the Service of Mass Murder: The Deutsche Reichsbahn and the Holocaust," *Holocaust and Genocide Studies* 15 (spring 2001), 34. Mierzejewski is also the author of *The Most Valuable Asset of the Reich: A History of the German National Railway*, 2 vols. (Chapel Hill: University of North Carolina Press, 2000).

19. Mierzejewski, "A Public Enterprise," 36.

20. Hilberg, *The Destruction of the European Jews*, 2:411 and 2:428–29.

21. Mierzejewski, "A Public Enterprise," 41.

22. Ibid., 34.

23. Ibid., 41–42.

24. See Patrick Hayden, ed., *The Philosophy of Human Rights* (St. Paul, Minn.: Paragon House, 2001), 353.

25. A helpful analysis of this trial is provided by Michael R. Marrus, *The Nuremberg War Crimes Trial: 1945–46: A Documentary History* (New York: St. Martin's Press, 1997).

26. Our account of the Nuremberg Trial draws on material prepared by John Roth for Roth et al., *The Holocaust Chronicle*.

27. Bradley F. Smith, *Reaching Judgment at Nuremberg* (New York: Basic Books, 1977), 14. Other helpful accounts of the Nuremberg trials include Eugene Davidson, *The Trial of the Germans: An Account of Twenty-two Defendants before the International Military Tribunal at Nuremberg* (New York: Macmillan, 1966); Stephen Goodell et al., *In Pursuit of Justice: Examining the Evidence of the Holocaust* (Washington, D.C.: United States Holocaust Memorial Museum, 1996); Michael R. Marrus, *The Nuremberg War Crimes Trial;* Joseph E. Persico, *Nuremberg: Infamy on Trial* (New York: Viking Penguin, 1994); Bradley F. Smith, *The Road to Nuremberg* (New York: Basic Books, 1981); and John and Ann Tusa, *The*

*Nuremberg Trial* (New York: Atheneum Publishers, 1984). For important pretrial background and documentation, including interrogations of some of the defendants at Nuremberg, see Richard Overy, *Interrogations: The Nazi Elite in Allied Hands, 1945* (New York: Viking, 2001).

28. Smith, *Reaching Judgment at Nuremberg*, 14.

29. Hilberg, *The Destruction of the European Jews*, 3:1077 n.72 and 3:1159 n.72. See also Borkin, *The Crime and Punishment of I. G. Farben*.

30. For more detail on these matters, see Adams and Balfour, *Unmasking Administrative Evil* and Allan A. Ryan Jr., *Quiet Neighbors: Prosecuting Nazi War Criminals in America* (San Diego: Harcourt Brace Jovanovich, 1984), 344. Between 1979 and the time of this writing, the Office of Special Investigations (OSI), an arm of the U.S. Justice Department that began operations in 1979, has sought to bring former Nazis to justice. At the time of this writing, the OSI's work includes the following results: about 70 people implicated in Nazi persecutions have had their American citizenship revoked, more than 50 others have been deported for similar reasons, and approximately 160 suspected Nazis have been refused entry to the United States. The remaining ex-Nazis are aging; their numbers dwindle. Racing against time, the OSI's work continues.

31. Ferencz, *Less Than Slaves*, 156.

32. Ibid., 155.

33. Rubenstein, *The Cunning of History*, 65.

34. For instructive sociopsychological discussions about rationalizations and interpersonal dynamics that expedited the Holocaust and facilitate the potential for future genocides, see Browning, *Ordinary Men*; Ervin Staub, *The Roots of Evil: The Origins of Genocide and Other Group Violence* (Cambridge: Cambridge University Press, 1989); and James Waller, *Becoming Evil: How Ordinary People Commit Genocide and Mass Killing* (New York: Oxford University Press, 2002).

35. For a useful discussion of the various defense mechanisms employed by Nazis to justify their actions in the Holocaust, see Hilberg, "The Nature of the Process," in *Survivors, Victims, and Perpetrators,* ed. Dimsdale, 5–54. See also Robert Wolfe, "Putative Threat to National Security as Nuremberg Defense for Genocide," in *Reflections on the Holocaust,* ed. Shur, Littell, and Wolfgang, 46–67. As he sized up the excuses that German industrialists offered, Benjamin Ferencz, an American prosecutor at the Nuremberg trials, added that as far as German business leaders were concerned, "it was only those who had nothing to be ashamed of who expressed a sense of guilt and culpability." See Ferencz, *Less Than Slaves*, 192.

36. G. W. F. Hegel, *Philosophy of Right*, trans. T. M. Knox (New York: Oxford University Press, 1967), 12–13.

37. The quotation is from Littell's concluding plenary speech at Remembering for the Future 2000, a major international conference on the Holocaust held in Oxford, England, 16–23 July 2000. See *Remembering for the Future*, ed. Roth and Maxwell, 3:8–9.

38. On these points, see Bauman, *Modernity and the Holocaust* and Glover, *Humanity: A Moral History of the Twentieth Century*.

39. Calel Perechodnik, *Am I a Murderer? Testament of a Jewish Ghetto Policeman*, ed. and trans. Frank Fox (Boulder, Colo.: Westview Press, 1996).

40. Ibid., 9.

41. Richard L. Rubenstein, *The Cunning of History*, 91. The italics are Rubenstein's.

42. Ibid., 78.

43. For an important study of bystanders during the Holocaust, see Barnett, *Bystanders*, which eloquently makes the case that the inaction and indifference of the bystander—a category containing vastly more human beings than the categories of perpetrator, victim, or rescuer—is extremely important when the

questions are "Why did the Holocaust happen?" and "Will genocide ever end?" Omer Bartov complements Barnett's account when he writes, "The majority of the estimated 300 million people under German rule during the Holocaust were neither victims of the camps nor perpetrators. They were bystanders of various degrees and types. Some belonged to Greater Germany, and their kin were either fighting for Hitler or running his camps. Others belonged to Germany's allies, and more likely than not were more supportive of the partnership with the Third Reich in the early phases of the war than toward the end. Others still belonged to the occupied nations, and stood a good chance of becoming victims themselves, especially if they resisted Nazi policies or tried to protect those slated for extermination. But by and large, those who did not carry out genocide and related atrocities, and those who were not subjected to these policies, namely, the vast majority of German-occupied Europe's population, mostly watched in silence or did their best not to see at all. . . . Genocide cannot take place without a majority of passive bystanders." See Bartov, ed., *The Holocaust*, 204. Points akin to those emphasized by Barnett and Bartov are effectively amplified in Gordon J. Horowitz, "Places Far Away, Places Very Near: Mauthausen, the Camps of the Shoah, and the Bystanders," in *The Holocaust and History*, ed. Berenbaum and Peck, 409–20. See also Gordon J. Horowitz, *In the Shadow of Death: Living Outside the Gates of Mauthausen* (New York: Free Press, 1990). For Hilberg's discussion of bystanders—neighbors, as he calls them—see *The Destruction of the European Jews* (2003), 3:1119–26.

44. Berenbaum, *The World Must Know*, 220.
45. An insightful study of rescue during the Holocaust is David P. Gushee, *The Righteous Gentiles of the Holocaust: A Christian Interpretation*, rev. ed. (St. Paul, Minn.: Paragon House, 2003).
46. Gerald Fleming, "Engineers of Death," *New York Times*, 18 July 1993, E19. In our discussion of Fleming's findings, all the quotations are from this same source and page.
47. Three especially significant works on Auschwitz are Gutman and Berenbaum, eds. *Anatomy of the Auschwitz Death Camp*; Dwork and Robert Jan van Pelt, *Auschwitz: 1270 to the Present*; and van Pelt, *The Case for Auschwitz*. In the context of this discussion, the following essays in *Anatomy of the Auschwitz Death Camp* are particularly relevant: Francisek Piper, "Gas Chambers and Crematoria," 157–82, and Jean-Claude Pressac with Robert Jan van Pelt, "The Machinery of Mass Murder at Auschwitz," 183–245. For further information about Kurt Prüfer and his associates, see *Auschwitz: 1270 to the Present*, esp. 269–71, and *The Case for Auschwitz*, esp. 296–97, 350.
48. For an important discussion of these themes, see Haas, *Morality after Auschwitz*. Related topics are discussed in John K. Roth, ed., *Ethics after the Holocaust: Perspectives, Critiques, and Responses* (St. Paul: Paragon House, 1999).
49. Even with respect to Berenbaum's appealing idea that the Holocaust is a negative absolute, this judgment remains valid. There is no guarantee that universal moral reason or intuition exists or that, if they do, they will automatically conclude without disagreement that the Holocaust is a negative absolute. In ethics, the human will is decisive in determining how good and evil, right and wrong are understood. Reason and intuition inform our willing and choosing, but without the latter, our senses of good and evil, right and wrong, lack the force that gives them full reality and makes them effective. Willing and choosing alone do not determine what is ethical, but in the fullest sense no determination of right and wrong takes place without them. For a careful and important ethical study that emphasizes rationality in a more universalistic way, see David H. Jones, *Moral*

*Responsibility in the Holocaust: A Study in the Ethics of Character* (Lanham, Md.: Rowman & Littlefield, 1999).

50. Rubenstein, *Cunning of History*, 90.
51. Ibid., 89.
52. Jean Améry, *At the Mind's Limits: Contemplations by a Survivor on Auschwitz and Its Realities*, trans. Sidney Rosenfeld and Stella P. Rosenfeld (New York: Schocken Books, 1986), 86. The book was originally published in 1966.
53. Ibid., 28.
54. Ibid., 94–95.
55. Ibid., 89.
56. Ibid., 30–31.
57. Ibid., 31.
58. Perechodnik, *Am I a Murderer?* 211.
59. Ibid., 209.
60. Ibid., 211.
61. Carl Friedman, *Nightfather,* trans. Arnold and Erica Pomerans (New York: Persea Books, 1994), 134.

# A CHRONOLOGY OF IMPORTANT HOLOCAUST-RELATED EVENTS
## 1933–1948

For additional chronological information, consult the following on-line sources: *www.yad-vashem.org.il; www.ushmm.org;* and *www.holocaustchronicle.org.*

**1933**

| | |
|---|---|
| 30 January | Hitler sworn in as chancellor of the German Republic. |
| 27 February | Reichstag fire. Hitler issues emergency decree suspending civil rights. |
| 5 March | Nazis win 44 percent of the vote in parliamentary elections. |
| 20 March | The Dachau concentration camp is established. |
| 23 March | The "Enabling Act" gives Hitler's government authority to enact emergency decrees. |
| 1 April | Nazi boycott of Jewish-owned businesses in Germany. |
| 10 May | Book burnings throughout Germany. |
| 14 July | Nazi Party declared the only legal political party in Germany. |
| 19 October | Germany leaves the League of Nations. |

**1934**

| | |
|---|---|
| 30 June | Hitler orders Himmler to purge the SA leadership. |
| 20 August | German officials and soldiers required to take an oath of personal loyalty to Hitler. |

**1935**

| | |
|---|---|
| 16 March | Military conscription reinstated in Germany. |
| 15 September | The Nuremberg Laws: Only persons of German blood can be citizens; marriage and extramarital relations between Jews and Germans prohibited. |
| 14 November | Supplementary decrees to the Nuremberg Laws define *Jew*. |

**1936**

| | |
|---|---|
| 17 June | Himmler appointed chief of German police. |
| 1–16 August | Summer Olympic games held in Berlin. |

**1937**

| | |
|---|---|
| 21 March | Pope Pius XI issues *Mit brennender Sorge* (With burning concern), an encyclical against racism and extreme nationalism. |
| 16 July | Buchenwald concentration camp opens. |

**1938**

| | |
|---|---|
| 13 March, *Anschluss* | Germany incorporates Austria into the Reich. |

| | |
|---|---|
| 16 May | Forced Jewish labor begins at the Mauthausen concentration camp in Austria. |
| 6–15 July | Evian Conference: International discussions about the European refugee problem produce few results. |
| 17 August | Jewish men and women required to add "Israel" or "Sarah" to their names. |
| 29 September | Munich Agreement: Nazi Germany allowed to annex parts of Czechoslovakia. |
| 28 October | Thousands of Polish-born Jews expelled from Germany. |
| 9–10 November, *Kristallnacht* | Massive pogrom throughout the Reich, provoked by Herschel Grynzpan's shooting of Ernest vom Rath in Paris. |
| 12 November | German Jewry fined 1 billion Reichsmarks in aftermath of *Kristallnacht*. |

**1939**

| | |
|---|---|
| 30 January | Hitler's Reichstag speech threatens Jewish extermination if war breaks out in Europe. |
| 2 March | Pius XII becomes pope. |
| 15 March | German forces occupy Prague. |
| 15 May | Ravensbrück concentration camp established for women. |
| 23 August | Nazi-Soviet nonaggression pact signed, which secretly provides for Poland's partition. |
| 1 September | German forces invade Poland; World War II begins. |
| 8 October | First Jewish ghetto established in Poland. |
| 23 November | All Jews in the *Generalgouvernement* ordered to wear yellow stars. |
| 2 December | Gassing of mental patients in Germany gets under way. |

**1940**

| | |
|---|---|
| 8 February | The Lodz ghetto established. |
| 9 April | German forces invade Denmark and Norway. |
| 27 April | Himmler orders the establishment of a concentration camp at Auschwitz. |
| 10 May | Germany invades Belgium, Luxembourg, and the Netherlands. |
| 17 May | Germany invades France. |
| 16 June | Vichy government established in France. |
| 19 July | Telephones confiscated from German Jews. |
| 12 October | Warsaw ghetto established. |

**1941**

| | |
|---|---|
| 1 March | Himmler orders the Birkenau camp established at Auschwitz. |
| 22 June, Operation Barbarossa | Germany invades the USSR. |

| 23 June | *Einsatzgruppen* killings begin in USSR. |
| 31 July | Göring authorizes Heydrich to plan for the so-called Final Solution. |
| 1 September | "Officially," the Nazi "euthanasia" program ends; more than 70,000 killed. |
| 3 September | First experimental gassings carried out at Auschwitz; Soviet POWs are killed. |
| 29–30 September | In massive shootings, more than 33,000 Jews are murdered at Babi Yar. |
| 15 October | Mass deportation of German Jews begins. |
| 1 November | Construction of the Belzec (Poland) extermination camp begins. |
| 24 November | Heydrich establishes Theresienstadt (Czechoslovakia) as a "model" ghetto. |
| 7 December | Japanese attack Pearl Harbor. |
| 8 December | U.S. declares war on Japan. Mobile gas vans are operational at Chelmno. |
| 11 December | Germany and Italy declare war on the U.S. |

**1942**

| 20 January | Heydrich convenes the Wannsee Conference. |
| 17 March | The Belzec extermination camp opens. |
| 20 March | Gas chambers are operational at a Birkenau farmhouse. |
| 7 May | The Sobibor extermination camp opens. |
| 16 July | Roundups of Jews in Paris begin. |
| 22 July | Treblinka extermination camp is operational. |
| 12 September | Battle of Stalingrad begins. |

**1943**

| 9 January | Himmler tours the Warsaw ghetto and orders further deportations. |
| 19 April | The Bermuda Conference explores rescue operations but produces no results. |
| 19 April–16 May | The Warsaw ghetto uprising takes place. |
| 18 May | The Germans declare Warsaw *judenrein*. |
| 11 June | Himmler orders the liquidation of all ghettos in Poland. |
| 28 June | Extensive gassing and crematoria facilities are completed and operational at Birkenau. |
| 2 August | Prisoners revolt at Treblinka. |
| 1 October | The Danes rescue more than 7,000 Danish Jews from deportation. |
| 14 October | Prisoner uprising at Sobibor. |
| 3 November, *Erntefest* | Massive shooting campaign slaughters Jews at Majdanek and other sites. |

**1944**

| | |
|---|---|
| 26 January | President Roosevelt establishes the U.S. War Refugee Board. |
| 19 March | German forces take control of Hungary; destruction of Hungarian Jewry begins soon thereafter. |
| 6 June, D day | Allied forces land at Normandy. |
| 20 July | Assassination plot against Hitler. |
| 24 July | Soviet forces liberate the concentration/death camp at Majdanek. |
| 7–30 August | Liquidation of the Lodz ghetto. |
| 25 August | Allies liberate Paris. |
| 7 October | Prisoner uprising at Auschwitz. |
| 25–26 November | German dismantling of Birkenau is under way. |

**1945**

| | |
|---|---|
| 18 January | The Nazis evacuate some 66,000 prisoners from Auschwitz; thousands perish in the death march. |
| 27 January | Auschwitz liberated by the Red Army. |
| 11 April | Buchenwald liberated by American troops. |
| 12 April | Franklin Roosevelt dies; Harry Truman becomes U.S. president. |
| 15 April | Bergen-Belsen liberated by British army. |
| 25 April | American and Soviet troops meet at the Elbe River. |
| 29 April | Dachau liberated by Americans. Ravensbrück liberated by Soviet forces. |
| 30 April | Hitler commits suicide. |
| 7 May | Germany surrenders. |
| 8 May | V-E day (Victory in Europe). |
| 6 August | U.S. drops atomic bomb on Hiroshima. |
| 2 September | Japan surrenders, ending World War II. |
| 20 November | The Nuremberg War Crimes Trials begin. |

**1948**

| | |
|---|---|
| 14 May | The state of Israel is proclaimed. |

# Select Bibliography

As this book's endnotes indicate, many sources have informed our work. Listed below are books, primarily recent ones, that have most influenced our interpretation of the Holocaust and its legacy in this revised, second edition of *Approaches to Auschwitz*.

Aly, Götz. *"Final Solution": Nazi Population Policy and the Murder of the European Jews.* Translated by Belinda Cooper and Allison Brown. London: Arnold, 1999.

Améry, Jean. *At the Mind's Limits: Contemplations by a Survivor on Auschwitz and Its Realities.* Translated by Sidney Rosenfeld and Stella P. Rosenfeld. New York: Schocken Books, 1986.

Apel, Dora. *Memory Effects: The Holocaust and the Art of Secondary Witnessing.* New Brunswick, N.J.: Rutgers University Press, 2002.

Barnett, Victoria. *Bystanders: Conscience and Complicity during the Holocaust.* Westport, Conn.: Praeger, 2000.

———. *For the Soul of the People: Protestant Protest against Hitler.* New York: Oxford University Press, 1992.

Bartov, Omer. *Hitler's Army: Soldiers, Nazis, and War in the Third Reich.* New York: Oxford University Press, 1992.

———. *Mirrors of Destruction: War, Genocide, and Modern Identity.* New York: Oxford University Press, 2000.

Bartov, Omer, and Phyllis Mack, eds. *In God's Name: Genocide and Religion in the Twentieth Century.* New York: Berghahn Books, 2001.

Bauer, Yehuda. *A History of the Holocaust.* Rev. ed. New York: Franklin Watts, 2001.

———. *Rethinking the Holocaust.* New Haven, Conn.: Yale University Press, 2001.

Benz, Wolfgang. *The Holocaust.* Translated by Jane Sydenham-Kwiet. New York: Columbia University Press, 1999.

Berenbaum, Michael, ed. *Witness to the Holocaust.* New York: HarperCollins, 1997.

Berenbaum, Michael, and Abraham J. Peck, eds. *The Holocaust and History: The Known, the Unknown, the Disputed, and the Reexamined.* Bloomington: Indiana University Press, 1998.

Bergen, Doris L. *Twisted Cross: The German Christian Movement in the Third Reich.* Chapel Hill: University of North Carolina Press, 1996.

Browning, Christopher R. *Nazi Policy, Jewish Workers, German Killers.* Cambridge: Cambridge University Press, 2000.

Burleigh, Michael. *The Third Reich: A New History.* New York: Hill & Wang, 2000.

Burns, Michael. *France and the Dreyfus Affair: A Documentary History.* New York: St. Martin's, 1999.

Burrin, Philippe. *Hitler and the Jews: The Genesis of the Holocaust*. Translated by Patsy Southgate. London: Edward Arnold, 1994

Carroll, James. *Constantine's Sword: The Church and the Jews*. Boston: Houghton Mifflin, 2001.

Czech, Danuta. *The Auschwitz Chronicle 1939–1945*. Translated by Barbara Harshav, Martha Humphries, and Stephen Shearier. New York: Henry Holt, 1990.

Delbo, Charlotte. *Auschwitz and After*. Translated by Rosette C. Lamont. New Haven, Conn.: Yale University Press, 1995.

Dwork, Debórah, and Robert Jan van Pelt. *Auschwitz: 1270 to the Present*. New York: W. W. Norton, 1996.

Ericksen, Robert P., and Susannah Heschel, eds. *Betrayal: German Churches and the Holocaust*. Minneapolis: Fortress Press, 1999.

Friedlander, Henry. *The Origins of Nazi Genocide: From Euthanasia to the Final Solution*. Chapel Hill: University of North Carolina Press, 1995.

Friedländer, Saul. *Nazi Germany and the Jews*, vol. 1, *The Years of Persecution, 1933–1939*. New York: HarperCollins, 1997.

Gellately, Robert. *Backing Hitler: Consent and Coercion in Nazi Germany*. New York: Oxford University Press, 2001.

Gellately, Robert, and Nathan Stoltzfus, eds. *Social Outsiders in Nazi Germany*. Princeton: Princeton University Press, 2002.

Gerlach, Wolfgang. *And the Witnesses Were Silent: The Confessing Church and the Persecution of the Jews*. Translated and edited by Victoria J. Barnett. Lincoln: University of Nebraska Press, 2000.

Glover, Jonathan. *Humanity: A Moral History of the Twentieth Century*. New Haven, Conn.: Yale University Press, 2000.

Goldhagen, Daniel Jonah. *Hitler's Willing Executioners: Ordinary Germans and the Holocaust*. New York: Alfred A. Knopf, 1996.

———. *A Moral Reckoning: The Role of the Catholic Church in the Holocaust and Its Unfulfilled Duty of Repair*. New York: Alfred A. Knopf, 2002.

Gordon, Sarah. *Hitler, Germans, and the "Jewish Question."* Princeton: Princeton University Press, 1984.

Gutman, Yisrael, and Michael Berenbaum, eds. *Anatomy of the Auschwitz Death Camp*. Bloomington: Indiana University Press, 1994.

Haas, Peter J. *Morality after Auschwitz: The Radical Challenge of the Nazi Ethic*. Philadelphia: Fortress Press, 1988.

Haynes, Stephen. *Reluctant Witnesses: Jews and the Christian Imagination*. Louisville, Ky.: Westminster John Knox Press, 1995.

Herbert, Ulrich, ed. *National Socialist Exterminationist Policies: Contemporary German Perspectives and Controversies*. New York: Berghahn Books, 2000.

Hilberg, Raul. *The Destruction of the European Jews*. 3 vols. New York: Holmes & Meier, 1985; New Haven, Conn.: Yale University Press, 2003.

———. *Perpetrators, Victims, Bystanders: The Jewish Catastrophe 1933–1945*. New York: HarperCollins, 1992.

———. *Sources of Holocaust Research: An Analysis*. Chicago: Ivan R. Dee, 2001.

Hirschfeld, Gerhard, ed. *The Policies of Genocide: Jews and Soviet Prisoners of War in Nazi Germany*. London: Allen & Unwin, 1986.

Kershaw, Ian. *Hitler, 1889–1936: Hubris*. New York: W. W. Norton, 1999.

———. *Hitler, 1936–1945: Nemesis*. New York: W. W. Norton, 2000.

Klemperer, Victor. *I Will Bear Witness: A Diary of the Nazi Years*. 2 vols. Translated by Martin Chalmers. New York: Random House, 1998, 1999.

Langer, Lawrence L. *Holocaust Testimonies: The Ruins of Memory*. New Haven, Conn.: Yale University Press, 1991.

Laqueur, Walter, ed. *The Holocaust Encyclopedia*. New Haven, Conn.: Yale University Press, 2001.

Levi, Primo. *The Drowned and the Saved*. Translated by Raymond Rosenthal. New York: Summit Books, 1988.

———. *Survival in Auschwitz*. Translated by Stuart Wolff. New York: Collier Books, 1976.

Mendes-Flohr, Paul, and Yehuda Reinharz, eds. *The Jew in the Modern World: A Documentary History*. 2d ed. New York: Oxford University Press, 1995.

Müller, Ingo. *Hitler's Justice: The Courts of the Third Reich*. Translated by Deborah Lucas Schneider. Cambridge, Mass.: Harvard University Press, 1991.

Noakes, J., and G. Pridham, eds. *Nazism: A History in Documents and Eyewitness Accounts, 1919–1945*. 2 vols. New York: Schocken Books, 1990.

Phayer, Michael. *The Catholic Church and the Holocaust, 1930–1965*. Bloomington: Indiana University Press, 2000.

Rhodes, Richard. *Masters of Death: The SS-Einsatzgruppen and the Invention of the Holocaust*. New York: Alfred A. Knopf, 2002.

Roseman, Mark. *The Wannsee Conference and the Final Solution: A Reconsideration*. New York: Henry Holt, 2002.

Roth, John K., and Elisabeth Maxwell, eds. *Remembering for the Future: The Holocaust in an Age of Genocide*. 3 vols. New York: Palgrave, 2001.

Scholder, Klaus. *The Churches and the Third Reich*. Translated by John Bowden. London: SCM Press, 1988.

Weinberg, Gerhard L. *A World at Arms: A Global History of World War II*. Cambridge: Cambridge University Press, 1994.

Wistrich, Robert S. *Hitler and the Holocaust*. New York: Modern Library, 2001.

Zuccotti, Susan. *Under His Very Windows: The Vatican and the Holocaust in Italy*. New Haven, Conn.: Yale University Press, 2001.

# Index

*The Abandonment of the Jews,* 432 nn.160–63
Abdul-Hammid II, Sultan, 18
Abel, 249
*Absence/Presence,* 298, 437 n.21
Absolute, the, 343
    negative, 450 n.49
Abraham, 26, 27
Abzug, Robert H.
    *America Views the Holocaust,* 432 n.163, 435
        n.7
    *Inside the Vicious Heart,* 416 n.88, 435 n.7
*Accounting for Genocide,* 383 n.26, 384 nn.33,
        36, 423 n.86
*Actes et Documents du Saint Siège relatifs à Sec-
        ond Guerre mondiale,* 429 n.88
*Action Française,* 91, 390 nn.42, 44
Adalian, Rouben Paul, 384 n.35
Adam and Eve, 25, 301
Adams, Guy B. and Danny L. Balfour
    *Unmasking Administrative Evil,* 447 n.5, 449
        n.30
Adam, Uwe Dietrich, 145
    *Judenpolitik in Dritten Reich,* 401 n.11
Adenauer, Konrad, 168
Adler, Hans-Günther, 137
    *Der verwaltete Mensch,* 399 nn.49, 50
*Admitting the Holocaust,* 418 n.32, 439 n.60
*Adolf Hitler,* 395 nn.38, 41
Adorno, Theodore, 291, 297, 329
    *Accounting for Genocide,* 383 n.26, 384
        nn.33, 36, 423 n.86
*adversus judaeus* tradition, 51
*Affair, The,* 389 n.23
Africa
    German East, 164
    South, 399 n.44
*After Auschwitz,* 335, 343, 385 n.23, 390 n.29,
        443 n.27, 443 n.36
*Against Silence,* 414 n.58
*Against the Apocalypse,* 442 n.2
*Against the Stream,* 427 n.62
*Age of Triage, The,* 382 n.18, 389 n.7, 390 n.2,
        395 n.43, 442 n.1

aid, mutual, 423 n.92
Akedah, 342, 444 n.48
*Aktion 14f13,* 156, 404 n.61
*Aktion Reinhard.* See Operation Reinhard
*Al-Akhbar,* 345, 445 n.59
Alexander the Great, 29–30, 31
Alexander II, Czar, 98, 424 n.8
Alexandria, 31–32
aliens, resident (*metics*), 91
Allen, Michael Thad
    *The Business of Genocide,* 422 n.85
*All Rivers Run to the Sea,* 319
*Alma Rosé,* 436 n.13
*Almstadtstrasse 43,* 437 n.15
*Along the Edge of Annihilation,* 439 n.58
Alsace, 75, 80, 83, 91, 163
Alsace-Lorraine, 405 n.89
Althaus, Paul, 387 n.31
*The Altruistic Personality,* 434 n.173
Aly, Götz, 6, 159, 164, 186, 401 n.13, 402
        nn.27, 29, 31, 35, 37–38, 404 n.68
    *"Final Solution,"* 383 n.21, 399 n.49, 52,
        402 nn.29, 37, 404 n.69, 405 nn.76, 83
Aly, Götz and Susanne Heim
    *Architects of Annihilation,* 447 n.5
    *Vordenker der Vernichtung,* 406 n.97
Ambros, Otto, 364
*Amen* (play), 423 n.1
American Joint Distribution Committee, 139
American War Refugee Board, 276, 284
*America Views the Holocaust,* 432 n.163, 435
        n.7
Améry, Jean, 304, 374, 376
    *At the Mind's Limits,* 451 n.52
*Am I a Murderer?,* 449 n.39
Amos (prophet), 43
Amsterdam, 2
*Anatomie des SS-Staates,* 407 n.8
*Anatomy of the Auschwitz Death Camp,* 414
        n.60, 450 n.47
*ancien Régime,* 73, 75, 80
*Ancun de nous ne reviendra* (None of us will
        return), 310–11

461

*And the Crooked Shall Be Made Straight,* 447 n.3
*And the Witnesses Were Silent,* 425 n.14, 426
    n.34
"angel of Death," *See* Mengele, Josef
Angier, Carole
    *The Double Bond: Primo Levi,* 435 n.1
*Angriff, Der* (The attack), 1
Anielewicz, Mordecai, 233
Anissimov, Myrian
    *Primo Levi,* 435 n.1
Annas, George J. and Michael A. Grodin, eds.
    *The Nazi Doctors and the Nuremberg Code,*
    447 n.8
*Anne Frank Remembered,* 436 n.9
annihilation. *See* Final Solution; *Vernichtung*
Anschluss, 130, 140
*Anselm Kiefer and the Philosophy of Martin Hei-*
    *degger,* 437 n.17
anti-Communism, 269, 287
anti-immigration sentiment, 432 n.167
anti-Judaism, 173
    in Christianity, 5, 51, 69, 384 n.8, 386 n.2
    in France, 72
    in Greco-Roman world, 29–33
*Anti-Judaism and the Fourth Gospel,* 385 n.22
antiman, 375
Antiochus IV Epiphanes, 31
"antipartisan," 171
antisemitism, 30, 71, 90–93, 115, 260, 361,
    381 n.14, 386 n.2
    Catholic, 81–82, 90, 268–69
    Christian, 252–53, 289, 332, 386 n.2, 387
    n.20
        eradication efforts, 289
        opposition to, 254
        roots of, 332, 386 n.1
    condemnation of, 271
    eliminationist, 71, 107, 382 n.20, 392 n.11
    French, 74, 76, 81, 388 n.4, 389 n.13, 393
    n.22
    genocidal, 380 n.3
    German, 388 n.2, 392 n.11
    Hitler's, 382 n.20, 396 n.47
    "insufficient," 258
    legitimate/illegitimate, 270
    modern, 94–95
    national, 121–25
    Nazi, 3, 15, 66, 72, 103, 105, 107, 183,
        193, 221, 236, 323, 370
    passive, 123
    Polish, 109–10, 131, 386 n.6
    political, 10
    racism and, 124, 236, 270, 370
    religious, 7, 33, 253
    Russian, 303
    socialist, 251, 389 n.11
    student, 123
*Anti-Semitism and Schooling under the Third*
    *Reich,* 448 n.11

*Antisemitism in France,* 389 nn.13, 17–18,
    20–21
*Antisemitism: The Longest Hatred,* 384 n.6, 386
    nn.4, 9, 388 n.4
Apel, Dora, 303
    *Memory Effects,* 436 n.14
apostasy, 258–59
*Appeasers, The,* 398 n.22
Aquinas, Thomas. *See* Thomas Aquinas
Arab-Israeli Conflict. *See* Israel, Six Day War
Arabs, 345, 382 n.14
Arad, Yitzhak, 413 n.45
    *Belzec, Sobibor, Treblinka,* 413 n.45
Arajs, Viktors, 177
*Arbeit macht Frei,* 355, 370
*Architect of Genocide, The,* 399 n.42
*Architects of Annihilation,* 447 n.5
architecture. *See* Holocaust, architecture
Arendt, Hannah, 11, 220, 399 n.46, 442 n.4
    *Eichmann in Jerusalem,* 218, 406 n.92, 416
    n.7
    *The Jew as Pariah,* 382 n.19
    *The Origins of Totalitarianism,* 382 n.19, 389
    n.23
Argentina, 145, 416 n.7
Arlen, Michael
    *Passage to Ararat,* 444 n.54
Armageddon, 342, 346
Armenians, 18, 20, 327, 344
Arons, Mark and John Loftus
    *Unholy Trinity,* 434 n.176
Aronson, Elliot, 385 n.21
Aroust, François-Marie. *See* Voltaire
art. *See* Holocaust: art
*Art from the Ashes,* 438 n.33, 439 n.60
*Art, Ideology, and Economics in Nazi Germany,*
    436 n.13
*Art, Music, and Education as Strategies for Sur-*
    *vival,* 437 n.27
*Art of the Holocaust,* 437 n.27
"Aryan/non-Aryan," 30, 126, 255, 374, 380 n.3
"Aryan paragraph," 125, 256, 259
Aryanization, 113, 129, 130, 161, 251
Aschheim, Steven, 181, 410 n.52
"asocials," 106
Association of Jewish Veterans, 425 n.12
Assumptionist Fathers, 81, 90
Astor, Gerald
    *The Last Nazi,* 447 n.6
atheism, 342
Athens, 280
*At Memory's Edge,* 438 n.45
*At the Mind's Limits,* 451 n.52
Attie, Shimon, 296, 303
    *Almstadtstrasse 43,* 437 n.15
Augustine of Hippo, 53–54, 250
    *The City of God,* 53
Aulich, James and John Lynch, eds.
    *Critical Kitaj,* 437 n.18

*Aurore, L',* 390 n.36
Auschwitz (Oświęcim), 8, 163, 202–7, 307,
    372, 383 n.21, 414 n.58, 450 n.47
  architecture of, 396 n.45
  art studies at, 299
  Birkenau, 195, 238, 240, 327, 371, 379 n.4,
    414 n.67, 421 n.59
    October uprising, 420 n.42
  Central Building Authority, 371
  *Chronicle,* 237, 414 n.60
  development of, 202, 414 n.60
  emblematic of Holocaust, 203
  end of the line, 311
  escape from, 422 n.59
  final months, 414 n.67
  gas chambers at, 396 n.45, 415 n.63, 433
    n.167
  medical experiments. *See* human experi-
    ments
  Monowitz, 203, 204, 433, 433 n.167
  a rail hub, 414 n.62
  reconnaissance photographs, 433 n.167
  survivors, ix, xi, 310, 420 n.45
    *See also* survivors
  uprisings, 233–34
  women in, 235, 310, 317, 421 n.53
*Auschwitz: 1270 to the Present,* 383 n.21, 414
    nn.60–61, 416 n.80, 450 n.47
*Auschwitz Album, The,* 239, 380 n.4, 421 n.59
*Auschwitz: Beginning of a New Era?,* 387, n.30
*Auschwitz et après* (Auschwitz and after),
    310–14, 379 n.2, 420 n.45
*Auschwitz: Nazi Death Camp,* 414 n.60
*Auschwitz: True Tales from a Grotesque Land,* 8
Austria, 130, 139, 140
Austria-Hungary, 170, 414 n.66
*Auswanderung,* 99, 151
Authers, John and Richard Wolffe
  *The Victim's Fortune,* 423 n.85
Avenue of the Righteous, 282–86, 433 n.172
Avisar, Ilan
  *Screening the Holocaust,* 435 n.8
*Axis Rule in Occupied Europe,* 383 n.24

babies. *See* children
baby carriages. *See* strollers
Babi Yar, 179, 283, 296
Bach-Zelewski, Erich von dem, 181
*Backing Hitler,* 6, 97, 392 n.11, 396 nn.49–50,
    399 n.45
badges. *See* clothing, distinctive
Baeck, Leo, 221, 223
Baer, Elizabeth R. and Myrna Goldenberg, eds.
  *Experience and Expression,* 420 nn.41, 45
Baigel, Matthew, 437 n.21
Bak, Samuel, 298, 300, 301, 438 n.37
  *Painted in Words,* 438 n.37
Bak, Samuel and Lawrence L. Langer
  *Landscapes of Jewish Experience,* 438 n.37

Baldwin, Neil
  *Henry Ford and the Jews,* 387 n.26
Balfour Declaration, 141
baptismal
  certificates, 280
  registers, 255, 370
Baranowski, Shelly, 256
barbarians, 30
Barbarossa, Operation. *See* Operation Bar-
  barossa
Barkan, Elazar
  *The Guilt of Nations,* 423 n.85
Barker, George, 281
Bar Kochba War, 32
Barmen Declaration, 259
Barnett, Victoria, 7, 252, 356
  *Bystanders,* 355, 447 n.4, 449 n.43
  *For the Soul of the People,* 397 n.7, 426 n.31
Barth, Karl, 254, 259–61, 264, 427 nn.58–62
  *Against the Stream,* 427 n.62
Bartov, Omer, 103–4, 450 n.43
  *The Eastern Front, 1941–45,* 408 n.32
  *The Holocaust,* 411 n.14
  *Hitler's Army,* 407 n.8, 408 nn.21, 23, 408
    n.35
  *Mirrors of Destruction,* 393 nn.15, 18–23
Bartov, Omer and Phyllis Mack
  *In God's Name,* 426 n.39
Battle of the Somme. *See* Somme, Battle of
Bauer, Yehuda, 17, 107, 396 n.46, 418 n.28
  *A History of the Holocaust,* 7, 383 n.28, 386
    n.6, 388 nn.42–43, 394 n.25, 418 n.28
  *The Holocaust in Historical Perspective,* 383
    n.30, 398 n.20
  *Rethinking the Holocaust,* 7, 217, 383 nn.29,
    30, 394 n.31
  *Rewriting the Holocaust,* 418 nn.28–29, 419
    n.35
Bauer, Yehuda, and Nathan Rotenstreich
  *The Holocaust as Historical Experience,* 416
    n.2, 418 n.29
Baumel, Judith Tydor, 400 n.55
Baumn, Zygmunt
  *Modernity and the Holocaust,* 388 n.38
Baum, Rainer C.
  *The Holocaust and the German Elite,* 447 n.5
Bavaria, 277
Bazyler, Michael
  *Holocaust Justice,* 423 n.85
*Bearing Witness,* 400 nn.54–55
Beck, Norman A.
  *Mature Christianity in the Twenty-first Cen-
    tury,* 385 n.22
*Becoming Evil,* 449 n.34
*Behandlung des Nichtjuden nach dem Talmud,
  Die,* 427 n.40
*Behandlung sowjetischer Kriegsgefangenen in
  "Fall Barbarossa," Die,* 408 n.23
*Bekennende Kirche. See* Confessing Churches

Belgium, 226
Belgrade, 170
Belorussia, 172–73, 174, 177, 408 n.28
Belzec,186, 187, 197,198–200, 413 nn.47–48,
    414 n.51, 424 n.1
*Belzec, Sobibor, Treblinka,* 413 n.45
Belzin, 147
Benigni, Robert
    *Life Is Beautiful,* 436 n.11
Ben-Sasson, H. H., ed.
    *A History of the Jewish People,* 384 n.2
Benz, Wolfgang, 6, 213, 381 n.6
    *The Holocaust,* 381 n.6, 398 n.28, 398
    nn.30, 33
Benzler, Felix, 170
Berehovo, 379 n.4
Berenbaum, Michael, 203, 228, 241, 368, 370,
    414 n.62
    *A Mosaic of Victims,* 381 n.8
    *Witness to the Holocaust,* 388 n. 34, 396
    n.48, 398 n.29, 400 nn.2–3, 401 nn.12,
    14, 402 n.32, 405 n.80, 418 n.24
    *The World Must Know,* 7, 414 n.62
Berenbaum, Michael and Abraham J. Peck, ed.
    *The Holocaust and History,* 446 n.2
Bergen-Belsen, 2, 209, 278
Bergen, Diego von, 270, 271
Bergen, Doris L., 7, 152, 257–58, 427 n.44
    *Twisted Cross,* 426 nn.30–31
    *War and Genocide,* 7, 143, 400 n.1
Berger, Alan L.
    *Crisis and Covenant,* 439 n.60
Berlin, 137, 147, 188, 237, 256, 337
    Jews in, 302, 303, 308, 412 n.34
    *Sportpalast. See* Sportpalast
Bermuda conference, 281
Bernberg, 156, 200
Bernstein, Leonard
    *Kaddish,* 296
Bernstein, Richard J.
    *Hannah Arendt and the Jewish Question,* 417
    n.7
    *Radical Evil,* 442 n.4
*Between Worlds,* 438 n.37
Beschloss, Michael
    *The Conquerors: Roosevelt, Truman, and the
    Destruction of Hitler's Germany,* 433 n.167
*Best: Biographische Studien über Radikalismus,*
    397 nn.8, 11
Bethge, Eberhard, 259, 427 n.56
    *Dietrich Bonhoeffer,* 428 n.68
Beth Shalom, Nottinghamshire, 379 n.4
*Betrayal: German Churches and the Holocaust,*
    387 n.32, 397 n.7
*Between Dignity and Despair,* 420 n.45
*Between Worlds,* 438 n.37
Beyerchen, Alan, 448 n.14
    *Scientists under Hitler,* 448 n.14
*Beyond Auschwitz,* 444 n.49

*Beyond Belief,* 432 n.163
Bialystok, 232
Biberstein, Ernst, 174, 282–83
Bible, 255, 289–90, 346, 353
    *See also* New Testament; Old Testament;
    Scripture
Biebow, Hans, 228
Bienert, Walter
    *Martin Luther und die Juden,* 387 nn.14, 27
Bikerniski, Forest, 177
Binding, Karl, 154
Binding, Karl and Alfred Hoche
    *Die Freigabe der Vernichtung Lebensunwerten
    Lebens,* 403 n.48
"biomedical vision," 152
Birkenau *See* Auschwitz-Birkenau
Biro, Matthew
    *Anselm Kiefer and the Philosophy of Martin
    Heidegger,* 437 n.17
*Bishop von Galen,* 404 n.64
Bismarck, Otto von, 11, 71, 99, 265
    *Kulturkampf,* 265
*Bitter Wounds,* 393 n.18
Blackburn, Gilmer W.
    *Education in the Third Reich,* 448 n.12
Black, Edwin
    *The Transfer Agreement,* 397 n.14, 400 n.57
Blair, Jon
    *Anne Frank Remembered,* 436 n.9
    *Schindler,* 436 n.9
Blake, Robert, ed.
    *The Private Papers of Douglas Haig
    1914–1918,* 393 n.16
Blanchot, Maurice, 241–43
    *The Writing of the Disaster,* 241
Blatter, Janet and Sybil Milton
    *Art of the Holocaust,* 437 n.27
*Blitzkrieg,* 173, 182
Blobel, Paul, 193, 197, 419 n.38
blood
    and soil, German, 113, 134
    Jewish, 193
    libel. *See* ritual murder
    "purity" (*limpieza de sangre*), 65–66, 388
    n.35
"Bloody Wednesday." *See* mass murder: *Ernte-
    fest*
Bloom, Harold, ed.
    *Elie Wiesel's Night,* 441 n.111
Bloom, Jack H., 343
    *The Rabbi as Symbolic Exemplar,* 444 n.52
"boat people," 138–39
Boer War, 399 n.44
Böhme, Franz, 170
Bolshevism, 65, 105, 114, 143, 144, 167, 172,
    176, 190, 211, 251–52, 267, 276–77,
    407 n.4, 408 n.30
Boltanski, Christian
    *The Storehouse (La Grande Reserve),* 436 n.15

Bonhoeffer, Dietrich, 259, 262–65, 425 n.19,
    428 nn.69–70, 73–81
    *No Rusty Swords,* 425 n.19
Bonhoeffer, Karl, 428 n.68
*Bonhoeffer Phenomenon, The,* 428 n.68
Bonhoeffer, Renate, 428 n.70
Bonnet, Georges, 163
Bontoux, Eugene, 81
book burning, 125
Borchert, H. H. and George Merz, eds.
    *Martin Luther,* 387 n.30
Borkin, Joseph
    *The Crime and Punishment of I. G. Farben,*
    446 n.1, 449 n.29
Bormann, Martin, 189, 190, 363–64, 408
    n.20
Borowski, Tadeusz, 305, 315–19
    *This Way for the Gas, Ladies and Gentlemen,*
    8, 315–16
Bosnia, 17
Bouhler, Philipp, 155, 189
bourgeoise, 76
boycotts, 122, 134
Boys, Mary, 51
Bracher, Karl Dietrich
    *The German Dictatorship,* 391 n.4
Brack, Viktor, 155, 157, 199
Braiterman, Zachary, 341, 348, 351
    (*God*) *after Auschwitz,* 443 n.37, 444 nn.45,
    49
Brandenburg, 156, 157, 198, 200
    Synod, 256
Brandon, S. G. F.
    *The Fall of Jerusalem and the Christian
    Church,* 385 nn.17, 19
Brandt, Karl, 148, 155
Brazil, 201
Bredin, Jean-Denis
    *The Affair,* 389 n.23
Breitman, Richard
    *The Architect of Genocide,* 399 n.42
    *Official Secrets,* 401 n.10
Breslau, 188
*Britain and the Jews of Europe,* 400 n.58
Broszat, Martin, 186, 187
Brown, Daniel Patrick
    *The Camp Women,* 421 n.48
Browning, Christopher, 150, 175, 187–88,
    382 n.20, 412–13 n.37
    *The Final Solution and the German Foreign
    Office,* 405 n.86, 448 n.16
    *Fearful Months,* 395 n.45
    *Ordinary Men,* 6, 401 n.16, 408 n.35
    *Nazi Policy, Jewish Workers, German Killers,*
    6, 402 nn.28, 33, 405 nn.79, 86, 408
    n.29, 411 n.56
    *The Path to Genocide,* 395 n.45
Brownlow, Donald Grey and John Eluthère Du
    Pont

*Hell Was My Home,* 401 n.21
Brown, Robert McAfee, 332
    *Elie Wiesel: Messenger to All Humanity,* 441
    n.111
Bruch, Max
    *Kol Nidre,* 296
Bru, Frederico Laredo, 141
Brüning, Heinrich, 253, 269
Brunner, Alois, 287
Brussels, 298
Brzezinka. *See* Auschwitz-Birkenau
Buber, Martin
    *Eclipse of God,* 341, 444 nn.40–41
Buchenwald, 132, 195, 208, 414 n.56
Buchheim, Hans, ed.
    *Anatomie des SS-Staates,* 407 n.8
Budapest, 226
Bühler, Josef, 190, 197
*Build-Up of German Military Aggression, The,*
    407 n.8
Bulgaria, 201, 279
Bullock, Alan
    *Hitler: A Study in Tyranny,* 391 n.4, 397
    n.51
Bultmann, Rudolf, 260
Buna, 204
*Bundeswehr,* 168
bureaucracy, 15, 127, 357, 370
burial. *See* corpse disposal
Burleigh, Michael, 126, 167, 406 n.1
    *The Third Reich,* 7, 380 n.1, 395 nn.38, 40,
    397 nn.12, 17, 406 n.1
Burleigh, Michael and Wolfgang Wipperman
    *The Racial State,* 415 n.72
Burns, Michael
    *Dreyfus,* 389 n.23, 390 n.47
    *France and the Dreyfus Affair,* 390 n.25, 390
    nn.32, 36, 40–41, 45
Burrin, Philippe 114, 382 n.20
    *Hitler and the Jews,* 396 n.47
Burzio, Giusseppe, 273
Busch, Eberhard
    *Karl Barth,* 427 nn.58–61
business, 13
    Jewish liquidated, 129
*Business of Genocide, The,* 422 n.85
*Butcher's Tale, The,* 388 n.2
Byrnes, Robert F., 80
    *Antisemitism in France,* 389 nn.13, 17–18,
    20–21
    *Pobedonostsev,* 391 n.3
bystanders, 449–50 n.43
*Bystanders,* 355, 447 n.4, 449 n.43
*By Words Alone,* 439 n.60

Cain, 249
*Call to Revolution,* 424 n.7
Calvin, John, 56
Cambodia, 20

*Cambridge Companion to the Bible,* 384 n.3
"camouflage and rationalization," 188
Campert, Remeo, 377
camps
  concentration, 132, 135, 163, 171, 195,
    202, 207, 208–9, 399 n.44, 421 n.46
  death, 159, 163, 195, 408 n.14, 447 n.3
    administrators of, 413 n.45, 421 n.48
    layout, 198
    location factor, 198
    revolts, 201, 233
    *See also* killing centers
  DP (displaced persons), 240
  forced labor, 355
  internment, 170
  liberation of, 299, 302, 416 n.88, 435 n.7
  photography of, 297
  prison, 195
  transit, 272, 285, 299
  *See also individual place names*
*Camp Women, The,* 421 n.48
Camus, Albert, 25
  *The Rebel,* 384 n.1
Canaan, 26, 29
"Canada," 237, 422 n.59
Canaris, Wilhelm, 428 n.81
capitalism, 40, 55, 68
Caprivi, Leo von, 99
*Captain Dreyfus,* 389 nn.23–24, 390
  nn.26–27, 38
Caraffa, Gian Pietro (Cardinal), 66
carbon monoxide gas, 157, 196, 424 n.1, 447
  n.3
Cargas, Harry James, 7, 332
  *Harry James Cargas in Conversation with Elie
    Wiesel,* 441 n.111
Caritas Catholica, 278
*Carnet de P. J. Proudhon,* 389 n.14
Carroll, James, 66
  *Constantine's Sword,* 49, 386 nn.1, 3, 9, 388
    nn.35–37, 389 nn.22, 23, 390 n.47
Carr-Saunders, Am M.
  *World Population,* 389 n.19, 391 n.7
Carter, Jimmy, 293
*Case for Auschwitz, The,* 396 n.45, 414 n.60,
  450 n.47
Catholic Center Party, 111, 253, 265, 269
*Catholic Church and Nazi Germany, The,* 399
  n.38
*Catholic Church and the Holocaust,
  The,1930–1965,* 399 n.38
*Catholic Teaching on the Shoah,* 434 n.187
Cavaignac, Godefroy, 90
Center for Holocaust and Genocide Studies, 298
Central Office for Jewish Emigration, 130
Cévenol School, 284
Chalk, Frank and Kurt Jonassohn
  *The History and Sociology of Genocide,* 384
    nn.31, 32, 442 n.1

Chamberlain, Neville, 129
Chambon-sur-Lignon, Le, 284–86, 294, 434
  n.174
chaplains, 257–58, 427 n.44
Chapman, Guy
  *The Dreyfus Case,* 389 n.23, 390 nn.31, 37
Charlesworth, James H., ed.
  *Jesus Two Thousand Years Later,* 385 n.22
Chelmno (Kulmhof), 163, 186, 187, 196,
  227, 447 n.3
  burial pits, 197
  gas vans, 159, 163, 196, 447 n.3
children('s), 234, 338
  in Auschwitz, 237, 436 n.11
  burning, 446 n.70
  emigration for, 274
  expelled, 133
  experiments on, 358, 447 n.7
  French, 285
  gassed, 172
  handicapped, 158, 381 n.7
  Jews as murders of, 54, 92, 268–69, 279
  legislation, 282
  murder of, 186, 258, 410 n.53
  rescue efforts, 294
  saved from Vilna, 284
  smuggled food, 420 n.44
  songs, 295
  starvation of, 157
  of survivors. *See* survivors: children of
  teaching of, 360
  treatment of, 200
*Children and Play in the Holocaust,* 420 n.44
*Children's Literature in Hitler's Germany,* 448
  n.12
*Children of a Vanished World,* 435 n.6
*Children of the Flames,* 447 n.7
*Children with a Star,* 420 n.44
chlorine gas. *See* gas: chlorine
Chmialnicki, Bogdan, 55
"choiceless choices," 225, 242, 293, 417 n.24
Chorover, Stephan L.
  *From Genesis to Genocide,* 403 nn.44, 49–51
chosen people. *See* Jews: as chosen people; witness-people myth
Christian(s)
  annihilation, 9
  anti-Jewish policies, 9
  attitudes toward Jews, 20, 49, 51, 250–51,
    252, 386 n.1
  complicity, 12
  expulsion by, 9
  Jewish relationships. *See* Jewish-Christian
    relationships
  missionary zeal of, 36
  press, 281, 282
  reaction to Hitler, 254
  responses to the Holocaust, 287
  supersessionism. *See* supersessionism

triumphalism, 49, 332
and war crimes, 287
*Christian Anti-Semitism and Paul's Theology,*
    385 n.9
*Christian Century,* 282, 433 n.168
*Christian Faith and Public Choices,* 427 n.56
Christianity
    American, 281–82, 342, 354, 432 n.163
    conversion to, 9, 19, 52, 69, 251, 264, 338,
        344
        Hungarians, 414 n.66
    dejudaization of, 257
    Gentile, 40
    "positive," 265
    relation to Judaism. *See* Jewish-Christian
        relationships; Judaism: Christian
        influence on
    as religion of love, 289
    self-understanding, 51
*Christianity and the Holocaust of Hungarian
    Jewry,* 424 n.5
*Christianity in Jewish Terms,* 435 n.187
"Chronicle of Shame," 264
*Chronicle of the Lodz Ghetto, 1941–1944, The,*
    418 nn.30–31
*Chronik des Zweiten Weltkrieges,* 399–400, n.51
Chrysostom, St. John. *See* John Chrysostom
church fathers, 51
    *See also individual names*
churches
    attitudes toward Jews, 249–51, 252–62
    Bulgarian Orthodox, 279
    Confessing. *See* Confessing Churches
    early Christian, 41
    Evangelical, 337, 426 n.32, 443 n.34
        Church of the Old Prussian Union
            (Brown Synod), 256
        Evangelical Reich, 253
        German, 60, 64, 255–62, 265–72, 426
            n.30
        as "persecuted victims," 425 n.18
        *See also Bekennende Kirche*
    Greek Orthodox, 280
    Lutheran, 254, 256, 387 n.30
        Danish, 279
        Norwegian, 280
        in North America, 60
        German, 65, 387 n.32, 434 n.175
        and nationalism, 252
    Polish, 110
    Protestant
        American, 424 n.3
        reaction to Hitler, 12
    Reformed, 256
        Dutch, 279
    Roman Catholic, 75, 279, 265–77, 278,
        280, 289, 386 n.1, 434 n.187
        depolitization of, 269–70
        *See also* papacy; Vatican

Romanian Orthodox, 280
    silence of, 250
    and state, 256, 259, 263
    in the United States, 251
    as victims of Social Nationalism, 254
*Churches and Politics in Germany, The,* 426
    n.30
Churchill, Ward, 384 n.31
Churchill, Winston
    *The World Crisis,* 393 n.12
*Church's Confession under Hitler, The,* 426 n.30
citizenship, 64, 68, 128
*City of God, The,* 53
civilization, x, 247, 369, 371
civil
    liberties, 67
    service, German, 256, 361
*Civilization and Its Discontents,* 2, 22, 380 n.2
civilizations, clash of, 351, 377
*Civiltà Cattolica, La,* 90, 251, 267–68, 390
    n.38
*Claims of Memory, The,* 398, 437 n.25
Clay, Lucius B., 288
*Cleansing the Fatherland,* 402 n.39
Clemenceau, Georges, 93
Clendinnen, Inga
    *Reading the Holocaust,* 439 n.61
Clermont-Tonnerre, Stanislas de, 68
Clinton, Bill, 301
clothing, distinctive, 54, 66, 250, 306, 307
Cochrane, Arthur C.
    *The Church's Confession under Hitler,* 426
        n.30
cognitive dissonance. *See* dissonance, cognitive
Cohn, Norman
    *Warrant for Genocide,* 387 n.25
Cohn-Sherbok, Dan
    *Holocaust Theology,* 379 n.1
Cold War, 287, 365
collaboration, 86, 91, 92, 280, 294, 419 n.35
*Collaboration in the Holocaust,* 408 n.31, 410
    n.45
colonization, 392 n.8
"commanding Voice," 348, 349–50
commandments, 353, 445 n.69
    614th, 348–50
*Commentary,* 340, 342
commerce, Jewish role in, 40, 54
Commission for Religious Relations with the
    Jews, 434 n.187
Committee of Union and Progress (CUP),
    18–19
communism, 267–68, 272, 276
    Jews as agents of, 410 n.42
Communist Red Front Fighters' League, 1
Communists, 170, 220
community of suffering, 104
competition
    economic, 113–14

*Composers of the Nazi Era,* 436 n.13
*Complete Black Book of Russian Jewry, The,* 410
    n.53
compliance, 12, 28, 221, 222, 226, 228–29
concentration camps
    *See* camps: concentration
    *See also individual place names*
Confessing Churches (*Bekennende Kirche*), 251,
    259–61, 338, 423 n.1
*Conquerors: Roosevelt, Truman, and the Destruc-
    tion of Hitler's Germany, The,* 433 n.167
conscription, military, 127
*Conspiracy* (film), 294
conspiracy theory, 11, 87–89, 125, 136, 267,
    345
    of silence, 145
Constantine, 50
*Constantine's Sword,* 49, 386 nn.1, 3, 9, 388
    nn.35–37, 389 nn.22, 23, 390 n.47
*Consuming Fire, A,* 441 n.111
*Contesting Sacrifice,* 389 n.23
*Contract of Mutual Indifference, The,* 423 n.92
conversion of Jews. *See* Christianity: conversion
    to
Conway, John S.
    *The Nazi Persecution of the Churches,
    1933–45,* 387 n.31, 425 n.18
"Copies Workshop," 299
Cornwell, John
    *Hitler's Pope,* 249
corporations, 356
    Allianz, 245
    Bayer, 245
    BMW, 245
    I.G. Farben, 204
    Krupp, 245
    Mitteldeutsche Stahlwerke, 365
    pharmaceutical, 358
    Saurer, 447 n.3
    Siemens, 245
    Topf und Söhne, 371
    Volkswagen, 245
corpse disposal, 196–97, 201
    by open air burning, 205
    *See also* crematoria
Costa-Garvas, Constantin, 423 n.1
Costanza, Mary S.
    *The Living Witness,* 438 n.30
Council of Jewish Elders. *See Judenräte*
Council of Lateran. *See* Lateran Council
Counter-Reformation, 65
*Courage to Care, The,* 434 n.173
*Courage under Siege,* 417 n.20
*Course of Modern Jewish History, The,* 390 n.2
covenant, 28–29, 330, 335–48, 352–53, 385
    n.9
Cracow, 148, 149, 165, 226, 232
    liberation of, 208

cremation, 152
crematoria, 157, 181, 205, 207, 233, 299,
    371–72, 450 n.47
*Cries in the Night,* 420 n.45
crime(s)
    against humanity, 245, 363–64
    war. *See* war: crime trials
Crimea, 174, 178
*Crime and Punishment of I. G. Farben, The,*
    446 n.1, 449 n.29
*Crisis and Covenant,* 439 n.60
*Critical Kitaj,* 437 n.18
Croatia, 272, 287
*Croix, La,* 81, 83, 85, 90
Crossan, John Dominic
    *Who Killed Jesus?,* 384 n.7
Crowe, David M.
    *A History of the Gypsies of Eastern Europe and
    Russia,* 415 n.72
*Crucifixion of the Jews, The,* 382 n.15
crusades, 54
Cuba, 141, 399 n.44
*Cum Nimis Absurdum,* 66
*Cunning of History, The,* 369, 373, 382 n.18,
    383 n.22
*Cup of Tears, A,* 418 n.25
Czech, Danuta, 237–38, 414 n.60
Czechoslovakia, 129–30, 147
Czerniakow, Adam, 225, 418 n.25
    *The Warsaw Diary of Adam Czerniakow,* 418
    n.25

Dachau, 116, 132, 135, 195, 208, 261, 315,
    399 n.38
Daladier, Édouard, 129–30
Daluege, Kurt, 146
*Daniel Libeskind: Jewish Museum in Berlin,* 438
    n.47
Dannatt, Adrian
    *United States Holocaust Memorial Museum,*
    438 n.40
Danzig, 161
*dar-al-harb,* 347
*dar-al-Islam,* 347
*dar-al-sulh,* 445 n.65
Darcissac, Roger, 285
*Dark Continent,* 7
*Darkness We Carry, The,* 439 n.60
*Dark Soliloquy,* 51
Darmstadt, 60, 338
Darwin, Charles, 152
Darwinists, social, 152, 153, 403 n.45
David, King, 29
*David Olère,* 438 n.29
Davidson, Eugene
    *The Trial of the Germans,* 448 n.27
Davidson, John
    *Haig,* 393 n.12

Davies, W. D.
  *The Setting of the Sermon on the Mount,* 385
    n.17
Davis, Stephen T., ed.
  *Encountering Evil,* 442 n.6
Dawidowicz, Lucy, 382 n.20
  *A Holocaust Reader,* 397 n.1
  *The War Against the Jews,* 7, 396 n.46
Dean, Martin
  *Collaboration in the Holocaust,* 408 n.31, 410
    n.45
*Death by Government,* 391 n.8
death marches. *See* forced marches
*Death of God Movement and the Holocaust, The,*
    444 n.51
"Death's Head," Order of the, 134–35
death-with-life, 311, 313
  squadrons. *See* Einsatzgruppen
  with dignity, 230
"Declaration of the Evangelical Lutheran
    Church in America to the Jewish Com-
    munity," 387 n.20
defenseless people, 2–3, 13, 22, 39, 127, 210,
    213, 234, 358, 376
defense mechanisms, 367, 449 n.35
*Degesch (Deutsche Gesellschaft für Schädlings-
    bekämpfung),* 206
deicide, 250, 269, 270
Deist, Wilhelm, ed.
  *The Build-Up of German Military Aggression,*
    407 n.8
  *The German Military in the Second World
    War,* 407 n.8
Delarbre, Leon, 299
Delbo, Charlotte, ix, 8, 242, 305, 420 n.45
  *Ancun de nous ne reviendra* (None of us will
    return), 310–11
  *Auschwitz et après* (Auschwitz and after),
    310–14, 379 n.2, 420 n.45
  *Le mémoire et les jours* (Days and memory), 310
  *Mesure de nos jours* (The measure of our
    days), 310, 313
  *Une connaissance inutile* (Useless knowledge),
    310, 312
demographic engineering, 150
Denange, Edgar, 84
Denmark, 279
*Denying the Holocaust,* 396 n.45
*Departing from Egypt,* 436 n.15
deportation, 150–51, 185, 399 n.38
  not secret, 276, 412 n.34
  statistics of, 399 n.50
depression, 139, 282
*Deputy, The. See Stellvertreter, Der*
Derfler, Leslie
  *The Dreyfus Affair,* 389 n.23
despair, 17, 321, 323, 341, 349, 444 n.46
  not yield to, 320, 348

Des Pres, Terrence, 415–16 n.80
  *The Survivor: An Anatomy of Life in the
    Death Camps,* 415 n.80
destruction, creative, 336
*Destruction of the European Jews, The,* 6, 145,
    381 n.6, 382 n.17, 401 n.7, 402 n.32,
    406 n.98, 407 n.4, 408 nn.16, 18, 408
    n.32, 410 nn.45–46, 412 n.34
*Destruction of the Jewish Community in Jed-
    wabne, Poland, The,* 395 n.37
*Deutsche Arbeitspartei* (DAP). *See* German
    Worker's Party
*Deutsche Bank and the Nazi Economic War
    Against the Jews, The,* 447 n.5
*Deutsche Christen,* 254, 255–59
*Deutschenhochschulring,* 123
*Deutsche Reichsbahn. See* railroads *(Deutsche
    Reichsbahn)*
*Deutsche Reich und der Zweite Weltkrieg, Das,*
    407 n.9
*deutschfeindlich,* 148
*Deuxièma Bureau,* 88, 90
devil, 40, 45, 88
  Jews identified with, 40, 46, 52, 61, 63, 64,
    246, 278–79
diaries, 142, 225, 304–9, 392 n.11, 400 n.60,
    439 n.58
*Diary of a Young Girl,* 380 n.4
Diaspora, 345, 351
Dibelius, Otto, 63, 255, 387 n.31
Dieckmann, Christoph, 176, 183, 409 n.38,
    411 n.58
*Dietrich Bonhoeffer,* 428 n.68
*Different Drummers,* 436 n.13
*Different Trains,* 296
*Different Voices,* 420 nn.41, 45, 421 n.47
dignity, 363, 374
Dimsdale, Joel E., ed.
  *Survivors, Victims, and Perpetrators,* 397 n.18
disconfirming evidence, 44
discrimination, 65, 124, 129, 140, 279
disease, 151, 153, 157, 163, 165–66, 178, 202,
    223, 311, 316
  typhus, 166, 314
disjunction, 311
dispensationalists, premillennial, 342, 354
dissonance, 51, 53
  cognitive, 44–45, 385 n.21
  reduction, 63, 329
divine-human relationship, 328
Divine Presence, 350
Dobroszycki, Lucjan, ed.
  *The Chronicle of the Lodz Ghetto,
    1941–1944,* 418 nn.30–31
doctors, 356–59, 370, 406 n.98, 447 nn.6–9
  Jewish, 129, 358, 395 n.44
*Doctors of Infamy,* 447 n.6
*Doctors Under Hitler,* 395 n.44, 403 n.39

Dohnanyi, Hans von, 264–65, 428 n.81
*Dolchstoss. See* "stab in the back"
Dollfuss, Engelbert, 136
domination, 5, 12, 15, 30, 34, 108, 127, 228, 234, 242, 267, 316, 358
Donat, Alexander, 225
Doneson, Judith E., 293
  *The Holocaust in American Film,* 435 n.8, 436 n.9
Dora, 379 n.4
Dörr, Alois, 209–10
*Double Bond: Primo Levi, The,* 435 n.1
*Double Dying, A,* 439 n.60
Drancy, 285
Dresden, xi, 306–7, 308–9, 392 n.11, 433 n.167
Drexler, Anton, 105
Dreyfus
  affair, 72, 84–93, 389 n.23
  Alfred, 72, 83–87
  family, 390 n.47
  Lucie, 86
  Mathieu, 86, 87, 89, 93
*Dreyfus,* 389 n.23, 390 n.47
*Dreyfus Affair, The,* 389 n.23
*Dreyfus Case,* 389 n.23, 390 nn.31, 37
Drobisch, Klaus
  *Juden unterm Hakenkreuz,* 398 n.27
*Drowned and the Saved, The,* 295
Drumont, Édouard, 81, 83, 90, 92
  *La France Juive,* 81
  *La Libre Parole,* 92
dualism rejected, 328
DuBois, Josiah E. Jr.
Dudach, Georges, 310
Dumbach, Annette E. and Jud Newborn
  *Shattering the German Night,* 433 n.170
Dürrfeld, Walter, 364
Dutlinger, Anne D., ed.
  *Art, Music, and Education as Strategies for Survival,* 437 n.27
Dwork, Debórah
  *Children with a Star,* 420 n.44
Dwork, Debórah and Robert Jan van Pelt, 134, 205, 383 n.20
  *Auschwitz: 1270 to the Present,* 383 n.21, 414 nn.60–61, 416 n.80, 450 n.47
  *Holocaust: A History,* 7, 399 n.40, 411 n.6, 413 n.38

*Eastern Front, The, 1941–45,* 408 n.32
Ebensee, 299
Eberl, Irmfried, 157, 200
ecclesiastical records. *See* records: ecclesiastical
Eckardt, Alice and A. Roy, 7, 332
*Eclipse of God,* 341, 444 nn.40–41
*Economic Origins of Antisemitism,* 386 n.6
economics
  capitalist, 98

cost-effective, 14
  medieval, 54–55
  modern, 69, 73
  *See also* commerce
education in Germany, 448 nn.11–13
educators. *See* teachers; university professors
Edwards, Mark U.
  *Luther's Last Battles,* 386 n.9
efficiency calculations, 447 n.3
Ehrenburg, Ilya and Vasily Grossman
  *The Complete Black Book of Russian Jewry,* 410 n.53
Eichmann, Adolf, ix, 130, 135–37, 150, 151, 187, 190, 276, 399 n.46, 402 n.32, 405 n.88
  death, 419 n.38
  escape of, 287
  notes, 401 n.14
  trial, 131, 145, 191, 192, 338, 416 n.7, 427 n.64, 447 n.3
*Eichmann in Jerusalem,* 218, 406 n.92, 416 n.7
*Eichmann Interrogated,* 399 n.45
Eicke, Theodor, 116, 135
*Einsatzgruppen,* 12, 147–49, 170, 173–75, 178, 197, 207, 230, 283, 365, 402 n.32, 419 n.37
Einstein, Albert, 282, 360
Eisen, George
  *Children and Play in the Holocaust,* 420 n.44
Eishyshok, 302, 438 n.44
Eizenstat, Stuart
  *Imperfect Justice,* 423 n.85
Eleazar ben Yair, 39
elect, Jews as. *See* Jews: as chosen people
election, 335–48
  Christian inheritance of, 353
Eliach, Yaffa
  *Hasidic Tales of the Holocaust,* 439 n.59
  *There Once Was a World,* 438 n.44
*Elie Wiesel: Between Memory and Hope,* 441 n.112
*Elie Wiesel: Messenger to All Humanity,* 441 n.112
*Elie Wiesel's Night,* 441 n.112
Eliot, Gil
  *The Twentieth-Century Book of the Dead,* 391 n.8, 392 n.9
Elkes, Elchanan, 418 n.27
Elkes, Joel
  *Values, Belief, and Survival,* 418 n.27
Ellis, Marc H.
  *Ending Auschwitz,* 444 n.55
emancipation. *See* Jewish: emancipation
emigration
  figures, 398 n.20
  forced, 382 n.20
  *See also* Jewish: emigration
Enabling Act, 111, 125
*Encountering Evil,* 442 n.6

*Encyclopedia of Holocaust Literature,* 439 n.60
*Ending Auschwitz,* 444 n.55
*Endlösung, Die. See* Final Solution
end-timers, 342, 346, 354
*Enduring Covenant, The,* 386 n.3
enemies, 347
engineers, 360
Enlightenment, 10, 66–67, 73–74, 388 n.41
*Entfernung,* 114, 121
epidemics, 205–6, 394 n.24, 406 n.98
equality. *See* human equality
Erasmus, 55
Ericksen, Robert P., 257
 *Theologians under Hitler,* 387 n.31, 425 n.22
Ericksen, Robert P. and Susannah Heschel, eds.
 *Betrayal: German Churches and the Holocaust,*
 387 n.32, 397 n.7
*Erntefest* (Harvest Festival). *See* mass murder:
 *Erntefest*
Esterhazy, Ferdinand Walsin-, 86, 88, 89, 90,
 390 n.31
Estonia, 149, 191–92
ethics, post-Holocaust, 355–56, 365–77, 450
 n.49
*Ethics after the Holocaust,* 450 n.48
ethnic
 cleansing, 15, 54, 150, 399 n.49, 403 n.41
  of Poland, 148, 408 n.31
eugenics movement, 150, 153, 392 n.8
euphemisms, 366
euthanasia program ("mercy killings"), 152,
 154–58, 181, 402 n.39, 403 nn.40–41,
 423 n.1
 cost-benefit analyses, 404 n.58
 front organizations, 404 n.55
 linked to Final Solution, 156, 198, 413 n.45
 protests against, 157–58
 replaced sterilization, 403–4 n.52
Evian conference, 139–40, 400 nn.54–55
evil
 overcoming, 328
 problem of, 348
 radical, 327, 345, 442 n.4
 resistance to, 284
*Evil in Modern Thought,* 442 n.4
exclusivism, 64
excremental assault, 209, 415 n.80
excuses, 365
exile and return, 345
existentialism, 343
Exodus, 26–29, 34
*Experience and Expression,* 420 nn.41, 45
experiments
 extermination, 186
 human. *See* human experiments
*Explaining Hitler,* 391 n.4
expulsion
 from England, 54
 from France, 54

from Poland, 148
from Saxony, 62
from Spain, 54
extermination, 272–73, 281, 328, 392 n.11
 marches. *See* forced marches
 policy, 397 n.4
 state-sponsored, 64, 69
 war of. *See Vernichtung*
Ezergalis, Andrew, 410 n.44
 *The Holocaust in Latvia,* 410 nn.44, 49
Ezrahi, Sidra Dekoven
 *By Words Alone,* 439 n.60

*Face of God after Auschwitz, The,* 335
Fackenheim, Emil, 7, 17, 328, 348–52,
 445–46 n.69
 *God's Presence in History,* 382 n.16, 446
  n.69, 446 n.80
 *The Jewish Return into History,* 446 n.69
 *Tikkun,* 350–52
 *To Mend the World,* 350, 427 n.62
Falkenhayn, Erik von, 101, 392 n.10
Falk, Harvey
 *Jesus the Pharisee,* 384 n.8
*Fall of Jerusalem and the Christian Church, The,*
 385 nn.17, 19
Farben, I.G. *See* corporations: I.G. Farben
fascism, 11
*Fathers According to Rabbi Nathan, The,* 385
 n.14
Faulhaber, Michael Cardinal von
*Faustian Bargain, The,* 398 n.34, 423 n.85
*Fear and Trembling,* 444 n.48
*Fearful Months,* 395 n.45
Fedier, Francois, 329
Fein, Helen, 19, 423 n.86
 *Accounting for Genocide,* 383 n.26, 384
  nn.33, 36, 423 n.86
Feingold, Henry L.
 *Bearing Witness,* 400 nn.54–55
 *The Politics of Rescue,* 400 n.54
Feinstein, Stephen C.
 *Absence/Presence,* 298, 437 n.21
 *Witness and Legacy,* 298, 437 n.21
Felstiner, Mary Lowenthal, 298
Fenelon, Fania
 *Playing for Time,* 296
Fensch, Thomas, ed.
 *Oskar Schindler and His List,* 436 n.9
Ferdinand and Isabella, 46, 65
Ferencz, Benjamin B., 449 n.35
 *Less Than Slaves,* 446 n.1, 449 n.35
Festinger, Leon, 385 n.21
Fest, Joachim
 *Hitler,* 391 n.4, 393 n.23
Fest, Joachim C., 391 n.4
feudalism, 336
 *See also* economics: feudal
*Figaro, La,* 87

film. *See* Holocaust: film
Final Solution ("*Die Endlösung*"), 3–8, 15, 47,
    114, 136, 137, 144, 183, 199, 276, 370,
    382 n.20, 408 n.29
  ended by defeat, 372
  evolved, 187
  as first phase, 150
  Hitler's role in, 175, 194, 212, 382 n.20,
    396 n.45
  as just deserts, 212
  leaders in, 157, 235
  and moral norms, 373
  as "new solution," 191
  not documented, 114
  numbers targeted, 146
  plan solicited, 188
  as problem-solving, 288
  statistics of, 213
  suppression of truth about, 381 n.12
  "territorial," 163, 165
*"Final Solution"*, 383 n.21, 399 n.49, 52, 402
    nn.29, 37, 404 n.69, 405 nn.76, 83
*Final Solution and the German Foreign Office,*
    *The,* 405 n.86, 448 n.16
*fin du voyage, La,* 436 n.15
Fink, Ida, 8
*First Day on the Somme, The,* 393 n.12
Fischer, Eugen, 391 n.8
Fischer, Klaus
    *Nazi Germany,* 397 n.51
Fischer, Ruth
    *Stalin and German Communism,* 424 n.7
Fleischner, Eva, 332
Fleming, Gerald, 371–72, 382 n.20, 450 n.46
    *Hitler and the Final Solution,* 391 n.4, 401
    n.10, 410 n.48
Flick, Friedrich, 364–65, 367
Flossenbürg, 209, 262
*Focusing on the Holocaust and Its Aftermath,* 414
    n.48
food allocations, 165, 183
    *See also* starvation
forced
    labor, 202, 203, 205, 209, 235, 244, 355,
    370, 421 n.53, 446 n.1
    marches, 208–11, 299
Ford, Henry, 62, 387 n.26
*Forgotten Holocaust, The,* 394 n.36
*For the Soul of the People,* 397 n.7, 426 n.31
Fortunoff Video Archive for Holocaust Testi-
    monies, 241
Fourier, Charles, 76–77, 389 n.12
*Fourteen Stations,* 297
Fox, Frank, 369
*Frailty of Goodness, The,* 432 n.159
France, 280, 392 n.10
    *See also* antisemitism: French; Jews: French
*France and the Dreyfus Affair,* 389 n.23, 390
    n.47

*France Juive, La,* 81
Frank, Anne, 2, 22, 309
    *Diary of a Young Girl,* 380 n.4
Frankfurt, 188
Frank, Hans, 149, 160, 165, 189
Fredrickson, George M.
    *Racism,* 388 n.35
Freed, James Ingo, 301–2, 438 n.39
freedom, 333
    and bread campaign, 110
    burden of, 335
Freemasons, 80, 87, 91, 136
*Freigabe der Vernichtung Lebensunwerten Lebens,*
    *Die,* 403 n.48
*Freikorps,* 401 n.17
Freisler, Roland, 190
French
    Republic, Third, 78, 85
    Revolution, 68, 72, 73, 76, 80, 82, 250
    of 1789, 91
*French Enlightenment and the Jews, The,* 389
    nn.8–9
*Fresh Wounds,* 417 n.10
Freud, Sigmund, 2, 5
    *Civilization and Its Discontents,* 2, 22, 380
    n.2
    *The Future of an Illusion,* 4, 381 n.11
Friedenthal, Charlotte, 428 n.81
Friedlander, Henry, 403 nn.40, 52, 437 n.27
    *The Origins of Nazi Genocide,* 392 n.8, 394
    n.30, 402 n.39, 403 n.40, 404 nn.52–54,
    58, 63, 67, 415 n.72
Friedländer, Saul, 107, 298, 398 n.20
    *Kurt Gerstein: The Ambiguity of Good,* 424
    n.1
    *Nazi Germany and the Jews,* 7, 397 n.3, 398
    nn.20, 32, 399 nn.35–37, 46, 400 n.56
    *Probing the Limits of Representation,* 437
    n.24
    *When Memory Comes,* 437 n.24
Friedman, Carl, 377
    *Nightfather,* 8, 377
Fritta. *See* Taussign, Fritz
Fritzsche, Hans, 364
*From Politics to Piety,* 385 n.11
*From Prejudice to Destruction,* 388 n.41, 389
    nn.6, 8, 12
*From the Kingdom of Memory,* 414 n.59
*Front National, Le,* 72
Führer order (*Führerbefehl*), 186
Fukuyama, Francis, 445 n.57
Fulda Bishops Conference, 266
*Future of an Illusion, The,* 4, 381 n.11

Gager, John, 385 n.9
    *The Origins of Anti-Semitism,* 386 n.4
    *Reinventing Paul,* 385 n.9
Galen, Clemens August Graf von, 157, 288,
    404 n.64, 434 n.184

Galle, Arie
  *Fourteen Stations,* 297
*Galut,* 246
Gancwajch, Abraham, 419 n.35
Gardelegen, 211, 416 n.88
Gargzdai, 176
Garibaldi, Giuseppe, 82
gas
  chambers, 181, 202, 207, 396 n.45, 421
    n.53, 450 n.47
  chlorine (mustard gas), 102
Gaspari, Pietro, 266
gassing, 152, 156, 197, 370
  mobile/portable units, 159, 172, 179, 181,
    196, 371, 401 n.15
  *See also* Chelmno: gas vans
Gaston, Lloyd, 385 n.9
*Geheime Staatspolizei. See* Gestapo
Gellately, Robert, 115, 135, 212
  *Backing Hitler,* 6, 97, 392 n.11, 396
    nn.49–50, 399 n.45
Gellately, Robert and Nathan Stoltzfus
  *Social Outsiders in Nazi Germany,* 381 n.7,
    412 n.34, 421 n.47
*Gemeinnützige Stiftung für Heil und Anstalt-*
  *spflege,* 404 n.55
Gemlich, Adolf, 121, 397 n.1
General Government. *See* Poland: General
  Government
Genesis, 25–29
*From Genesis to Genocide,* 403 nn.44, 49–51
Geneva Convention, 144
genocide(s), 15, 17, 146, 324, 357, 383 n.23,
    392 n.8, 399 n.49, 403 n.41, 408 n.29
  active core, 123
  Armenian, 18–19, 20–21, 327, 344, 384
    n.35, 444 n.54
  Bosnian, 383 n.23
  Cambodian, 17, 383 n.23
  definition of, 16, 423 n.86
  government sponsored, 19
  Gypsy, 207
  Namibia, 391 n.8
  national, 19
  perpetrators, 410 n.51
  post-Holocaust, 17, 383 n.23, 442 n.1
  prevention of, 367
  Rwanda, 327, 383 n.23, 442 n.1
  Southwest Africa, 391 n.8
  types of, 16–17
*Genocide and the Modern Age,* 442 n.1
Gens, Jacob, 219
Gentiles, 228
Geras, Norman
  *The Contract of Mutual Indifference,* 423 n.92
Gerhard, Wolfgang, 357
Gerlach, Christian, 6, 188–89, 190, 193–94,
    212, 408 n.28, 411 n.14, 412–13 n.37
Gerlach, Wolfgang, 253, 256

*And the Witnesses Were Silent,* 425 n.14, 426
  n.34
*German Army and Genocide, The,* 402 n.25,
    407 nn.9–11
"German Army and Genocide" (exhibit), 169,
    171
*German Big Business and the Rise of Hitler,* 447 n.5
German Christians. *See Deutsche Christen*
*German Churches under Hitler, The,* 426 n.30
*German Dictatorship, The,* 391 n.4
German East Africa. *See* Africa: German East
*German Military in the Second World War, The,*
    407 n.8
*German Slump, The,* 395 n. 38
German-Soviet pact. *See* Soviet-German pact
*German Church Struggle and the Holocaust, The,*
    394 n.28, 427 n.56
German Workers' Party, 1, 105
Germany
  as *Altreich,* 398 n.20
  unification (1871), 112
Gerstein, Kurt, 423–24 n.1
*Gesamtlösung,* 136
*Gesellschaftskrise und Judenfeindschaft in*
  *Deutschland,* 397 n.7
Gestapo, 116, 124, 131, 132, 135, 146, 174,
    264–65, 412 n.34
  spies for, 419 n.35
Getter, Matylda, 278
ghettoization, 12, 161, 165, 178, 223–25, 268
ghettos, 95, 402 n.32, 405 n.81
  administration (internal), 218, 417 nn.23, 27
  Bialystok, 299
  "clearing," 178
  *Eishyshok,* 438 n.44
  epidemics in, 164
  establishment of, 66, 150
  Kovno, 176, 330, 412 n.37, 418 n.27
  Lodz, xi, 161–63, 196, 223, 228, 232, 405
    nn.81, 85, 412 n.37, 418 n.30
  Minsk, 412 n.37
  Otwock, 369
  Piotrkow Tribunalski, 405 n.81
  police. *See* Order Police
  'Reich,' 150
  Riga, 307, 412 n.37
  Terezin, 296, 438 n.33
  Theresienstadt, 223, 299, 437 n.27
  Vilna, 217–19, 223, 232, 284, 300, 416 n.1,
    416 n.4
  Warsaw, 201, 202, 223, 224, 225, 232–33,
    295, 303, 406 nn.98–99, 417 n.20,
    419 n.35
  children in, 420 n.44
  history, 417 n.19
  testimonies from, 418 n.25
  uprisings, 232, 416 n.4, 418 n.25, 420
    n.41
  women in. *See* women

Gilbert, Martin
  *The Holocaust: A History of the Jews of
    Europe,* 7
  *The Righteous,* 434 n.173
Gilbert, Martin and Richard Gott
  *The Appeasers,* 398 n.22
Giles, Geoffrey J.
  *Students and National Socialism in Germany,*
    448 n.13
Glazar, Richard, 201, 414 n.54
  *Trap with a Green Fence,* 414 n.54
Globocnik, Odilo, 197, 198–99, 202
Glover, Jonathan, 383 n.30
  *Humanity: A Moral History of the Twentieth
    Century,* 7, 384 n.30, 391 n.8, 393 n.17
  *Never Again: A History of the Holocaust,* 7
Glücks, Richard, 135
Gnesen, 159
God
  action in history, 21, 42, 327, 332, 334,
    337–39, 345, 347–48, 353
  authority of, 76
  author of Holocaust, 339
  biblical/rabbinic image of, 343, 346, 349,
    352
  and catastrophic events, 320
  covenant with. *See* covenant
  and creation, 324
  cruelty of, 341
  death of, 14, 444 n.51
  as defendant, 322
  denial of, 348
  election. *See* election; Jews: as Chosen People
  as empty space, 301
  existence of, 13, 334, 344, 376
  freedom of, 334
  goodness, 334
  Jewish concept of, 329
  justice of, 20, 328, 342
  kingdom of, 348
  love of, 334
  omnipotence/power, 327, 328, 334, 342
  permitted Holocaust, 320
  plan of, 330
  power for salvation, 443 n.38
  providence of, 347
  punishment of, 20, 42, 253, 263, 330–31,
    338, 340
  rejection of Jews, 44, 60, 384 n.9
  silence of, 14, 322, 333
  suffering of, 333
  will of, 252
*(God) after Auschwitz,* 443 n.37, 444 nn.45, 49
Godfrey, William, 274
*God's Presence in History,* 382 n.16, 446 n.69,
  446 n.80
*God, the Holocaust, and the Children of Israel,*
  441 n.111
Goebbels, Joseph, 1–2, 107, 189, 257, 361

  diary of, 8, 142, 400 n.60
  speech of, 132, 412 n.34
*Goebbels Diaries 1942–43, The,* 400 n.60
Goldenberg, Myrna, 235, 420 n.45
Goldhagen, Daniel Jonah, 71, 107, 208–9,
  211, 254, 289–90, 382 n.20, 392 n.11
  *Hitler's Willing Executioners,* 6, 181, 388 n.2,
    392 n.11, 394 n.32, 408 n.35
  *A Moral Reckoning,* 424 n.3
Goldin, Judah, ed.
  *The Fathers According to Rabbi Nathan,* 385
    n.14
Goldschmidt, Dietrich and Hans-Joachim
  Kraus, eds.
  *Der Ungekündigte Bund,* 387 n.19
Goldsmith, Martin
  *The Inextinguishable Symphony,* 436 n.13
Gollwitzer, Helmut, 252–53
good and evil, 347, 450 n.49
Goodell, Stephen, ed.
  *In Pursuit of Justice,* 448 n.27
*"Good News" after Auschwitz?,* 434 n.187
*Good Old Days, The,* 402 n.25, 408 n.35, 409
  n.41
Good Samaritan. *See* Jesus: parables: Good
  Samaritan
Gordon, Sarah, 108
  *Hitler, Germans, and the "Jewish Question,"*
    391 n.4, 394 n.34
Gorecki, Henryk
  *Third Symphony,* 296
Göring, Hermann, 105, 107, 133, 135, 136,
  149, 173, 187, 364, 391 n.8, 411 n.8
  condemned, 101, 363
gospels. *See* New Testament: Gospels
Gottlieb, Roger S., ed.
  *Thinking the Unthinkable,* 420 n.45
Gougenot des Mousseaux, Henri. *See*
  Mousseau
Graebe, Hermann Friedrich, 230, 419 n.37
Graf, Willi, 283
Grafeneck, 156
Graham, Robert, 287
"gray zone," 315
*Great Powers and Poland 1919–1945, The,* 394
  n.36
Greco-Roman world, 9, 29–33, 74
Greenberg, Clement, 301
Greenberg, Irving, 442 n.11
  working principle of, 446 n.70
Greenberg, Yitzhak, 330
Greene, Joshua M. and Shiva Kumar, eds.
  *Witness: Voices from the Holocaust,* 417 n.10
Greenspan, Henry
  *On Listening to Holocaust Survivors,*
    417 n.10
Gregory of Nyssa, 52
Greiser, Arthur, 196
*Grey Zone, The,* 295

Griech-Polelle, Beth A.
  *Bishop von Galen,* 404 n.64
Gross, John T.
  *The Destruction of the Jewish Community in
    Jedwabne, Poland,* 395 n.37
Gross-Rosen, 208–9
Ground of Being, 347
Grüber, Heinrich, 261, 337–40, 427 nn.63–64
"Grüber office," 261, 427 n.63, 443 n.32
Grünberg, 209
Grunberger, Richard
  *Red Rising in Bavaria,* 424 n.7
  *The 12-Year Reich,* 447 nn.6, 10, 448 n.11
Grundmann, Walter, 257, 426 n.38
Grynbert, Michal, ed.
  *Words to Outlive Us,* 439 n.58
Grynzpan, Herschel, 132
guilt, 247
*Guilt of Nations, The,* 423 n.85
Gurewitsch, Brana, ed.
  *Mothers, Sisters, Resisters,* 420 n.45
Gurs, 163, 405 n.90, 428 n.81
Gushee, David P.
  *The Righteous Gentiles of the Holocaust,* 450
    n.45
Gush Emunim (Bloc of the Faithful), 332
Gutman, Yisrael
  *Encyclopedia of the Holocaust,* 381 n.6
  *The Jews of Warsaw, 1939–1943,* 417 n.19
Gutman, Yisrael and Michael Berenbaum, eds.
  *Anatomy of the Auschwitz Death Camp,* 414
    n.60, 450 n.47
Gutman, Yisrael and Shmuel Krakowski
  *Poles and Jews between the Wars,* 394 n.36
Gutteridge, Richard
  *Open Thy Mouth for the Dumb,* 426 n.30
Gypsies, 3, 170–71, 195, 196, 206–7, 381 n.7,
    405 n.83, 408 n.14, 415 nn.63, 71–72,
    447 n.8
*Gypsies under the Swastika,* 415 n.72

Haas, Leo, 300, 438 n.33
Haas, Pavel, 296
Haas, Peter, 160
  *Morality after Auschwitz,* 405 n.74, 450 n.48
Haavara Agreements, 140, 141, 400 n.57
Hadamar, 156
Haeckel, Ernst, 154
  *Die Lebenswunder,* 403 n.47
Hafner, Sebastian
  *The Meaning of Hitler,* 391 n.4
Hagi, Douglas, 102–3, 393 n.12
  *Captain Dreyfus,* 389 nn.23–24, 390
    nn.26–27, 38
*Haig,* 393 n.12
Haig, Douglas, 101–2, 393 nn.12, 16
Halder, Franz, 406 n.1, 406 n.1
Halevi, Yehuda, 351
Hall III, Sidney G., 385 n.9

*Christian Anti-Semitism and Paul's Theology,*
    385 n.9
Hallie, Philip P.
  *Lest Innocent Blood Be Shed,* 434 n.174
Halter, Roman, xi, 379 n,4
  *The Last Journey,* xi
Hamann, Brigitte
  *Hitler's Vienna,* 391 n.4
Hamas, 445 n.58, 446 n.80
handicapped, 3, 152, 196
Handlin, Oscar
  *The Uprooted,* 391 n.6
*Hannah Arendt and the Jewish Question,* 417
    n.7
Hanser, Richard
  *A Noble Treason,* 433 n.170
Hanukkah, 31
Hapsburg Empire, 100
Haran, 26
Harlan, Veit
  *Jud Süss,* 292
Harris, Mark Jonathan and Deborah Oppen-
    heimer
  *Into the Arms of Strangers,* 294, 295
*Harry James Cargas in Conversation with Elie
    Wiesel,* 441 n.111
Hart-Davis, Duff
  *Hitler's Games,* 398 n.21
Hartheim, 156
Hartman, Geoffrey H.
  *The Longest Shadow,* 439 n.61
Harvest Festival. See mass murder: *Erntefest*
*Harvest of Hate,* 404 n.57
*Has God Rejected His People?,* 384 n.8
*Hasidic Tales of the Holocaust,* 439 n.59
Haubtmann, Pierre, ed.
  *Carnet de P. J. Proudhon,* 389 n.14
Hayden, Patrick, ed.
  *The Philosophy of Human Rights,* 448 n.24
Hayes, Peter, 446 n.2
  *Industry and Ideology: I. G. Farben in the
    Nazi Era,* 415 n.68
Haynes, Stephen R., 20, 262, 265, 332
  *Reluctant Witnesses,* 25, 384 n.37, 386 nn. 5,
    9
Haynes Stephen R. and John K. Roth, eds.
  *The Death of God Movement and the Holo-
    caust,* 444 n.51
Hebrews, 26–27
Hebrew Sheltering and Aid Society of America,
    109
Hebrew Union College, 340
Hegel, G. F. W., 328–29, 367, 442 n.4, 445
    n.57
  *Philosophy of Right,* 449 n.36
Heidegger, Martin, 329, 442 n.8
Heidenreich, Richard, 169
*Heim-ins-Reich. See* resettlement
Heim, Susanna, 164

Heinemann, Elizabeth
  "Sexuality and Nazism," 421 n.47
Heller, Celia S.
  On the Edge of Destruction, 394 n.36
Hellig, Jocelyn
  The Holocaust and Antisemitism, 384 n.6
Hellman, Peter
  The Auschwitz Album, 380 n.4, 421 n.59
Hell Was My Home, 401 n.21
Helmbrechts, 209–10
Helmreich, Ernst Christian
  The German Churches under Hitler, 426 n.30
Henry Ford and the Jews, 387 n.26
Henry, Hubert, 83, 87, 91
  faux Henry, 87, 89, 90
Herbert, Ulrich, 6, 123–24, 145, 176, 401 n.8
  Best: Biographische Studien über Radikalis-
    mus, 397 nn.8, 11
  National Socialist Extermination Policies, 397
    n.4, 398 n.30, 399 n.39, 52, 401 n.13407
    n.13, 408 n.28, 409 n.38
Herczl, Moshe Y.
  Christianity and the Holocaust of Hungarian
    Jewry, 424 n.5
Hereros, 391 n.8
Hermanns, William
  The Holocaust: From a Survivor of Verdun,
    392 n.10
Hertzberg, Arthur, 74
  The French Enlightenment and the Jews, 389
    nn.8–9
Herzl, Theodor, 85, 94–95, 97, 390 n.46
Heschel, Abraham Joshua, 340, 341, 443 n.39,
    444 n.46
  Israel: An Echo in Eternity, 341, 444 n.45
  A Passion for Truth, 341, 444 n.44
Heschel, Susannah, 7, 387 n.32, 426 n.38
Hess, Rudolf, 256
Heyde, Werner, 155
Heydrich, Reinhard, 132, 133, 134–35, 136,
    146–47, 150, 151, 161, 164, 187, 189,
    190, 197, 222, 398 n.29, 402 n.32, 405
    nn.79–80, 88, 407 n.4, 408 n.36
Hidden Encyclical of Pius XI, The, 430
    nn.112–13
Hidden History of the Kovno Ghetto, 418 n.27
Hilberg, Raul, x, 9, 127, 137, 144, 198, 201,
    213, 219–20, 221, 294, 362, 365–66,
    381 n.6, 397 n.18
  The Destruction of the European Jews, 6, 145,
    381 n.6, 382 n.17, 401 n.7, 402 n.32,
    406 n.98, 407 n.4, 408 nn.16, 18, 408
    n.32, 410 nn.45–46, 412 n.34
  Perpetrators Victims Bystanders, 420 n.44
  Sources of Holocaust Research, 1, 379 n.3
Hildebrandt, Richard, 171
Hillesum, Etty, 8
Hillgruber, Andreas and Gerhard Hüm-
    melchen

Chronik des Zweiten Weltkrieges, 399–400,
    n.51
Himmler, Heinrich, 107, 116, 133, 135, 146,
    151, 160–61, 167, 175, 181, 182, 195,
    203, 206–7, 236, 383 n.21, 399 n.42,
    401 n.15, 410 n.47
  calendars of, 8
  decree about SS, 414 n.56
  former teacher, 359
  halts transports, 412–13 n.37
  speeches, 421 n.50
Hindenburg, Paul von, 110, 115, 253, 255
Hindenburg, Oskar von, 425 n.16
Hirsch, Emmanuel, 387 n.31
Hirschfeld, Gerhard, ed.
  The Policies of Genocide, 406 n.1, 409 n.38
history, 328, 332
  end of, 445 n.57
  God and. See God: action in history
  Jewish, 345–46
  reason in, 442 n.4, 450 n.49
  used to discredit Jews, 61
History and Memory after Auschwitz, 437 n.20
History and Sociology of Genocide, The, 384
    nn.31, 32, 442 n.1
History of Anti-Semitism, The, 386 nn.4, 7
History of the Gypsies of Eastern Europe and Rus-
    sia, A, 415 n.72
History of the Holocaust, A, 7, 383 n.28, 386
    n.6, 388 nn.42–43, 394 n.25, 418 n.28
Hitler, Adolf, 99–100, 105, 185, 397 n.1
  agent of God, 327, 330, 340
  as anti-Christ, 262
  anti-Jewish tirades, 114, 137, 292, 396 n.47
  assassination attempts on, 265, 410 n.54
  authority of, 382 n.20
  Beer Hall Putsch, 132
  biographies of, 8, 391 n.4
  charismatic mystique of, 292
  concordat with Vatican. See Vatican concor-
    dat with Nazi Germany
  interest in opera, 413 n.38
  Mein Kampf. See Mein Kampf
  paranoia, 185, 190
  political testament of, 212, 400 n.3
  posthumous victories, 348–50, 446 n.69
  racial hierarchy of, 12
  racism, 265, 270
  resistance to. See resistance
  rise to power, 110–12, 116–17, 253
  speeches
    to Düsseldorf Industry Club, 397 n.3
    to Hamburg National Club, 397 n.3
    See also Reichstag: speeches
  strategies, 413 n.38
  suicide, 143, 240
  underlings, 411 n.6, 413 n.38
  victory euphoria, 187, 188
  writing about Jews, 121, 122

young, 295
*Zweites Buch* (*Hitler's Secret Book*), 394 n.29
*Hitler,* 8, 391 n.4, 393 n.23, 397 n.4
*Hitler and Nazi Germany,* 393 n.23
*Hitler and the Final Solution,* 391 n.4, 401 n.10, 410 n.48
*Hitler and the Holocaust,* 7, 389 n.5
*Hitler and the Jews,* 396 n.47
*Hitler: A Study in Tyranny,* 391 n.4, 397 n.51
*Hitler, Germans, and the "Jewish Question,"* 391 n.4, 394 n.34
*Hitler of History, The,* 391 n.4
Hitler-Stalin Non-Aggression Pact. *See* Soviet-German pact
*Hitler's Army,* 407 n.8, 408 nn.21, 23, 408 n.35
*Hitler's Games,* 398 n.21
*Hitler's Pope,* 249
*Hitler's Vienna,* 391 n.4
*Hitler's Weltanschauung,* 391 n.4
*Hitler's Willing Executioners,* 6, 181, 388 n.2, 392 n.11, 394 n.32, 408 n.35
Hittites, 28
Hlond, August, 272
Hobbes, Thomas
  *Leviathan,* 352
Hoche, Alfred, 154
Hochhuth, Rolf
  *Der Stellvertreter* (The deputy), 249, 423 n.1
Hoffman, Robert L.
  *More Than a Trial,* 389 n.23
Höfle, Hermann, 198
Hofman, Otto, 191
Hofstadter, Richard
  *Social Darwinism in American Thought,* 403 n.45
Höhler, Ali, 1
Höhne, Heinz, 134
  *The Order of the Death's Head,* 396 n.51, 399 n.41, 408 n.32
Holland/Netherlands, 226, 309
*Hollow Years, The,* 393 n.22
Holocaust, 381 n.12, 420 n.41
  American responses, 281–82, 432 n.167
  American views of, 435 n.7
  architecture, 298–99, 301–3, 437 n.26, 438 n.40
  art and, 14, 296–303, 436 nn.14–15, 437 nn.16–25, 27, 439 n.56
  Christian response to, 46, 332–35
  consciousness, 344
  continuity with other genocides, x, 240, 442 n.1
  counter-testimony to faith, 350
  defeated love, 312
  as a crime, 13, 288
  definition of, 5, 16, 17
  denials of, 345

  distinctiveness of, 17
  as divine punishment, 60, 261
  documentaries about, 292, 435 nn.7–8
  "epoch-making event," 17, 348
  as a fabrication, 445 n.59
  fiction about, 8, 293, 421 n.49
  films about, 14, 292–93, 295, 435 nn.7–8
    documentary, 294, 436 n.9
    military, 292
    music in, 295, 436 n.13
    original role, 292
  functionalists, 382 n.20
  historiography of, 382–83 n.20
  and human memory, 323
  as human failure, 368
  humanity as victim of, 217
  as indispensable, 332
  as inexplicable, 321
  intentionalists, 382 n.20
  interpretations of, 6–8, 9–14
  as intervention of God, 335–36
  Jewish downgrading of, 444 n.55
  literature of, 14, 292–93, 303–24, 435 n.4, 439 n.60
    novels. *See* Holocaust: fiction
  memorials to, 301, 379 n.4
    *See also individual names and places*
  metaphors inadequate for, 304
  mocking life, 317
  moral significance of, 293
  music and, 436 n.13
  oral testimonies. *See* oral histories
  perpetrators, 380 n.3
  photography of, 292, 302, 303, 379 n.4, 416 n.88
    military, 292, 297, 407 n.12
    still, 435 n.6
  poetry, 421 n.51
  President's Commission on. *See* President's Commission
  rationalism of, 13, 449 n.34
  religious interpretation of, 19–20, 327–35, 442 n.2
  representation of, 439 n.61
  research, 145
  responses to, 12, 282, 352
  signification of, 2–6
  and State of Israel, 446 n.80
  statistics of, 137, 144, 149, 175–77, 213, 285, 306, 381 n.6, 414 n.63, 415 n.67
  stories, 439 n.59
  survivors of. *See* survivors
  theology of, 42–43, 332–35, 336–48, 352–54
  uniqueness, 383 nn.25, 27
  *See also* Final Solution
*Holocaust, The,* 411 n.14
*Holocaust, The,* 381 n.6, 398 n.28, 398 nn.30, 33

*Holocaust* (miniseries), 293
*Holocaust: A History of the Jews of Europe, The,*
    7, 399 n.40, 411 n.6, 413 n.38
*Holocaust and Antisemitism,* 384 n.6
*Holocaust and Genocide Studies,* 409 n.38, 410
    n.51
*Holocaust and History, The,* 446 n.2
*Holocaust and Other Genocides, The,* 435 n.6
*Holocaust and the Christian World, The,* 434
    n.187
*Holocaust and the Crisis of Human Behavior,*
    *The,* 419 n.39, 423 n.87
*Holocaust and the German Elite, The,* 447 n.5
*Holocaust and the Literary Imagination, The,*
    439 n.60
*Holocaust as Historical Experience, The,* 416 n.2,
    418 n.29
*Holocaust Chronicle, The,* 381 n.6, 394 n.27,
    396 n.51, 397 n.15
*Holocaust Fiction,* 439 n.60
*Holocaust: From a Survivor of Verdun, The,* 392
    n.10
*Holocaust in American Film, The,* 435 n.8, 436
    n.9
*Holocaust in Historical Perspective, The,* 383
    n.30, 398 n.20
*Holocaust in History, The,* 71
*Holocaust in Latvia, The,* 410 nn.44, 49
*Holocaust Justice,* 423 n.85
*Holocaust Literature,* 439 n.60
*Holocaust Museum in Washington, The,* 438
    n.40
*Holocaust Reader, A,* 397 n.1
*Holocaust: Religious and Philosophical Implica-*
    *tions,* 418 n.24
*Holocaust Representation,* 439 n.61
*Holocaust Testimonies,* 241–44, 417 n.10
*Holocaust: The Fate of European Jewry, The,* 398
    n.23
*Holocaust, the French, and the Jews, The,* 393 n.22
*Holocaust Theology,* 379 n.1
home, sense of, 375–77
homosexuals, 3, 116, 381 n.7
hope, 353
Horn, Alistair
    *The Price of Glory,* 392 n.10
Horowitz, Gordon J.
    *In the Shadow of Death,* 450 n.43
Horowitz, Sara R.
    *Voicing the Void,* 439 n.60
Horthy, Regent, 276
Höss, Rudolf Franz Ferdinand, 8, 203, 205,
    299, 367
Howe, Irving, 437 n.27
Huber, Kurt, 283
Hudal, Alois C., 287, 434 nn.177, 181
    *Römische Tagebücher,* 434 n.180
Huguenots, 92, 284
human/humanity

amorality, 341
    common, 374
    definition of, 246
    equality, 67, 74
    experiments, 13, 195, 235, 358, 370, 487
        nn.8–9
    freedom, 333
    progress. *See* progress
    rights, 11, 14, 352, 363, 365, 373–74, 377
    will, 450 n.49
*Humani Generis Unitas* (encyclical), 270, 430
    n.112
*Humanity at the Limit,* 435 n.187
Huneke, Douglas K.
    *The Moses of Rovno,* 419 n.37
Hungary, 272, 273, 276, 277, 414 n.66
    anti-Jewish laws in, 424 n.5
Huntington, Samuel, 351
Hussein, Saddam, 17, 446 n.80
hydrogen cyanide, 210
*Hyping the Holocaust,* 388 n.2

*I Cannot Forgive,* 422 n.59
*The Idea of Usury,* 423 n.91
identity, 220
    Jewish, 344
    religious, 126
    unity of communal and religious, 27
*Ideology of Death,* 7, 388n.2
*If Not, Not,* 297
I.G. Auschwitz, 204, 364
I.G. Farben. *See* corporations: I.G.Farben
illusion exposed, 319
Immigration Act of 1924 (U.S.), 109, 281,
    403 n.46
*Imperfect Justice,* 423 n.85
*In a Different Light,* 438 n.37
incarnation, 67
*Indelible Shadows,* 435 n.8
individualism, possessive, 76
industrialists' trials, 364
industry, 244, 449 n.30
    *See also* corporations
*Industry and Ideology: I. G. Farben in the Nazi*
    *Era,* 415 n.68
*Inextinguishable Symphony, The,* 436 n.13
inferiors, 404 n.52
*In God's Name,* 426 n.39
*Inherit the Truth,* 436 n.13
*In Pursuit of Justice,* 448 n.27
Inquisition, 65, 66, 277
Insdorf, Annette
    *Indelible Shadows,* 435 n.8
*Inside the Vicious Heart,* 416 n.88, 435 n.7
Institute for Military History (*Mil-*
    *itärgeschichtliches Forschungamt*), 168
Institute for the Study and Eradication of
    Jewish Influence in German Church/Reli-
    gious Life, 257, 426 n.38

intellectuals, overproduction of, 78
intermarriage
   dissolved, 307, 344
   prohibited, 54
   *See also Mischlinge*
International Criminal Court, 368
International Military Tribunal. *See* Nuremberg: International Military Tribunal
*Interrogations: The Nazi Elite in Allied Hands,* 449 n.27
*In the Days of Destruction and Revolt,* 419 n.41
*In the Name of Eugenics,* 403 n.43
*In the Shadow of Death,* 450 n.43
*Intimate Journal of the Dreyfus Case, An,* 390 n.28
*Into the Arms of Strangers,* 294, 295
*Into That Darkness,* 404 n.65
Iran, 445 n.62
Irving, David, 396 n.45
*Irving Judgment, The,* 415 n.68
Isaac, 26, 27, 342
Isaac, Jules, 385–86, n.1
   *Jesus and Israel,* 385 n.1
   *The Teaching of Contempt,* 385 n.1
Isaiah, 328, 442 n.3
Islam, 343, 346
   criminalized in Spain, 65
Islamic fundamentalism, 388 n. 33
Israel, 20, 342
   as Holy Land, 346–47
   Kingdom of, 61
   mission of, 335–36
   Six-Day War, 341, 352
   State of, 328, 332, 333–34, 345, 351
      and Holocaust, 446 n.80
      plan for, 390 n.46
   unbelief of, 446 n.81
*Israel: An Echo in Eternity,* 341, 444 n.45
*Is the Holocaust Unique?,* 383 nn.25, 27; 384 n.31, 442 n.1
Italy, 280
*I Will Bear Witness,* 8, 306, 392 n.11

Jäckel, Eberhard, 383 n.30
   *Hitler's Weltanschauung,* 391 n.4
   *Remembering for the Future,* 381 n.12, 428 n.70
Jacob, 26, 27
Jacob, Lili, 379 n.4
Jacobs, Helen, 338
Jacobs, Steven L., ed.
   *Raphael Lemkin's Thoughts on Genocide,* 383 n.24
Jaenicke, Erna, 1
James, Harold
   *The Deutsche Bank and the Nazi Economic War Against the Jews,* 447 n.5
   *The German Slump,* 395 n. 38
Jasenovac camp complex, 408 n.14

Jaurès, Jean, 92
jazz, 296
*Jazz in the Culture of Nazi Germany,* 436 n.13
Jeckeln, Friedrich, 179, 410 n.47
Jedwabne, 395 n.37
Jehovah's Witnesses, 3, 235, 255, 426 n.30
Jena, University of, 257
Jeremiah, 331
Jerusalem, 43, 52
   as *al-Quds,* 347, 445 n.62
   destruction/fall of, 20, 35,37–39, 41–44, 46, 60, 331
   Temple, 31, 32, 34–35, 37, 41, 43, 52, 60
      reestablishment of, 342
Jesus, 34
   as Aryan, 257
   crucifixion, 35–36, 263, 334, 336, 338, 339
      *See also* deicide
   as divine, 49
   Jewish rejection of, 20, 45–46, 52, 252, 274, 289
   as Messiah. *See* Messiah: Jesus as
   as (observant) Jew, 35, 260, 353, 384 n.8
   parables of, 41
      Good Samaritan, 278, 286
   resurrection, 334
   trial, 35
*Jesus and Israel,* 385 n.1
*Jesus Connection, The,* 384 n.8
*Jesus, Judaism, and Christian Anti-Judaism,* 385 n.22
*Jesus the Pharisee,* 384 n.8
*Jesus Two Thousand Years Later,* 385 n.22
*Jew as Pariah, The,* 382 n.19
*Jew in the Modern World, The,* 388 nn.39–40, 388 n.1, 390 n.46
Jewish
   assimilation, 68, 330
   -Christian relationships, 7, 33–37, 50, 228, 263, 278, 289, 332
   civility, 419 n.38
   conspiracy. *See* conspiracy theory
   councils. *See Judenräte*
   death brigade, 199
   emancipation, 68, 95, 98–99, 277
      irony of, 71–75
      opposition to, 75–78, 252, 267
   emigration, 39, 79, 82, 99–100, 109, 133, 261
      of Austrian, 130
      of Eastern, 112
      ended, 187
      failure of, 138–42
      forced, 133, 138
      Grüber office for, 261
      increased antisemitism, 146
      to North and South American, 112, 247
         United States, 281
      Reich Central Office for, 137

Jewish (*continued*)
  ethical demands, 31
  exclusion from activities, 127, 250
  "experts," 361
  expulsion. *See* expulsion
  extermination, 374, 399 n.39
    threat of, 247
    *See also* Final Solution
  failures, 323
  history. *See* history, Jewish
  identiy, 68, 220, 231, 246, 344, 354
    German definitions of, 126
  intellectuals, 324
  labor, 162–63
  leadership
  liturgy, 331, 344, 444 n.56
  malnourishment of, 199
  "menace," 286
  monotheism, 31
  Museum (Berlin), 298, 301–2, 438 n.45
  Museum (New York), 298
  musicians, 295–96
  mysticism, 444 n.46
  nationalism, 220
  police force. *See* Order Police
  "Question/Problem," 3–4, 26, 95, 107, 114,
    121, 123, 150, 171, 175, 252, 254, 262,
    272–73, 382 n.20, 387 n.19, 398 n.26,
    402 n.32, 443 n.34
    Eichmann assigned, 136
    knowledge of, 13
    precedents, 144
    as priority, 185
    Russian, 99
    territorial solution, 405 n.88
      *See also* Madagascar Plan
    Wayrsch's methods, 149
    *See also* Wannsee Conference
  rationalization, 229, 385 n.21, 449 n.34
  resistance. *See* resistance: Jewish
  responsibility for failure, 351
  separatism, 33
  state. *See* Israel: state of
  survival, 350
  survivors. *See* survivors
  Theological Seminary, 340
  visibility, 220
  women. *See* women
*Jewish Chronicle,* 390 n.46
*Jewish Responses to Nazi Persecution,* 419 n.38
*Jewish Return into History, The,* 446 n.69
Jews
  accused of ritual murder. *See* ritual murder
  as alien presence, 9
  of Alsace-Lorraine, 163
  Austrian, 130–31, 398 n.20
  baptized, 259, 270, 273, 276, 338, 428 n.81
  Belgian, 389 n.4, 399 n.50
  Bohemian, 399 n.50

Bulgarian, 279, 432 n.159
children. *See* children
as chosen people, 7, 20, 28, 246, 263,
  330–31, 344, 352–53
communal life. *See* ghetto
and communism, 251
as converts. *See* Christianity: conversion to
as criminals, 212
Croatian, 408 n.14
Danish, 279, 399 n.50
Dresden, 309
Dutch, 226, 279, 309, 389 n.4, 399 n.50
as enemies of Christians, 288
English, 54, 79, 146
"evils," 330
European, 413 n.37
"expropriation" of goods, 162
expulsion of, 12
French, 54, 72–77, 201, 272, 285, 310, 393
  n.22, 399 n.50, 405 n.90
German, 113, 389 n.4, 399 n.50, 412 n.34
  deprived of rights, 123
as non-believers, 250
population, 11
Greek, 201, 233
Hasidic, 303
Hungarian, 205–6, 226, 251, 260, 275,
  276, 280, 284, 319, 379 n.4, 414 n.66
Italian, 238, 273, 275
Latvian, 177, 410 n.43
Lithuanian, ix, 175–76, 218, 223, 341, 409
  n.38, 409 n.42, 411 n.58, 416 n.1
Luxembourg, 389 n.4, 399 n.50
of Moravia, 399 n.50
Nazi extermination of, 16
  *See also* extermination
"new," 74
Norwegian, 280, 399 n.50
Orthodox, 220, 330, 351
pariah people, 11, 21, 82
Polish, 11, 55, 109, 112, 137, 147, 150,
  161–63, 223, 272, 375, 394 n.36, 399
  n.50, 406 n.2
  murdered by Poles, 395 n.37
portrayal of, 403 n.41
refugees, 389 n.4
rescue of, 278, 338, 434 n.173, 450 n.45
of Rome, 275–76, 287
Russian, 112, 144, 175, 177, 410 nn.53–54
as sacrificial victims, 339
as satanic, 46, 246, 250
as scapegoat, 104
secular, 350–351
Serbian, 171, 407 n.13
Slovakian, 226, 273–74, 399 n.50
Spanish (Marranos), 46, 54, 65, 73, 146
Swedish, 146
Swiss, 146
Turkish, 146

Ukranian, 283
Yugoslavian, 407 n.13
Zionist. *See* Zionism
*Jews of Warsaw, 1939–1943, The,* 417 n.19
*Jew Today, A,* 320–21
*jihad,* 345, 347
Job, 340
Jochmann, Werner
    *Gesellschaftskrise und Judenfeindschaft in
        Deutschland,* 397 n.7
Jodl, Alfred, 101, 144, 364
John Chrysostom, 52
John Hyrcanus, 31
John Paul II, Pope
John XXIII, Pope, 386 n.1
    *See also* Roncalli, Angelo
*John Chrysostom and the Jews* 386 n.4
Johnson, Eric A.
    *Nazi Terror,* 393 n.11
Johnson-Reed Act. *See* Immigration Act of
    1924
John the Baptist, 433 n.172
Jonca, Karol, 398 n.30
Jones, David H.
    *Moral Responsibility in the Holocaust,*
        450–51, n.49
Josephus, 37, 39
    *The Jewish War,* 385 nn.10, 15
Joshua, 29
"journey toward nothingness," 291
Judaism, 344
    American, 354
    Christian influence on, 353–54
    Orthodox, 337, 341, 442 nn.12–14
    post-Holocaust, 336
    Rabbinic, 40, 336
    Reconstructionist, 443 n.38
    Reform, 330, 335, 337, 339
Judas, 394 n.26
    Jews as, 40, 83, 84–85, 87, 91, 252, 279,
        390 n.29, 394 n.26
Judas Maccabaeus/ Judas the Maccabee, 31
*Judenfrage. See* Jewish: "Question/Problem"
*Judenhass,* 30, 265
*Judenpolitik in Dritten Reich,* 401 n.11
*Judenrat,* 417 nn.22–23
Judenräte (Jewish councils), 162, 178, 219,
    222–23, 223–26, 402 n.32, 417 nn.9,
    22–23, 418 n.27
    corruption, 232
*judenrein,* 21, 128, 131, 138, 177, 191, 196,
    223, 237, 307, 380 n.3, 402 n.32, 410
    n.47, 412 n.34
*Judenreservat,* 160
"*Juden sind unser Unglück, Die,*" 113, 388n.2
*Judensuppe,* 210
*Juden unterm Hakenkreuz,* 398 n.27
Judeo-Roman War, 33, 331, 345
*Jud Süss,* 292

Juergensmeyer, Mark
    *Terror in the Mind of God,* 388 n. 33
*Juif, le judaisme, et le judaisation, Le,* 80
*Juifs rois de l'epoque, Les,* 80
jurisprudence, 359
    *See also* lawyers
justification of actions, 366, 449 n.35
*Just War and Jihad,* 445 n.64

Kaas, Ludwig, 111
Kaddish, 297, 323
Kafka, Franz, 74, 246
    *The Trial,* 74, 246
Kaltenbrunner, Ernst, 147, 363
*Kampfgemeinschaft,* 104
Kampuchea, 327
Kant, Immanuel, 442 n.4
Kaplan, Chaim A., 303–4
    *Scroll of Agony,* 418 n.25, 439 n.57
Kaplan, Marion A., 235
    *Between Dignity and Despair,* 420 n.45
Kaplan, Mordecai, 340, 443 n.38
Kappler, Herbert, 275
*Karl Barth,* 427 nn.58–61
Karski, Jan, 394 n.36
    *The Great Powers and Poland 1919–1945,*
        394 n.36
Kater, Michael H.
    *Composers of the Nazi Era,* 436 n.13
    *Different Drummers,* 436 n.13
    *Doctors Under Hitler,* 395 n.44, 403 n.39
    *Jazz in the Culture of Nazi Germany,* 436
        n.13
    *Twisted Music,* 436 n.13
Katowice, 147–48, 150
Katz, Jacob
    *From Prejudice to Destruction,* 388 n.41, 389
        nn.6, 8, 12
    *Out of the Ghetto,* 389 n.6
Katz, Steven T., 7, 383 n.27
Kaufbeuren, 158
Kazik (Simha Rotem)
    *Memoirs of a Warsaw Ghetto Fighter,* 418
        n.25
*Kehillah,* 222
*Keine Kameraden,* 408 n.23
Keitel, Wilhelm, 101, 364
Kellenbach, Katharina von, 434 n.175
Kelsay, John and James Turner Johnson
    *Just War and Jihad,* 445 n.64
Kemenetsky, Christa
    *Children's Literature in Hitler's Germany,* 448
        n.12
Kenrich, Donald and Grattan Puxon
    *Gypsies under the Swastika,* 415 n.72
Kepel, Gilles
    *The Revenge of God,* 388 n. 33
Kershaw, Ian, 8, 253
    *Hitler,* 8, 391 n.4, 397 n.4

Kertész, Imre
    *Fateless,* 8
Kertzer, David I., 268
    *The Kidnapping of Edgardo Mortara,* 389
        n.22
Kevles, Daniel J.
    *In the Name of Eugenics,* 403 n.43
KGB, 410 n.42
Khmer Rouge, 17
*Kiddush ha-Shem,* 330
*Kidnapping of Edgardo Mortara, The,* 389 n.22
Kiefer, Anselm
    *Departing from Egypt,* 297, 436 n.15
    *Sulamith,* 437 n.17
Kierkegaard, Søren, 444 n.48
    *Fear and Trembling,* 444 n.48
Kiernan, Ben, 392 n.8
Kiev, 179, 187
killing
    centers, 8, 195, 197
    methods. *See* gassing; mass murder
*Kindertransport,* 294
Kirk, Tim, 394 n.33
Kitaj, R. B., 437 n.18
    *If Not, Not,* 297
Kitos War, 32
Kittel, Gerhard, 257, 387 n.31, 426–27
        nn.39–41, 49
    *Die Behandlung des Nichtjuden nach dem
        Talmud,* 427 n.40
Klarsfeld, Serge
    *David Olère,* 438 n.29
*KL Auschwitz Seen by the SS,* 414 n.60
Kleeblatt, Norman L., ed.
    *Mirroring Evil, Nazi Imagery/Recent Art,* 437
        n.23
Klein, Gerda, 8
Klein, Gideon, 296
Klemperer, Victor, 305–9, 392 n.11, 440
        nn.63–64
    *I Will Bear Witness,* 8, 306, 392 n.11
    *The Language of the Third Reich,* 440 n.64
    *LTI-Notizbuch eines Philologen,* 306
Klopfer, Gertrud, 237
Knappe, Siegfried, 185, 187
knowledge
    useless. *See* useless knowledge
    of wrongdoing, 366
Koch, Ilse, 414 n.56
Koch, Karl, 202, 414 n.56
Koch, Werner, 262
Koerner, Henry, 3001, 301
    *My Parents II,* 438 n.36
    *Unfinished Sentence,* 438 n.36
Kohn, Mara Vishniac
    *Children of a Vanished World,* 435 n.6
Kolbert, Jack
    *The Worlds of Elie Wiesel,* 441 n.111
Kolmar, Gertrud, 237

*Dark Soliloquy,* 51
    *My Gaze is Turned Inward,* 421 n.51
*Kol Nidre,* 296
*Kommissarbefehl,* 172
Konitz, 388 n.2,
Koontz, Claudia
    *Mothers in the Fatherland,* 421 n.47
Korczak, Janusz, 304
Koskull, Andreas von, 159
Kossover, Paltiel, 324–25
Kovály, Heda Margolis, 304
Kovner, Abba, 2117, 218, 416 nn.2, 5
Kovno, 176, 188, 226, 409 n.41, 412 n.37
Krakow. *See* Cracow
Krakowski, Shmuel, 355, 446 n.1
Krauch, Carl, 364
Krause, Reinhold, 256
Kreidl, Paul, 307
Kremer, Lillian
    *Women's Holocaust Writing,* 420 n.45
Kren, George M. and Leon Rapport
    *The Holocaust and the Crisis of Human
        Behavior,* 419 n.39, 423 n.87
*Kreuz und Hakenkreuz im Dritten Reich,* 425 n.18
Kripo, 146, 174
*Kristallnach,* 63, 131–33, 136, 139, 149, 260,
        271, 306
Kritzinger, Friedrich, 191
Krüger, Friedrich Wilhelm, 405 n.83
Kruk, Herman
    *The Last Days of the Jerusalem of Lithuania,*
        416 n.1
Krupka, 169
Krupp, Alfried, 364
Krupp, Gustav, 363
Kühl, Stefan
    *The Nazi Connection,* 403 n.44
Ku Klux Klan, 109, 281
Kulka, Otto Dov, 398 n.26
Kulmhof. *see* Chelmno
*Kurt Gerstein: The Ambiguity of Good,* 424 n.1
Kweit, Konrad, 409 n.38

labor. *See* forced labor
LaCapra, Dominick, 298
    *History and Memory after Auschwitz,* 437 n.20
    *Writing History, Writing Trauma,* 410 n.52,
        439 n.61
LaFarge, John, 270
Lagerwey, Mary
    *Reading Auschwitz,* 420 n.45
Lagnado, Lucette Matalon and Sheila Cohn
        Dekel
    *Children of the Flames,* 447 n.7
Laks, Szymon
    *Music of Another World,* 436 n.13
*Landscapes of Jewish Experience,* 438 n.37
Lang, Berel
    *Holocaust Representation,* 439 n.61

Lange, Herbert, 196
Lange, Rudolf, 191
Langer, Lawrence L., 311, 417–18 n.24, 439
  n.60
  *Admitting the Holocaust*, 418 n.32, 439 n.60
  *Art from the Ashes*, 438 n.33, 439 n.60
  *The Holocaust and the Literary Imagination*,
    439 n.60
  *Holocaust Testimonies*, 241–44, 417 n.10
  *In a Different Light*, 438 n.37
  *Preempting the Holocaust*, 438 n.37, 439
    n.60
  *Versions of Survival*, 418 n.24
Lang, Jochen von, ed.
  *Eichmann Interrogated*, 399 n.45
*Language and Silence*, 435 n.5
language, "Aryan" and "Semitic" roots, 30
*Language of the Third Reich, The*, 440 n.64
  Lanzmann, Claude, 197, 296–97, 419 n.41
  *La fin du voyage*, 436 n.15
  *Sobibor, Oct. 14, 1943*, 294
  *Shoah*, 197, 293–94, 296, 399 n.48, 400
    n.54, 419 n.41, 437 n.16, 441 n.110
Laqueur, Walter, 5, 381 n.13
  *The Holocaust Encyclopedia*, 398 n.30, 401
    n.16
  *The Terrible Secret*, 381 n.12, 401 n.6
Lasker-Wallfisch, Anita
  *Inherit the Truth*, 436 n.13
*Last Album, The*, 435 n.6
*Last Days of the Jerusalem of Lithuania, The*,
  416 n.1
*Last Journey, The*, xi
*Last Nazi, The*, 447 n.6
Lateran Council, Fourth, 54, 66
Lateran Treaty, 269
Latvia, 149, 177, 179–80, 191–92, 410 nn.44,
  47
law, 376
  beyond political boundaries, 13, 15
  *See also* jurisprudence
Law for Restoration of the Professional Civil
  Service, 125, 395 n.44
Law for the Prevention of Hereditarily Dis-
  eased Offspring, 206
Law for the Protection of German Blood and
  Honor (Reich Citizenship Law), 128
lawyers, 54, 129, 357, 359, 370, 447 n.10
League of Nations, 111
  German withdrawal from, 111
*Lebensraum*, 106, 112, 146, 150, 172, 253–54,
  383 n.21, 392 n.8, 394 n.29
"legends of our time," 321
*Legislating the Holocaust*, 398 n.19
legislation, 125, 127
  anti-Jewish, 125
Leibbrandt, Georg, 190
Leitner, Isabella, 304
Lemkin, Raphael, 15–16

*Axis Rule in Occupied Europe*, 383 n.24
Leo XIII, Pope, 80, 92
Le Pen, Jean-Marie, 72
*Lessons and Legacies*, 400 n.5
*Less Than Slaves*, 446 n.1, 449 n.35
*Lest Innocent Blood Be Shed*, 434 n.174
Levinas, Emmanuel, 442 n.4
Levine, Hillel
  *Economic Origins of Antisemitism*, 386 n.6
Leviné-Meyer, Rosa
  *Leviné the Spartacist*, 424 n.7
Levi, Primo, 245–46, 302, 304, 315, 435 n.1
  *The Drowned and the Saved*, 295
  *Survival in Auschwitz*, 8, 291, 435 n.1
Lévy, Madeleine Dreyfus, 95
Lewin, Abraham
  *A Cup of Tears*, 418 n.25
Lewis, Bryan F., 435 n.66
Lewy, Guenter, 207
  *The Catholic Church and Nazi Germany*, 399
    n.38
  *The Nazi Persecution of the Gypsies*, 381 n.7,
    415 n.69
Ley, Robert, 363
*Libre Parole, La*, 83–84, 390 n.25
Lichtenberg, Bernhard, 399 n.38, 432
  nn.152–53
Lichtheim, George, 77, 389 nn.11–12, 14–15
Lichtenberg, Bernard, 277
Liebermann-Shiber, Ella
  *On the Edge of the Abyss*, 437 n.28
Liebeskind, Daniel, 298, 302–3, 437 n.26
Liebhold, Gerhard and Sabine, 262
life
  compartmentalization of, 366
  sacredness of, 10
*Life Is Beautiful*, 436 n.11
"life unworthy of life," 152, 160, 370
Lifton, Robert J.
  *The Nazi Doctors*, 402 n.39, 403 nn.41, 44
*limpieza* law *See* "blood purity"
Lindqvish, Sven
  *"Exterminate All the Brutes,"* 403 n.42
Lipstadt, Deborah E., 396 n.45
  *Beyond Belief*, 432 n.163
  *Denying the Holocaust*, 396 n.45
List, Wilhelm, 148
literature. *See* Holocaust: literature
Lithuania, 149, 175–76, 192, 272, 302, 409
  n.42, 443 n.38
  Soviet occupation of, 410 n.42
  *See also* Jews: Lithuanian
Littell, Franklin H., 7, 332, 368, 449 n.37
  *The Crucifixion of the Jews*, 382 n.15
  *Hyping the Holocaust*, 388 n.2
Littell, Franklin H. and Hubert G. Locke, eds.
  *The German Church Struggle and the Holo-
    caust*, 394 n.28, 427 n.56
*Living Witness, The*, 438 n.30

Lochner, Louis P.
  *The Goebbels Diaries 1942–43,* 400 n.60
Lodz (Litzmannstadt), 161–63, 188, 226, 405
  n.85
  *See also* ghettos: Lodz
Löesner, Bernhard, 127, 398 n.19
logic, 13, 15
  *See also* rationality
Longerich, Peter, 6, 395–96 n.45, 401 n.16
  *The Unwritten Order,* 395 n.45, 399 n.49
*Longest Shadow, The,* 439 n.61
Loshitzky, Yosefa, ed.
  *Spielberg's Holocaust,* 436 n.9
Loubet, Émile, 93
Louis XIV, King, 73
Louis Napoleon, 80
Lovin, Robin W.
  *Christian Faith and Public Choices,* 427 n.56
Lubetkin, Zivia, 419–20 n.41
  *In the Days of Destruction and Revolt,* 419
  n.41
Lubin, 137, 160, 165, 199, 202, 226
Lucas, Scott, 281
Luckner, Gertrud, 278
Lukas, John
  *The Hitler of History,* 391 n.4
Lukas, Richard C.
  *The Forgotten Holocaust,* 394 n.36
Luther, Martin, 53, 56–65, 263, 386 n.9, 387
  n.20
  *Against the Sabbatarians,* 58
  *On the Jews and Their Lies,* 57–59, 63, 387
  nn.12, 16–18, 21–24, 28–29
Luther, Martin (Foreign Officer), 191
Lutheran churches *see* churches: Lutheran
*Luther's Last Battles,* 386 n.9
Lvov, 199

MacPherson, C. B.
  *The Political Theory of Possessive Individual-
  ism,* 389 n.10
MacQueen, Michael, 409 n.38
Madagascar Plan, 137–38, 163–65, 405
  nn.86–88
magic, 269
Maglione, Luigi, 273–74, 430 nn.127, 130
Mahler, Gustav, 295
Mahmoud, Fatma Abdallaj, 445 n.59
Maier, Hans, 373
Maimonides, 219
Majdanek, 195, 202, 286, 339, 414 n.56
Mandell, Richard D.
  *The Nazi Olympics,* 398 n.21
Manning, Henry, 390 n.43
Mann, Michael, 180, 410 n.51
Manoshek, Walter, 407 nn.13, 15–17, 22, 25
Marcuse, Herbert, 329, 442 n.8
Marius, Richard
  *Martin Luther,* 386 n.9

*Marranos. See* Jews: Spanish
  marriages, mixed. *See Mischlinge*
Marrus, Michael R., 383 n.20
  *The Holocaust in History,* 71
  *The Nuremberg War Crimes Trial,* 448 nn.25,
  27
  *The Politics of Assimilation,* 389 n.23
  *The Unwanted,* 382 n.19, 400 n.54
Marrus, Michael R. and Robert O. Paxton
  *Vichy France and the Jews,* 393 n.22, 405
  n.90
Marr, Wilhelm, 30, 384 n.5
*Martin Luther und die Juden,* 387 nn.14, 27
martyrdom, grammar of, 243
Marxism, 220, 253
  French hostility to, 76
Marx, Karl, 76, 251, 389 n.13
Masada, 3, 39, 232
masking, 366
mass murder, 54, 100, 104, 170, 178–80, 317,
  371, 382 n.20, 410 n.47, 424 n.1, 450
  n.47
  appetite for, 207
  *Erntefest,* 202, 455
  feasibility study for, 187
  first targets of, 152
  incomprehensibility of, 419 n.38
  knowledge of, 145, 412 n.34
  at Krupka, 169
  ongoing relationship with, 310
  as policy, 183
  primarily by firearms and deprivation, 181
  by shooting, 419 n.37
  of Soviets, 407 n.8
  state-sponsored, 4, 64–65, 69, 154–57, 362,
  370
  statistics of, 171, 213
  weapons of, 324, 346
*Masters of Death,* 392 n.8, 401 n.16, 402 n.30,
  408 n.32, 410 n.48, 410 n.53, 419 n.38
*Mature Christianity in the Twenty-first Century,*
  385 n.22
Maurer, Charles B.
  *Call to Revolution,* 424 n.7
Maurras, Charles, 90–91, 92, 94, 390 n.41
*Maus: A Survivor's Tale,* 297, 436–37 n.15, 437
  n.20
Mauthausen, 208, 450 n.43
Maxwell, Elisabeth, 381 n.12
Maybaum, Ignaz, 328, 336–37, 339
  *The Face of God after Auschwitz,* 335
Mayer, Josef, 158
"May laws," 98
Mazower, Mark
  *Dark Continent,* 7
McCloy, John J., 365
meaning, 353
*Meaning of Hitler, The,* 391 n.4
medical

experiments. *See* human experiments
personnel, 152
    *See also* doctors
*Medicine and Medical Ethics in Nazi Germany,*
    447 n.6
Meed, Vladka
    *On Both Sides of the Wall,* 418 n.25
Meier, Kurt
    *Kreuz und Hakenkreuz im Dritten Reich,* 425
    n.18
Meier, Lili Jacob, 379 n.4
    *Auschwitz Album,* 239, 380 n.4
*Mein Kampf,* 106, 111, 122, 346, 391–92 n.8,
    394 n.28, 395 n.42, 397 n.2
melancholy, 242
Méline, Félix-Jules, 90
Melvern, Linda R.
    *A People Betrayed,* 442 n.1
*mémoire et les jours, Le* (Days and memory), 310
*Memoirs of a Warsaw Ghetto Fighter,* 418 n.25
memory, 323–24, 348
*Memory Effects,* 436 n.14
Mendelssohn, Felix, 295
Mendes-Flohr, Paul and Jehuda Reinharz, eds.
    *The Jew in the Modern World,* 388 nn.39–40,
    388 n.1, 390 n.46
Mengele, Josef, 357–58, 447 nn.6–7
Mennecke, Friedrich, 1 55
mentally ill, 152
Mercier, Auguste, 84, 85, 86, 93
"mercy killings." *See* euthanasia program
Messiah, 45, 330, 331, 342–43, 442 n.12
    birth pangs of, 337
    Jesus as, 34–35, 49, 50, 58, 271, 346
    Jewish rejection of, 52, 271, 384 n.9
*Mesure de nos jours* (The measure of our days),
    310, 313
Meyer, Alfred, 190
Meyer, Franz, 131
Meyjes, Menno
    *Max,* 295
Micah (prophet), 43
Michelangelo, 300
Middlebrook, Martin
    *The First Day on the Somme,* 393 n.12
middle class, 112–13
    indigenous, 98
"middle-man minority," 39–40
Mierzejewski, Alfred, 362–63, 448 n.18
    *The Most Valuable Asset of the Reich,* 448
    n.18
*Minderwertige. See* inferiors
Ministry of Public Enlightenment and Propa-
    ganda, 124
    *See also* Nazi: propaganda
Minsk, 181, 188, 226, 410 n.53, 412 n.37
Mintz, Alan
    *Popular Culture and the Shaping of Holocaust
    Memory in America,* 436 n.9

*Mirroring Evil, Nazi Imagery/Recent Art,* 298
*Mirrors of Destruction,* 393 nn.15, 18–23
miscegenation, 391 n.8
*Mischlinge,* 126, 138, 192–93, 206, 273,
    307–8, 398 n.19, 412 n.34
    statistics of, 412 n.34
*Mit brennender Sorge* (encyclical), 270
Mitchell, Allan
    *Revolution in Bavaria, 1918–1919,* 424 n.7
Mitscherlich, Alexander and Fred Mielke
    *Doctors of Infamy,* 447 n.6
mobile
    death squadrons *See* Einsatzgruppen
    gas vans. *See* gassing
*Modernity and the Holocaust,* 388 n.38
modernization/moderity, 10, 8, 113, 266
Mommsen, Hans, 409 n.38
Monowitz, 203, 204
Montini, Giovanni Battista, 430 n.134
moral/morality, 13, 14, 15
    absolutes, 368, 372
    dualism in, 328
    law, Christian, 399 n.38
    obligaton, 247, 278, 286
    political and social, 76
    post-Holocaust, 450 n.48
    reflection, 367
    restitution of, 289
*Moral Reckoning, A,* 424 n.3
*Moral Responsibility in the Holocaust,* 450–51,
    n.49
*Morality after Auschwitz,* 405 n.74, 450 n.48
Moreno, Jonathan D.
    *Under Risk: Secret State Experiments on
    Humans,* 447 n.9
*More Than a Trial,* 389 n.23
Morgan, Michael L.
    *Beyond Auschwitz,* 444 n.49
Morrison, Charles Clayton, 433 n.168
Morrison, Jack G.
    *Rabensbrück,* 421 n.46
Morse, Arthur D.
    *While Six Million Died,* 400 n.59
*A Mosaic of Victims,* 381 n.8
Moscow, 371
*Moscow—the Turning Point,* 411 n.57
Moses, 26–29, 43
*Moses of Rovno, The,* 419 n.37
Moslems
    *See* Islam; Muslims
Mosse, George L., 72
    *Toward the Final Solution,* 388n.3
*Most Valuable Asset of the Reich, The,* 448 n.18
*Mothers in the Fatherland,* 421 n.47
*Mothers, Sisters, Resisters,* 420 n.45
Mount Sinai, 26, 28
Mousseaux, Henri Gougenot des
    *Le Juif, le judaisme, et le judaisation,* 80
Muhammad, 347

Müller, Heinrich, 191
Müller, Ingo, 395 n.44
Müller, Ludwig, 256
Müller, Stefan, 438 n.47
Munich, 105, 132, 188, 251, 267, 283, 401
    n.17, 433 n.170
  agreement, 129–30
  Red revolution in, 424 n.7
murder. *See* mass murder
Museum of Modern Art (MOMA), 296–98,
    436 n.15
music, 295–96, 436 n.13
*Music of Another World,* 436 n.13
Muslims, 334, 345. ˆ´ʿ -47, 445 nn.59–62,
    64–65
  propaganda, 347
  *See also* Islam
Mussolini, Benito, 129, 267, 269, 413 n.38
mustard gas. *See* gas: chlorine
mutual indifference. *See* contract of mutual
    indifference
*"My Brother's Keeper?",* 394 n.36
*My Gaze Is Turned Inward,* 421 n.51
*My Parents II,* 438 n.36
mysticism, 134
  Jewish, 350
myth, 327
*Myth of Rescue, The,* 53
*Myth of Ritual Murder, The,* 429 n.101
*Myth of the Twentieth Century, The,* 166

Napoleon, 72
Napoleon III, 82
nationalism, 15, 69
  racial, 113
  secular, 330
National Socialism, 116, 167, 244, 260, 276,
    428 n.68
  Church's endorsement of, 270, 425 n.22
  ideology, 103, 113, 350
  Jewish policy, 161
  nature of, 260
  origins, 105
  policies, 62–63
*National Socialist Extermination Policies,* 397
    n.4, 398 n.30, 399 n.39, 52, 407 n.13,
    408 n.28, 409 n.38
*Nationalsozialistische Deutsche Arbeiterpartei*
    (NSDAP). See Nazi: party (NSDAP)
Native Americans, 17–18, 384 n.31
"nature reserve," 150
Nazi(s), 380 n.3
  anti-Christian racists, 20
  anti-Jewish program 122, 271, 401 n.18
  antisemitism. *See* antisemitism: Nazi
    definition of "Jewish," 126
  doctors. *See* doctors
  "ethic," 160, 372–73
  euthanasia program. *See* euthanasia program

"good," 293
Hitler's control of, 108
Hungarian, 276
ideology, 106–7, 115, 130, 242, 360, 380
    n.3, 382 n.20, 403 n.41
"kleptocracy," 423 n.85
party (NSDAP), 1, 108, 111, 195, 252
policies, 149, 191, 272, 356, 382 n.20
propaganda, 3, 16, 106–7, 124, 236, 347,
    366, 370, 403 n.41
rally, 388 n.2
scientific research. *See* human experiments
slavery. *See* forced labor
Student Organization, 211, 309, 360
tactics, 3
Teachers' Association, 359
"violent socialization," 419 n.38
*Nazi Connection, The,* 403 n.44
*Nazi Doctors, The,* 402 n.39, 403 nn.41, 44
*Nazi Doctors and the Nuremberg Code, The,* 447
    n.8
*Nazi Germany,* 397 n.51
*Nazi Germany and the Jews,* 7, 397 n.3, 398
    nn.20, 32, 399 nn.35–37, 46, 400 n.56
*Nazi Olympics, The,* 398 n.21
*Nazi Persecution of the Churches, The, 1933–45,*
    387 n.31, 425 n.18
*Nazi Persecution of the Gypsies, The,* 381 n.7,
    415 n.69
*Nazi Policy, Jewish Workers, German Killers,* 6,
    402 nn.28, 33, 405 nn.79, 86, 408 n.29,
    411 n.56
*Nazi Terror,* 393 n.11
*Nazi War on Cancer, The,* 403 n.41
*Nazi Years, The,* 404 nn.62, 64
*Nazism 1919–1945,* 399 n.47, 402 nn.32, 34,
    405 nn.77, 86, 88, 91, 406 nn.1, 99–100,
    411 n.8
Nebe, Arthur, 174, 181, 410 n.54
Nebuchadnezzar, 331
negative, the, 328
  absolute, 368–72, 450 n.49
Neiman, Susan
  *Evil in Modern Thought,* 442 n.4
Nelson, Benjamin, 247
  *The Idea of Usury,* 423 n.91
Nelson, Tim Blake
  *The Grey Zone,* 295
Netherlands. *See* Holland/Netherlands
Neufeld, Michael and Michael Berenbaum, ed.
  *The Bombing of Auschwitz,* 433 n.167
Neumann, Erich, 191
Neusner, Jacob
  *First-Century Judaism in Crisis,* 385 nn.12,
    14, 20
  *From Politics to Piety,* 385 n.11
"New Christians," 73
Newhouse, Victoria
  *Towards a New Museum,* 437 n.26

Newman, Barnett, 301
Newman, Richard
 *Alma Rosé,* 436 n.13
New Testament, 33, 289
 anti-Judaism in, 289–90
 Gospels, 33–34, 41–43
 John, 44–45
 *See also* Paul, Saint
Nicholas I, Czar, 18
Nicosia, Francis R. and Jonathan Huener, eds.
 *Medicine and Medical Ethics in Nazi Germany,* 447 n.6
Niebuhr, Reinhold, 264, 282, 433 n.169
Niemöller, Martin, 261, 427 n.65
Nietzsche, Friedrich, 442 n.4
Niewyk, Donald, ed.
 *Fresh Wounds,* 417 n.10
*Night,* 8, 319, 321, 441 n.110, 441 n.111
*Night and Fog,* 292
*Nightfather,* 8, 377
"Night of the Gypsies," 206
Night of the Long Knives, 115
Nikolayev, Vladimir, 159
Nisko plan, 150–51, 402 n.32
NKVD (Soviet secret police), 410 n.42
*Noble Treason, A,* 433 n.170
Nobs, Ernst, 260
Nomberg-Przytyk, Sara
 *Auschwitz: True Tales from a Grotesque Land,* 8
"non-person," 65, 244–47, 423 n.87
*No Rusty Swords,* 425 n.19
*Notes from the Warsaw Ghetto,* 418 n.25
Norway, 280
November Pogrom, 131–32
 *See also Kristallnacht*
Nuremberg
 city, 132
 International Military Tribunal, 101, 168, 363–64, 406 n.101, 407 n.6
 Laws, 128, 190, 192, 221, 373, 398 n.19, 417 n.14
 rally, 202
 trials, 8, 239, 363–64, 421 n.59, 448–49 nn.25–28
*Nuremberg: Infamy on Trial,* 448 n.27
*Nuremberg Trial, The,* 448 n.27
*Nuremberg War Crimes Trial, The,* 448 nn.25, 27
Nussbaum, Felix, 298–99

Oberman, Heiko A.
 *The Origins of Anti-Semitism in the Age of Renaissance and Reformation,* 386 nn.4, 9
Ofer, Dalia, 235
Ofer, Dalia and Lenore J. Weitzman, eds.
 *Women in the Holocaust,* 420 nn.41, 45, 421 n.47
*Official Secrets,* 401 n.10

O'Hare, Padraic, 51
 *The Enduring Covenant,* 386 n.3
Ohlendorf, Otto, 174, 288
Old Testament, 255, 256, 270
 *See also* Bible; Torah
Olère, David, 299, 438 n.29
Oliver, Samuel P. and Pearl M.
 *The Altruistic Personality,* 434 n.173
Olympic Games, 128, 398 n.21
*On Both Sides of the Wall,* 418 n.25
*One Generation After,* 327
*Oneg Shabbat,* 304
*On Listening to Holocaust Survivors,* 417 n.10
*On the Edge of Destruction,* 394 n.36
*On the Edge of the Abyss,* 437 n.28
*On the Jews and Their Lies,* 57–59, 63, 387 nn.12, 16–18, 21–24, 28–29
"Open Ends" exhibit, 296
*Open Thy Mouth for the Dumb,* 426 n.30
Operation 7, 264–65
Operation Barbarossa, 167, 172–75, 182, 406 n.1, 407 n.4, 408 n.29
Operation Ratline, 279, 287
Operation Reinhard, 197–201, 413 nn.45, 47
Oppenheimer, Deborah. *See* Harris, M. J.
oral histories, 8, 243, 294
*Order of the Death's Head, The,* 396 n.51, 399 n.41, 408 n.32
Order Police, 178, 369, 419 n.35
*Ordinary Men,* 6, 401 n.16, 408 n.35
Oreglia di San Stephano, Guiseppe, 268
*Origins of Anti-Semitism in the Age of Renaissance and Reformation, The,* 386 nn.4, 9
*Origins of Nazi Genocide, The,* 392 n.8, 394 n.30, 402 n.39, 403 n.40, 404 nn.52–54, 58,63, 67, 415 n.72
*Origins of Totalitarianism, The,* 382 n.19, 389 n.23
Orsenigo, Cesare, 158, 277, 432 n.153
*Oskar Schindler and His List,* 436 n.9
*Osservatore Cattolico, L',* 268
*Osservatore Romano, L',* 158, 266, 268
Ostrau, 150
Oświęcim. *See* Auschwitz
Ottoman Empire, 18
Otwock, 369, 375
*Out of the Ghetto,* 389 n.6
ovens. *See* crematoria
Overy, Richard
 *Interrogations: The Nazi Elite in Allied Hands,* 449 n.27

Pacelli, Eugenio Cardinal (later Pius XII), 105, 111, 266–67, 270, 424 n.3
*Painted in Words,* 438 n.37
Pakula, Alan J.
 *Sophie's Choice,* 293
Paldiel, Mordecai, 428–29 n.81

Paléologue, Maurice
    *An Intimate Journal of the Dreyfus Case,* 390
        n.28
Palestine, 110, 136, 140–41, 220, 275, 334,
        351–52
    British concern for emigration to, 281, 400
        n.58
    Jewish agency for, 274
    Jewish immigration to, 351
    White Paper on, 141
Panizzardi, Alesandro, 85, 86–87, 89
papacy/pope, 66, 91, 266, 287
    infallibility, 289
    *See also individual popes by name*
papal encyclicals. *See under individual titles*
    States, 82, 250, 277, 289
Papen, Franz von, 364, 425 n.16
paper violence, 11, 125–26
*Paper Walls,* 400 n.54
parables. *See* Jesus: parables
pariah people
    Armenians as, 21
    protected, 82
    *See also* Jews: pariah people
Paris, 72, 77, 272
    Commune, 80
Pasha, Enver, 18
Pasha, Jemal, 18
Pasha, Taalat, 18–19
*Passage to Ararat,* 444 n.54
*Passchendaele,* 393 n.13
Passchendaele. *See* Ypres, Battle of
Passelecq, Georges and Bernard Suchecky
    *The Hidden Encyclical of Pius XI,* 430
        nn.112–13
*Passion for Truth, A,* 341, 444 n.44
passion plays, 394 n.26
Passover, 34–35, 54, 268
Pastor's Emergency League (PEL), 259
*Path to Genocide, The,* 395 n.45
Patterson, David
    *Along the Edge of Annihilation,* 439 n.58
    *The Shriek of Silence,* 439 n.60
Paul, Saint, 33, 36, 250, 256, 271, 384 n.9,
        446 n.81
Paul IV, Pope, 66, 388 n.35
Paul VI, Pope, 430 n.134
Paulsson, Gunnar S.
    *Secret City,* 417 n.19
Pauwels, Jacques R.
    *Women, Nazis, and Universities,* 448 n.13
Pavelić, Ante, 408 n.14
*Pavement of Hell, The,* 417 n.8
Pawiak prison, 315
Pawlikowski, John T., 7, 332
Peckmann, Wilhelm von, 254
Pellieux, Georges de, 89
Pelt, Robert. *See* van Pelt
*People Betrayed, A,* 442 n.1

Perechodnik, Calel, 369–70, 373, 375–76, 377
    *Am I a Murderer?,* 449 n.39
Peretz, Ahron, ix, 379 n.1
*Perpetrators Victims Bystanders,* 420 n.44
Perrin, Norman, 41
    *The New Testament,* 385 n.16
    *Rediscovering the Teaching of Jesus,* 385 n.18
persecution, 36, 258
Persians, 387 n.24
Persico, Joseph E.
    *Nuremberg: Infamy on Trial,* 448 n.27
*persona,* 245
Pétain, Henri Philippe, 94, 272, 285, 393 n.22
Peter the Great, 390 n.1
Petrie, Jon, 381 n.12
Petropoulos, Jonathan
    *The Faustian Bargain,* 398 n.34, 423 n.85
Pfannmüller, Hermann, 155
Pharisees, 37, 46, 278, 384 n.8, 385 n.11
"phalansteries," 77
Phayer, Michael, 276, 288
    *The Catholic Church and the Holocaust,
        1930–1965,* 399 n.38
Phayer, Michael and Eva Fleischner
    *Cries in the Night,* 420 n.45
philosophy, 327, 445 n.57
*Philosophy of Human Rights, The,* 448 n.24
*Philosophy of Right,* 449 n.36
photographs. *See* Holocaust: photographs
physicians. *See* doctors
*Pianist, The,* 295, 417 n.21
Picquart, Georges, 86, 89, 93
Piotrkow Tribunalski, 405 n.81
Piper, Franciszek, 450 n.47
Piper, Franciszek and Teresa Swiebocka, eds.
    *Auschwitz: Nazi Death Camp,* 414 n.60
Pipes, Richard, 251
Pius IX, Pope, 266
Pius XI, Pope, 82
Pius XII, Pope, 249, 271–72, 274, 275, 288,
        289, 404 n.65, 424 n.3, 434 n.187
    wartime speech of, 431 nn.138–39
*Pius XII and the Holocaust,* 424 n.3, 434 n.187
*Playing for Time,* 296
Pobedonostsev, Konstantin Petrovich, 99, 391
        n.3
*Pobedonostsev,* 391 n.3
Po-chia Hsia, R.
    *The Myth of Ritual Murder,* 429 n.101
Podchlebnik, Mordechaï, 197
pogroms, 131, 322
    in Poland, 408 n.31
    Roman, 32
    Russian, 10–11, 18, 98
Pohl, Dieter, 6
Pohl, Oswald, 135, 202, 288
*Poles and Jews between the Wars,* 394 n.36
*Policies of Genocide, The,* 406 n.1, 409 n.38
*Politics of Assimilation, The,* 389 n.23

*Politics of Rescue, The,* 400 n.54
politics, power, 14
Pol Pot, 17, 20, 327
Poland, 147, 151, 167, 195, 406 n.2
   division of, 149
   General Government/*Generalgouvernement,*
      149, 160–62, 186, 223, 405 n.83, 408
      n.30
   invasion of, 144, 146
   Polish-Jewish relations, 395 n.37
   resettlement plan, 150
   Wartheland/Wartegau, 149, 160, 164, 186,
      196, 223
Polanski, Roman
   *The Pianist,* 295
Poliakov, Léon
   *Harvest of Hate,* 404 n.57
   *The History of Anti-Semitism,* 386 nn.4, 7
*Polin: Studies in Polish Jewry,* 414 n.48
*Political Theory of Possessive Individualism, The,*
   389 n.10
politics
   biologically-based, 15
   rationalization of, 73
Polke, Sigmar
   *Watchtower,* 297, 437 n.15
Polonsky, Antony, ed.
   *Focusing on the Holocaust and Its Aftermath,*
      414 n.48
   *"My Brother's Keeper?",* 394 n.36
Ponary, 217–18
Poniatowa, 202
Pontius Pilate, 34, 35, 42, 50
pope. *See* papacy
*Popular Culture and the Shaping of Holocaust*
   *Memory in America,* 436 n.9
population(s)
   decimation, 408 n.29
   elimination, 153
      state-sponsored, 15
      *See also* genocide
   Germany's Jewish, 398 n.20
   indigenous, 153
   movement of, 383 n.21
      *See also Lebensraum*
   surplus, 162, 370
      factors leading to, 15
   target, 220
   unwanted, 15, 112
Posen, 175
Posner, Gerald L. and John Ware
   *Mengele,* 447 n.6
possessive individualism. *See* individualism,
   possessive
"Postards," 83–84, 94
Powell, Glen, 379 n.4
power, 14
   of state, 15, 377
Power, Samantha

*"A Problem from Hell,"* 383 nn.23, 24
powerlessness, 351
Powiercie, 196
Prague, 13
   Heydrich assassinated in, 193
*Preempting the Holocaust,* 438 n.37, 439 n.60
prejudice, 30
   education as bulwark against, 360
press, 286
   *See also* United States: press *and individual*
      *names of publications*
Preysing, Konrad, 158, 404 n.65
*Price of Glory, The,* 392 n.10
*Primo Levi,* 435 n.1
Prior, Robin and Trevor Wilson
   *Passchendaele,* 393 n.13
prisoners
   of war. *See* war: prisoners of
   political, 204, 235
   revolt, 201
   Soviet, 381 n.8, 414 n.63
prisons. *See* camps: prison
*Private Papers of Douglas Haig 1914–1918,*
   *The,* 393 n.16
*Probing the Limits of Representation,* 437 n.24
Probst, Christoph, 283
Proctor, Robert N.
   *The Nazi War on Cancer,* 403 n.41
   *Racial Hygiene,* 403 n.41
"progress," 15, 339, 369
propaganda. *See* Nazi: propaganda
prophets, 60
   *See also names of individual prophets*
prostitution, compulsory, 274
Protestant
   American, 281
   French, 286
      *See also* Huguenots
   Reformation. *See* Reformation
*Protocols of the Elders of Zion,* 62, 87, 105, 123,
   136, 251, 346, 387 n.25, 424 n.8, 445
   n.61
"proto-Israelites," 384 n.4
Proudhon, Pierre-Joseph, 77
Prüfer, Kurt, 369, 371–72
prussic acid. *See* Zyklon B
Przemysl, 148
purges. *See* pogroms
Purim, 322
purity. *See* racial purity

*Quiet Neighbors: Prosecuting Nazi War Crimi-*
   *nals in America,* 449 n.30
Quisling, Vidkun, 280

rabbis, 38–39, 42, 278, 323, 331, 353
   as symbolic exemplar, 343, 444 n.52
*Rabbi as Symbolic Exemplar, The,* 444 n.52
*Rabensbrück,* 421 n.46

race
  hygiene, 392 n.8, 403 n.41
  and space, 143
  *stirpe* and, 431 n.138
racial
  purification. *See Judenrein*
  purity, 15, 106, 130, 143, 236, 392 n.8
  struggle, 167
  transformation, 400 n.5
*Racial Hygiene,* 403 n.39
"racial inferiors," 206, 392 n.8, 406 n.2
*Racial State, The,* 415 n.72
racism, 74, 153, 236, 251, 270
  antisemitic, 66, 259
  Jewishness defined as, 108, 121, 263, 397
    n.16
  *See also* antisemitism: Nazi
*Racism: A Short History,* 388 n.35
Raczkiewicz, Wladislaw, 431 n.139
Rademacher, Franz, 163, 405 nn.86, 88
*Radical Evil,* 442 n.4
Rafsanjani, Ali Akhbar Hashemi, 445 n.62
rage, German, 211
railroads (*Deutsche Reichsbahn*), 199, 200, 296,
    362–63, 370, 448 n.17
  proximity to, 195, 402 n.32
  *Sonderzüge,* 362
  special spurs, 205
Rampolla, Mariano, 90
*Raphael Lemkin's Thoughts on Genocide,* 383
    n.24
Rasch, Emil Otto, 147–48, 174
Rath, Ernst vom, 132
rationality, 13, 15, 113, 328, 449 n.34, 450
    n.49
rationalization, 14, 188, 193, 385 n.21
Ratti, Achille. *See* Pius XI, Pope
Ratzel, Friedrich, 392 n.8
Rauff, Walter, 287
Ravensbrück, 235, 278, 310, 420 n.45, 421
    n.46
*Reaching Judgment at Nuremberg,* 448 n.27
*Reader, The,* 421 n.49
*Reading Auschwitz,* 420 n.45
*Reading the Holocaust,* 439 n.61
reason. *See* rationality
*Reasoning after Revelation,* 444 n.55
*Rebel, The,* 384 n.1
records, ecclesiastical, 126
  *See also* baptismal registers
Red Cross, 300, 310, 316
Reder, Rudolf, 199, 413 n.48, 414 n.51
*Rediscovering the Teaching of Jesus,* 385 n.18
Redlich, Fritz
  *Hitler,* 391 n.4
*Red Rising in Bavaria,* 424 n.7
*Reference Guide to Holocaust Literature,* 439
    n.60
*Reflections on the Holocaust,* 396 n.46

Reformation, 56, 64–66, 252, 265
refugees, 105, 382 n.19, 393 n.22, 433 n.167
Reich Citizenship Law, 126, 128
Reichenau, Walter von, 258
Reichsbruderrat der Evangelischen Kirche in
    Deutschland, 443 n.34
*Reichskirche,* 256
*Reichskonkordat. See* Vatican: concordat with
    Nazi Germany
Reich's Physicians' League, 359
*Reichssicherheitshauptamt. See* RSHA
*Reichstag,* 255
  Enabling Act. *See* Enabling Act
  speech (of 30 January 1939), 114, 212, 401
    n.12
  speech (of 30 June 1939), 65, 143
  speech (of 6 October 1939), 150, 159
Reich, Steve
  *Different Trains,* 296
*Reichsvereinigung,* 222–23
*Reichsvertretung der Deutschen Juden,* 221–222,
    417 n.14
Reinecke, Herman, 407 n.4
Reinhardt, Klaus
  *Moscow—the Turning Point,* 411 n.57
*Reinventing Paul,* 385 n.9
religion, 327, 344, 348
  *See also* Christianity; Islam; Judaism
*Reluctant Witnesses,* 25, 384 n.37, 386 nn.5, 9
Remak, Joachim, ed.
  *The Nazi Years,* 404 nn.62, 64
*Remembering for the Future,* 381 n.12, 424 n.3,
    428 n.70, 435 n.6
Remembering for the Future 2000 (confer-
    ence), 449 n.37
*Remembering to Forget,* 435 n.6
remnant, 39, 353
remorse, 247
reparations, 422–23 n.85
*Requiem for Hitler and Other New Perspectives
    on the German Church Struggle, A,* 431
    n.151
rescue-through-work. *See* work: salvation
    through
research on miscegenation, 391 n.8
resettlement, 225, 382 n.20, 401 n.13, 402
    nn.27,29, 31, 35–36, 38, 404 n.68, 405
    nn.72, 75
  commission, 227
  of ethnic Germans, 152, 402 n.32
  as euphemism, 163, 192
  of nationalities, 150–51, 159–60
*Resilience and Courage,* 420 n.45
resistance, 308, 377
  Christian, 262, 278, 280
  French, 95, 420 n.45
  German, 262, 283, 315, 370
  Jewish, 217, 226, 231–34, 296, 418 n.29,
    419 n.35, 420 n.41

in ghettos. *See* ghettos: uprisings
nonviolent, 230–31, 284
  through art, 299
  Polish, 394 n.36
*Resistance of the Heart,* 412 n.34
Resnais, Alain
  *Night and Fog,* 292
responsibility, group, 367
*Rethinking the Holocaust,* 7, 217, 383 nn.29,
  30, 394 n.31
revelation, inseparable from interpretation, 349
*Revenge of God, The,* 388 n. 33
*Revolution in Bavaria, 1918–1919,* 424 n.7
*Rewriting the Holocaust,* 418 nn.28–29, 419
  n.35
Rhodes, Richard, 150, 180–81, 191, 213, 410
  n.53, 419 n.38
  *Masters of Death,* 392 n.8, 401 n.16, 402
    n.30, 408 n.32, 410 n.48, 410 n.53, 419
    n.38
Ribentrop, Joachim von, 163, 170
Rich, Sara, 437 n.17
Riefenstahl, Levi, 370
  *Triumph of the Will,* 292
Riegner, Gerhart, 272, 43 n.126
Riga, 177, 179, 410 n.47, 412 n.37
  Trial, 410 n.48
Riggs, Thomas, ed.
  *Reference Guide to Holocaust Literature,* 439
    n.60
right and wrong, 368
  *See also* ethics
*Righteous, The,* 434 n.173
Righteous Gentiles, 265, 283, 395 n.36, 428
  n.81, 433 n.172
  *See also* Avenue of the Righteous
*Righteous Gentiles of the Holocaust, The,* 450
  n.45
rights. *See* human rights
Ringelblum, Emmanuel, 304
  *Notes from the Warsaw Ghetto,* 418 n.25
Ringelheim, Joan, 235
Rittner, Carol, 235, 383 n.23
  *Elie Wiesel: Between Memory and Hope,* 441
    n.111
Rittner, Carol and John K. Roth, eds.
  *Different Voices,* 420 nn.41, 45, 421 n.47
  *"Good News" after Auschwitz?,* 434 n.187
  *Pius XII and the Holocaust,* 424 n.3, 434
    n.187
Rittner, Carol and Sondra Myers, eds.
  *The Courage to Care,* 434 n.173
Rittner, Roth, and Smith
  *Will Genocide Ever End?,* 383 n.23, 392 n.8,
    442 n.1
ritual murder, 54, 92, 268–69, 279
Rivers, Larry, 298,, 301
*Road to Nuremberg, The,* 448 n.27
Robertson, Edwin H., 428 n.70

Robinson, Jacob
  *And the Crooked Shall Be Made Straight,* 447
    n.3
Rodina, Saverio, 268
Rogers, Edith, 282
Röhm, Ernst, 105, 115–16, 396 n.51
Roland, Charles G.
  *Courage under Siege,* 417 n.20
Roma and Sinti. *See* Gypsies
Roman authority, 32, 49, 52
  Hitler heir to, 46
  Jewish submission to, 46
Roman Catholic Church. *See* churches: Roman
  Catholic
Roman Empire, 32–33, 35
Romania, 273
Rome, 41, 44, 276
  bishop of, 50
  march on, 82
*Römische Tagebücher,* 434 n.180
Roncalli, Angelo (Pope John XXIII), 274, 280
Roosevelt, Franklin D., 139, 275, 394 n.36,
  431 n.137, 432 n.167, 433 n.167
  New Deal/"Jew Deal," 282
Roseman, Mark, 191
  *The Wannsee Conference and the Final Solu-
    tion,* 411 n.14
Rosenbaum, Alan S., ed.
  *Is the Holocaust Unique?,* 383 nn.25, 27, 384
    n.31, 442 n.1
Rosenbaum, Ron
  *Explaining Hitler,* 391 n.4
Rosenberg, Alfred, 166, 406 n.101
  *The Myth of the Twentieth Century,* 166
Rosenfeld, Alvin H.
  *A Double Dying,* 439 n.60
  *Thinking about the Holocaust,* 439 n.61
Rosenstrasse Protest, 412 n.34
Roskies, David G.
  *Against the Apocalypse,* 442 n.2
Rossino, Alexander, 148, 401 n.18, 402
  nn.21–16, 26
Ross, Robert W., 281
  *So It Was True,* 432 n.163
Rost, Nella, 413 n.48
Rothberg, Michael
  *Traumatic Realism,* 436 n.9, 437 n.20
Roth, John K., 332, 381 n.12, 383 n.23
  *A Consuming Fire,* 441 n.111
  *Ethics after the Holocaust,* 450 n.48
  *The Holocaust Chronicle,* 381 n.6, 394 n.27,
    396 n.51, 397 n.15
Roth, John K. and Elizabeth Maxell, ed.
  *Remembering for the Future,* 381 n.12, 424
    n.3, 428 n.70, 435 n.6
Roth, John K. and Michael Berenbaum
  *Holocaust: Religious and Philosophical Impli-
    cations,* 418 n.24
Rothko, Marc, 301

Rothmund, Heinrich, 260
Rotta, Angello, 276
Rousseau, René Waldeck-, 93
*Roz Al-Youssuf,* 445 n.61
Rozett, Robert, 213, 381 n.6
Rozycki, Stanislav, 406 n.100
RSHA (*Reichssicherheitshauptamt*), 137, 147,
    150, 173, 402 n.32
Rubel, Margaret M., 199, 413 n.48
Rubenstein, Betty Rogers and Michael Beren-
    baum
    *What Kind of God?,* 426 n.31
Rubenstein, Richard L., 261, 328, 337–38,
    340–44, 353, 371, 443 n.39, 444
    nn.50–51
    *After Auschwitz,* 335, 343, 385 n.23, 390
        n.29, 443 n.27, 443 n.36
    *The Age of Triage,* 382 n.18, 389 n.7, 390
        n.2, 395 n.43, 442 n.1
    *The Cunning of History,* 369, 373, 382 n.18,
        383 n.22
Rubenstein, William D.
    *The Myth of Rescue,* 53
Rumkowski, Mordecai Chaim, 162, 226–28,
    418 nn.30–32
Rummel, R. J.
    *Death by Government,* 391 n.8
Russia, invasion of, 17, 172–74
    *See also Blitzkrieg;* Soviet Union
Russian Revolution, 144, 251
Russians, 144
Rwanda, 17
Ryan Jr., Allan A.
    *Quiet Neighbors: Prosecuting Nazi War Crim-
        inals in America,* 449 n.30
Ryan, Michael D., 394 n.28
Ryder, A. J.
    *Twentieth-Century Germany from Bismarck to
        Brandt,* 391 n.5

SA (*Sturmabteilung*), 105, 115–16, 124–25,
    134–35, 256
Sabac, 170
Sachar, Howard Morley
    *The Course of Modern Jewish History,* 390 n.2
Sachsenhausen, 132, 159, 208, 262, 338, 348
sacrifice, 342
Sajništi, 171
Saldern, Adelheid von
    "Victims or Perpetrators," 421 n.47
Salomon, Charlotte, 437 n.22
    *Life? Or Theater?,* 298
Saltzman, Lisa
    *Anselm Kiefer and Art after Auschwitz,* 437
        n.17
*Salvaged Pages,* 439 n.58
Sander, Fritz, 369, 372
Sandherr, Jean, 83–84
Sao Paulo, 357

"sardine method," 179
Satan, 54, 322
    *See also* devil; Jews: as satanic
Saul, 29
Sauvage, Pierre
    *Conspiracy,* 294
    *Weapons of the Spirit,* 294
Schacht, Hjalmar, 364
Scheurer-Kestner, Auguste, 87
Schilling, Donald G., ed.
    *Lessons and Legacies,* 400 n.5
Schindler, Emilie, 436 n.9
    *Where Light and Shadow Meet,* 436 n.9
Schindler, Oskar, 284, 293
*Schindler's List* (film), 293, 436 n.9
Schlachta, Margit, 278
Schlesiersee, 209
Schleunes, Karl A., 4, 114
    *Legislating the Holocaust,* 398 n.19
    *The Twisted Road to Auschwitz,* 381 n.9, 395
        n.45, 398 nn.24–25, 31, 399 n.43, 400
        n.52
Schlick zu Falkenau, Wolf (Count), 58
Schlink, Bernhard
    *The Reader,* 421 n.49
Schmäling, Julius, 285–86
Schmitz, Hanna, 421 n.49
Schneersohn, Joseph Isaac, 330, 337, 442 n.14
Schneider, Bernard, 438 n.47
Scholder, Klaus, 252, 254, 265
    *The Reader,* 421 n.49
    *A Requiem for Hitler and Other New Perspec-
        tives on the German Church Struggle,* 431
        n.151
Scholem, Gershom, 340
Scholl, Hans, 283
Scholl, Inge
    *The White Rose,* 433 n.170
Scholl, Sophie, 283
Schonberg, Arnold
    *A Survivor from Warsaw,* 296
Schöngarth, Eberhard, 191
Schön, Waldemar, 406 n.99
Schorske, Carl
    *Fin-de-Siècle Vienna,* 390 n.30
Schreiber, Jurgen, 171
Schulkind, Nina, 303
Schwartzkopppen, Maximillian von, 83,
    85–87, 89
scientific experiments. *See* human experiments
scientists, 357, 370, 448 n.14
*Scientists under Hitler,* 448 n.14
*Screening the Holocaust,* 435 n.8
Scripture, 270, 340
    *See also* Bible; Old Testament; New Testa-
        ment; Torah
*Scroll of Agony,* 418 n.25, 439 n.57
SD (*Sicherheitsdienst*), 116, 132, 146, 174, 397
    n.12, 399 n.46

*Sea is Never Full, The,* 319
*Secret City,* 417 n.19
Sedlmeier, Hans, 357
Segal, George, 301, 438 n.39
Seidman, Naomi, 441 n.111
Semite, 382 n.14
Serbia, 169–70, 408 n.15
Seredi, Justinian, 276, 280, 431 nn.143–44
Sereny, Gitta
    *Into That Darkness,* 404 n.65
serfs, 98
Seti I, 27
*Setting of the Sermon on the Mount, The,* 385
    n.17
Shahn, Ben, 298
Shamgorod, 322
Shandler, Jeffrey
    *While America Watches,* 435 n.7
Shandley, Robert R.
    *Unwilling Germans?,* 388n.2
*Shape of Theriesienstadt, The,* 300
*Shattering the German Night,* 433 n.170
Shay, Arnold, 401 n.21
Shechem, 26
Shimaite, Anna, 284
*Shoah* (the), 4–5, 329, 344, 381 n.10, 424 n.3,
    450 n.43
    Roman Catholic teaching on, 434 n.187
    sacrificial interpretation of, 336
*Shoah,* 197, 293–94, 296, 399 n.48, 400 n.54,
    419 n.41, 437 n.16, 441 n.110
Shoah Visual History Foundation, 8, 241, 417
    n.10
Shostakovich, Dmitry
    *Thirteenth Symphony,* 296
*Shriek of Silence, The,* 439 n.60
*Sicherheitspolizei* (security police), 146–47
Sidor, Charles, 273, 430 n.130
Siemens. *See* corporations: Siemens
Signer, Michael A., ed.
    *Humanity at the Limit,* 435 n.187
Siirala, Aarne, 387 n.30
Silberner, Edmund
    *Sozialisten zur Judenfrage,* 389 nn.11–12
silence. *See* conspiracy: of silence
Silesia, Upper, 147
Sinai, Mount. *See* Mount Sinai
Skloot, Robert
    *The Darkness We Carry,* 439 n.60
slave labor. *See* forced labor
slavery, 13, 245
Slovakia, 272, 273, 280
Smith, Bradley F.
    *Reaching Judgment at Nuremberg,* 448 n.27
    *The Road to Nuremberg,* 448 n.27
Smith, Helmut Walser
    *The Butcher's Tale,* 388 n.2
    *The Holocaust and Other Genocides,*
        435 n.6

Smith, James M., 379 n.4, 383 n.23
Smith, Stephen, 379 n.4
*Smoke over Birkenau,* 421 n.59
Sobibor, 197–98, 200, 233, 234
*Sobibor, October 14, 1943, 4 p.m.,* 294
social
    contract, 346
    reality, 397 n.16
*Social Darwinism in American Thought,* 403
    n.45
Social Darwinists, 152, 153, 403 n.45
*Social Teachings of the Christian Churches, The,*
    387 nn.10, 13
socialism, 77, 220, 267
society, new, 316, 356
sociology, 346, 373
Sodom, 324
*So It Was True,* 432 n.163
"soldier's glory," 103–4
Soloveitchik, Joseph B., 340, 341–42, 443
    n.38, 444 nn.47–48
Solomon, 29
Somme, Battle of, 100, 102, 393 n.12
Sommer, Margarete, 278
*Sonderbehandlung 14f13,* 156, 404 n.61
*Sonderkommandos,* 173, 196, 304
    at Auschwitz-Birkenau, 295, 299
    in concentration and death camps, 234
    Latvian, 177
*Sonderzüge. See* railroads: *Sonderzüge*
Sonnenstein, 156
*Sophie's Choice* (film), 293
Soumerai, Eve Nussbaum and Carol D. Schulz
    *Daily Life during the Holocaust,* 417 n.10
*Sources of Holocaust Research,* 1, 379 n.3
Soviet Army, 208
    partisan groups, 231
Soviet
    -German Pact, 148, 149
Soviet Union, 146, 148, 167, 175, 182, 275
    German campaign, 399 n.51, 406 nn.1–2,
        409 n.30
    invasion by, 272
    *Wehrmacht,* attack of, 172
*Sozialisten zur Judenfrage,* 389 nn.11–12
Spain, 46, 65
Speer, Albert, 363
Spiegelman, Art
    *Maus: A Survivor's Tale,* 297, 436–37 n.15,
        437 n.20
*Spielberg's Holocaust,* 436 n.9
Spielberg, Steven
    *Schindler's List,* 293, 436 n.9
*Sportpalast,* 2
    rally, 256
Spotts, Frederic
    *The Churches and Politics in Germany,* 426
        n.30
Srebnik, Simon, 296

SS (*Schutzstaffel*), 116, 134–35, 145, 168
   controlled by Himmler, 401 n.15
   murder of Polish priests, 271
   officers, 244
"stab in the back," 11, 104, 130, 393 n.24
Stahl, Heinrich, 222
Stahlecker, Franz Walter, 174, 177, 409 n.41
*Stalin and German Communism,* 424 n.7
Stalin, Joseph, 272, 324, 327
Stangl, Franz, 157, 200, 201, 287, 367, 434
   n.181
Stannard, David E., 384 n.31
starvation, 157, 159, 173, 183
star, yellow. *See* clothing: distinctive
state, the, 247
   Jewish. *See* Israel: State of
Steiner, George, 291, 447 n.5
   *Language and Silence,* 435 n.5
Steinweis, Alan E.
   *Art, Ideology, and Economics in Nazi Ger-
      many,* 436 n.13
*Stellvertreter, Der* (The deputy), 249, 423 n.1
Stendahl, Krister, 385 n.9
sterilization, 153–54, 192, 206, 235, 403
   nn.41, 52
*St. Louis* (ship), 141, 400 n.59
Stoltzfus, Nathan, 412 n.34
   *Resistance of the Heart,* 412 n.34
*Storehouse, The* (*La Grande Reserve*), 436 n.15
Stowers, Stanley, 385 n.9
Streicher, Julius, 359
Streim, Alfred
   *Die Behandlung sowjetischer Kriegsgefangenen
      in "Fall Barbarossa,"* 408 n.23
Streit, Christian, 381 n.8, 406 n.1
   *Keine Kameraden,* 408 n.23
Strenski, Ivan
   *Contesting Sacrifice,* 389 n.23
strollers, 237–38, 239, 422 n.59
Stuckart, Wilhelm, 190
students, 123
*Sturmabteilung* [SA]/storm troopers, 1, 105,
   115
Styron, William
   *Sophie's Choice,* 293
Sudetenland. *See* Czechoslovakia
suffering, problem of, 348
Suffering Servant, 339
Suhard, Célestin, 272
*Sulamith,* 437 n.17
*Summi Pontificatus* (encyclical), 271
supersessionism, 51, 332
*Surplus of Memory, A,* 418 n.25
surplus people, 78
*Surrender of Breda, The,* 101
survival, 348
   meaning of, 310
   odds for and against, 231

strategies, 12
*Survival in Auschwitz,* 8, 291, 435 n.1
*Surviving the Holocaust,* 418 n.27
*Survivor: An Anatomy of Life in the Death
   Camps, The,* 415 n.80
*Survivor from Warsaw, A,* 296
survivors, xi, 8, 197, 223, 225, 240–44, 296,
   300, 301, 303, 304, 315, 369, 373,
   377, 401 n.21, 419 n.41, 420 n.45, 422
   n.59
   children of, 377
   hostility to, 286
   religious attitudes of, 321, 331–32
   reparations for, 422 n.85
   testimonies, 417 n.10
*Survivors, Victims, and Perpetrators,* 397 n.18
Sutthof, xi, 208
"symbolic exemplar," 343
synagogues, burning/desecration of, 123, 132,
   133, 147–48, 161
Szmaglewska, Seweryna, 421–22 n.59
   *Smoke over Birkenau,* 421 n.59
   *United in Wrath,* 421 n.59
Szpilman, Wladyslaw, 295
   *The Pianist,* 295, 417 n.21
Szyk, Arthur, 298

T4 operation, 155–57, 158, 198–99, 207
Tadeusz, Vorarbeiter, 315–16
Talmud, 37, 287
Tal, Uriel, 4, 381 n.10
Tardini, Dominico, 274, 430 n.134
Taussig, Fritz
   *The Shape of Theriesienstadt,* 300
Taylor, Myron C., 273, 275, 430 n.127
teachers, 357, 359–60, 370
"teaching of contempt," 51, 385–86 n.1
*Teaching of Contempt, The,* 385–86 n.1
Tec, Nechama
   *Resilience and Courage,* 420 n.45
Tedeschi, Giuliana, 238–40
   *There Is a Place on Earth,* 238
Temple. *See* Jerusalem: Temple
Temple, William, 281
Ten Commandments, 28, 300
   *See also* commandments
Terezin, 299, 300
*Terrible Secret, The,* 381 n.12, 401 n.6
territorial
   claims, 347–48
   expansion, 143
*Terror in the Mind of God,* 388 n. 33
terrorism, 324
*Testament, The,* 324
Tewes, Father, 258
*Texture of Memory, The,* 438 n.39
Theis, Édouard, 284–85
theodicy, 328

*Theologians under Hitler,* 387 n.31, 425 n.22
theology, Jewish, 340
    *See also* God; Holocaust: theology of
*There Is a Place on Earth,* 238
*There Once Was a World,* 438 n.44
Theresienstadt, 223, 299, 437 n.27
*Thinking about the Holocaust,* 439 n.61
*Thinking the Unthinkable,* 420 n.45
Third French Republic. *See* French Republic:
    Third
Third Reich, 9, 254, 372, 392 n.11
    appraisal of church life in, 332
    *See also* Nazis
*Third Reich, The,* 7, 380 n.1, 395 nn.38, 40,
    397 nn.12, 17, 406 n.1
Thirteen, The. *See* Trzynastka
*This Way for the Gas, Ladies and Gentlemen,* 8,
    315–16
Thomalla, Richard, 198
Thomas Aquinas, 53
Tiegenhof, 159
*Tikkun,* 350–52
Tillich, Ernst, 262
Tillich, Paul, 254
Tiso, Josef, 273
Tittman, Harold, 276
Toderov, Tzvetan
    *The Frailty of Goodness,* 432 n.159
*Todesmärchen. See* forced marches
Toland, John
    *Adolf Hitler,* 395 nn.38, 41
Toledo, Statute of, 65
toleration, 113
    religious, 67
Toll, Nelly
    *Without Surrender,* 437 n.28
*To Mend the World,* 350, 427 n.62
Torah, 52, 330, 344, 385 n.9
torture, 374
Tory, Avraham
    *Surviving the Holocaust,* 418 n.27
*Totenkopfverbände,* 135
Toussenel, Allphonse, 80
    *Les Juifs rois de l'epoque,* 80
*Towards a New Museum,* 437 n.26
*Toward the Final Solution,* 388n.3
*Transfer Agreement, The,* 397 n.14, 400 n.57
transports, 137, 199, 201, 237, 278, 405 n.83,
    412 n.37
    *See also* railroads
*Traumatic Realism,* 436 n.9, 437 n.20
Trawniki, 202
Treblinka, 8, 197–98, 200–201, 232, 233,
    234, 367, 369, 375, 414 n.54
Treitschke, Heinrich von, 71, 388n.2
    *"Ein Wort über unser Judentum,"* 71
*Trial of God, The,* 322
*Trial of the Germans, The,* 448 n.27

*Trial of the Major War Criminals before the
    International Military Tribunal,* 422 n.59
trials, post-war, 13, 258, 364
    *See also* Nuremberg: trials
*Triumph of the Will,* 292
Trocmé, André, 284, 286
Trocmé, Daniel, 286
Trocmé, Magda, 284–85
Troeltsch, Ernst, 57
    *The Social Teachings of the Christian
        Churches,* 387 nn.10, 13
Trotha, Lothar von, 391 n.8
Trunk, Isaiah, 230
    *Jewish Responses to Nazi Persecution,* 419 n.38
    *Judenrat,* 417 nn.22–23
trust, 374, 376
truth, 243, 244, 329
    disillusionment's, 318
    of moral claims, 368
Trzynastka (The Thirteen), 419 n.35
"Turkification" process, 18
Turkey, 18–19, 21
Turner, Harold, 171
Turner Jr., Henry Ashby
    *German Big Business and the Rise of Hitler,*
        447 n.5
Tusa, John and Ann
    *The Nuremberg Trial,* 448 n.27
Tushnet, Leonard
    *The Pavement of Hell,* 417 n.8
*12-Year Reich, The,* 447 nn.6, 10, 448 n.11
*Twentieth-Century Book of the Dead, The,* 391
    n.8, 392 n.9
*Twentieth-Century Germany from Bismarck to
    Brandt,* 391 n. 5
Twersky, Isadore, 341
*Twisted Cross,* 426 nn.30–31
*Twisted Music,* 436 n.13
*Twisted Road to Auschwitz, The,* 381 n.9, 395
    n.45, 398 nn.24–25, 31, 399 n.43,
    400 n.52
Tyas, Stephen, 413 n.47

Übelhoer, Frederick, 161
Ukraine, 173, 177, 283, 288, 419 n.37
Ullmann, Viktor, 296
*Under His Very Windows,* 431 n.138
*Under Risk: Secret State Experiments on
    Humans,* 447 n.9
*Une connaissance inutile* (Useless knowledge),
    310, 312
unemployment, 108
*Unfinished Sentence,* 438 n.36
*Ungekündigte Bund, Der,* 387 n.19
Unger, Michael, 405 n.85
*Unholy Trinity,* 434 n.176
*Unit 731: Japan's Secret Biological Warfare in
    World War II,* 447 n.9

*United in Wrath,* 421 n.59
United Nations (U.N.), 281, 363, 367
United States
    Congressional Committee on Immigration,
       109, 394 n.35
    eugenics movement, 403 n.43
    Genocide Convention, 16
    Holocaust Memorial Museum, 293, 298,
       301, 400 n.59, 417 n.10, 418 n.27, 438
       n.40
    Immigration Act. *See* Immigration Act of
       1924
    immigration limitation, 281, 403 n.46
    Jewish immigration to, 281
       census figures, 384 n.331
    Office of Special Investigations (OSI), 449
       n.30
    press, 281, 182
    refugees allowed, 432 n.167
    State Department, 432 n.167
    War Refugee Board, 432 n.167
Universal Declaration of Rights, 363, 367
universe of obligation. *See* moral obligation
university professors, 260, 359–60
    Jewish, of law, 395 n.44
    *See also* teachers
*Unmasking Administrative Evil,* 447 n.5, 449
    n.30
*Unwanted, The,* 382 n.19, 400 n.54
*Unwilling Germans?,* 388 n.2
*Unwritten Order, The,* 395 n.45, 399 n.49
*Uprooted, The,* 391 n.6
"useless eaters," 152, 157, 12, 292, 404 n.58
useless knowledge, 242, 301, 312
Ustasa, 287, 408 n.14
usury, 40
utopia, 342
    sanitary, 403 n.41

Vainshtein, Marina, 303
values, 368
*Values, Belief, and Survival,* 418 n.27
Van Buren, Paul M., 7, 208, 328, 332–34
*Vanished World, A,* 435 n.6
van Pelt, Robert Jan., x, 208, 396 n.45
    *The Case for Auschwitz,* 396 n.45, 414 n.60,
       450 n.47
    *See also* Dwork, Debórah
vans, gas. *See* Chelmno: gas vans
Vatican, 274, 276, 424 n.3, 429 n.88
    archives, 249
    attitude of, 266, 431 n.136
    blanket pardon sought by, 288
    concordats
       with Fascist Italy. *See* Lateran Treaty
       with Nazi Germany, 266, 269, 403 n.52
    policies, 431 n.139
    response to euthanasia program, 157–58

Vatican II, 274, 289
Veesenmayer, Edmund, 170
Velasquez, Diego de, 101
    *The Surrender of Breda,* 101
Vélodrome d'Hiver, 285
Verdun, 101–2, 392 n.10, 393 n.12
*Vernichtung,* 114, 143, 167–68, 169
*Vernichtungsbefehl,* 391 n.8
Versailles Treaty, 104, 252, 253–54
*Versions of Survival,* 418 n.24
*Der verwaltete Mensch,* 399 nn.49, 50
Vespasian, 38, 47
Vice, Sue
    *Holocaust Fiction,* 439 n.60
Vichy France, 72, 91, 94, 272, 285–86, 405
    n.90
*Vichy France and the Jews,* 393 n.22, 405 n.90
victim as non-person. *See* non-person
*Victim's Fortune, The,* 423 n.85
Vienna, 150
villains, 347
Vilna, 176, 217–19, 232, 416 n.1
violence
    religiously inspired, 388 n.33
    sadistic, 410 n.53
Vishniac, Roman and Elie Wiesel
    *A Vanished World,* 435 n.6
*Visual Culture and the Holocaust,* 436 n.9, 437
    n.17
*Voicing the Void,* 439 n.60
*Völkischer Beobachter,* 140
*Volksdienst, N.S.,* 155
*Volksgemeinschaft,* 104, 112, 142
*Volksgerichtshof* (People's Court), 190
*Volkskirche. See Reichskirche*
Voltaire, (François-Marie Arouet de), 68,
    73–74, 388 n.39
von Bismarck. *See* Bismarck, Otto von
*Vordenker der Vernichtung,* 406 n.97
Vrba, Rudolf, 422 n.59, 441 n.110
Vrba, Rudolf and Alan Bestic
    *I Cannot Forgive,* 422 n.59

*Waffen-SS,* 174, 401 n.15, 424 n.1
Wagner, Eduard, 409 n.36
Wagner family, 436 n.12
Wagner, Gerhard, 155
Wagner, Gottfried
    *Twilight of the Wagners,* 436 n.12
Wagner, Gustav, 287
Wagner, Richard, 295, 413 n.38, 436 n.12
Wagner, Robert, 282
Wagner-Rogers Child Refugee Bill, 282
Waite, Robert G. L.
    *Hitler and Nazi Germany,* 393 n.23
    *The Psychopathic God: Adolf Hitler*
Waldeck-Rousseau, Rene. *See* Rousseau
Wallenberg, Raoul, 284

Waller, James
    *Becoming Evil,* 449 n.34
Wallimann, Isidor and Michael Dobkowski,
    ed.
    *Genocide and the Modern Age,* 442 n.1
Walsin-Esterhazy, Ferdinand. *See* Esterhazy
Wannsee Conference, 188–94, 294, 307, 401
    n.14, 411 n.14–22, 24–28, 413 n.37
    Protocol, 191, 192
*Wannsee Conference and the Final Solution, The,*
    411 n.14
war, 130
    Cold. *See* Cold War
    crime trials, 288, 363
        *See also* Nuremberg Trials
    criminals, 101, 287, 288, 406 n.101
        to U.S., 364
    declared vs. U.S., 185, 189
    Eastern front, 408 n.27
    of extermination. *See* Vernichtung
    holy, 343, 445 n.64
    posture of, 352
    preventative, 366
    prisoners of, 3, 195
        Catholic, 287
        gassed, 186
    Soviet, 204, 407 n.4
        Jewish murdered, 407 n.4
    purpose of, 400 n.5
    "total," 412 n.34
*War Against the Jews, The,* 7, 396 n.46
*War and Genocide,* 7, 143, 400 n.1
*Warrant for Genocide,* 387 n.25
War Refugee Board, 432 n.167
Warsaw, 149, 165, 166, 209, 295, 318, 375,
    406 n.98
    archives at, 304
    liberation of, 208
    quarantine of Jewish quarter, 406 n.98
    resistance, 232
*Warsaw Diary of Adam Czerniakow, The,* 418
    n.25
Wartegau/Wartheland. *See* Poland: Wartegau
Wassermann, Elchonon, 330, 442 n.12
Wasserstein, Bernard
    *Britain and the Jews of Europe,* 400 n.58
*Watchtower,* 297, 437 n.15
wealth, 15
*Weapons of the Spirit* (film), 294
Weber, Eugen Joseph., 94
    *Action Française,* 91, 390 nn.42, 44
    *The Hollow Years,* 393 n.22
Weber, Max, 11, 127, 247, 390 n.35
Wegner, Gregory Paul
    *Anti-Semitism and Schooling under the Third
        Reich,* 448 n.11
*Wehrmacht,* 148, 168, 175, 402 n.25, 406 n.2,
    407 n.5

opposition to SS, 150
    in Serbia, 169–72, 408 n.15
Weimar Republic, 79, 80, 85, 105, 108,
    110
Weinberg, Gerhard L., 400 n.5
    *A World at Arms,* 7, 408 n.27
Weinberg, Jehiel Jacob, 331, 443 n.16
Weinberg, Jeshajahu and Rina Elieli
    *The Holocaust Museum in Washington,* 438
    n.40
Weiss, Ann
    *The Last Album,* 435 n.6
Weiss, John
    *Ideology of Death,* 7, 388 n.2
Weissler, Friedrich, 262
Weitzman, Lenore, 235
*We Remember: A Reflection on the Shoah,* 434
    n.187
Wessel, Horst, 1, 5
    *"Die Fahne hoch,"* 1, 4, 22
Wetzler, Alfred, 441 n.110
Wewelsburg conference, 182
Weyler, Valeriano, 399 n.44
Whalen, Robert Weldon
    *Bitter Wounds,* 393 n.18
*What Kind of God?,* 426 n.31
*When Biology Became Destiny,* 421 n.47
*When Memory Comes,* 437 n.24
*When Prophecy Fails,* 385 n.21
*Where Light and Shadow Meet,* 436 n.9
*While America Watches,* 435 n.7
*While Six Million Died,* 400 n.59
White Paper on Palestine, 110, 141
White Rose, The, 283, 433 n.170
*Who Killed Jesus?,* 384 n.7
Wiedmer, Caroline
    *The Claims of Memory,* 398, 437 n.25
Wiesel, Elie, 202–3, 293, 301, 305, 319–25,
    441 nn.110–28
    *Against Silence,* 414 n.58
    *All Rivers Run to the Sea,* 319
    dialogues, 320
    *From the Kingdom of Memory,* 414 n.59
    *A Jew Today,* 320–21
    *Night,* 8, 319, 321, 441 nn.110, 111
    *One Generation After,* 327
    *The Sea is Never Full,* 319
    *The Testament,* 324
    *The Trial of God,* 322
Wiesel, Elie and Richard D. Heffner
    *Conversation with Elie Wiesel,* 441 n.111
Wilcox, Larry D., 435 n.7
Wilczek, Pastor, 258
Wilhelm I, Kaiser, 71
Wilhelm II, Kaiser, 255
*Wilhelm Marr,* 384 n.5
Wilkin, Robert L.
    *John Chrysostom and the Jews* 386 n.4

*Will Genocide Ever End?,* 383 n.23, 392 n.8,
    442 n.1
Will, George, 302
Williamson, Clark M.
    *Has God Rejected His People?,* 384 n.8
Williams, Peter and David Wallace
    *Unit 731: Japan's Secret Biological Warfare in
        World War II,* 447 n.9
Wirth, Christian, 157, 198
Wistrich, Robert, 7, 72
    *Antisemitism: The Longest Hatred,* 384 n.6,
        386 nn.4, 9, 388 n.4
    *Hitler and the Holocaust,* 7, 389 n.5
*Without Surrender,* 437 n.28
Witkin, Jerome, 298, 301
*Witness and Legacy,* 298, 437 n.21
*Witness to the Holocaust,* 388 n. 34, 396 n.48,
        398 n.29, 400 nn.2–3, 401 nn.12, 14,
        402 n.32, 405 n.80, 418 n.24
"witness-people myth," 20, 265
*Witness: Voices from the Holocaust,* 417 n.10
Witte, Peter, 411 n.9, 413 n.47
women, 234–38, 245, 318
    in Birkenau uprising, 420 n.42
    as camp administrators, 421 nn.48–49
    education of, 448 n.13
    French, 310
    gassed, 172
    German, 235, 421 n.47
    in ghettos, 420 n.41
    not executed, 170
    memoirs by, 235, 420 n.45
    murdered, 186
    at Schlesiersee, 209–10
    treatment of, 200
*Women in the Holocaust,* 420 nn.41, 45, 421
    n.47
*Women, Nazis, and Universities,* 448 n.13
*Women's Holocaust Writing,* 420 n.45
*Words to Outlive Us,* 439 n.58
work
    permits, 218
    salvation through, 224, 228
*World at Arms, A,* 7, 408 n.27
World Council of Churches, 63
*World Crisis, The,* 393 n.12
World Jewish Congress, 272
*World Must Know, The,* 7, 414 n.62
*Worlds of Elie Wiesel, The,* 441 n.111
*World Reacts to the Holocaust, The,* 433 n.167
World War I, 250, 277, 393 n.22
    Jews banned, 211
    Serbs blamed for, 170
    statistics of, 424–25 n.9
World War II, 12, 244
    death statistics, 381 n.5
    German goals of, 143
    as "holy" struggle, 12

necessary for Holocaust, 143
    post-war analysis, 145
    as two wars, 144
    U.S. entry, 185, 188, 212, 431 n.136
"worthless" people, 154
Woyrsch, Udo von, 147–48, 402 n.22
*Writing and Rewriting the Holocaust,* 439 n.61
*Writing History, Writing Trauma,* 410 n.52, 439
    n.61
*Writing of the Disaster, The,* 241
Wroclaw. *See* Warsaw
Wurm, Theophil, 157, 254, 255, 425–26 n.27
WVHA (*Wirtschafts-Verwaltungshauptamt*),
    202, 203, 356
Wyman, David S., 281
    *The Abandonment of the Jews,* 432
        nn.160–63
    *Paper Walls,* 400 n.54
Wyman, David S. and Charles H. Rosenzveig,
    eds.
    *The World Reacts to the Holocaust,* 433
        n.167

Yad Vashem, 283–84, 395 n.36, 417 n.10, 429
    n.81, 433 n.172
Yahill, Leni
    *The Holocaust: The Fate of European Jewry,*
        398 n.23
Yahweh, 27–29
    *See also* God
Yale University. *See* Fortunoff Video Archive
Yaseen, Leonard C.
    *The Jesus Connection,* 384 n.8
Yavneh, 38
yellow star/armband. *See* clothing: distinctive
Yeshiva University (N.Y.), 341–42
Yochanan ben Zakkai, 32, 37–38, 42, 46, 385
    n.12
Yom Kippur, 165, 296, 307
Young, James E., 298
    *At Memory's Edge,* 438 n.45
    *The Texture of Memory,* 438 n.39
    *Writing and Rewriting the Holocaust,* 439
        n.61
Ypres, Battle of, 102, 393 n.14
Yugoslavia, 169

Zagreb, 408 n.14
Zapruder, Alexandra, ed.
    *Salvaged Pages,* 439 n.58
Zawistowska, Sophie, 293
Zealots, 32, 37, 39, 233
Zelizer, Barbie
    *Remembering to Forget,* 435 n.6
    *Visual Culture and the Holocaust,* 436 n.9,
        437 n.17
Zellner, Emil, 148
Zimmerman, Michael, 415 n.71

Zimmerman, Moshe
  *Wilhelm Marr,* 384 n.5
Zionism, 85, 97, 136, 228, 282, 336
Zionist
  agencies, 139, 140
  factions, 218, 220, 232
Zola, Émile, 89, 94, 390 n.36
Zuccotti, Susan, 275

*The Holocaust, the French, and the Jews,* 393 n.22
*Under His Very Windows,* 431 n.138
Zuckerman, Itzhak, 419 n.41
Zuckerman, Yitzak
  *A Surplus of Memory,* 418 n.25
Zyklon B, 186, 204, 205–6, 237, 298, 371, 415 n.68, 423–24 n.1